SECOND EDITION

INQUIRY

Questioning, Reading, Writing

EDITED BY

LYNN Z. BLOOM
University of Connecticut, Storrs

EDWARD M. WHITE
University of Arizona, Tucson

with SHANE BORROWMAN
Gonzaga University, Spokane

PEARSON

Prentice
Hall

Upper Saddle River, NJ 07458

Library of Congress Cataloging-in-Publication Data

Inquiry: questioning, reading, writing [edited by] Lynn Z. Bloom, Edward M. White, with Shane Borrowman.

   p. cm.

Includes index.

   ISBN 0-13-182371-X

   1. College readers. 2. English language—Rhetoric. 3. Interdisciplinary approach in education. 4. Academic writing. I. Bloom, Lynn Z. - II. White, Edward M. (Edward Michael) III. Borrowman, Shane.

PE1417.I56 2004
808′.0427—dc21

2003042999

Senior Acquisitions Editor: Corey Good
Editor-in-Chief: Leah Jewell
Editorial Assistant: Steve Kyritz
Executive Marketing Manager: Brandy Dawson
Production Liaison: Joanne Hakim
Manufacturing Buyer: Mary Ann Gloriande
Cover Art Director: Jayne Conte
Cover Design: Kiwi Design
Cover Illustration/Photo: Renè Magritte (1898-1967) Belgian, "La Lunette d'approche" (The Telescope) 1963, oil on canvas, 69-5/16 x 45-1/4 inches, 176 x 115 cm. Photographer: Hickey-Robertson, Houston. The Menil Collection, Houston
Composition/Full-Service Project Management: Fran Daniele/Preparé Inc.
Printer/Binder: R.R. Donnelly & Sons

Credits and acknowledgments borrowed from other sources and reproduced, with permission, in this textbook appear on appropriate page within text.

Pearson Education Ltd., London
Pearson Education Singapore, Pte. Ltd
Pearson Education, Canada, Ltd
Pearson Education–Japan
Pearson Education Australia PTY, Limited

Pearson Education North Asia Ltd
Pearson Educación de Mexico, S.A. de C.V.
Pearson Education Malaysia, Pte. Ltd
Pearson Education, Upper Saddle River, New Jersey

10 9 8 7 6 5 4 3 2 1

ISBN 0-13-182371-X

PREFACE

The title of this book, *Inquiry*, reflects the process at its heart. In *Inquiry*, a wide variety of writers are searching, from a wide range of academic and social perspectives, for answers to important questions. The book, in fact, is filled with questions: Questions define and organize the chapters, questions stimulate thought before and after the readings, and questions call for connections at the chapters' ends. Inquiry is, by definition, a process of asking questions and trying out answers. Active reading demands the same kind of process. So does writing. Our hope is that students using this book will produce writing that is worth reading, because it will be writing based on inquiry. Long after the completion of the course using *Inquiry*, the process of inquiry, so central to reading and writing, should remain with the students.

Organization

Good questions are at the heart of good reading and writing. Thus, this book focuses on key issues for writers by posing six major questions of perennial interest:

1. Identity: How do I know who I am?
2. Thinking: How do we know what we know?
3. Ethics: What principles do—and should—govern our personal lives?
4. Values: What are human rights and responsibilities?
5. Reinterpretations/Contexts: What can we learn from the past?
6. Predictions: What will the future be like?

These questions differ significantly from many questions we common-ly ask, because they have no right answers. The questions are intended to stimulate critical thinking, to encourage thoughtful examination of what others have to say, and to help develop independent ideas. Each chapter's readings, by significant writers—from Plato to Stephen Hawking, from Frederick Douglass to Leslie Marmon Silko—approach a central question, from many different fields of study and many different social perspectives. Students pursuing the ideas that the ques-tions pose will be considering their own views in light of what these other writers have had to say.

The central question of each chapter is subdivided into three more specific subquestions. Thus, Chapter 1—"Identity: How Do I Know Who I Am?"—has three groups of readings centered on the following subquestions: (1) What is my physical self? (2) Who am I in relation to others? (3) How do language and literacy affect my identity? The read-ings grouped under each subquestion present different approaches to the topic, different perspectives and positions. Active readers will need to examine not only the readings, but their own lives for possible an-swers, perspectives, and parallels.

Readings

Inquiry by definition is open to many methods of pursuit and many individual perspectives; therefore, we have included a wide variety of authors taking differing approaches to the specific chapter ques-tions. In our choice of readings, we have been particularly attentive to the various discourse communities that make up the American university. Although some readings do not fit neatly into such cate-gories, of course, and some fit approximately into several, almost every student will find some readings in or very close to his or her major field of study. Approximately half of the readings are from the humanities, including philosophical and reflective writing and such literature as autobiography and personal essays. Many of the read-ings are from the social and behavioral sciences, including anthro-pology, economics, history, political science, psychology, and sociology. Likewise, the natural sciences are well represented, with readings from astronomy, physics, biology, chemistry, environmen-tal studies, computer science, and medicine. In fact, in preparing this book, we have consulted with our colleagues in a variety of disci-plines to ensure cross-curricular perspectives, although we have in-cluded only readings appropriate to our audience of undergraduate students.

Inquiry also represents the diversity of American culture. Almost half of our authors are women, and we have strong representation from many of the ethnic communities that make up the United States today. Issues of ethnicity and gender recur throughout, as is appropriate for a book whose opening chapter asks, "How Do I Know Who I Am?"

Chapter Introductions

The introduction to each of the six chapters provides background for the question and subquestions, an overview of that chapter's readings, a discussion of a specific rhetorical concept for writers, and preliminary questions for discussion and writing. Each of these four sections has a distinct purpose.

"Why Consider This Question?" opens each chapter introduction by discussing the meaning of the chapter question. For example, the second chapter asks, "How Do I Know What I Know?"—very different from alternative and simpler versions of the question such as "What Do I Know?" We begin each introduction by emphasizing the complexity and challenge of its central question, which governs not only the choice of reading selections, but also the direction of all the other questions in the chapter.

The second section of each introduction presents the three subquestions that shape the chapter, with a brief commentary about each reading. Here, we give an overview of the chapter's contents and discuss how the readings relate to one another and to the chapter's questions.

Rhetorical concepts are best taught in context, as a way of addressing the reading and writing problems that emerge from engagement with a text; therefore, the third section of each introduction defines and exemplifies a rhetorical concept appropriate to the chapter question. Notice how the sequence of six rhetorical concepts, each loosely related to the central question of its chapter, covers the rhetorical issues associated with most college writing courses:

1. writing for an audience
2. writing as a means of learning: the writing processes
3. definition
4. argument and evidence
5. use of sources
6. discourse communities

The "Questions for Discovery and Discussion" that conclude each introduction ask students to begin thinking about the central question of the chapter in light of what they already know. Students who discuss or write about the question prior to their reading are in a better position to read actively; the readings become encounters with the ways other writers have dealt with the same ideas and issues.

Questions

The "Responding to Reading" questions that follow each reading are also meant to be used for discussion or writing. Some of these are designed to deepen students' understanding of the particular reading, while others ask students to make connections between that reading and other readings, or between that reading and their own lives. At the end of each chapter are "Questions for Reflection and Writing," pertinent to the entire chapter, that ask students to consider the ways that the selections have enriched and deepened their own thoughts. In keeping with the concept of inquiry, the book contains over four hundred questions of one sort or another; our hope is that every instructor will find ample materials for discussion and writing, whatever the level of the students and goals of the class.

Headnotes

We have taken special care with the headnotes that precede readings. Each headnote provides a ready biographical reference to the author (concise, incisive, and humanizing) and key concepts and terms associated with that author's work. The headnote also serves as an introduction to the reading, identifying its significant intellectual and rhetorical features and providing a lead-in to the "Responding to Reading" questions that follow.

Alternative Ways to Use This Book

The movement from chapter to chapter is a natural one, outward, from one's physical self to the future of the world. Nonetheless, instructors using this book may want to make reading and writing assignments in a different order. Our purpose is to create a textbook that presents a clear curriculum, but that also allows a considerable amount of flexibility to instructors with different students, different curricular goals, and different amounts of class time. Instructors interested in grouping the selections by field of study or by rhetorical concept will find alternative listings at the back of the book to support such rearrangements. We know that many instructors share our belief that inquiry must lie behind both reading and writing, and we urge these colleagues to use the book imaginatively, to ask their own questions, to explore their own answers.

Acknowledgments

No book, even a collaborative work, is the product of its authors alone. Over the years we have listened to many voices; our teachers, our students, and a host of writers—some of whom appear in this book, others whose thinking informs more generally our culture and our profession. Specifically, colleagues who have read and commented on *Inquiry*, in various drafts, include Laura Brady, West Virginia University; Christine Cetrulo, University of Kentucky; Kristine Hansen, Brigham Young University; Susie Paul Johnson, Auburn University, Montgomery; and Laura Stokes, University of California, Davis. Martin Bloom, Beth Borrowman, and Volney White aided our collaboration at long and short distance, cheerfully providing many perspectives on inquiry amidst the comforts of home. Research assistants Kathrine Aydelott, Matthew Simpson, and Lori Corsini–Nelson of the University of Connecticut, have helped *Inquiry* come out on time, with accuracy. We reserve special thanks for Nancy Perry, our creative publisher's editor of the first edition, and Corey Good, editor of this new edition for Prentice-Hall. They both have helped us keep our balance between vision and revision, writing and respite and writing again. Finally, we welcome Shane Borrowman of Gonzaga University, who has contributed information, headnotes and study questions, and who has mounted the Website that contains the instructor's manual and continues our dialogue with our readers. Thirteen years after we began collaborating on the first edition, we remain friends, still fascinated with the joys and complexities of inquiry—and of collaboration.

Lynn Z. Bloom
University of Connecticut Storrs, Connecticut

Edward M. White
University of Arizona, Tucson, Arizona

CONTENTS

CHAPTER 2

THINKING: HOW DO WE KNOW WHAT WE KNOW?   117

WHAT IS THE PROCESS OF THINKING?   131

WHAT ARE SOME WAYS OF UNDERSTANDING NATURE?   163

HOW CAN WE EXPLAIN WHAT WE KNOW?   193

CHAPTER 3

ETHICS: WHAT PRINCIPLES DO—AND SHOULD— GOVERN OUR PERSONAL LIVES?   223

Chapter 4

Values: What Are Human Rights and Responsibilities?   340

all right one night [handwritten annotation]

CHAPTER 5

REINTERPRETATIONS/CONTEXTS:
WHAT CAN WE LEARN FROM THE PAST?   478

Chapter 6

Predictions: What Will the Future Be Like?   604

Introduction

We write, as we read, for a variety of reasons. We also write for a variety of audiences. In saying, "I write for myself and strangers," Gertrude Stein identifies two sets of readers: the author and everyone else. She also implies that there are two major areas of concern for any writer: the need to preserve material for oneself and the need to communicate it to others. Yet no matter what we say or how we say it, we are reacting to what is in the world: reacting on paper, in our minds, and in our hearts. What we write provides some point of view or interpretation for ourselves, our friends, teachers, prospective employers, and strangers. Even something as seemingly arbitrary as a list is rarely random. We choose what to put on the list (our friends, say, on a Christmas card list), what to leave off (former friends), and how to arrange the list (in alphabetical order, or from the most to the least important in case we run out of time or stamps).

Sometimes we write simply to *list facts,* for our own reference or others': people to invite to a party; things to do today or to be put off till tomorrow. Or we write *to record or summarize others' opinions and our own reactions to events, experiences, or reading*: class notes, a reading journal, or a travel diary. At times, we write *to convey information*: directions on how to get downtown or to Bali ("You can get there from here!"); instructions on how to assemble a bicycle or write a computer program; recipes for pasta, potpourri, or the perfect friendship. Or we write *to clarify or interpret information or ideas*: letters to friends and family, final examinations, or job applications.

This book emphasizes *writing as thinking, or inquiry*. Novelist E. M. Forster described his own writing as a process of inquiry: "How do I know what I think until I see what I say?" Writing about the ideas of others enables us not only to understand what they mean, but also to focus our own thoughts: Does the author make sense? What are the essay's main points? Subordinate points? Does its organization reinforce the logic or help the argument to develop? What are the illustrations or supporting information? Does the author tell me something I did not know before? Enable me to see the issue in new ways? Shake up beliefs I have taken for granted? Make me angry, delighted, or inspired to protest the way things are and want to change the world?

Inquiry also raises other questions: Will the issue still look the same if I compare one author with another? Or another? Where do I now stand on the issue? Why? Through sorting out the implications and wrestling with the ideas (reacting to, reaffirming, or taking issue with them), it is possible to enter into a dialogue, spoken or written, with the authors of this book, individually or in combination. As we do so, we are forced to think, to try out ideas, to take a stand. We can find out why we are right, where we are wrong, or what the implications of our thinking are. In this way, we become authors ourselves.

Writing as inquiry has a number of significant features:

- Writing as inquiry needs a *question worth asking*, an issue worth exploring as a starting place. But such value may start only in the mind of the beholder; millions of apples fell, insignificantly, before Isaac Newton asked what principle that implied. Through writing, the question's significance emerges to the writer and readers alike.

- Writing as inquiry is *thought in action*. As your ideas develop, you can expect to make a number of drafts, in your head or on paper. Writing as inquiry is never really finished, since one's thinking is continually in process. Any given draft of a paper, even the "final" one, shows where one's thinking is at one point in time.

- Writing as inquiry requires writers *to have a voice and point of view* of their own; it can never merely report what others have said.

- Writing as inquiry cannot occur in a vacuum. It requires *taking other people's ideas, research, speculations, and disagreements into account*, whether one discounts, disagrees with, or incorporates them into one's own writing.

- Writing as inquiry ultimately requires *a controlling idea or thesis, whether it is stated overtly or implied*. What point (or points) do you want to make? Can you make your point(s) most effectively through an argument that marshalls facts and other evidence selected to lead to an apparently inevitable conclusion? (For example, "We should/should not sacrifice market efficiency to protect the environment.") Or will another mode of writing work better—

a narration, a poem, a satire, or a parody perhaps? (Does Italo Calvino, in Chapter 5, really mean that there was a cleaning woman on the "point" of matter about to become the universe?)

At the heart of *Inquiry* is the premise that *a good question can lead to all sorts of answers.* A good question has intellectual vitality; to answer it may lead to a fundamental understanding about human nature, the quality of life, or the importance of one value or set of values over another. Or it may lead to still more questions, some with answers, some that represent stages in an ongoing dialogue that can never be fully resolved. As editors of this book, we think it is more important to ask exciting questions and explore their possibilities than to define the issues so narrowly that they lead to predictable, safe discussions. Therefore, we have organized *Inquiry* around six fundamental issues, each defined by major questions. That these questions have provoked a variety of lively discussions is indicated by the essays that follow each topic and that resonate with others throughout the book. The questions, with their identifying themes, are as follows:

1. Identity: How do I know who I am?
2. Thinking: How do we know what we know?
3. Ethics: What principles do—and should—govern our personal lives?
4. Values: What are human rights and responsibilities?
5. Reinterpretations/Contexts: What can we learn from the past?
6. Predictions: What will the future be like?

These issues have not yet been resolved and may never be, but they provide a wealth of opportunity for you to express your own point of view, which is, after all, the basic task for every writer. Joan Didion claims that all writers are fundamentally subversive, that they approach the subject and their readers saying, *"Listen to me. See it my way. Change your mind."*

We invite you to participate in this subversive activity. A good way to start your inquiry is by doing some exploratory writing about the given questions as you begin to think about them, before you do much reading. The introduction to each chapter presents a few writing topics to help you focus on the subject. Your thinking and writing will be more interesting if you keep the questions as complex (and messy) as they really are; avoid making them overly simple in search of tidy answers. For example, if you change "How do I know who I am?" into "Who am I?" the revised question can be much less complicated than the first. *"How* do I know who I am?" asks you to focus on how people come to understand themselves and the human condition. That is, the questions in *Inquiry* are concerned with the nature of learning about an issue ("What does it mean to be a member of the human race or of a particular gender?"), rather than going exploring for or finding a specific answer applicable only to a single individual. Such writing, even if it is about yourself, thus becomes of interest to others, since it is not *only* about yourself. Writing at this stage, before you have read much on the subject, can help you start thinking about the subject, asking questions that will be addressed as you read further in the chapter or elsewhere in *Inquiry*. The questions not only are complex, but also ask you to reflect on your own thinking and knowing process. Sometimes this way of approaching issues is called *critical thinking*, since it asks you to examine how that process take place.

The introductions to the chapters, with their discussions of the central question of the chapter, explanations of related rhetorical issues, and exploratory writing assignments, are followed by clusters of readings arranged around three related subquestions. The subquestions allow us to focus the selections on specific issues that generate debate and to illustrate what and how writers from various scholarly perspectives think about the issues. Space limitations permit us to include in *Inquiry* only a few of the many ways of looking at a subject. So we have chosen the writings of major thinkers and influential commentators, people who write well and whose work is not overly specialized and can be understood by general readers. In addition, we have sought writers whose disagreements will lead to continuing debate by those working with the book. The questions following each selection and at the end of each chapter ask not only for careful reading, but also for connections, comparisons, contrasts, and critical thinking.

In order to consider writing as inquiry, you will need to undertake reading as inquiry. As with writing, it is possible to read in many different ways. Sometimes we read passively, to memorize information, such as French verb tenses or vital statistics. Sometimes we read essentially to be able to understand the author's subject matter (What is multiple sclerosis anyway?) or point of view (What are the effects of working mothers on families?). Such reading is valuable, but *Inquiry* expects you to go beyond passive, uncritical ways of reading. Although you will need to read carefully, you should also read with an alert and critical mind. You will be looking for the writer's underlying—and often unstated—definitions and assumptions; you will be examining the evidence and testing it against what you know and what other writers claim. As you form your own opinions, test and challenge the ideas in each essay. Since many of the essays disagree with each other, you will not be able simply to accept what one authority has to say without taking into account conflicting points of view. You will need to understand why their opinions differ, what the grounds for their differences are, and what you find of value in each essay—and what you reject. Write in the margins of the book, argue with the authors, and notice when, where, and why they disagree with one another. Only strong, active readers can become strong, active writers.

None of the writers you read in *Inquiry* has the last word. In this forum, *you* have that privilege—and that responsibility. You might consider your writing as an *evolving interpretation*, a series of drafts that enable you to think through the questions and possible answers raised by your reading. As you write, you will incorporate some of the ideas or perspectives you have read, dispute others, give some opinions and evidence greater weight than others, and dismiss still others out of hand. As you bring later reading and thinking to bear on the issues, your own inquiry should become more knowledgeable and more complicated than your initial writing was—and, possibly, more certain. You may find the question itself to be more interesting than any of the known answers. When Gertrude Stein was dying, her lifelong companion, Alice B. Toklas, is said to have asked, "What is the answer?" To which Stein allegedly replied, "What is the question?" To be able to ask good questions as you read and as you write is ultimately to understand the importance of inquiry in all learning.

Identity
How Do I Know Who I Am?

> *A biography is considered complete if it merely accounts
> for six or seven selves, whereas a person may have as many
> as a thousand.*
> VIRGINIA WOOLF

Why Consider This Question?

We are our most fascinating subjects, for thinking about and for writing. Living intimately with ourselves as we do, we seldom seek to escape or transcend the self, but rather strive to know ourselves more fully. Indeed, "know thyself" might be the motto of our contemporary society. But, what is that self we are to know? If each of us has a core self, what is it? Our genetic makeup remains constant, but old photographs of ourselves, as babies or even five years ago, reveal changes that may overwhelm the continuities—the "family" build, or ears, or set of the smile.

Who is this self we seek to understand, this changing entity that takes its coloration and configuration from changing contexts? Because that self shifts in significant ways according to the roles we choose or have assigned to us throughout our lives, the person we are in class is both the same as and different from the person with the same name, same size, and same shape outside of class. Who is the version of our self who lives in our dorm room or apartment, holds down a job after class, plays music, watches TV, cooks, swims, hangs out with friends? Is the self who votes the same self who pays taxes, worships, makes love (or war)? Who are we, or will we be, when and if we marry, become parents, in-laws, adults with elderly parents, or aged persons

1

ourselves? Will our selves be determined by our roles, our jobs, or our personalities—and chance and luck—or some combination of these?

How, indeed, do we know when we have attained even a partial understanding of the numerous selves that, like Benjamin Franklin's many roles as tradesman, businessman, author, publisher, public citizen, inventor, scholar, statesman, husband, father, and flirt, comprise our essence? By what means can we come to even the limited self-understanding that we will have to live with? One way is by reading others' explorations of themselves. Because we understand what we read, in part, through analogy with our own lives, as we learn about others we can come to understand ourselves.

To examine the question, "How do I know who I am?", this chapter focuses on three clusters of writings that explore the physical self, the social self, and the self that is both expressed and created through language. As these writings make clear, these selves are inextricably intertwined. For instance, the physical self (male or female; gay or straight; black, white, or some other "color") is as much a construct of social interpretation and language as of one's genetic constitution.

What Is My Physical Self?

Many contemporary Americans are concerned with having perfect health and obsessed with having perfect bodies. Many of us have in mind an ideal of what we should look like, even if that ideal is an unreal image constructed and reinforced by the media. We spend considerable effort, worry, and money in trying to make our bodies attain the ideal that fewer than five percent conform to naturally.

If we don't like the way we look, for whatever reason, we can change it. We can exercise and diet for a fit, muscular, or slender body. We can curl, straighten, dye or bleach our hair, shave it off, or wear wigs. We can tan, bleach, and tattoo our skin; straighten our teeth; surgically pare our noses, bellies, and buttocks; use steroids or other drugs to increase our strength, height, and fighting spirit; even alter our sex or cure congenital defects of our offspring in utero. We want to believe that these changes are for the better, notwithstanding the existence of skin cancer, anorexia, bulimia, sterility, and other potentially devastating consequences.

Once we have altered our bodies, with their innumerable surface manifestations that send messages to those who see us (Do blondes *really* have more fun?), are we the same people underneath? Well, yes and no, say the authors in this chapter as they consider the question of identity: "What is my physical self?" All, however, take issue with the conventional conception of the self as an autonomous, coherent, unchanging entity.

Our physical selves gain meaning from the social and political contexts in which we live. Even our most rudimentary biology is not fixed. Many people contend that even gender does not automatically carry with it a cluster of distinctively "male" or "female" characteristics unless society affirms what these are. Maxine Hong Kingston's Tang Ao of "On Discovery," transformed through bound feet, pierced ears, diet, and dress from "male" to "female," is a case in point. Natalie Angier, in "Estrogen, Desire, and Puberty," explores the chemistry behind our identity, but finds us wonderfully complex both because of and despite our hormones. All the essays in this section demonstrate that, in some way, the shape and condition of one's body reflect the possessor's state of mind. And when change occurs, mutation does not have to mean mutilation; it can be a source of new and powerful self-definition, as Nancy Mairs demonstrates in "On Being a Cripple." Here she breaks the taboos of reticence, propriety, and social expectations to face publicly the "brutal truth" of her life as a victim of multiple sclerosis. "As a cripple, I swagger." The last essay in this section, Shelby Steele's "The Age of White Guilt and the Disappearance of the Black Individual," insists that "the age of racism" is past and that it is time to reconsider the social meaning of dark skin. The unconventional perspectives of Steele, Mairs, Kingston, and Angier challenge readers' comfortable assumptions about body shape, size, condition, gender, class, and race; they question their readers' values and shake them up.

Who Am I in Relation to Others?

To be human is to be inextricably involved with other people. The English renaissance poet John Donne, in a famous phrase, said no man, or woman, "is an island, entire of itself." All of us are assigned, and assume, particular roles that are continually changing in response to the way others play their parts: child, parent, student, friend, lover, spouse, in-law, someone at work or at play, or citizen—of a community, a state, a country, the world.

As citizens or residents of the United States, our expectations are influenced by the ideal of the American dream—work hard and you will succeed, not as the member of a team, but as an individual making an extraordinary personal effort. Schoolchildren learn about Benjamin Franklin, striding confidently down the streets of Philadelphia with a large puffy roll in his hands, on his way to success, or Abraham Lincoln shivering and studying before the fireplace in his log cabin on the frontier. In "Resurrection," Frederick Douglass explains how he singlehandedly fought his way out of slavery, defying his overseer with strength, intelligence, and ingenuity. Only then was he able to become an independent human being; his fate was literally in his own hands, as he explains throughout his autobiography.

But even in this land of opportunity, not everyone will be as successful as Benjamin Franklin (who tells us how to "arrive at moral perfection" in Chapter 3) or Frederick Douglass. Some people tailor their expectations to the reality rather than the dream. In "I Just Wanna Be Average," Mike Rose shows how high schools slot students into particular tracks, academic and vocational. "Students will float to the mark you set," he says. If a curriculum does not free its students to aspire to the best, they may "just wanna be average," no better or worse than anyone else, and no different. Joan Didion is even more insistent on the need to be an individual, inner-directed, without regard to one's social context. That crucial component of what she calls "character," *self-respect*, "has nothing to do with the approval of others," she tells us—making an argument that many students will want to challenge.

Finally, Eric Liu and Gloria Anzaldúa examine the way that racism affects their identities as an Asian–American male and as a Hispanic feminist. Each of them agrees in part, but only in part, with Steele; to be an individual in a society that, however friendly, considers you to be (always) foreign, is to be shaped inevitably by others' perceptions. How the individual responds to those perceptions then becomes the test of the self.

How Does My Writing Relate to My Self?

All writing involves some representation of the writer. The writer must decide what to include or leave out and how to arrange the items—a reflection not only of taste, but also of a way to order the world. While lists merely hint at the writer behind them, other writings reveal their authors more explicitly—diaries, letters, personal essays, self-sketches, and autobiographies. Like snapshots, each writing "frames" the writer, highlighting some features, shadowing others, and cropping out others altogether. As writers, we choose the image and we choose our frame. To the extent that we can, we try to control how readers will respond to the self or selves that we have presented.

When writers discuss the ways in which their writing expresses profoundly moving experiences, they disclose an intimate relationship between their words and themselves. Amy Tan, in "Mother Tongue," approaches with love and respect the English dialect that her mother speaks. Tan calls it "her impeccable broken English"; some linguists will call it "international English." But until Tan comes to terms with outside and inner perceptions of that accent, she is not able to write or to come to a full sense of who she really is.

Eudora Welty is another writer who credits her family language experience with shaping her identity and direction. In "Listening," she describes "one writer's beginnings" in her family home in Jackson, Mississippi. Her essay is filled with the sounds of that house, with its clocks ticking and tolling, with its toy trains rushing and clicking, and, above all, with the echoes of words and reading. Unlike Welty's, the childhood of Richard Wright, Welty's contemporary, was marked by poverty, violence, and racial discrimination—some of it in the very same hometown where Welty knew such joy. But Wright too writes about himself as shaped by words. Words, he realizes, can be used "as weapons." As he starts his self-education, he is overcome by words and "the new moods and ideas" that books contain. The books that he must lie to obtain transform his sense of who he is and what he can accomplish.

Finally, Richard Rodriguez provides a case history of his own literacy in "Aria," analyzing his bicultural childhood as a Mexican–American who spoke Spanish at home and English in school. Through this personal example, he argues against bilingual education; rather than being taught first in their native language and then in English, schoolchildren, he argues from his own experience, should be taught in English right from the start to give them the "public identity" that they will need as American citizens. But with the acquisition of that public identity come some wrenching losses, most particularly the silence of his parents and the disappearance of gentle Spanish vowels. As the soft sounds of Ricardo yield to the harsher public sound of Richard, Rodriguez determines who he is and will be.

The authors in this section define themselves through the aspects of their lives that they choose to emphasize in their writing. In all cases, their individual presentations transcend the personal and demonstrate their connections with others: families, members of their community or culture, and the human race. As writers, we can understand from these examples how to use writing not only to discover who we are, but also to disclose some of our various selves to readers, who interpret our experiences and point of view through analogy with their own.

Rhetorical Issues: Writing for an Audience

"I write for myself and strangers," said Gertrude Stein, making explicit the understood principle that guides the writing of most skilled authors, professional or otherwise. In contrast, "I write for myself alone" or "I write for myself and people who know and love me" appears to guide the composition of many less skilled writers who are unaware of or indifferent to what outside readers need to know to understand their writing.

The Audience

Writers aware of an audience ask themselves such questions as, "Who would want to read this?" "Why?" "So what?" Although the questions may sound cynical, the answers are not. Unless our writing is deliberately private, we can expect others to read it. The audience may be specific and predetermined, such as one's teacher, boss, or friends. Or it may be the "strangers" to whom Gertrude Stein referred, anyone who might want to read the work or an imaginary reader to keep in mind as one writes. No writer can anticipate everything that a reader will bring to a given work. Nevertheless, all writers need to consider some characteristics of anticipated readers, for instance, their level of knowledge, cultural heritage, values, and biases. All of us have to consider the same features about ourselves as writers, in order to ensure the intended reception for our writing. We return to this matter of audience in Chapter 6, but for now consider what it means to share your inquiry with others.

Knowledge, general and specialized: As writers, we must consider how much the readers already know about the subject. What else do they need to know in order to understand what I'm saying? What background information will I need to supply? What terms must I define? How simple or technical, general or specialized can my language be? In addition to common sense and common knowledge, do I expect my readers to know as much as an eighth grader (the reading level of many American newspapers), a high-school graduate, or a college student? Do my readers have a hobbyist's interests or a professional-level education in the specialized field my writing addresses? Do I expect my readers to know more about the subject than I do (as would a teacher reading a student's exam), less simply or complexly than I do, or the same amount?

The writer's expectations will determine how to present one's ideas, and in what language; which terms to define, and how much background information—of what sort—and other explanations to include. However, even if we're explaining something elementary, we can avoid condescension by treating our readers as collaborators in the process of gaining an understanding, rather than as an audience to a lecture. Notice, for instance, how Amy Tan helps us see and hear her mother. Her characterization of her mother helps us understand why as an adult Tan has come to respect her mother, and indeed uses her as the imagined audience for the books Tan now writes.

Cultural heritage: If you are an American writing for other Americans, you can assume some aspects of a common cultural heritage. You will not need to explain Oprah or the Alamo or Washington—as long as it is clear whether you are talking about George or Booker T., the District of Columbia, or the state. If you are a typical member of the group for which you are writing, you can use yourself as a reference point. Assume that what you know and take for granted your audience will also understand (whether pom-pom girls or Prohibition, Elvis Presley or the Promised Land). What is strange or difficult for you will be likely to present problems for your readers.

Values: All of us hold values, regardless of whether we explicitly label them as such. We may openly or subtly approve of (or reject) marriage, having children, equal employment opportunities for minorities and women, regular exercise, suburban living, and a host of other aspects of our lives that we take for granted—or question. Our values unavoidably influence the way we treat a topic; even when we try to be even-handed, it is hard not to speak more glowingly of what we approve than of what we disapprove ("Vote the rascals out!" "Never! They're the noble leaders I know and love!"). To accommodate divergent views, try to imagine your subject as some disparate readers might. Suppose that you were writing on dual-career marriages. What would a feminist—man or woman—assume about these? Would a conservative male agree with any of the feminist's assumptions about the role of each wage-earner? Each partner's responsibilities as a parent? As a member of a household? If so, what might be the points of agreement? Of disagreement? Would any of these views coincide with those of a conservative female over 40? Between 25 and 40? Under 25? Each aspect of the issue can assume a different perspective, as revealed in the essays on "How Does Family Heritage Affect Who We Are" in the first section of Chapter 5.

Persona

All writers speak through a persona, the mask or created character they invent to talk to their readers. Readers often believe that because a piece of writing sounds personal—if the author uses *I* or appears as a conspicuous character in the work—it is unaltered autobiography. Nothing could be farther from the truth; a piece of writing intended for an external audience should be as carefully cultivated as a well-tended garden—planted, arranged, pruned, weeded, and shaped to accommodate the aims of both writer and audience.

When scientists write about the natural world, for instance, the authorial persona may be self-effacing, subdued. But even here an authorial character is present through the tone of voice, the presentation of data, and the organization—someone who is authoritative, rigorous, keen-minded, logical, and yet cares deeply about the subject. This persona is "scientific"—but with a heart—see Nathalie Angier (this chapter), Rachel Carson and Stephen Hawking (Chapter 5), or W. French Anderson (Chapter 6).

Writing that seems to be more personal, where the writer's persona more closely and conspicuously corresponds to the known facts of the author's real life, is also shaped to enhance the author's aims. As Joan Didion says in an essay about her work, all writing is "the act of saying *I*, of imposing yourself upon other people, of saying *listen to me, see it my way, change your mind*." In "On Being a Cripple," Nancy Mairs compels an audience of physically able people to experience her version of what it means to be a "cripple," the word she chooses to define herself instead of "disabled," "handicapped," or "differently able." Her persona is quite different from both the objective medical textbook definitions of multiple sclerosis as a collection of symptoms and the smiling-through-tears public persona that often characterizes poster children. Mairs shows herself in action, grotesque ("one arm bent in front of me, the fingers curled into a claw"), clumsy (dropping cans, falling over backward in a public toilet), and fearful of others' pity ("always the terror that people are kind to me only because I'm a cripple"). In exposing her frailties, admitting that she is grouchy and surly, and in laughing at herself, Mairs gives her readers permission to regard her on the same human terms as they regard themselves. In forcing her audience to confront her illness head on, as she does, without evasive delicacy, Mairs forces them to understand it on her terms, in her way. This deeply human persona is no less shaped and crafted than the scientific one.

We have only to think of the different selves that we present in our letters to different people, even on the same subject, to realize how we select and shape evidence, mood, motives, and foreground and background information to render the same experience in different ways on different occasions. As victims of discrimination, Shelby Steele, Frederick Douglass, Eric Liu, Amy Tan, Richard Wright, and Richard Rodriguez offer very different presentations of their subject. If you were to write as a victim of discrimination, for instance, how would you tell your story to your grandparents, your best friends (male or female), your English teacher, a court of law, or the local newspapers? Depending on what you chose to emphasize and suppress, you would probably be a somewhat different character in each account. Your purpose, your audience, and the type of story you decide to tell—a sermon, a cautionary tale, a plea for sympathy or social action, or even a joke—would determine whether you presented yourself as a hero, either bold or unassuming; a victim of circumstances; a rebel bent on revenge; or the embodiment of noble forgiveness.

The language of our writing needs to reinforce our persona, the self we present to our audience. In informal writing, we can imagine ourselves composing a letter to a friend; the friendly, casual, conversational tone incorporating contractions, our everyday vocabulary, and the use of the first person will resemble our actual conversations with that person. If we want to sound more formal, we will choose a less intimate approach to the subject; longer sentences and the more technical vocabulary found in more specialized writings on the subject will communicate a more serious approach.

Finding a Focus

All writing intended for an audience needs to have a focus; readers cannot be expected to come along for the ride until the writer provides the directions. The focus of a paper, like a camera's focus, sharpens one's perspective on a subject, confines it within identifiable boundaries, and presents the resulting interpretation for the readers' response. As Joan Didion says, the writer urges the reader to "see it my way;" keep that image of the focused picture in mind no matter what your other "takes" on the subject may be.

As you examine your subject from all the possible perspectives to find just the right angle, you will be looking for ways to make it your own. It helps to think of the subject as presenting a problem and the paper to be written as offering one or more ways of clarifying or solving the problem. When examining a subject area as a problem, you could look at it in some of the following ways:

- *Define the problem.* What is it? What major issue(s) does it contain? Are there any minor issues or other ways of subdividing a large or vague subject to make it more manageable? Suppose that you want to write about discrimination—a broad topic. What do you want to say about it? One major issue might be whether legislation can effectively address or remedy the problem. But it is first necessary to define and explain the kind of discrimination—such as religious, racial, or gender.

- *Explain the key terms pertinent to the problem.* Sometimes a clarification of terms focuses or even resolves the issue. What exactly do you mean by discrimination? Refusing to rent an apartment to a non-white couple or a single mother? Or, as Shelby Steele sees it, giving a minority candidate or a woman preferential treatment in hiring? Suppose that you chose to focus on the problem as Steele presents it. Just what does "preferential treatment" mean? Or "affirmative action"? Are these synonyms? Do they have the same meaning in all circumstances?

- *Explain the problem.* What are its causes? What are its effects, short-term and in the long-run? Do people (who? what groups?) disagree about the alleged causes or effects? If so, what is the disagreement? For instance, does affirmative action undercut either a merit or a seniority system of hiring and retention? Does it lead to the stereotyping of minorities? Or does it enhance equal opportunity?

- *What is the solution to the problem?* Are there alternative solutions? Can the problem be resolved at all? Would preferential treatment in hiring actually solve the problems that it is intended to remedy? Or would it lead to earlier firings ("last hired, first fired") or to reverse-discrimination suits? Are other solutions feasible or only different ways of perpetuating inequality?

- *Which solutions are most necessary? Desirable? Feasible? Likely to be put into effect?* Why? How can the possible solutions be effected? Are there conflicts, actual or potential, among the alternatives? For example, what is the relation of a quota system to merit hiring or retention?

- *Which individuals or groups favor which solutions?* Why? Which stand(s) to gain or lose the most from which solutions? Why? Whose views should be given precedence? Under what circumstances?

- *What will be the consequences of any given solution?* On what basis can these be predicted? Will they be permanent? Temporary? Are they contingent on still other factors, controllable or uncontrollable?

- *Are some consequences preferable to others?* On what basis? Ethical? Political? Social? Economic? Religious? Expediency?

Here are some other perspectives from which to examine your subject. For instance, you might consider its *static* or *dynamic characteristics*. If you regard something as static, you will be treating it at a particular moment in time. Although if might be possible to freeze an object, such as a car, in time, anything that involves policy, values, or activity (for instance, affirmative action) is a dynamic part of a process that changes over time, space, and circumstances. Is the "desegregation" of the 1960s, manifested through integrated schools and lunch counters, the same as affirmative action of the twenty-first century, giving women in the military the opportunity to serve in front-line combat or employees who test HIV positive for AIDS the right to keep this information confidential?

You could consider the dynamics of the subject in relation to the various ways you view it, from *psychological, chronological,* or *physical distance.* Would you have seen affirmative action differently when you were a child from the way you do now as an adult? How close you are to the subject will undoubtedly affect your views; familiarity breeds understanding. If you or people you know have been the victims of discrimination, these experiences will probably be more important than those less immediate; the more recent or profound the experience, the more memorable it appears.

It is also useful to consider your subject from the perspective of *figure/ground*. How does the issue appear in isolation? How does it appear in relation to others like itself? In relation to things different from itself? To what extent is it influenced by its context? And, perhaps most importantly, how has the process of your thinking about the subject changed your views even as you contemplated it? How can you compel your readers to care about the subject as much as you do—and to see it your way?

Finally, writing for an audience is a human relationship that shares many elements with the other human relationships you engage in all of the time. You want to remain aware of your audience and of how you present yourself and your ideas to that audience. Your choice and use of words tell your readers who you are.

QUESTIONS FOR DISCOVERY AND DISCUSSION

1. Compose three brief descriptions of yourself, from your own point of view.
   A. Describe yourself physically, so precisely that a stranger in the room could pick you out from everyone else in the room.
   B. Now describe yourself as a member of your family or some other group.
   C. Then describe the person you would like to be ten years from now. Notice that you will be creating this person through your writing.

   Review your three descriptions, and find the relationship among them. For what audience have you written? Who are you really? How do you know who you are?

2. Compose three brief descriptions of yourself, from an outside point of view.
   A. Describe yourself as might someone who has just met you for the first time.
   B. Follow this with a description of yourself as you appear to most people who know you.
   C. Then, describe yourself the way your best friend or your favorite family member would.

   Review your three descriptions, and reflect on what they say about you. How do they relate to your responses to Question 1? Have you written for the same audience? How do other people know who you are?

What Is My Physical Self?

On Discovery

MAXINE HONG KINGSTON

Maxine Hong Kingston was the first of her parents' six children who were born in America—in Stockton, California, in 1940. Her book *Woman Warrior: Memories of a Girlhood Among Ghosts* (1975) was in 1990 "the most widely taught book by a living writer in U.S. colleges and universities." It is, according to reviewer William Mc Pherson of the *Washington Post Book World*, "a strange, sometimes savagely terrifying . . . wonderful story of growing up caught between two . . . alien cultures." In an interview she commented on the subject of her writing: "My family is more imaginative and brave than most people. They've had more adventures, more triumphs and defeats. They've traveled half-way round the world. They're people with big lives. And I guess I think this about all Chinese people: They have an amazing amalgam of practicality and imagination. Maybe that's the Chinese spirit—to embody those two wildly different world views."

"On Discovery," from Kingston's second book, *China Men* (1980), expresses the dual vision of this Chinese–American writer, educated in Chinese and American schools and holding a B.A. from the University of California at Berkeley. At home she spoke Chinese, her only language until she started first grade. She also learned Chinese customs from stories exchanged in her parents' laundry. As this passage from *Woman Warrior* illustrates, discrimination against women pervaded the traditional Chinese culture, including the selling of girls into slavery: "Eight-year-olds were about twenty dollars. Five-year-olds were ten dollars and up. Two-year-olds were about five dollars. Babies were free."

Kingston's writing reflects her experience with both racial and sexual stereotyping. Tang Ao's transformation in the Land of Women, as recounted in "On Discovery," presents a contemporary interpretation of the values embedded in traditional roles of Chinese men and women. Although on one level Kingston's writings can be read as a feminist protest against sex discrimination in China, on other levels they can be seen as a celebration of the complexity, vitality, and endurance of the ancient Chinese culture in contemporary America, with women as vigorous participants.

1   Once upon a time, a man, named Tang Ao, looking for the Gold Mountain, crossed an ocean, and came upon the Land of Women. The women immediately captured him, not on guard against ladies. When they asked Tang Ao to come along, he followed; if he had had male companions, he would've winked over his shoulder.

12

"We have to prepare you to meet the queen," the women said. They locked him in a canopied apartment equipped with pots of make-up, mirrors, and a woman's clothes. "Let us help you off with your armor and boots," said the women. They slipped his coat off his shoulders, pulled it down his arms, and shackled his wrists behind him. The women who kneeled to take off his shoes chained his ankles together.

A door opened, and he expected to meet his match, but it was only two old women with sewing boxes in their hands. "The less you struggle, the less it'll hurt," one said, squinting a bright eye as she threaded her needle. Two captors sat on him while another held his head. He felt an old woman's dry fingers trace his ear; the long nail on her little finger scraped his neck. "What are you doing?" he asked. "Sewing your lips together," she joked, blackening needles in a candle flame. The ones who sat on him bounced with laughter. But the old women did not sew his lips together. They pulled his earlobes taut and jabbed a needle through each of them. They had to poke and probe before puncturing the layers of skin correctly, the hole in the front of the lobe in line with the one in back, the layers of skin sliding about so. They worked the needle through—a last jerk for the needle's wide eye ("needle's nose" in Chinese). They strung his raw flesh with silk threads; he could feel the fibers.

The women who sat on him turned to direct their attention to his feet. They bent his toes so far backward that his arched foot cracked. The old ladies squeezed each foot and broke many tiny bones along the sides. They gathered his toes, toes over and under one another like a knot of ginger root. Tang Ao wept with pain. As they wound the bandages tight and tighter around his feet, the women sang foot-binding songs to distract him: "Use aloe for binding feet and not for scholars."

During the months of a season, they fed him on women's food: the tea was thick with white chrysanthemums and stirred the cool female winds inside his body; chicken wings made his hair shine; vinegar soup improved his womb. They drew the loops of thread through the scabs that grew daily over the holes in his earlobes. One day they inserted gold hoops. Every night they unbound his feet, but his veins had shrunk, and the blood pumping through them hurt so much, he begged to have his feet re-wrapped tight. They forced him to wash his used bandages, which were embroidered with flowers and smelled of rot and cheese. He hung the bandages up to dry, streamers that dropped and draped wall to wall. He felt embarrassed; the wrappings were like underwear, and they were his.

One day his attendants changed his gold hoops to jade studs and strapped his feet to shoes that curved like bridges. They plucked out each hair on his face, powdered him white, painted his eyebrows like a moth's wings, painted his cheeks and lips red. He served a meal at the queen's court. His hips swayed and his shoulders swiveled because of his shaped feet. "She's pretty, don't you agree?" the diners said, smacking their lips at his dainty feet as he bent to put dishes before them.

7   In the Women's Land there are no taxes and no wars. Some scholars say that the country was discovered during the reign of Empress Wu (A.D. 694–705), and some say earlier than that, A.D. 441, and it was in North America.

RESPONDING TO READING

1. By what process(es) is Tang Ao transformed from a man to a woman, physically, psychologically, and socially?
2. What is Tang Ao's personality like before, during, and after this process? Why does he willingly submit to his captors, even to the painful process of foot binding?
3. What definition of woman emerges from this parable? Why is this definition a feminist protest? Against what? What else does the parable protest?
4. Is this parable fair to men? Does it, or any parable or other literary work, have to be fair, to provide equal representation of all likely stands on an issue?
5. How does the reader of a parable know to read the work not as a literal truth, but as analogous to real life? In what way does Kingston let her readers know they are reading a parable rather than a literally true story?

Estrogen, Desire, and Puberty

NATALIE ANGIER

Natalie Angier, born in 1958, graduated from Barnard College in 1978. Angier has worked as a journalist and staff writer for *Discover, Savvy,* and *Time* and has also taught journalism at New York University. She is currently a science writer for the *New York Times.* To do the research for her first book, *Natural Obsessions: The Search for Oncogene* (1988), an exploration of the world of cancer cell research, Angier spent several months shadowing medical researchers at the Whitehead Institute of the Massachusetts Institute of Technology. Angier's second book, *The Beauty of the Beastly: New Views on the Nature of Life* (1995), is a collection of essays on "all levels of life forms from roundworms to dolphins." Her most recent book, the well-received *Woman: An Intimate Geography* (1999), offers a feminist perspective on major aspects of female biology—beginning with cells and chromosomes, moving on to various aspects of the body (in "Default Line," for instance, Angier asks, "Is the Female Body a Passive Construct?"), to muscle structure, the chemistry of love, and evolutionary psychology. "Estrogen, Desire, and Puberty" is drawn from the chapter "Venus in Furs" in this text.

In "Estrogen, Desire, and Puberty," Angier writes that "Hormones change everything" when we examine the motivations behind behavior, particularly when human free will (or the lack thereof) is discussed. Specifically, Angier explores the maelstrom of adolescence through which women must navigate as they leave childhood behind—a journey made more difficult by both biology and culture. She writes, "Girls learn from women: fake women, amalgamated women, real women," and they must, therefore, learn to see through the world—and through the biological forces acting upon them.

... The moment a young girl enters adolescence, she begins   1
dwelling on sex, consciously, unconsciously, in her dreams, alone in the bath—however or wherever it happens, it happens. Her desire is aroused. The changes of puberty are largely hormonal changes. The shifting of the chemical setting stirs desire. Intellectually, we accept the idea that sexuality is a hormonally inflected experience, but we still resent the connection. If hormones count, we worry that they count too much and that therefore we have no free will, and so we deny that they count, all the while knowing that they count, because we see it in our teenage children and we remember, please goddess, our teenage greed.

Rather than denying the obvious, we should try to appreciate the   2
ways in which estrogen and other hormones affect behavior. Granted, our knowledge of neurobiology is primitive, presimian. We don't understand how estrogen or any other substance works on the brain to elicit desire, or feed a fantasy, or muffle an impulse. But there are enough indirect strands of evidence to knit a serviceable thinking cap with which to mull over estrogen's meaning.

Desires and emotions can be fleeting, mayflies in the brain. They're   3
born and they're gone. But they can also be persistent. They can change from whims to obsessions. If an emotion or drive is going to persist and resonate, a hormone is a useful object to turn to for the task. In the brain, steroid hormones generally work together with one or more of the neuropeptides. A neuropeptide is quick and transient. A steroid hormone is resilient and insistent. They work synergistically on neural circuits that subserve motive and behavior, integrating psyche with body. Take the sensation of thirst. When your body is low in water and salt, it reacts vigorously, because we all once dwelled in the sea and our cells still must be bathed in salty water to survive. Among the responses is the activation of the adrenal glands, which secrete steroid hormones such as aldosterone. Aldosterone is a practical hormone, and it seeks to conserve the supplies that exist—for instance, by reabsorbing salt from urine or gastric juice and returning it to the fluid between cells. Aldosterone also infiltrates the brain, where it galvanizes the activity of a neuropeptide, angiotensin. The neuropeptide in turn arouses the brain's circuitry of thirst. You feel thirsty. You have an urge to drink.

The sensation can usually be satisfied with ease, with a glass of water, and the adrenals and the thirst locus settle down. But if your requirements for fluid and sodium are unusually large, as they are during breastfeeding, you will be awash in aldosterone and very efficient in your use of water and salt, but you will also feel chronically parched, and you will wonder if the Nile itself is large enough to slake you, and you will love salty foods as you never did before.

4   An emotion is a piece of information. It is a signal of need, of a temporary lapse in homeostasis. It is the body's way of encouraging or inhibiting behaviors, which the body hopes will fulfill the need and restore balance. We don't usually think of thirst as an emotion, but that's what it is, an emotion of the body's interstitial spaces. As an emotion, thirst can be disregarded or overruled by competing demands. If you are running a race in the heat and feel thirsty, you might ignore the desire rather than stop to drink and lose precious time and weigh your belly down with fluids. Panic can bring on enormous thirst, in part because the adrenal activity that comes with fear unleashes the flow of angiotensin in the brain; but panic can also clench the throat and stomach and make the thought of drink or food repulsive. Still, thirst gives you a comparatively short leash. You can only ignore it so long—a week without water, and you will die of dehydration. The synergistic impact of neuropeptide and steroid hormone on the circuitry overseeing the behavior of fluid acquisition is therefore quite extreme. The longer you refuse to engage in the requested behavior, drinking, the more exaggerated your adrenal output becomes and the more overwhelming the desire is. At some point, as you near death, you will drink anything—poisoned water, sea water that is too salty for your body to use. Even Jesus could not conquer thirst, and died with vinegar moistening his lips.

5   If, however, you don't reproduce during a particular cycle, it won't kill you. Humans are long-lived creatures who operate on the implicit assumption that they will have many opportunities to breed and can afford to override the whims and impulses of Eros for months, years, decades, and, oops, a lifetime if conditions of the moment are not quite optimal. Animals in whom reproductive drives are as relentless as thirst are short-lived species who may have only one or two breeding seasons in which to leave their Mendelian badge on the world. A corollary of longevity is a rich emotional life and a complex sexuality. We mistakenly equate emotionality with the primitive and rationality with the advanced, but in fact the more intelligent the animal, the deeper its passions. The greater the intelligence, the greater the demand on the emotions, the portmanteaus of information, to expand their capacity and multiply their zippers and compartments.

6   We impugn emotions, but we are lucky to be so thick with them. They give us something to think about and decode. We are brilliant be-

cause of them, not in spite of them. Hormones are part of the suitcase, and they are part of the contents. They relay information about themselves, and they carry information about others. They do not make us do anything, but they may make the doing of something easier or more pleasurable when all else conspires in favor of it.

Estrogen, puckish estrogen, works through many intermediaries   7
in the brain, many neuropeptides and neurotransmitters. It works through nerve growth factor, and it works through serotonin, a neuropeptide best known for its role in depression. It works through natural opiates and it works through oxytocin. It may be thought of as a conjoiner or a facilitator, or as leavening, like yeast or baking soda. Estrogen has no particular emotion in mind, yet it permits emoting. For years researchers have sought to link estrogen levels to women's sexual behavior. The assumption is logical. Estrogen concentrations rise steadily as the egg follicle grows each month, peaking with the moment of ovulation, when the egg is released into the fallopian tube. If the egg has a need, a desire to be fertilized, in theory it could make the need known to the brain through estrogen, and estrogen would then stimulate a neuropeptide to encourage a particular behavior—to wit, seeking a sexual partner like a thirsty pedestrian seeks a water fountain.

The difficulties of correlating estrogen to human sexual behavior   8
are considerable. What sort of behavior are you looking at? What are the relevant data points? Frequency of intercourse? Frequency of orgasm? Frequency of masturbation or sexual fantasy? The sudden urge to buy *Cosmopolitan*? Here is what we know. There is no association between rate of intercourse and where a woman is in her ovulatory cycle. Women do not have sex more often during ovulation than they do at any other time of the month, unless they're consciously on the fertility quest. But the completion of a behavior tells you little about the subliminal provocations of that behavior. If you plot the incidence of intercourse among couples, you'll see an amazing statistical high point, and it's called the weekend—not because people necessarily feel sexy each Sunday, but because people have sex when it's convenient, when they're not exhausted by work, and when they have the whole day to toy with. A hormone may lead you to water, but it can't make you drink.

There is also no correlation between estrogen levels and physical   9
arousability—the tendency of the genitals to swell and lubricate in response to an overt sexual stimulus, such as a lovemaking scene in a movie. Women have been shown to be fairly invariate in their display of physiological arousal, regardless of their cycle. But physiological arousal says little about meaningful sexual motivation or hunger, for some women will lubricate during rape, and Ellen Laan, of the University of Amsterdam, has shown that women's genitals congest robustly

when they watch pornography that the women later describe as stupid, trite, and distinctly unerotic.

10   We get a somewhat better kinship between hormones and sexuality when we look at desire rather than at genital performance. Some studies have taken female initiation of sex as the marker of desire. The results have varied considerably, depending on the type of birth control used, but they list in the predicted direction. Women on oral contraceptives, which interfere with normal hormonal oscillations, are no more likely to come on to their partners at the middle of the cycle than they are at other times. When the birth control method is reliable but nonhormonal—a vasectomized husband, for example—women show a tendency to be the initiators of sex at the peak of ovulation more than they are during other times of the month, suggesting that the estrogen high is beckoning to them. Add in the complicating factor of a less trustworthy barrier, such as a diaphragm or condom, and the likelihood of midpeak propositioning subsides. No great enigma there: if you don't want to get pregnant, you might not be eager to fool around when you think you're at your most fertile. In a study of lesbian couples, who have no fear of pregnancy, don't use birth control, and are free of supposedly confounding factors of male expectations and manipulations, psychologists found that women were about 25 percent more likely to initiate sex and had twice as many orgasms during the midpoint of their cycle than at other times of the month.

11   The strongest correlations between hormones and sexuality are seen when pure, disembodied desire is the object of scrutiny. In one large study, five hundred women were asked to take their basal temperatures every day for several months and to mark down the day of the month when they first noticed the stirrings of sexual desire. The pooled results show an extraordinary concordance between the onset of sexual hunger and the time that basal temperature readings suggest the women were at or nearing ovulation. Women may even express desire through unconscious body language. In a study of young women who spent a lot of time dancing in nightclubs, the scientists found that as the women approached the day of ovulation, their outfits became progressively skimpier, more flaunting of flesh: the hemlines rose with estrogen levels as if with a bull market. (Of course, it doesn't hurt that midcycle is also the best time to wear your tightest and most revealing clothing, as that is when you are free of premenstrual water retention and blemishes and any fear of leaking menstrual blood.)

12   A number of researchers lately have suggested that it is testosterone, not estrogen, that is the "true" hormone of libido, in men and women alike. They point out that the ovaries generate testosterone as well as estrogen and that androgen levels spike at midcycle just as estrogen levels do. How can we neglect testosterone when men have so

much of it and men love sex so madly, don't they? Many textbooks on human sexuality declare flatly that testosterone is the source of all lust, and some women have added testosterone to their hormone replacement regimens in an effort to shore up their ebbing libido. But if testosterone is relevant to female lust, evidence suggests that it is as a handmaiden to estrogen rather than as Eros descended. As it happens, some proteins in the blood will cling to both testosterone and estrogen and in so clinging prevent the hormones from penetrating the barrier between blood and brain. Estrogen accelerates the production of these binding proteins, but the proteins have a slight preference for testosterone. Hence, as the levels of sex hormones and binding proteins climb with the menstrual cycle, the binding proteins seek out testosterone prejudicially, defusing it in the blood below before it can accomplish much of psychodynamic interest above. The testosterone proves useful indirectly, though: by occupying the binding proteins, it frees estrogen to reach the brain unimpeded. This power of distraction could explain why testosterone therapy works for some women with low libidos: it keeps the blood proteins busy and lets estrogen breaststroke straight to the brain.

But to view estrogen as the hormone of libido is to overstate it and   13 underrate it. If estrogen is the messenger of the egg, we should expect the brain to pay attention, but not in any simple, linear fashion. Just as the mechanics of our genitals have been released from the hormonal chokehold, so have our motives and behaviors. We would not appreciate a hormonal signal that is a blind nymphomaniac, an egg groupie, telling us we're horny and must fornicate. We do not want to indulge an egg just because it is there. We live in the world, and we have constraints and desires of our own. What we might like, though, is a pair of well-appointed glasses, to read the fine print better. Estrogen's basic behavioral strategy is to hone the senses. It pinches us and says, Pay attention. A number of studies have suggested that a woman's vision and sense of smell are heightened at ovulation. So too do the senses shine at other times of high estrogenicity, such as right before menstruation, when your progesterone levels have dropped way down and left estrogen to act unopposed. During pregnancy, you can smell a dirty cat box from two flights away, and you can see dim stars and the pores on every face you meet. It must be emphasized that we don't *need* estrogen to pay attention or to smell a thing, but there it is, coursing from blood to brain and lending the brain a mild buzz, just as it does the bones and heart and breast and little gray basket.

If estrogen is to help at all, it should help us best when our minds   14 must be wonderfully concentrated. Ovulation is a time of danger and of possibility. Estrogen is like hunting magic, the hallucinogenic drug that Amazonian Indians extract from the skin of the poison-dart frog to lend them the sensorial strength of heroes. The more we are of the world, the greater are our chances of meeting others who suit us, but the more incumbent it is on us to notice and assess those around us. If there is such a thing as feminine intuition, it may lie in the occasional gift of a really sweet estrogen high, the great emulsifier, bringing together disparate observations. But estrogen is also at the behest of history and current affairs. If you are in a sour, reclusive mood to begin with, the hump of estrogen at ovulation, or its unopposed premenstrual energy, may make you feel more rather than less reclusive. Estrogen is a promoter, not an initiator. We can understand this by considering how estrogen contributes to breast cancer. The hormone is not, strictly speaking, a carcinogen. It does not crack or destabilize the genetic material of breast cells, in the way radioactivity or toxins such as benzene can. Yet if an abnormal cell exists, estrogen may stoke and stimulate it, abetting its growth until a minor aberration that might otherwise regress or be cleaned up by the immune system survives and expands to malignant dimensions.

15   The strength of estrogen lies in its being context-dependent. It does not make us do anything, but it may make us notice certain things we might otherwise neglect. Estrogen may enhance sensory perception, giving us a slight and fluctuating advantage overlaid on the background of the self. If we are good, we may have our moments of being very, very good, and if we are mediocre, well, we can blame it on our hormones. They are there to be used.

16   As a lubricant for learning, estrogen is of greatest benefit in young women, who are sorting themselves out and gathering cues and experiences. Young women may reap advantages from intuition for lack of anything better to draw on as they assess the motives and character of another. But we can become too enamored of our intuitive prowess, our insight into others, and believe too unshakably in the correctness of our snap judgments. The older we get, the softer the peaks and valleys of our estrogen cycles are, and the less we need them and their psychotogglings. Experience, after all, is a trustworthier friend than intuition. How many times do you have to encounter a man who reminds you of your cold, aloof, angry, hypercritical, and infinitely alluring father before you can recognize the phenotype in your sleep and know enough to keep your eyes and nose and hormones far, far away? . . .

17   We each of us have but one chemistry set and brain to explore, and the effects of estrogen will vary from head to head. Yet if there is a principle to be drawn from the general recognition that hormones can stimulate and emulsify the brain and sensitize it to experience and input, it is this: puberty counts. Under the influence of steroid hormones, the brain in early adolescence is a brain expanding, a Japanese flower

dropped in water. It is also vulnerable to the deposition of dreck and pain, which can take a lifetime to dump back out again. The plasticity of the pubertal mind is grievously underestimated. We've obsessed over the brain of early childhood and the brain of the fetus, and though those brains matter deeply to the development of all-round intelligence, character, and skill, the adolescent brain counts in another way. As the brain stumbles toward maturity, and as it is buffeted by the output of the adrenal glands at age ten and of the gonads a year or two later, it seeks to define itself sexually and socially. The brain of a prepubertal girl is primed to absorb the definitions of womanness, of what counts and what doesn't, of what power is and how she can get it or how she will never get it. We've all heard about the crisis of self-confidence that supposedly strikes girls as they leave childhood and climb the Bunker Hill of junior high, but what has been less recognized is the correspondence between this period of frailty, this tendency for the personality to mutate beyond recognition, and the hormonal squall in the head. The pubertal brain is so aware of the world that it throbs, it aches, it wants to find the paths to calm it down and make sense of the world. It is an exposed brain, as tender as a molted crab, and it can be seared deeply. Who can forget adolescence? And who has ever recovered from it?

At the same time that hormones challenge the pubertal brain, they 18
change the body. A girl's high estrogen content helps in the deposition of body fat on the breasts, hips, thighs, and buttocks, subcutaneously, everywhere. Because of estrogen and auxiliary hormones, women have more body fat than men. The body of the average woman is 27 percent fat, that of the average man 15 percent fat. The leanest elite female athletes may get their body fat down to 11 or 12 percent, but that is nearly double the percentage of body fat found on the elite male athlete, who is as spare as a pronghorn antelope. We can look at the deposition of body fat that comes with womanhood and say it's natural for girls to fatten up when they mature, but what *natural* means is subject to cultural definition, and our culture still hasn't figured out how to handle fat. On the one hand, we're getting fatter by the year, we westerners generally and North Americans particularly, and why should we expect otherwise? We are stapled to our desks; food is never far from our hands and mouths, and that food tends to be starchy and fatty and overrich; and we get exercise only if we exert willpower, not because sustained body movement is an integrated feature of work, social life, or travel. On the other hand, we are intolerant of fatness, we are repulsed by it, and we see it as a sign of weak character and sloth. Contradictory messages assail us from all sides: we must work all the time, the world is a competitive place, and technology requires that our

work be sedentary, cerebral, but we must not get too fat, because fat is unhealthy and looks self-indulgent. So we must exercise and control our bodies, because our natural lives won't do it for us.

19   Girls, poor girls, are in the thick of our intolerance and vacillation. Girls put on body fat as they pass into adulthood. They put on fat more easily than boys do, thank you very much, Lady Estradiol. And then they are subject to the creed of total control, the idea that we can subdue and discipline our bodies if we work very very hard at it. The message of self-control is amplified by the pubescent brain, which is flailing about for the tools to control and soothe itself and to find what works, how to gather personal and sexual power. Dieting becomes a proxy for power, not simply because girls are exposed through the media to a smothering assemblage of slender, beautiful models, but because adolescent girls today are laying down a bit of fat in an era when fat is creeping up everywhere and is everywhere despised. How is a girl to know that her first blush of fatness will ever stop, when we're tearing our hair out over how the national fat index keeps on rising and we must wrestle it to the ground right *now*?

20   There are other, obvious reasons that a girl's brain might decide that a fixation on appearance is the swiftest route to power. There are too many of these *Beauty 'n' You, Beast* magazines around, far more than when I was a prepubescent girl circa 1970. (There were too many of them back then.) Supermarkets now offer no-candy checkout aisles for parents who don't want their children screaming for Mars bars as they wait in line. Where are the no-women's-magazine aisles? Where are the aisles to escape from the fascism of the Face? Any sane and observant girl is bound to conclude that her looks matter and that she can control her face as she controls her body, through makeup and the proper skin care regimen and parsing her facial features and staying on guard and paying attention and thinking about it, really thinking about it. No wonder a girl loses confidence. If she is smart, she knows that it is foolish to obsess over her appearance. It is depressing and disappointing; for this she learned to read, speak passable Spanish, and do calculus? But if she is smart, she has observed the ubiquitous Face and knows of its staggering power and wants that power. A girl wants to learn the possible powers. By all indications, a controlled body and a beautiful face practically guarantee a powerful womanhood.

21   I'm not saying anything new here, but I argue that people should see adolescence as an opportunity, a fresh coat of paint on the clapboards of the brain. Girls learn from women: fake women, amalgamated women, real women. The Face is inescapable, but it can be raspberried, sabotaged, emotionally exfoliated. Repetition helps. Reas-

suring a girl that she is great and strong and gorgeous helps. The exhilarating, indoctrinating rah-rah spirit of the new girl-power movement helps. Girls helping each other helps, because girls take cues from other girls as well as from women. Ritual helps, and anti-ritual helps. We can denude totemic objects and reinfuse them with arbitrary mania. Girls can use lipstick to draw scarification patterns on each other's backs or faces, or a line of supernumerary nipples from armpit to pelvis. Build a hammock with brassieres and fill it with doughnuts and Diet Coke. Combine the covers of women's magazines with cut-out parts from nature magazines to make human-animal chimerical masks: Ellephant MacPherson, Naomi Camel. Glue rubber insects and Monopoly hotels onto the top of a bathroom scale. Girls can imagine futures for each other, with outrageous careers and a string of extraordinary lovers, because it is easier to be generous to another than to yourself, but imagining greatness for a friend makes it thinkable for yourself. Sports help. Karate helps. Sticking by your girlfriends helps. Writing atonal songs with meaningless lyrics helps more than you might think. Learn to play the drums. The world needs more girl drummers. The world needs your wild, pounding, dreaming heart.

RESPONDING TO READING

1. How does Angier's focus on young girls entering puberty, establish a foundation for the arguments she makes about motivation, biology, and desire?

2. What comparisons and contrasts is Angier making, either implicitly or explicitly, between humans and other animals? Between men and women? What purpose do these comparisons/contrasts serve in her argument?

3. In what ways does Angier balance arguments between human free will and biological programming? Does this balance reinforce or refute the observations that she makes about other primates?

4. Either in an essay or in a discussion with other students, come up with possible definitions of "emotion." How does Angier's definition of an emotion as "a piece of information" contradict the definitions you generate? How does her nontraditional definition serve to advance her argument—or yours?

5. Write an essay in which Angier's defininition of the "fascism of the Face" figures prominently in your discussion. (You may feel free to disagreee with her.) What connections does Angier make between this definition and her arguments about the role of cultural behavior and sexuality? Illustrate your essay with examples from your own behavior or the behavior of a friend or two. Do you approve of this behavior, or does it present problems for you or others?

On Being a Cripple

NANCY MAIRS

In her writing, Nancy Mairs (born 1943) aims "to speak the unspeakable [and] to expose ways in which [her] personal experiences inscribe cultural values dangerous to women and other creatures worth preserving." She chose as the epigraph to her book, *Remembering the Bone House* (1989), a quotation from Gaston Bachelard's *The Poetics of Space*: "Not only our memories, but the things we have forgotten are 'housed.' Our soul is an abode. And by remembering 'houses' and 'rooms,' we learn to 'hide' within ourselves." In conceiving of her self, body and soul, as a "bone house," Mairs writes about her life as framed and determined by her body.

As she reveals in *Plaintext* (1986), the collection of autobiographical essays she wrote when earning her doctorate in creative writing at the University of Arizona, Mairs is afflicted with multiple sclerosis. In addition, she has been plagued by allergies, headaches, clinical depression, infections, and fatigue that made her feel as if her bones were changing "from porous calcium to solid granite." Nevertheless, as "On Being a Cripple," from *Plaintext*, makes clear, Mairs's illness governs but does not dominate her life. In this essay, as in some of her other writings, this utterly candid writer presents herself as bitchy, whiny, self-indulgent—but with a redeeming sense of wry humor. We ultimately come to admire her gritty and abrasive personality, but with difficulty, for she succeeds in making her life just as hard for her readers as it has been for her.

> *To escape is nothing. Not to escape is nothing.*
>
> LOUISE BOGAN

1   The other day I was thinking of writing an essay on being a cripple. I was thinking hard in one of the stalls of the women's room in my office building, as I was shoving my shirt into my jeans and tugging up my zipper. Preoccupied, I flushed, picked up my book bag, took my cane down from the hook, and unlatched the door. So many movements unbalanced me, and as I pulled the door open I fell over backward, landing fully clothed on the toilet seat with my legs splayed in front of me: the old beetle-on-its-back routine. Saturday afternoon, the building deserted, I was free to laugh aloud as I wriggled back to my feet, my voice bouncing off the yellowish tiles from all directions. Had anyone been there with me, I'd have been still and faint and hot with chagrin. I decided that it was high time to write the essay.

2   First, the matter of semantics. I am a cripple. I choose this word to name me. I choose from among several possibilities, the most common of which are "handicapped" and "disabled." I made the choice a number of years ago, without thinking, unaware of my motives for doing

so. Even now, I'm not sure what those motives are, but I recognize that they are complex and not entirely flattering. People—crippled or not—wince at the word "cripple," as they do not at "handicapped" or "disabled." Perhaps I want them to wince. I want them to see me as a tough customer, one to whom the fates/gods/viruses have not been kind, but who can face the brutal truth of her existence squarely. As a cripple, I swagger.

But, to be fair to myself, a certain amount of honesty underlies my   3 choice. "Cripple" seems to me a clean word, straightforward and precise. It has an honorable history, having made its first appearance in the Lindisfarne Gospel in the tenth century. As a lover of words, I like the accuracy with which it describes my condition: I have lost the full use of my limbs. "Disabled," by contrast, suggests any incapacity, physical or mental. And I certainly don't like "handicapped," which implies that I have deliberately been put at a disadvantage, by whom I can't imagine (my God is not a Handicapper General), in order to equalize chances in the great race of life. These words seem to me to be moving away from my condition, to be widening the gap between word and reality. Most remote is the recently coined euphemism "differently abled," which partakes of the same semantic hopefulness that transformed countries from "undeveloped" to "underdeveloped," then to "less developed," and finally to "developing" nations. People have continued to starve in those countries during the shift. Some realities do not obey the dictates of language.

Mine is one of them. Whatever you call me, I remain crippled. But   4 I don't care what you call me, so long as it isn't "differently abled," which strikes me as pure verbal garbage designed, by its ability to describe anyone, to describe no one. I subscribe to George Orwell's thesis that "the slovenliness of our language makes it easier for us to have foolish thoughts." And I refuse to participate in the degeneration of the language to the extent that I deny that I have lost anything in the course of this calamitous disease; I refuse to pretend that the only differences between you and me are the various ordinary ones that distinguish any one person from another. But call me "disabled" or "handicapped" if you like. I have long since grown accustomed to them; and if they are vague, at least they hint at the truth. Moreover, I use them myself. Society is no readier to accept crippledness than to accept death, war, sex, sweat, or wrinkles. I would never refer to another person as a cripple. It is the word I use to name only myself.

I haven't always been crippled, a fact for which I am soundly grate-   5 ful. To be whole of limb is, I know from experience, infinitely more pleasant and useful than to be crippled; and if that knowledge leaves me open to bitterness at my loss, the physical soundness I once enjoyed (though I did not enjoy it half enough) is well worth the occasional stab of regret. Though never any good at sports, I was a normally active child and young adult. I climbed trees, played hopscotch, jumped rope, skated, swam, rode my bicycle, sailed. I despised team sports, spending some of the wretchedest afternoons of my life, sweaty and humiliated, behind a field-hockey stick and under a basketball hoop. I tramped alone for miles along the bridle paths that webbed the woods behind the house I grew up in. I swayed through countless dim hours in the arms of one man or another under the scattered shot of light from mirrored balls, and gyrated through countless more as Tab Hunter and Johnny Mathis gave way to the Rolling Stones, Creedence Clearwater Revival, Cream. I walked down the aisle. I pushed baby carriages, changed tires in the rain, marched for peace.

6   When I was twenty-eight I started to trip and drop things. What at first seemed my natural clumsiness soon became too pronounced to shrug off. I consulted a neurologist, who told me that I had a brain tumor. A battery of tests, increasingly disagreeable, revealed no tumor. About a year and a half later I developed a blurred spot in one eye. I had, at last, the episodes "disseminated in space and time" requisite for a diagnosis: multiple sclerosis. I have never been sorry for the doctor's initial misdiagnosis, however. For almost a week, until the negative results of the tests were in, I thought that I was going to die right away. Every day for the past nearly ten years, then, has been a kind of gift. I accept all gifts.

7   Multiple sclerosis is a chronic degenerative disease of the central nervous system, in which the myelin that sheathes the nerves is somehow eaten away and scar tissue forms in its place, interrupting the nerves' signals. During its course, which is unpredictable and uncontrollable, one may lose vision, hearing, speech, the ability to walk, control of bladder and/or bowels, strength in any or all extremities, sensitivity to touch, vibration, and/or pain, potency, coordination of movements—the list of possibilities is lengthy and yes, horrifying. One may also lose one's sense of humor. That's the easiest to lose and the hardest to survive without.

8   In the past ten years, I have sustained some of these losses. Characteristic of MS are sudden attacks, called exacerbations, followed by remissions, and these I have not had. Instead, my disease has been slowly progressive. My left leg is now so weak that I walk with the aid of a brace and a cane; and for distances I use an Amigo, a variation on the electric wheelchair that looks rather like an electrified kiddie car. I no longer have much use of my left hand. Now my right side is weakening as well. I still have the blurred spot in my right eye. Overall, though, I've been lucky so far. My world has, of necessity, been circumscribed by my losses, but the terrain left me has been ample enough for me to continue many of the activities that absorb me: writing, teaching, rais-

ing children and cats and plants and snakes, reading, speaking publicly about MS and depression, even playing bridge with people patient and honorable enough to let me scatter cards every which way without sneaking a peek.

Lest I begin to sound like Pollyana, however, let me say that I don't   9 like having MS. I hate it. My life holds realities—harsh ones, some of them—that no right-minded human being ought to accept without grumbling. One of them is fatigue. I know of no one with MS who does not complain of bone-weariness; in a disease that presents an astonishing variety of symptoms, fatigue seems to be a common factor. I wake up in the morning feeling the way most people do at the end of a bad day, and I take it from there. As a result, I spend a lot of time *in extremis* and, impatient with limitation, I tend to ignore my fatigue until my body breaks down in some way and forces rest. Then I miss picnics, dinner parties, poetry readings, the brief visits of old friends from out of town. The offspring of a puritanical tradition of exceptional venerability, I cannot view these lapses without shame. My life often seems a series of small failures to do as I ought.

I lead, on the whole, an ordinary life, probably rather like the one I   10 would have led had I not had MS. I am lucky that my predilections were already solitary, sedentary, and bookish—unlike the world-famous French cellist I have read about, or the young woman I talked with one long afternoon who wanted only to be a jockey. I had just begun graduate school when I found out something was wrong with me, and I have remained, interminably, a graduate student. Perhaps I would not have if I'd thought I had the stamina to return to a full-time job as a technical editor; but I've enjoyed my studies.

In addition to studying, I teach writing courses. I also teach med-   11 ical students how to give neurological examinations. I pick up free-lance editing jobs here and there. I have raised a foster son and sent him into the world, where he has made me two grandbabies, and I am still escorting my daughter and son through adolescence. I go to Mass every Saturday. I am a superb, if messy, cook. I am also an enthusiastic laundress, capable of sorting a hamper full of clothes into five subtly differentiated piles, but a terrible housekeeper. I can do italic writing and, in an emergency, bathe an oil-soaked cat. I play a fiendish game of Scrabble. When I have the time and the money, I like to sit on my front steps with my husband, drinking Amaretto and smoking a cigar, as we imagine our counterparts in Leningrad and make sure that the sun gets down once more behind the sharp childish scrawl of the Tucson Mountains.

This lively plenty has its bleak complement, of course, in all the   12 things I can no longer do. I will never run again, except in dreams, and one day I may have to write that I will never walk again. I like to go camping, but I can't follow George and the children along the trails that wander out of a campsite through the desert or into the mountains. In fact, even on the level I've learned never to check the weather or try to hold a coherent conversation: I need all my attention for my wayward feet. Of late, I have begun to catch myself wondering how people can propel themselves without canes. With only one usable hand, I have to select my clothing with care not so much for style as for ease of ingress and egress, and even so, dressing can be laborious. I can no longer do fine stitchery, pick up babies, play the piano, braid my hair. I am immobilized by acute attacks of depression, which may or may not be physiologically related to MS but are certainly its logical concomitant.

13   These two elements, the plenty and the privation, are never pure, nor are the delight and wretchedness that accompany them. Almost every pickle that I get into as a result of my weakness and clumsiness—and I get into plenty—is funny as well as maddening and sometimes painful. I recall one May afternoon when a friend and I were going out for a drink after finishing up at school. As we were climbing into opposite sides of my car, chatting, I tripped and fell, flat and hard, onto the asphalt parking lot, my abrupt departure interrupting him in mid-sentence. "Where'd you go?" he called as he came around the back of the car to find me hauling myself up by the door frame. "Are you all right?" Yes, I told him, I was fine, just a bit rattly, and we drove off to find a shady patio and some beer. When I got home an hour or so later, my daughter greeted me with "What have you done to yourself?" I looked down. One elbow of my white turtleneck with the green froggies, one knee of my white trousers, one white kneesock were blood-soaked. We peeled off the clothes and inspected the damage, which was nasty enough but not alarming. That part wasn't funny: The abrasions took a long time to heal, and one got a little infected. Even so, when I think of my friend talking earnestly, suddenly, to the hot thin air while I dropped from his view as though through a trap door, I find the image as silly as something from a Marx Brothers movie.

14   I may find it easier than other cripples to amuse myself because I live propped up by the acceptance and the assistance and, sometimes, the amusement of those around me. Grocery clerks tear my checks out of my checkbook for me, and sales clerks find chairs to put into dressing rooms when I want to try on clothes. The people I work with make sure I teach at times when I am least likely to be fatigued, in places I can get to, with the materials I need. My students, with one anonymous exception (in an end-of-the-semester evaluation), have been unperturbed by my disability. Some even like it. One was immensely cheered by the information that I paint my own fingernails; she decided, she told me, that if I could go to such trouble over fine details, she could keep on

writing essays. I suppose I became some sort of bright-fingered muse. She wrote good essays, too.

The most important struts in the framework of my existence, of 15 course, are my husband and children. Dismayingly few marriages survive the MS test, and why should they? Most twenty-two- and nineteen-year-olds, like George and me, can vow in clear conscience, after a childhood of chickenpox and summer colds, to keep one another in sickness and in health so long as they both shall live. Not many are equipped for catastrophe: the dismay, the depression, the extra work, the boredom that a degenerative disease can insinuate into a relationship. And our society, with its emphasis on fun and its association of fun with physical performance, offers little encouragement for a whole spouse to stay with a crippled partner. Children experience similar stresses when faced with a crippled parent, and they are more helpless, since parents and children can't usually get divorced. They hate, of course, to be different from their peers, and the child whose mother is tacking down the aisle of a school auditorium packed with proud parents like a Cape Cod dinghy in a stiff breeze jolly well stands out in a crowd. Deprived of legal divorce, the child can at least deny the mother's disability, even her existence, forgetting to tell her about recitals and PTA meetings, refusing to accompany her to stores or church or the movies, never inviting friends to the house. Many do.

But I've been limping along for ten years now, and so far George 16 and the children are still at my left elbow, holding tight. Anne and Matthew vacuum floors and dust furniture and haul trash and rake up dog droppings and button my cuffs and bake lasagne and Toll House cookies with just enough grumbling so I know that they don't have brain fever. And far from hiding me, they're forever dragging me by racks of fancy clothes or through teeming school corridors, or welcoming gaggles of friends while I'm wandering through the house in Anne's filmy pink babydoll pajamas. George generally calls before he brings someone home, but he does just as many dumb thankless chores as the children. And they all yell at me, laugh at some of my jokes, write me funny letters when we're apart—in short, treat me as an ordinary human being for whom they have some use. I think they like me. Unless they're faking. . . .

Faking. There's the rub. Tugging at the fringes of my consciousness 17 always is the terror that people are kind to me only because I'm a cripple. My mother almost shattered me once, with that instinct mothers have—blind, I think, in this case, but unerring nonetheless—for striking blows along the fault-lines of their children's hearts, by telling me, in an attack of my selfishness, "We all have to make allowances for you, of course, because of the way you are. "From the distance of a couple of years, I have to admit that I haven't any idea just what she meant, and I'm not sure that she knew either. She was awfully angry. But at the time, as the words thudded home, I felt my worst fear, suddenly realized. I could bear being called selfish: I am. But I couldn't bear the corroboration that those around me were doing in fact what I'd always suspected them of doing, professing fondness while silently putting up with me because of the way I am. A cripple. I've been a little cracked ever since.

18   Along with this fear that people are secretly accepting shoddy goods comes a relentless pressure to please—to prove myself worth the burdens I impose, I guess, or to build a substantial account of goodwill against which I may write drafts in times of need. Part of the pressure arises from social expectations. In our society, anyone who deviates from the norm had better find some way to compensate. Like fat people, who are expected to be jolly, cripples must bear their lot meekly and cheerfully. A grumpy cripple isn't playing by the rules. And much of the pressure is self-generated. Early on I vowed that, if I had to have MS, by God I was going to do it well. This is a class act, ladies and gentlemen. No tears, no recriminations, no faint-heartedness.

19   One way and another, then, I wind up feeling like Tiny Tim, peering over the edge of the table at the Christmas goose, waving my crutch, piping down God's blessing on us all. Only sometimes I don't want to play Tiny Tim. I'd rather be Caliban, a most scurvy monster. Fortunately, at home no one much cares whether I'm a good cripple or a bad cripple as long as I make vichyssoise with fair regularity. One evening several years ago, Anne was reading at the dining-room table while I cooked dinner. As I opened a can of tomatoes, the can slipped in my left hand and juice spattered me and the counter with bloody spots. Fatigued and infuriated, I bellowed, "I'm so sick of being crippled!" Anne glanced at me over the top of her book. "There now," she said, "do you feel better?" "Yes," I said, "yes, I do. "She went back to her reading. I felt better. That's about all the attention my scurviness ever gets.

20   Because I hate being crippled, I sometimes hate myself for being a cripple. Over the years I have come to expect—even accept—attacks of violent self-loathing. Luckily, in general our society no longer connects deformity and disease directly with evil (though a charismatic once told me that I have MS because a devil is in me) and so I'm allowed to move largely at will, even among small children. But I'm not sure that this revision of attitude has been particularly helpful. Physical imperfection, even freed of moral disapprobation, still defies and violates the ideal, especially for women, whose confinement in their bodies as objects of desire is far from over. Each age, of course, has its ideal, and I doubt that ours is any better or worse than any other. Today's ideal woman, who lives on the glossy pages of dozens of magazines, seems

to be between the ages of eighteen and twenty-five; her hair has body, her teeth flash white, her breath smells minty, her underarms are dry; she has a career but is still a fabulous cook, especially of meals that take less than twenty minutes to prepare; she does not ordinarily appear to have a husband or children; she is trim and deeply tanned; she jogs, swims, plays tennis, rides a bicycle, sails, but does not bowl; she travels widely, even to out-of-the-way places like Finland and Samoa, always in the company of the ideal man, who possesses a nearly identical set of characteristics. There are a few exceptions. Though usually white and often blonde, she may be black, Hispanic, Asian, or Native American, so long as she is unusually sleek. She may be old, provided she is selling a laxative or is Lauren Becall. If she is selling a detergent, she may be married and have a flock of strikingly messy children. But she is never a cripple.

Like many women I know, I have always had an uneasy relation- 21 ship with my body. I was not a popular child, largely, I think now, because I was peculiar: intelligent, intense, moody, shy, given to unexpected actions and inexplicable notions and emotions. But as I entered adolescence, I believed myself unpopular because I was homely: my breasts too flat, my mouth too wide, my hips too narrow, my clothing never quite right in fit or style. I was not, in fact, particularly ugly, old photographs inform me, though I was well off the ideal; but I carried this sense of self-alienation with me into adulthood, where it regenerated in response to the depredations of MS. Even with my brace I walk with a limp so pronounced that, seeing myself on the videotape of a television program on the disabled, I couldn't believe that anything but an inchworm could make progress humping along like that. My shoulders droop and my pelvis thrusts forward as I try to balance myself upright, throwing my frame into a bony S. As a result of contractures, one shoulder is higher than the other and I carry one arm bent in front of me, the fingers curled into a claw. My left arm and leg have wasted into pipe-stems, and I try always to keep them covered. When I think about how my body must look to others, especially to men, to whom I have been trained to display myself, I feel ludicrous, even loathsome.

At my age, however, I don't spend much time thinking about my 22 appearance. The burning egocentricity of adolescence, which assures one that all the world is looking all the time, has passed, thank God, and I'm generally too caught up in what I'm doing to step back, as I used to, and watch myself as though upon a stage. I'm also too old to believe in the accuracy of self-image. I know that I'm not a hideous crone, that in fact, when I'm rested, well dressed, and well made up, I look fine. The self-loathing I feel is neither physically nor intellectually substantial. What I hate is not me but a disease.

23   I am not a disease.

24   And a disease is not—at least not singlehandedly—going to determine who I am, though at first it seemed to be going to. Adjusting to a
chronic incurable illness, I have moved through a process similar to
that outlined by Elizabeth Kübler-Ross in *On Death and Dying*. The
major difference—and it is far more significant than most people recognize—is that I can't be sure of the outcome, as the terminally ill cancer
patient can. Research studies indicate that, with proper medical care, I
may achieve a "normal" life span. And in our society, with its vision of
death as the ultimate evil, worse even than decrepitude, the response
to such news is, "Oh well, at least you're not going to *die*." Are there
worse things than dying? I think that there may be.

25   I think of two women I know, both with MS, both enough older
than I to have served me as models. One took to her bed several years
ago and has been there ever since. Although she can sit in a high-
backed wheelchair, because she is incontinent she refuses to go out at
all, even though incontinence pants, which are readily available at any
pharmacy, could protect her from embarrassment. Instead, she stays at
home and insists that her husband, a small quiet man, a retired civil
servant, stay there with her except for a quick weekly foray to the supermarket. The other woman, whose illness was diagnosed when she
was eighteen, a nursing student engaged to a young doctor, finished
her training, married her doctor, accompanied him to Germany when
he was in the service, bore three sons and a daughter, now grown and
gone. When she can, she travels with her husband; she plays bridge,
embroiders, swims regularly; she works, like me, as a symptomatic-
patient instructor of medical students in neurology. Guess which
woman I hope to be.

26   At the beginning, I thought about having MS almost incessantly.
And because of the unpredictable course of the disease, my thoughts
were always terrified. Each night I'd get into bed wondering whether
I'd get out again the next morning, whether I'd be able to see, to speak,
to hold a pen between my fingers. Knowing that the day might come
when I'd be physically incapable of killing myself, I thought perhaps I
ought to do so right away, while I still had the strength. Gradually
I came to understand that the Nancy who might one day lie inert under
a bedsheet, arms and legs paralyzed, unable to feed or bathe herself,
unable to reach out for a gun, a bottle of pills, was not the Nancy I was
at present, and that I could not presume to make decisions for that future Nancy, who might well not want in the least to die. Now the only
provision I've made for the future Nancy is that when the time
comes—and it is likely to come in the form of pneumonia, friend to the
weak and the old—I am not to be treated with machines and medica-

tions. If she is unable to communicate by then, I hope she will be satisfied with these terms.

Thinking all the time about having MS grew tiresome and intrusive, especially in the large and tragic mode in which I was accustomed to considering my plight. Months and even years went by without catastrophe (at least without one related to MS), and really I was awfully busy, what with George and children and snakes and students and poems, and I hadn't the time, let alone the inclination, to devote myself to being a disease. Too, the richer my life became, the funnier it seemed, as though there were some connection between largesse and laughter, and so my tragic stance began to waver until, even with the aid of a brace and cane, I couldn't hold it for very long at a time. 27

After several years I was satisfied with my adjustment. I had suffered my grief and fury and terror, I thought, but now I was at ease with my lot. Then one summer day I set out with George and the children across the desert for a vacation in California. Part way to Yuma I became aware that my right leg felt funny. "I think I've had an exacerbation," I told George. "What shall we do?" he asked. "I think we'd better get the hell to California," I said, "because I don't know whether I'll ever make it again." So we went on to San Diego and then to Orange, and up the Pacific Coast Highway to Santa Cruz, across to Yosemite, down to Sequoia and Joshua Tree, and so back over the desert to home. It was a fine two-week trip, filled with friends and fair weather, and I wouldn't have missed it for the world, though I did in fact make it back to California two years later. Nor would there have been any point in missing it, since in MS, once the symptoms have appeared, the neurological damage has been done, and there's no way to predict or prevent that damage. 28

The incident spoiled my self-satisfaction, however. It renewed my grief and fury and terror, and I learned that one never finishes adjusting to MS. I don't know now why I thought one would. One does not, after all, finish adjusting to life, and MS is simply a fact of my life—not my favorite fact, of course—but as ordinary as my nose and my tropical fish and my yellow Mazda station wagon. It may at any time get worse, but no amount of worry or anticipation can prepare me for a new loss. My life is a lesson in losses. I learn one at a time. 29

And I had best be patient in the learning, since I'll have to do it like it or not. As any rock fan knows, you can't always get what you want. Particularly when you have MS. You can't, for example, get cured. In recent years researchers and the organizations that fund research have started to pay MS some attention even though it isn't fatal; perhaps they have begun to see that life is something other than a quantitative phenomenon, that one may be very much alive for a very long time in 30 a life that isn't worth living. The researchers have made some progress toward understanding the mechanism of the disease: It may well be an autoimmune reaction triggered by a slow-acting virus. But they are nowhere near its prevention, control, or cure. And most of us want to be cured. Some, unable to accept incurability, grasp at one treatment after another, no matter how bizarre: megavitamin therapy, gluten-free diet, injections of cobra venom, hypothermal suits, lymphocytopharesis, hyperbaric chambers. Many treatments are probably harmless enough, but none are curative.

31   The absence of a cure often makes MS patients bitter toward their doctors. Doctors are, after all, the priests of modern society, the new shamans, whose business is to heal, and many an MS patient roves from one to another, searching for the "good" doctor who will make him well. Doctors too think of themselves as healers, and for this reason many have trouble dealing with MS patients, whose disease in its intransigence defeats their aims and mocks their skills. Too few doctors, it is true, treat their patients as whole human beings, but the reverse is also true. I have always tried to be gentle with my doctors, who often have more at stake in terms of ego than I do. I may be frustrated, maddened, depressed by the incurability of my disease, but I am not diminished by it, and they are. When I push myself up from my seat in the waiting room and stumble toward them, I incarnate the limitation of their powers. The least I can do is refuse to press on their tenderest spots.

32   This gentleness is part of the reason that I'm not sorry to be a cripple. I didn't have it before. Perhaps I'd have developed it anyway—how could I know such a thing?—and I wish I had more of it, but I'm glad of what I have. It has opened and enriched my life enormously, this sense that my frailty and need must be mirrored in others, that in searching for and shaping a stable core in a life wrenched by change and loss, change and loss, I must recognize the same process, under individual conditions, in the lives around me. I do not deprecate such knowledge, however I've come by it.

33   All the same, if a cure were found, would I take it? In a minute. I may be a cripple, but I'm only occasionally a loony and never a saint. Anyway, in my brand of theology God doesn't give bonus points for a limp. I'd take a cure; I just don't need one. A friend who also has MS startled me once by asking, "Do you ever say to yourself, 'Why me, Lord?'" "No, Michael, I don't," I told him, "because whenever I try, the only response I can think of is 'Why not?'" If I could make a cosmic deal, who would I put in my place? What in my life would I give up in exchange for sound limbs and a thrilling rush of energy? No one. Nothing. I might as well do the job myself. Now that I'm getting the hang of it.

RESPONDING TO READING

1. Why does Mairs deliberately label herself a "cripple" (paragraphs 2–4) and reject the more euphemistic alternatives of "disabled," "handicapped," "differently abled"? Why does she use that loaded word in her title?

2. Identify some of the many illustrations that Mairs uses to define "being a cripple." Given the fact that these physical difficulties and failures represent a condition that will only get worse, how do you account for the essay's essentially positive, affirmative attitude ("I'm not sorry to be a cripple," paragraph 32)?

3. Throughout the essay, Mairs makes numerous comparisons and contrasts, overt and implied, between being crippled and "whole of limb." Why is it important for her to let her readers know that she "was a normally active child and young adult" (paragraph 5) and that she actively functions in a variety of roles, as friend, wife, mother, writer, and teacher?

4. Mairs is very candid about her body ("When I think about how my body must look to others, especially to men . . . I feel ludicrous, even loathsome," paragraph 21), even though she is careful not to equate her body with her illness ("I am not a disease," paragraph 23.) Might her "uneasy relationship" with her physical condition be a mirror of Americans' general dissatisfaction with their bodies? Is this as true of adults as of teenagers, of men as well as women? What features of American society contribute to this dissatisfaction?

5. "On Being a Cripple" shows the positive as well as the negative consequences of being different, and how many of those differences can be transcended, in spirit and in action. If you have ever felt sufficiently different from your peers to be uncomfortable or isolated, write a definition of "On Being Different" in which you discuss the positive as well as the negative consequences. If you can generalize from your individual experience, do so.

The Age of White Guilt and the Disappearance of the Black Individual

SHELBY STEELE, JR.

The political background of Shelby Steele, Jr. (born in Chicago in 1946), arguably America's most visible conservative black analyst of society, is impeccably liberal. Since 1994, Steele has been a research fellow at the conservative Hoover Institution, specializing in the study of race relations, multiculturalism, and affirmative action.

His personal history might have predicted a different direction. Steele's parents, a black truck driver and a white social worker, met while working for the activist Congress of Racial Equality (CORE); Steele considers his mixed parentage an amazing gift, which served to demystify race for him. At Coe College in Cedar Rapids, Iowa,

Steele—one of eighteen black students in his class—continued his parents' pursuit of social justice through working with SCOPE, an affiliate of the Southern Christian Leadership Conference (SCLC), where he also met Rita, his future wife. After graduating in 1968, Steele earned a master's in sociology from Southern Illinois University, followed by a Ph.D. in English from the University of Utah in 1974, where he taught black literature. Encountering hostility to their interracial marriage in Utah, the couple moved to California, where Steele taught English at San Jose State University from 1974 to 1991.

Although Steele's conservative point of view angers many liberals, white as well as black, he earned an Emmy in 1990 for *Seven Days in Bensonhurst*, a PBS "Frontline" documentary examining the racially motivated killing of Yusef Hawkins in Brooklyn. In 1999, he published *A Dream Deferred: The Second Betrayal of Black Freedom in America*, where he argues that many contemporary civil rights policies are dictated by whites' desires for moral redemption or self-satisfaction, rather than for real improvement in the lives of blacks. Steele won the National Book Critics Circle Award in 1991 for *The Content of Our Character: A New Vision of Race in America*, a collection of essays on race. Steele's assertions here, that the black American citizen is as "free as he or she wants to be" and that the path to advancement is self-help and integration into the American mainstream, stake out the stance against Affirmative Action that he takes in "The Age of White Guilt and the Disappearance of the Black Individual," published in *Harper's*, November 2002.

1   One day back in the late fifties, when I was ten or eleven years old, there was a moment when I experienced myself as an individual—as a separate consciousness—for the first time. I was walking home from the YMCA, which meant that I was passing out of the white Chicago suburb where the Y was located and crossing Halsted Street back into Phoenix, the tiny black suburb where I grew up. It was a languid summer afternoon, thick with the industrial-scented humidity of south Chicago that I can still smell and feel on my skin, though I sit today only blocks from the cool Pacific and more than forty years removed.

2   Into Phoenix no more than a block and I was struck by a thought that seemed beyond me. I have tried for years to remember it, but all my effort only pushes it further away. I do remember that it came to me with the completeness of an aphorism, as if the subconscious had already done the labor of crafting it into a fine phrase. What scared me a little at the time was its implication of a separate self with independent thoughts—a distinct self that might distill experience into all sorts of ideas for which I would then be responsible. That feeling of responsibility was my first real experience of myself as an individual—as someone who would have to navigate a separate and unpredictable consciousness though a world I already knew to be often unfair and always tense.

Of course I already knew that I was black, or "Negro," as we said   3
back then. No secret there. The world had made this fact quite clear by
imposing on my life all the elaborate circumscriptions of Chicago-style
segregation. Although my mother was white, the logic of segregation
meant that I was born in the hospital's black maternity ward. I grew up
in a black neighborhood and walked to a segregated black school as
white children in the same district walked to a white school. Kindness
in whites always came as a mild surprise and was accepted with a gratitude that I later understood to be a bit humiliating. And there were
many racist rejections for which I was only partly consoled by the
knowledge that racism is impersonal.

Back then I thought of being black as a fate, as a condition I shared   4
with people as various as Duke Ellington and the odd-job man who
plowed the neighborhood gardens with a mule and signed his name
with an X. And it is worth noting here that never in my life have I met
a true Uncle Tom, a black who identifies with white racism as a truth.
The Negro world of that era believed that whites used our race against
our individuality and, thus, our humanity. There was no embrace of a
Negro identity, because that would have weakened the argument for
our humanity. "Negroness" or "blackness" would have collaborated
with the racist lie that we were different and, thus, would have been
true Uncle Tomism. To the contrary, there was an embrace of the individual *and* assimilation.

My little experience of myself as an individual confirmed the mes-   5
sage of the civil-rights movement itself, in which a favorite picket sign
read, simply, "I am a man." The idea of the individual resonated with
Negro freedom—a freedom not for the group but for the individuals
who made up the group. And assimilation was not a self-hating mimicry of things white but a mastery by Negro individuals of the modern
and cosmopolitan world, a mastery that showed us to be natural members of that world. So my experience of myself as an individual made
me one with the group.

Not long ago C-SPAN carried a Harvard debate on affirmative ac-   6
tion between conservative reformer Ward Connerly and liberal law
professor Christopher Edley. During the Q and A a black undergraduate rose from a snickering clump of black students to challenge Mr.
Connerly, who had argued that the time for racial preferences was past.
Once standing, this young man smiled unctuously, as if victory were so
assured that he must already offer consolation. But his own pose
seemed to distract him, and soon he was sinking into incoherence.
There was impatience in the room, but it was suppressed. Black students play a role in campus debates like this and they are indulged.

The campus forum of racial confrontation is a ritual that has   7
changed since the sixties in only one way. Whereas blacks and whites

confronted one another back then, now black liberals and black conservatives do the confronting while whites look on—relieved, I'm sure—from the bleachers. I used to feel empathy for students like this young man, because they reminded me of myself at that age. Now I see them as figures of pathos. More than thirty years have passed since I did that sort of challenging, and even then it was a waste of time. Today it is perseveration to the point of tragedy.

8   Here is a brief litany of obvious truths that have been resisted in the public discourse of black America over the last thirty years: a group is no stronger than its individuals; when individuals transform themselves they transform the group; the freer the individual, the stronger the group; social responsibility begins in individual responsibility. Add to this an indisputable fact that has also been unmentionable: that American greatness has a lot to do with a culturally ingrained individualism, with the respect and freedom historically granted individuals to pursue their happiness—this despite many egregious lapses and an outright commitment to the oppression of black individuals for centuries. And there is one last obvious but unassimilated fact: ethnic groups that have asked a lot from their individuals have done exceptionally well in America even while enduring discrimination.

9   Now consider what this Harvard student is called upon by his racial identity to argue in the year 2002. All that is creative and imaginative in him must be rallied to argue the essential weakness of his own people. Only their weakness justifies the racial preferences they receive decades after any trace of anti-black racism in college admissions. The young man must *not* show faith in the power of his people to overcome against any odds; he must show faith in their inability to overcome without help. As Mr. Connerly points to far less racism and far more freedom and opportunity for blacks, the young man must find a way, against all the mounting facts, to argue that black Americans simply cannot compete without preferences. If his own forebears seized freedom in a long and arduous struggle for civil rights, he must argue that his own generation is unable to compete on paper-and-pencil standardized tests.

10   It doesn't help that he locates the cause of black weakness in things like "structural racism" and "uneven playing fields," because there has been so little correlation between the remedies for such problems and actual black improvement. Blacks from families that make $100,000 a year or more perform worse on the SAT than whites from families that make $10,000 a year or less. After decades of racial preferences blacks remain the lowest performing student group in American higher education. And once they are out of college and in professions, their own children also underperform in relation to their white and Asian peers.

Thus, this young man must also nurture the idea of a black psychological woundedness that is baroque in its capacity to stifle black aspiration. And all his faith, his proud belief, must be in the truth of this woundedness and the injustice that caused it, because this is his only avenue to racial pride. He is a figure of pathos because his faith in racial victimization is his only release from racial shame.

Right after the sixties' civil-rights victories came what I believe to   11
be the greatest miscalculation in black American history. Others had oppressed us, but this was to be the first "fall" to come by our own hand. We allowed ourselves to see a greater power in America's liability for our oppression than we saw in ourselves. Thus, we were faithless with ourselves just when we had given ourselves reason to have such faith. We couldn't have made a worse mistake. We have not been the same since.

To go after America's liability we had to locate real transformative   12
power outside ourselves. Worse, we had to see our fate as contingent on America's paying off that liability. We have been a contingent people ever since, arguing our weakness and white racism in order to ignite the engine of white liability. And this has mired us in a protest-group identity that mistrusts individualism because free individuals might jeopardize the group's effort to activate this liability.

Today I would be encouraged to squeeze my little childhood experience of individuality into a narrow group framework that would not   13
endanger the group's bid for white intervention. I would be urged to embrace a pattern of reform that represses our best hope for advancement—our individuals—simply to keep whites "on the hook."

Mr. Connerly was outnumbered and outgunned at that Harvard   14
debate. The consensus finally was that preferences would be necessary for a while longer. Whites would remain "on the hook." The black student prevailed, but it was a victory against himself. In all that his identity required him to believe, there was no place for him . . .

The greatest problem in coming from an oppressed group is the   15
power the oppressor has over your group. The second greatest problem is the power your group has over you. Group identity in oppressed groups is always very strategic, always a calculation of advantage. The humble black identity of the Booker T. Washington era—"a little education spoiled many a good plow hand"—allowed blacks to function as tradesmen, laborers, and farmers during the rise of Jim Crow, when hundreds of blacks were being lynched yearly. Likewise, the black militancy of the late sixties strategically aimed for advantage in an America suddenly contrite over its long indulgence in racism.

One's group identity is always a mask—a mask replete with a pol-   16
itics. When a teenager in East Los Angeles says he is Hispanic, he is

thinking of himself within a group strategy pitched at larger America. His identity is related far more to America than to Mexico or Guatemala, where he would not often think of himself as Hispanic. In fact, "Hispanic" is much more a political concept than a cultural one, and its first purpose is to win power within the fray of American identity politics. So this teenager must wear the mask that serves his group's ambitions in these politics.

17   With the civil-rights victories, black identity became more carefully calculated around the pursuit of power, because black power was finally possible in America . . . In the late forties, [the black American writer James] Baldwin went to Paris, like his friend and mentor Richard Wright, to escape America's smothering racism and to find himself as a writer and as an individual. He succeeded dramatically and quickly on both counts. His first novel, the minor masterpiece *Go Tell It on the Mountain*, appeared in 1953 and was quickly followed by another novel and two important essay collections.

18   It was clearly the remove of Europe that gave Baldwin the room to find his first important theme: self-acceptance. In a Swiss mountain village in winter, against an "absolutely alabaster landscape" and listening to Bessie Smith records, he accepts that he is black, gay, talented, despised by his father, and haunted by a difficult childhood. From this self-acceptance emerges an individual voice and one of the most unmistakable styles in American writing.

19   Then, in 1957, Baldwin did something that changed him—and his writing—forever. He came home to America. He gave up the psychological remove of Europe and allowed himself to become once again fully accountable as a black American. And soon, in blatant contradiction of his own powerful arguments against protest writing, he became a protest writer. There is little doubt that this new accountability weakened him greatly as an artist. Nothing he wrote after the early sixties had the human complexity, depth, or literary mastery of what he wrote in those remote European locales where children gawked at him for his color.

20   The South African writer Nadine Gordimer saw the black writer in her own country as conflicted between "a deep, intense, private view" on the one hand and the call to be a spokesman for his people on the other. This classic conflict—common to writers from oppressed groups around the world—is really a conflict of authority. In Europe, Baldwin enjoyed exclusive authority over his own identity. When he came back to America he did what in Western culture is anathema to the artist: he submitted his artistic vision—his "private view"—to the authority of his group. From *The Fire Next Time* to the end of his writing life, he allowed protest to be the framing authority of his work.

What Baldwin did was perhaps understandable, because his group   21
was in a pitched battle for its freedom. The group had enormous moral
authority, and he had a splendid rhetorical gift the group needed. Baldwin was transformed in the sixties into an embodiment of black
protest, an archetypal David—frail, effeminate, brilliant—against a
brutish and stupid American racism. He became a celebrity writer on
the American scene, a charismatic presence with huge, penetrating
eyes that were fierce and vulnerable at the same time. People who had
never read him had strong opinions about him. His fame was out of
proportion to his work, and if all this had been limited to Baldwin himself, it might be called the Baldwin phenomenon. But, in fact, his ascendancy established a pattern that would broadly define, and in many
ways corrupt, an entire generation of black intellectuals, writers, and
academics. And so it must be called the Baldwin model.

The goal of the Baldwin model is to link one's intellectual reputa-   22
tion to the moral authority—the moral glamour—of an oppressed
group's liberation struggle. In this way one ceases to be a mere individual with a mere point of view and becomes, in effect, the embodiment
of a moral imperative. This is rarely done consciously, as a Faustian
bargain in which the intellectual knowingly sells his individual soul to
the group. Rather the group identity is already a protest-focused identity, and the intellectual simply goes along with it. Adherence to the
Baldwin model is usually more a sin of thoughtlessness and convenience than of conscious avarice, though it is *always* an appropriation
of moral power, a stealing of thunder.

The protest intellectual positions himself in the pathway of the   23
larger society's march toward racial redemption. By allowing his work
to be framed by the protest identity, he articulates the larger society's
moral liability. He seems, therefore, to hold the key to how society must
redeem itself. Baldwin was called in to advise Bobby Kennedy on the
Negro situation. It is doubtful that the Baldwin of *Go Tell It on the Mountain* would have gotten such a call. But the Baldwin of *The Fire Next
Time* probably expected it. Ralph Ellison, a contemporary of Baldwin's
who rejected the black protest identity but whose work showed a far
deeper understanding of black culture than Baldwin's, never had this
sort of access to high places. By insisting on his individual autonomy as
an artist, Ellison was neither inflated with the moral authority of his
group's freedom struggle nor positioned in the pathway of America's
redemption.

Today the protest identity is a career advantage for an entire gener-   24
ation of black intellectuals, particularly academics who have been virtually forced to position themselves in the path of their university's
obsession with "diversity." Inflation from the moral authority of

protest, added to the racial preference policies in so many American institutions, provides an irresistible incentive for black America's best
minds to continue defining themselves by protest. Professors who resist the Baldwin model risk the Ellisonian fate of invisibility.

25   What happened in America to make the Baldwin model possible?

26   The broad answer is this: America moved from its long dark age of
racism into an age of white guilt. I saw this shift play out in my own
family.

27   I grew up watching my parents live out an almost perpetual
protest against racial injustice. When I was five or six we drove out of
our segregated neighborhood every Sunday morning to carry out the
grimly disciplined business of integrating a lily-white church in the
next town. Our family was a little off-color island of quiet protest
amidst rows of pinched white faces. And when that battle was lost
there was a long and successful struggle to create Chicago's first fully
integrated church. And from there it was on to the segregated local
school system, where my parents organized a boycott against the elementary school that later incurred the first desegregation lawsuit in the
North.

28   Amidst all this protest, I could see only the price people were paying. I saw my mother's health start to weaken. I saw the white minister
who encouraged us to integrate his church lose his job. There was a
time when I was sent away to stay with family friends until things
"cooled down." Black protest had no legitimacy in broader America in
the 1950s. It was subversive, something to be repressed, and people
who indulged in it were made to pay.

29   And then there came the sunny day in the very late sixties when I
leaned into the window of my parents' old powder-blue Rambler and,
inches from my mother's face, said wasn't it amazing that I was making $13,500 a year. They had come to visit me on my first job out of col-
lege, and had just gotten into the car for their return trip. I saw my
mistake even as the words tumbled out. My son's pride had blinded
me to my parents' feelings. This was four or five thousand dollars more
than either of them had ever made in a single year. I had learned the
year before that my favorite professor—a full professor with two books
to his credit—had fought hard for a raise to $10,000 a year. Thirteen five
implied a different social class, a different life than we had known as a
family.

30   "Congratulations," they said. "That's very nice."

31   The subtext of this role reversal was President Johnson's Great Society, and beneath that an even more profound shift in the moral plates
of society. The year was 1969, and I was already employed in my fourth
Great Society program—three Upward Bound programs and now a ju-

nior college-level program called Experiment in Higher Education, in East St. Louis, Illinois. America was suddenly spending vast millions to end poverty "in our time," and, as it was for James Baldwin on his return from Paris, the timing was perfect for me.

I was chosen for my first Upward Bound job because I was the   32 leader of the campus civil-rights group. This engagement with black protest suddenly constituted a kind of aptitude, in my employers' minds, for teaching disadvantaged kids. It inflated me into a person who was gifted with young people. The protesting that had gotten me nowhere when I started college was serving me as well as an advanced degree by the time I was a senior.

Two great, immutable forces have driven America's attitudes, cus-   33 toms, and public policies around race. The first has been white racism, and the second has been white guilt. The civil-rights movement was the dividing line between the two. Certainly there was some guilt before this movement, and no doubt some racism remains after it. But the great achievement of the civil-rights movement was that its relentless moral witness finally defeated the legitimacy of racism as propriety—a principle of social organization, manners, and customs that defines decency itself. An idea controls culture when it achieves the invisibility of propriety. And it must be remembered that racism was a propriety, a form of decency. When, as a boy, I was prohibited from entering the fine Christian home of the occasional white playmate, it was to save the household an indecency. Today, thanks to the civil-rights movement, white guilt is propriety—an utterly invisible code that defines decency in our culture with thousands of little protocols we no longer even think about. We have been living in an age of white guilt for four decades now.

What is white guilt? It is not a personal sense of remorse over past   34 wrongs. White guilt is literally a vacuum of moral authority in matters of race, equality, and opportunity that comes from the association of mere white skin with America's historical racism. It is the stigmatization of whites and, more importantly, American institutions with the sin of racism. Under this stigma white individuals and American institutions must perpetually *prove a negative*—that they are not racist—to gain enough authority to function in matters of race, equality, and opportunity. If they fail to prove the negative, they will be seen as racists. Political correctness, diversity policies, and multiculturalism are forms of deference that give whites and institutions a way to prove the negative and win reprieve from the racist stigma.

Institutions especially must be proactive in all this. They must en-   35 gineer a demonstrable racial innocence to garner enough authority for simple legitimacy in the American democracy. No university today, private or public, could admit students by academic merit alone if that meant no black or brown faces on campus. Such a university would be seen as racist and shunned accordingly. White guilt has made social engineering for black and brown representation a condition of legitimacy.

36   People often deny white guilt by pointing to its irrationality—"I never owned a slave," "My family got here eighty years after slavery was over." But of course almost nothing having to do with race is rational. That whites are now stigmatized by their race is not poetic justice; it is simply another echo of racism's power to contaminate by mere association.

37   The other common denial of white guilt has to do with motive: "I don't support affirmative action because I'm guilty; I support it because I want to do what's fair." But the first test of sincere support is a demand that the policy be studied for effectiveness. Affirmative action went almost completely unexamined for thirty years and has only recently been briefly studied in a highly politicized manner now that it is under threat. The fact is that affirmative action has been a very effective racial policy in garnering moral authority and legitimacy for institutions, and it is now institutions—not individual whites or blacks—that are fighting to keep it alive.

38   The real difference between my parents and myself was that they protested in an age of white racism and I protested in an age of white guilt. They were punished; I was rewarded. By my time, moral authority around race had become a great and consuming labor for America. Everything from social programs to the law, from the color of TV sitcom characters to the content of school curricula, from college admissions to profiling for terrorists—every aspect of our culture—now must show itself redeemed of the old national sin. Today you cannot credibly run for president without an iconography of white guilt: the backdrop of black children, the Spanish-language phrases, the word "compassion" to separate conservatism from its associations with racism.

39   So then here you are, a black American living amidst all this. Every institution you engage—the government, universities, corporations, public and private schools, philanthropies, churches—faces you out of a deficit of moral authority. Your race is needed everywhere. How could you avoid the aggressions, and even the bigotries, of white guilt? What institution could you walk into without having your color tallied up as a credit to the institution? For that matter, what political party or ideological direction could you pursue without your race being plundered by that party or ideology for moral authority?

40   Because blacks live amidst such hunger for the moral authority of their race, we embraced protest as a *permanent* identity in order to capture the fruits of white guilt on an ongoing basis. Again, this was our first fall by our own hand. Still, it is hard to imagine any group of individuals coming out of four centuries of oppression and not angling their identity toward whatever advantage seemed available. White

guilt held out the promise of a preferential life in recompense for past injustice, and the protest identity seemed the best way to keep that promise alive.

An obvious problem here is that we blacks fell into a group identi-   41
ty that has absolutely no other purpose than to collect the fruits of white guilt. And so the themes of protest—a sense of grievance and vic- timization—evolved into a sensibility, an attitude toward the larger world that enabled us always and easily to feel the grievance whether it was there or not. Protest became the mask of identity, because it de- fined us in a way that kept whites "on the hook." Today the angry rap singer and Jesse Jackson and the black-studies professor are all joined by an unexamined devotion to white guilt.

To be black in my father's generation, when racism was rampant,   42
was to be a man who was very often victimized by racism. To be black in the age of white guilt is to be a victim who is very rarely victimized by racism. Today in black life there is what might be called "identity grievance"—a certainty of racial grievance that is entirely disconnected from actual grievance. And the fervor of this symbiosis with white guilt has all but killed off the idea of the individual as a source of group strength in black life. All is group and unity, even as those minority groups that ask much of their individuals thrive in America despite any discrimination they encounter.

I always thought that James Baldwin on some level knew that he   43
had lost himself to protest. His work grew narrower and narrower when age and experience should have broadened it. And, significantly, he spent the better part of his last decades in France, where he died in 1987. Did he again need France in those years to be himself, to be out from under the impossible demands of a symbiotically defined black identity, to breathe on his own?

There is another final and terrible enemy of the black individual. I   44
first saw it in that Great Society program in which my salary was so sweetened by white guilt. The program itself quickly slid into banana republic-style corruption, and I was happy to get away to graduate- student poverty. But on the way out certain things became clear. The program was not so much a program as it was an idea of the social "good," around which there was an intoxicating enthusiasm. It was my first experience with the utter thrill of untested good intentions. On the way out I realized that thrill had been the point. That feeling is what we sent back to Washington, where it was received as an end in itself.

Now I know that white guilt is a moral imperative that can be sat-   45
isfied by good intentions alone. In my own lifetime, racial reform in America changed from a struggle for freedom to a struggle for "the good." A new metaphysics of the social good replaced the principles of freedom. Suddenly "diversity," "inclusion," "tolerance," "pluralism," and "multiculturalism" were all conjure words that aligned you with a

social good so compelling that you couldn't leave it to mere freedom. In certain circumstances freedom could be the outright enemy of "the good." If you want a "diverse" student body at your university, for example, the individualistic principles of freedom might be a barrier. So usually "the good" has to be imposed from above out of a kind of moral imperialism by a well-meaning white elite.

46   In the sixties, black identity also shifted its focus from freedom to "the good" to better collect the fruits of white guilt. Thus it was a symbiosis of both white and black need that pushed racial reform into a totalitarian model where schemes of "the good" are imposed by coercion at the expense of freedom. The Franco-Czech writer Milan Kundera says that every totalitarianism is "also the dream of paradise." And when people seem to stand in its way, the rulers "build a little gulag on the side of Eden." In this good-driven age of white guilt, with all its paradises of diversity, a figurative gulag has replaced freedom's tradition of a respected and loyal opposition. Conservatives are automatically relegated to this gulag because of their preference for freedom over ideas of "the good."

47   But there is another "little gulag" for the black individual. He lives in a society that needs his race for the good it wants to do more than it needs his individual self. His race makes him popular with white institutions and unifies him with blacks. But he is unsupported everywhere as an individual. Nothing in his society asks for or even allows his flowering as a full, free, and responsible person. As is always the case when "the good" becomes ascendant over freedom, and coercion itself becomes a good thing, the individual finds himself in a gulag. . . .

48   In the age of racism there were more powerful black intellectuals, because nobody wanted them for their race. Richard Wright, Ralph Ellison, Zora Neale Hurston, W.E.B. Du Bois, and many others were fully developed, self-made individuals, no matter their various political and ideological bents. Race was not a "talent" that falsely inflated them or won them high position. Today no black intellectual in America, including this writer, is safe from this sort of inflation. The white world is simply too hungry for the moral authority our skins carry. And this is true on both the political left and right. . . .

49   James Baldwin once wrote: "What Europe still gives an American is the sanction, if one can accept it, to become oneself." If America now gives this sanction to most citizens, its institutions still fiercely deny it to blacks. And this society will never sanction blacks in this way until it drops all the mechanisms by which it tries to appease white guilt. Guilt can be a very civilizing force, but only when it is simply carried as a kind of knowledge. Efforts to appease or dispel it will only engage the society in new patterns of dehumanization against the same people who inspired guilt in the first place. This will always be true.

Restraint should be the watchword in racial matters. We should   50
help people who need help. There are, in fact, no races that need help;
only individuals, citizens. Over time maybe nothing in the society, not
even white guilt, will reach out and play on my race, bind me to it for
opportunity. I won't ever find in America what Baldwin found in Europe, but someday maybe others will.

RESPONDING TO READING

1. How does Steele's point that "racism is impersonal" affect your reading of his argument? How does an essay based on personal experience support or refute this idea of racism as an impersonal experience?

2. Do you agree with Steele that those who support the preferences extended to certain minority groups by affirmative action policies must, by definition, argue for the inability of their ethnic group to succeed without help? Is the figure of the black individual who argues in favor of affirmative action truly a figure of pathos, as Steele suggests, or is this figure a straw man Steele only constructs in order to further his own argument?

3. Discuss with classmates whether the identity of an individual is more important than the identity of the group. Do you agree or disagree with Steele's arguments about individual and group identity? Why? In what ways is an individual's identification of him/herself with a group a political act? List the main points of your argument, and feel free to develop these into an essay.

4. How does Steele use personal experience and discussion of the lives of writers such as James Baldwin to build his argument? How does he define the "Baldwin model," and what part does it play in his argument?

5. Steele argues that white guilt has overtaken white racism as the marker of propriety in America, as "a principle of social organization, manners, and customs that defines decency itself." In an essay, explain whether you agree or disagree with his argument. Identify one or two other proprieties that Americans live under, in addition to white guilt. Do these make society a better place in which to live? If they present problems, identify and illustrate some of these and explain why they are problematic.

Who Am I in Relation to Others?

Resurrection

FREDERICK DOUGLASS

Frederick Douglass (1817–85), born a slave in Talbot County, Maryland, devoted much of his life to interpreting and revising his public image, as revealed in the four very different versions of his autobiography that were published at intervals during his lifetime. Taken together, the various selves represent a black version of Benjamin Franklin's *Autobiography*, for they show the rise from slavery to freedom, from dependence to independence, from illiteracy to extraordinary command over the spoken and written word. As Douglass, too, fulfilled the American Dream, he became a national spokesperson for the abolitionist movement, serving as an advisor to Harriet Beecher Stowe and to President Abraham Lincoln, among others. His postbellum activities included campaigning for civil rights for blacks and women. Public acknowledgment of his stature culminated in his appointment as Minister to Haiti in 1890.

The episode recounted in "Resurrection," which was taken from the first version of *The Narrative of the Life of Frederick Douglass, An American Slave* (1845), explains the incident that was "the turning point in [his] career as a slave," for it enabled him to make the transformation from slave to human being. Douglass's autobiography, an abolitionist document like many other slave narratives, is exceptional in its forthright language and absence of stereotyping of either whites or blacks. His people are multidimensional, although the overseer, Mr. Covey, might have been the original of Harriet Beecher Stowe's arch villain, Simon Legree.

1   I have already intimated that my condition was much worse, during the first six months of my stay at Mr. Covey's, than in the last six. The circumstances leading to the change in Mr. Covey's course toward me form an epoch in my humble history. You have seen how a man was made slave; you shall see how a slave was made a man. On one of the hottest days of the month of August, 1833, Bill Smith, William Hughes, a slave named Eli, and myself, were engaged in fanning wheat. Hughes was clearing the fanned wheat from before the fan. Eli was turning, Smith was feeding, and I was carrying wheat to the fan. The work was simple, requiring strength rather than intellect; yet, to one entirely unused to such work, it came very hard. About three o'clock of that day, I broke down; my strength failed me; I was seized with a violent aching of the head, attended with extreme dizziness; I trembled in every limb.

Finding what was coming, I nerved myself up, feeling it would never do to stop work. I stood as long as I could stagger to the hopper with grain. When I could stand no longer, I fell, and felt as if held down by an immense weight. The fan of course stopped; every one had his own work to do; and no one could do the work of the other, and have his own go on at the same time.

Mr. Covey was at the house, about one hundred yards from the treading-yard where we were fanning. On hearing the fan stop, he left immediately, and came to the spot where we were. He hastily inquired what the matter was. Bill answered that I was sick, and there was no one to bring wheat to the fan. I had by this time crawled away under the side of the post and rail-fence by which the yard was enclosed, hoping to find relief by getting out of the sun. He then asked where I was. He was told by one of the hands. He came to the spot, and, after looking at me awhile, asked me what was the matter. I told him as well as I could, for I scarce had strength to speak. He then gave me a savage kick in the side, and told me to get up. I tried to do so, but fell back in the attempt. He gave me another kick, and again told me to rise. I again tried, and succeeded in gaining my feet; but, stooping to get the tub with which I was feeding the fan, I again staggered and fell. While down in this situation, Mr. Covey took up the hickory slat with which Hughes had been striking off the half-bushel measure, and with it gave me a heavy blow upon the head, making a large wound, and the blood ran freely; and with this again told me to get up. I made no effort to comply, having now made up my mind to let him do his worst. In a short time after receiving this blow, my head grew bigger. Mr. Covey had now left me to my fate. At this moment I resolved, for the first time, to go to my master, enter a complaint, and ask his protection. In order to do this, I must that afternoon walk seven miles; and this, under the circumstances, was truly a severe undertaking. I was exceedingly feeble; made so as much by the kicks and blows which I received, as by the severe fit of sickness to which I had been subjected. I, however, watched my chance, while Covey was looking in an opposite direction, and started for St. Michael's: I succeeded in getting a considerable distance on my way to the woods, when Covey discovered me, and called after me to come back, threatening what he would do if I did not come. I disregarded both his calls and his threats, and made my way to the woods as fast as my feeble state would allow; and thinking I might be overhauled by him if I kept to the road, I walked through the woods, keeping far enough from the road to avoid detection, and near enough to prevent losing my way. I had not gone far before my little strength again failed me. I could go no farther. I fell down, and lay for a considerable time. The blood was yet oozing from the wound on my head. For a time I thought I should bleed to death; and think now that I should have done so, but that the blood so matted my hair as to stop the wound. After lying there about three quarters of an hour, I nerved myself up again, and started on my way, through bogs and briers, barefooted and bareheaded, tearing my feet sometimes at nearly every step; and after a journey of about seven miles, occupying some five hours to perform it, I arrived at master's store. I then presented an appearance enough to affect any but a heart of iron. From the crown of my head to my feet, I was covered with blood. My hair was all clotted with dust and blood; my shirt was stiff with blood. My legs and feet were torn in sundry places with briers and thorns, and were also covered with blood. I suppose I looked like a man who had escaped a den of wild beasts, and barely escaped them. In this state I appeared before my master, humbly entreating him to interpose his authority for my protection. I told him all the circumstances as well as I could, and it seemed, as I spoke, at times to affect him. He would then walk the floor, and seek to justify Covey by saying he expected I deserved it. He asked me what I wanted. I told him, to let me get a new home; that as sure as I lived with Mr. Covey again, I should live with but to die with him; that Covey would surely kill me; he was in a fair way for it. Master Thomas ridiculed the idea that there was any danger of Mr. Covey's killing me, and said that he knew Mr. Covey, that he was a good man, and that he could not think of taking me from him; that, should he do so, he would lose the whole year's wages; that I belonged to Mr. Covey for one year, and that I must go back to him, come what might; and that I must not trouble him with any more stories, or that he would himself *get hold of me.* After threatening me thus, he gave me a very large dose of salts, telling me that I might remain in St. Michael's that night, (it being quite late,) but that I must be off back to Mr. Covey's early in the morning; and that if I did not, he would *get hold of me,* which meant that he would whip me. I remained all night, and, according to his orders, I started off to Covey's in the morning, (Saturday morning,) wearied in body and broken in spirit. I got no supper that night, or breakfast that morning. I reached Covey's about nine o'clock; and just as I was getting over the fence that divided Mrs. Kemp's fields from ours out ran Covey with his cowskin, to give me another whipping. Before he could reach me, I succeeded in getting to the cornfield; and as the corn was very high, it afforded me the means of hiding. He seemed very angry, and searched for me a long time. My behavior was altogether unaccountable. He finally gave up the chase, thinking, I suppose, that I must come home for something to eat; he would give himself no further trouble in looking for me. I spent that day mostly in the woods, having the alternative before me—to go home and be whipped to death, or stay in the woods and be starved to death. That night, I fell in with Sandy Jenkins, a slave with whom I was somewhat acquainted.

Sandy had a free wife who lived about four miles from Mr. Covey's; and it being Saturday, he was on his way to see her. I told him my circumstances, and he very kindly invited me to go home with him. I went home with him, and talked this whole matter over, and got his advice as to what course it was best for me to pursue. I found Sandy an old adviser. He told me, with great solemnity, I must go back to Covey; but that before I went, I must go with him into another part of the woods, where there was a certain *root*, which, if I would take some of it with me, carrying it *always on my right side*, would render it impossible for Mr. Covey, or any other white man, to whip me. He said he had carried it for years; and since he had done so, he had never received a blow, and never expected to while he carried it. I at first rejected the idea, that the simple carrying of a root in my pocket would have any such effect as he had said, and was not disposed to take it; but Sandy impressed the necessity with much earnestness, telling me it could do no harm, if it did no good. To please him, I at length took the root, and, according to his direction, carried it upon my right side. This was Sunday morning. I immediately started for home; and upon entering the yard gate, out came Mr. Covey on his way to meeting. He spoke to me very kindly, bade me drive the pigs from a lot near by, and passed on towards the church. Now, this singular conduct of Mr. Covey really made me begin to think that there was something in the *root* which Sandy had given me; and had it been on any other day than Sunday, I could have attributed the conduct to no other cause than the influence of that root; and as it was, I was half inclined to think the *root* to be something more than I at first had taken it to be. All went well till Monday morning. On this morning, the virtue of the *root* was fully tested. Long before daylight, I was called to go and rub, curry, and feed, the horses. I obeyed, and was glad to obey. But whilst thus engaged, whilst in the act of throwing down some blades from the loft, Mr. Covey entered the stable with a long rope; and just as I was half out of the loft, he caught hold of my legs, and was about tying me. As soon as I found what he was up to, I gave a sudden spring, and as I did so, he holding to my legs, I was brought sprawling on the stable floor. Mr. Covey seemed now to think he had me, and could do what he pleased; but at this moment—from whence came the spirit I don't know—I resolved to fight; and, suiting my action to the resolution, I seized Covey hard by the throat; and as I did so, I rose. He held on to me, and I to him. My resistance was so entirely unexpected, that Covey seemed taken all aback. He trembled like a leaf. This gave me assurance, and I held him uneasy, causing the blood to run where I touched him with the ends of my fingers. Mr. Covey soon called out to Hughes for help. Hughes came, and while Covey held me, attempted to tie my right hand. While he was in the act of doing so, I watched my chance, and gave him a heavy kick close under the ribs. This kick fairly sickened Hughes, so that he left me in the hands of Mr. Covey. This kick had the effect of not only weakening Hughes, but Covey also. When he saw Hughes bending over with pain, his courage quailed. He asked me if I meant to persist in my resistance. I told him I did, come what might; that he had used me like a brute for six months, and that I was determined to be used so no longer. With that, he strove to drag me to a stick that was lying just out of the stable door. He meant to knock me down. But just as he was leaning over to get the stick, I seized him with both hands by his collar, and brought him by a sudden snatch to the ground. By this time, Bill came. Covey called upon him for assistance. Bill wanted to know what he could do. Covey said, "Take hold of him, take hold of him!" Bill said his master hired him out to work, and not to help whip me; so he left Covey and myself to fight our own battle out. We were at it for nearly two hours. Covey at length let me go, puffing and blowing at a great rate, saying that if I had not resisted, he would not have whipped me half so much. The truth was, that he had not whipped me at all. I considered him as getting entirely the worst end of the bargain; for he had drawn no blood from me, but I had from him. The whole six months afterwards, that I spent with Mr. Covey, he never laid the weight of his finger upon me in anger. He would occasionally say, he didn't want to get hold of me again. "No," thought I, "you need not; for you will come off worse than you did before."

3   This battle with Mr. Covey was the turning-point in my career as a slave. It rekindled the few expiring embers of freedom, and revived within me a sense of my own manhood. It recalled the departed self-confidence, and inspired me again with a determination to be free. The gratification afforded by the triumph was a full compensation for whatever else might follow, even death itself. He only can understand the deep satisfaction which I experienced, who has himself repelled by force the bloody arm of slavery. I felt as I never felt before. It was a glorious resurrection, from the tomb of slavery, to the heaven of freedom. My long-crushed spirit rose, cowardice departed, bold defiance took its place; and I now resolved that, however long I might remain a slave in form, the day had passed forever when I could be a slave in fact. I did not hesitate to let it be known of me, that the white man who expected to succeed in whipping, must also succeed in killing me.

RESPONDING TO WRITING

1. Douglass's *Narrative*, from which this section is reprinted, is in whole and in part an example of "witnessing," that is, dramatizing an experience fully for an audience. How does Douglass attempt to have his readers vicariously "witness" the experience?

2. Who was Douglass's original audience for this section from his autobiography, first published in 1845? Would slave owners have been likely to read his autobiography? Blacks or whites, Northern or Southern, after the Civil War? Find passages that indicate the audiences Douglass had in mind.

3. What, if anything, does Douglass expect members of any of the previously mentioned audiences to do about slavery as a consequence of having read his narrative?

4. Explain and justify Douglass's use of the following rhetorical strategies: a very long second paragraph and some long sentences; emphasizing some events and scarcely mentioning others that occur between the Friday afternoon and Monday morning of his narrative; using literary language to discuss an experience he had long before he become a writer and orator.

5. Douglass identifies his defiance of Mr. Covey as "the turning-point in my career as a slave," a watershed experience in establishing his self-identity. Write a narrative in which you recount and explain the significance of a comparable experience in which you attained an important change of self-image or status in others' eyes.

"I Just Wanna Be Average"

MIKE ROSE

In his award-winning *Lives on the Boundary* (1989), Mike Rose (born 1944) explains his understanding of the book's subtitle, *The Struggles and Achievements of America's Underprepared*. Growing up in Los Angeles, in a poor neighborhood near Watts, Rose remembers his early years as "a peculiar mix of physical warmth and barrenness." His father was ill and disabled, his mother worked nights as a waitress; his childhood days were "quiet, lazy, lonely." Only reading "opened up the world," but a mixup in high school placement tests put Rose in the vocational track, a euphemism for the bottom level. There he was labeled "slow" and placed in a curriculum designed not to liberate the students but to occupy their time.

Prodded by a challenging teacher of sophomore biology, Rose switched to the college prep track and in 1966 graduated from Loyola University in Los Angeles. There he learned that learning meant more than merely memorizing. Ultimately he earned three more degrees, an M.S. in education from the University of Southern California (1970), an M.A. in English (1970), and a Ph.D. in educational psychology (1981) from UCLA. Rose has remained at UCLA as a professor of education. His experiences in tutoring veterans and Chicano, Asian, and black students provided firsthand research not only for *Lives on the Boundary*, but also for his investigation of the writing processes of anxious writers, explained in *Writer's Block: The Cognitive Dimension* (1984). For his 1999 book *Possible Lives*, Rose spent four years visiting the public-school classrooms of America where he repeatedly found students and teachers succeeding against all odds and in spite of the apocryphal images of both groups prevalent in the news media.

1   My rhapsodic and prescientific astronomy carried me into my teens, consumed me right up till high school, losing out finally, and only, to the siren call of pubescence—that endocrine hoodoo that transmogrifies nice boys into gawky flesh fiends. My mother used to bring home *Confidential* magazine, a peep-show rag specializing in the sins of the stars, and it beckoned me mercilessly: Jayne Mansfield's cleavage, Gina Lollobrigida's eyes, innuendos about deviant sexuality, ads for Frederick's of Hollywood—spiked heels, lacy brassieres, the epiphany of silk panties on a mannequin's hips. Along with Phil Everly, I was through with counting the stars above.

2   Budding manhood. Only adults talk about adolescence budding. Kids have no choice but to talk in extremes; they're being wrenched and buffeted, rabbit-punched from inside by systemic thugs. Nothing sweet and pastoral here. Kids become ridiculous and touching at one and the same time: passionate about the trivial, fixed before the mirror, yet traversing one of the most important rites of passage in their lives— liminal people, silly and profoundly human. Given my own expertise, I fantasized about concocting the fail-safe aphrodisiac that would bring Marianne Bilpusch, the cloakroom monitor, rushing into my arms or about commanding a squadron of bosomy, linguistically mysterious astronauts like Zsa Zsa Gabor. My parents used to say that their son would have the best education they could afford. Maybe I would be a doctor. There was a public school in our neighborhood and several Catholic schools to the west. They had heard that quality schooling meant private, Catholic schooling, so they somehow got the money together to send me to Our Lady of Mercy, fifteen or so miles southwest of Ninety-first and Vermont. So much for my fantasies. Most Catholic secondary schools then were separated by gender.

3   I took two buses to get to Our Lady of Mercy. The first started deep in South Los Angeles and caught me at midpoint. The second drifted through neighborhoods with trees, parks, big lawns, and lots of flowers. The rides were long but were livened up by a group of South L.A. veterans whose parents also thought that Hope had set up a shop in the west end of the county. There was Christy Biggars, who, at sixteen, was dealing and was, according to rumor, a pimp as well. There were Bill Cobb and Johnny Gonzales, grease-pencil artists extraordinaire, who left Nembutal-enhanced swirls of "Cobb" and "Johnny" on the corrugated walls of the bus. And then there was Tyrell Wilson. Tyrrell was the coolest kid I knew. He ran the dozens like a metric halfback, laid down a rap that outrhymed and outpointed Cobb, whose rap was good

but not great—the curse of a moderately soulful kid trapped in white skin. But it was Cobb who would sneak a radio onto the bus, and thus underwrote his patter with Little Richard, Fats Domino, Chuck Berry, the Coasters, and Ernie K. Doe's mother-in-law, an awful woman who was "sent from down below." And so it was that Christy and Cobb and Johnny G. and Tyrrell and I and assorted others picked up along the way passed our days in the back of the bus, a funny mix brought together by geography and parental desire.

Entrance to school brings with it forms and releases and assessments. Mercy relied on a series of tests, mostly the Stanford-Binet, for placement, and somehow the results of my tests got confused with those of another student named Rose. The other Rose apparently didn't do very well, for I was placed in the vocational track, a euphemism for the bottom level. Neither I nor my parents realized what this meant. We had no sense that Business Math, Typing, and English-Level D were dead ends. The current spate of reports on the schools criticizes parents for not involving themselves in the education of their children. But how would someone like Tommy Rose, with his two years of Italian schooling, know what to ask? And what sort of pressure could an exhausted waitress apply? The error went undetected, and I remained in the vocational track for two years. What a place.   4

My homeroom was supervised by Brother Dill, a troubled and unstable man who also taught freshman English. When his class drifted away from him, which was often, his voice would rise in paranoid accusations, and occasionally he would lose control and shake or smack us. I hadn't been there two months when one of his brisk, face-turning slaps had my glasses sliding down the aisle. Physical education was also pretty harsh. Our teacher was a stubby ex-lineman who had played old-time pro ball in the Midwest. He routinely had us grabbing our ankles to receive his stinging paddle across our butts. He did that, he said, to make men of us. "Rose," he bellowed on our first encounter; me standing geeky in line in my baggy shorts. "'Rose'? What the hell kind of name is that?"   5

"Italian, sir," I squeaked.   6

"Italian! Ho. Rose, do you know the sound a bag of shit makes when it hits the wall?"   7

"No, sir."   8

"Wop!"   9

Sophomore English was taught by Mr. Mitropetros. He was a large, bejeweled man who managed the parking lot at the Shrine Auditorium. He would crow and preen and list for us the stars he'd brushed against. We'd ask questions and glance knowingly and snicker, and all that fueled the poor guy to brag some more. Parking cars was his night job. He had little training in English, so his lesson plan for his day work had us reading the district's required text, *Julius Caesar*, aloud for the   10 semester. We'd finish the play way before the twenty weeks was up, so he'd have us switch parts again and again and start again: Dave Snyder, the fastest guy at Mercy, muscling through Caesar to the breathless squeals of Calpurnia, as interpreted by Steve Fusco, a surfer who owned the school's most envied paneled wagon. Week ten and Dave and Steve would take on new roles, as would we all, and render a water-logged Cassius and a Brutus that are beyond my powers of description.

11   Spanish I—taken in the second year—fell into the hands of a new recruit. Mr. Montez was a tiny man, slight, five foot six at the most, soft-spoken and delicate. Spanish was a particularly rowdy class, and Mr. Montez was as prepared for it as a doily maker at a hammer throw. He would tap his pencil to a room in which Steve Fusco was propelling spitballs from his heavy lips, in which Mike Deetz was taunting Billy Hawk, a half-Indian, half-Spanish, reed-thin, quietly explosive boy. The vocational track at Our Lady of Mercy mixed kids traveling in from South L.A. with South Bay surfers and a few Slavs and Chicanos from the harbors of San Pedro. This was a dangerous miscellany: surfers and hodads and South-Central blacks all ablaze to the metronomic tapping of Hector Montez's pencil.

12   One day Billy lost it. Out of the corner of my eye I saw him strike out with his right arm and catch Dweetz across the neck. Quick as a spasm, Dweetz was out of his seat, scattering desks, cracking Billy on the side of the head, right behind the eye. Snyder and Fusco and others broke it up, but the room felt hot and close and naked. Mr. Montez's tenuous authority was finally ripped to shreds, and I think everyone felt a little strange about that. The charade was over, and when it came down to it, I don't think any of the kids really wanted it to end this way. They had pushed and pushed and bullied their way into a freedom that both scared and embarrassed them.

13   Students will float to the mark you set. I and the others in the vocational classes were bobbing in pretty shallow water. Vocational education has aimed at increasing the economic opportunities of students who do not do well in our schools. Some serious programs succeed in doing that, and through exceptional teachers—like Mr. Gross in *Horace's Compromise*—students learn to develop hypotheses and troubleshoot, reason through a problem, and communicate effectively—the true job skills. The vocational track, however, is most often a place for those who are just not making it, a dumping ground for the disaffected. There were a few teachers who worked hard at education; young Brother Slattery, for example, combined a stern voice with weekly quizzes to try to pass along to us a skeletal outline of world history. But mostly the teachers had no idea of how to engage the imaginations of us kids who were scuttling along at the bottom of the pond.

And the teachers would have needed some inventiveness, for none   14
of us was groomed for the classroom. It wasn't just that I didn't know
things—didn't know how to simplify algebraic fractions, couldn't
identify different kinds of clauses, bungled Spanish translations—but
that I had developed various faulty and inadequate ways of doing algebra and making sense of Spanish. Worse yet, the years of defensive
tuning out in elementary school had given me a way to escape quickly
while seeming at least half alert. During my time in Voc. Ed., I developed further into a mediocre student and a somnambulant problem
solver, and that affected the subjects I did have the wherewithal to handle: I detested Shakespeare; I got bored with history. My attention flit-
ted here and there. I fooled around in class and read my books
indifferently—the intellectual equivalent of playing with your food. I
did what I had to do to get by, and I did it with half a mind.

But I did learn things about people and eventually came into my   15
own socially. I liked the guys in Voc. Ed. Growing up where I did, I understood and admired physical prowess, and there was an abundance
of muscle here. There was Dave Snyder, a sprinter and halfback of true
quality. Dave's ability and his quick wit gave him a natural appeal, and
he was welcome in any clique, though he always kept a little independent. He enjoyed acting the fool and could care less about studies, but
he possessed a certain maturity and never caused the faculty much
trouble. It was a testament to his independence that he included me
among his friends—I eventually went out for track, but I was no jock.
Owing to the Latin alphabet and a dearth of Rs and Ss., Snyder sat behind Rose, and we started exchanging one-liners and became friends.

There was Ted Richard, a much-touted Little League pitcher. He   16
was chunky and had a baby face and came to Our Lady of Mercy as a
seasoned street fighter. Ted was quick to laugh and he had a loud,
jolly laugh, but when he got angry he'd smile a little smile, the kind
that simply raises the corner of the mouth a quarter of an inch. For
those who knew, it was an eerie signal. Those who didn't found themselves in big trouble, for Ted was very quick. He loved to carry on
what we would come to call philosophical discussions: What is
courage? Does God exist? He also loved words, enjoyed picking up
big ones like *salubrious* and *equivocal* and using them in our conversations—laughing at himself as the word hit a chuckhole rolling off his
tongue. Ted didn't do all that well in school—baseball and parties
and testing the courage he'd speculated about took up his time. His
textbooks were *Argosy* and *Field and Stream*, whatever newspapers
he'd find on the bus stop—from *The Daily Worker* to pornography—
conversations with uncles or hobos or businessmen he'd meet in a
coffee shop, *The Old Man and the Sea*. With hindsight, I can see that
Ted was developing into one of those rough-hewn intellectuals whose

sources are a mix of the learned and the apocryphal, whose discussions are both assured and sad.

17   And then there was Ken Harvey. Ken was good-looking in a puffy way and had a full and oily ducktail and was a car enthusiast . . . a hodad. One day in religion class, he said the sentence that turned out to be one of the most memorable of the hundreds of thousands I heard in those Voc. Ed. years. We were talking about the parable of the talents, about achievement, working hard, doing the best you can do, blah-blah-blah, when the teacher called on the restive Ken Harvey for an opinion. Ken thought about it, but just for a second, and said (with studied, minimal affect), "I just wanna be average." That woke me up. Average?! Who wants to be average? Then the athletes chimed in with the clichés that make you want to laryngectomize them, and the exchange became a platitudinous melee. At the time, I thought Ken's assertion was stupid, and I wrote him off. But his sentence has stayed with me all these years, and I think I am finally coming to understand it.

18   Ken Harvey was gasping for air. School can be a tremendously disorienting place. No matter how bad the school, you're going to encounter notions that don't fit with the assumptions and beliefs that you grew up with—maybe you'll hear these dissonant notions from teachers, maybe from the other students, and maybe you'll read them. You'll also be thrown in with all kinds of kids from all kinds of backgrounds, and that can be unsettling—this is especially true in places of rich ethnic and linguistic mix, like the L.A. basin. You'll see a handful of students far excel you in courses that sound exotic and that are only in the curriculum of the elite: French, physics, trigonometry. And all this is happening while you're trying to shape an identity, your body is changing, and your emotions are running wild. If you're a working-class kid in the vocational track, the options you'll have to deal with this will be constrained in certain ways: You're defined by your school as "slow"; you're placed in a curriculum that isn't designed to liberate you but to occupy you, or, if you're lucky, train you, though the training is for work the society does not esteem; other students are picking up the cues from your school and your curriculum and interacting with you in particular ways. If you're a kid like Ted Richard, you turn your back on all this and let your mind roam where it may. But youngsters like Ted are rare. What Ken and so many others do is protect themselves from such suffocating madness by taking on with a vengeance the identity implied in the vocational track. Reject the confusion and frustration by openly defining yourself as the Common Joe. Champion the average. Rely on your own good sense. Fuck this bullshit. Bullshit, of course, is everything you—and the others—fear is beyond you:

books, essays, tests, academic scrambling, complexity, scientific reasoning, philosophical inquiry.

The tragedy is that you have to twist the knife in your own gray 19 matter to make this defense work. You'll have to shut down, have to reject intellectual stimuli or diffuse them with sarcasm, have to cultivate stupidity, have to convert boredom from a malady into a way of confronting the world. Keep your vocabulary simple, act stoned when you're not or act more stoned than you are, flaunt ignorance, materialize your dreams. It is a powerful and effective defense—it neutralizes the insult and the frustration of being a vocational kid and, when perfected, it drives teachers up the wall, a delightful secondary effect. But like all strong magic, it exacts a price.

My own deliverance from the Voc. Ed. world began with sopho- 20 more biology. Every student, college prep to vocational, had to take biology, and unlike the other courses, the same person taught all sections. When teaching the vocational group, Brother Clint probably slowed down a bit or omitted a little of the fundamental biochemistry, but he used the same book and more or less the same syllabus across the board. If one class got tough, he could get tougher. He was young and powerful and very handsome, and looks and physical strength were high currency. No one gave him any trouble.

I was pretty bad at the dissecting table, but the lectures and the 21 textbook were interesting: plastic overlays that, with each turned page, peeled away skin, then veins and muscle, then organs, down to the very bones that Brother Clint, pointer in hand, would tap out on our hanging skeleton. Dave Snyder was in big trouble, for the study of life—versus the living of it—was sticking in his craw. We worked out a code for our multiple-choice exams. He'd poke me in the back: once for the answer under A, twice for B, and so on; and when he'd hit the right one, I'd look up to the ceiling as though I were lost in thought. Poke: cytoplasm. Poke, poke: methane. Poke, poke, poke: William Harvey. Poke, poke, poke, poke: islets of Langerhans. This didn't work out perfectly, but Dave passed the course, and I mastered the dreamy look of a guy on a record jacket. And something else happened. Brother Clint puzzled over this Voc. Ed. kid who was racking up 98s and 99s on his tests. He checked the school's records and discovered the error. He recommended that I begin my junior year in the College Prep program. According to all I've read since, such a shift, as one report put it, is virtually impossible. Kids at that level rarely cross tracks. The telling thing is how chancy both my placement into and exit from Voc. Ed. was; neither I nor my parents had anything to do with it. I lived in one world during spring semester, and when I came back to school in the fall, I was living in another.

22   Switching to College Prep was a mixed blessing. I was an erratic student. I was undisciplined. And I hadn't caught onto the rules of the game: Why work hard in a class that didn't grab my fancy? I was also hopelessly behind in math. Chemistry was hard; toying with my chemistry set years before hadn't prepared me for the chemist's equations. Fortunately, the priest who taught both chemistry and second-year algebra was also the school's athletic director. Membership on the track team covered me; I knew I wouldn't get lower than a C. U.S. history was taught pretty well, and I did okay. But civics was taken over by a football coach who had trouble reading the textook aloud—and reading aloud was the centerpiece of his pedagogy. College Prep at Mercy was certainly an improvement over the vocational program—at least it carried some status—but the social science curriculum was weak, and the mathematics and physical sciences were simply beyond me. I had a miserable quantitative background and ended up copying some assignments and finessing the rest as best I could. Let me try to explain how it feels to see again and again material you should once have learned but didn't.

23   You are given a problem. It requires you to simplify algebraic fractions or to multiply expressions containing square roots. You know this is pretty basic material because you've seen it for years. Once a teacher took some time with you, and you learned how to carry out these operations. Simple versions, anyway. But that was a year or two or more in the past, and these are more complex versions, and now you're not sure. And this, you keep telling yourself, is ninth- or even eighth-grade stuff.

24   Next it's a word problem. This is also old hat. The basic elements are as familiar as story characters: trains speeding so many miles per hour or shadows of buildings angling so many degrees. Maybe you know enough, have sat through enough explanations, to be able to begin setting up the problem: "If one train is going this fast . . ." or "This shadow is really one line of a triangle. . . ." Then: "Let's see . . ." "How did Jones do this?" "Hmmmm." "No." "No, that won't work." Your attention wavers. You wonder about other things: a football game, a dance, that cute new checker at the market. You try to focus on the problem again. You scribble on paper for a while, but the tension wins out and your attention flits elsewhere. You crumple the paper and begin daydreaming to ease the frustration.

25   The particulars will vary, but in essence this is what a number of students go through, especially those in so-called remedial classes. They open their textbooks and see once again the familiar and impenetrable formulas and diagrams and terms that have stumped them for years. There is no excitement here. *No* excitement. Regardless of what the teacher says, this is not a new challenge. There is, rather, embar-

rassment and frustration and, not surprisingly, some anger in being reminded once again of long-standing inadequacies. No wonder so many students finally attribute their difficulties to something inborn, organic: "That part of my brain just doesn't work." Given the troubling histories many of these students have, it's miraculous that any of them can lift the shroud of hopelessness sufficiently to make deliverance from these classes possible.

RESPONDING TO READING

1. Rose re-creates the ambience and context of a parochial California high school in the 1960s. To what extent is Our Lady of Mercy in Los Angeles representative of high school as you and your peers have experienced it? What has remained constant over time? What has changed?

2. Analyze the following passage to show how Rose creates a composite character, "the Common Joe," to express a point of view and a range of behavior that create more educational and personal and social problems than they solve.

> The tragedy is that you have to twist the knife in your own gray matter to make this defense work. You'll have to shut down, have to reject intellectual stimuli or diffuse them with sarcasm, have to cultivate stupidity, have to convert boredom from a malady into a way of confronting the world. . . . It is a powerful and effective defense—it neutralizes the insult and the frustration of being a vocational kid and, when perfected, it drives teachers up the wall. . . . But like all strong magic, it exacts a price. [paragraph 19]

How does this description differ from conventional explanations of why students in the low track do not learn? What evidence does Rose present to support his view? What is his attitude toward the students he describes? How convincing do you find his explanation?

3. Why would a student "just wanna be average," rather than to excel? What aspects of the school itself—student placement, courses, attitudes of teachers and students, for instance—contribute to the students' expectations of themselves? What is the influence of the home? The outside culture? What does it take for a student to move beyond the average?

4. Describe your group in high school, with particular attention to their expectations, and yours, and how these expectations developed.

On Self-Respect

JOAN DIDION

"People with self-respect," says Joan Didion in the following essay, "exhibit a certain toughness, a kind of moral nerve; they display what was once called *character* . . . the willingness to accept responsibility for one's own life." In one way or another, Didion's collections of essays, *Slouching Towards Bethlehem* (1968) and *The White Album* (1979), and her novels focus on people who lack character, struggle with self-respect, and, too often, lose the struggle. Many of the major characters in the novels *Run River* (1963), *Play It As It Lays* (1971), *A Book of Common Prayer* (1977), *Democracy* (1984), and *The Last Thing He Wanted* (1996) and in the essays in *After Henry* (1992) are estranged from the traditional values of religion, family, and society. They do not know what to do or where to turn to find the stability, peace, and certainty they seek. These themes find their most extreme expression in works such as *Salvador* (1983), which deals with the ghastly and pointless frenzy of killing in El Salvador's ongoing civil war.

Didion was born in Sacramento, California, in 1934, and educated at the University of California, Berkeley. In 1964 she married writer John Gregory Dunne, and the couple moved to Los Angeles to collaborate on screenplays (*Panic in Needle Park* [1971], *A Star is Born* [1976]) and to try to forge a family and community "in the face of what many people believe to be a moral vacuum." In response to an interviewer's suggestion that "You seem to live your life on the edge, or, at least, on the literary idea of the edge," Didion replied, "Again, it's a literary idea, and it derives from what engaged me imaginatively as a child. I can recall disapproving of the golden mean, always thinking there was more to be learned from the dark journey. The dark journey engaged me more." The dark journey is what passionate writers take, and life on the edge is where they live; to do so demands the character and self-respect required to compel readers to, as Didion says, "*listen to me, see it my way, change your mind.*"

1   Once, in a dry season, I wrote in large letters across two pages of a notebook that innocence ends when one is stripped of the delusion that one likes oneself. Although now, some years later, I marvel that a mind on the outs with itself should have nonetheless made painstaking record of its every tremor, I recall with embarrassing clarity the flavor of those particular ashes. It was a matter of misplaced self-respect.

2   I had not been elected to Phi Beta Kappa. This failure could scarcely have been more predictable or less ambiguous (I simply did not have the grades), but I was unnerved by it; I had somehow thought myself a kind of academic Raskolnikov, curiously exempt from the cause-effect relationships which hampered others. Although even the humorless nineteen-year-old that I was must have recognized that the situation lacked real tragic stature, the day that I did not make Phi Beta Kappa nonetheless marked the end of something, and innocence may well be the word for it. I lost the conviction that lights would always turn green for me, the pleasant certainty that those rather passive virtues which had won me approval as a child automatically guaranteed me not only Phi Beta Kappa keys but happiness, honor, and the love of a good man;

lost a certain touching faith in the totem power of good manners, clean hair, and proven competence on the Stanford-Binet scale. To such doubtful amulets had my self-respect been pinned, and I faced myself that day with the nonplused apprehension of someone who has come across a vampire and has no crucifix at hand.

Although to be driven back upon oneself is an uneasy affair at best, rather like trying to cross a border with borrowed credentials, it seems to me now the one condition necessary to the beginnings of real self-respect. Most of our platitudes notwithstanding, self-deception remains the most difficult deception. The tricks that work on others count for nothing in that very well-lit back alley where one keeps assignations with oneself: no winning smiles will do here, no prettily drawn lists of good intentions. One shuffles flashily but in vain through one's marked cards—the kindness done for the wrong reason, the apparent triumph which involved no real effort, the seemingly heroic act into which one had been shamed. The dismal fact is that self-respect has nothing to do with the approval of others—who are, after all, deceived easily enough; has nothing to do with reputation, which, as Rhett Butler told Scarlett O'Hara, is something people with courage can do without. 3

To do without self-respect, on the other hand, is to be an unwilling audience of one to an interminable documentary that details one's failings, both real and imagined, with fresh footage spliced in for every screening. *There's the glass you broke in anger, there's the hurt on X's face; watch now, this next scene, the night Y came back from Houston, see how you muff this one.* To live without self-respect is to lie awake some night, beyond the reach of warm milk, phenobarbital, and the sleeping hand on the coverlet, counting up the sins of commission and omission, the trusts betrayed, the promises subtly broken, the gifts irrevocably wasted through sloth or cowardice or carelessness. However long we postpone it, we eventually lie down alone in that notoriously uncomfortable bed, the one we make ourselves. Whether or not we sleep in it depends, of course, on whether or not we respect ourselves. 4

To protest that some fairly improbable people, some people who *could not possibly respect themselves,* seem to sleep easily enough is to miss the point entirely, as surely as those people miss it who think that self-respect has necessarily to do with not having safety pins in one's underwear. There is a common superstition that "self-respect" is a kind of charm against snakes, something that keeps those who have it locked in some unblighted Eden, out of strange beds, ambivalent conversations, and trouble in general. It does not at all. It has nothing to do with the face of things, but concerns instead a separate peace, a private reconciliation. Although the careless, suicidal Julian English in 5

Appointment in Samarra and the careless, incurably dishonest Jordan Baker in *The Great Gatsby* seem equally improbable candidates for self-respect, Jordan Baker had it, Julian English did not. With that genius for accommodation more often seen in women than in men, Jordan took her own measure, made her own peace, avoided threats to that peace: "I hate careless people," she told Nick Carraway. "It takes two to make an accident."

6   Like Jordan Baker, people with self-respect have the courage of their mistakes. They know the price of things. If they choose to commit adultery, they do not then go running, in an access of bad conscience, to receive absolution from the wronged parties; nor do they complain unduly of the unfairness, the undeserved embarrassment, of being named co-respondent. In brief, people with self-respect exhibit a certain toughness, a kind of moral nerve; they display what was once called *character*, a quality which, although approved in the abstract, sometimes loses ground to other, more instantly negotiable virtues. The measure of its slipping prestige is that one tends to think of it only in connection with homely children and United States senators who have been defeated, preferably in the primary, for reelection. Nonetheless, character—the willingness to accept responsibility for one's own life—is the source from which self-respect springs.

7   Self-respect is something that our grandparents, whether or not they had it, knew all about. They had instilled in them, young, a certain discipline, the sense that one lives by doing things one does not particularly want to do, by putting fears and doubts to one side, by weighing immediate comforts against the possibility of larger, even intangible, comforts. It seemed to the nineteenth century admirable, but not remarkable, that Chinese Gordon put on a clean white suit and held Khartoum against the Mahdi; it did not seem unjust that the way to free land in California involved death and difficulty and dirt. In a diary kept during the winter of 1846, an emigrating twelve-year-old named Narcissa Cornwall noted coolly: "Father was busy reading and did not notice that the house was being filled with strange Indians until Mother spoke about it." Even lacking any clue as to what Mother said, one can scarcely fail to be impressed by the entire incident: the father reading, the Indians filing in, the mother choosing the words that would not alarm, the child duly recording the event and nothing further that those particular Indians were not, "fortunately for us," hostile. Indians were simply part of the *donnée*.

8   In one guise or another, Indians always are. Again, it is a question of recognizing that anything worth having has its price. People who respect themselves are willing to accept the risk that the Indians will be hostile, that the venture will go bankrupt, that the liaison may not turn out to be one in which *every day is a holiday because you're married to me.*

They are willing to invest something of themselves; they may not play at all, but when they do play, they know the odds.

That kind of self-respect is a discipline, a habit of mind that can   9
never be faked but can be developed, trained, coaxed forth. It was once suggested to me that, as an antidote to crying, I put my head in a paper bag. As it happens, there is a sound physiological reason, something to do with oxygen, for doing exactly that, but the psychological effect alone is incalculable: it is difficult in the extreme to continue fancying oneself Cathy in *Wuthering Heights* with one's head in a Food Fair bag. There is a similar case for all the small disciplines, unimportant in themselves; imagine maintaining any kind of swoon, commiserative or carnal, in a cold shower.

But those small disciplines are valuable only insofar as they repre-   10
sent larger ones. To say that Waterloo was won on the playing fields of Eton is not to say that Napoleon might have been saved by a crash pro-gram in cricket; to give formal dinners in the rain forest would be pointless did not the candlelight flickering on the liana call forth deep-er, stronger disciplines, values instilled long before. It is a kind of ritu-al, helping us to remember who and what we are. In order to remember it, one must have known it.

To have that sense of one's intrinsic worth which constitutes self-   11
respect is potentially to have everything: the ability to discriminate, to love and to remain indifferent. To lack it is to be locked within oneself, paradoxically incapable of either love or indifference. If we do not re-spect ourselves, we are on the one hand forced to despise those who have so few resources as to consort with us, so little perception as to re-main blind to our fatal weaknesses. On the other, we are peculiarly in thrall to everyone we see, curiously determined to live out—since our self-image is untenable—their false notions of us. We flatter ourselves by thinking this compulsion to please others an attractive trait: a gist for imaginative empathy, evidence of our willingness to give. *Of course* I will play Francesca to your Paolo, Helen Keller to anyone's Annie Sul-livan: no expectation is too misplaced, no role too ludicrous. At the mercy of those we cannot but hold in contempt, we play roles doomed to failure before they are begun, each defeat generating fresh despair at the urgency of divining and meeting the next demand made upon us.

It is the phenomenon sometimes called "alienation from self." In its   12
advanced stages, we no longer answer the telephone, because someone might want something; that we could say *no* without drowning in self-reproach is an idea alien to this game. Every encounter demands too much, tears the nerves, drains the will, and the specter of something as small as an unanswered letter arouses such disproportionate guilt that answering it becomes out of the question. To assign unanswered letters their proper weight, to free us from the expectations of others, to give

us back to ourselves—there lies the great, the singular power of self-respect. Without it, one eventually discovers the final turn of the screw: one runs away to find oneself, and finds no one at home.

RESPONDING TO READING

1. What, in Didion's view, differentiates self-respect from reputation? Do you agree with Didion that self-respect is far more important than reputation? Why or why not?

2. Explain Didion's observation "people with self-respect have the courage of their mistakes. They know the price of things." (paragraph 6).

3. What is the relation of risk-taking to self-respect (*see* paragraphs 7–8)? Illustrate your answer with reference to your own experience, or that of someone you know or have read about. The risk might be physical (in war, in sports, or in using dangerous machines), intellectual (experimenting with new, daring, shocking, or otherwise radical ideas in any discipline), economic (quitting or changing jobs, investing in an impossible dream or scheme), or some other sort. What "price," if any, was paid?

4. How are self-discipline and self-respect interrelated? How can a person develop either, or both? Why, in Didion's view, are they worth the effort? Do you agree? To illustrate your answer, interpret an experience or life pattern of your own or someone you know well—for instance, the discipline and practice required to become a champion athlete, or a successful musician or writer, or to overcome or accommodate to a physical, mental, or emotional disability. (*See*, for instance, Nancy Mairs, "On Being a Cripple.") Does fighting discrimination, as explained by Frederick Douglass, Sojourner Truth, and Martin Luther King, Jr., require comparable self-discipline? In what ways does such effort enhance self-respect?

Notes of a Native Speaker

ERIC LIU

Born (1968) in Poughkeepsie, New York, Eric Liu fit easily into the suburban environment of his youth. The fact that he was assimilating his Chinese racial background into "white" culture was not an issue. His mother and father, immigrants from Taiwan and professionals in the computer industry, set a challenging pace: "I grew up feeling that my life was Book II of an ongoing saga," write Liu, "or that I was running the second leg of a relay race." The race included a degree at Yale (B.A., *summa cum laude*, 1990), an internship with Senator Daniel Patrick Moynihan, and two summers at Marine Officer Candidate School in Quantico, Virginia. Liu became a speechwriter, first for Secretary of State Warren Christopher and then for President Bill Clinton (1993), and after attending Harvard Law School (J.D., *cum laude*, 1999), he served as deputy domestic policy adviser at the White House (2000). Simultaneously, his interest in American culture led him to edit *Next: Young American Writers on the New Generation* (1994), a volume of essays about his peers in "Generation X." Contemplating the path he had followed, Liu then wrote *The Accidental Asian: Notes of a Native Speaker* (1998). A combination of autobiography and cultural analysis, the book asks how much is lost when people adapt to their surroundings and whether Asians should be forced to choose between total assimilation and total racial identification.

In "Notes of a Native Speaker," an essay from *The Accidental Asian*, Liu confronts the choices he made in his youth. Aware that his natural indifference to race would cause many Asian–Americans to label him as a "banana"—yellow on the outside, but white on the inside—he looks back on his high school and college years with honesty and humor.

1.

Here are some of the ways you could say I am "white":   1

I listen to National Public Radio.

I wear khaki Dockers.

I own brown suede bucks.

I eat gourmet greens.

I have few close friends "of color."

I married a white woman.

I am a child of the suburbs.

I furnish my condo à la Crate & Barrel.

I vacation in charming bed-and-breakfasts.

I have never once been the victim of blatant discrimination.

I am a member of several exclusive institutions.

I have been in the inner sanctums of political power.

I have been there as something other than an attendant.

I have the ambition to return.

I am a producer of the culture.

I expect my voice to be heard.

I speak flawless, unaccented English.

I subscribe to *Foreign Affairs*.

I do not mind when editorialists write in the first person plural.

I do not mind how white television casts are.

I am not too ethnic.

I am wary of minority militants.

I consider myself neither in exile nor in opposition.

I am considered "a credit to my race."

I never asked to be white. I am not literally white. That is, I do not have white skin or white ancestors. I have yellow skin and yellow ancestors, hundreds of generations of them. But like so many other Asian Americans of the second generation, I find myself now the bearer of a strange new status: white, by acclamation. Thus it is that I have been described as an "honorary white," by other whites, and as a "banana," by other Asians. Both the honorific and the epithet take as a given this idea: to the extent that I have moved away from the periphery and toward the center of American life, I have become white inside. *Some are born white, others achieve whiteness, still others have whiteness thrust upon them.* This, supposedly, is what it means to assimilate.

2   There was a time when assimilation did quite strictly mean whitening. In fact, well into the first half of this century, mimicry of the stylized standards of the WASP gentry was the proper, dominant, perhaps even sole method of ensuring that your origins would not be held against you. You "made it" in society not only by putting on airs of anglitude, but also by assiduously bleaching out the marks of a darker, dirtier past. And this bargain, stifling as it was, was open to European immigrants almost exclusively; to blacks, only on the passing occasion; to Asians, hardly at all.

3   Times have changed, and I suppose you could call it progress that a Chinaman, too, may now aspire to whiteness. But precisely because the times have changed, that aspiration—and the *imputation* of the aspiration—now seems astonishingly outmoded. The meaning of "American" has undergone a revolution in the twenty-nine years I have been alive, a revolution of color, class, and culture. Yet the vocabulary of "assimilation" has remained fixed all this time: fixed in whiteness, which is still our metonym for power; and fixed in shame, which is what the colored are expected to feel for embracing the power.

4   I have assimilated. I am of the mainstream. In many ways I fit the psychological profile of the so-called banana: imitative, impressionable, rootless, eager to please. As I will admit in this essay, I have at times gone to great lengths to downplay my difference, the better to penetrate the "establishment" of the moment. Yet I'm not sure that what I did was so cut-and-dried as "becoming white." I plead guilty to the charges above: achieving, learning the ways of the upper middle class, distancing myself from radicals of any hue. But having confessed, I still do not know my crime.

5   To be an accused banana is to stand at the ill-fated intersection of class and race. And because class is the only thing Americans have more trouble talking about than race, a minority's climb up the social

ladder is often willfully misnamed and wrongly portrayed. There is usually, in the portrayal, a strong whiff of betrayal: the assimilist is a traitor to his kind, to his class, to his own family. He cannot gain the world without losing his soul. To be sure, something *is* lost in any migration, whether from place to place or from class to class. But something is gained as well. And the result is always more complicated than the monochrome language of "whiteness" and "authenticity" would suggest.

My own assimilation began long before I was born. It began with   6
my parents, who came here with an appetite for Western ways already whetted by films and books and music and, in my mother's case, by a father who'd been to the West. My parents, who traded Chinese formality for the more laissez-faire stance of this country. Who made their way by hard work and quiet adaptation. Who fashioned a comfortable life in a quiet development in a second-tier suburb. Who, unlike your "typical" Chinese parents, were not pushy, status-obsessed, rigid, disciplined, or prepared. Who were haphazard about passing down ancestral traditions and "lessons" to their children. Who did pass down, however, the sense that their children were entitled to mix and match, as they saw fit, whatever aspects of whatever cultures they encountered.

I was raised, in short, to assimilate, to claim this place as mine. I   7
don't mean that my parents told me to act like an American. That's partly the point: they didn't tell me to do anything except to be a good boy. They trusted I would find my way, and I did, following their example and navigating by the lights of the culture that encircled me like a dome. As a function of my parents' own half-conscious, half-finished acculturation, I grew up feeling that my life was Book II of an ongoing saga. Or that I was running the second leg of a relay race. *Slap!* I was out of the womb and sprinting, baton in hand. Gradually more sure of my stride, my breathing, the feel of the track beneath me. Eyes forward, never backward.

Today, nearly seven years after my father's death and two years   8
after my marriage into a large white family, it is as if I have come round a bend and realized that I am no longer sure where I am running or why. My sprint slows to a trot. I scan the unfamiliar vista that is opening up. I am somewhere else now, somewhere far from the China that yielded my mother and father; far, as well, from the modest horizons I knew as a boy. I look at my limbs and realize I am no longer that boy; my gait and grasp exceed his by an order of magnitude. Now I want desperately to see my face, to see what time has marked and what it has erased. But I can find no mirror except the people who surround me. And they are mainly pale, powerful.

How did I end up here, standing in what seems the very seat of   9
whiteness, gazing from the promontory of social privilege? How did I

cover so much ground so quickly? What was it, in my blind journey, that I felt I should leave behind? And what *did* I leave behind? This, the jettisoning of one mode of life to send another aloft, is not only the immigrant's tale; it is the son's tale, too. By coming to America, my parents made themselves into citizens of a new country. By traveling the trajectory of an assimilist, so did I.

2.

10   As a child, I lived in a state of "amoebic bliss," to borrow the felicitous phrase of the author of *Nisei Daughter*, Monica Sone. The world was a gossamer web of wonder that began with life at home, extended to my friendships, and made the imaginary realm of daydream seem as immediate as the real. If something or someone was in my personal web of meaning, then color or station was irrelevant. I made no distinctions in fourth grade between my best friend, a black boy named Kimathi, and my next-best friend, a white boy named Charlie—other than the fact that one was number one, the other number two. I did not feel, or feel for, a seam that separated the textures of my Chinese life from those of my American life. I was not "bicultural" but omnicultural, and omnivorous, too. To my mind, I differed from others in only two ways that counted: I was a faster runner than most, and a better student. Thus did work blend happily with play, school with home, Western culture with Eastern: it was all the same to a self-confident boy who believed he'd always be at the center of his own universe.

11   As I approached adolescence, though, things shifted. Suddenly, I could no longer subsume the public world under my private concept of self. Suddenly, the public world was more complicated than just a parade of smiling teachers and a few affirming friends. Now I had to contend with the unstated, inchoate, but inescapable standards of *cool*. The essence of cool was the ability to conform. The essence of conformity was the ability to anticipate what was cool. And I wasn't so good at that. For the first time, I had found something that did not come effortlessly to me. No one had warned me about this transition from happy amoeboid to social animal; no one had prepared me for the great labors of fitting in.

12   And so in three adjoining arenas—my looks, my loves, my manners—I suffered a bruising adolescent education. I don't mean to over-dramatize: there was, in these teenage banalities, usually something humorous and nothing particularly tragic. But in each of these realms, I came to feel I was not normal. And obtusely, I ascribed the difficulties of that age not to my age but to my color. I came to suspect that there was an order to things, an order that I, as someone Chinese, could perceive but not quite crack. I responded not by exploding in rebellion but

by dedicating myself, quietly and sometimes angrily, to learning the order as best I could. I was never ashamed of being Chinese; I was, in fact, rather proud to be linked to a great civilization. But I was mad that my difference should matter now. And if it had to matter, I did not want it to defeat me.

Consider, if you will, my hair. For the first eleven years of my life, I 13 sported what was essentially the same hairstyle: a tapered bowl cut, the handiwork of my mother. For those eleven joyful years, this low-maintenance do was entirely satisfactory. But in my twelfth year, as sixth grade got under way, I became aware—gradually at first, then urgently—that bangs were no longer the look for boys. This was the year when certain early bloomers first made the height-weight-physique distribution in our class seem startlingly wide—and when I first realized that I was lingering near the bottom. It was essential that I compensate for my childlike mien by cultivating at least a patina of teenage style.

This is where my hair betrayed me. For some readers the words 14 "Chinese hair" should suffice as explanation. For the rest, particularly those who have spent all your lives with the ability to comb back, style, and part your hair *at will*, what follows should make you count your blessings. As you may recall, 1980 was a vintage year for hair that was parted straight down the middle, then feathered on each side, feathered so immaculately that the ends would meet in the back like the closed wings of angels. I dreamed of such hair. I imagined tossing my head back casually, to ease into place the one or two strands that had drifted from their positions. I dreamed of wearing the fluffy, tailored locks of the blessed.

Instead, I was cursed. My hair was straight, rigid, and wiry. Not 15 only did it fail to feather back; it would not even bend. Worse still, it grew the wrong way. That is, it all emanated from a single swirl near the rear edge of my scalp. Parting my hair in any direction except back to front, the way certain balding men stage their final retreat, was a physical impossibility. It should go without saying that this was a disaster. For the next three years, I experimented with a variety of hairstyles that ranged from the ridiculous to the sublimely bad. There was the stringy pothead look. The mushroom do. Helmet head. Bangs folded back like curtains. I enlisted a blow-dryer, a Conair set on high heat, to force my hair into stiff postures of submission. The results, though sometimes innovative, fell always far short of cool.

I feigned nonchalance, and no one ever said anything about it. But 16 make no mistake: this was one of the most consuming crises of my inner life as a young teen. Though neither of my parents had ever had such troubles, I blamed this predicament squarely on my Chinese genes. And I could not abide my fate. At a time when homogeneity was the highest virtue, I felt I stood out like a pigtailed Manchu.

17 My salvation didn't come until the end of junior high, when one of my buddies, in an epiphany as we walked past the Palace of Hair Design, dared me to get my head shaved. Without hesitation, I did it—to the tearful laughter of my friends and, soon afterward, the tearful horror of my mother. Of course, I had moments of doubt the next few days as I rubbed my peach-fuzzed skull. But what I liked was this: I had managed, without losing face, to rid myself of my greatest social burden. What's more, in the eyes of some classmates, I was now a bold (if bald) iconoclast. I've worn a crew cut ever since.

18 Well-styled hair was only one part of a much larger preoccupation during the ensuing years: wooing girls. In this realm I experienced a most frustrating kind of success. I was the boy that girls always found "sweet" and "funny" and "smart" and "nice." Which, to my highly sensitive ear, sounded like "leprous." Time and again, I would charm a girl into deep friendship. Time and again, as the possibility of romance came within reach, I would smash into what I took to be a glass ceiling.

19 The girls were white, you see; such were the demographics of my school. I was Chinese. And I was convinced that this was the sole obstacle to my advancement. It made sense, did it not? I was, after all, sweet and funny and smart and nice. Hair notwithstanding, I was not unattractive, at least compared with some of the beasts who had started "going out" with girls. There was simply no other explanation. Yet I could never say this out loud: it would have been the whining of a loser. My response, then, was to secretly scorn the girls I coveted. It was *they* who were subpar, whose small-mindedness and veiled prejudice made them unworthy.

20 My response, too, was to take refuge in my talents. I made myself into a Renaissance boy, playing in the orchestra but also joining the wrestling team, winning science prizes but also editing the school paper. I thought I was defying the stereotype of the Asian American male as a one-dimensional nerd. But in the eyes of some, I suppose, I was simply another "Asian overachiever."

21 In hindsight, it's hard to know exactly how great a romantic penalty I paid for being Chinese. There may have been girls who would have had nothing to do with me on account of my race, but I never knew them. There were probably girls who, race aside, simply didn't like me. And then there were girls who liked me well enough but who also shied from the prospect of being part of an interracial couple. With so many boys out there, they probably reasoned, why take the path of greater resistance? Why risk so many status points? Why not be "just friends" with this Chinese boy?

22 Maybe this stigma was more imagined than real. But being an ABC ("American-born Chinese," as our parents called us) certainly affected me another way. It made me feel like something of a greenhorn, a social immigrant. I wanted so greatly to be liked. And my earnestness,

though endearing, was not the sort of demeanor that won girls' hearts. Though I was observant enough to notice how people talked when flirting, astute enough to mimic the forms, I was oblivious to the subterranean levels of courtship, blind to the more subtle rituals of "getting chicks" by spurning them. I held the view that if you were manifestly a good person, eventually someone of the opposite sex would do the rational thing and be smitten with you. I was clueless. Many years would pass before I'd wise up.

3.

I recently dug up a photograph of myself from freshman year of 23 college that made me smile. I have on the wrong shoes, the wrong socks, the wrong checkered shirt tucked the wrong way into the wrong slacks. I look like what I was: a boy sprung from a middlebrow burg who affected a secondhand preppiness. I look nervous. Compare that image to one from my senior-class dinner: now I am attired in a gray tweed jacket with a green plaid bow tie and a sensible button-down shirt, all purchased at the Yale Co-op. I look confident, and more than a bit contrived.

What happened in between those two photographs is that I experi- 24 enced, then overcame, what the poet Meena Alexander has called "the shock of arrival." When I was deposited at the wrought-iron gates of my residential college as a freshman, I felt more like an outsider than I'd thought possible. It wasn't just that I was a small Chinese boy standing at a grand WASP temple; nor simply that I was a hayseed neophyte puzzled by the refinements of college style. It was *both*: color and class were all twisted together in a double helix of felt inadequacy.

For a while I coped with the shock by retreating to a group of my 25 own kind—not fellow Asians, but fellow marginal public-school grads who resented the rah-rah Yalies to whom everything came so effortlessly. Aligning myself this way was bearable—I was hiding, but at least I could place myself in a long tradition of underdog exiles at Yale. Aligning myself by race, on the other hand, would have seemed too inhibiting.

I know this doesn't make much sense. I know also that college, in 26 the multicultural era, is supposed to be where the deracinated minority youth discovers the "person of color" inside. To a point, I did. I studied Chinese, took an Asian American history course, a seminar on race politics. But ultimately, college was where the unconscious habits of my adolescent assimilation hardened into self-conscious strategy.

I still remember the moment, in the first week of school, when I 27 came upon a table in Yale Station set up by the Asian American Student Association. The upperclassman staffing the table was pleasant enough. He certainly did not strike me as a fanatic. Yet, for some reason, I flashed immediately to a scene I'd witnessed days earlier, on the corner outside. Several Lubavitcher Jews, dressed in black, their faces bracketed by dangling side curls, were looking for fellow travelers at this busy crossroads. Their method was crude but memorable. As any vaguely Jewish-looking male walked past, the zealots would quickly approach, extend a pamphlet, and ask, "Excuse me, sir, are you Jewish?" Since most were not, and since those who were weren't about to stop, the result was a frantic, nervous, almost comical buzz all about the corner: Excuse me, are you Jewish? Are you Jewish? Excuse me. Are you Jewish?

28   I looked now at the clean-cut Korean boy at the AASA table (I think I can distinguish among Asian ethnicities as readily as those Hasidim thought they could tell Gentile from Jew), and though he had merely offered an introductory hello and was now smiling mutely at me, in the back of my mind I heard only this: *Excuse me, are you Asian? Are you Asian? Excuse me. Are you Asian*? I took one of the flyers on the table, even put my name on a mailing list, so as not to appear impolite. But I had already resolved not to be active in any Asians-only group. I thought then: I would never *choose* to be so pigeonholed.

29   This allergic sensitivity to "pigeonholing" is one of the unhappy hallmarks of the banana mentality. What does the banana fear? That is, what did *I* fear? The possibility of being mistaken for someone more Chinese. The possibility of being known only, or even primarily, for being Asian. The possibility of being written off by whites as a self-segregating ethnic clumper. These were the threats—unseen and, frankly, unsubstantiated—that I felt I should keep at bay.

30   I didn't avoid making Asian friends in college or working with Asian classmates; I simply never went out of my way to do so. This distinction seemed important—it marked, to my mind, the difference between self-hate and self-respect. That the two should have been so proximate in the first place never struck me as odd, or telling. Nor did it ever occur to me that the reasons I gave myself for dissociating from Asians as a group—that I didn't want to be part of a clique, that I didn't want to get absorbed and lose my individuality—were the very developments that marked my own assimilation. I simply hewed to my ideology of race neutrality and self-reliance. I didn't need that crutch, I told myself nervously, that crutch of racial affinity. What's more, I was vaguely insulted by the presumption that I might.

31   But again: Who was making the presumption? Who more than I was taking the mere existence of Korean volleyball leagues or Taiwanese social sets or pan-Asian student clubs to mean that *all* people of Asian descent, myself included, needed such quasi-kinship groups?

And who more than I interpreted this need as infirmity, as a failure to fit in? I resented the faintly sneering way that some whites regarded Asians as an undifferentiated mass. But whose sneer, really, did I resent more than my own?

I was keenly aware of the unflattering mythologies that attach to 32 Asian Americans: that we are indelibly foreign, exotic, math and science geeks, numbers people rather than people people, followers and not leaders, physically frail but devious and sneaky, unknowable and potentially treacherous. These stereotypes of Asian otherness and inferiority were like immense blocks of ice sitting before me, challenging me to chip away at them. And I did, tirelessly. All the while, though, I was oblivious to rumors of my *own* otherness and inferiority, rumors that rose off those blocks like a fog, wafting into my consciousness and chilling my sense of self.

As I had done in high school, I combated the stereotypes in part by 33 trying to disprove them. If Asians were reputed to be math and science geeks, I would be a student of history and politics. If Asians were supposed to be feeble subalterns, I'd lift weights and go to Marine officer candidate school. If Asians were alien, I'd be ardently patriotic. If Asians were shy and retiring, I'd try to be exuberant and jocular. If they were narrow-minded specialists, I'd be a well-rounded generalist. If they were perpetual outsiders, I'd join every establishment outfit I could and show that I, too, could run with the swift.

I overstate, of course. It wasn't that I chose to do all these things 34 with no other purpose than to cut against a supposed convention. I was neither so Pavlovian nor so calculating that I would simply remake myself into the opposite of what people expected. I actually *liked* history, and wasn't especially good at math. As the grandson of a military officer, I *wanted* to see what officer candidates school would be like, and I enjoyed it, at least once I'd finished. I am *by nature* enthusiastic and allegiant, a joiner, and a bit of a jingo.

At the same time, I was often aware, sometimes even hopeful, that 35 others might think me "exceptional" for my race. I derived satisfaction from being the "atypical" Asian, the only Chinese face at OCS or in this club or that.

The irony is that in working so duteously to defy stereotype, I be- 36 came a slave to it. For to act self-consciously against Asian "tendencies" is not to break loose from the cage of myth and legend; it is to turn the very key that locks you inside. What spontaneity is there when the value of every act is measured, at least in part, by its power to refute a presumption about why you act? The *typical Asian* I imagined, and the *atypical Asian* I imagined myself to be, were identical in this sense: neither was as much a creature of free will as a human being ought to be.

37   Let me say it plainly, then: I am not proud to have had this mentality. I believe I have outgrown it. And I expose it now not to justify it but to detoxify it; to prevent its further spread.

38   Yet it would be misleading, I think, to suggest that my education centered solely on the discomfort caused by race. The fact is, when I first got to college I felt deficient compared with people of *every* color. Part of why I believed it so necessary to achieve was that I lacked the connections, the wealth, the experience, the sophistication that so many of my classmates seemed to have. I didn't get the jokes or the intellectual references. I didn't have the canny attitude. So in addition to all my coursework, I began to puzzle over this, the culture of the influential class.

39   Over time, I suppose, I learned the culture. My interests and vocabulary became ever more worldly. I made my way onto what Calvin Trillin once described as the "magic escalator" of a Yale education. Extracurriculars opened the door to an alumni internship, which brought me to Capitol Hill, which led to a job and a life in Washington after commencement. Gradually, very gradually, I found that I was not so much of an outsider anymore. I found that by almost any standard, but particularly by the standards of my younger self, I was actually beginning to "make it."

40   It has taken me until now, however, to appraise the thoughts and acts of that younger self. I can see now that the straitening path I took was not the only or even the best path. For while it may be possible to transcend race, *it is not always necessary to try.* And while racial identity is sometimes a shackle, it is not *only* a shackle. I could have spared myself a great deal of heartache had I understood this earlier, that the choice of race is not simply "embrace or efface."

41   I wonder sometimes how I would have turned out had I been, from the start, more comfortable in my own skin. What did I miss by distancing myself from race? What friendships did I forgo, what self-knowledge did I defer? Had certain accidents of privilege been accidents of privation or exclusion, I might well have developed a different view of the world. But I do not know just how my view would have differed.

42   What I know is that through all those years of shadow-dancing with my identity, something happened, something that had only partially to do with color. By the time I left Yale I was no longer the scared boy of that freshman photo. I had become more sure of myself and of my place—sure enough, indeed, to perceive the folly of my fears. And in the years since, I have assumed a sense of expectation, of access and *belonging*, that my younger self could scarcely have imagined. All this happened incrementally. There was no clear tipping point, no obvious moment of mutation. The shock of arrival, it would seem, is simply that I arrived.

RESPONDING TO READING

1. Why does Liu begin his essay with a list of stereotypical statements about being "white" and then explain that he is, in fact, an "honorary white"? How do this list and this revelation give him authority to write on the topic of race?

2. Does Liu believe that a nonwhite "cannot gain the world without losing his soul"? How do readers know that this is or is not his position?

3. Liu often defines himself both through what he does and does not do: "If Asians were reputed to be math and science geeks, I would be a student of history and politics. If Asians were supposed to be feeble subalterns, I'd lift weights and go to Marine officer candidate school." (See paragraph 33.) How do these binary definitions connect with his disparaging definition of himself as a "banana"?

4. Why does Liu describe his life as "omnicultural" rather than "bicultural" (paragraph 10)? What difference does he see between the two terms? How is being "omnicultural" connected with Liu's being a "social immigrant"? What does it mean to you to be either "bicultural" or "omnicultural"? Explain your answer in an essay intended for an audience different from the designation you've selected.

5. For Liu, his hair is the greatest bane of his teenage years. Discuss with other students how his solution—shaving his head—is part of his argument about assimilation. Make a list of other ways in which each of us balances our individuality with our assimilation during our teenage years, and—either individually or as part of a team—write an essay about one of these ways.

Beyond Traditional Notions of Identity

GLORIA ANZALDÚA

One way to understand identity is through the metaphors writers use to convey their sense of selfhood; for Chicana writer Gloria Anzaldúa, it's the "Borderlands," an image that expresses her sense of being both at the margins of the American majority culture and also at the productive intersection of several sources of identity—Mexican, American, feminist, English speaking, and Spanish speaking. Anzaldúa was born on a ranch for migrant workers in south Texas (1942). Her parents, both fieldworkers, could barely support the family, but encouraged their children to concentrate on their education. When she was fifteen her father died, leaving the family in dire circumstances; yet she attended Pan American University—coming home to work the fields on weekends and vacations—and received her B.A. in 1969. Embarking on a career as a teacher and creative writer while continuing her education, she earned her M.A. in English and education at University of Texas in Austin (1972) and studied at the University of California at Santa Cruz. The fusion of cultures in her writing is part of her mestiza status—a mixture of Spanish and Indian culture; "mestiza consciousness" traverses languages and cultures to combat oppression. Her best known works are *This Bridge Called My Back: Radical Writings by Women of Color* (coedited with Cherríe Morgana, 1981), and particularly *Borderlands/LaFrontera: The New Mestiza* (1987), which reveals Anzaldúa's struggle to transform her world. Language and ideas intertwine to traverse the borders drawn by gender and cultural stereotypes. Personal anecdotes lead into linguistic analysis, and passages of Spanish challenge her readers to cross over into the alienation and mystery that she lives with every day. A collection of interviews with Anzaldúa was recently published as *Interviews = Entrevistas*, edited by AnaLouise Keating (2000). Keating and Anzaldúa also edited a collection of essays, *This Bridge We Call Home: Radical Visions for Transformation* (2000), in which "Beyond Traditional Notions of Identity" (first published in *The Chronicle of Higher Education*, 11 Oct., 2002) appears. Here Anzaldúa shifts focus from the well-known *Borderlands*, which "struggled with the recognition of difference within the context of commonality" to grapple instead "with the recognition of commonality within the context of difference," questioning "the terms *white* and *women of color* by showing that whiteness may not be applied to all whites, because some possess women-of-color consciousness, just as some women of color bear white consciousness."

1   At sunset I walk along the bluffs gazing at the shifting sea, a hammered sheet of silver. A full moon rises over the cliffs of Natural Bridges State Beach in California like an opalescent ball. Under my feet pressure and heat are continuously changing the layers of sedimentary rock formed 100,000 years ago. It took the waves thousands of years to cut out remnant headlands and thousands more to wear holes or arches through its flanks and shape three stone bridges. Year after year these same waves expanded the arches, until the weight of the overlying rock collapsed the outermost bridge 21 years ago. In a few seconds the 1989 Loma Prieta earthquake brought down the innermost bridge. Today only the middle one remains, a lone, castlelike seastack with an arched hole for an eye.

2   Whenever I glimpse the arch of this bridge my breath catches. Bridges are thresholds to other realities, archetypal, primal symbols of shifting consciousness. They connote transitioning, crossing borders, and changing perspectives. Transformations occur in this in-between space, an unstable, unpredictable, precarious, always-in-transition space lacking clear boundaries.

3   Most of us dwell in this space so much of the time that it's become a sort of "home." Though it links us to other ideas, people, and worlds, we feel threatened by these new connections and the change they engender. I think of how feminist ideas and movements are attacked, called unnatural by the ruling powers, when in fact they are ideas

whose time has come, ideas as relentless as the waves carving and later eroding stone arches. Change is inevitable; no bridge lasts forever.

More than two decades ago, Cherríe Moraga and I edited a multi-   4
genre collection giving voice to radical women of color, *This Bridge Called My Back*. Every generation that reads *This Bridge Called My Back* rewrites it. Like the trestle bridge, and other things that have reached their zenith, it will decline unless we attach it to new growth or append new growth to it. In a new collection of writings and art, *this bridge we call home*, AnaLouise Keating and I, together with our contributors, attempt to continue the dialogue of the past 21 years, rethink the old ideas, and germinate new theories. We move from focusing on what has been done to us (victimhood) to a more extensive level of agency, one that questions what we're doing to each other, to those in distant countries, and to the earth's environment.

Twenty-one years ago we struggled with the recognition of differ-   5
ence within the context of commonality. Today we grapple with the recognition of commonality within the context of difference. While *This Bridge Called My Back* displaced whiteness, *this bridge we call home* carries that displacement further. It questions the terms *white* and *women of color* by showing that whiteness may not be applied to all whites, because some possess women-of-color consciousness, just as some women of color bear white consciousness. We intend to change notions of identity, viewing it as part of a more complex system covering a larger terrain, and demonstrating that the politics of exclusion based on traditional categories diminishes our humanness.

Today categories of race and gender are more permeable and flexi-   6
ble than they were for those of us growing up before the 1980s. Today we need to move beyond separate and easy identifications, creating bridges that cross race and other classifications among different groups via intergenerational dialogue. Rather than legislating and restricting racial identities, we hope to make them more pliant.

We must learn to incorporate additional underrepresented voices;   7
we must attempt to break the impasse between women of color and other groups. By including women and men of different "races," nationalities, classes, sexualities, genders, and ages in our discussions, we complicate the debates within feminist theory both inside and outside the academy and inside and outside the United States.

Our goal is not to use differences to separate us from others, but   8
neither is it to gloss over those differences. Many of us identify with groups and social positions not limited to our ethnic, racial, religious, class, gender, and national classifications. Though most people self-define by what they exclude, we define who we are by what we include—what I call the new tribalism. I fear that many mujeres de color will not want whites or men to join the dialogue. We risk the

displeasure of those women. There are no safe spaces. "Home" can be unsafe and dangerous because it bears the likelihood of intimacy and thus thinner boundaries.

9   I recall the internal strife that flared in the postings of the listserv that we had set up for contributors to our book. I think the online conflict, too, masked feelings of fear—this supposedly safe space was no longer safe. The contentious debates among Palestinian women and Jews of Latina, Native, and European ancestry churned a liquid fire in our guts.

10   Conflict, with its fiery nature, can trigger transformation, depending on how we respond to it. Often, delving deeply into conflict, instead of fleeing from it, can bring an understanding (conocimiento) that will turn things around.

11   A bridge is not just about one set of people crossing to the other side; it's also about those on the other side crossing to this side. And ultimately, it's about doing away with demarcations like "ours" and "theirs." Diversity of perspectives expands and alters the dialogue, not in an add-on fashion but through a multiplicity that's transformational, such as in mestiza consciousness. To include whites is not an attempt to restore the privilege of white writers, scholars, and activists; it is a refusal to continue walking the color line. To include men is to collapse the gender line. These inclusions challenge conventional identities and promote more expansive configurations of identities—some of which will, in turn, soon become cages and have to be dismantled.

12   Ours is the responsibility of marking the journey and passing on the torches left by those who have already crossed many types of bridges. We honor those whose backs are the bedrock we stand on, even as our shoulders become the ground for the generations that follow, and their bodies then become the next layer.

13   I descend down the steep bluffs to the tide-pool terraces between sea and cliffs. Squatting, I stare at a sea anemone in a pocket of water on the pitted rock. I prod the anemone; it shudders and shakes, contracting into a protective ball. We all respond to pain and pleasure in similar ways. Imagination, a function of the soul, has the capacity to extend us beyond the confines of our skin, situation, and condition so we can choose our responses. It enables us to reimagine our lives, rewrite the self, and create guiding myths for our times. As I walk back home along the cliffs, a westerly wind buffeting my back, the crashing breakers scour the shoulders of the bluffs, slowly hewing out keyholes, fledgling bridges in the making.

14   You struggle each day to know the world you live in, to come to grips with the problems of life. Motivated by the need to understand, you crave to be what and who you are.

Many are witnessing a major cultural shift in their understanding   15
of what knowledge consists of and how we come to know, a shift from
the kinds of knowledge valued now to the kinds that will be desired in
the 21st century, a shift away from knowledge contributing to both military and corporate technologies and the colonization of our lives by
TV and the Internet, to the inner exploration of the meaning and purpose of life. You attribute this shift to the feminization of knowledge, a
way of knowing and acting on ese saber you call *conocimiento*. Those
carrying conocimiento refuse to accept spirituality as a devalued form
of knowledge, and instead elevate it to the same level occupied by science and rationality.

You're strolling downtown. Suddenly the sidewalk buckles and   16
rises before you. Bricks fly through the air. Your thigh muscles tense to
run, but shock holds you in check. Dust rains down all around you,
dimming your sight, clogging your nostrils, coating your throat. In
front of you the second story of a building caves into the ground floor.
Just as suddenly the earth stops trembling. People with pallid faces
gather before the collapsed building. Near your feet a hand sticks out
of the rubble.

Coasting over the cracked bridge and pits in the pavement, you   17
drive home at five miles an hour. The apartment manager comes to
check and tells you, "No te puedes quedar aquí. You have to evacuate,
the gas lines are not secure, there's no electricity, and the water's contaminated." You want to salvage your books, your computer, and three
years' worth of writing. "I'm staying home," you reply.

You boil water, sweep up the broken cups and plates. Just when   18
you think the ground beneath your feet is stable, the two plates again
grind together along the San Andreas Fault. The seismic rupture moves
the Monterey Peninsula three inches north. It shifts you into the crack
between the worlds, shattering the mythology that grounds you.

Three weeks after the doctor confirms your diagnosis, you cross   19
the trestle bridge near the wharf, your shortcut to downtown Santa
Cruz. As you listen to your footsteps echoing on the timber, the reality
of having a disease that could cost you your feet . . . your eyes . . . your
creativity . . . the life of the writer you've worked so hard to build
. . . life itself . . . finally penetrates, arresting you in the middle del
puente.

You're furious with your body for limiting your artistic activities,   20
for its slow crawl toward the grave. You're infuriated with yourself for
not living up to your expectations, not living your life fully. You realize
that you use the whip of your ideals to flagellate yourself, and the
masochist in you gets pleasure from your suffering.

21   Tú, la consentida, the special one, thought yourself exempt from living like ordinary people. Self-pity swamps you, que suerte maldita! Self-absorbed, you're unable to climb out of the pit that's yourself. Feeling helpless, you draft the script of victimization and retreat from the world, withdraw from your body. You count the bars of your cage, refusing to name your demons.

22   Taking a deep breath, you close your eyes and sense parts of your soul returning to your body. Challenging the old self's orthodoxy is never enough; you must submit a sketch of an alternative self.

23   You fly in from another speaking gig on the East Coast, arriving at the feminist academic conference late. Hayas un desmadre. A racist incident has unleashed flames of anger held in check for decades. Like most feminist conferences, this one begins as a bridge, a place of mutual access where thousands crisscross, network, share ideas, and struggle together to resolve women's issues. After 15 years of struggle, of putting their trust on this common space, of waiting for the organization to deal with racism as it's promised, the women of color and some Jewish, working-class, and progressive white allies feel betrayed by their white middle-class sisters.

24   They're tired of being treated as outsiders. They feel that whites still view issues of racism as the concern of women of color alone, anti-Semitism the concern only of Jewish women, homophobia the concern of lesbians, and class the concern of working-class and poor women. White women accuse women of color and their allies of emotionalism—after all, this is the academy. Feeling unjustly attacked, they adamantly proclaim they're not racist.

25   Caught in the middle of the power struggle, you're forced to take sides, forced to negotiate another identity crisis. Being coerced to turn your back on one group/person and favor the other feels like a knife to the heart. It reminds you of the '70s when other lesbians reprimanded you and urged you to abandon your friendships with men.

26   What takes a bashing is not so much you but who you think you are, an illusion you're hellbent on protecting and preserving at all costs. You think you've made progress, gained a new awareness, found a new version of reality, created a workable story, fulfilled an obligation, and followed your own conscience. But when you cast to the world what you've created and put your ideals into action, the contradictions explode in your face.

27   When creating a personal narrative, you also co-create the group/cultural story. You examine the description handed to you of the world, picking holes in the paradigms currently constructing reality. You doubt that traditional Western science is the best knowledge

system, the only true, impartial arbiter of reality. You turn the established narrative on its head, seeing through, resisting, and subverting its assumptions. Again, it's not enough to denounce the culture's old account—you must provide new narratives embodying alternative potentials.

You examine the contentions accompanying the old cultural narratives: Your ethnic tribe wants you to isolate, insisting that you remain within race and class boundaries. The dominant culture prefers that you abandon your roots and assimilate, insisting that you leave your Indianness behind and seek shelter under the Hispanic or Latino umbrella.   28

The temptation to succumb to these assimilationist tactics and escape the stigma of being Mexican stalls you on the bridge between isolation and assimilation. But both are debilitating. How can you step outside ethnic and other labels while cleaving to your identity? Your identity has roots you share with all people and other beings—spirit, feeling, and body compose a greater identity category.   29

Reframing the old story points to another option besides assimilation and separation—a "new tribalism." You pick and choose views, cultures with transformational potential—a partially conscious selection, not a mestizaje imposed on you, but one whose process you can control. A retribalizing mestizaje becomes your coping mechanism, your strategy of resistance to both acculturating and inculturating pressures.   30

Tussling con remolinos (whirlwinds) of different belief systems builds the muscles of mestiza consciousness, enabling it to stretch. Being Chicana (or indigenous, Mexican, Basque, Spanish, Berber-Arab, Gypsy) is no longer enough; being female, woman of color, patlache (queer) no longer suffices. Your resistance to identity boxes leads you to a different tribe, a different story (of mestizaje), enabling you to rethink yourself in global-spiritual terms instead of conventional categories of color, class, career.   31

It calls you to retribalize your identity to a more inclusive one, redefining what it means to be una mexicana de este lado, an American in the United States, a citizen of the world, classifications reflecting an emerging planetary culture. In this narrative, national boundaries dividing us from the "others" (nos/otras) are porous, and the cracks between worlds serve as gateways.   32

Through the act of writing you call, like the ancient chamana, the scattered pieces of your soul back to your body. You commence the arduous task of rebuilding yourself, composing a story that more accurately expresses your new identity. You seek out allies and, together, begin building spiritual/political communities that struggle for personal growth and social justice. By compartiendo historias, ideas,   33 we forge bonds across race, gender, and other lines, creating a new tribalism.

34   For you, writing is an archetypal journey home to the self, un proceso de crear puentes (bridges) to the next phase, next place, next culture, next reality. The thrust toward spiritual realization, health, freedom, and justice propels you to help rebuild the bridge to the world when you return "home." You realize that "home" is that bridge, the in-between place of constant transition, the most unsafe of all spaces. You remove the old bridge from your back, and though afraid, allow diverse groups to collectively rebuild it, to buttress it with new steel plates, girders, cable bracing, and trusses.

RESPONDING TO READING

1. How does Anzaldúa use her opening narrative to introduce her focus on "feminist ideas"? How does the metaphor she builds concerning bridges affect her argument?

2. What does Anzaldúa consider "traditional notions of identity"? According to Anzaldúa, has the concept of identity itself changed over time? If so, in what ways?

3. In Anzaldúa's view, what part do race and gender play in the formation of an individual's identity? What does she mean in her assertion that "Today categories of race and gender are more permeable and flexible than they were for those of us growing up before the 1980s" (paragraph 6)?

4. Anzaldúa writes that "What takes a bashing [in life's confrontations] is not so much you but who you think you are, an illusion you're hellbent on protecting and preserving at all costs." Is there, as Anzaldúa posits, a difference between "you" and your image of yourself? Does the "you" that forms the core of your individual identity change over time or in radically different situations? Is there a "you" in you, or are there only illusions of "you" built around a single physical being?

5. In an essay, consider the image of yourself you project in a specific situation and to a specific audience—other students in a particular class, coworkers at your place of employment, listserv members in an online discussion, friends in your neighborhood or dormitory, etc. What image of yourself do you project, and how do you project it? Are there ways of acting or speaking that you only employ in this particular situation? How do the reactions of the other members of the group influence your image of yourself?

How Do Language and Literacy Affect My Identity?

Mother Tongue

AMY TAN

Amy Tan's talent for capturing human relationships in words is one example of her lifelong engagement with language and the speaking voice. Born (1952) and raised by her Chinese mother in Oakland, California, she grew up immersed in Chinese–American culture. After earning both her B.A. and M.A. in linguistics (1973, 1974) at San Jose State University, Tan worked as a language development specialist and freelanced as a corporate speech writer. In her first novel, *The Joy Luck Club* (1989), characters such as traditional Chinese matriarchs and Americanized teenagers were defined not only by what they said, but also by the perfect pitch of their words. Tan earned a wide readership and the book was a finalist for the National Book Award. Tan based her second novel, *The Kitchen God's Wife* (1991), on themes from her mother's difficult life in pre-World War II China. Her third book, *The Hundred Secret Senses* (1995), emphasized Tan's interest in the supernatural along with the intricacies of sisterhood, motherhood, and marriages that spanned cultures. *The Bonesetter's Daughter* (2001) returned to mother–daughter themes. Although her readers have received an education in Chinese–American culture, Tan told a *Salon* interviewer that she shuns the designation of role model: "Placing on writers the responsibility to represent a culture is an onerous burden. Someone who writes fiction is not necessarily writing a depiction of any generalized group, they're writing a very specific story."

In "Mother Tongue," using an intimate style that treats serious matters with a light touch, Tan describes how her life was shaped by her mother's language. The "many Englishes" that she learned revolved around her mother's adaptations to a foreign world; yet while the speech she heard at home caused her to be stigmatized as different, Tan used her creativity to turn problems into advantages.

1   I am not a scholar of English or literature. I cannot give you much more than personal opinions on the English language and its variations in this country or others.

2   I am a writer. And by that definition, I am someone who has always loved language. I am fascinated by language in daily life. I spend a great deal of my time thinking about the power of language—the

way it can evoke an emotion, a visual image, a complex idea, or a simple truth. Language is the tool of my trade. And I use them all—all the Englishes I grew up with.

3   Recently, I was made keenly aware of the different Englishes I do use. I was giving a talk to a large group of people, the same talk I had already given to half a dozen other groups. The nature of the talk was about my writing, my life, and my book, *The Joy Luck Club*. The talk was going along well enough, until I remembered one major difference that made the whole talk sound wrong. My mother was in the room. And it was perhaps the first time she had heard me give a lengthy speech, using the kind of English I have never used with her. I was saying things like, "The intersection of memory upon imagination" and "There is an aspect of my fiction that relates to thus-and-thus"—a speech filled with carefully wrought grammatical phrases, burdened, it suddenly seemed to me, with nominalized forms, past perfect tenses, conditional phrases, all the forms of standard English that I had learned in school and through books, the forms of English I did not use at home with my mother.

4   Just last week, I was walking down the street with my mother, and I again found myself conscious of the English I was using, the English I do use with her. We were talking about the price of new and used furniture and I heard myself saying this: "Not waste money that way." My husband was with us as well, and he didn't notice any switch in my English. And then I realized why. It's because over the twenty years we've been together I've often used that same kind of English with him, and sometimes he even uses it with me. It has become our language of intimacy, a different sort of English that relates to family talk, the language I grew up with.

5   So you'll have some idea of what this family talk I heard sounds like, I'll quote what my mother said during a recent conversation which I videotaped and then transcribed. During this conversation, my mother was talking about a political gangster in Shanghai who had the same last name as her family's, Du, and how the gangster in his early years wanted to be adopted by her family, which was rich by comparison. Later, the gangster became more powerful, far richer than my mother's family, and one day showed up at my mother's wedding to pay his respects. Here's what she said in part:

6   "Du Yusong having business like fruit stand. Like off the street kind. He is Du like Du Zong—but not Tsung-ming Island people. The local people call putong, the river east side, he belong to that side local people. That man want to ask Du Zong father take him in like become own family. Du Zong father wasn't look down on him, but didn't take seriously, until that man big like become a mafia. Now important person, very hard to inviting him. Chinese way, came only to show respect, don't stay for dinner. Respect for making big celebration, he

shows up. Mean give lots of respect. Chinese custom. Chinese social life that way. If too important won't have to stay too long. He come to my wedding. I didn't see, I heard it. I gone to boy's side, they have YMCA dinner. Chinese age I was nineteen."

You should know that my mother's expressive command of English belies how much she actually understands. She reads the *Forbes* report, listens to *Wall Street Week*, converses daily with her stockbroker, reads all of Shirley MacLaine's books with ease—all kinds of things I can't begin to understand. Yet some of my friends tell me they understand 50 percent of what my mother says. Some say they understand 80 to 90 percent. Some say they understand none of it, as if she were speaking pure Chinese. But to me, my mother's English is perfectly clear, perfectly natural. It's my mother tongue. Her language, as I hear it, is vivid, direct, full of observation and imagery. That was the language that helped shape the way I saw things, expressed things, made sense of the world. 7

Lately, I've been giving more thought to the kind of English my mother speaks. Like others, I have described it to people as "broken" or "fractured" English. But I wince when I say that. It has always bothered me that I can think of no way to describe it other than "broken," as if it were damaged and needed to be fixed, as if it lacked a certain wholeness and soundness. I've heard other terms used, "limited English," for example. But they seem just as bad, as if everything is limited, including people's perceptions of the limited English speaker. 8

I know this for a fact, because when I was growing up, my mother's "limited" English limited *my* perception of her. I was ashamed of her English. I believed that her English reflected the quality of what she had to say. That is, because she expressed them imperfectly her thoughts were imperfect. And I had plenty of empirical evidence to support me: the fact that people in department stores, at banks, and at restaurants did not take her seriously, did not give her good service, pretended not to understand her, or even acted as if they did not hear her. 9

My mother has long realized the limitations of her English as well. When I was fifteen, she used to have me call people on the phone to pretend I was she. In this guise, I was forced to ask for information or even to complain and yell at people who had been rude to her. One time it was a call to her stockbroker in New York. She had cashed out her small portfolio and it just happened we were going to go to New York the next week, our very first trip outside California. I had to get on the phone and say in an adolescent voice that was not very convincing, "This is Mrs. Tan." 10

And my mother was standing in the back whispering loudly, "Why he don't send me check, already two weeks late. So mad he lie to me, losing me money." 11

12   And then I said in perfect English, "Yes, I'm getting rather con-cerned. You had agreed to send the check two weeks ago, but it hasn't arrived."

13   Then she began to talk more loudly. "What he want, I come to New York tell him front of his boss, you cheating me?" And I was trying to calm her down, make her be quiet, while telling the stockbroker, "I can't tolerate any more excuses. If I don't receive the check immediate-ly, I am going to have to speak to your manager when I'm in New York next week." And sure enough, the following week there we were in front of this astonished stockbroker, and I was sitting there red-faced and quiet, and my mother, the real Mrs. Tan, was shouting at his boss in her impeccable broken English.

14   We used a similar routine just five days ago, for a situation that was far less humorous. My mother had gone to the hospital for an appoint-ment, to find out about a benign brain tumor a CAT scan had revealed a month ago. She said she had spoken very good English, her best Eng-lish, no mistakes. Still, she said, the hospital did not apologize when they said they had lost the CAT scan and she had come for nothing. She said they did not seem to have any sympathy when she told them she was anxious to know the exact diagnosis, since her husband and son had both died of brain tumors. She said they would not give her any more information until the next time and she would have to make an-other appointment for that. So she said she would not leave until the doctor called her daughter. She wouldn't budge. And when the doctor finally called her daughter, me, who spoke in perfect English—lo and behold—we had assurances the CAT scan would be found, promises that a conference call on Monday would be held, and apologies for any suffering my mother had gone through for a most regrettable mistake.

15   I think my mother's English almost had an effect on limiting my possibilities in life as well. Sociologists and linguists probably will tell you that a person's developing language skills are more influenced by peers. But I do think that the language spoken in the family, especially in immigrant families which are more insular, plays a large role in shaping the language of the child. And I believe that it affected my re-sults on achievement tests, IQ tests, and the SAT. While my English skills were never judged as poor, compared to math, English could not be considered my strong suit. In grade school I did moderately well, getting perhaps B's, sometimes B-pluses, in English and scoring per-haps in the sixtieth or seventieth percentile on achievement tests. But those scores were not good enough to override the opinion that my true abilities lay in math and science, because in those areas I achieved A's and scored in the ninetieth percentile or higher.

16   This was understandable. Math is precise; there is only one correct answer. Whereas, for me at least, the answers on English tests were al-

ways a judgment call, a matter of opinion and personal experience. Those tests were constructed around items like fill-in-the-blank sentence completion, such as, "Even though Tom was _____, Mary thought he was _____." And the correct answer always seemed to be the most bland combinations of thoughts, for example "Even though Tom was shy, Mary thought he was charming," with the grammatical structure "even though" limiting the correct answer to some sort of semantic opposites, so you wouldn't get answers like, "Even though Tom was foolish, Mary thought he was ridiculous." Well, according to my mother, there were very few limitations as to what Tom could have been and what Mary might have thought of him. So I never did well on tests like that.

The same was true with word analogies, pairs of words in which   17 you were supposed to find some sort of logical, semantic relationship—for example, "*Sunset* is to *nightfall* as _____ is to _____." And here you would be presented with a list of four possible pairs, one of which showed the same kind of relationship: *red* is to *spotlight, bus* is to *arrival, chills* is to *fever, yawn* is to *boring*. Well, I could never think that way. I knew what the tests were asking, but I could not block out of my mind the images already created by the first pair, "*sunset* is to *nightfall*"—and I would see a burst of colors against a darkening sky, the moon rising, the lowering of a curtain of stars. And all the other pairs of words—red, bus, spotlight, boring—just threw up a mass of confusing images, making it impossible for me to sort out something as logical as saying: "A sunset precedes nightfall" is the same as "a chill precedes a fever." The only way I would have gotten that answer right would have been to imagine an associative situation, for example, my being disobedient and staying out past sunset, catching a chill at night, which turns into feverish pneumonia as punishment, which indeed did happen to me.

I have been thinking about all this lately, about my mother's Eng-   18 lish, about achievement tests. Because lately I've been asked as a writer, why there are not more Asian Americans represented in American literature. Why are there few Asian Americans enrolled in creative writing programs? Why do so many Chinese students go into engineering? Well, these are broad sociological questions I can't begin to answer. But I have noticed in surveys—in fact, just last week—that Asian students, as a whole, always do significantly better on math achievement tests than in English. And this makes me think that there are other Asian-American students whose English spoken in the home might also be described as "broken" or "limited." And perhaps they also have teachers who are steering them away from writing and into math and science, which is what happened to me.

Fortunately, I happen to be rebellious in nature and enjoy the chal-   19 lenge of disproving assumptions made about me. I became an English major my first year in college, after being enrolled as premed. I started writing nonfiction as a freelancer the week after I was told by my former boss that writing was my worst skill and I should hone my talents toward account management.

20   But it wasn't until 1985 that I finally began to write fiction. And at first I wrote using what I thought to be wittily crafted sentences, sentences that would finally prove I had mastery over the English language. Here's an example from the first draft of a story that later made its way into *The Joy Luck Club*, but without this line: "That was my mental quandary in its nascent state." A terrible line, which I can barely pronounce.

21   Fortunately, for reasons I won't get into today, I later decided I should envision a reader for the stories I would write. And the reader I decided upon was my mother, because these were stories about mothers. So with this reader in mind—and in fact she did read my early drafts—I began to write stories using all the Englishes I grew up with: the English I spoke to my mother, which for lack of a better term might be described as "simple"; the English she used with me, which for lack of a better term might be described as "broken"; my translation of her Chinese, which could certainly be described as "watered down"; and what I imagined to be her translation of her Chinese if she could speak in perfect English, her internal language, and for that I sought to preserve the essence, but neither an English nor a Chinese structure. I wanted to capture what language ability tests can never reveal: her intent, her passion, her imagery, the rhythms of her speech and the nature of her thoughts.

22   Apart from what any critic had to say about my writing, I knew I had succeeded where it counted when my mother finished reading my book and gave me her verdict: "So easy to read."

RESPONDING TO READING

1. Working in a small group, consider why Tan begins by defining herself by what she is not. What tone does this set? How does this establish her authority to argue on this subject? Do all of us, as individuals who are also members of groups, sometimes define ourselves by what we are and by what we are not? When do we do this? Why?

2. What link does Tan make between her mother's English and the perceptions other people have of the mother? How does the mother's English connect to Tan's poor performance on standardized tests?

3. At the beginning of her essay, Tan worries over the fact that her mother is listening to her discuss *The Joy Luck Club*, yet at the end of the essay, Tan explains that she wrote the book with her mother in mind. To what degree is this a contradiction? How can she both worry about communicating with her mother and, at the same time, write for that same person?

4. Tan uses two main illustrations to develop her essay—her mother's confrontation with the stockbroker and her mother's difficulties with the doctor who performed her CAT scan. What purposes do these two illustrations serve? How do they develop Tan's argument and connect with her title?

5. How does Tan explain the differences in the Englishes that she speaks? Are there different versions of your language that you speak in different situations? Write an essay in which you describe those differences to an outsider, and explain the reasons for using more than one English.

Listening

EUDORA WELTY

Eudora Welty lived, wrote, and gardened in her hometown of Jackson, Mississippi, from the time of her birth (1909) until her death in 2001. Although she graduated from the University of Wisconsin in 1929 and studied advertising for a year at Columbia University, the depression and her father's death in 1931 prompted her return to the South. Significant in her development as a writer were the three years she spent in the 1930s writing feature stories for the Works Progress Administration, based on her visits to Mississippi's eighty-two counties, where she met, photographed, and interpreted the lives of a great variety of people in small towns and rural areas. These individuals, communities, and landscapes fed her imagination for years, forming the basis of much of her fiction, including the short stories collected in *A Curtain of Green* (1941) and *The Wide Net* (1943), and her novels, *Delta Wedding* (1946), *The Ponder Heart* (1954), and *Losing Battles* (1970). Her novel *The Optimist's Daughter* (1972) won the Pulitzer Prize. Other works include *One Time, One Place* (revised edition 1996), a collection of stories illustrated with Welty's own photographs, and *Writer's Eye* (1994), a collection of book reviews.

"Listening" is from Welty's autobiography *One Writer's Beginnings* (1983), derived from three lectures at Harvard that demonstrated the importance of "Listening," "Learning to See," and "Finding a Voice." Although in 1972 she was "discouraged at the very thought" of writing her autobiography because, she told an interviewer, "to me a writer's work should be everything. A writer's whole feeling, the force of his whole life, can go into a story. . . . [But one's] private life should be kept private. My own I don't think would particularly interest anybody." The appeal of Welty's endearing autobiography contradicts her modest assertion. Part of its charm derives from the sense of a strong, cohesive family that Welty conveys, in part by her avoidance of both intimate matters and familial difficulties. Both parents consistently nurtured their young child, teaching her through their own example and through the shared activities of stargazing, playing with puzzles and toys, reading, and singing. No wonder the adult writer was content to live happily for decades with her widowed mother in the family home.

1   In our house on North Congress Street in Jackson, Mississippi, where I was born, the oldest of three children, in 1909, we grew up to the striking of clocks. There was a mission-style oak grandfather clock standing in the hall, which sent its gong-like strokes through the living-room, diningroom, kitchen, and pantry, and up the sounding board of the stairwell. Through the night, it could find its way into our ears; sometimes, even on the sleeping porch, midnight could wake us up. My parents' bedroom had a smaller striking clock that answered it. Though the kitchen clock did nothing but show the time, the dining room clock was a cuckoo clock with weights on long chains, on one of which my baby brother, after climbing on a chair to the top of the china closet, once succeeded in suspending the cat for a moment. I don't know whether or not my father's Ohio family, in having been Swiss back in the 1700s before the first three Welty brothers came to America, had anything to do with this; but we all of us have been time-minded all our lives. This was good at least for a future fiction writer, being able to learn so penetratingly, and almost first of all, about chronology. It was one of a good many things I learned almost without knowing it; it would be there when I needed it.

2   My father loved all instruments that would instruct and fascinate. His place to keep things was the drawer in the "library table" where lying on top of his folded maps was a telescope with brass extensions, to find the moon and the Big Dipper after supper in our front yard, and to keep appointments with eclipses. There was a folding Kodak that was brought out for Christmas, birthdays, and trips. In the back of the drawer you could find a magnifying glass, a kaleidoscope, and a gyro-scope kept in a black buckram box, which he would set dancing for us on a string pulled tight. He had also supplied himself with an assort-ment of puzzles composed of metal rings and intersecting links and keys chained together, impossible for the rest of us, however patiently shown, to take apart; he had an almost childlike love of the ingenious.

3   In time, a barometer was added to our diningroom wall; but we didn't really need it. My father had the country boy's accurate knowl-edge of the weather and its skies. He went out and stood on our front steps first thing in the morning and took a look at it and a sniff. He was a pretty good weather prophet.

4   "Well, I'm *not*," my mother would say with enormous self-satisfaction.

5   He told us children what to do if we were lost in a strange country. "Look for where the sky is brightest along the horizon," he said. "That reflects the nearest river. Strike out for a river and you will find habita-

tion." Eventualities were much on his mind. In his care for us children he cautioned us to take measures against such things as being struck by lightning. He drew us all away from the windows during the severe electrical storms that are common where we live. My mother stood apart, scoffing at caution as a character failing. "Why, I always loved a storm! High winds never bothered me in West Virginia! Just listen at that! I wasn't a bit afraid of a little lightning and thunder! I'd go out on the mountain and spread my arms wide and *run* in a good big storm!"

So I developed a strong meteorological sensibility. In years ahead   6
when I wrote stories, atmosphere took its influential role from the start. Commotion in the weather and the inner feelings aroused by such a hovering disturbance emerged connected in dramatic form. (I tried a tornado first, in a story called "The Winds.")

From our earliest Christmas times, Santa Claus brought us toys   7
that instruct boys and girls (separately) how to build things—stone blocks cut to the castle-building style, Tinker Toys, and Erector sets. Daddy made for us himself elaborate kites that needed to be taken miles out of town to a pasture long enough (and my father was not afraid of horses and cows watching) for him to run with and get up on a long cord to which my mother held the spindle, and then we children were given it to hold, tugging like something alive at our hands. They were beautiful, sound, shapely box kites, smelling delicately of office glue for their entire short lives. And of course, as soon as the boys attained anywhere near the right age, there was an electric train, the engine with its pea-sized working headlight, its line of cars, tracks equipped with switches, semaphores, its station, its bridges, and its tunnel, which blocked off all other traffic in the upstairs hall. Even from downstairs, and through the cries of excited children, the elegant rush and click of the train could be heard through the ceiling, running around and around its figure eight.

All of this, but especially the train, represents my father's fondest   8
beliefs—in progress, in the future. With these gifts, he was preparing his children.

And so was my mother with her different gifts.   9

I learned from the age of two or three that any room in our house,   10
at any time of day, was there to read in, or to be read to. My mother read to me. She'd read to me in the big bedroom in the mornings, when we were in her rocker together, which ticked in rhythm as we rocked, as though we had a cricket accompanying the story. She'd read to me in the dining room on winter afternoons in front of the coal fire, with our cuckoo clock ending the story with "Cuckoo," and at night when I'd got in my own bed. I must have given her no peace. Sometimes she read to me in the kitchen while she sat churning, and the churning sobbed along with *any* story. It was my ambition to have her read to me while *I* churned; once she granted my wish, but she read off my story

before I brought her butter. She was an expressive reader. When she was reading "Puss in Boots," for instance, it was impossible not to know that she distrusted *all* cats.

11   It had been startling and disappointing to me to find out that story books had been written by *people*, that books were not natural wonders, coming up of themselves like grass. Yet regardless of where they came from, I cannot remember a time when I was not in love with them— with the books themselves, cover and binding and the paper they were printed on, with their smell and their weight and with their possession in my arms, captured and carried off to myself. Still illiterate, I was ready for them, committed to all the reading I could give them.

12   Neither of my parents had come from homes that could afford to buy many books, but though it must have been something of a strain on his salary, as the youngest officer in a young insurance company, my father was all the while carefully selecting and ordering away for what he and Mother thought we children should grow up with. They bought first for the future.

13   Besides the bookcase in the livingroom, which was always called "the library," there were the encyclopedia tables and dictionary stand under windows in our dining room. Here to help us grow up arguing around the dining room table were the Unabridged Webster, the Columbia Encyclopedia, Compton's Pictured Encyclopedia, the Lincoln Library of Information, and later the Book of Knowledge. And the year we moved into our new house, there was room to celebrate it with the new 1925 edition of the Britannica, which my father, his face always deliberately turned toward the future, was of course disposed to think better than any previous edition.

14   In "the library," inside the mission-style bookcase with its three diamond-latticed glass doors, with my father's Morris chair and the glass-shaded lamp on its table beside it, were books I could soon begin on—and I did, reading them all alike and as they came, straight down their rows, top shelf to bottom. There was the set of Stoddard's Lectures, in all its late nineteenth-century vocabulary and vignettes of peasant life and quaint beliefs and customs, with matching halftone illustrations: Vesuvius erupting, Venice by moonlight, gypsies glimpsed by their campfires. I didn't know then the clue they were to my father's longing to see the rest of the world. I read straight through his other love-from-afar: the Victrola Book of the Opera, with opera after opera in synopsis, with portraits in costume of Melba, Caruso, Galli-Curci, and Geraldine Farrar, some of whose voices we could listen to on our Red Seal records.

15   My mother read secondarily for information; she sank as a hedonist into novels. She read Dickens in the spirit in which she would have eloped with him. The novels of her girlhood that had stayed on in her

imgination, besides those of Dickens and Scott and Robert Louis Stevenson, were *Jane Eyre, Trilby, The Woman in White, Green Mansions, King Solomon's Mines*. Marie Corelli's name would crop up but I understood she had gone out of favor with my mother, who had only kept *Ardath* out of loyalty. In time she absorbed herself in Galsworthy, Edith Wharton, above all in Thomas Mann of the *Joseph* volumes.

St.Elmo was not in our house; I saw it often in other houses. This   16 wildly popular Southern novel is where all the Edna Earles in our population started coming from. They're all named for the heroine, who succeeded in bringing a dissolute, sinning roué and atheist of a lover (St.Elmo) to his knees. My mother was able to forgo it. But she remembered the classic advice given to rose growers on how to water their bushes long enough: "Take a chair and *St.Elmo*."

To both my parents I owe my early acquaintance with a beloved   17 Mark Twain. There was a full set of Mark Twain and a short set of Ring Lardner in our bookcase, and those were the volumes that in time united us all, parents and children.

Reading everything that stood before me was how I came upon a   18 worn old book without a back that had belonged to my father as a child. It was called *Sanford and Merton*. Is there anyone left who recognizes it, I wonder? It is the famous moral tale written by Thomas Day in the 1780s, but of him no mention is made on the title page of *this* book; here it is *Sanford and Merton in Words of One Syllable* by Mary Godolphin. Here are the rich boy and the poor boy and Mr. Barlow, their teacher and interlocutor, in long discourses alternating with dramatic scenes—danger and rescue allotted to the rich and the poor respectively. It may have only words of one syllable, but one of them is "quoth." It ends with not one but two morals, both engraved on rings: "Do what you ought, come what may," and "If we would be great, we must first learn to be good."

This book was lacking its front cover, the back held on by strips of   19 pasted paper, now turned golden, in several layers, and the pages stained, flecked, and tattered around the edges; its garish illustrations had come unattached but were preserved, laid in. I had the feeling even in my heedless childhood that this was the only book my father as a little boy had had of his own. He had held onto it, and might have gone to sleep on its coverless face: he had lost his mother when he was seven. My father had never made any mention to his own children of the book, but he had brought it along with him from Ohio to our house and shelved it in our bookcase.

My mother had brought from West Virginia that set of Dickens;   20 those books looked sad, too—they had been through fire and water before I was born, she told me, and there they were, lined up—as I later realized, waiting for *me*.

21   I was presented, from as early as I can remember, with books of my
own, which appeared on my birthday and Christmas morning. Indeed,
my parents could not give me books enough. They must have sacrificed to give me on my sixth or seventh birthday—it was after I became
a reader for myself—the ten-volume set of Our Wonder World. These
were beautifully made, heavy books I would lie down with on the floor
in front of the dining room hearth, and more often than the rest volume
5, *Every Child's Story Book*, was under my eyes. There were the fairy
tales—Grimm, Andersen, the English, the French, "Ali Baba and the
Forty Thieves"; and there was Aesop and Reynard the Fox; there were
the myths and legends, Robin Hood, King Arthur, and St. George and
the Dragon, even the history of Joan of Arc; a whack of *Pilgrim's
Progress* and a long piece of *Gulliver*. They all carried their classic illustrations. I located myself in these pages and could go straight to the stories and pictures I loved; very often "The Yellow Dwarf" was first
choice, with Walter Crane's Yellow Dwarf in full color making his terrifying appearance flanked by turkeys. Now that volume is as worn and
backless and hanging apart as my father's poor *Sanford and Merton*. The
precious page with Edward Lear's "Jumblies" on it has been in danger
of slipping out for all these years. One measure of my love for Our
Wonder World was that for a long time I wondered if I would go
through fire and water for it is as my mother had done for Charles
Dickens; and the only comfort was to think I could ask my mother to
do it for me.

22   I believe I'm the only child I know of who grew up with this treasure in the house. I used to ask others, "Did you have Our Wonder
World?" I'd have to tell them The Book of Knowledge could not hold a
candle to it.

23   I live in gratitude to my parents for initiating me—and as early as I
begged for it, without keeping me waiting—into knowledge of the
word, into reading and spelling, by way of the alphabet. They taught it
to me at home in time for me to begin to read before starting to school.
I believe the alphabet is no longer considered an essential piece of
equipment for traveling through life. In my day it was the keystone to
knowledge. You learned the alphabet as you learned to count to ten, as
you learned "Now I lay me" and the Lord's Prayer and your father's
and mother's name and address and telephone number, all in case you
were lost.

24   My love for the alphabet, which endures, grew out of reciting it
but, before that, out of seeing the letters on the page. In my own story
books, before I could read them for myself, I fell in love with various
winding, enchanted-looking initials drawn by Walter Crane at the
heads of fairy tales. In "Once upon a time," an "O" had a rabbit running it as a treadmill, his feet upon flowers. When the day came, years

later, for me to see the Book of Kells, all the wizardry of letter, initial, and word swept over me a thousand times over, and the illumination, the gold, seemed a part of the word's beauty and holiness that had been there from the start.

Learning stamps you with its moments. Childhood's learning is 25
made up of moments. It isn't steady. It's a pulse.

In a children's art class, we sat in a ring on kindergarten chairs and 26
drew three daffodils that had just been picked out of the yard; and while I was drawing, my sharpened yellow pencil and the cup of the yellow daffodil gave off whiffs just alike. That the pencil doing the drawing should give off the same smell as the flower it drew seemed part of the art lesson—as shouldn't it be? Children, like animals, use all their senses to discover the world. Then artists come along and discover it the same way, all over again. Here and there, it's the same world. Or now and then we'll hear from an artist who's never lost it.

In my sensory education I include my physical awareness of the 27
word. Of a certain word, that is; the connection it has with what it stands for. At around age six, perhaps, I was standing by myself in our front yard waiting for supper, just at that hour in a late summer day when the sun is already below the horizon and the risen full moon in the visible sky stops being chalky and begins to take on light. There comes the moment, and I saw it then, when the moon goes from flat to round. For the first time it met my eyes as a globe. The word "moon" came into my mouth as though fed to me out of a silver spoon. Held in my mouth the moon became a word. It had the roundness of a Concord grape Grandpa took off his vine and gave me to suck out of its skin and swallow whole, in Ohio.

This love did not prevent me from living for years in foolish error 28
about the moon. The new moon just appearing in the west was the rising moon to me. The new should be rising. And in early childhood the sun and moon, those opposite reigning powers, I just as easily assumed rose in east and west respectively in their opposite sides of the sky, and like partners in a reel they advanced, sun from the east, moon from the west, crossed over (when I wasn't looking) and went down on the other side. My father couldn't have known I believed that when, bending behind me and guiding my shoulder, he positioned me at our telescope in the front yard and, with careful adjustment of the focus, brought the moon close to me.

The night sky over my childhood Jackson was velvety black. I 29
could see the full constellations in it and call their names; when I could read, I knew their myths. Though I was always waked for eclipses, and indeed carried to the window as an infant in arms and shown Halley's Comet in my sleep, and though I'd been taught at our dining room

table about the solar system and knew the earth revolved around the sun, and our moon around us, I never found out the moon didn't come up in the west until I was a writer and Herschel Brickell, the literary critic, told me after I misplaced it in a story. He said valuable words to me about my new profession: "Always be sure you get your moon in the right part of the sky."

30   My mother always sang to her children. Her voice came out just a little bit in the minor key. "Wee Willie Winkie's" song was wonderfully sad when she sang the lullabies.

31   "Oh, but now there's a record. She could have her own record to listen to," my father would have said. For there came a Victrola record of "Bobby Shafftoe" and "Rock-a-Bye Baby," all of Mother's lullabies, which could be played to take her place. Soon I was able to play her my own lullabies all day long.

32   Our Victrola stood in the dining room. I was allowed to climb onto the seat of a dining room chair to wind it, start the record turning, and set the needle playing. In a second I'd jumped to the floor, to spin or march around the table as the music called for—now there were all the other records I could play too. I skinned back onto the chair just in time to lift the needle at the end, stop the record and turn it over, then change the needle. That brass receptacle with a hole in the lid gave off a metallic smell like human sweat, from all the hot needles that were fed it. Winding up, dancing, being cocked to start and stop the record, was of course all in one the act of *listening*—to "Overture to *Daughter of the Regiment*," "Selections from *The Fortune Teller*," "Kiss Me Again," "Gypsy Dance from *Carmen*," "Stars and Stripes Forever," "When the Midnight Choo-Choo Leaves for Alabam," or whatever came next. Movement must be at the very heart of listening.

33   Ever since I was first read to, then started reading to myself, there has never been a line read that I didn't *hear*. As my eyes followed the sentence, a voice was saying it silently to me. It isn't my mother's voice, or the voice of any person I can identify, certainly not my own. It is human, but inward, and it is inwardly that I listen to it. It is to me the voice of the story or the poem itself. The cadence, whatever it is that asks you to believe, the feeling that resides in the printed word, reaches me through the reader-voice. I have supposed, but never found out, that this is the case with all readers—to read as listeners—and with all writers, to write as listeners. It may be part of the desire to write. The sound of what falls on the page begins the process of testing it for truth, for me. Whether I am right to trust so far I don't know. By now I don't know whether I could do either one, reading or writing, without the other.

34   My own words, when I am at work on a story, I hear too as they go, in the same voice that I hear when I read in books. When I write and

the sound of it comes back to my ears, then I act to make my changes. I have always trusted this voice.

RESPONDING TO READING

1. This memoir, like Pauli Murray's in Chapter 5, is a series of "scenes" from family history. But here the child herself is at the center of the stories and the essay has to do with the way childhood learning works: "Childhood's learning is made up of moments. It isn't steady. It's a pulse." Explain what Welty means by this "pulse" and show how "Listening" exemplifies it.

2. "Listening" begins with the child listening to clocks and then presents a series of her other experiences as a listener. Identify them and explain why Welty finds listening to be a powerful, even central experience, in her own learning.

3. Examine closely the passage in which the young Welty connects the sight of the moon and the word "moon" (paragraph 27). What does she mean when she says the word "had the roundness of a Concord grape"? What does the literary critic mean when he cautions her as an adult, "Always be sure you get your moon in the right part of the sky"? Find another passage in which a childhood scene resonates with meaning into adult life and show how it works.

4. Tell the story of how you learned to read, or the first time you realized you could read. What were you reading, and how did you feel about your accomplishment? Be sure to characterize the person or people who taught you and the circumstances under which you learned; re-create a typical scene, if you can. What does that scene, that experience mean to you now, as you reflect upon this as an adult?

5. What, as a child, did you most enjoy doing with a parent, or grandparent, either on a single occasion or repeated over time? What ramifications has this experience for you now? When you explain this, try to re-create the experience, characterizing yourself and the other person through actions, thoughts, possibly dialogue, in the scene as you experienced it and as you see it again in your mind's eye.

The Power of Books

RICHARD WRIGHT

It is a tribute to the power of literature that Richard Wright (1908–60), born on a sharecropper's farm in the rural, racist, Jim Crow south, could become one of the most prominent African–American intellectuals of the twentieth century. Henry Louis Gates, Jr., calls Wright and the publication of his novel *Native Son* (1940) "the single most influential shaping force in black literary history." The grandson of former slaves, Wright was born on a plantation near Natchez, Mississippi, to a sharecropper father and a schoolteacher mother; his two acclaimed autobiographies, *Black Boy* (1945) and *American Hunger* (1977)—intended as the second half of *Black Boy*—bear angry witness to his hungry and chaotic early years. Discovering that books offered a way out of his limited circumstances, Wright pursued literature with a vengeance—words were "weapons." With only an eighth grade education, he relocated to Chicago, worked at the post office, and became a key figure in the Chicago Renaissance. A social activist, Wright was drawn to the American Communist Party, which promised to rid society of racism and chronic poverty. After stints writing for radical publications, Wright moved to New York City to pursue literature full time, and in 1938 his first publication, *Uncle Tom's Children*, appeared. Then *Native Son* surprised the publishing world by becoming a bestseller. After breaking with the Communist Party, Wright moved his family to Paris, France (1947) in search of intellectual openness and freedom from bigotry. As an expatriate, his literary fortunes declined, but his autobiographies and early novels have become American classics.

"The Power of Books," a key episode from *Black Boy*, describes how a white coworker helped Wright gain access to the public library. There Wright discovered hard-hitting, naturalistic American novels by Sinclair Lewis and Theodore Dreiser that spoke directly to him. It is a story about the reality of fiction, the first stirrings of a writer's ambition, and the survival of an independent self.

1   One morning I arrived early at work and went into the bank lobby where the Negro porter was mopping. I stood at a counter and picked up the Memphis *Commercial Appeal* and began my free reading of the press. I came finally to the editorial page and saw an article dealing with one H. L. Mencken. I knew by hearsay that he was the editor of the *American Mercury*, but aside from that I knew nothing about him. The article was a furious denunciation of Mencken, concluding with one, hot, short sentence: Mencken is a fool.

2   I wondered what on earth this Mencken had done to call down upon him the scorn of the South. The only people I had ever heard denounced in the South were Negroes, and this man was not a Negro. Then what ideas did Mencken hold that made a newspaper like the *Commercial Appeal* castigate him publicly? Undoubtedly he must be advocating ideas that the South did not like. Were there, then, people other than Negroes who criticized the South? I knew that during the Civil War the South had hated northern whites, but I had not encountered such hate during my life. Knowing no more of Mencken than I did at that moment, I felt a vague sympathy for him. Had not the South, which had assigned me the role of a nonman, cast at him its hardest words?

3   Now, how could I find out about this Mencken? There was a huge library near the riverfront, but I knew that Negroes were not allowed to

patronize its shelves any more than they were the parks and playgrounds of the city. I had gone into the library several times to get books for the white men on the job. Which of them would now help me to get books? And how could I read them without causing concern to the white men with whom I worked? I had so far been successful in hiding my thoughts and feelings from them, but I knew that I would create hostility if I went about this business of reading in a clumsy way.

I weighed the personalities of the men on the job. There was Don, a   4
Jew; but I distrusted him. His position was not much better than mine and I knew that he was uneasy and insecure; he had always treated me in an offhand, bantering way that barely concealed his contempt. I was afraid to ask him to help me to get books; his frantic desire to demonstrate a racial solidarity with the whites against Negroes might make him betray me.

Then how about the boss? No, he was a Baptist and I had the sus-   5
picion that he would not be quite able to comprehend why a black boy would want to read Mencken. There were other white men on the job whose attitudes showed clearly that they were Kluxers or sympathizers, and they were out of the question.

There remained only one man whose attitude did not fit into an   6
anti-Negro category, for I had heard the white men refer to him as a "Pope lover." He was an Irish Catholic and was hated by the white Southerners. I knew that he read books, because I had got him volumes from the library several times. Since he, too, was an object of hatred, I felt that he might refuse me but would hardly betray me. I hesitated, weighing and balancing the imponderable realities.

One morning I paused before the Catholic fellow's desk.   7
"I want to ask you a favor," I whispered to him.   8
"What is it?"   9
"I want to read. I can't get books from the library. I wonder if you'd   10
let me use your card?"

He looked at me suspiciously.   11
"My card is full most of the time," he said.   12
"I see," I said and waited, posing my question silently.   13
"You're not trying to get me into trouble, are you, boy?" he asked,   14
starting at me.

"Oh, no, sir."   15
"What book do you want?"   16
"A book by H.L. Mencken."   17
"Which one?"   18
"I don't know. Has he written more than one?"   19
"He has written several."   20
"I didn't know that."   21
"What makes you want to read Mencken?"   22

23   "Oh, I just saw his name in the newspaper," I said.

24   "It's good of you to want to read," he said. "But you ought to read the right things."

25   I said nothing. Would he want to supervise my reading?

26   "Let me think," he said. "I'll figure out something."

27   I turned from him and he called me back. He stared at me quizzically.

28   "Richard, don't mention this to the other white men," he said.

29   "I understand," I said, "I won't say a word."

30   A few days later he called me to him.

31   "I've got a card in my wife's name," he said. "Here's mine."

32   "Thank you, sir."

33   "Do you think you can manage it?"

34   "I'll manage fine," I said.

35   "If they suspect you, you'll get in trouble," he said.

36   "I'll write the same kind of notes to the library that you wrote when you sent me for books," I told him. "I'll sign your name."

37   He laughed.

38   "Go ahead. Let me see what you get," he said.

39   That afternoon I addressed myself to forging a note. Now, what were the names of books written by H.L. Mencken? I did not know any of them. I finally wrote what I thought would be a foolproof note: *Dear Madam: Will you please let this nigger boy*—I used the word "nigger" to make the librarian feel that I could not possibly be the author of the note—*have some books by H.L. Mencken?* I forged the white man's name.

40   I entered the library as I had always done when on errands for whites, but I felt that I would somehow slip up and betray myself. I doffed my hat, stood a respectful distance from the desk, look as unbookish as possible, and waited for the white patrons to be taken care of. When the desk was clear of people, I still waited. The white librarian looked at me.

41   "What do you want, boy?"

42   As though I did not possess the power of speech, I stepped forward and simply handed her the forged note, not parting my lips.

43   "What books by Mencken does he want?" she asked.

44   "I don't know, ma'am," I said, avoiding her eyes.

45   "Who gave you this card?"

46   "Mr. Falk," I said.

47   "Where is he?"

48   "He's at work, at the M _____ Optical Company," I said. "I've been in here for him before."

49   "I remember," the woman said. "But he never wrote notes like this."

Oh, God, she's suspicious. Perhaps she would not let me have the   50
books? If she had turned her back at that moment, I would have
ducked out the door and never gone back. Then I thought of a bold
idea.

"You can call him up, ma'am," I said, my heart pounding.   51

"You're not using these books, are you?" she asked pointedly.   52

"Oh, no, ma'am. I can't read."   53

"I don't know what he wants by Mencken," she said under her   54
breath.

I knew now that I had won; she was thinking of other things and   55
the race question had gone out of her mind. She went to the shelves.
Once or twice she looked over her shoulder at me, as though she was
still doubtful. Finally she came forward with two books in her hand.

"I'm sending him two books," she said. "But tell Mr. Falk to come   56
in next time, or send me the names of the books he wants. I don't know
what he wants to read."

I said nothing. She stamped the card and handed me the books.   57
Not daring to glance at them, I went out of the library, fearing that the
woman would call me back for further questioning. A block away from
the library I opened one of the books and read a title: _A Book of Prefaces_.
I was nearing my nineteenth birthday and I did not know how to pronounce the word _preface_. I thumbed the pages and saw strange words
and strange names. I shook my head, disappointed. I looked at the
other book; it was called _Prejudices_. I knew what that word meant; I had
heard it all of my life. And right off I was on guard against Mencken's
books. Why would a man want to call a book _Prejudices_? The word was
so stained with all my memories of racial hate that I could not conceive
of anybody using it for a title. Perhaps I had made a mistake about
Mencken? A man who had prejudices must be wrong.

When I showed the books to Mr. Falk, he looked at me and   58
frowned.

"That librarian might telephone you," I warned him.   59

"That's all right," he said. "But when you're through reading those   60
books, I want you to tell me what you get out of them."

That night in my rented room, while letting the hot water run over   61
my can of pork and beans in the sink, I opened _A Book of Prefaces_ and
began to read. I was jarred and shocked by the style, the clear, clean,
sweeping sentences. Why did he write like that? And how did one
write like that? I pictured the man as a raging demon, slashing with his
pen, consumed with hate, denouncing everything American, extolling
everything European or German, laughing at the weaknesses of people, mocking God, authority. What was this? I stood up, trying to realize what reality lay behind the meaning of the words. . . . Yes, this man

was fighting, fighting with words. He was using words as a weapon, using them as one would use a club. Could words be weapons? Well, yes, for here they were. Then, maybe, perhaps, I could use them as a weapon? No. It frightened me. I read on and what amazed me was not what he said, but how on earth anybody had the courage to say it.

62   Occasionally I glanced up to reassure myself that I was alone in the room. Who were these men about whom Mencken was talking so passionately? Who was Anatole France? Joseph Conrad? Sinclair Lewis, Sherwood Anderson, Dostoevski, George Moore, Gustave Flaubert, Maupassant, Tolstoy, Frank Harris, Mark Twain, Thomas Hardy, Arnold Bennett, Stephen Crane, Zola, Norris, Gorky, Bergson, Ibsen, Balzac, Bernard Shaw, Dumas, Poe, Thomas Mann, O. Henry, Dreiser, H. G. Wells, Gogol, T. S. Eliot, Gide, Baudelaire, Edgar Lee Masters, Stendhal, Turgenev, Huneker, Nietzsche, and scores of others? Were these men real? Did they exist or had they existed? And how did one pronounce their names?

63   I ran across many words whose meanings I did not know, and I either looked them up in a dictionary or, before I had a chance to do that, encountered the word in a context that made its meaning clear. But what strange world was this? I concluded the book with the conviction that I had somehow overlooked something terribly important in life. I had once tried to write, had once reveled in feeling, had let my crude imagination roam, but the impulse to dream had been slowly beaten out of me by experience. Now it surged up again and I hungered for books, new ways of looking and seeing. It was not a matter of believing or disbelieving what I read, but of feeling something new, of being affected by something that made the look of the world different.

64   As dawn broke I ate my pork and beans, feeling dopey, sleepy. I went to work, but the mood of the book would not die; it lingered, coloring everything I saw, heard, did. I now felt that I knew what the white men were feeling. Merely because I had read a book that had spoken of how they lived and thought, I identified myself with that book, I felt vaguely guilty. Would I, filled with bookish notions, act in a manner that would make the whites dislike me?

65   I forged more notes and my trips to the library became frequent. Reading grew into a passion. My first serious novel was Sinclair Lewis's *Main Street*. It made me see my boss, Mr. Gerald, and identify him as an American type. I would smile when I saw him lugging his golf bags into the office. I had always felt a vast distance separating me from the boss, and now I felt closer to him, though still distant. I felt now that I knew him, that I could feel the very limits of his narrow life. And this had happened because I had read a novel about a mythical man called George F. Babbitt.

66   The plots and stories in the novels did not interest me so much as the point of view revealed. I gave myself over to each novel without re-

serve, without trying to criticize it; it was enough for me to see and feel something different. And for me, everything was something different. Reading was like a drug, a dope. The novels created moods in which I lived for days. But I could not conquer my sense of guilt, my feeling that the white men around me knew that I was changing, that I had begun to regard them differently.

Whenever I brought a book to the job, I wrapped it in newspaper— 67 a habit that was to persist for years in other cities and under other circumstances. But some of the white men pried into my packages when I was absent and they questioned me.

"Boy, what are you reading those books for?"   68
"Oh, I don't know, sir."   69
"That's deep stuff you're reading, boy."   70
"I'm just killing time, sir."   71
"You'll addle your brains if you don't watch out."   72

I read Dreiser's *Jennie Gerhardt* and *Sister Carrie* and they revived in 73 me a vivid sense of my mother's suffering; I was overwhelmed, I grew silent, wondering about the life around me. It would have been impossible for me to have told anyone what I derived from these novels, for it was nothing less than a sense of life itself. All my life had shaped me for the realism, the naturalism of the modern novel, and I could not read enough of them.

Steeped in new moods and ideas, I bought a ream of paper and 74 tried to write; but nothing would come, or what did come was flat beyond telling. I discovered that more than desire and feeling were necessary to write and I dropped the idea. Yet I still wondered how it was possible to know people sufficiently to write about them? Could I ever learn about life and people? To me, with my vast ignorance, my Jim Crow station in life, it seemed a task impossible of achievement. I now knew what being a Negro meant. I could endure the hunger. I had learned to live with hate. But to feel that there were feelings denied me, that the very breath of life itself was beyond my reach, that more than anything else hurt, wounded me. I had a new hunger.

In buoying me up, reading also cast me down, made me see what 75 was possible, what I had missed. My tension returned, new, terrible, bitter, surging, almost too great to be contained. I no longer *felt* that the world about me was hostile, killing; I *knew* it. A million times I asked myself what I could do to save myself, and there were no answers. I seemed forever condemned, ringed by walls.

I did not discuss my reading with Mr. Falk, who had lent me his li- 76 brary card; it would have meant talking about myself and that would have been too painful. I smiled each day, fighting desperately to maintain my old behavior, to keep my disposition seemingly sunny. But some of the white men discerned that I had begun to brood.

"Wake up there, boy!" Mr. Olin said one day.   77

78   "Sir!" I answered for the lack of a better word.

79   "You act like you've stolen something," he said.

80   I laughed in the way I knew he expected me to laugh, but I resolved to be more conscious of myself, to watch my every act, to guard and hide the new knowledge that was dawning within me.

81   If I went north, would it be possible for me to build a new life then? But how could a man build a life upon vague, unformed yearnings? I wanted to write and I did not even know the English language. I bought English grammars and found them dull. I felt that I was getting a better sense of the language from novels than grammars. I read hard, discarding a writer as soon as I felt that I had grasped his point of view. At night the printed page stood before my eyes in sleep.

82   Mrs. Moss, my landlady, asked me one Sunday morning:

83   "Son, what is this you keep on reading?"

84   "Oh, nothing. Just novels."

85   "What you get out of 'em?"

86   "I'm just killing time," I said.

87   "I hope you know your own mind," she said in a tone which implied that she doubted if I had a mind.

88   I knew of no Negroes who read the books I liked and I wondered if any Negroes ever thought of them. I knew that there were Negro doctors, lawyers, newspapermen, but I never saw any of them. When I read a Negro newspaper I never caught the faintest echo of my preoccupation in its pages. I felt trapped and occasionally, for a few days, I would stop reading. But a vague hunger would come over me for books, books that opened up new avenues of feeling and seeing, and again I would forge another note to the white librarian. Again I would read and wonder as only the naive and unlettered can read and wonder, feeling that I carried a secret, criminal burden about with me each day.

89   That winter my mother and brother came and we set up housekeeping, buying furniture on the installment plan, being cheated and yet knowing no way to avoid it. I began to eat warm food and to my surprise found the regular meals enabled me to read faster. I may have lived through many illnesses and survived them, never suspecting that I was ill. My brother obtained a job and we began to save toward the trip north, plotting our time, setting tentative dates for departure. I told none of the white men on the job that I was planning to go north; I knew that the moment they felt I was thinking of the North they would change toward me. It would have made them feel that I did not like the life I was living, and because my life was completely conditioned by what they said or did, it would have been tantamount to challenging them.

90   I could calculate my chances for life in the South as a Negro fairly clearly now.

I could fight the southern whites by organizing with other Ne-   91
groes, as my grandfather had done. But I knew that I could never win
that way; there were many whites and there were but few blacks. They
were strong and we were weak. Outright black rebellion could never
win. If I fought openly I would die and I did not want to die. News of
lynchings were frequent.

I could submit and live the life of a genial slave, but that was im-   92
possible. All of my life had shaped me to live by my own feelings and
thoughts. I could make up to Bess and marry her and inherit the house.
But that, too, would be the life of a slave; if I did that, I would crush to
death something within me, and I would hate myself as much as I
knew the whites already hated those who had submitted. Neither
could I ever willingly present myself to be kicked, as Shorty had done.
I would rather have died than do that.

I could drain off my restlessness by fighting with Shorty and Har-   93
rison. I had seen many Negroes solve the problem of being black by
transferring their hatred of themselves to others with a black skin and
fighting them. I would have to be cold to do that, and I was not cold
and I could never be.

I could, of course, forget what I had read, thrust the whites out of   94
my mind, forget them; and find release from anxiety and longing in sex
and alcohol. But the memory of how my father had conducted himself
made that course repugnant. If I did not want others to violate my life,
how could I voluntarily violate it myself?

I had no hope whatever of being a professional man. Not only had   95
I been so conditioned that I did not desire it, but the fulfillment of such
an ambition was beyond my capabilities. Well-to-do Negroes lived in a
world that was almost as alien to me as the world inhabited by whites.

What, then, was there? I held my life in my mind, in my conscious-   96
ness each day, feeling at times that I would stumble and drop it, spill it
forever. My reading had created a vast sense of distance between me
and the world in which I lived and tried to make a living, and that
sense of distance was increasing each day. My days and nights were
one long, quiet, continuously contained dream of terror, tension, and
anxiety. I wondered how long I could bear it.

RESPONDING TO READING

1. As he reads through Mencken's work, Wright is amazed not by what Menck-
   en says but by the fact that he "had the courage to say it." How does this
   amazement connect with Wright's discussion of his own fears—of being betrayed by a coworker, interrogated by the librarian, etc.?

2. Wright argues that, for him, "Reading was like a drug, a dope," [See paragraph 66.] Why does he describe it with such a comparison? Why does the
   act of reading make him feel guilty?

3. As he reads more and more novels, why is it harder for Wright to continue to act as he always has? How is this difficulty connected with his ongoing plans to travel north?

4. Near the end of his essay, Wright uses the repetition of "I could" to begin five paragraphs in a row. In an essay, explain how this careful weighing of his options connects with his earlier plans to gain access to the library. Does it increase or decrease the hopelessness of the final paragraph?

5. Consider this question as the basis for an essay: Identify and analyze three or four ways in which stereotypes influence the way people react to one another, for worse—and, if possible, for better. You might begin by examining the tone Wright takes in his narrative, particularly as he stereotypes the men with whom he works according to either their religion—Jewish, Baptist, or Catholic—or their affiliation with the Ku Klux Klan (all four groups labeled by Wright as "anti-Negro"). But broaden your discussion out to include your own experiences, or those of people you know well.

Aria: Memoir of a Bilingual Childhood

RICHARD RODRIGUEZ

Richard Rodriguez was born in San Francisco in 1944, the son of Mexican immigrants. His writing often uses the example of his own life to argue against bilingual education and to question affirmative action. In "Aria: Memoir of a Bilingual Childhood," from his autobiography *Hunger of Memory: The Education of Richard Rodriguez* (1982), Rodriguez focuses on the double burden of expulsion from the Eden of his warm and loving Spanish-speaking family and integration into the wider, harsher public world of English-speaking American life. Although to speak English was to become remote from his parents and estranged from their culture, it was not too high a price to pay, he argues, for obtaining public identity in the mainstream culture—an identity reinforced in Rodriguez's case by a Ph.D. in Renaissance literature from the University of California at Berkeley. In his most recent work, *Brown: The Last Discovery of America* (2002), Rodriguez explores topics ranging from minstrel shows and puritanism to the influence that sharing part of a name with Richard Nixon has had on his own life.

Known to his family as "Mr. Secrets"—he did not come out as gay until some years after *Hunger of Memory* was published—Rodriguez, now an educational consultant and freelance writer, comments on the self he presents in *Hunger of Memory*: "Autobiography is simply one version of a life. The woman who runs the cheese store on California Street used to say, 'I know all about you because I've read your autobiography.' But in fact, she *doesn't* know all about me. What is on those pages is a very selective and a very partial view of who I am. Many times readers of autobiography forget how much is missing. Writers withhold as much as they tell."

Supporters of bilingual education today imply that students like   1
me miss a great deal by not being taught in their family's language.
What they seem not to recognize is that, as a socially disadvantaged
child, I considered Spanish to be a private language. What I needed to
learn in school was that I had the right—and the obligation—to speak
the public language of *los gringos*. The odd truth is that my first-grade
classmates could have become bilingual, in the conventional sense of
that word, more easily than I. Had they been taught (as upper-middle-
class children are often taught early) a second language like Spanish or
French, they could have regarded it simply as that: another public language. In my case such bilingualism could not have been so quickly
achieved. What I did not believe was that I could speak a single public
language.

Without question, it would have pleased me to hear my teachers   2
address me in Spanish when I entered the classroom. I would have felt
much less afraid. I would have trusted them and responded with ease.
But I would have delayed—for how long postponed?—having to learn
the language of public society. I would have evaded—and for how long
could I have afforded to delay?—learning the great lesson of school,
that I had a public identity.

Fortunately, my teachers were unsentimental about their responsi-   3
bility. What they understood was that I needed to speak a public language. So their voices would search me out, asking me questions. Each
time I'd hear them, I'd look up in surprise to see a nun's face frowning
at me. I'd mumble, not really meaning to answer. The nun would persist, 'Richard, stand up. Don't look at the floor. Speak up. Speak to the
entire class, not just to me!' But I couldn't believe that the English language was mine to use. (In part, I did not want to believe it.) I continued to mumble. I resisted the teacher's demands. (Did I somehow
suspect that once I learned public language my pleasing family life
would be changed?) Silent, waiting for the bell to sound, I remained
dazed, diffident, afraid.

Because I wrongly imagined that English was intrinsically a public   4
language and Spanish an intrinsically private one, I easily noted the
difference between classroom language and the language of home. At
school, words were directed to a general audience of listeners. ('Boys
and girls.') Words were meaningfully ordered. And the point was not
self-expression alone but to make oneself understood by many others.
The teacher quizzed: 'Boys and girls, why do we use that word in this
sentence? Could we think of a better word to use there? Would the sentence change its meaning if the words were differently arranged? And
wasn't there a better way of saying much the same thing?' (I couldn't
say. I wouldn't try to say.)

Three months. Five. Half a year passed. Unsmiling, ever watchful,   5
my teachers noted my silence. They began to connect my behavior with

the difficult progress my older sister and brother were making. Until one Saturday morning three nuns arrived at the house to talk to our parents. Stiffly, they sat on the blue living room sofa. From the doorway of another room, spying the visitors, I noted the incongruity—the clash of two worlds, the faces and voices of school intruding upon the familiar setting of home. I overheard one voice gently wondering, 'Do your children speak only Spanish at home, Mrs. Rodriguez?' While another voice added, 'That Richard especially seems so timid and shy.'

6   *That Rich-heard*!

7   With great tact the visitors continued, 'Is it possible for you and your husband to encourage your children to practice their English when they are home?' Of course, my parents complied. What would they not do for their children's well-being? And how could they have questioned the Church's authority which those women represented? In an instant, they agreed to give up the language (the sounds) that had revealed and accentuated our family's closeness. The moment after the visitors left, the change was observed. '*Ahora*, speak to us *en inglés*,' my father and mother united to tell us.

8   At first, it seemed a kind of game. After dinner each night, the family gathered to practice 'our' English. (It was still then *inglés*, a language foreign to us, so we felt drawn as strangers to it.) Laughing, we would try to define words we could not pronounce. We played with strange English sounds, often overanglicizing our pronunciations. And we filled the smiling gaps of our sentences with familiar Spanish sounds. But that was cheating, somebody shouted. Everyone laughed. In school, meanwhile, like my brother and sister, I was required to attend a daily tutoring session. I needed a full year of special attention. I also needed my teachers to keep my attention from straying in class by calling out, *Rich-heard*—their English voices slowly prying loose my ties to my other name, its three notes, *Ri-car-do*. Most of all I needed to hear my mother and father speak to me in a moment of seriousness in broken—suddenly heartbreaking—English. The scene was inevitable: One Saturday morning I entered the kitchen where my parents were talking in Spanish. I did not realize that they were talking in Spanish however until, at the moment they saw me, I heard their voices change to speak English. Those *gringo* sounds they uttered startled me. Pushed me away. In that moment of trivial misunderstanding and profound insight, I felt my throat twisted by unsounded grief. I turned quickly and left the room. But I had no place to escape to with Spanish. (The spell was broken.) My brother and sisters were speaking English in another part of the house.

9   Again and again in the days following, increasingly angry, I was obliged to hear my mother and father: 'Speak to us *en inglés*.' (Speak.) Only then did I determine to learn classroom English. Weeks after, it happened: One day in school I raised my hand to volunteer an answer.

I spoke out in a loud voice. And I did not think it remarkable when the entire class understood. That day, I moved very far from the disadvantaged child I had been only days earlier. The belief, the calming assurance that I belonged in public, had at last taken hold.

Shortly after, I stopped hearing the high and loud sounds of *los*   10 *gringos*. A more and more confident speaker of English, I didn't trouble to listen to *how* strangers sounded, speaking to me. And there simply were too many English-speaking people in my day for me to hear American accents anymore. Conversations quickened. Listening to persons who sounded eccentrically pitched voices, I usually noted their sounds for an initial few seconds before I concentrated on *what* they were saying. Conversations became content-full. Transparent. Hearing someone's *tone* of voice—angry or questioning or sarcastic or happy or sad—I didn't distinguish it from the words it expressed. Sound and word were thus tightly wedded. At the end of a day, I was often bemused, always relieved, to realize how 'silent,' though crowded with words, my day in public had been. (This public silence measured and quickened the change in my life.)

At last, seven years old, I came to believe what had been technical-   11 ly true since my birth: I was an American citizen.

But the special feeling of closeness at home was diminished by   12 then. Gone was the desperate, urgent, intense feeling of being at home; rare was the experience of feeling myself individualized by family intimates. We remained a loving family, but one greatly changed. No longer so close; no longer bound tight by the pleasing and troubling knowledge of our public separateness. Neither my older brother nor sister rushed home after school anymore. Nor did I. When I arrived home there would often be neighborhood kids in the house. Or the house would be empty of sounds.

Following the dramatic Americanization of their children, even my   13 parents grew more publicly confident. Especially my mother. She learned the names of all the people on our block. And she decided we needed to have a telephone installed in the house. My father continued to use the word *gringo*. But it was no longer charged with the old bitterness or distrust. (Stripped of any emotional content, the word simply became a name for those Americans not of Hispanic descent.) Hearing him, sometimes, I wasn't sure if he was pronouncing the Spanish word *gringo* or saying gringo in English.

Matching the silence I started hearing in public was a new quiet at   14 home. The family's quiet was partly due to the fact that, as we children learned more and more English, we shared fewer and fewer words with our parents. Sentences needed to be spoken slowly when a child addressed his mother or father. (Often the parent wouldn't understand.) The child would need to repeat himself. (Still the parent misunderstood.) The young voice, frustrated, would end up saying,

'Never mind'—the subject was closed. Dinners would be noisy with the clinking of knives and forks against dishes. My mother would smile softly between her remarks; my father at the other end of the table would chew and chew at his food, while he stared over the heads of his children.

15   *My mother! My father!* After English became my primary language, I no longer knew what words to use in addressing my parents. The old Spanish words (those tender accents of sound) I had used earlier— *mamá* and *papá*—I couldn't use anymore. They would have been too painful reminders of how much had changed in my life. On the other hand, the words I heard neighborhood kids call *their* parents seemed equally unsatisfactory. *Mother* and *Father; Ma, Papa, Pa, Dad, Pop* (how I hated the all-American sound of that last word especially)—all these terms I felt were unsuitable, not really terms of address for *my* parents. As a result, I never used them at home. Whenever I'd speak to my parents, I would try to get their attention with eye contact alone. In public conversations, I'd refer to 'my parents' or 'my mother and father.'

16   My mother and father, for their part, responded differently, as their children spoke to them less. She grew restless, seemed troubled and anxious at the scarcity of words exchanged in the house. It was she who would question me about my day when I came home from school. She smiled at small talk. She pried at the edges of my sentences to get me to say something more. (What?) She'd join conversations she overheard, but her intrusions often stopped her children's talking. By contrast, my father seemed reconciled to the new quiet. Though his English improved somewhat, he retired into silence. At dinner he spoke very little. One night his children and even his wife helplessly giggled at his garbled English pronunciation of the Catholic Grace before Meals. Thereafter he made his wife recite the prayer at the start of each meal, even on formal occasions, when there were guests in the house. Hers became the public voice of the family. On official business, it was she, not my father, one would usually hear on the phone or in stores, talking to strangers. His children grew so accustomed to his silence that, years later, they would speak routinely of his shyness. (My mother would often try to explain: Both his parents died when he was eight. He was raised by an uncle who treated him like little more than a menial servant. He was never encouraged to speak. He grew up alone. A man of few words.) But my father was not shy, I realized, when I'd watch him speaking Spanish with relatives. Using Spanish, he was quickly effusive. Especially when talking with other men, his voice would spark, flicker, flare alive with sounds. In Spanish, he expressed ideas and feelings he rarely revealed in English. With firm Spanish sounds, he conveyed confidence and authority English would never allow him.

The silence at home, however, was finally more than a literal si- 17
lence. Fewer words passed between parent and child, but more profound was the silence that resulted from my inattention to sounds. At
about the time I no longer bothered to listen with care to the sounds of
English in public, I grew careless about listening to the sounds family
members made when they spoke. Most of the time I heard someone
speaking at home and didn't distinguish his sounds from the words
people uttered in public. I didn't even pay much attention to my parents' accented and ungrammatical speech. At least not at home. Only
when I was with them in public would I grow alert to their accents.
Though, even then, their sounds caused me less and less concern. For I
was increasingly confident of my own public identity.

I would have been happier about my public success had I not 18
sometimes recalled what it had been like earlier, when my family had
conveyed its intimacy through a set of conveniently private sounds.
Sometimes in public, hearing a stranger, I'd hark back to my past. A
Mexican farmworker approached me downtown to ask directions to
somewhere. '¿ Hijito . . . ?' he said. And his voice summoned deep longing. Another time, standing beside my mother in the visiting room of a
Carmelite convent, before the dense screen which rendered the nuns
shadowy figures, I heard several Spanish-speaking nuns—their busy,
singsong overlapping voices—assure us that yes, yes, we were remembered, all our family was remembered in their prayers. (Their voices
echoed faraway family sounds.) Another day, a dark-faced old
woman—her hand light on my shoulder—steadied herself against me
as she boarded a bus. Her Spanish voice came near, like the face of a
never-before-seen relative in the instant before I was kissed. Her voice,
like so many of the Spanish voices I'd hear in public, recalled the gold-
en age of my youth. Hearing Spanish then, I continued to be a careful,
if sad, listener to sounds. Hearing a Spanish-speaking family walking
behind me, I turned to look. I smiled for an instant, before my glance
found the Hispanic-looking faces of strangers in the crowd going by.

RESPONDING TO READING

1. What distinctions does Rodriguez make between private and public language? How do his quotations, in dialogue and dialect, reinforce his point?

2. Rodriguez says, "At last, seven years old, I came to believe what had been
technically true since my birth: I was an American citizen." [para-
graph 11] What does "citizenship" mean for Rodriguez? How is it related
to bilingualism?

3. What is the effect of the bilingualism of the Rodriguez children on their
home life? On their parents? What does Rodriguez think of the dilution or
subduing of their Hispanic culture? How convincing is his interpretation?

4. In his outspoken opposition to bilingual education, Rodriguez has publicly and consistently advocated monolingualism in the schools. How does "Aria" reinforce his stance? Do you agree? Why or why not?

5. Rodriguez, like many other authors, uses himself and examples from his own life as evidence for an argument, here concerning the education that he would like applied to the entire bilingual student population. To what extent is Rodriguez, or any author, justified in using this technique? How convincing is it here? In other writings?

6. Like many authors writing about their childhoods, Rodriguez re-creates himself as a child character who changes over time in his narrative. To better understand this technique, try to make a point presenting your childhood self as a character in an incident that you narrate from your current perspective. How does language shape your identity?

QUESTIONS FOR REFLECTION AND WRITING

What Is My Physical Self?

1. In what ways do Kingston and Angier agree on what it means to be female? In what ways do they disagree?

2. Imagine a conversation on individuality between Mairs and Steele. What points of agreement and disagreement would emerge? Where might they fail to understand each other? To what degree would their disagreements and misunderstandings be based on their sex? Their race? Their social class?

3. Imagine that you have been transformed into someone of the opposite sex. What might it be like? How would it change who you are?

4. If you have had the experience of filling a role customarily played by someone of a different gender, age, cultural group, or social class, describe it and how it affected you. You might, for example, have been the only female in an all-male class in engineering, or a middle-aged returning freshman in a class of eighteen-year-olds, or a college student working in construction.

5. We might see Angier and Mairs arguing for the "self as body" while Kingston and Steele present the self as largely determined by social construction of class, gender, and race. Write an essay in which you define your physical self with reference to the approaches of these writers.

Who Am I in Relation to Others?

1. Douglass and Rose both describe young men in deprived circumstances making decisions about their future. Why do the decisions turn out to be so different? Suppose that Douglass were writing today; in what ways might his essay be different? For instance, what might his language sound like? Would he be more or less angry?

2. How does school affect a child's sense of who he or she is? Write an essay in which you evaluate the relationship between education and self-discovery.

3. To what degree does Liu have self respect, according to Didion's definitions?

4. Write an essay on who you are in relation to another person (such as a parent, grandparent, friend, lover, spouse, child, or boss) or in relation to a group (such as your family, living group, coworkers, or fellow citizens). To what extent does this relationship shape your personality, character, or development, either by enhancing or interfering with it? Are you "really" yourself in this context?

How Do Language and Literacy Affect My Identity?

1. Try to remember how you learned to read and to write. What were the first words you read? The first words you wrote? Compare your own experiences to some of those narrated by Tan, Welty, Wright, and Rodriguez, and show how your developing literacy related to your developing sense of self.

2. Tell the story of a significant language experience you have had—positive, negative, or a mixture—in a way that enables you to affirm who you are. Make clear from the start why you chose that particular experience.

3. Compare Rodriguez's account of his growth through language, and the decline in family intimacy that occurred at the same time, with Tan's account of her language growth. To what degree is Rodriguez's experience special to second language learners, as opposed to the general experience of children educated beyond their parents' level?

4. Select two essays from this or the previous sections and write an essay showing how writers use words and their understanding of words as an important means of self-definition.

5. Locate a piece of writing of your own in which you have described and analyzed a personal experience. Read it carefully, reflecting on how you shaped that experience in your writing.

   Then, using that reflection as a start, write an essay on the following question: In presenting themselves, to what extent can writers be trusted to tell the truth? The whole truth? What kind of truth: Literal? Psychological? Or some other kind entirely?

Identity: How Do I Know Who I Am?

1. Write an essay on some of the ways you have discovered who you are. Include at least one key aspect of your physical self, one important relationship to someone else, and your sense of who you are as a student and writer. What are the most essential elements of your identity? What aspects may change? What aspects do you see as permanent?

2. Tell about an important moment in your past that let you see clearly something about yourself that was, until that moment, obscure. Some writers call such a moment an "epiphany," an almost religious insight; others speak of the "aha!" experience which reveals truth. Your writing will both capture the moment for yourself and help your audience see what you have seen.

Thinking
How Do We Know What We Know?

*A man woke up from a dream in which he dreamed he was a
cat, but could never be sure if he were a man who had
dreamt about being a cat or was actually a cat continuing
to dream of being a man. He drank some milk and went
about his business.*
PERSIAN FOLKTALE

Why Consider This Question?

Most of what we think we know is a matter of believing what we
have been told to believe by those with more power or greater authority than ourselves. As children, we usually trust this way of knowing.
However, as adults, unless we examine how we have come to know
what we know, we forfeit our right to think independently and to
know things for ourselves.

What are the sources of our knowledge? While much of what we
know does indeed come from others—parents, books, teachers, television, websites—we also accumulate knowledge from other sources that
are less external, such as an intuition that we believe. We also trust the
knowledge that we derive from our own observation and experience,
which accumulates as we grow older. By the time we enter college,
most of us combine our own intuitions and observations with what we
have been taught. But sometimes what we know conflicts directly with
what someone else knows or even with other things that we know. Perhaps the science we learned in school conflicts with the religion we absorbed at home, or maybe the way we have learned to treat men or
women turns out to be offensive to people we admire or to people we

want to admire us. When conflicts occur, we need to question the adequacy of our sources of knowledge.

Where does intuition come from, and what do we do when our "just knowing" differs from the intuitions of someone else? We probably need to go beyond intuition to resolve the issues. Observation sometimes seems more reliable, since many of us like to believe that there is an objective reality "out there" that needs only to be recorded accurately in order to create knowledge. But not all observers wind up seeing the same things, and even those who see the same things sometimes interpret them differently. No authorities, intuitions, or observations are absolute or conclusive. We cannot really rest securely with what we know until we have thought about and assessed how we have come to know what we do and until we have come to terms with the problems that lie behind different ways of knowing.

We cannot, however, be forever waiting for final knowledge; we must live our lives. Perhaps the best we can do is to remain aware of the sources of our knowledge, whatever they may be, and to allow the possibility that new knowledge or new perspectives on old knowledge will arise. Even then, like the dreamer in the Persian folktale, we must still go about our business.

Our business, in this case, turns out to be reading and writing—our principal means of inquiry into problems. The readings that follow deal with the ways we come to know things. The first section presents some ways of thinking about thinking. The second section offers some ways of knowing about nature—the plants and animals with whom we share our planet. The third section asks us to consider the patterns of thought and language that we use to understand what we observe. Although we may not end our reading of this chapter with a conclusive answer to how we have come to know what we know, the variety of answers we discover through our reading and writing should enrich the question.

What Is the Process of Thinking?

The first set of readings focuses on the way we see and understand reality. The underlying issue here is not knowing or learning about something so much as it is thinking about the ways we acquire and process any kind of knowledge. Thinking about thinking has concerned many fields of study. Psychology, philosophy, linguistics, biology, and anthropology look at a given issue from substantially different angles. The psychologist may observe how children mature, the philosopher will ask about the relation of learning to truth, the linguist might argue that language determines thought, the biologist or medical researcher could investigate the purposes of different regions of the brain, and the anthropologist would inquire into the learning and language of our earliest ancestors. While there are many ways of thinking about thinking, the essays in this section raise some fundamental questions about the way our language and our perceptions lead to knowledge.

Susanne Langer, in "Signs and Symbols," sees the central distinction between the human race and the "animal mind" as our ability to use symbols. The human mind, she argues, does not merely mediate "between an event in the outer world and a creature's responsive action," but instead "transforms or, if you will, distorts the event into an image to be looked at, retained, and contemplated." For Langer, symbolic language is not merely essential for thinking; it is the defining characteristic of our species, the single trait that makes us human rather than animal.

Plato's "Allegory of the Cave" questions our usual acceptance of what we see as "real." He is not concerned with the language of perception, as Langer is, but with our perception of reality itself: Only the wisest of us, he says, can see what is real in "the region of the intelligible" or "the world of knowledge." What most people take to be real is not real, according to this allegory, despite the convictions and passions of those with limited vision.

Isaac Asimov, in "Those Crazy Ideas," seeks the sources of creative thinking in science. He first examines his own scientific creativity, then analyzes Darwin's discovery of "a new and revolutionary scientific principle," and finally presents a series of criteria for identifying scientific creativity in general. In a conversational tone, Asimov defines and describes five specific criteria, culminating in "luck"—all them necessary for the scientific breakthroughs that can change the way people imagine the world.

Frank Conroy, in "Think about It," shows the complexity of apparently ordinary ideas: "I thought about the words 'clear and present danger,' and the fact that if you looked at them closely they might not be as simple as they had first appeared." Through his accidental association with two judges, he learned that even complicated legal rulings do not interpret themselves; like simple terms, they require thought and time to develop meaning: "Documents alone do not keep democracy alive, nor maintain the state of law . . . Living men and women, generation after generation, must continually remake democracy and the law." Referring to what we think we know, Conroy suggests that we must continue to "think about it," using our own experiences, contexts, and understanding of the past.

Finally, Anne Fadiman, in "Under Water," reflects on a wilderness tragedy, trying to explore the meaning of a fellow student's drowning many years ago. The incident, still vivid in all of its details, never leaves the mind, though its meaning changes over time. Whether we reflect on apparently simple and familiar concepts or vividly remembered tragedies, such meanings must be negotiated anew as one gets older. What we know about our own experience changes as we change.

What Are Some Ways of Understanding Nature?

Charles Darwin opens this section with "Understanding Natural Selection," a portion of the landmark work examined by Asimov in the previous section. Here, we can test Asimov's interpretation of Darwin against our own experience of reading Darwin. Darwin's clear and accessible style almost hides the fact that his work changed the way the scientific community understands nature.

Stephen Jay Gould follows with "Evolution as Fact and Theory," an essay arguing for definitions and distinctions that allow us to think clearly about a controversial subject: "Well, evolution is a theory. It is also a fact. And facts and theories are different things, not rungs in a hierarchy of increasing certainty." His definitions are crucial to his argument; if we agree with his definitions, we are likely to agree with his conclusions. As a natural scientist and a writer, Gould delights in the intellectual game of creating possible explanations for observed phenomena, and he asks his readers to join in the play. For both Darwin and Gould, we learn about the external world by observing it and then thinking about it. If we contrast them with Conroy, in the previous section, we notice that Conroy is ready to use his personal experience and intuitions, in addition to his observations, in ways that Darwin and Gould are not. Do we understand nature better by interacting with it or by standing outside of it?

Jane van Lawick-Goodall's account of her many years observing the behavior of chimpanzees in their natural habitat suggests that the apparently irreconcilable positions we have just encountered might, in fact, be put together by an intuitive and personal observer of natural phenomena. Her discoveries about chimpanzees have raised many questions about the distinctiveness of human beings. For instance, if her approach to animals is valid, what can we say about Langer's emphasis on language as distinguishing humans from other animal life? As we experience with Goodall the touch of a female bushbuck or her fear of the leopard, we come to trust the observations she makes as a source of knowledge—and problems.

Finally, Michael Pollan's "Playing God in the Garden" provides more questions than answers about genetically engineered foods, "human control of nature . . . taking a giant step forward." "Truly," he says with some irony, "we have stepped out onto new ground. Or have we?" What happens, he later asks, "when people begin approaching the genes of our food plants as software"? In our new millennium, he suggests, we must develop a fresh relationship with the very food we eat if we are to understand what it is and how much of our own selves is embedded in it.

We are likely to argue with any one of the positions taken by these essays, and we might be unable to resolve the questions raised by the four of them taken together. But, as we test our own assumptions about ways of knowing by what these writers have to say, we are bound to deepen and complicate our own views. How, we would ask, does our way of knowing affect or determine what we know?

How Can We Explain What We Know? Thomas Kuhn opens this section with "The Route to Normal Science," that is, by arguing for the necessity of established norms and patterns (such as the right way to conduct a laboratory experiment) within which scientific (or other) discoveries can take place. He calls this pattern a "paradigm"—the shared fundamentals under which scientists operate, the "rules and standards for scientific practice." But Kuhn does not take these paradigms to be truth; they are rather working agreements that change from time to time, a temporary "research consensus" that defines a field of study at a particular time. Without such a consensus, he argues, research and knowledge cannot go forward; but no paradigm can explain all observations. In fact, as new observations and theories appear, paradigms shift and new ones come to the fore, neither more nor less true than the previous ones. Nevertheless, they are powerful lenses through which to view reality.

Deborah Tannen focuses on student conversational styles in the classroom, pointing out one particular sex-related phenomenon: males are much more willing to compete for time to speak and to challenge others than are females. She then describes her own experiment to demonstrate this difference and goes on to explore its implications. A conversational style is also a learning style, and how we learn is important for what we learn. Benjamin Lee Whorf has explored the relation of language to learning in great depth and, in "An American Indian Model of the Universe," focuses on how certain grammatical features of the Hopi language (such as a lack of tenses for its verbs and the absence of any word that conveys time) lead to a special view of time and space. Our language, Whorf suggests here and elsewhere in his writing, determines our reality; we know what we know through the prism of our words.

Finally, Perri Klass, writing as an advanced medical student completing a residency in a hospital, focuses on the way the language of medicine is both a means of learning about and dealing with a harsh reality, as well as a device for gaining membership in the closed club of the medical community. This "linguistic separation between doctors and patients" is what "Learning the Language" is all about; furthermore, the language helps to define the profession and those who "belong" to it. As do the other writers in this section, Klass suggests that a way of speaking is an entire way of thinking and acting.

Rhetorical Issues: Writing as a Means of Learning: The Writing Process

If we think of writing as inquiry—as an important and essential part of thinking and learning—we will value the time we spend planning, drafting, revising, and editing our own work. This time is not to be given grudgingly to polishing a finished work; rather, it is creative thinking time to deepen and broaden our knowledge. Pages discarded (or recycled) from early drafts do not represent wasted time; the material is now rethought and incorporated into new and better ideas. A wholly new thesis statement, arrived at through rethinking and rewriting, does make us discard the old one, but we should feel no regret for the loss, which is really a gain.

When any one of us talks about "the writing process," we are likely to mean whatever we do to produce a particular paper—some sequence of thinking, writing, rethinking, rewriting, and editing. But just as no two fingerprints are the same, neither are two writing processes; we might write a poem in a very different way from a lab report, a memo, or a letter to the editor. We might even write an essay on one topic differently from the way we would write another essay on a different topic. Likewise, different people have different styles of composing. Some compose writing the way Mozart composed music, thinking it through carefully—perhaps for a very long time—and then writing a fairly clean draft in a single sitting. As novelist and essayist Joyce Carol Oates says, "If you are a writer, you can locate yourself behind a wall of silence and no matter what you are doing, driving a car or walking or doing housework . . . you can still be writing." This mental writing process works best with short pieces that can be easily kept in mind—a brief poem focused on a single metaphor, a short essay with a single major point, or a narrative that proceeds chronologically, one point leading to the next in a direct time sequence. Writing in the head is difficult and exhausting for most of us. Mozart was exceptional; even as a young child, he was able to hear long and complex musical performances and write all the parts down perfectly when he got back home.

Other writers make many messy starts, using a first draft to explore the subject, to find connections among ideas, and to discover a point of view and the right language. With persistence, every draft may bring them closer to the final product that continues to emerge. Most writers have to go through this painful process of revision after revision to produce their best work. Ernest Hemingway says casually that he wrote the last page of *Farewell to Arms* thirty-nine times, "getting the words right." Regardless of whether he was actually counting, he rewrote over and over again.

Computer word processing has made life a lot easier for all writers, particularly the most experienced ones, who become tinkerers, seldom satisfied with a "final" draft. Computers make it easy to add, delete, and move words, sentences, or larger blocks of text under revision. Computers can save time and effort, because you are always working with a clean screen or printout, so you do not have to labor to decipher handwritten text. The spell and grammar checkers make it easier to fix mechanical matters, and once you are done, you do not have to recopy the passages that were right the first time or retype the entire work, as was common a generation ago. But there is a danger: Computers always print out nice, clean-looking text, even if the contents are intellectually messy. Our technology makes the writing process easier to undergo, but does not relieve us of the burden or responsibility of thinking through and expressing carefully what we want to say.

Planning

Choosing a subject: Suppose that you are writing an essay in response to question 4 on page 130: Explain how the *way* you have come to know your subject has affected *what* you know about it.

Your first task will be to focus on a subject. What will you choose, and how will you decide? In keeping with the spirit of *Inquiry*, you will write a better paper if you pick a topic that interests you, that grows from what you have been reading and thinking about, or that comes from your own experience. The topic should be sufficiently complicated so that you will be able to learn more about it from new perspectives. You will get bored if you simply rehash what you already know—and so will your readers.

Suppose that you have just been through a bad experience and found that several of your friends and family have stood by you in a way you never quite expected. Then you have come to understand friendship in a way that is different from how you have defined it in the past. The paper gives you a chance to explore that issue, and, right now, it is more important to you than the other possible topics. So you decide that your paper will be on how you have come to learn about the meaning of friendship. It will be in part an essay focused on definition, but you will expect to illustrate your complex definition partly by means of a personal narrative.

Taking an inventory of your knowledge: Your second task, determining what you know about the subject and what you need to find out about it, will probably influence the direction the paper will take. What have you learned from your parents, from your siblings and other relations when you were young, and from good and bad friends of yours and of other people? What have you read about friendship? You can examine some of the ways of knowing what you know; you might, for instance, examine what you were told or have read about friendship in the light of what you have experienced. As you think about your topic, you could jot down your answers in the form of key words, in clusters or lists. Or you can brainstorm with a classmate, taking notes as you talk. Or talk into a tape recorder. Or take notes—single key words or phrases—on your reading. Some areas you might explore in determining the bases for your opinions, for example, are as follows:

A. Personal experience
   1. Participating in an activity or event: my own friendships—some casual, some intimate, some new, some long standing, some outgrown.
   2. Knowing someone intimately (oneself, a parent, a friend): Parents' friendship deepened into romantic love (or, sadly, did not); my own first love.
   3. Getting to know the people and the territory of my surroundings: neighbors in my hometown, roommates in my dorm, friends at work.
   4. Experiencing a condition (needing help), the law (the effects of school desegregation), a circumstance (a new roommate), a crisis (a fight with my best friend), a natural phenomenon (interests and attachments change as we grow older).
   5. Intuition

B. Others' views on the subject
   1. Habit, custom, folk wisdom: the general belief that friendship is good; friends should be loyal; till death do us part.
   2. Rebellion against habit or custom: friends my parents did not approve of.
   3. Readings
      a. philosophy: Plato, platonic friendships.
      b. religion: the Bible—do unto others; if I have not charity, I am nothing.
      c. classics: Shakespeare—Mark Antony and Caesar, Hamlet and Laertes, King Lear and Kent.
      d. literature and fine arts: fiction, poetry, sculpture, music, photographs.
      e. *Inquiry*, other textbooks: Richard Rodriguez, "Aria: Memoir of a Bilingual Childhood," gradual distancing from Spanish-

speaking parents as he went to school and learned English; Robert S. Weiss, "Marriage as Partnership."
  f. other disciplines, where relevant: business, economics, education, engineering, geography, history, psychology, and sociology, each with a different perspective on friendship. Consider a variety of documents in addition to articles and books, such as interviews, speeches, policy statements, statistical tables and analyses, graphs, public records, surveys, institutional analyses, research reports, case studies, stock market reports, and business forecasts.
  g. mass media: films, TV, newspapers, and radio.

When you start to examine what you know, you'll probably be surprised to realize that you know a lot more than you thought you did. As you focus on a particular aspect of friendship—say, the friendship adult children can develop with their parents or the possibility of a nonsexual friendship between young men and young women—you will start to find your reading, your observation, and your experience coming together to give you a topic worth pursuing.

Focusing

Clustering: Some people work well with charts, maps, and other spatial arrangements of thought. If you are comfortable with this mode of learning, you might plan your writing by using a visual picture of the ideas for your paper. While there are many forms of mapping, the most popular is a procedure called *clustering*.

To use clustering, select unlined paper and start with a topic that looks promising to you, writing it in the middle of the page. Suppose that you have written "adult friendships" as the topic for your paper. Put a circle around the phrase, and let your mind search for words associated with it.

Writers use clustering to tap their unconscious knowledge and interests. Unlocking a mental treasure chest, they will put words anywhere on the page as they occur, not concerning themselves with connections, logic, or anything except the discovery of ideas. This process is brainstorming by association. One might wind up with a dozen or more words or phrases on the page, perhaps going every which way: casual acquaintances, lovers. Uncle Charley, biblical David and Jonathan, loyalty, AIDS support, Twain's Huck and Jim, friendship over time, and so on. The idea here is to free one's mind from restrictions, even from the necessity of writing in straight lines, so that the fullest kind of creativity can take place.

The next stage is to connect and arrange the ideas on the page. In clustering, you draw large and winding circles around words that seem related to each other. Thus, you might connect one group of words that has to do with kinds of friends, another that has to do with levels of friendship, still another that deals with your personal experience of friendship, and yet another that lists famous friends.

If the assigned paper is relatively short, you cannot cover all the topics. So you must ask, which one is likely to be the most interesting? What will you focus on? What will you say about that topic?

At this point, some writers will go back to a new clustering exercise, now restricted to the topic that seems most worth pursuing. Or it may be time to get to the library or to use a Web search engine such as Google to determine whether you can find more information that you need, before you start organizing your paper in too detailed a way. Or you might even want to start writing a discovery draft to see the ideas actually develop through sentences and paragraphs.

Outlining: For other writers, a simple list will achieve the same purpose as clustering, or a formal outline will stimulate, as well as organize, ideas. A list of possible ideas is a good place to start. Begin jotting down childhood experiences with friendship and how you learned about friendship. Next, you might list some experiences with teenage friends. Perhaps you could write down some headings of what you have read or been taught about friendship. Maybe a section of the list could focus on friendships with the opposite sex, even leading into headings on the differences (if any) from same-sex friendships. What do you gain and give in such relationships? What do you lose?

After some careful reading and notetaking, you will be ready to turn the list into a topical outline, one that arranges headings in a logical sequence and begins to focus the material. Perhaps you have decided that the best way to meet the assignment is to write about the way you have learned that you can be friends with people of the opposite sex, without attempting or needing a sexual relationship. Some of the material on the list that you first wrote will have to be discarded to make room for the detail that will be needed to develop the new and more focused topic. Your outline might look something like this:

  I. Childhood friends: some examples
 II. Childhood learning about sex and friendship
III. Requirements for friendship
     a. Common interests
     b. Common values
     c. Acceptance
     d. Mutuality
     e. Time

IV. What do men and women seek, want, or need in friendships
   a. Power
   b. Self-definition
   c. Caring
   d. Sensuality, etc.
 V. Can friendship with the opposite sex exist?
   a. Famous examples, pro and con
   b. My experience
VI. Adult definitions of friendship

As you begin to move from planning to drafting—and these stages frequently overlap—you may develop still other, more detailed outlines for your work. Perhaps topics I and II will blend into a single one; maybe you will need to abbreviate the material from childhood so you have enough room for your more mature learning. You will need to guard against mere repetition of experience for its own sake, so that you meet the demands of the assignment—which asked you to focus upon the process of coming to know and understand something—and renewed outlining will help keep you on track.

Other kinds of outlining will become more valuable as you start drafting. The sentence outline, for example, which we will look at shortly, is a particularly valuable way to help you see what needs to be changed in early drafts. But there is one danger in using outlining for planning: It is important not to be trapped by outlines into premature decisions about your topic; the outline exists to help you shape your inquiry, not to shut it down or close off possibilities you had not thought of at the time.

Other Planning and Focusing Activities: In addition to clustering and outlining, you may find that reading and notetaking, talking with others about the topic, writing notes or journal entries, and imagining metaphors, analogies, or stories can help you create and shape your ideas. For some people, the best planning emerges from sitting quietly and thinking; still others awake at night with brilliant ideas that must be written down on the spot, for they will be gone by morning.

Planning activities are a crucial part of the writing processes of most good writers. If you neglect to plan and just plunge into drafting, trusting to inspiration and luck, you are not likely to come out with an organized or convincing essay. Most good writers never stop planning as long as the paper is in process, and some planning activities may go on even at the last minute; but, obviously, the earlier you plan, the more efficiently you will work. Whatever planning techniques or approach you find suitable, you will save time and produce better work if you write out ideas, group them, and focus your thoughts before you start producing the drafts that lead to your finished work.

Drafting and Revising: Planning leads naturally to drafting—to the production of writing. But these stages are not wholly distinct. Writing out drafts and revising them is in one sense the next step in most writing processes, but in another sense it is the most powerful part of the planning stage. Planning does not stop when drafting begins; the creation of initial drafts (or "discovery drafts") tests the planning and often refines it.

How many drafts should you produce? Sometimes, as on a timed essay exam, you have no time to produce more than one. All you can do is plan carefully, write your response, and save a few moments at the end for editing. By contrast, we have pointed out that professional writers often will put an important piece of writing through twenty or thirty drafts, an exhausting routine few students will want, or have the time, to emulate. Most students probably turn out one or two drafts for most of their college papers, even though another draft or two might make their writing much more satisfying and result in higher grades.

Professional writers not only revise much more than less experienced writers do, but they revise differently, with a firmer understanding of writing processes. The professionals will throw away much of what they write in early drafts, as they revise, plan, and revise again. Many less experienced writers find it hard to throw away anything; they tend to edit for correctness rather than to revise and reshape. Thus, while it is impossible to say how many drafts you should produce, it is clear that you will write better if you use the professional approach to writing, in which early drafting is more likely to be a form of planning than a way to produce a finished product. The more revising you can do, the better off you will be.

One reasonable way to combine revising and drafting is to use a sentence outline as a way to read and improve your initial draft. The sentence outline differs from the topic outline by containing complete sentences, rather than topic headings. Try abstracting your draft into one sentence for each paragraph, so that a twelve-paragraph paper can be outlined in twelve numbered sentences on a single page. The sentence outline has two distinct advantages: (1) It helps you notice what each paragraph is saying and hence leads you to revise certain paragraphs, and (2) it helps you see the movement of your thoughts from paragraph to paragraph. You may find that the central idea of the paper is most clearly stated in the tenth paragraph, suggesting that it should be moved to the front of the paper. Or you may discover that you say the same thing in the seventh paragraph that you said in the second paragraph, which suggests that these two sections should be combined or one of them should be eliminated. Most importantly, you can determine whether your focused topic has been set out clearly and that everything in the paper relates to it.

Many professional writers allot about half of the time available for writing a paper to revising it. That is, if you can spend twenty hours on a paper, it should exist in draft form after ten hours, so you can spend another ten hours revising and reworking the draft. This introduction talks more about planning than revising, simply because there is no room to give examples of revising here. But do not be misled: Careful revision ("re-vision," a new seeing of the topic) is half of the writing process for most successful writers. When you are convinced that your paper is well focused on an interesting topic, that it is organized effectively, that you have convincing evidence for what you have to say, and that you have demonstrated as well as stated your ideas, you are ready for the final, cleanup, stage.

Editing: Do not confuse editing with revising. Sometimes it is easy to think that going through a paper with an eye to such matters as vocabulary, punctuation, and spelling is really revising. In fact, sometimes a change in mechanics actually does develop into more substantial revision; for example, a badly constructed sentence will often reflect an idea that needs more thought to become clear. But careful editing of a discovery draft does not usually lead to a final draft; rather, it leads just to a clean discovery draft which fools you into thinking that it is finished because it looks so neat. But beware: The tidiness that premature editing can impose on your paper may make you reluctant to make necessary changes in the focus, organization, or development of ideas. If you keep in mind the general principle *revise before you edit*, you'll be less likely to spend time laboring over the spelling of words that you may delete later on or tinkering with the style of paragraphs that will be dropped. Editing before revising is like eating dessert first: It gives you a false sense of completion when you may only have begun.

But the final stage every writer, no matter how experienced, must go through is editing the writing. This means, for example, cleaning up the inevitable spelling errors and other mechanical slips, making sure that the subjects agree with the verbs and the sentences are complete, checking to be sure that the quotations are accurate, and making sure that the paper presents you as a careful person who wants the writing to be taken seriously. We have cautioned against premature editing, a common problem, but now we must warn even more seriously about failing to edit at all. To ignore the editing stage of the writing process can be a serious mistake, for appearances count on a paper they way they do on a person. A sloppy appearance makes it hard for others to respect what you have to say.

Finally, we must admit that some mystery still remains about writing. On some occasions, the most careful planning and endless revision still fail to produce a good essay. Some writers can work so efficiently in their heads that the writing process can be abbreviated, and every now and then someone turns out a superb first draft. But most of us, most of the time, find writing to be hard work, and our early drafts usually need to be revised or even thrown away as we struggle to define and develop our best ideas while our work slowly improves. We often find ourselves coming to know much more about our topic as we go through the writing process, developing our thoughts as we develop our writing. So we might as well take advantage of what experienced writers have learned and develop our ideas through a writing process that allows time for multiple revisions and careful rethinking of the topic.

QUESTIONS FOR DISCOVERY AND DISCUSSION

1. Choose a subject of any sort (it does not have to be a school subject; chess or baking will work as well as chemistry) about which you know more than many other people do. Identify the subject, and explain how you have come to know about it.

2. Identify other possible ways of learning (from books, experience, a parent, and so on) about the subject you have just discussed. What might you know or not know about the subject if you had followed one of these other routes? Why?

3. Imagine someone of a different sex, skin color, period of history, or educational level learning about the subject you have described. What is that person likely to know about it? Why?

4. Explain how *the way* you have come to know your subject has affected *what* you know about it.

What Is the Process of Thinking?

Signs and Symbols

Susanne K. Langer

In Susanne Langer's view, the unique ability of humans to symbolize is what distinguishes our species from animals. This conviction led Langer (1895–1985), a philosopher, to a lifetime of research in which asking the right questions was more important than coming up with a right answer. Langer, who earned three degrees from Radcliffe (Ph.D., 1926), taught at Columbia University from 1945 to 1950 and thereafter at Connecticut College until her retirement in 1952.

Langer's focus on symbolic behavior integrates her research on topics as seemingly different as aesthetics (*Feeling and Form: A Theory of Art*, 1953); the nature of the human mind (*Mind: An Essay on Human Feelings*, 3 vols., 1967–82); and symbolic logic (*Philosophy in a New Key: A Study in the Symbols of Reason, Rite, and Art*, 1942). Although the latter included "Signs and Symbols," that essay was also published in *Fortune* in 1944. It is a good example of how a specialist can convey abstractions and complicated concepts to a general audience. "Signs and Symbols" epitomizes the view that language is the "most amazing achievement of the symbolistic human mind" and that the ability to use language distinguishes humans from other animals. Without language, it is impossible to think or reason, contends Langer. Given the recent experiments in which chimpanzees and gorillas "talk" in American Sign Language or by pressing symbol or word keys on special typewriters, and even transmit their knowledge to others of their species, it will be interesting to see whether this animal behavior threatens the long-established definition of humankind as the exclusive user of symbols.

The trait that sets human mentality apart from every other is its 1 preoccupation with symbols, with images and names that *mean* things, rather than with things themselves. This trait may have been a mere sport of nature once upon a time. Certain creatures do develop tricks and interests that seem biologically unimportant. Pack rats, for instance, and some birds of the crow family take a capricious pleasure in bright objects and carry away such things for which they have, presumably, no earthly use. Perhaps man's tendency to see certain forms as *images*, to hear certain sounds not only as signals but as expressive tones, and to be excited by sunset colors or starlight, was originally just a peculiar sensitivity in a rather highly developed brain. But whatever its cause, the ultimate destiny of this trait was momentous; for all human activity is based on the appreciation and use of symbols. Language, religion, mathematics, all learning, all science and superstition, even right and wrong, are products of symbolic expression rather than direct experience. Our commonest words, such as "house" and "red" and "walking," are symbols; the pyramids of Egypt and the mysterious circles of Stonehenge are symbols; so are dominions and empires and astronomical universes. We live in a mind-made world, where the things of prime importance are images or words that embody ideas and feelings and attitudes.

2   The animal mind is like a telephone exchange; it receives stimuli from outside through the sense organs and sends out appropriate responses through the nerves that govern muscles, glands, and other parts of the body. The organism is constantly interacting with its surroundings, receiving messages and acting on the new state of affairs that the messages signify.

3   But the human mind is not a simple transmitter like a telephone exchange. It is more like a great projector; for instead of merely mediating between an event in the outer world and a creature's responsive action, it transforms or, if you will, distorts the event into an image to be looked at, retained, and contemplated. For the images of things that we remember are not exact and faithful transcriptions even of our actual sense impressions. They are made as much by what we think as by what we see. It is a well-known fact that if you ask several people the size of the moon's disk as they look at it, their estimates will vary from the area of a dime to that of a barrel top. Like a magic lantern, the mind projects its ideas of things on the screen of what we call "memory"; but like all projections, these ideas are transformations of actual things. They are, in fact, *symbols* of reality, not pieces of it.

4   A symbol is not the same thing as a sign; that is a fact that psychologists and philosophers often overlook. All intelligent animals use signs; so do we. To them as well as to us sounds and smells and motions are signs of food, danger, the presence of other beings, or of rain or storm. Furthermore, some animals not only attend to signs but produce them for the benefit of others. Dogs bark at the door to be let in; rabbits thump to call each other; the cooing of doves and the growl of a wolf defending his kill are unequivocal signs of feelings and intentions to be reckoned with by other creatures.

5   We use signs just as animal do, though with considerably more elaboration. We stop at red lights and go on green; we answer calls and bells, watch the sky for coming storms, read trouble or promise or anger in each other's eyes. That is animal intelligence raised to the human level. Those of us who are dog lovers can probably all tell won-

derful stories of how high our dogs have sometimes risen in the scale of clever sign interpretation and sign using.

A sign is anything that announces the existence or the imminence 6 of some event, the presence of a thing or a person, or a change in a state of affairs. There are signs of the weather, signs of danger, signs of future good or evil, signs of what the past has been. In every case a sign is closely bound up with something to be noted or expected in experience. It is always a part of the situation to which it refers, though the reference may be remote in space and time. In so far as we are led to note or expect the signified event we are making correct use of a sign. This is the essence of rational behavior, which animals show in varying degrees. It is entirely realistic, being closely bound up with the actual objective course of history—learned by experience, and cashed in or voided by further experience.

If man had kept to the straight and narrow path of sign using, he 7 would be like the other animals, though perhaps a little brighter. He would not talk, but grunt and gesticulate and point. He would make his wishes known, give warnings, perhaps develop a social system like that of bees and ants, with such a wonderful efficiency of communal enterprise that all men would have plenty to eat, warm apartments— all exactly alike and perfectly convenient—to live in, and everybody could and would sit in the sun or by the fire, as the climate demanded, not talking but just basking, with every want satisfied, most of his life. The young would romp and make love, the old would sleep, the middle-aged would do the routine work almost unconsciously and eat a great deal. But that would be the life of a social, superintelligent, purely sign-using animal.

To us who are human, it does not sound very glorious. We want to 8 go places and do things, own all sorts of gadgets that we do not absolutely need, and when we sit down to take it easy we want to talk. Rights and property, social position, special talents and virtues, and above all our ideas, are what we live for. We have gone off on a tangent that takes us far away from the mere biological cycle that animal generations accomplish; and that is because we can use not only signs but symbols.

A symbol differs from a sign in that it does not announce the pres- 9 ence of the object, the being, condition, or whatnot, which is its meaning, but merely *brings this thing to mind*. It is not a mere "substitute sign" to which we react as though it were the object itself. The fact is that our reaction to hearing a person's name is quite different from our reaction to the person himself. There are certain rare cases where a symbol stands directly for its meaning: in religious experience, for instance, the Host is not only a symbol but a Presence. But symbols in the ordinary sense are not mystic. They are the same sort of thing that ordinary signs are; only they do not call our attention to something necessarily present or to be physically dealt with—they call up merely a conception of the thing they "mean."

10   The difference between a sign and a symbol is, in brief, that a sign causes us to think or act *in face of* the thing signified, whereas a symbol causes us to think *about* the thing symbolized. Therein lies the great importance of symbolism for human life, its power to make this life so different from any other animal biography that generations of men have found it incredible to suppose that they were of purely zoological origin. A sign is always embedded in reality, in a present that emerges from the actual past and stretches to the future; but a symbol may be divorced from reality altogether. It may refer to what is *not* the case, to a mere idea, a figment, a dream. It serves, therefore, to liberate thought from the immediate stimuli of a physically present world; and that liberation marks the essential difference between human and nonhuman mentality. Animals think, but they think *of* and *at* things; men think primarily *about* things. Words, pictures, and memory images are symbols that may be combined and varied in a thousand ways. The result is a symbolic structure whose meaning is a complex of all their respective meanings, and this kaleidoscope of *ideas* is the typical product of the human brain that we call the "stream of thought."

11   The process of transforming all direct experience into imagery or into that supreme mode of symbolic expression, language, has so completely taken possession of the human mind that it is not only a special talent but a dominant, organic need. All our sense impressions leave their traces in our memory not only as signs disposing our practical reactions in the future but also as symbols, images representing our *ideas* of things; and the tendency to manipulate ideas, to combine and abstract, mix and extend them by playing with symbols, is man's outstanding characteristic. It seems to be what his brain most naturally and spontaneously does. Therefore his primitive mental function is not judging reality, but *dreaming his desires.*

12   Dreaming is apparently a basic function of human brains, for it is free and unexhausting like our metabolism, heartbeat, and breath. It is easier to dream than not to dream, as it is easier to breathe than to refrain from breathing. The symbolic character of dreams is fairly well established. Symbol mongering, on this ineffectual, uncritical level, seems to be instinctive, the fulfillment of an elementary need rather than the purposeful exercise of a high and difficult talent.

13   The special power of man's mind rests on the evolution of this special activity, not on any transcendently high development of animal in-

telligence. We are not immeasurably higher than other animals; we are different. We have a biological need and with it a biological gift that they do not share.

Because man has not only the ability but the constant need of *conceiving* what has happened to him, what surrounds him, what is demanded of him—in short, of symbolizing nature, himself, and his hopes and fears—he has a constant and crying need of *expression*. What he cannot express, he cannot conceive; what he cannot conceive is chaos, and fills him with terror.   14

If we bear in mind this all-important craving for expression we get a new picture of man's behavior; for from this trait spring his powers and his weaknesses. The process of symbolic transformation that all our experiences undergo is nothing more nor less than the process of *conception*, which underlies the human faculties of abstraction and imagination.   15

When we are faced with a strange or difficult situation, we cannot react directly, as other creatures do, with flight, aggression, or any such simple instinctive pattern. Our whole reaction depends on how we manage to conceive the situation—whether we cast it in a definite dramatic form, whether we see it as a disaster, a challenge, a fulfillment of doom, or a fiat of the Divine Will. In words or dreamlike images, in artistic or religious or even in cynical form, we must *construe* the events of life. There is great virtue in the figure of speech, "I can *make* nothing of it," to express a failure to understand something. Thought and memory are processes of *making* the thought content and the memory image; the pattern of our ideas is given by the symbols through which we express them. And in the course of manipulating those symbols we inevitably distort the original experience, as we abstract certain features of it, embroider and reinforce those features with other ideas, until the conception we project on the screen of memory is quite different from anything in our real history.   16

Conception is a necessary and elementary process; what we do with our conceptions is another story. That is the entire history of human culture—of intelligence and mortality, folly and superstition, ritual, language, and the arts—all the phenomena that set man apart from, and above, the rest of the animal kingdom. As the religious mind has to make all human history a drama of sin and salvation in order to define its own moral attitudes, so a scientist wrestles with the mere presentation of "the facts" before he can reason about them. The process of *envisaging* facts, values, hopes, and fears underlies our whole behavior pattern; and this process is reflected in the evolution of an extraordinary phenomenon found always, and only, in human societies—the phenomenon of language.   17

18   Language is the highest and most amazing achievement of the symbolistic human mind. The power it bestows is almost inestimable, for without it anything properly called "thought" is impossible. The birth of language is the dawn of humanity. The line between man and beast—between the highest ape and the lowest savage—is the language line. Whether the primitive Neanderthal man was anthropoid or human depends less on his cranial capacity, his upright posture, or even his use of tools and fire, than on one issue we shall probably never be able to settle—whether or not he spoke.

19   In all physical traits and practical responses, such as skills and visual judgments, we can find certain continuity between animal and human mentality. Sign using is an ever evolving, ever improving function throughout the whole animal kingdom, from the lowly worm that shrinks into his hole at the sound of an approaching foot, to the dog obeying his master's command, and even to the learned scientist who watches the movements of an index needle.

20   This continuity of the sign-using talent has led psychologists to the belief that language is evolved from the vocal expressions, grunts and coos and cries, whereby animals vent their feelings or signal their fellows; that man has elaborated this sort of communication to the point where it makes a perfect exchange of ideas possible.

21   I do not believe that this doctrine of the origin of language is correct. The essence of language is symbolic, not significant; we use it first and most vitally to formulate and hold ideas in our own minds. Conception, not social control, is its first and foremost benefit.

22   Watch a young child that is just learning to speak play with a toy; he says the name of the object, e.g.: "Horsey! horsey! horsey!" over and over again, looks at the object, moves it, always saying the name to himself or to the world at large. It is quite a time before he talks to anyone in particular; he talks first of all to himself. This is his way of forming and fixing the *conception* of the object in his mind, and around this conception all his knowledge of it grows. *Names* are the essence of language; for the *name* is what abstracts the conception of the horse from the horse itself, and lets the mere idea recur at the speaking of the name. This permits the conception gathered from one horse experience to be exemplified again by another instance of a horse, so that the notion embodied in the name is a general notion.

23   To this end, the baby uses a word long before he *asks for* the object; when he wants his horsey he is likely to cry and fret, because he is reacting to an actual environment, not forming ideas. He use the animal language of *signs* for his wants; talking is still a purely symbolic process—its practical value has not really impressed him yet.

24   Language need not be vocal; it may be purely visual, like written language, or even tactual, like the deaf-mute system of speech; but it

must be denotative. The sounds, intended or unintended, whereby animals communicate do not constitute a language, because they are signs, not names. They never fall into an organic pattern, a meaningful syntax of even the most rudimentary sort, as all language seems to do with a sort of driving necessity. That is because signs refer to actual situations, in which things have obvious reactions to each other that require only to be noted; but symbols refer to ideas, which are not physically there for inspection, so their connections and features have to be represented. This gives all true language a natural tendency toward growth and development, which seems almost like a life of its own. Languages are not invented; they grow with our need for expression.

In contrast, animal "speech" never has a structure. It is merely an   25
emotional response. Apes may greet their ration of yams with a shout of "Nga!" But they do not say "Nga" between meals. If they could *talk about* their yams instead of just saluting them, they would be the most primitive men instead of the most anthropoid of beasts. They would have ideas, and tell each other things true or false, rational or irrational; they would make plans and invent laws and sing their own praises, as men do.

RESPONDING TO READING

1. How does Langer define signs? Symbols? Where does Langer, a philosopher, use evidence from anthropology and biology for her definitions? To what degree do you agree with Langer's way of distinguishing humans from animals?

2. How do you know when you are responding to signs? Give some examples of human behavior that reflects the use of *signs*, in Langer's sense. Is this, as Langer says, evidence of "animal intelligence raised to the human level" (paragraph 5)?

3. Analyze some of your significant *symbolic* behavior to show how you think about what you do. Are signs and symbols ever intermingled in your thinking? Explain.

4. Define, in discussion or in writing, an abstract term—a quality or concept that can be explained in terms of its causes, effects, or other nonphysical aspects, such as love, peace, sophistication, beauty, maturity, or riskiness. How do you know what you know about the term you have chosen? Illustrate your definition with two or three specific examples from your own experience.

5. Does a particular term (such as "peace" or "love") have the same meaning for a historian as for a psychologist? A biologist? A novelist? A parent? A child? A teenager? Will this term have the same meaning for all people of a given group (historians, parents)? Why or why not? Explain. Write an essay defining the various meanings of the term you have chosen.

The Allegory of the Cave
PLATO

Plato (c. 427–c. 347 B.C.), Greek educator, literary artist, and philosopher of ethics, politics, aesthetics, and rhetoric, perfected the Socratic dialogue, a verbal exchange of ideas that enables the participants to get at the essentials of the truth through its question and answer format. Socratic dialogues, as in "The Allegory of the Cave" that follows, involve a cast of characters, some more fully delineated than they are here, discussing, sometimes arguing, about an issue in an effort to reach the truth. The dominant character, Socrates (although he is not identified by name in the pages that follow), invariably has the broadest, deepest understanding of the issues under debate. His penetrating logic ultimately compels both understanding and consensus, leaving the other characters little choice but to agree with him. Thus, Glaucon's brief responses in "The Allegory of the Cave"—"I see," "Of course," and "Necessarily"—echo and reaffirm Socrates's main points, but do not dispute them.

The Republic, in which "The Allegory of the Cave" appears, presents the first Utopia, an ideal state which according to Plato is a static, closed society whose major groups are the guardians, the military, and the workers. When all work in harmony, justice prevails. Despite their aristocratic status, the guardians must live in a state of Spartan communism, lest they succumb to the temptations of wealth and the exercise of military power. If the poverty-stricken masses revolt, democracy (undesirable) or even tyranny (even worse) could result. (But Plato's views were not static; ever self-critical, in a later dialogue, *The Laws*, he greatly modified the *Republic*'s political doctrines.)

Thus, the education of guardians in *The Republic* is crucial. "The Allegory of the Cave" uses an extended analogy to show how the unphilosophical person is at the mercy of sense impressions, transient, finite, and fickle. It is as if one sees flickering shadows of objects reflected on a cave wall, and hears echos, and mistakes these for reality. In contrast, the genuinely philosophical person attains true knowledge, apprehending universal forms as timeless and unchanging; these contain the essence of the subject.

1   Next, said I, here is a parable to illustrate the degrees in which our nature may be enlightened or unenlightened. Imagine the condition of men living is a sort of cavernous chamber underground, with an entrance open to the light and a long passage all down the cave. Here they have been from childhood, chained by the leg and also by the neck, so that they cannot move and can see only what is in front of them, because the chains will not let them turn their heads. At some distance higher up is the light of a fire burning behind them; and between the prisoners and the fire is a track with a parapet built along it,

like the screen at a puppet-show, which hides the performers while they show their puppets over the top.

I see, said he.   2

Now behind this parapet imagine persons carrying along various   3
artificial objects, including figures of men and animals in wood or stone or other materials, which project above the parapet. Naturally, some of these persons will be talking, others silent.

It is a strange picture, he said, and a strange sort of prisoners.   4

Like ourselves, I replied; for in the first place prisoners so confined   5
would have seen nothing of themselves or of one another, except the shadows thrown by the fire-light on the wall of the Cave facing them, would they?

Not if all their lives they had been prevented from moving their   6
heads.

And they would have seen as little of the objects carried past.   7

Of course.   8

Now, if they could talk to one another, would they not suppose   9
that their words referred only to those passing shadows which they saw?

Necessarily.   10

And suppose their prison had an echo from the wall facing them?   11
When one of the people crossing behind them spoke, they could only suppose that the sound came from the shadow passing before their eyes.

No doubt.   12

In every way, then, such prisoners would recognize as reality noth-   13
ing but the shadows of those artificial objects.

Inevitably.   14

Now consider what would happen if their release from the chains   15
and the healing of their unwisdom should come about in this way. Sup-pose one of them were set free and forced suddenly to stand up, turn his head, and walk with eyes lifted to the light; all these movements would be painful, and he would be too dazzled to make out the objects whose shadows he had been used to see. What do you think he would say, if someone told him that what he had formerly seen was meaning-less illusion, but now, being somewhat nearer to reality and turned to-wards more real objects, he was getting a truer view? Suppose further that he were shown the various objects being carried by and were made to say, in reply to questions, what each of them was. Would he not be perplexed and believe the objects now shown him to be not so real as what he formerly saw?

Yes, not nearly so real.   16

And if he were forced to look at the fire-light itself, would not his   17
eyes ache, so that he would try to escape and turn back to the things

which he could see distinctly, convinced that they really were clearer than these other objects now being shown to him?

18 Yes.

19 And suppose someone were to drag him away forcibly up the steep and rugged ascent and not let him go until he had hauled him out into the sunlight, would he not suffer pain and vexation at such treatment, and, when he had come out into the light, find his eyes so full of its radiance that he could not see a single one of the things that he was now told were real?

20 Certainly he would not see them all at once.

21 He would need, then, to grow accustomed before he could see things in that upper world. At first it would be easiest to make out shadows, and then the images of men and things reflected in water, and later on the things themselves. After that, it would easier to watch the heavenly bodies and the sky itself by night, looking at the light of the moon and stars rather than the Sun and the Sun's light in the day-time.

22 Yes, surely.

23 Last of all, he would be able to look at the Sun and contemplate its nature, not as it appears when reflected in water or any alien medium, but as it is in itself in its own domain.

24 No doubt.

25 And now he would begin to draw the conclusion that it is the Sun that produces the seasons and the course of the year and controls everything in the visible world, and moreover is in a way the cause of all that he and his companions used to see.

26 Clearly he would come at last to that conclusion.

27 Then if he called to mind his fellow prisoners and what passed for wisdom in his former dwelling-place, he would surely think himself happy in the change and be sorry for them. They may have had a practice of honouring and commending one another, with prizes for the man who had the keenest eye for the passing shadows and the best memory for the order in which they followed or accompanied one another, so that he could make a good guess as to which was going to come next. Would our released prisoner be likely to covet those prizes or to envy the men exalted to honour and power in the Cave? Would he not feel like Homer's Achilles, that he would far sooner 'be on earth as a hired servant in the house of landless man' or endure anything rather than go back to his old beliefs and live in the old way?

28 Yes, he would prefer any fate to such a life.

29 Now imagine what would happen if he went down again to take his former seat in the Cave. Coming suddenly out of the sunlight, his eyes would be filled with darkness. He might be required once more to deliver his opinion on those shadows, in competition with the prisoners who had never been released, while his eyesight was still dim and

unsteady; and it might take some time to become used to the darkness. They would laugh at him and say that he had gone up only to come back with his sight ruined; it was worth no one's while even to attempt the ascent. If they could lay hands on the man who was trying to set them free and lead them up, they would kill him.

Yes, they would.   30

Every feature in this parable, my dear Glaucon, is meant to fit our   31 earlier analysis. The prison dwelling corresponds to the region revealed to us through the sense of sight, and the fire-light within it to the power of the Sun. The ascent to see the things in the upper world you may take as standing for the upward journey of the soul into the region of the intelligible; then you will be in possession of what I surmise, since that is what you wish to be told. Heaven knows whether it is true; but this, at any rate, is how it appears to me. In the world of knowledge, the last thing to be perceived and only with great difficulty is the essential Form of Goodness. Once it is perceived, the conclusion must follow that, for all things, this is the cause of whatever is right and good; in the visible world it gives birth to light and to the lord of light, while it is itself sovereign in the intelligible world and the parent of intelligence and truth. Without having had a vision of this Form no one can act with wisdom, either in his own life or in matters of state.

RESPONDING TO READING

1. Try drawing or describing in your own words Plato's picture of the men in the cave. Why do they not turn around to see the light? Why do they not notice that the figures they take for reality are only "puppets"? Why are the men "prisoners"? Why are they "like ourselves"?

2. The next scene shows us one man set free, trying to cope with the new vision of reality that freedom brings. What is the first reaction? The second?

3. The third scene shows one of the men forcibly "hauled out into the sun." What is the sequence of his reactions? Why? What is his response now to those left behind in the cave? What is the response of those in the cave to his new vision?

4. The last paragraph details Plato's explanation of the meaning of his parable. What does he mean by "the region of the intelligible," "the world of knowledge," and "the essential Form of Goodness"?

5. To what degree does your present vision of reality correspond to Plato's? Do you agree that there are "essential forms" of goodness and the like that exist in a reality beyond daily experience? Are you willing to accept that your day-to-day experiences are a world of shadows, distorted reflections of some other world? What would such a concept suggest about the way you should act in the world? Construct an allegory to explain your version of reality.

6. How did you learn about "reality"? How firmly convinced are you that your version of reality is the true one? How do you feel about Plato, or anyone

else, disputing the reality of your reality? Plato says that "no one can act with wisdom, either in his own life or in matters of state" (paragraph 31) without a vision of essential forms. How would a different sense of reality affect the way you lead your life?

Those Crazy Ideas

ISAAC ASIMOV

Isaac Asimov (1920–92) was an astonishingly prolific writer of nearly five hundred volumes, notably of science and science fiction. He wrote seven days a week, from 7:30 A.M. until 10:00 P.M.; his demanding schedule allowed two—and only two—drafts of everything, the first on a typewriter and, in recent years, the second on a computer. Over the course of fifty years, he averaged a book every six weeks. "Nightfall" was chosen by the Science Fiction Writers of America as "the best science fiction work of all time."

Called by astronomer Carl Sagan "the greatest explainer of the age," Asimov earned a Ph.D. in chemistry from Columbia in 1948 and won numerous awards for his science writing as well as for his science fiction. He said, "I'm on fire to explain, and happiest when it's something reasonably intricate which I can make clear step by step." Three things, he claims, are essential in explaining technical subjects for general readers. "One is an understanding of what it is you're trying to explain." Another is "an understanding of the position of those to whom you're trying to explain it." Many scientists, Asimov observes, cannot remember what it is like to be a newcomer to a field, and their writing is too technical, too complicated for lay readers to understand. The third quality science writers need is self assurance, so they can write simply without worrying about sounding ignorant. "In my case," said Asimov, "since I'm an extaordinarily self-assured person, I'm not afraid."

Asimov's writing is considered by reviewers such as Ray Sokolov and Alfred Bester as "encyclopedic, witty, with a gift for colorful and illuminating examples and explanations"—qualities apparent in "Those Crazy Ideas." There he explains the creative processes by which two scientists, Charles Darwin and Alfred Russel Wallace, arrived independently at the theory of evolution. He then analyzes how they worked, to illustrate the common characteristics of the creative process: a combination of education, intelligence, intuition, courage, and luck.

1   Time and time again I have been asked (and I'm sure others who have, in their time, written science fiction have been asked too): "Where do you get your crazy ideas?"

2   Over the years, my answers have sunk from flattered confusion to a shrug and a feeble smile. Actually, I don't really know, and the lack of

knowledge doesn't really worry me, either, as long as the ideas keep coming.

But then some time ago, a consultant firm in Boston, engaged in a sophisticated space-age project for the government, got in touch with me.

What they needed, it seemed, to bring their project to a successful conclusion were novel suggestions, startling new principles, conceptual breakthroughs. To put it into the nutshell of a well-turned phrase, they needed "crazy ideas."

Unfortunately, they didn't know how to go about getting crazy ideas, but some among them had read my science fiction, so they looked me up in the phone book and called me to ask (in essence), "Dr. Asimov, where do you get your crazy ideas?"

Alas, I still didn't know, but as speculation is my profession, I am perfectly willing to think about the matter and share my thoughts with you.

The question before the house, then, is: How does one go about creating or inventing or dreaming up or stumbling over a new and revolutionary scientific principle?

For instance—to take a deliberately chosen example—how did Darwin come to think of evolution?

To begin with, in 1831, when Charles Darwin was twenty-two, he joined the crew of a ship called the *Beagle*. This ship was making a five-year voyage about the world to explore various coast lines and to increase man's geographical knowledge. Darwin went along as ship's naturalist, to study the forms of life in far-off places.

This he did extensively and well, and upon the return of the *Beagle* Darwin wrote a book about his experiences (published in 1840) which made him famous. In the course of this voyage, numerous observations led him to the conclusion that species of living creatures changed and developed slowly with time; that new species descended from old. This, in itself was not a new idea. Ancient Greeks had had glimmerings of evolutionary notions. Many scientists before Darwin, including Darwin's own grandfather, had theories of evolution.

The trouble, however, was that no scientist could evolve an explanation for the *why* of evolution. A French naturalist, Jean Baptiste de Lamarck, had suggested in the early 1800s that it came about by a kind of conscious effort or inner drive. A tree-grazing animal, attempting to reach leaves, stretched its neck over the years and transmitted a longer neck to its descendants. The process was repeated with each generation until a giraffe in full glory was formed.

The only trouble was that acquired characteristics are not inherited and this was easily proved. The Lamarckian explanation did not carry conviction.

13   Charles Darwin, however, had nothing better to suggest after several years of thinking about the problem.

14   But in 1798, eleven years before Darwin's birth, an English clergyman named Thomas Robert Malthus had written a book entitled *An Essay on the Principle of Population*. In this book Malthus suggested that the human population always increased faster than the food supply and that the population had to be cut down by either starvation, disease, or war; that these evils were therefore unavoidable.

15   In 1838 Darwin, still puzzling over the problem of the development of species, read Malthus's book. It is hackneyed to say "in a flash" but that, apparently, is how it happened. In a flash, it was clear to Darwin. Not only human beings increased faster than the food supply; all species of living things did. In every case, the surplus population had to be cut down by starvation, by predators, or by disease. Now no two members of any species are exactly alike; each has slight individual variations from the norm. Accepting this fact, which part of the population was cut down?

16   Why—and this was Darwin's breakthrough—those members of the species who were less efficient in the race for food, less adept at fighting off or escaping from predators, less equipped to resist disease, went down.

17   The survivors, generation after generation, were better adapted, on the average, to their environment. The slow changes toward a better fit with the environment accumulated until a new (and more adapted) species had replaced the old. Darwin thus postulated the reason for evolution as being the action of *natural selection*. In fact, the full title of his book is *On the Origin of Species by Means of Natural Selection, or the Preservation of Favoured Races in the Struggle for Life*. We just call it *The Origin of Species* and miss the full flavor of what it was he did.

18   It was in 1838 that Darwin received this flash and in 1844 that he began writing his book, but he worked on for fourteen years gathering evidence to back his thesis. He was a methodical perfectionist and no amount of evidence seemed to satisfy him. He always wanted more. His friends read his preliminary manuscripts and urged him to publish. In particular, Charles Lyell (whose book *Principles of Geology*, published in 1830–1833, first convinced scientists of the great age of the earth and thus first showed there was *time* for the slow progress of evolution to take place) warned Darwin that someone would beat him to the punch.

19   While Darwin was working, another and younger English naturalist, Alfred Russel Wallace, was traveling in distant lands. He too found copious evidence to show that evolution took place and he too wanted to find a reason. He did not know that Darwin had already solved the problem.

He spent three years puzzling, and then in 1858, he too came across 20
Malthus's book and read it. I am embarrassed to have to become hackneyed again, but in a flash he saw the answer. Unlike Darwin, however, he did not settle down to fourteen years of gathering and arranging
evidence.

Instead, he grabbed pen and paper and at once wrote up his theo- 21
ry. He finished this in two days.

Naturally, he didn't want to rush into print without having his no- 22
tions checked by competent colleagues, so he decided to send it to
some well-known naturalist. To whom? Why, to Charles Darwin. To
whom else?

I have often tried to picture Darwin's feeling as he read Wallace's 23
essay which, he afterward stated, expressed matters in almost his own
words. He wrote to Lyell that he had been forestalled "with a vengeance."

Darwin might easily have retained full credit. He was well known 24
and there were many witnesses to the fact that he had been working on
his project for a decade and a half. Darwin, however, was a man of the
highest integrity. He made no attempt to suppress Wallace. On the contrary, he passed on the essay to others and arranged to have it published along with a similar essay of his own. The year after, Darwin
published his book.

Now the reason I chose this case was that here we have two men 25
making one of the greatest discoveries in the history of science independently and simultaneously and under precisely the same stimulus.
Does that mean *anyone* could have worked out the theory of natural selection if they had but made a sea voyage and combined that with reading Malthus?

Well, let's see. Here's where the speculation starts. 26

To begin with, both Darwin and Wallace were thoroughly ground- 27
ed in natural history. Each had accumulated a vast collection of facts in
the field in which they were to make their breakthrough. Surely this is
significant.

Now every man in his lifetime collects facts, individual pieces of 28
data, items of information. Let's call these "bits" (as they do, I think, in
information theory). The "bits" can be of all varieties: personal memories, girls' phone numbers, baseball players' batting averages, yesterday's weather, the atomic weights of the chemical elements.

Naturally, different men gather different numbers of different vari- 29
eties of "bits." A person who has collected a larger number than usual
of those varieties that are held to be particularly difficult to obtain—
say, those involving the sciences and the liberal arts—is considered
"educated."

There are two broad ways in which the "bits" can be accumulated. 30
The more common way, nowadays, is to find people who already

possess many "bits" and have them transfer those "bits" to your mind in good order and in predigested fashion. Our schools specialize in this transfer of "bits" and those of us who take advantage of them receive a "formal education."

31   The less common way is to collect "bits" with a minimum amount of live help. They can be obtained from books or out of personal experience. In that case you are "self-educated." (It often happens that "self-educated" is confused with "uneducated." This is an error to be avoided.)

32   In actual practice, scientific breakthroughs have been initiated by those who were formally educated, as for instance by Nicolaus Copernicus, and by those who were self-educated, as for instance by Michael Faraday.

33   To be sure, the structure of science has grown more complex over the years and the absorption of the necessary number of "bits" has become more and more difficult without the guidance of someone who has already absorbed them. The self-educated genius is therefore becoming rarer, though he has still not vanished.

34   However, without drawing any distinction according to the manner in which "bits" have been accumulated, let's set up the first criterion for scientific creativity:

35   1) The creative person must possess as many "bits" of information as possible; i.e., he must be educated.

36   Of course, the accumulation of "bits" is not enough in itself. We have probably all met people who are intensely educated, but who manage to be abysmally stupid, nevertheless. They have the "bits," but the "bits" just lie there.

37   But what is there one can do with "bits"?

38   Well, one can combine them into groups of two or more. Everyone does that; it is the principle of the string on the finger. You tell yourself to remember *a* (to buy bread) when you observe *b* (the string). You enforce a combination that will not let you forget *a* because *b* is so noticeable.

39   That, of course, is a conscious and artificial combination of "bits." It is my feeling that every mind is, more or less unconsciously, continually making all sorts of combinations and permutations of "bits," probably at random.

40   Some minds do this with greater facility than others; some minds have greater capacity for dredging the combinations out of the unconscious and becoming consciously aware of them. This results in "new ideas," in "novel outlooks."

41   The ability to combine "bits" with facility and to grow consciously aware of the new combinations is, I would like to suggest, the measure of what we call "intelligence." In this view, it is quite possible to be educated and yet not intelligent.

Obviously, the creative scientist must not only have his "bits" on 42
hand but he must be able to combine them readily and more or less
consciously. Darwin not only observed data, he also made deductions—clever and far-reaching deductions—from what he observed.
That is, he combined the "bits" in interesting ways and drew important
conclusions.

So the second criterion of creativity is: 43

2) The creative person must be able to combine "bits" with facil- 44
ity and recognize the combinations he has formed; i.e., he must be
intelligent.

Even forming and recognizing new combinations is insufficient 45
in itself. Some combinations are important and some are trivial. How
do you tell which are which? There is no question but that a person
who cannot tell them apart must labor under a terrible disadvantage.
As he plods after each possible new idea, he loses time and his life
passes uselessly.

There is also no question but that there are people who somehow 46
have the gift of seeing the consequences "in a flash" as Darwin and
Wallace did; of feeling what the end must be without consciously going
through every step of the reasoning. This, I suggest, is the measure of
what we call "intuition."

Intuition plays more of a role in some branches of scientific knowl- 47
edge than others. Mathematics, for instance, is a deductive science in
which, once certain basic principles are learned, a large number of
items of information become "obvious" as merely consequences of
those principles. Most of us, to be sure, lack the intuitive powers to see
the "obvious."

To the truly intuitive mind, however, the combination of the few 48
necessary "bits" is at once extraordinarily rich in consequences. Without too much trouble they see them all, including some that have not
been seen by their predecessors.[1]

It is perhaps for this reason that mathematics and mathematical 49
physics have seen repeated cases of first-rank breakthroughs by youngsters. Evariste Galois evolved group theory at twenty-one. Isaac Newton worked out calculus at twenty-three. Albert Einstein presented the
theory of relativity at twenty-six, and so on.

In those branches of science which are more inductive and require 50
larger numbers of "bits" to begin with, the average age of the scientists
at the time of the breakthrough is greater. Darwin was twenty-nine at
the time of his flash, Wallace was thirty-five.

---

[1]The Swiss mathematician, Leonhard Euler, said that to the true mathematician, it is at once obvious that $e^{\pi i} = -1$.

51   But in any science, however inductive, intuition is necessary for creativity. So:

52   3) The creative person must be able to see, with as little delay as possible, the consequences of the new combinations of "bits" which he has formed; i.e., he must be intuitive.

53   But now let's look at this business of combining "bits" in a little more detail. "Bits" are at varying distances from each other. The more closely related two "bits" are, the more apt one is to be reminded of one by the other and to make the combination. Consequently, a new idea that arises from such a combination is made quickly. It is a "natural consequence" of an older idea, a "corollary." It "obviously follows."

54   The combination of less related "bits" results in a more startling idea; if for no other reason than that it takes longer for such a combination to be made, so that the new idea is therefore less "obvious." For a scientific breakthrough of the first rank, there must be a combination of "bits" so widely spaced that the random chance of the combination being made is small indeed. (Otherwise, it will be made quickly and be considered but a corollary of some previous idea which will then be considered the "breakthrough.")

55   But then, it can easily happen that two "bits" sufficiently widely spaced to make a breakthrough by their combination are not present in the same mind. Neither Darwin nor Wallace, for all their education, intelligence, and intuition, possessed the key "bits" necessary to work out the theory of evolution by natural selection. Those "bits" were lying in Malthus's book, and both Darwin and Wallace had to find them there.

56   To do this, however, they had to read, understand, and appreciate the book. In short, they had to be ready to incorporate other people's "bits" and treat them with all the ease with which they treated their own.

57   It would hamper creativity, in other words, to emphasize intensity of education at the expense of broadness. It is bad enough to limit the nature of the "bits" to the point where the necessary two would not be in the same mind. It would be fatal to mold a mind to the point where it was incapable of accepting "foreign bits."

58   I think we ought to revise the first criterion of creativity, then, to read:

59   1) The creative person must possess as many "bits" as possible, falling into as wide a variety of types as possible; i.e., he must be broadly educated.

60   As the total amount of "bits" to be accumulated increases with the advance of science, it is becoming more and more difficult to gather enough "bits" in a wide enough area. Therefore, the practice of "brain-busting" is coming into popularity; the notion of collecting thinkers

into groups and hoping that they will cross-fertilize one another into startling new breakthroughs.

Under what circumstances could this conceivably work? (After all, 61 anything that will stimulate creativity is of first importance to humanity.)

Well, to begin with, a group of people will have more "bits" on 62 hand than any member of the group singly since each man is likely to have some "bits" the others do not possess.

However, the increase in "bits" is not in direct proportion to the 63 number of men, because there is bound to be considerable overlapping. As the group increases, the smaller and smaller addition of completely new "bits" introduced by each additional member is quickly outweighed by the added tensions involved in greater numbers; the longer wait to speak, the great likelihood of being interrupted, and so on. It is my (intuitive) guess that five is as large a number as one can stand in such a conference.

Now of the three criteria mentioned so far, I feel (intuitively) that 64 intuition is the least common. It is more likely that none of the group will be intuitive than that none will be intelligent or none educated. If no individual in the group is intuitive, the group as a whole will not be intuitive. You cannot add non-intuition and form intuition.

If one of the group is intuitive, he is almost certain to be intelligent 65 and educated as well, or he would not have been asked to join the group in the first place. In short, for a brain-busting group to be creative, it must be quite small and it must possess at least one creative individual. But in that case, does that one individual need the group? Well, I'll get back to that later.

Why did Darwin work fourteen years gathering evidence for a the- 66 ory he himself must have been convinced was correct from the beginning? Why did Wallace send his manuscript to Darwin first instead of offering it for publication at once?

To me it seems that they must have realized that any new idea is 67 met by resistance from the general population who, after all, are not creative. The more radical the new idea, the greater the dislike and distrust it arouses. The dislike and distrust aroused by a first-class breakthrough are so great that the author must be prepared for unpleasant consequences (sometimes for expulsion from the respect of the scientific community; sometimes, in some societies, for death).

Darwin was trying to gather enough evidence to protect himself by 68 convincing others through a sheer flood of reasoning. Wallace wanted to have Darwin on his side before proceeding.

It takes courage to announce the results of your creativity. The 69 greater the creativity, the greater the necessary courage in much more than direct proportion. After all, consider that the more profound the breakthrough, the more solidified the previous opinions;

the more "against reason" the new discovery seems, the more against cherished authority.

70   Usually a man who possesses enough courage to be a scientific genius seems odd. After all, a man who has sufficient courage or irreverence to fly in the face of reason or authority *must* be odd, if you define "odd" as "being not like most people." And if he is courageous and irreverent in such a colossally big thing, he will certainly be courageous and irreverent in many small things so that being odd in one way, he is apt to be odd in others. In short, he will seem to the noncreative, conforming people about him to be a "crackpot."

71   So we have the fourth criterion:

72   4) The creative person must possess courage (and to the general public may, in consequence, seem a crackpot).

73   As it happens, it is the crackpottery that is most often most noticeable about the creative individual. The eccentric and absentminded professor is a stock character in fiction; and the phrase "mad scientist" is almost a cliché.

74   (And be it noted that I am never asked where I get my interesting or effective or clever or fascinating ideas. I am invariably asked where I get my *crazy* ideas.)

75   Of course, it does not follow that because the creative individual is usually a crackpot, that any crackpot is automatically an unrecognized genius. The chances are low indeed, and failure to recognize that the proposition cannot be so reversed is the cause of a great deal of trouble.

76   Then, since I believe that combinations of "bits" take place quite at random in the unconscious mind, it follows that it is quite possible that a person may possess all four of the criteria I have mentioned in superabundance and yet may never happen to make the necessary combination. After all, suppose Darwin had never read Malthus. Would he ever have thought of natural selection? What made him pick up the copy? What if someone had come in at the crucial time and interrupted him?

77   So there is a fifth criterion which I am at a loss to phrase in any other way than this:

78   5) A creative person must be lucky.

79   To summarize:

80   A creative person must be 1) broadly educated, 2) intelligent, 3) intuitive, 4) courageous, and 5) lucky.

81   How, then, does one go about encouraging scientific creativity? For now, more than ever before in man's history, we must; and the need will grow constantly in the future.

82   Only, it seems to me, by increasing the incidence of the various criteria among the general population.

Of the five criteria, number 5 (luck) is out of our hands. We can 83 only hope; although we must also remember Louis Pasteur's famous statement that "Luck favors the prepared mind." Presumably, if we have enough of the four other criteria, we shall find enough of number five as well.

Criterion 1 (broad education) is in the hands of our school system. 84 Many educators are working hard to find ways of increasing the quality of education among the public. They should be encouraged to continue doing so.

Criterion 2 (intelligence) and 3 (intuition) are inborn and their inci- 85 dence cannot be increased in the ordinary way. However, they can be more efficiently recognized and utilized. I would like to see methods devised for spotting the intelligent and intuitive (particularly the latter) early in life and treating them with special care. This, too, educators are concerned with.

To me, though, it seems that it is criterion 4 (courage) that receives 86 the least concern, and it is just the one we may most easily be able to handle. Perhaps it is difficult to make a person more courageous than he is, but that is not necessary. It would be equally effective to make it sufficient to be less courageous; to adopt an attitude that creativity is a permissible activity.

Does this mean changing society or changing human nature? I 87 don't think so. I think there are ways of achieving the end that do not involve massive change of anything, and it is here that brain-busting has its greatest chance of significance.

Suppose we have a group of five that includes one creative indi- 88 vidual. Let's ask again what that individual can receive from the non-creative four.

The answer to me, seems to be just this: Permission! 89

They must permit him to create. They must tell him to go ahead 90 and be a crackpot.[2]

How is this permission to be granted? Can four essentially non-cre- 91 ative people find it within themselves to grant such permission? Can the one creative person find it within himself to accept it?

I don't know. Here, it seems to me, is where we need experimenta- 92 tion and perhaps a kind of creative breakthrough about creativity. Once we learn enough about the whole matter, who knows—I may even find out where I get those crazy ideas.

---

[2]Always with the provision, of course, that the crackpot creation that results survives the test of hard inspection. Though many of the products of genius seem crackpot at first, very few of the creations that seem crackpot turn out, after all, to be products of genius.

RESPONDING TO READING

1. When is a "crazy idea" a good idea (i.e., a "new and revolutionary scientific principle") and not simply the crackpot notion of a mad scientist?
2. What five qualities does Asimov say are necessary for creativity? In what ways do these operate in people with different "styles" of creativity, such as Charles Darwin and Alfred Russel Wallace?
3. To what extent must a good idea find a receptive climate? What happens to "crazy ideas" that are ahead of the times?
4. What is your style of creativity? Is it the same under all circumstances, or do you exercise different types of creativity in different areas that call for different skills, understanding, and performance (such as writing, cooking, playing the piano, playing tennis, or being a good friend)?
5. How do you know when you have a good idea? How can you decide whether one idea—of your own or from someone else—is better than another? When does creativity involve risk-taking? What is the relation of risk-taking to what Asimov calls "courage"?

Think About It

FRANK CONROY

Frank Conroy (born 1936) leads a life to which many writers aspire, alternating between Massachusetts and Washington, D.C. In 1981 he was appointed director of the literature program for the National Endowment for the Arts. His literary reputation began with the nomination of his first book, the autobiographical *Stop-time* (1967), for a National Book Award. His second book, *Midair* (1985), is a collection of short stories similar in form, technique, and subject to his autobiography. Other works include *Body and Soul* (1998), the fictional story of Claude Rawlings set in 1940s New York, and *Dogs Bark, but the Caravan Rolls on* (2002), a collection of Conroy's journalistic musings on music, writing, and everyday life. Conroy publishes widely in periodicals such as the *New Yorker* and *Harper's*, in which "Think About It" originally appeared. Since graduation from Haverford College in 1958, Conroy has also taught writing at the University of Iowa, the Massachusetts Institute of Technology, and Brandeis University.

"Think About It" has the same deceptively easy pace and casual anecdotal tone that pervades Conroy's other autobiographical writing. His wondering, awkward but curious, teenage self is the consciousness and semi-consciousness through which growing knowledge and understanding are filtered, patiently sought, but not always understood at the time. Only later, does something else happen—a chance remark, a new experience—that triggers the dormant understanding and makes meaning from the fragments stored away. If we think about it, much thinking works that way.

When I was sixteen I worked selling hot dogs at a stand in the   1
Fourteenth Street subway station in New York City, one level above the
trains and one below the street, where the crowds continually flowed
back and forth. I worked with three Puerto Rican men who could not
speak English. I had no Spanish, and although we understood each
other well with regard to the tasks at hand, sensing and adjusting to
each other's body movements in the extremely confined space in
which we operated, I felt isolated with no one to talk to. On my break I
came out from behind the counter and passed the time with two old
black men who ran a shoeshine stand in a dark corner of the corridor. It
was a poor location, half hidden by columns, and they didn't have
much business. I would sit with my back against the wall while they
stood or moved around their ancient elevated stand, talking to each
other or to me, but always staring into the distance as they did so.

As the weeks went by I realized that they never looked at anything   2
in their immediate vicinity—not at me or their stand or anybody who
might come within ten or fifteen feet. They did not look at approaching
customers once they were inside the perimeter. Save for the instant it
took to discern the color of the shoes, they did not even look at what
they were doing while they worked, but rubbed in polish, brushed,
and buffed by feel while looking over their shoulders, into the distance,
as if awaiting the arrival of an important person. Of course there was-
n't all that much distance in the underground station, but their behavior was so focused and consistent they seemed somehow to transcend
the physical. A powerful mood was created, and I came almost to believe that these men could see through walls, through girders, and
around corners to whatever hyperspace it was where whoever it was
they were waiting and watching for would finally emerge. Their scattered talk was hip, elliptical, and hinted at mysteries beyond my white
boy's ken, but it was the staring off, the long, steady staring off, that
had me hypnotized. I left for a better job, with handshakes from both of
them, without understanding what I had seen.

Perhaps ten years later, after playing jazz with black musicians in   3
various Harlem clubs, hanging out uptown with a few young artists
and intellectuals, I began to learn from them something of the extraordinarily varied and complex riffs and rituals embraced by different
people to help themselves get through life in the ghetto. Fantasy of all
kinds—from playful to dangerous—was in the very air of Harlem. It
was the spice of uptown life.

Only then did I understand the two shoeshine men. They were   4
trapped in a demeaning situation in a dark corner in an underground
corridor in a filthy subway system. Their continuous staring off was a
kind of statement, a kind of dance. Our bodies are here, went the statement, but our souls are receiving nourishment from distant sources

only we can see. They were powerful magic dancers, sorcerers almost, and thirty-five years later I can still feel the pressure of their spell.

5   The light bulb may appear over your head, is what I'm saying, but it may be a while before it actually goes on. Early in my attempts to learn jazz piano, I used to listen to recordings of a fine player named Red Garland, whose music I admired. I couldn't quite figure out what he was doing with his left hand, however; the chords eluded me. I went uptown to an obscure club where he was playing with his trio, caught him on his break, and simply asked him. "Sixths," he said cheerfully. And then he went away.

6   I didn't know what to make of it. The basic jazz chord is the seventh, which comes in various configurations, but it is what it is. I was a self-taught pianist, pretty shaky on theory and harmony, and when he said sixths I kept trying to fit the information into what I already knew, and it didn't fit. But it stuck in my mind—a tantalizing mystery.

7   A couple of years later, when I began playing with a bass player, I discovered more or less by accident that if the bass played the root and I played a sixth based on the fifth note of the scale, a very interesting chord involving both instruments emerged. Ordinarily, I suppose I would have skipped over the matter and not paid much attention, but I remembered Garland's remark and so I stopped and spent a week or two working out the voicings, and greatly strengthened my foundations as a player. I had remembered what I hadn't understood, you might say, until my life caught up with the information and the light bulb went on.

8   I remember another, more complicated example from my sophomore year at the small liberal-arts college outside Philadelphia. I seemed never to be able to get up in time for breakfast in the dining hall. I would get coffee and a doughnut in the Coop instead—a basement area with about a dozen small tables where students could get something to eat at odd hours. Several mornings in a row I noticed a strange man sitting by himself with a cup of coffee. He was in his sixties, perhaps, and sat straight in his chair with very little extraneous movement. I guessed he was some sort of distinguished visitor to the college who had decided to put in some time at a student hangout. But no one ever sat with him. One morning I approached his table and asked if I could join him.

9   "Certainly," he said. "Please do." He had perhaps the clearest eyes I had ever seen, like blue ice, and to be held in their steady gaze was not, at first, an entirely comfortable experience. His eyes gave nothing away about himself while at the same time creating in me the eerie impression that he was looking directly into my soul. He asked a few quick questions, as if to put me at my ease, and we fell into conversation. He was William O. Douglas from the Supreme Court, and when he saw how startled I was he said, "Call me Bill. Now tell me what

you're studying and why you get up so late in the morning." Thus began a series of talks that stretched over many weeks. The fact that I was an ignorant sophomore with literary pretensions who knew nothing about the law didn't seem to bother him. We talked about everything from Shakespeare to the possibility of life on other planets. One day I mentioned that I was going to have dinner with Judge Learned Hand. I explained that Hand was my girlfriend's grandfather. Douglas nodded, but I could tell he was surprised at the coincidence of my knowing the chief judge of the most important court in the country save the Supreme Court itself. After fifty years on the bench Judge Hand had become a famous man, both in and out of legal circles—a living legend, to his own dismay. "Tell him hello and give him my best regards," Douglas said.

Learned Hand, in his eighties, was a short, barrel-chested man 10
with a large, square head, huge, thick, bristling eyebrows, and soft brown eyes. He radiated energy and would sometimes bark out remarks or questions in the living room as if he were in court. His humor was sharp, but often leavened with a touch of self-mockery. When something caught his funny bone he would burst out with explosive laughter—the laughter of a man who enjoyed laughing. He had a large repertoire of dramatic expressions involving the use of his eyebrows— very useful, he told me conspiratorially, when looking down on things from behind the bench. (The court stenographer could not record the movement of his eyebrows.) When I told him I'd been talking to William O. Douglas, they first shot up in exaggerated surprise, and then lowered and moved forward in a glower.

"*Justice* William O. Douglas, young man," he admonished. "Justice 11
Douglas, if you please." About the Supreme Court in general, Hand insisted on a tone of profound respect. Little did I know that in private correspondence he had referred to the Court as "The Blessed Saints, Cherubim and Seraphim," "The Jolly Boys," "The Nine Tin Jesuses," The Nine Blameless Ethiopians," and my particular favorite, "The Nine Blessed Chalices of the Sacred Effluvium."

Hand was badly stooped and had a lot of pain in his lower back. 12
Martinis helped, but his strict Yankee wife approved of only one before dinner. It was my job to make the second and somehow slip it to him. If the pain was particularly acute he would get out of his chair and lie flat on the rug, still talking, and finish his point without missing a beat. He flattered me by asking for my impression of Justice Douglas, instructed me to convey his warmest regards, and then began talking about the Dennis case, which he described as a particularly tricky and difficult case involving the prosecution of eleven leaders of the Communist party. He had just started in on the First Amendment and free speech when we were called in to dinner.

13   William O. Douglas loved the outdoors with a passion, and we fell into the habit of having coffee in the Coop and then strolling under the trees down toward the duck pond. About the Dennis case, he said something to this effect: "Eleven Communists arrested by the government. Up to no good, said the government; dangerous people, violent overthrow, etc. First Amendment, said the defense, freedom of speech, etc." Douglas stopped walking. "Clear and present danger."

14   "What?" I asked. He often talked in a telegraphic manner, and one was expected to keep up with him. It was sometimes like listening to a man thinking out loud.

15   "Clear and present danger," he said. "That was the issue. Did they constitute a clear and present danger? I don't think so. I think everybody took the language pretty far in Dennis." He began walking, striding along quickly. Again, one was expected to keep up with him. "The FBI was all over them. Phones tapped, constant surveillance. How could it be clear and present danger with the FBI watching every move they made? That's a ginkgo," he said suddenly, pointing at a tree. "A beauty. You don't see those every day. Ask Hand about clear and present danger."

16   I was in fact reluctant to do so. Douglas's argument seemed to me to be crushing—the last word, really—and I didn't want to embarrass Judge Hand. But back in the living room, on the second martini, the old man asked about Douglas. I sort of scratched my nose and recapitulated the conversation by the ginkgo tree.

17   "What?" Hand shouted. "Speak up, sir, for heaven's sake."

18   "He said the FBI was watching them all the time so there couldn't be a clear and present danger," I blurted out, blushing as I said it.

19   A terrible silence filled the room. Hand's eyebrows writhed on his face like two huge caterpillars. He learned forward in the wing chair, his face settling, finally, into a grim expression. "I am astonished," he said softly, his eyes holding mine, "at Justice Douglas's newfound faith in the Federal Bureau of Investigation." His big, granite head moved even closer to mine, until I could smell the martini. "I had understood him to consider it a politically corrupt, incompetent organization, directed by a power-crazed lunatic." I realized I had been holding my breath throughout all of this, and as I relaxed, I saw the faintest trace of a smile cross Hand's face. Things are sometimes more complicated than they first appear, his smile seemed to say. The old man leaned back. "The proximity of the danger is something to think about. Ask him about that. See what he says."

20   I chewed the matter over as I returned to campus. Hand had pointed out some of Douglas's language about the FBI from other sources that seemed to bear out his point. I thought about the words "clear and present danger," and the fact that if you looked at them closely they

might not be as simple as they had first appeared. What degree of danger? Did the word "present" allude to the proximity of the danger, or just the fact that the danger was there at all—that it wasn't an anticipated danger? Were there other hidden factors these great men were weighing of which I was unaware?

But Douglas was gone, back to Washington. (The writer in me is 21 tempted to create a scene here—to invent one for dramatic purposes—but of course I can't do that.) My brief time as a messenger boy was over, and I felt a certain frustration, as if, with a few more exchanges, the matter of *Dennis v. United States* might have been resolved to my satisfaction. They'd left me high and dry. But, of course, it is precisely because the matter did not resolve that has caused me to think about it, off and on, all these years. "The Constitution," Hand used to say to me flatly, "is a piece of paper. The Bill of Rights is a piece of paper." It was many years before I understood what he meant. Documents alone do not keep democracy alive, nor maintain the state of law. There is no particular safety in them. Living men and women, generation after generation, must continually remake democracy and the law, and that involves an ongoing state of tension between the past and the present which will never completely resolve.

Education doesn't end until life ends, because you never know when 22 you're going to understand something you hadn't understood before. For me, the magic dance of the shoeshine men was the kind of experience in which understanding came with a kind of click, a resolving kind of click. The same with the experience at the piano. What happened with Justice Douglas and Judge Hand was different, and makes the point that understanding does not always mean resolution. Indeed, in our intellectual lives, our creative lives, it is perhaps those problems that will never resolve that rightly claim the lion's share of our energies. The physical body exists in a constant state of tension as it maintains homeostasis, and so too does the active mind embrace the tension of never being certain, never being absolutely sure, never being done, as it engages the world. That is our special fate, our inexpressibly valuable condition.

RESPONDING TO READING

1. Information comes quickly, Conroy says, but understanding only much later: "The light bulb may appear over your head . . . but it may be a while before it actually goes on." Explain this idea by describing how the jazz musicians helped Conroy understand the shoeshine men.

2. How did the experience of conveying messages between the two justices help Conroy understand the role of "living men and women" in the making of democracy? What did he come to know and how did he come to know it?

3. Think about something you have come to understand a long time after you experienced it. Describe what happened in the first place and what led to your later knowledge.

4. Knowledge, according to Conroy, "does not always mean resolution." Indeed, this ability to know while "never being certain, never being absolutely sure, never being done," is "our inexpressibly valuable condition." This high value for uncertainty conflicts with what most people think about knowledge, that it gives answers. Consider the degree of certainty in the other essays in this section. How much uncertainty can you tolerate in your knowledge?

Under Water

ANNE FADIMAN

When Anne Fadiman began working as a columnist for *Civilization*, the magazine of the Library of Congress (now defunct), her editor told her to write personal essays—not reportage. "He insisted that the characters in my essays be drawn entirely from my own circle of family and friends, something I would have never done on my own, thinking it would be much too narcissistic," she told an *Atlantic Unbound* interviewer (1998). She had been well prepared for this challenge, however. Born in New York City (1953), she was raised by a family in love with books; her father was Clifton Fadiman, a prolific editor, reviewer, and author; her mother was Annalee Whitmore Jacoby Fadiman, a World War II correspondent who cowrote *Thunder Out of China*. After earning her B.A. at Harvard (1975), Fadiman worked as an editor and staff writer for *Life* magazine, then took the job with *Civilization*, and since 1998 has edited the *American Scholar* (the national magazine of Phi Beta Kappa), in which her essays appear under the pseudonym Philonoë—"a lover of things of the mind." Her first book, *The Spirit Catches You and You Fall Down: A Hmong Child, Her American Doctors, and the Collision of Two Cultures* (1997), won a National Book Critics Circle Award. Her most recent book, *Ex Libris: Confessions of a Common Reader* (1998), is a collection of personal essays about reading that gives full range to her bibliophilia and encyclopedic mind.

"Under Water," published in the *New Yorker*, takes us out of Fadiman's familiar world of books and culture and into the wilderness of Wyoming, where a canoeing trip turns into a disaster. As events unfold, the writing seems to take place in real time. This disturbing essay points two ways, saying as much about Fadiman's habits of perception as it does about the catastrophe she witnessed.

1   WHEN I WAS EIGHTEEN, I was a student on a month-long wilderness program in western Wyoming. On the third day, we went canoeing on the Green River, a tributary of the Colorado that begins in the glaciers

of the Wind River Range and flows south across the sagebrush plains. Swollen by warm-weather runoff from an unusually deep snowpack, the Green was higher and swifter that month—June of 1972—than it had been in forty years. A river at flood stage can have strange currents. There is not enough room in the channel for the water to move downstream in an orderly way, so it collides with itself and forms whirlpools and boils and souse holes. Our instructors decided to stick to their itinerary nevertheless, but they put in at a relatively easy section of the Green, one that the flood had merely upgraded, in the international system of white-water classification, from Class I to Class II. There are six levels of difficulty, and Class II was not an unreasonable challenge for novice paddlers.

The Green River did not seem dangerous to me. It seemed magnif- 2
icently unobstructed. Impediments to progress—the rocks and stranded trees that under normal conditions would protrude above the surface—were mostly submerged. The river carried our aluminum canoe high and lightly, like a child on a broad pair of shoulders. We could rest our paddles on the gunwales and let the water do our work. The sun was bright and hot. Every few minutes, I dipped my bandanna in the river, draped it over my head, and let an ounce or two of melted glacier run down my neck.

I was in the bow of the third canoe. We rounded a bend and saw, 3
fifty feet ahead, a standing wave in the wake of a large black boulder. The students in the lead canoe were backferrying, slipping crabwise across the current by angling their boat diagonally and stroking backward. Backferrying allows paddlers to hover midstream and carefully plan their course instead of surrendering to the water's pace. But if they lean upstream—a natural inclination, for few people choose to lean toward the difficulties that lie ahead—the current can overflow the lowered gunwale and flip the boat. And that is what happened to the lead canoe.

I wasn't worried when I saw it go over. Knowing that we might 4
capsize in the fast water, our instructors had arranged to have our gear trucked to our next campsite. The packs were all safe. The water was little more than waist-deep, and the paddlers were both wearing life jackets. They would be fine. One was already scrambling onto the right-hand bank.

But where was the second paddler? Gary, a local boy from Rawl- 5
ins, a year or two younger than I, seemed to be hung up on something. He was standing at a strange angle in the middle of the river, just downstream from the boulder. Gary was the only student on the course who had not brought sneakers, and one of his mountaineering boots had become wedged between two rocks. The other canoes would come around the bend in a moment, and the instructors would pluck him out.

6   But they didn't come. The second canoe pulled over to the bank and ours followed. Thirty seconds passed, maybe a minute. Then we saw the standing wave bend Gary's body forward at the waist, push his face underwater, stretch his arms in front of him, and slip his orange life jacket off his shoulders. The life jacket lingered for a moment at his wrists before it floated downstream, its long white straps twisting in the current. His shirtless torso was pale and undulating, and it changed shape as hills and valleys of water flowed over him, altering the curve of the liquid lens through which we watched him. I thought, He looks like the flayed skin of St. Bartholomew in the Sistine Chapel. As soon as I had the thought, I knew that it was dishonorable. To think about anything outside the moment, outside Gary, was a crime of inattention. I swallowed a small, sour piece of self-knowledge: I was the sort of person who, instead of weeping or shouting or praying during a crisis, thought about something from a textbook (H. W. Janson's *History of Art*, page 360).

7   Once the flayed man had come, I could not stop the stream of images: Gary looked like a piece of seaweed, Gary looked like a waving handkerchief, Gary looked like a hula dancer. Each simile was a way to avoid thinking about what Gary was, a drowning boy. To remember these things is dishonorable, too, for I have long since forgotten Gary's last name and the color of his hair and the sound of his voice.

8   I do not remember a single word that anyone said. Somehow, we got into one of the canoes, all five of us, and tried to ferry the twenty feet or so to the middle of the river. The current was so strong, and we were so incompetent, that we never got close. Then we tried it on foot, linking arms to form a chain. The water was so cold that it stung. And it was noisy—not the roar and crash of white water but a groan, a terrible bass grumble, from the stones that were rolling and leaping down the riverbed. When we got close to Gary, we couldn't see him; all we could see was the reflection of the sky. A couple of times, groping blindly, one of us touched him, but he was as slippery as soap. Then our knees buckled and our elbows unlocked, and we rolled downstream, like the stones. The river's rocky load, moving invisibly beneath its smooth surface, pounded and scraped us. Eventually, the current heaved us, blue-lipped and panting, onto the bank. In that other world above the water, the only sounds were the buzzing of bees and flies. Our wet sneakers kicked up red dust. The air smelled of sage and rabbitbrush and sunbaked earth.

9   We tried again and again, back and forth between the worlds. Wet, dry, cold, hot, turbulent, still.

10   At first, I assumed that we would save him. He would lie on the bank and the sun would warm him while we administered mouth-to-

mouth resuscitation. If we couldn't get him out, we would hold him upright in the river, and maybe he could still breathe. But the Green River was flowing at nearly three thousand cubic feet—about ninety tons—per second. At that rate, water can wrap a canoe around a boulder like tinfoil. Water can uproot a tree. Water can squeeze the air out of a boy's lungs, undo knots, drag off a life jacket, lever a boot so tightly into the riverbed that even if we had had ropes—the ropes that were in the packs that were in the trucks—we could never have budged him.

We kept going in, not because we had any hope of rescuing Gary   11 after the first ten minutes, but because we had to save face. It would have been humiliating if the instructors came around the bend and found us sitting in the sagebrush, a docile row of five with no hypothermia and no skinned knees. Eventually, they did come. The boats had been delayed because one had nearly capsized, and the instructors had made the other students stop and practice backferrying until they learned not to lean upstream. Even though Gary had already drowned, the instructors did all the same things we had done, more competently but no more effectively, because they, too, would have been humiliated if they hadn't skinned their knees. Men in wet suits, belayed with ropes, pried the body out the next morning.

When I was eighteen, I wanted to hurry through life as fast as I   12 could. Twenty-seven years have passed, and my life now seems too fast. I find myself wanting to backferry, to hover midstream, suspended. I might then avoid many things: harsh words, foolish decisions, moments of inattention, regrets that wash over me, like water.

RESPONDING TO READING

1. In her narrative about Gary becoming trapped in the river, how does Fadiman build tension? What details does she use to achieve this effect? What comparisons does she make?

2. How does Fadiman's title reflect and refract on the story she relates. How does it relate to her use of irony and symbolism, particularly in the last two paragraphs?

3. How, in the final paragraph, does the image of paddling a canoe upon a river become symbolic? Is this symbolism supported by the narrative of Gary's death?

4. Why does Fadiman feel shame as she thinks about Gary and images from *History of Art*? How does this early shame connect to her later statement that "We kept going in, not because we had any hope of rescuing Gary after the first ten minutes, but because we had to save face"? Have you ever done anything to save face? Are you embarrassed about this now? Would you still

have acted this way now? If it's not too problematic to revisit in an essay this experience and the issues it involves, feel free to do so. But don't confess to anything you want to keep private.

5. Discuss with a response group Fadiman's reactions to the death she witnesses. In what ways are her reactions similar to those that any of us would experience in a similar situation? How are her reactions different from those we might have—or perhaps have had—in similar situations? Expand your discussion into an essay in which you identify and analyze the principles for appropriate behavior in a crisis. Be sure to specify the type of crisis you're talking about.

What Are Some Ways
of Understanding Nature?

―――

Understanding Natural Selection
Charles Darwin

During his lukewarm study of medicine at Edinburgh University from 1825 to 1828, and equally desultory preparation for the clergy at Cambridge (B.A., 1831), Charles Darwin (1809–82) was most alert when studying natural phenomena, particularly beetles. He was even known to pop a rare specimen into his mouth to preserve it when his hands were full of other newly collected insects. Ultimately, this naturalist and biologist was to have over a hundred species of animals and plants named after him, ranging from a water beetle to a giant tortoise, as well as sea channels and bays, mountains, towns, a volcano, and Darwin College at his alma mater.

In 1859 Darwin published his major work, *On the Origin of Species by Means of Natural Selection, or the Preservation of Favoured Races in the Struggle for Life*. This book was based on his painstaking observations of animals and plants that were begun during his voyage to South America aboard the *Beagle*, 1831–36. The scientific world has not been the same since. "Understanding Natural Selection," a small portion of this work, contains the essence of Darwin's best known and most revolutionary principles, that in natural selection those variations, "infinitesimally small inherited modifications," endure if they aid in survival. The claim that these modifications occur gradually, rather than being produced at a single stroke by a Divine Creator, is the basis for Darwin's theory of evolution, which antagonized Victorian clergy and continues to challenge contemporary creationists.

Darwin's work prevailed, in part, because of his clear and elegant literary style. Using the techniques of popular literature to explain sophisticated scientific concepts and to present mountains of detailed information, Darwin is a highly engaging writer, making extensive use of the first person, metaphors, anecdotes, and illustrations. "I never study style," he said, "all that I do is to try to get the subject as clear as I can in my own head, and express it in the commonest language which occurs to me. But I generally have to think a good deal before the simplest arrangement and words occur to me."

It may be said that natural selection is daily and hourly scrutinizing, throughout the world, every variation, even the slightest; rejecting that which is bad, preserving and adding up all that is good; silently and insensibly working, whenever and wherever opportunity offers, at 1 the improvement of each organic being in relation to its organic and inorganic conditions of life. We see nothing of these slow changes in progress, until the hand of time has marked the long lapses of ages, and then so imperfect is our view into long past geological ages, that we only see that the forms of life are now different from what they formerly were.

2   Although natural selection can act only through and for the good of each being, yet characters and structures, which we are apt to consider as of very trifling importance, may thus be acted on. When we see leaf-eating insects green, and bark-feeders mottled-grey; the alpine ptarmigan white in winter, the red-grouse the color of heather, and the black-grouse that of peaty earth, we must believe that these tints are of service to these birds and insects in preserving them from danger. Grouse, if not destroyed at some period of their lives, would increase in countless numbers; they are known to suffer largely from birds of prey; and hawks are guided by eyesight to their prey—so much so, that on parts of the Continent persons are warned not to keep white pigeons, as being the most liable to destruction. Hence I can see no reason to doubt that natural selection might be most effective in giving the proper color to each kind of grouse, and in keeping that color, when once acquired, true and constant. Nor ought we to think that the occasional destruction of an animal of any particular color would produce little effect: we should remember how essential it is in a flock of white sheep to destroy every lamb with the faintest trace of black. In plants the down on the fruit and the color of the flesh are considered by botanists as characters of the most trifling importance: yet we hear from an excellent horticulturist, Downing, that in the United States smooth-skinned fruits suffer far more from a beetle, a curculio, than those with down; that purple plums suffer far more from a certain disease than yellow plums; whereas another disease attacks yellow-fleshed peaches far more than those with other colored flesh. If, with all the aids of art, these slight differences make a great difference in cultivating the several varieties, assuredly, in a state of nature, where the trees would have to struggle with other trees and with a host of enemies, such differences would effectually settle which variety, whether a smooth or downy, a yellow or purple fleshed fruit, should succeed.

3   In looking at many small points of difference between species, which, as far as our ignorance permits us to judge, seem to be quite unimportant, we must not forget that climate, food, and so on probably produce some slight and direct effect. It is, however, far more necessary to bear in mind that there are many unknown laws of correlation to growth, which, when one part of the organization is modified through variation, and the modifications are accumulated by natural selection

for the good of the being, will cause other modifications, often of the most unexpected nature.

As we see that those variations which under domestication appear   4
at any particular period of life, tend to reappear in the offspring of the same period; for instance, in the seeds of the many varieties of our culinary and agricultural plants; in the caterpillar and cocoon stages of the varieties of the silkworm; in the eggs of poultry, and in the color of the down of their chickens; in the horns of our sheep and cattle when nearly adult; so in a state of nature, natural selection will be enabled to act on and modify organic beings at any age, by the accumulation of profitable variations at that age, and by their inheritance at a corresponding age. If it profit a plant to have its seeds more and more widely disseminated by the wind, I can see no greater difficulty in this being effected through natural selection, than in the cotton-planter increasing and improving by selection the down in the pods on his cotton-trees. Natural selection may modify and adapt the larva of an insect to a score of contingencies, wholly different from those which concern the mature insect. These modifications will no doubt affect, through the laws of correlation, the structure of the adult; and probably in the case of those insects which live only for a few hours, and which never feed, a large part of their structure is merely the correlated result of successive changes in the structure of their larvae. So, conversely, modifications in the adult will probably often affect the structure of the larva; but in all cases natural selection will ensure that modifications consequent on other modifications at a different period of life, shall not be in the least degree injurious: for if they became so, they would cause the extinction of the species.

Natural selection will modify the structure of the young in relation   5
to the parent, and of the parent in relation to the young. In social animals it will adapt the structure of each individual for the benefit of the community; if each in consequence profits by the selected change. What natural selection cannot do, is to modify the structure of one species, without giving it any advantage, for the good of another species; and though statements to this effect may be found in works of natural history, I cannot find one case which will bear investigation. A structure used only once in an animal's whole life, if of high importance to it, might be modified to any extent by natural selection; for instance, the great jaws possessed by certain insects, and used exclusively for opening the cocoon—or the hard tip to the beak of nestling birds, used for breaking the egg. It has been asserted, that of the best short-beaked tumbler-pigeons more perish in the egg than are able to get out of it; so that fanciers assist in the act of hatching. Now, if nature had to make the beak of a full-grown pigeon very short for the

bird's own advantage, the process of modification would be very slow, and there would be simultaneously the most rigorous selection of the young birds within the egg, which had the most powerful and hardest beaks, for all with weak beaks would inevitably perish: or, more delicate and more easily broken shells might be selected, the thickness of the shell being known to vary like every other structure.

Sexual Selection

6   Inasmuch as peculiarities often appear under domestication in one sex and become hereditarily attached to that sex, the same fact probably occurs under nature, and if so, natural selection will be able to modify one sex in its functional relations to the other sex, or in relation to wholly different habits of life in the two sexes, as is sometimes the case with insects. And this leads me to say a few words on what I call sexual selection. This depends, not on a struggle for existence, but on a struggle between the males for possession of the females; the result is not death to the unsuccessful competitor, but few or no offspring. Sexual selection is, therefore, less rigorous than natural selection. Generally, the most vigorous males, those which are best fitted for their places in nature, will leave most progeny. But in many cases, victory will depend not on general vigor, but on having special weapons, confined to the male sex. A hornless stag or spurless cock would have a poor chance of leaving offspring. Sexual selection by always allowing the victor to breed might surely give indomitable courage, length to the spur, and strength to the wing to strike in the spurred leg, as well as the brutal cock-fighter, who knows well that he can improve his breed by careful selection of the best cocks. How low in the scale of nature this law of battle descends, I know not; male alligators have been described as fighting, bellowing, and whirling round, like Indians in a war dance, for the possession of the females; male salmons have been seen fighting all day long; male stag-beetles often bear wounds from the huge mandibles of other males. The war is, perhaps, severest between the males of polygamous animals, and these seem oftenest provided with special weapons. The males of carnivorous animals are already well armed; though to them and to others, special means of defence may be given through means of sexual selection, as the mane to the lion, the shoulder-pad to the boar, and the hooked jaw to the male salmon; for the shield may be as important for victory, as the sword or spear.

7   Amongst birds, the contest is often of a more peaceful character. All those who have attended to the subject, believe that there is the severest rivalry between the males of many species to attract by singing to the females. The rock-thrush of Guiana, birds of Paradise, and some others, congregate; and successive males display their gorgeous plumage and

perform strange antics before the females, which standing by as spectators, at last choose the most attractive partner. Those who have closely attended to birds in confinement well know that they often take individual preferences and dislikes: thus Sir R. Heron has described how one pied peacock was eminently attractive to all his hen birds. It may appear childish to attribute any effect to such apparently weak means: I cannot here enter on the details necessary to support this view; but if man can in a short time give elegant carriage and beauty to his bantams, according to his standard of beauty, I can see no good reason to doubt that female birds, by selecting, during thousands of generations, the most melodious or beautiful males, according to their standard of beauty, might produce a marked effect. I strongly suspect that some well-known laws with respect to the plumage of male and female birds, in comparison with the plumage of the young, can be explained on the view of plumage having been chiefly modified by sexual selection, acting when the birds have come to the breeding age or during the breeding season; the modifications thus produced being inherited at corresponding ages or seasons, either by the males alone, or by the males and females; but I have not space here to enter on this subject.

    Thus it is, as I believe, that when the males and females of any animal have the same general habits of life, but differ in structure, color, or ornament, such differences have been mainly caused by sexual selection; that is, individual males have had, in successive generations, some slight advantage over other males, in their weapons, means of defence, or charms; and have transmitted these advantages to their male offspring. Yet, I would not wish to attribute all such sexual differences to this agency: for we see peculiarities arising and becoming attached to the male sex in our domestic animals (as the wattle in male carriers, horn-like protuberances in the cocks of certain fowls, and so on), which we cannot believe to be either useful to the males in battle, or attractive to the females. We see analogous cases under nature, for instance, the tuft of hair on the breast of the turkey-cock, which can hardly be either useful or ornamental to this bird; indeed, had the tuft appeared under domestication, it would have been called a monstrosity.

8

Illustration of the Action of Natural Selection

[. . .] Let us take the case of a wolf, which preys on various animals, securing some by craft, some by strength, and some by fleetness; and let us suppose that the fleetest prey, a deer for instance, had from any change in the country increased in numbers, or that other prey had decreased in numbers, during that season of the year when the wolf is hardest pressed for food. I can under such circumstances see no reason

9

to doubt that the swiftest and slimmest wolves would have the best chance of surviving, and so be preserved or selected—provided always that they retained strength to master their prey at this or at some other period of the year, when they might be compelled to prey on other animals. I can see no more reason to doubt this, than that man can improve the fleetness of his greyhounds by careful and methodical selection, or by that unconscious selection which results from each man trying to keep the best dogs without any thought of modifying the breed.

10   Even without any change in the proportional numbers of the animals on which our wolf preyed, a cub might be born with an innate tendency to pursue certain kinds of prey. Nor can this be thought very improbable; for we often observe great differences in the natural tendencies of our domestic animals; one cat, for instance, taking to catch rats, another mice; one cat [. . .] bringing home winged game, another hares or rabbits, and another hunting on marshy ground and almost nightly catching woodcocks or snipes. The tendency to catch rats rather than mice is known to be inherited. Now, if any slight innate change of habit or of structure benefited an individual wolf, it would have the best chance of surviving and of leaving offspring. Some of its young would probably inherit the same habits or structure, and by the repetition of this process, a new variety might be formed which would either supplant or coexist with the parent-form of wolf. Or, again, the wolves inhabiting a mountainous district, and those frequenting the lowlands, would naturally be forced to hunt different prey; and from the continued preservation of the individuals best fitted for the two sites, two varieties might slowly be formed. These varieties would cross and blend where they met; but to this subject of intercrossing we shall soon have to return. I may add, that [. . .] there are two varieties of the wolf inhabiting the Catskill Mountains in the United States, one with a light greyhound-like form, which pursues deer, and the other more bulky, with shorter legs, which more frequently attacks the shepherd's flocks.

RESPONDING TO READING

1. Notice that Darwin does not use the term "evolution" nor does he speak of the origin of the human race. What does he mean by "natural selection," and how did that concept lead into the controversy about evolution of humans?

2. Refer to Stephen Jay Gould's "Evolution as Fact and Theory." Is Darwin speaking about what Gould calls evolution as fact? As theory? Or both, or neither?

3. Compare the way Darwin proceeds in his argument with the way Gould does. Notice the differences in style, kinds of evidence, force of conclusions, and personal involvement. Which differences do you attribute to stylistic and

rhetorical changes over the century that separates the two writers and which are essential differences in approach?

4. Darwin later dropped much of his interest in what he here calls "sexual selection." Compare the strength of that argument with that of the argument for natural selection. Which has better supporting evidence? Which is the better idea? Why?

5. Is it a good idea for scientists to look closely at the origin of humanity and of the earth, or should they leave such matters to philosophers and theologians? Do you see science and religion as fundamentally incompatible, or as partners in a quest for knowledge and understanding, or as related in some other way? In your discussion of these matters, refer to some of the other selections in this book, such as those by Gould, Goodall, and Pollan in Chapter 2; Hawking in Chapter 5; and Turner and Armstrong in Chapter 6.

2.2.2 *Evolution as Fact and Theory*

STEPHEN JAY GOULD

After earning his Ph.D. from Columbia in 1967, Gould (1941-2002) taught paleontology, biology, and history of science at Harvard, explaining his ideas in "surprisingly new ways" to students, peers, and general readers of his columns in *Natural History*. These columns have been collected in *Ever Since Darwin* (1977); *The Panda's Thumb* (1980); *Hen's Teeth and Horse's Toes* (1983); *Bully for Brontosaurus* (1991); and other volumes. A prolific author, Gould published two books in 2002, the year of his death: *I Have Landed: The End of a Beginning in Natural History* and *The Structure of Evolutionary Theory*.

Gould's reinterpretations of scientific history favor the underdogs, as is evident in *The Mismeasure of Man* (1981). There Gould reinterprets the research methods and philosophy behind nineteenth- and twentieth-century IQ testing and other quantitiatve methods of determining intelligence, showing how flawed measurement procedures and wrong interpretations of information invariably favored educated white Anglo–Saxon males and contributed to the oppression of everyone else. Gould's perceptive writing and critical thinking have been rewarded with the American Book Award in Science (1981) and numerous other academic prizes.

Science, like any other body of knowledge, is ever changing. Facts can be reassessed, reinterpreted; intellectual constructs can be re-configured. New contexts can provide new ways to understand familiar information, as Stephen Jay Gould shows in his discussion of "Evolution as Fact and Theory," originally published in *Discover*, a journal of popular science. The greatest fun of science, or any subject, according to Gould, is "when it plays with interesting ideas, examines

their implications, and recognizes that old information may be explained in surprisingly new ways." Thus, in his refutation of Creationism, Gould deals not only with the facts and theory of evolution,
but with the chilling wish "to mute the healthy debate about theory
that has brought new life to evolutionary biology."

1   Kirtley Mather, who died last year at age 89, was a pillar of both
science and the Christian religion in America and one of my dearest
friends. The difference of half a century in our ages evaporated before
our common interests. The most curious thing we shared was a battle
we each fought at the same age. For Kirtley had gone to Tennessee with
Clarence Darrow to testify for evolution at the Scopes trial of 1925.
When I think that we are enmeshed again in the same struggle for one
of the best documented, most compelling and exciting concepts in all of
science, I don't know whether to laugh or cry.

2   According to idealized principles of scientific discourse, the
arousal of dormant issues should reflect fresh data that give renewed
life to abandoned notions. Those outside the current debate may therefore be excused for suspecting that creationists have come up with
something new, or that evolutionists have generated some serious internal trouble. But nothing has changed; the creationists have not a single new fact or argument. Darrow and Bryan were at least more
entertaining than we lesser antagonists today. The rise of creationism is
politics, pure and simple; it represents one issue (and by no means the
major concern) of the resurgent evangelical right. Arguments that
seemed kooky just a decade ago have re-entered the mainstream.

Creationism Is Not Science

3   The basic attack of the creationists falls apart on two general
counts before we even reach the supposed factual details of their
complaints against evolution. First, they play upon a vernacular misunderstanding of the word "theory" to convey the false impression
that we evolutionists are covering up the rotten core of our edifice.
Second, they misuse a popular philosophy of science to argue that
they are behaving scientifically in attacking evolution. Yet the same
philosophy demonstrates that their own belief is not science, and that
"scientific creationism" is therefore meaningless and self-contradictory, a superb example of what Orwell called "newspeak."

4   In the American vernacular, "theory" often means "imperfect
fact"—part of a hierarchy of confidence running downhill from fact to
theory to hypothesis to guess. Thus the power of the creationist argument: evolution is "only" a theory, and intense debate now rages about
many aspects of the theory. If evolution is less than a fact, and scientists
can't even make up their minds about the theory, then what confidence

can we have in it? Indeed, President Reagan echoed this argument before an evangelical group in Dallas when he said (in what I devoutly hope was campaign rhetoric): "Well, it is a theory. It is a scientific theory only and it has in recent years been challenged in the world of science—that is, not believed in the scientific community to be as infallible as it once was."

Well, evolution *is* a theory. It is also a fact. And facts and theories 5 are different things, not rungs in a hierarchy of increasing certainty. Facts are the world's data. Theories are structures of ideas that explain and interpret facts. Facts do not go away when scientists debate rival theories to explain them. Einstein's theory of gravitation replaced Newton's, but apples did not suspend themselves in mid-air pending the outcome. And human beings evolved from apelike ancestors whether they did so by Darwin's proposed mechanism or by some other, yet to be discovered.

Moreover, "fact" does not mean "absolute certainty." The final 6 proofs of logic and mathematics flow deductively from stated premises and achieve certainty only because they are *not* about the empirical world. Evolutionists make no claim for perpetual truth, though creationists often do (and then attack us for a style of argument that they themselves favor). In science, "fact" can only mean "confirmed to such a degree that it would be perverse to withhold provisional assent." I suppose that apples might start to rise tomorrow, but the possibility does not merit equal time in physics classrooms.

Evolutionists have been clear about this distinction between fact 7 and theory from the very beginning, if only because we have always acknowledged how far we are from completely understanding the mechanisms (theory) by which evolution (fact) occurred. Darwin continually emphasized the difference between his two great and separate accomplishments: establishing the fact of evolution, and proposing a theory—natural selection—to explain the mechanism of evolution. He wrote in *The Descent of Man*: "I had two distinct objects in view; firstly, to show that species had not been separately created, and secondly, that natural selection had been the chief agent of change . . . Hence if I had erred in . . . having exaggerated its [natural selection's] power . . . I have at least, as I hope, done good service in aiding to overthrow the dogma of separate creations."

Thus Darwin acknowledged the provisional nature of natural se- 8 lection while affirming the act of evolution. The fruitful theoretical debate that Darwin initiated has never ceased. From the 1940s through the 1960s, Darwin's own theory of natural selection did achieve a temporary hegemony that it never enjoyed in his lifetime. But renewed debate characterizes our decade, and, while no biologist questions the importance of natural selection, many now doubt its ubiquity. In particular, many evolutionists argue that substantial amounts of genetic change may not be subject to natural selection and may spread through populations at random. Others are challenging Darwin's linking of natural selection with gradual, imperceptible change through all intermediary degrees; they are arguing that most evolutionary events may occur far more rapidly than Darwin envisioned.

9   Scientists regard debates on fundamental issues of theory as a sign of intellectual health and a source of excitement. Science is—and how else can I say it?—most fun when it plays with interesting ideas, examines their implications, and recognizes that old information may be explained in surprising new ways. Evolutionary theory is now enjoying this uncommon vigor. Yet amidst all this turmoil no biologist has been led to doubt the fact that evolution occurred; we are debating *how* it happened. We are all trying to explain the same thing: the tree of evolutionary descent linking all organisms by ties of genealogy. Creationists pervert and caricature this debate by conveniently neglecting the common conviction that underlies it, and by falsely suggesting that we now doubt the very phenomenon we are struggling to understand.

10   Using another invalid argument, creationists claim that "the dogma of separate creations," as Darwin characterized it a century ago, is a scientific theory meriting equal time with evolution in high school biology curricula. But a prevailing viewpoint among philosophers of science belies this creationist argument. Philosopher Karl Popper has argued for decades that the primary criterion of science is the falsifiability of its theories. We can never prove absolutely, but we can falsify. A set of ideas that cannot, in principle, be falsified is not science.

11   The entire creationist argument involves little more than a rhetorical attempt to falsify evolution by presenting supposed contradictions among its supporters. Their brand of creationism, they claim, is "scientific" because it follows the Popperian model in trying to demolish evolution. Yet Popper's argument must apply in both directions. One does not become a scientist by the simple act of trying to falsify another scientific system; one has to present an alternative system that also meets Popper's criterion—it too must be falsifiable in principle.

12   "Scientific creationism" is a self-contradictory, nonsense phrase precisely because it cannot be falsified. I can envision observations and experiments that would disprove any evolutionary theory I know, but I cannot imagine what potential data could lead creationists to abandon their beliefs. Unbeatable systems are dogma, not science. Lest I seem harsh or rhetorical, I quote creationism's leading intellectual, Duane Gish, Ph.D., from his recent (1978) book *Evolution? The Fossils Say No!* "By creation we mean the bringing into being by a supernatural Creator of the basic kinds of plants and animals by the process of sudden, or fiat, creation. We do not know how the Creator created, what processes He used, *for He used processes which are not now operating anywhere in the natural universe* [Gish's italics]. This is why we

refer to creation as special creation. We cannot discover by scientific investigations anything about the creative processes used by the Creator." Pray tell, Dr. Gish, in the light of your last sentence, what then is "scientific" creationism?

The Fact of Evolution

Our confidence that evolution occurred centers upon three general 13
arguments. First, we have abundant, direct, observational evidence of evolution in action, from both the field and the laboratory. It ranges from countless experiments on change in nearly everything about fruit flies subjected to artificial selection in the laboratory to the famous British moths that turned black when industrial soot darkened the trees upon which they rest. (The moths gain protection from sharp-sighted bird predators by blending into the background.) Creationists do not deny these observations; how could they? Creationists have tightened their act. They now argue that God only created "basic kinds," and allowed for limited evolutionary meandering within them. Thus toy poodles and Great Danes come from the dog kind and moths can change color, but nature cannot convert a dog to a cat or a monkey to a man.

The second and third arguments for evolution—the case for major 14
changes—do not involve direct observation of evolution in action. They rest upon inference, but are no less secure for that reason. Major evolutionary change requires too much time for direct observation on the scale of recorded human history. All historical sciences rest upon inference, and evolution is no different from geology, cosmology, or human history in this respect. In principle, we cannot observe processes that operated in the past. We must infer them from results that still survive: living and fossil organisms for evolution, documents and artifacts for human history, strata and topography for geology.

The second argument—that the imperfection of nature reveals evo- 15
lution—strikes many people as ironic, for they feel that evolution should be most elegantly displayed in the nearly perfect adaptation expressed by some organisms—the chamber of a gull's wing, or butterflies that cannot be seen in ground litter because they mimic leaves so precisely. But perfection could be imposed by a wise creator or evolved by natural selection. Perfection covers the tracks of past history. And past history—the evidence of descent—is our mark of evolution.

Evolution lies exposed in the *imperfections* that record a history of 16
descent. Why should a rat run, a bat fly, a porpoise swim, and I type this essay with structures built of the same bones unless we all inherited them from a common ancestor? An engineer, starting from scratch, could design better limbs in each case. Why should all the large native

mammals of Australia be marsupials, unless they descended from a common ancestor isolated on this island continent? Marsupials are not "better," or ideally suited for Australia; many have been wiped out by placental mammals imported by man from other continents. This principle of imperfection extends to all historical sciencies. When we recognize the etymology of September, October, November, and December (seventh, eighth, ninth, and tenth, from the Latin), we know that two additional items (January and February) must have been added to an original calendar of ten months.

17   The third argument is more direct: transitions are often found in the fossil record. Preserved transitions are not common—and should not be, according to our understanding of evolution (see next section)—but they are not entirely wanting, as creationists often claim. The lower jaw of reptiles contains several bones, that of mammals only one. The non-mammalian jawbones are reduced, step by step, in mammalian ancestors until they become tiny nubbins located at the back of the jaw. The "hammer" and "anvil" bones of the mammalian ear are descendants of these nubbins. How could such a transition be accomplished? the creationists ask. Surely a bone is either entirely in the jaw or in the ear. Yet paleontologists have discovered two transitional lineages or therapsids (the so-called mammal-like reptiles) with a double jaw joint—one composed of the old quadrate and articular bones (soon to become the hammer and anvil), the other of the squamosal and dentary bones (as in modern mammals). For that matter, what better transitional form could we desire than the oldest human, *Australopithecus afarensis*, with its apelike palate, its human upright stance, and a cranial capacity larger than any ape's of the same body size but a full 1,000 cubic centimeters below ours? If God made each of the half dozen human species discovered in ancient rocks, why did he create in an unbroken temporal sequence of progressively more modern features—increasing cranial capacity, reduced face and teeth, larger body size? Did he create to mimic evolution and test our faith thereby?

An Example of Creationist Argument

18   Faced with these facts of evolution and the philosophical bankruptcy of their own position, creationists rely upon distortion and innuendo to buttress their rhetorical claim. If I sound sharp or bitter, indeed I am—for I have become a major target of these practices.

19   I count myself among the evolutionists who argue for a jerky, or episodic, rather than a smoothly gradual, pace of change. In 1972 my colleague Niles Eldredge and I developed the theory of punctuated equilibrium [*Discover*, October]. We argued that two outstanding facts

of the fossil record—geologically "sudden" origin of new species and failure to change thereafter (stasis)—reflect the predictions of evolutionary theory, not the imperfections of the fossil record. In most theories, small isolated populations are the source of new species, and the process of speciation takes thousands or tens of thousands of years. This amount of time, so long when measured against our lives, is a geological microsecond. It represents much less than 1 per cent of the average life span for a fossil invertebrate species—more than 10 million years. Large, widespread, and well-established species, on the other hand, are not expected to change very much. We believe that the inertia of large populations explains the stasis of most fossil species over millions of years.

We proposed the theory of punctuated equilibrium largely to provide a different explanation for pervasive trends in the fossil record. Trends, we argued, cannot be attributed to gradual transformation within lineages, but must arise from the differential success of certain kinds of species. A trend, we argued, is more like climbing a flight of stairs (punctuations and stasis) than rolling up an inclined plane.   20

Since we proposed punctuated equilibria to explain trends, it is infuriating to be quoted again and again by creationists—whether through design or stupidity, I do not know—as admitting that the fossil record includes no transitional forms. Transitional forms are generally lacking at the species level, but are abundant between larger groups. The evolution from reptiles to mammals, as mentioned earlier, is well documented. Yet a pamphlet entitled "Harvard Scientists Agree Evolution Is a Hoax" states: "The facts of punctuated equilibrium which Gould and Eldredge . . . are forcing Darwinists to swallow fit the picture that Bryan insisted on, and which God has revealed to us in the Bible."   21

Continuing the distortion, several creationists have equated the theory of punctuated equilibrium with a caricature of the beliefs of Richard Goldschmidt, a great early geneticist. Goldschmidt argued, in a famous book published in 1940, that new groups can arise all at once through major mutations. He referred to these suddenly transformed creatures as "hopeful monsters." (I am attracted to some aspects of the non-caricatured version, but Goldschmidt's theory still has nothing to do with punctuated equilibrium.) Creationist Luther Sunderland talks of the "punctuated equilibrium hopeful monster theory" and tells his hopeful readers that "it amounts to tacit admission that anti-evolutionists are correct in asserting there is no fossil evidence supporting the theory that all life is connected to a common ancestor." Duane Gish writes, "According to Goldschmidt, and now apparently according to Gould, a reptile laid an egg from which the first bird, feathers and all, was produced." Any evolutionist who believed such nonsense would rightly   22 be laughed off the intellectual stage; yet the only theory that could ever envision such a scenario for the evolution of birds is creationism—God acts in the egg.

Conclusion

23   I am both angry at and amused by the creationists; but mostly I am deeply sad. Sad for many reasons. Sad because so many people who respond to creationist appeals are troubled for the right reason, but venting their anger at the wrong target. It is true that scientists have often been dogmatic and elitist. It is true that we have often allowed the white-coated, advertising image to represent us—"Scientists say that Brand X cures bunions ten times faster than . . . " We have not fought it adequately because we derive benefits from appearing as a new priesthood. It is also true that faceless bureaucratic state power intrudes more and more into our lives and removes choices that should belong to individuals and communities. I can understand that requiring that evolution be taught in the schools might be seen as one more insult on all these grounds. But the culprit is not, and cannot be, evolution or any other fact of the natural world. Identify and fight your legitimate enemies by all means, but we are not among them.

24   I am sad because the practical result of this brouhaha will not be expanded coverage to include creationism (that would also make me sad), but the reduction or excision of evolution from high school curricula. Evolution is one of the half dozen "great ideas" developed by science. It speaks to the profound issues of genealogy that fascinate all of us—the "roots" phenomenon writ large. Where did we come from? Where did life arise? How did it develop? How are organisms related? It forces us to think, ponder, and wonder. Shall we deprive millions of this knowledge and once again teach biology as a set of dull and unconnected facts, without the thread that weaves diverse material into a supple unity.

25   But most of all I am saddened by a trend I am just beginning to discern among my colleagues. I sense that some now wish to mute the healthy debate about theory that has brought new life to evolutionary biology. It provides grist for creationist mills, they say, even if only by distortion. Perhaps we should lie low and rally round the flag of strict Darwinism, at least for the moment—a kind of old-time religion on our part.

26   But we should borrow another metaphor and recognize that we too have to tread a straight and narrow path, surrounded by roads to perdition. For if we ever begin to suppress our search to understand

nature, to quench our own intellectual excitement in a misguided effort
to repesent a united front where it does not and should not exist, then
we are truly lost.

RESPONDING TO READING

1. Give the two different definitions Gould cites of the word "theory"—the sci-
    entific one and the vernacular (everyday) one. Then define what he means by
    a "fact." Using these definitions, explain what he means when he says,
    "Well, evolution *is* a theory. It is also a fact." How does he differentiate be-
    tween evolution as a fact and evolution as a theory?

2. What is the subject of scientific debate over evolution, the "fun" and "play" Gould
    refers to? What is the misunderstanding of that debate that Gould seeks to refute?
    Does his own writing reveal the sense of "fun" (paragraph 9) that he advocates?

3. What does Gould mean by insisting that any set of scientific ideas must be
    able to be falsified? Name some "unbeatable systems" that cannot be falsi-
    fied, besides Creationism, and decide what characterizes them. From this se-
    quence of definitions, come up with the rules for scientific debate according
    to Gould. Does Gould himself follow these rules?

4. Why have Gould's antagonists reacted to his theories with what he calls "distor-
    tion and innuendo"? Why would religious people do such things? Are the legit-
    imate complaints about science that Gould lists in his "Conclusion" sufficient
    reason? Is this the kind of debate that Kuhn calls "normal science" (p. 193)?
    How do you respond to Gould's assertion in his second paragraph that "the
    rise of creationism is politics, pure and simple"?

5. Reflect upon how you have come to know about evolution and what it
    means. If Gould's perspective is new to you, discuss the source of his knowl-
    edge and the source of yours. Is this a matter of conflicting belief systems, of
    different definitions, of different paradigms of knowledge, or what?

First Observations

JANE GOODALL

Although Jane Goodall was born (1934) and reared in London, she
has lived in Africa since she was eighteen, when she served as an assistant to Dr. Louis Leakey, an anthropologist and paleontologist
studying human origins in Kenya. Her research since 1960 has been
conducted in Tanzania at the Gombe Stream Chimpanzee Reserve, a
rugged area with steep mountains and dense jungles on the shore of
Lake Tanganyika. Her careful observation of chimpanzees, not only
only in groups, but as individuals ("David Graybeard," "Goliath")
in their native habitat over many years has made her a respected
world expert. She is only the eighth person in the history of Cambridge University to have received a Ph.D. without first earning an

undergraduate degree; her thesis, *Behavior of the Free-Ranging Chimpanzee*, consolidated five years' work at Gombe.

In "First Observations," from *In the Shadow of Man* (1971), Goodall describes how she watched chimpanzees at Gombe, with patience, perseverance, and unquenchable excitement. She also explains two of her numerous discoveries about animal behavior that have dramatically changed the knowledge of the field. One is her conclusive discovery that chimpanzees, previously believed to be vegetarian, eat meat. The other is that, in addition to using tools—in this case, blades of grass to "fish" for termites—chimpanzees make their own tools and stockpile them for future use. Such observations as these have forced anthropologists to redefine "man" in a more complex manner than simply as "a tool making and using animal." In recent years, Goodall has become a spokesperson for the humane treatment of chimpanzees in both scientific research and entertainment, the subject of *Visions of Caliban* (1993), written with Dale Peterson.

1   For about a month I spent most of each day either on the Peak or overlooking Mlinda Valley where the chimps, before or after stuffing themselves with figs, ate large quantities of small purple fruits that tasted, like so many of their foods, as bitter and astringent as sloes or crab apples. Piece by piece, I began to form my first somewhat crude picture of chimpanzee life.

2   The impression that I had gained when I watched the chimps at the msulula tree of temporary, constantly changing associations of individuals within the community was substantiated. Most often I saw small groups of four to eight moving about together. Sometimes I saw one or two chimpanzees leave such a group and wander off on their own or join up with a different association. On other occasions I watched two or three small groups joining to form a larger one.

3   Often, as one group crossed the grassy ridge separating the Kasekela Valley from the fig trees on the home valley, the male chimpanzee, or chimpanzees, of the party would break into a run, sometimes moving in an upright position, sometimes dragging a fallen branch, sometimes stamping or slapping the hard earth. These charging displays were always accompanied by loud pant-hoots and afterward the chimpanzee frequently would swing up into a tree overlooking the valley he was about to enter and sit quietly, peering down and obviously listening for a response from below. If there were chimps feeding in the fig trees they nearly always hooted back, as though in answer. Then the new arrivals would hurry down the steep slope and, with more calling and screaming, the two groups would meet in the fig trees. When groups of females and youngsters with no males present joined other feeding chimpanzees, usually there was none of this excitement; the newcomers merely climbed up into the

trees, greeted some of those already there, and began to stuff themselves with figs.

While many details of their social behavior were hidden from me by the foliage, I did get occasional fascinating glimpses. I saw one female, newly arrived in a group, hurry up to a big male and hold her hand toward him. Almost regally he reached out, clasped her hand in his, drew it toward him, and kissed it with his lips. I saw two adult males embrace each other in greeting. I saw youngsters having wild games through the treetops, chasing around after each other or jumping again and again, one after the other, from a branch to a springy bough below. I watched small infants dangling happily by themselves for minutes on end, patting at their toes with one hand, rotating gently from side to side. Once two tiny infants pulled on opposite ends of a twig in a gentle tug-of-war. Often, during the heat of midday or after a long spell of feeding, I saw two or more adults grooming each other, carefully looking through the hair of their companions.

At that time of year the chimps usually went to bed late, making their nests when it was too dark to see properly through binoculars, but sometimes they nested earlier and I could watch them from the Peak. I found that every individual, except for infants who slept with their mothers, made his own nest each night. Generally this took about three minutes: the chimp chose a firm foundation such as an upright fork or crotch, or two horizontal branches. Then he reached out and bent over smaller branches onto this foundation, keeping each one in place with his feet. Finally he tucked in the small leafy twigs growing around the rim of his nest and lay down. Quite often a chimp sat up after a few minutes and picked a handful of leafy twigs, which he put under his head or some other part of his body before settling down again for the night. One young female I watched went on and on bending down branches until she had constructed a huge mound of greenery on which she finally curled up.

I climbed up into some of the nests after the chimpanzees had left them. Most of them were built in trees that for me were almost impossible to climb. I found that there was quite complicated interweaving of the branches in some of them. I found, too, that the nests were fouled with dung; and later, when I was able to get closer to the chimps, I saw how they were always careful to defecate and urinate over the edge of their nests, even in the middle of the night.

During that month I really came to know the country well, for I often went on expeditions from the Peak, sometimes to examine nests, more frequently to collect specimens of the chimpanzees' food plants, which Bernard Verdcourt had kindly offered to identify for me. Soon I could find my way around the sheer ravines and up and down the steep slopes of three valleys—the home valley, the Pocket, and Mlinda

Valley—as well as a taxi driver finds his way about in the main streets
and byways of London. It is a period I remember vividly, not only because I was beginning to accomplish something at last, but also because of the delight I felt in being completely by myself. For those who
love to be alone with nature I need add nothing further; for those who
do not, no words of mine could ever convey, even in part, the almost
mystical awareness of beauty and eternity that accompanies certain
treasured moments. And, though the beauty was always there, those
moments came upon me unaware: when I was watching the pale flush
preceding dawn; or looking up through the rustling leaves of some
giant forest tree into the greens and browns and black shadows that occasionally ensnared a bright fleck of the blue sky; or when I stood, as
darkness fell, with one hand on the still-warm trunk of a tree and
looked at the sparkling of an early moon on the never still, sighing
water of the lake.

8   One day, when I was sitting by the trickle of water in Buffalo
Wood, pausing for a moment in the coolness before returning from a
scramble in Mlinda Valley, I saw a female bushbuck moving slowly
along the nearly dry streambed. Occasionally she paused to pick off
some plant and crunch it. I kept absolutely still, and she was not aware
of my presence until she was little more than ten yards away. Suddenly
she tensed and stood staring at me, one small forefoot raised. Because I
did not move, she did not know what I was—only that my outline was
somehow strange. I saw her velvet nostrils dilate as she sniffed the air,
but I was downwind and her nose gave her no answer. Slowly she
came closer, and closer—one step at a time, her neck craned forward—
always poised for instant flight. I can still scarcely believe that her nose
actually touched my knee; yet if I close my eyes I can feel again, in
imagination, the warmth of her breath and the silken impact of her
skin. Unexpectedly I blinked and she was gone in a flash, bounding
away with loud barks of alarm until the vegetation hid her completely
from my view.

9   It was rather different when, as I was sitting on the Peak, I saw a
leopard coming toward me, his tail held up straight. He was at a slightly lower level than I, and obviously had no idea I was there. Ever since
arrival in Africa I had had an ingrained, illogical fear of leopards. Already, while working at the Gombe, I had several times nearly turned
back when, crawling through some thick undergrowth, I had suddenly
smelled the rank smell of cat. I had forced myself on, telling myself that
my fear was foolish, that only wounded leopards charged humans
with savage ferocity.

10   On this occasion, though, the leopard went out of sight as it started
to climb up the hill—the hill on the peak of which I sat. I quickly hastened to climb a tree, but halfway there I realized that leopards can

climb trees. So I uttered a sort of halfhearted squawk. The leopard, my logical mind told me, would be just as frightened of me if he knew I was there. Sure enough, there was a thudding of startled feet and then silence. I returned to the Peak, but the feeling of unseen eyes watching me was too much. I decided to watch for the chimps in Mlinda Valley. And, when I returned to the Peak several hours later, there, on the very rock which had been my seat, was a neat pile of leopard dung. He must have watched me go and then, very carefully, examined the place where such a frightening creature had been and tried to exterminate my alien scent with his own.

As the weeks went by the chimpanzees became less and less afraid.   11
Quite often when I was on one of my food-collecting expeditions I came across chimpanzees unexpectedly, and after a time I found that some of them would tolerate my presence provided they were in fairly thick forest and I sat still and did not try to move closer than sixty to eighty yards. And so, during my second month of watching from the peak, when I saw a group settle down to feed I sometimes moved closer and was thus able to make more detailed observations.

It was at this time that I began to recognize a number of different   12
individuals. As soon as I was sure of knowing a chimpanzee if I saw it again, I named it. Some scientists feel that animals should be labeled by numbers—that to name them is anthropomorphic—but I have always been interested in the *differences* between individuals, and a name is not only more individual than a number but also far easier to remember. Most names were simply those which, for some reason or other, seemed to suit the individuals to whom I attached them. A few chimps were named because some facial expression or mannerism reminded me of human acquaintances.

The easiest individual to recognize was old Mr. McGregor. The   13
crown of his head, his neck, and his shoulders were almost entirely devoid of hair, but a slight fill remained around his head rather like a monk's tonsure. He was an old male—perhaps between thirty and forty years of age (the longevity record of a captive chimp is forty-seven years). During the early months of my acquaintance with him, Mr. McGregor was somewhat belligerent. If I accidentally came across him at close quarters he would threaten me with an upward and backward jerk of his head and a shaking of branches before climbing down and vanishing from my sight. He reminded me, for some reason, of Beatrix Potter's old gardener in *The Tale of Peter Rabbit*.

Ancient Flo with her deformed, bulbous nose and ragged ears was   14
equally easy to recognize. Her youngest offspring at that time were two-year-old Fifi, who still rode everywhere on her mother's back, and her juvenile son, Figan, who was always to be seen wandering around with his mother and little sister. He was then about six years old; it was

approximately a year before he would attain puberty. Flo often traveled with another old mother, Olly. Olly's long face was also distinctive; the fluff of hair on the back of her head—though no other feature—reminded me of my aunt, Olwen. Olly, like Flo, was accompanied by two children, a daughter younger than Fifi, and an adolescent son about a year older than Figan.

15   Then there was William, who, I am certain, must have been Olly's blood brother. I never saw any special signs of friendship between them, but their faces were amazingly alike. They both had long upper lips that wobbled when they suddenly turned their heads. William had the added distinction of several thin, deeply etched scar marks running down his upper lip from his nose.

16   Two of the other chimpanzees I knew well by sight at that time were David Graybeard and Goliath. Like David and Goliath in the Bible, these two individuals were closely associated in my mind because they were very often together. Goliath, even in those days of his prime, was not a giant, but he had a splendid physique and the springy movements of an athlete. He probably weighed about one hundred pounds. David Graybeard was less afraid of me from the start than were any of the other chimps. I was always pleased when I picked out his handsome face and well-marked silvery beard in a chimpanzee group, for with David to calm the others, I had a better chance of approaching to observe them more closely.

17   Before the end of my trial period in the field I made two really exciting discoveries—discoveries that made the previous months of frustration well worth while. And for both of them I had David Graybeard to thank.

18   One day I arrived on the Peak and found a small group of chimps just below me in the upper branches of a thick tree. As I watched I saw that one of them was holding a pink-looking object from which he was from time to time pulling pieces with his teeth. There was a female and a youngster and they were both reaching out toward the male, their hands actually touching his mouth. Presently the female picked up a piece of the pink thing and put it to her mouth: it was at this moment that I realized the chimps were eating meat.

19   After each bite of meat the male picked off some leaves with his lips and chewed them with the flesh. Often, when he had chewed for several minutes on this leafy wad, he spat out the remains into the waiting hands of the female. Suddenly, he dropped a small piece of meat, and like a flash the youngster swung after it to the ground. Even as he reached to pick it up the undergrowth exploded and an adult bushpig charged toward him. Screaming, the juvenile leaped back into the tree. The pig remained in the open, snorting and moving backward and forward. Soon I made out the shapes of three small striped piglets.

Obviously the chimps were eating a baby pig. The size was right and later, when I realized that the male was David Graybeard, I moved closer and saw that he was indeed eating piglet.

For three hours I watched the chimps feeding. David occasionally let the female bite pieces from the carcass and once he actually detached a small piece of flesh and placed it in her outstretched hand. When he finally climbed down there was still meat left on the carcass; he carried it away in one hand, followed by the others.

Of course I was not sure, then, that David Graybeard had caught the pig for himself, but even so, it was tremendously exciting to know that these chimpanzees actually ate meat. Previously scientists had believed that although these apes might occasionally supplement their diet with a few insects or small rodents and the like they were primarily vegetarians and fruit eaters. No one had suspected that they might hunt larger mammals.

It was within two weeks of this observation that I saw something that excited me even more. By then it was October and the short rains had begun. The blackened slopes were softened by feathery new grass shoots and in some places the ground was carpeted by a variety of flowers. The Chimpanzees' Spring, I called it. I had had a frustrating morning, tramping up and down three valleys with never a sign or sound of a chimpanzee. Hauling myself up the steep slope of Mlinda Valley I headed for the Peak, not only weary but soaking wet from crawling through dense undergrowth. Suddenly I stopped, for I saw a slight movement in the long grass about sixty yards away. Quickly focusing my binoculars I saw that it was a single chimpanzee, and just then he turned in my direction. I recognized David Graybeard.

Cautiously I moved around so that I could see what he was doing. He was squatting beside the red earth mound of a termite nest, and as I watched I saw him carefully push a long grass stem down into a hole in the mound. After a moment he withdrew it and picked something from the end with his mouth. I was too far away to make out what he was eating, but it was obvious that he was actually using a grass stem as a tool.

I knew that on two occasions casual observers in West Africa had seen chimpanzees using objects as tools: one had broken open palmnut kernels by using a rock as a hammer, and a group of chimps had been observed pushing sticks into an underground bees' nest and licking off the honey. Somehow I had never dreamed of seeing anything so exciting myself.

For an hour David feasted at the termite mound and then he wandered slowly away. When I was sure he had gone I went over to examine the mound. I had found a few crushed insects strewn about, and a swarm of worker termites sealing the entrances of the nest passages into which David had obviously been poking his stems. I picked up one of his discarded tools and carefully pushed it into a hole myself. Immediately I felt the pull of several termites as they seized the grass, and when I pulled it out there were a number of workers termites and a few soldiers, with big red heads, clinging on with their mandibles. There they remained, sticking out at right angles to the stem with their legs waving in the air.

26   Before I left I trampled down some of the tall dry grass and constructed a rough hide—just a few palm fronds leaned up against the low branch of a tree and tied together at the top. I planned to wait there the next day. But it was another week before I was able to watch a chimpanzee "fishing" for termites again. Twice chimps arrived, but each time they saw me and moved off immediately. Once a swarm of fertile winged termites—the princes and princesses, as they are called—flew off on their nuptial flight, their huge white wings fluttering frantically as they carried the insects higher and higher. Later I realized that it is at this time of year, during the short rains, when the worker termites extend the passages of the nest to the surface, preparing for these emigrations. Several such swarms emerge between October and January. It is principally during these months that the chimpanzees feed on termites.

27   On the eighth day of my watch David Graybeard arrived again, together with Goliath, and the pair worked there for two hours. I could see much better: I observed how they scratched open the sealed-over passage entrances with a thumb or forefinger. I watched how they bit the end off their tools when they became bent, or used the other end, or discarded them in favor of new ones. Goliath once moved at least fifteen yards from the heap to select a firm-looking piece of vine, and both males often picked three or four stems while they were collecting tools, and put the spares beside them on the ground until they wanted them.

28   Most exciting of all, on several occasions they picked small leafy twigs and prepared them for use by stripping off the leaves. This was the first recorded example of a wild animal not merely *using* an object as a tool, but actually modifying an object and thus showing the crude beginnings of tool*making*.

29   Previously man had been regarded as the only tool-making animal. Indeed, one of the clauses commonly accepted in the definition of man was that he was a creature who "made tools to a regular and set pattern." The chimpanzees, obviously, had not made tools to any set pattern. Nevertheless, my early observations of their primitive toolmaking abilities convinced a number of scientists that it was necessary to redefine man in a more complex manner than before. Or else, as Louis Leakey put it, we should by definition have to accept the chimpanzee as Man.

RESPONDING TO READING

1. Goodall uses metaphors from human life to help readers interpret her description of chimpanzee life. Find some of these metaphors and explain their effects. What do they tell you about Goodall's "way of knowing" the animals?

2. Goodall's love of nature is connected with being "completely by myself." She describes "the almost mystical awareness of beauty and eternity that accompanies certain treasured moments." The scene with the female bushbuck is an example. Which of the various ways of knowing in this section seems closest to what Goodall exemplifies?

3. Goodall describes two "exciting" discoveries about the chimpanzees. What are these discoveries and what do they have in common? Do these discoveries, and other aspects of her "first observations," suggest what kinds of things she was looking for?

4. Describe a particularly exciting observation you have made about human nature, an animal, a plant, or another part of the country or world, to someone who is unfamiliar with your subject. How did you know what to look for, what procedures to use, what to expect? Or was your discovery entirely accidental or serendipitous? How did you know when you were on to something significant? Compare the completeness and reliability of the kind of knowledge gained from firsthand observation with the knowledge you have gained in other ways.

Playing God in the Garden

MICHAEL POLLAN

Journalist, author, and environmentalist Michael Pollan traces his interest in gardening and nature back to when his father mowed his initials in the ragged grass in front of their home, to protest against suburban lawn conformity. Pollan graduated from Bennington College (B.A.), and earned an M.A. in English from Columbia. He has held the post of executive editor at *Harper's Magazine*, his articles have appeared in *Harper's, Best American Essays, Gardens Illustrated*, and *Orion Nature Quarterly*, and he regularly contributes to the *New York Times Magazine*. Pollan's books, written to appeal to gardening enthusiasts as well as scientists, have earned him a wide audience. *Second Nature: A Gardener's Education* (1991) is the story of his struggle to create a natural garden on a run-down Connecticut dairy farm that he had purchased. An autobiographical meditation on the inseparability of wildlife, plants, and human intervention, the book concludes that nature itself is a garden. *A Place of My Own: The Education of an Amateur Builder* (1997) is about Pollan's experience building a writing hut in the woods and explores issues ranging from construction problems to architectural theory. *The Botany of Desire: A Plant's Eye View of the World* (2001) investigates the cultural history of plants, focusing on the way human needs have influenced the propagation and hybridization of four domesticated species that satisfy particular desires: apples (sweetness), tulips (beauty), cannabis (intoxication), and potatoes (control).

In "Playing God in the Garden," from *Botany of Desire*, genetic engineering takes the human–plant dynamic to an entirely new level, as Pollan considers what happens when a corporation seeks to profit by altering plant genomes. As he narrates his first experience growing "NewLeaf" potatoes—spuds that have been genetically altered to produce their own insecticide—Pollan warns about the potentially harmful results of bypassing the normal processes of evolution.

1   The garden is still a site for experiment, a good place to try out new plants and techniques without having to bet the farm. Many of the methods employed by organic farmers today were first discovered in the garden. Attempted on the scale of a whole farm, the next New Thing is an expensive and risky proposition, which is why farmers have always been a conservative breed, notoriously slow to change. But for a gardener like me, with relatively little at stake, it's no big deal to try out a new variety of potato or method of pest control, and every season I do.

2   Admittedly, my experiments in the garden are unscientific and far from foolproof or conclusive. Is it the new neem tree oil I sprayed on the potatoes that's controlling the beetles so well this year, or the fact I planted a pair of tomatillos nearby, the leaves of which the beetles seem to prefer to potatoes? (My scapegoats, I call them.) Ideally, I'd control for every variable but one, but that's hard to do in a garden, a place that, like the rest of nature, seems to consist of nothing *but* variables. "Everything affecting everything else" is not a bad description of what happens in a garden or, for that matter, in any ecosystem.

3   In spite of these complexities, it is only by trial and error that my garden ever improves, so I continue to experiment. Recently I planted something new—something very new, as a matter of fact—and embarked on my most ambitious experiment to date. I planted a potato called "NewLeaf" that has been genetically engineered (by the Monsanto corporation) to produce its own insecticide. This it does in every cell of every leaf, stem, flower, root, and—this is the unsettling part— every spud.

4   The scourge of potatoes has always been the Colorado potato beetle, a handsome, voracious insect that can pick a plant clean of its leaves virtually overnight, starving the tubers in the process. Supposedly, any Colorado potato beetle that takes so much as a nibble of a NewLeaf leaf is doomed, its digestive tract pulped, in effect, by the bacterial toxin manufactured in every part of these plants.

5   I wasn't at all sure I really *wanted* the NewLeaf potatoes I'd be digging at the end of the season. In this respect my experiment in growing

them was very different from anything else I've ever done in my garden—whether growing apples or tulips or even pot. All of those I'd planted because I really wanted what the plants promised. What I wanted here was to gratify not so much a desire as a curiosity: Do they work? Are these genetically modified potatoes a good idea, either to plant or to eat? If not mine, then whose desire *do* they gratify? And finally, what might they have to tell us about the future of the relationship between plants and people? To answer these questions, or at least begin to, would take more than the tools of the gardener (or the eater); I'd need as well the tools of the journalist, without which I couldn't hope to enter the world from which these potatoes had come. So you could say there was something fundamentally artificial about my experiment in growing NewLeaf potatoes. But then, artificiality seems very much to the point.

Certainly my NewLeafs are aptly named. They're part of a new   6
class of crop plant that is transforming the long, complex, and by now largely invisible food chain that links every one of us to the land. By the time I conducted my experiment, more than fifty million acres of American farmland had already been planted to genetically modified crops, most of it corn, soybeans, cotton, and potatoes that have been engineered either to produce their own pesticide or to withstand herbicides. The not-so-distant future will, we're told, bring us potatoes genetically modified to absorb less fat when fried, corn that can withstand drought, lawns that don't ever have to be mowed, "golden rice" rich in Vitamin A, bananas and potatoes that deliver vaccines, tomatoes enhanced with flounder genes (to withstand frost), and cotton that grows in every color of the rainbow.

It's probably not too much to say that this new technology repre-   7
sents the biggest change in the terms of our relationship with plants since people first learned how to cross one plant with another. With genetic engineering, human control of nature is taking a giant step forward. The kind of reordering of nature represented by the rows in a farmer's field can now take place at a whole new level: within the genome of the plants themselves. Truly, we have stepped out onto new ground.

Or have we?   8

Just how novel these plants really are is in fact one of the biggest   9
questions about them, and the companies that have developed them give contradictory answers. The industry simultaneously depicts these plants as the linchpins of a biological revolution—part of a "paradigm shift" that will make agriculture more sustainable and feed the world—and, oddly enough, as the same old spuds, corn, and soybeans, at least so far as those of us at the eating end of the food chain should be concerned. The new plants are novel enough to be patented, yet not so novel as to warrant a label telling us what it is we're eating. It would

seem they are chimeras: "revolutionary" in the patent office and on the farm, "nothing new" in the supermarket and the environment.

10   By planting my own crop of NewLeafs, I was hoping to figure out which version of reality to believe, whether these were indeed the same old spuds or something sufficiently novel (in nature, in the diet) to warrant caution and hard questions. As soon as you start looking into the subject, you find that there are many questions about genetically modified plants that, fifty million acres later, remain unanswered and, more remarkable still, unasked—enough to make me think mine might not be the only experiment going on.

11   *May 2.* Here at the planter's end of the food chain, where I began my experiment after Monsanto agreed to let me test-drive its NewLeafs, things certainly look new and different. After digging two shallow trenches in my vegetable garden and lining them with compost, I untied the purple mesh bag of seed potatoes Monsanto had sent and opened the grower's guide tied around its neck. Potatoes, you will recall from kindergarten experiments, are grown not from actual seeds but from the eyes of other potatoes, and the dusty, stone-colored chunks of tuber I carefully laid at the bottom of the trench looked much like any other. Yet the grower's guide that comes with them put me in mind not so much of planting vegetables as booting up a new software release.

12   By "opening and using this product," the card informed me, I was now "licensed" to grow these potatoes, but only for a single generation; the crop I would water and tend and harvest was mine, yet also not mine. That is, the potatoes I would dig come September would be mine to eat or sell, but their genes would remain the intellectual property of Monsanto, protected under several U.S. patents, including 5,196,525; 5,164,316; 5,322,938; and 5,352,605. Were I to save even one of these spuds to plant next year—something I've routinely done with my potatoes in the past—I would be breaking federal law. (I had to wonder, what would be the legal status of any "volunteers"—those plants that, with no prompting from the gardener, sprout each spring from tubers overlooked during the previous harvest?) The small print on the label also brought the disconcerting news that my potato plants were *themselves* registered as a pesticide with the Environmental Protection Administration (U.S. EPA Reg. No. 524-474).

13   If proof were needed that the food chain that begins with seeds and ends on our dinner plates is in the midst of revolutionary change, the small print that accompanied my NewLeafs will do. That food chain has been unrivaled for its productivity: on average, an American farmer today grows enough food each year to feed a hundred people. Yet that achievement—that power over nature—has come at a price. The modern industrial farmer cannot grow that much food without

large quantities of chemical fertilizers, pesticides, machinery, and fuel. This expensive set of "inputs," as they're called, saddles the farmer with debt, jeopardizes his health, erodes his soil and ruins its fertility, pollutes the groundwater, and compromises the safety of the food we eat. Thus the gain in the farmer's power has been trailed by a host of new vulnerabilities.

All this I'd heard before, of course, but always from environmen-   14
talists or organic farmers. What is new is to hear the same critique from industrial farmers, government officials, and the agribusiness companies that sold farmers on all those expensive inputs in the first place. Taking a page from Wendell Berry, of all people, Monsanto declared in a recent annual report that "current agricultural technology is unsustainable."

What is to rescue the American food chain is a new kind of plant.   15
Genetic engineering promises to replace expensive and toxic chemicals with expensive but apparently benign genetic information: crops that, like my NewLeafs, can protect themselves from insects and diseases without the help of pesticides. In the case of the NewLeaf, a gene borrowed from one strain of a common bacterium found in the soil—*Bacillus thuringiensis*, or "Bt" for short—gives the potato plant's cells the information they need to manufacture a toxin lethal to the Colorado potato beetle. This gene is now Monsanto's intellectual property. With genetic engineering, agriculture has entered the information age, and Monsanto's aim, it would appear, is to become its Microsoft, supplying the proprietary "operating systems"—the metaphor is theirs—to run this new generation of plants.

The metaphors we use to describe the natural world strongly influ-   16
ence the way we approach it, the style and extent of our attempts at control. It makes all the difference in (and to) the world if one conceives of a farm as a factory or a forest as a farm. Now we're about to find out what happens when people begin approaching the genes of our food plants as software.

May 15. After several days of drenching rain, the sun appeared   17
this week, and so did my NewLeafs: a dozen deep green shoots pushed up out of the soil and commenced to grow—faster and more robustly than any of my other potatoes. Apart from their vigor, though, my NewLeafs looked perfectly normal—they certainly didn't beep or glow, as a few visitors to my garden jokingly inquired. (Not that the glowing notion is so far-fetched: I've read that plant breeders have developed a luminescent tobacco plant by inserting a gene from a firefly. I've yet to read *why* they would do this, except perhaps to prove it could be done: a demonstration of power.) Yet as I watched my NewLeafs multiply their lustrous, dark green leaves those first few days, eagerly awaiting the arrival of the first unwitting beetle, I

couldn't help thinking of them as existentially different from the rest of my plants.

18   All domesticated plants are in some sense artificial, living archives of both cultural and natural information that people have helped to "design." Any given type of potato reflects the human desires that have been bred into it. One that's been selected to yield long, handsome french fries or unblemished, round potato chips is the expression of a national food chain and a culture that likes its potatoes highly processed. At the same time, some of the more delicate European fingerlings growing beside my NewLeafs imply an economy of small-market growers and a cultural taste for eating potatoes fresh—for none of these varieties can endure much travel or time in storage. I'm not sure exactly what cultural values to ascribe to my Peruvian blues; perhaps nothing more than a craving for variety among a people who ate potatoes morning, noon, and night.

19   "Tell me what you eat," Anthelme Brillat-Savarin famously claimed, and "I will tell you what you are." The qualities of a potato—as of any domesticated plant or animal—are a fair reflection of the values of the people who grow and eat it. Yet all these qualities already existed in the potato, somewhere within the universe of genetic possibilities presented by the species *Solanum tuberosum*. And though that universe may be vast, it is not infinite. Since unrelated species in nature cannot be crossed, the breeder's art has always run up against a natural limit of what a potato is willing, or able, to do—that species' essential identity. Nature has always exercised a kind of veto over what culture can do with a potato.

20   Until now. The NewLeaf is the first potato to override that veto. Monsanto likes to depict genetic engineering as just one more chapter in the ancient history of human modifications of nature, a story going back to the discovery of fermentation. The company defines the word *biotechnology* so broadly as to take in the brewing of beer, cheese making, and selective breeding: all are "technologies" that involve the manipulation of life-forms.

21   Yet this new biotechnology has overthrown the old rules governing the relationship of nature and culture in a plant. Domestication has never been a simple one-way process in which our species has controlled others; other species participate only so far as their interests are served, and many plants (such as the oak) simply sit the whole game out. That game is the one Darwin called "artificial selection," and its rules have never been any different from the rules that govern natural selection. The plant in its wildness proposes new qualities, and then man (or, in the case of natural selection, nature) selects which of those qualities will survive and prosper. But about one rule Darwin was emphatic; as he wrote in *The Origin of Species*, "Man does not actually produce variability."

Now he does. For the first time, breeders can bring qualities at will   22
from anywhere in nature into the genome of a plant: from fireflies (the
quality of luminescence), from flounders (frost tolerance), from viruses
(disease resistance), and, in the case of my potatoes, from the soil bacterium known as *Bacillus thuringiensis*. Never in a million years of natural or
artificial selection would these species have proposed those qualities.
"Modification by descent" has been replaced by . . . something else.

Now, it is true that genes occasionally move between species; the   23
genome of many species appears to be somewhat more fluid than scientists used to think. Yet for reasons we don't completely understand,
distinct species do exist in nature, and they exhibit a certain genetic integrity—sex between them, when it does occur, doesn't produce fertile
offspring. Nature presumably has some reason for erecting these walls,
even if they are permeable on occasion. Perhaps, as some biologists believe, the purpose of keeping species separate is to put barriers in the
path of pathogens, to contain their damage so that a single germ can't
wipe out life on Earth at a stroke.

The deliberate introduction into a plant of genes transported not   24
only across species but across whole phyla means that the wall of that
plant's essential identity—its irreducible wildness, you might say—has
been breached, not by a virus, as sometimes happens in nature, but by
humans wielding powerful new tools.

For the first time the genome itself is being domesticated—brought   25
under the roof of human culture. This made the potato I was growing
slightly different from the other plants in this book, all of which had
been both the subjects and the objects of domestication. While the other
plants coevolved in a kind of conversational give-and-take with people, the NewLeaf potato has really only taken, only listened. It may or
may not profit from the gift of its new genes; we can't yet say. What we
can say, though, is that this potato is not the hero of its own story in
quite the same way the apple has been. It didn't come up with this Bt
scheme all on its evolutionary own. No, the heroes of the NewLeaf
story are scientists working for Monsanto. Certainly the scientists in
the lab coats have something in common with the fellow in the coffee
sack: both work, or worked, at disseminating plant genes around the
world. Yet although Johnny Appleseed and the brewers of beer and
makers of cheese, the high-tech pot growers and all the other "biotech-
nologists" manipulated, selected, forced, cloned, and otherwise altered
the species they worked with, the species themselves never lost their
evolutionary say in the matter—never became solely the objects of our
desires. Now the once irreducible wildness of these plants has
been . . . reduced. Whether this is a good or bad thing for the plants (or
for us), it is unquestionably a *new* thing.

What is perhaps most striking about the NewLeafs coming up in   26
my garden is the added human intelligence that the insertion of the

Bacillus thuringiensis gene represents. In the past that intelligence resided outside the plant, in the minds of the organic farmers and gardeners (myself included) who used Bt, commonly in the form of a spray, to manipulate the ecological relationship between certain insects and a certain bacterium in order to foil those insects. The irony about the new Bt crops (a similar gene has been inserted into corn plants) is that the cultural information they encode happens to be knowledge that's always resided in the heads of the very sorts of people—that is, organic growers—who most distrust high technology. Most of the other biotech crops—such as the ones Monsanto has engineered to withstand Roundup, the company's patented herbicide—encode a very different, more industrial sort of intelligence.

27   One way to look at genetic engineering is that it allows a larger portion of human culture and intelligence to be incorporated into the plants themselves. From this perspective, my NewLeafs are just plain smarter than the rest of my potatoes. The others will depend on my knowledge and experience when the Colorado potato beetles strike. The NewLeafs, already knowing what I know about bugs and Bt, will take care of themselves. So while my genetically engineered plants might at first seem like alien beings, that's not quite right; they're more like us than other plants because there's more of us in them.

RESPONDING TO READING

1. How is growing the NewLeaf potatoes different for Pollan than any other experiment he has attempted in his garden? Why does this particular experiment make him uneasy?

2. How does Pollan's garden—with its crop of NewLeaf potatoes—become part of his argument about human beings and their relationship to nature? What metaphor makes this argument work?

3. Discuss with classmates the ways in which Pollan links changes in farming and growing to dangerous changes in the relationship of humans to nature, particularly to the food chain. Do these links make his argument convincing? Are there other examples of such dangerous links that Pollan does not address? Either as an individual or as a group, write an essay on this topic addressed to people who either favor or disapprove of genetic engineering.

4. How does Pollan "read" potatoes as a means of discussing cultural differences between various groups of people? In an essay—for (pick one) anthropologists, cooks, or people from a culture different from yours—identify three or four foods (or dishes) typical of your culture, and "read" these for your audience. What do they reveal about your culture's values? geography? holidays or other occasions (even ordinary days) on which they are conventionally eaten?

How Can We Explain What We Know?

The Route to Normal Science

THOMAS S. KUHN

Thomas S. Kuhn (1922–96), who earned a doctorate in physics from Harvard University in 1949, taught at Harvard (1948–56); the University of California, Berkeley (1958–64); Princeton (1964–79); and the Massachusetts Institute of Technology (1979–91). As a professor of philosophy and history of science, Kuhn has studied the ways scientists think and work from a philosophical and humanistic perspective. Although he is the author of works ranging from *The Copernican Revolution: Planetary Astronomy in the Development of Western Thought* (1957) to *The Essential Tension* (1977), Kuhn is best known to readers outside the sciences for *The Structure of Scientific Revolutions* (1962), which includes "The Route to Normal Science." Since its first publication, this work has been translated into twenty-five languages and has sold more than one million copies in English alone.

Kuhn begins "The Route to Normal Science" by defining paradigms—structures or patterns that allow scientists to share a common set of assumptions, theories, laws, or applications as they look at their fields. If their research is based on shared paradigms and they "learned the bases of their field from the same concrete models," they are "committed to the same rules and standards for scientific practice" and do not disagree over the fundamentals. Kuhn devotes the rest of the essay to explaining how and why this is so. The concepts of "paradigm" and "paradigm shift" have become central, economical ways to conceptualize not only how scientists think and work (the focus of Kuhn's examples), but how knowledge is created and transmitted in a variety of fields.

In this essay, "normal science" means research firmly based upon one or more past scientific achievements, achievements that some particular scientific community acknowledges for a time as supplying the foundation for its further practice. Today such achievements are recounted, though seldom in their original form, by science textbooks, elementary and advanced. These textbooks expound the body of accepted theory, illustrate many or all of its successful applications, and compare these applications with exemplary observations and experiments. Before such books became popular early in the nineteenth century (and until even more recently in the newly matured sciences), many of the famous classics of science fulfilled a similar function. Aristotle's *Physica*, Ptolemy's *Almagest*, Newton's *Principia* and *Opticks*,

1

Franklin's *Electricity*, Lavoisier's *Chemistry*, and Lyell's *Geology*—these and many other works served for a time implicitly to define the legitimate problems and methods of a research field for succeeding generations of practitioners. They were able to do so because they shared two essential characteristics. Their achievement was sufficiently unprecedented to attract an enduring group of adherents away from competing modes of scientific activity. Simultaneously, it was sufficiently open-ended to leave all sorts of problems for the redefined group of practitioners to resolve.

2   Achievements that share these two characteristics I shall henceforth refer to as "paradigms," a term that relates closely to "normal science." By choosing it, I mean to suggest that some accepted examples of actual scientific practice—examples which include law, theory, application, and instrumentation together—provide models from which spring particular coherent traditions of scientific research. These are the traditions which the historian describes under such rubrics as "Ptolemaic astronomy" (or "Copernican"), "Aristotelian dynamics" (or "Newtonian"), "corpuscular optics" (or "wave optics"), and so on. The study of paradigms, including many that are far more specialized than those named illustratively above, is what mainly prepares the student for membership in the particular scientific community with which he will later practice. Because he there joins men who learned the bases of their field from the same concrete models, his subsequent practice will seldom evoke overt disagreement over fundamentals. Men whose research is based on shared paradigms are committed to the same rules and standards for scientific practice. That commitment and the apparent consensus it produces are prerequisites for normal science, i.e., for the genesis and continuation of a particular research tradition.

3   Because in this essay the concept of a paradigm will often substitute for a variety of familiar notions, more will need to be said about the reasons for its introduction. Why is the concrete scientific achievement, as a locus of professional commitment, prior to the various concepts, laws, theories, and points of view that may be abstracted from it? In what sense is the shared paradigm a fundamental unit for the student of scientific development, a unit that cannot be fully reduced to logically atomic components which might function in its stead? There can be a sort of scientific research without paradigms, or at least without any so unequivocal and so binding as the ones named above. Acquisition of a paradigm and of the more esoteric type of research it permits is a sign of maturity in the development of any given scientific field.

4   If the historian traces the scientific knowledge of any selected group of related phenomena backward in time, he is likely to encounter some minor variant of a pattern here illustrated from the history of physical optics. Today's physics textbooks tell the student that

light is photons, i.e., quantum-mechanical entities that exhibit some characteristics of waves and some of particles. Research proceeds accordingly, or rather according to the more elaborate and mathematical characterization from which this usual verbalization is derived. That characterization of light is, however, scarely half a century old. Before it was developed by Planck, Einstein, and others early in this century, physics texts taught that light was transverse wave motion, a conception rooted in a paradigm that derived ultimately from the optical writings of Young and Fresnel in the early nineteenth century. Nor was the wave theory the first to be embraced by almost all practitioners of optical science. During the eighteenth century the paradigm for this field was provided by Newton's *Opticks*, which taught that light was material corpuscles. At that time physicists sought evidence, as the early wave theorists had not, of the pressure exerted by light particles impinging on solid bodies.

These transformations of the paradigms of physical optics are sci-   5
entific revolutions, and the successive transition from one paradigm to another via revolution is the usual developmental pattern of mature science. It is not, however, the pattern characteristic of the period before Newton's work, and that is the contrast that concerns us here. No period between remote antiquity and the end of the seventeenth century exhibited a single generally accepted view about the nature of light. Instead there were a number of competing schools and subschools, most of them espousing one variant or another of Epicurean, Aristotelian, or Platonic theory. One group took light to be particles emanating from material bodies; for another it was a modification of the medium that intervened between the body and the eye; still another explained light in terms of an interaction of the medium with an emanation from the eye; and there were other combinations and modifications besides. Each of the corresponding schools derived strength from its relation to some particular metaphysic, and each emphasized, as paradigmatic observations, the particular cluster of optical phenomena that its own theory could do most to explain. Other observations were dealt with by *ad hoc* elaborations, or they remained as outstanding problems for further research.

At various times all these schools made significant contributions to   6
the body of concepts, phenomena, and techniques from which Newton drew the first nearly uniformly accepted paradigm for physical optics. Any definition of the scientist that excludes at least the more creative members of these various schools will exclude their modern successors as well. Those men were scientists. Yet anyone examining a survey of physical optics before Newton may well conclude that, though the field's practitioners were scientists, the net result of their activity was something less than science. Being able to take no common body of belief for granted, each writer on physical optics felt forced to build his

field anew from its foundations. In doing so, his choice of supporting observation and experiment was relatively free, for there was no standard set of methods or of phenomena that every optical writer felt forced to employ and explain. Under these circumstances, the dialogue of the resulting books was often directed as much to the members of other schools as it was to nature. That pattern is not unfamiliar in a number of creative fields today, nor is it incompatible with significant discovery and invention. It is not, however, the pattern of development that physical optics acquired after Newton and that other natural sciences make familiar today.

7   The history of electrical research in the first half of the eighteenth century provides a more concrete and better known example of the way a science develops before it acquires its first universally received paradigm. During that period there were almost as many views about the nature of electricity as there were important electrician experimenters, men like Haukshee, Gray, Desaguliers, Du Fay, Nollett, Watson, Franklin, and others. All their numerous concepts of electricity had something in common—they were partially derived from one or another version of the mechanico-corpuscular philosophy that guided all scientific research of the day. In addition, all were components of real scientific theories, of theories that had been drawn in part from experiment and observation that partially determined the choice and interpretation of additional problems undertaken in research. Yet though all the experiments were electrical and though most of the experimenters read each other's works, their theories had no more than a family resemblance.

8   One early group of theories, following seventeenth-century practice, regarded attraction and frictional generation as the fundamental electrical phenomena. This group tended to treat repulsion as a secondary effect due to some sort of mechanical rebounding and also to postpone for as long as possible both discussion and systematic research on Gray's newly discovered effect, electrical conduction. Other "electricians" (the term is their own) took attraction and repulsion to be equally elementary manifestations of electricity and modified their theories and research accordingly. (Actually, this group is remarkably small—even Franklin's theory never quite accounted for the mutual repulsion of two negatively charged bodies.) But they had as much difficulty as the first group in accounting simultaneously for any but the simplest conduction effects. Those effects, however, provided the starting point for still a third group, one which tended to speak of electricity as a "fluid" that could run through conductors rather than as an "effluvium" that emanated from non-conductors. This group, in its turn, had difficulty reconciling its theory with a number of attractive and repulsive effects. Only through the work of Franklin and his im-

mediate successors did a theory arise that could account with something like equal facility for very nearly all these effects and that therefore could and did provide a subsequent generation of "electricians" with a common paradigm for its research.

Excluding those fields, like mathematics and astronomy, in which   9 the first firm paradigms date from prehistory and also those, like biochemistry, that arose by division and recombination of specialties already matured, the situations outlined above are historically typical. Though it involves my continuing to employ the unfortunate simplification that tags an extended historical episode with a single and somewhat arbitrarily chosen name (e.g., Newton or Franklin), I suggest that similar fundamental disagreements characterized, for example, the study of motion before Aristotle and of statics before Archimedes, the study of heat before Black, of chemistry before Boyle and Boerhaave, and of historical geology before Hutton. In parts of biology—the study of heredity, for example—the first universally received paradigms are still more recent; and it remains an open question what parts of social science have yet acquired such paradigms at all. History suggests that the road to a firm research consensus is extraordinarily arduous.

History also suggests, however, some reasons for the difficulties   10 encountered on the road. In the absence of a paradigm or some candidate for paradigm, all of the facts that could possibly pertain to the development of a given science are likely to seem equally relevant. As a result, early fact-gathering is a far more nearly random activity than the one that subsequent scientific development makes familiar. Furthermore, in the absence of a reason for seeking some particular form of more recondite information, early fact-gathering is usually restricted to the wealth of data that lie ready to hand. The resulting pool of facts contains those accessible to casual observation and experiment together with some of the more esoteric data retrievable from established crafts like medicine, calendar making, and metallurgy. Because the crafts are one readily accessible source of facts that could not have been casually discovered, technology has often played a vital role in the emergence of new sciences.

But though this sort of fact-collecting has been essential to the   11 origin of many significant sciences, anyone who examines, for example, Pliny's encyclopedic writings or the Baconian natural histories of the seventeenth century will discover that it produces a morass. One somehow hesitates to call the literature that results scientific. The Baconian "histories" of heat, color, wind, mining, and so on, are filled with information, some of it recondite. But they juxtapose facts that will later prove revealing (e.g., heating by mixture) with others (e.g., the warmth of dung heaps) that will for some time remain too complex to be integrated with theory at all. In addition, since any description must be partial, the typical natural history often omits from its immensely circumstantial accounts just those details that later scientists will find sources of important illumination. Almost none of the early "histories" of electricity, for example, mention that chaff, attracted to a rubbed glass rod, bounces off again. That effect seemed mechanical, not electrical. Moreover, since the casual fact-gatherer seldom possesses the time or the tools to be critical, the natural histories often juxtapose descriptions like the above with others, say, heating by antiperistasis (or by cooling), that we are now quite unable to confirm.[1] Only very occasionally, as in the cases of ancient statics, dynamics, and geometrical optics, do facts collected with so little guidance from pre-established theory speak with sufficient clarity to permit the emergence of a first paradigm.

12   This is the situation that creates the schools characteristic of the early stages of a science's development. No natural history can be interpreted in the absence of at least some implicit body of intertwined theoretical and methodological belief that permits selection, evaluation, and criticism. If that body of belief is not already implicit in the collection of facts—in which case more than "mere facts" are at hand—it must be externally supplied, perhaps by a current metaphysic, by another science, or by personal and historical accident. No wonder, then, that in the early stages of the development of any science different men confronting the same range of phenomena, but not usually all the same particular phenomena, describe and interpret them in different ways. What is surprising, and perhaps also unique in its degree to the fields we call science, is that such initial divergences should ever largely disappear.

13   For they do disappear to a very considerable extent and then apparently once and for all. Furthermore, their disappearance is usually caused by the triumph of one of the pre-paradigm schools, which, because of its own characteristic beliefs and pre-conceptions, emphasized only some special part of the too sizable and inchoate pool of information. Those electricians who thought electricity a fluid and therefore gave particular emphasis to conduction provide an excellent case in point. Led by this belief, which could scarcely cope with the known multiplicity of attractive and repulsive effects, several of them conceived the idea of bottling the electrical fluid. The immediate fruit of their efforts was the Leyden jar, a device which might never have been discovered by a man exploring nature casually or at random, but which was in fact independently developed by at least two investiga-

---

[1]Bacon [in the *Novum Organum*] says, "Water slightly warm is more easily frozen than quite cold"; *antiperistasis*: means a reaction caused by an opposite action, in this case, heating by means of cooling. [Eds.]

tors in the early 1740's. Almost from the start of his electrical research-es, Franklin was particularly concerned to explain that strange and, in the event, particularly revealing piece of special apparatus. His success in doing so provided the most effective of the arguments that made his theory a paradigm, though one that was still unable to account for quite all the known cases of electrical repulsion.[2] To be accepted as a paradigm, a theory must seem better than its competitors, but it need not, and in fact never does, explain all the facts with which it can be confronted.

What the fluid theory of electricity did for the subgroup that held   14 it, the Franklinian paradigm later did for the entire group of electri-cians. It suggested which experiments would be worth performing and which, because directed to secondary or to overly complex manifesta-tions of electricity, would not. Only the paradigm did the job far more effectively, partly because the end of interschool debate ended the con-stant reiteration of fundamentals and partly because the confidence that they were on the right track encouraged scientists to undertake more precise, esoteric, and consuming sorts of work.[3] Freed from the concern with any and all electrical phenomena, the united group of electricians could pursue selected phenomena in far more detail, de-signing much special equipment for the task and employing it more stubbornly and systematically than electricians had ever done before. Both fact collection and theory articulation became highly directed ac-tivities. The effectiveness and efficiency of electrical research increased accordingly, providing evidence for a societal version of Francis Bacon's acute methodological dictum: "Truth emerges more readily from error than from confusion."

We shall be examining the nature of this highly directed or para-   15 digm-based research in the next section, but must first note briefly how the emergence of a paradigm affects the structure of the group that practices the field. When, in the development of a natural sci-ence, an individual or group first produces a synthesis able to attract most of the next generation's practitioners, the older schools gradual-

---

[2]The troublesome case was the mutual repulsion of negatively charged bodies.

[3]It should be noted that the acceptance of Franklin's theory did not end quite all debate. In 1759 Robert Symmer proposed a two-fluid version of that theory, and for many years thereafter electricians were divided about whether electricity was a single fluid or two. But the debates on this subject only confirm what has been said above about the manner in which a universally recognized achievement unites the profession. Electri-cians, though they continued divided on this point, rapidly concluded that no experi-mental tests could distinguish the two versions of the theory and that they were therefore equivalent. After that, both schools could and did exploit all the benefits that the Franklinian theory provided.

ly disappear. In part their disappearance is caused by their members' conversion to the new paradigm. But there are always some men who cling to one or another of the older views, and they are simply read out of the profession, which thereafter ignores their work. The new paradigm implies a new and more rigid definition of the field. Those unwilling or unable to accommodate their work to it must proceed in isolation or attach themselves to some other group.[4] Historically, they have often simply stayed in the departments of philosophy from which so many of the special sciences have been spawned. As these indications hint, it is sometimes just its reception of a paradigm that transforms a group previously interested merely in the study of nature into a profession or, at least, a discipline. In the sciences (though not in fields like medicine, technology, and law, of which the principal *raison d'être* is an external social need), the formation of specialized journals, the foundation of specialists' societies, and the claim for a special place in the curriculum have usually been associated with a group's first reception of a single paradigm. At least this was the case between the time, a century and a half ago, when the institutional pattern of scientific specialization first developed and the very recent time when the paraphernalia of specialization acquired a prestige of their own.

16   The more rigid definition of the scientific group has other consequences. When the individual scientist can take a paradigm for granted, he need no longer, in his major works, attempt to build his field anew, starting from first principles and justifying the use of each concept introduced. That can be left to the writer of textbooks. Given a textbook, however, the creative scientist can begin his research where it leaves off and thus concentrate exclusively upon the subtlest and most esoteric aspects of the natural phenomena that concern his group. And as he does this, his research communiqués will begin to change in ways whose evolution has been too little studied but whose modern end products are obvious to all and oppressive to many. No longer will his researchers usually be embodied in books addressed, like Franklin's *Experiments ... on Electricity* or Darwin's *Origin of Species*, to anyone

---

[4]The history of electricity provides an excellent example which could be duplicated from the careers of Priestley, Kelvin, and others. Franklin reports that Nollet, who at mid-century was the most influential of the Continental electricians, "lived to see himself the last of his Sect, except Mr. B.—his *Eleve* [pupil] and immediate Disciple." More interesting, however, is the endurance of whole schools in increasing isolation from professional science. Consider, for example, the case of astrology, which was once an integral part of astronomy. Or consider the continuation in the eighteenth, and early nineteenth centuries of a previously respected tradition of "romantic" chemistry. . . .

who might be interested in the subject matter of the field. Instead they will usually appear as brief articles addressed only to professional colleagues, the men whose knowledge of a shared paradigm can be assumed and who prove to be the only ones able to read the papers addressed to them.

Today in the sciences, books are usually either texts or retrospective reflections upon one aspect or another of the scientific life. The   17
scientist who writes one is more likely to find his professional reputation impaired than enhanced. Only in the earlier, pre-paradigm, stages of the development of the various sciences did the book ordinarily possess the same relation to professional achievement that it still retains in other creative fields. And only in those fields that still retain the book, with or without the article, as a vehicle for research communication are the lines of professionalization still so loosely drawn that the layman may hope to follow progress by reading the practitioners' original reports. Both in mathematics and astronomy, research reports had ceased already in antiquity to be intelligible to a generally educated audience. In dynamics, research became similarly esoteric in the latter Middle Ages, and it recaptured general intelligibility only briefly during the early seventeenth century when a new paradigm replaced the one that had guided medieval research. Electrical research began to require translation for the layman before the end of the eighteenth century, and most other fields of physical science ceased to be generally accessible in the nineteenth. During the same two centuries similar transitions can be isolated in the various parts of the biological sciences. In parts of the social sciences they may well be occurring today. Although it has become customary, and is surely proper, to deplore the widening gulf that separates the professional scientist from his colleagues in other fields, too little attention is paid to the essential relationship between that gulf and the mechanisms intrinsic to scientific advance.

Ever since prehistoric antiquity one field of study after another has   18
crossed the divide between what the historian might call its prehistory as a science and its history proper. These transitions to maturity have seldom been so sudden or so unequivocal as my necessarily schematic discussion may have implied. But neither have they been historically gradual, coextensive, that is to say, with the entire development of the fields within which they occurred. Writers on electricity during the first four decades of the eighteenth century possessed far more information about electrical phenomena than had their sixteenth-century predecessors. During the half-century after 1740, few new sorts of electrical phenomena were added to their lists. Nevertheless, in important respects, the electrical writings of Cavendish, Coulomb, and Volta in the last

third of the eighteenth century seem further removed from those of Gray, Du Fay, and even Franklin than are the writings of these early eighteenth-century electrical discoverers from those of the sixteenth century.[5] Sometime between 1740 and 1780, electricians were for the first time enabled to take the foundations of their field for granted. From that point they pushed on to more concrete and recondite problems, and increasingly they then reported their results in articles addressed to other electricians rather than in books addressed to the learned world at large. As a group they achieved what had been gained by astronomers in antiquity and by students of motion in the Middle Ages, of physical optics in the late seventeenth century, and of historical geology in the early nineteenth. They had, that is, achieved a paradigm that proved able to guide the whole group's research. Except with the advantage of hindsight, it is hard to find another criterion that so clearly proclaims a field a science.

RESPONDING TO READING

1. What is "normal science" (paragraph 1 and elsewhere), or by analogy, any other "normal" academic discipline? What is the relation of "paradigm" to "normal science" (paragraph 2 and elsewhere)?

2. Why don't textbooks make revolutionary breakthroughs in their presentation of the knowledge of the discipline they represent? Who reads textbooks? Who reads the cutting-edge articles or books? What use(s) do their respective readers make of the material they encounter?

3. Every field is full of disagreements and conflicting ways of interpreting and configuring the knowledge of its subject. For instance, critics read literature from a variety of perspectives—Freudian, Marxian, historical, feminist, moral, and many more. How can you, as the reader of a textbook, identify the authors' prevailing interpretation of the subject matter?

4. How can you decide which of a number of alternative, possibly conflicting, interpretations of a topic within a discipline is right? (For instance, some American historians see the white settlement of the West as fulfillment of America's "manifest destiny;" others interpret white settlement as exploitation of the Native American population. Who's right? See Frances FitzGerald, "America Revised,"in Chapter 5.)

5. How do you (or students in general) know when you know enough to disagree with what you read?

---

[5]The post-Franklinian developments include an immense increase in the sensitivity of charge detectors, the first reliable and generally diffused techniques for measuring charge, the evolution of the concept of capacity and its relation to a newly refined notion of electric tension, and the quantification of electrostatic force. . . .

2.3.2 *Conversational Styles*

DEBORAH TANNEN

Deborah Tannen was born in Brooklyn (1945) and had decided on a career in literature, but after graduating from SUNY Binghamton (B.A., 1966) and doing graduate work at Wayne State University (M.A., 1970), she became intrigued by a different field. While working on creative writing projects and teaching English in Greece, she became fascinated by interpersonal communication. She pursued an advanced degree in linguistics at Berkeley (Ph.D., 1979), and is currently a professor of linguistics at Georgetown. Her studies of the way verbal interactions structure relationships are read by both academic and general audiences. *That's Not What I Meant* (1986) looked at the effects of gender, power, and status on communication; *You Just Don't Understand: Women and Men in Conversation* (1990) focused primarily on gender. More recently she has examined discourse within institutions: *Talking from 9 to 5* (1994) looks at the language of the workplace, particularly in relation to "glass ceiling" issues—hidden barriers that prevent women from being promoted. In *The Argument Culture: Moving from Debate to Dialogue* (1998), Tannen questions whether our public discussions can move beyond "either/or" "win/lose" antagonistic models to a more cooperative and enlightening level. (See "The Roots of Debate" in Chapter 4.) *I Only Say This Because I Love You* (2001) is about communication within the family.

During her research, Tannen took a look at the setting in which much of her own conversations took place: the classroom. She concluded that academic discussions were affected by the same gender dynamics as in the other areas of the culture. In "Conversational Styles," published in the *Chronicle of Higher Education* (1991), she asserts that male and female students operate from different assumptions about debate and discussion. Gender influences not only who will speak in class, but also what they will say.

When I researched and wrote my latest book, *You just Don't Understand: Women and Men in Conversation,* the furthest thing from my mind was reevaluating my teaching strategies. But that has been one of the direct benefits of having written the book.   1

The primary focus of my linguistic research always has been the language of everyday conversation. One facet of this is conversational style: how different regional, ethnic, and class backgrounds, as well as age and gender, result in different ways of using language to communicate. *You Just Don't Understand* is about the conversational styles of women and men. As I gained more insight into typically male and female ways of using language, I began to suspect some of the causes of the troubling facts that women who go to single-sex schools do better in later life, and that when young women sit next to young men in classrooms, the males talk more. This is not to say that all men talk   2 in class, nor that no women do. It is simply that a greater percentage of discussion time is taken by men's voices.

3   The research of sociologists and anthropologists such as Janet Lever, Marjorie Harness Goodwin, and Donna Eder has shown that girls and boys learn to use language differently in their sex-separate peer groups. Typically, a girl has a best friend with whom she sits and talks, frequently telling secrets. It's the telling of secrets, the fact and the way that they talk to each other, that makes them best friends. For boys, activities are central: Their best friends are the ones they do things with. Boys also tend to play in larger groups that are hierarchical. High-status boys give orders and push low-status boys around. So boys are expected to use language to seize center stage: by exhibiting their skill, displaying their knowledge, and challenging and resisting challenges.

4   These patterns have stunning implications for classroom interaction. Most faculty members assume that participating in class discussion is a necessary part of successful performance. Yet speaking in a classroom is more congenial to boys' language experience than to girls', since it entails putting oneself forward in front of a large group of people, many of whom are strangers and at least one of whom is sure to judge speakers' knowledge and intelligence by their verbal display.

5   Another aspect of many classrooms that makes them more hospitable to most men than to most women is the use of debate-like formats as a learning tool. Our educational system, as Walter Ong argues persuasively in his book *Fighting for Life* (Cornell University Press, 1981), is fundamentally male in that the pursuit of knowledge is believed to be achieved by ritual opposition: public display followed by argument and challenge. Father Ong demonstrates that ritual opposition—what he calls "adversativeness" or "agonism"—is fundamental to the way most males approach almost any activity. (Consider, for example, the little boy who shows he likes a little girl by pulling her braids and shoving her.) But ritual opposition is antithetical to the way most females learn and like to interact. It is not that females don't fight, but that they don't fight for fun. They don't *ritualize* opposition.

6   Anthropologists working in widely disparate parts of the world have found contrasting verbal rituals for women and men. Women in completely unrelated cultures (for example, Greece and Bali) engage in ritual laments: spontaneously produced rhyming couplets that express their pain, for example, over the loss of loved ones. Men do not take part in laments. They have their own, very different verbal ritual: a contest, a war of words in which they vie with each other to devise clever insults.

7   When discussing these phenomena with a colleague, I commented that I see these two styles in American conversation: Many women bond by talking about troubles, and many men bond by exchanging

playful insults and put-downs, and other sorts of verbal sparring. He exclaimed: "I never thought of this, but that's the way I teach: I have students read an article, and then I invite them to tear it apart. After we've torn it to shreds, we talk about how to build a better model."

This contrasts sharply with the way I teach: I open the discussion   8
of readings by asking, "What did you find useful in this? What can we use in our own theory building and our own methods?" I note what I see as weaknesses in the author's approach, but I also point out that the writer's discipline and purposes might be different from ours. Finally, I offer personal anecdotes illustrating the phenomena under discussion and praise students' anecdotes as well as their critical acumen.

These different teaching styles must make our classrooms wildly   9
different places and hospitable to different students. Male students are more likely to be comfortable attacking the readings and might find the inclusion of personal anecdotes irrelevant and "soft." Women are more likely to resist discussion they perceive as hostile, and, indeed, it is women in my classes who are most likely to offer personal anecdotes.

A colleague who read my book commented that he had always   10
taken for granted that the best way to deal with students' comments is to challenge them; this, he felt it was self-evident, sharpens their minds and helps them develop debating skills. But he had noticed that women were relatively silent in his classes, so he decided to try beginning discussion with relatively open-ended questions and letting comments go unchallenged. He found, to his amazement and satisfaction, that more women began to speak up.

Though some of the women in his class clearly liked this better, per-   11
haps some of the men liked it less. One young man in my class wrote in a questionnaire about a history professor who gave students questions to think about and called on people to answer them: "He would then play devil's advocate . . . *i.e.,* he debated us. . . . That class *really* sharpened me intellectually. . . . We as students do need to know how to defend ourselves." This young man valued the experience of being attacked and challenged publicly. Many, if not most, women would shrink from such "challenge," experiencing it as public humiliation.

A professor at Hamilton College told me of a young man who was   12
upset because he felt his class presentation had been a failure. The professor was puzzled because he had observed that class members had listened attentively and agreed with the student's observations. It turned out that it was this very agreement that the student interpreted as failure: Since no one had engaged his ideas by arguing with him, he felt they had found them unworthy of attention.

So one reason men speak in class more than women is that many of   13
them find the "public" classroom setting more conducive to speaking, whereas most women are more comfortable speaking in private to a

small group of people they know well. A second reason is that men are more likely to be comfortable with the debate-like form that discussion may take. Yet another reason is the different attitudes toward speaking in class that typify women and men.

14   Students who speak frequently in class, many of whom are men, assume that it is their job to think of contributions and try to get the floor to express them. But many women monitor their participation not only to get the floor but to avoid getting it. Women students in my class tell me that if they have spoken up once or twice, they hold back for the rest of the class because they don't want to dominate. If they have spoken a lot one week, they will remain silent the next. These different ethics of participation are, of course, unstated, so those who speak freely assume that those who remain silent have nothing to say, and those who are reining themselves in assume that the big talkers are selfish and hoggish.

15   When I looked around my classes, I could see these differing ethics and habits at work. For example, my graduate class in analyzing conversation had 20 students, 11 women and 9 men. Of the men, four were foreign students: two Japanese, one Chinese, and one Syrian. With the exception of the three Asian men, all the men spoke in class at least occasionally. The biggest talker in the class was a woman, but there were also five women who never spoke at all, only one of whom was Japanese. I decided to try something different.

16   I broke the class into small groups to discuss the issues raised in the readings and to analyze their own conversational transcripts. I devised three ways of dividing the students into groups: one by the degree program they were in, one by gender, and one by conversational style, as closely as I could guess it. This meant that when the class was grouped according to conversational style, I put Asian students together, fast talkers together, and quiet students together. The class split into groups six times during the semester, so they met in each grouping twice. I told students to regard the groups as examples of interactional data and to note the different ways they participated in the different groups. Toward the end of the term, I gave them a questionnaire asking about their class and group participation.

17   I could see plainly from my observation of the groups at work that women who never opened their mouths in class were talking away in the small groups. In fact, the Japanese woman commented that she found it particularly hard to contribute to the all-woman group she was in because "I was overwhelmed by how talkative the female students were in the female-only group." This is particularly revealing because it highlights that the same person who can be "oppressed" into silence in one context can become the talkative "oppressor" in another. No one's conversational style is absolute; everyone's style changes in response to the context and others' styles.

Some of the students (seven) said they preferred the same-gender   18
groups; others preferred the same-style groups. In answer to the question "Would you have liked to speak in class more than you did?" six of
the seven who said Yes were women; the one man was Japanese. Most
startlingly, this response did not come only from quiet women; it came
from women who had indicated they had spoken in class never, rarely,
sometimes, and often. Of the 11 students who said the amount they
had spoken was fine, 7 were men. Of the four women who checked
"fine," two added qualifications indicating it wasn't completely fine:
One wrote in "maybe more," and one wrote, "I have an urge to participate but often feel I should have something more interesting/relevant/
wonderful/intelligent to say!!"

I counted my experiment a success. Everyone in the class found the   19
small groups interesting, and no one indicated he or she would have
preferred that the class not break into groups. Perhaps most instructive,
however, was the fact that the experience of breaking into groups, and
of talking about participation in class, raised everyone's awareness
about classroom participation. After we had talked about it, some of
the quietest women in the class made a few voluntary contributions,
though sometimes I had to insure their participation by interrupting
the students who were exuberantly speaking out.

Americans are often proud that they discount the significance of   20
cultural differences: "We are all individuals," many people boast. Ig-
noring such issues as gender and ethnicity becomes a source of pride:
"I treat everyone the same." But treating people the same is not equal
treatment if they are not the same.

The classroom is a different environment for those who feel com-   21
fortable putting themselves forward in a group than it is for those who
find the prospect of doing so chastening, or even terrifying. When a
professor asks, "Are there any questions?," students who can formulate statements the fastest have the greatest opportunity to respond.
Those who need significant time to do so have not really been given a
chance at all, since by the time they are ready to speak, someone else
has the floor.

In a class where some students speak out without raising hands,   22
those who feel they must raise their hands and wait to be recognized
do not have equal opportunity to speak. Telling them to feel free to
jump in will not make them feel free; one's sense of timing, of one's
rights and obligations in a classroom, are automatic, learned over years
of interaction. They may be changed over time, with motivation and effort, but they cannot be changed on the spot. And everyone assumes
his or her own way is best. When I asked my students how the class
could be changed to make it easier for them to speak more, the most
talkative woman said she would prefer it if no one had to raise hands,

and a foreign student said he wished people would raise their hands and wait to be recognized.

23   My experience in this class has convinced me that small-group interaction should be part of any class that is not a small seminar. I also am convinced that having the students become observers of their own interaction is a crucial part of their education. Talking about ways of talking in class makes students aware that their ways of talking affect other students, that the motivations they impute to others may not truly reflect others' motives, and that the behaviors they assume to be self-evidently right are not universal norms.

24   The goal of complete equal opportunity in class may not be attainable, but realizing that one monolithic classroom-participation structure is not equal opportunity is itself a powerful motivation to find more-diverse methods to serve diverse students—and every classroom is diverse.

RESPONDING TO READING

1. In paragraph 3, Tannen describes the ways in which young boys and girls use language differently. Do your own experiences in same-sex groups support or refute Tannen's observations?

2. Tannen argues, "It is not that females don't fight, but that they don't fight for fun." How does this argument connect with Tannen's belief that classrooms, and particularly class discussions, are more hospitable for men than for women?

3. Working with other students, describe your own conversation styles during class time. Does your style change from one class to another? What causes such changes? Where did each of you learn your pattern of conversational behavior for each of these classes?

4. In paragraph 13, Tannen summarizes her arguments about how men and women behave differently in classroom settings. Discuss these conclusions with a small group of fellow students, in two stages: The first group should be of the same sex as yourself. Then, summarize your group's discussion, and revisit these issues in a group that includes both men and women. What differences, if any, appear in the conclusions the group reaches? Are there significant differences in the style in which they conduct the discussion? Present your findings in a paper that supports or refutes Tannen's claims.

5. As you engage in informal conversations with different groups of people, observe both your behavior and that of the other participants. Do you behave the same way, conversationally, in same-sex groups? Do the other members behave as you do? How does this contrast with your behavior (and that of others) in gender-mixed conversation groups? In an essay, explain your observations and the conclusions you draw about the different behaviors that you see. If you've already participated in the discussion identified in Question 4, feel free to compare the conclusions reached in this classroom setting with behavior in more casual groups.

An American Indian Model of the Universe

BENJAMIN LEE WHORF

Benjamin Lee Whorf (1897–1941) had a hybrid career combining both business and linguistics, and although his premature death from cancer left much of his research unfinished, his ideas remain relevant to current debates about language and culture. He grew up in Winthrop, Massachusetts, earned a degree in chemical engineering from the Massachusetts Institute of Technology (B.S., 1918), and worked for the Hartford Fire Insurance Agency as a fire prevention inspector. Gifted with a powerful intellectual curiosity, Whorf devoted his off-hours to self-directed study. Seeking to reconcile his scientific background with his deeply felt Methodist religious beliefs, he undertook the study of Hebrew and investigated the biblical creation story. The project revealed that he had a talent for linguistics, and he went on to study Native American languages, tackling Mayan hieroglyphics in 1928 and corresponding with scholars in the field—including Edward Sapir, the most prominent American linguist of the period. When Sapir became chair of anthropology and linguistics at Yale, Whorf became a part-time graduate student there (1931–32). During leaves of absence from his insurance work, Whorf studied the Hopi language in Arizona and with a native speaker in New York City. He is best known today for his collaboration with Sapir; the Whorf–Sapir hypothesis—now highly controversial among contemporary linguists—argues that language structures the way a person perceives the world. Current versions of the theory include two basic varieties: The strong version argues that language rigidly locks people into the world-view of their culture, whereas the weak version views language as an influence, but not a determining one.

Whorf's articles and other writings were collected in the posthumous *Language, Thought, and Reality* (1956). "An American Indian Model of the Universe" maintains that the Hopi language embodies a world-view that varies significantly from the modern Western model, because its terms for fundamental ideas such as space and time are different. Translating back and forth between Hopi and English, Whorf argues that the Hopi language, from its basic vocabulary to its verb forms, refers to a different reality than ours.

I find it gratuitous to assume that a Hopi who knows only the Hopi 1 language and the cultural ideas of his own society has the same notions, often supposed to be intuitions, of time and space that we have, and that are generally assumed to be universal. In particular, he has no general notion or intuition of TIME as a smooth flowing continuum in which everything in the universe proceeds at an equal rate, out of a future, through a present, into a past; or, in which, to reverse the picture, the observer is being carried in the stream of duration continuously away from a past and into a future.

2   After long and careful study and analysis, the Hopi language is seen to contain no words, grammatical forms, constructions or expressions that refer directly to what we call "time," or to past, present, or future, or to enduring or lasting, or to motion as kinematic rather than dynamic (i.e., as a continuous translation in space and time rather than as an exhibition of dynamic effort in a certain process), or that even refer to space in such a way as to exclude that element of extension or existence that we call "time," and so by implication leave a residue that could be referred to as "time." Hence, the Hopi language contains no reference to "time," either explicit or implicit.

3   At the same time, the Hopi language is capable of accounting for and describing correctly, in a pragmatic or operational sense, all observable phenomena of the universe. Hence, I find it gratuitous to assume that Hopi thinking contains any such notion as the supposed intuitively felt flowing of "time," or that the intuition of a Hopi gives him this as one of its data. Just as it is possible to have any number of geometries other than the Euclidean[1] which give an equally perfect account of space configurations, so it is possible to have descriptions of the universe, all equally valid, that do not contain our familiar contrasts of time and space. The relativity viewpoint of modern physics is one such view, conceived in mathematical terms, and the Hopi Weltanschauung is another and quite different one, nonmathematical and linguistic.

4   Thus, the Hopi language and culture conceals a METAPHYSICS, such as our so-called naïve view of space and time does, or as the relativity theory does; yet it is a different metaphysics from either. In order to describe the structure of the universe according to the Hopi, it is necessary to attempt—insofar as it is possible—to make explicit this metaphysics, properly describable only in the Hopi language, by means of an approximation expressed in our own language, somewhat inadequately it is true, yet by availing ourselves of such concepts as we have worked up into relative consonance with the system underlying the Hopi view of the universe.

5   In this Hopi view, time disappears and space is altered, so that it is no longer the homogeneous and instantaneous timeless space of our supposed intuition or of classical Newtonian mechanics. At the same time, new concepts and abstractions flow into the picture, taking up the task of describing the universe without reference to such time or space—abstractions for which our language lacks adequate terms. These abstractions, by approximations of which we attempt to reconstruct for ourselves the metaphysics of the Hopi, will undoubtedly

---

[1]Euclid was a Greek mathematician who lived about 300 B.C. The geometry he developed is the one most commonly studied in North American schools.

appear to us as psychological or even mystical in character. They are ideas which we are accustomed to consider as part and parcel either of so-called animistic or vitalistic beliefs, or of those transcendental unifications of experience and intuitions of things unseen that are felt by the consciousness of the mystic, or which are given out in mystical and (or) so-called occult systems of thought. These abstractions are definitely given either explicitly in words—psychological or metaphysical terms—in the Hopi language, or, even more, are implicit in the very structure and grammar of that language, as well as being observable in Hopi culture and behavior. They are not, so far as I can consciously avoid it, projections of other systems upon the Hopi language and culture made by me in my attempt at an objective analysis. Yet, if MYSTICAL be perchance a term of abuse in the eyes of a modern Western scientist, it must be emphasized that these underlying abstractions and postulates of the Hopian metaphysics are, from a detached viewpoint, equally (or to the Hopi, more) justified pragmatically and experientially, as compared to the flowing time and static space of our own metaphysics, which are *au fond*[2] equally mystical. The Hopi postulates equally account for all phenomena and their interrelations, and lend themselves even better to the integration of Hopi culture in all its phases.

The metaphysics underlying our own language, thinking, and modern culture (I speak not of the recent and quite different relativity metaphysics of modern science) imposes upon the universe two grand COSMIC FORMS, space and time; static three-dimensional infinite space, and kinetic one-dimensional uniformly and perpetually flowing time—two utterly separate and unconnected aspects of reality (according to this familiar way of thinking). The flowing realm of time is, in turn, the subject of a threefold division: past, present, and future.   6

The Hopi metaphysics also has its cosmic forms comparable to these in scale and scope. What are they? It imposes upon the universe two grand cosmic forms, which as a first approximation in terminology we may call MANIFESTED and MANIFESTING (or, UNMANIFEST) or, again, OBJECTIVE and SUBJECTIVE. The objective or manifested comprises all that is or has been accessible to the senses, the historical physical universe, in fact, with no attempt to distinguish between present and past, but excluding everything that we call future. The subjective or manifesting comprises all that we call future, BUT NOT MERELY THIS; it includes equally and indistinguishably all that we call mental—everything that appears or exists in the mind, or, as the Hopi would prefer to say, in the HEART, not only the heart of man, but the heart of animals, plants, and things, and behind and within all the forms and appearances of nature in the heart of nature, and by an implication and extension which has been felt   7

---

[2]At bottom, fundamentally.

by more than one anthropologist, yet would hardly ever be spoken of by a Hopi himself, so charged is the idea with religious and magical awesomeness, in the very heart of the Cosmos, itself.[3] The subjective realm (subjective from our viewpoint, but intensely real and quivering with life, power, and potency to the Hopi) embraces not only our FUTURE, much of which the Hopi regards as more or less predestined in essence if not in exact form, but also all mentality, intellection, and emotion, the essence and typical form of which is the striving of purposeful desire, intelligent in character, toward manifestation—a manifestation which is much resisted and delayed, but in some form or other is inevitable. It is the realm of expectancy, of desire and purpose, of vitalizing life, of efficient causes, of thought thinking itself out from an inner realm (the Hopian HEART) into manifestation. It is in a dynamic state, yet not a state of motion—it is not advancing toward us out of a future, but ALREADY WITH US in vital and mental form, and its dynamism is at work in the field of eventuating or manifesting, i.e., evolving without motion from the subjective by degrees to a result which is the objective. In translating into English, the Hopi will say that these entities in process of causation "will come" or that they—the Hopi—"will come to" them, but, in their own language, there are no verbs corresponding to our "come" and "go" that mean simple and abstract motion, our purely kinematic concept. The words in this case translated "come" refer to the process of eventuating without calling it motion—they are "eventuates to here" (*pew'i*) or "eventuates from it" (*angqö*) or "arrived" (*pitu*, pl. *öki*) which refers only to the terminal manifestation, the actual arrival at a given point, not to any motion preceding it.

8   This realm of the subjective or of the process of manifestation, as distinguished from the objective, the result of this universal process, includes also—on its border but still pertaining to its own realm—an aspect of existence that we include in our present time. It is that which is beginning to emerge into manifestation; that is, something which is beginning to be done, like going to sleep or starting to write, but is not yet in full operation. This can be and usually is referred to by the same verb form (the EXPECTIVE form in my terminology of Hopi grammar) that refers to our future, or to wishing, wanting, intending, etc. Thus, this nearer edge of the subjective cuts across and includes a part of our present time, viz. the moment of inception, but most of our present belongs in the Hopi scheme to the objective realm and so is indistinguishable from our past. There is also a verb form, the INCEPTIVE which refers to this EDGE of emergent manifestation in the reverse

---

[3]This idea is sometimes alluded to as the "spirit of the Breath" (*hikwsu*) and as the "Mighty Something" (*?a?ne himu*), although these terms may have lower and less cosmic though always awesome connotations. [Whorf's note].

way—as belonging to the objective, as the edge at which objectivity is attained; this is used to indicate beginning or starting, and in most cases there is no difference apparent in the translation from the similar use of the expective. But, at certain crucial points, significant and fundamental differences appear. The inceptive, referring to the objective and result side, and not like the expective to the subjective and causal side, implies the ending of the work of causation in the same breath that it states the beginning of manifestation. If the verb has a suffix which answers somewhat to our passive, but really means that causation impinges upon a subject to effect a certain result—i.e. "the food is being eaten," then addition of the INCEPTIVE SUFFIX in such a way as to refer to the basic action produces a meaning of causal cessation. The basic action is in the inceptive state; hence whatever causation is behind it is ceasing; the causation explicitly referred to by the causal suffix is hence such as WE would call past time, and the verb includes this and the incepting and the decausating of the final state (a state of partial or total eatenness) in one statement. The translation is "it stops getting eaten." Without knowing the underlying Hopian metaphysics, it would be impossible to understand how the same suffix may denote starting or stopping.

If we were to approximate our metaphysical terminology more closely to Hopian terms, we should probably speak of the subjective realm as the realm of HOPE or HOPING. Every language contains terms that have come to attain cosmic scope of reference, that crystallize in themselves the basic postulates of an unformulated philosophy, in which is couched the thought of a people, a culture, a civilization, even of an era. Such are our words "reality, substance, matter, cause," and as we have seen "space, time, past, present, future." Such a term in Hopi is the word most often translated "hope"—*tunátya*—"it is in the action of hoping, it hopes, it is hoped for, it thinks or is thought of with hope," etc. Most metaphysical words in Hopi are verbs, not nouns as in European languages. The verb *tunátya* contains in its idea of hope something of our words "thought," "desire," and "cause," which sometimes must be used to translate it. The word is really a term which crystallizes the Hopi philosophy of the universe in respect to its grand dualism of objective and subjective; it is the Hopi term for SUBJECTIVE. It refers to the state of the subjective, unmanifest, vital and causal aspect of the Cosmos, and the fermenting activity toward fruition and manifestation with which it seethes—an action of HOPING; i.e., mental-causal activity, which is forever pressing upon and into the manifested realm. As anyone acquainted with Hopi society knows, the Hopi see this burgeoning activity in the growing of plants, the forming of clouds and their condensation in rain, the careful planning out of the communal activities of agriculture and architecture, and in all human hoping, wishing,

9

striving, and taking thought: and as most especially concentrated in prayer, the constant hopeful praying of the Hopi community, assisted by their exoteric communal ceremonies and their secret, esoteric rituals in the underground kivas—prayer which conducts the pressure of the collective Hopi thought and will out of the subjective into the objective. The inceptive form of *tunátya*, which is *tunátyava*, does not mean "begins to hope," but rather "comes true, being hoped for." Why it must logically have this meaning will be clear from what has already been said. The inceptive denotes the first appearance of the objective, but the basic meaning of *tunátya* is subjective activity or force; the inceptive is then the terminus of such activity. It might then be said that *tunátya* "coming true" is the Hopi term for objective, as contrasted with subjective, the two terms being simply two different inflectional nuances of the same verbal root, as the two cosmic forms are the two aspects of one reality.

10   As far as space is concerned, the subjective is a mental realm, a realm of no space in the objective sense, but it seems to be symbolically related to the vertical dimension and its poles the zenith and the underground, as well as to the "heart" of things, which corresponds to our word "inner" in the metaphorical sense. Corresponding to each point in the objective world is such a vertical and vitally INNER AXIS which is what we call the wellspring of the future. But to the Hopi there is no temporal future; there is nothing in the subjective state corresponding to the sequences and successions conjoined with distances and changing physical configurations that we find in the objective state. From each subjective axis, which may be thought of as more or less vertical and like the growth-axis of a plant, extends the objective realm in every physical direction, though these directions are typified more especially by the horizontal plane and its four cardinal points. The objective is the great cosmic form of extension; it takes in all the strictly extensional aspects of existence, and it includes all intervals and distances, all seriations and number. Its DISTANCE includes what we call time in the sense of the temporal relation between events which have already happened. The Hopi conceive time and motion in the objective realm in a purely operational sense—a matter of the complexity and magnitude of operations connecting events—so that the element of time is not separated from whatever element of space enters into the operations. Two events in the past occurred a long "time" apart (the Hopi language has no word quite equivalent to our "time") when many periodic physical motions have occurred between them in such a way as to traverse much distance or accumulate magnitude of physical display in other ways. The Hopi metaphysics does not raise the question whether the things in a distant village exist at the same present moment as those in one's own village, for it is frankly pragmatic on this

score and says that any "events" in the distant village can be compared to any events in one's own village only by an interval of magnitude that has both time and space forms in it. Events at a distance from the observer can only be known objectively when they are "past" (i.e., posited in the objective) and the more distant, the more "past" (the more worked upon from the subjective side). Hopi, with its preference for verbs, as contrasted to our own liking for nouns, perpetually turns our propositions about things into propositions about events. What happens at a distant village, if actual (objective) and not a conjecture (subjective) can be known "here" only later. If it does not happen "at this place," it does not happen "at this time"; it happens at "that" place and at "that" time. Both the "here" happening and the "there" happening are in the objective, corresponding in general to our past, but the "there" happening is the more objectively distant, meaning, from our standpoint, that it is further away in the past just as it is further away from us in space than the "here" happening.

As the objective realm displaying its characteristic attribute of extension stretches away from the observer toward that unfathomable remoteness which is both far away in space and long past in time, there comes a point where extension in detail ceases to be knowable and is lost in the vast distance, and where the subjective, creeping behind the scenes as it were, merges into the objective, so that at this inconceivable distance from the observer—from all observers—there is an all-encircling end and beginning of things where it might be said that existence, itself, swallows up the objective and the subjective. The borderland of this realm is as much subjective as objective. It is the abysm of antiquity, the time and place told about in the myths, which is known only subjectively or mentally—the Hopi realize and even express in their grammar that the things told in myths or stories do not have the same kind of reality or validity as things of the present day, the things of practical concern. As for the far distances of the sky and stars, what is known and said about them is supposititious, inferential—hence, in a way subjective—reached more through the inner vertical axis and the pole of the zenith than through the objective distances and the objective processes of vision and locomotion. So the dim past of myths is that corresponding distance on earth (rather than in the heavens) which is reached subjectively as myth through the vertical axis of reality via the pole of the nadir—hence it is placed BELOW the present surface of the earth, though this does not mean that the nadirland of the origin myths is a hole or cavern as we should understand it. It is *Palátkwapi* "At the Red Mountains," a land like our present earth, but to which our earth bears the relation of a distant sky—and similarly the sky of our earth is penetrated by the heroes of tales, who find another earthlike realm above it.

12   It may now be seen how the Hopi do not need to use terms that refer to space or time as such. Such terms in our language are recast into expressions of extension, operation, and cyclic process provided they refer to the solid objective realm. They are recast into expressions of subjectivity if they refer to the subjective realm—the future, the psychic-mental, the mythical period, and the invisibly distant and conjectural generally. Thus, the Hopi language gets along perfectly without tenses for its verbs.

RESPONDING TO READING

1. What tone does Whorf take as he discusses the superiority of Hopi metaphysics to that of other cultures? How is this tone established?

2. Working with other students, consider why *mystical* would be a "term of abuse in the eyes of a modern Western scientist." What connotations does *mystical* carry that the term *scientific* does not? How do the connotations of both words limit Western understanding of the world?

3. What are the properties of the Hopi metaphysics? How are they each defined in relation to the English language?

4. As Whorf describes it, how is Hopi grammar different from that of English? Why are these differences important in his argument?

5. Philosophically, what does it mean to think of distance—such as the distance between the Earth and a random star—as a subjective rather than objective concept? While Westerners have multiple ways to measure distance objectively (meters, inches, miles, etc.) and to measure time objectively (hours, decades, centuries, etc.), are there instances when these objective measures seem subjective? When does an hour feel longer than an hour should? Why do these objective measures sometimes seem subjective when we apply them? Explain your answer to these questions in a short essay. Since you'll be employing Whorfian concepts, you'll need to clarify these for your readers.

2.3.4 *Learning the Language*

PERRI KLASS

Although an American, Klass was born in Trinidad in 1958, where her father, an anthropologist, and her mother, a writer, were working at the time. These diverse and humanizing influences are reflected in the three major areas of Klass's life. Pediatrics: she earned an M.D. from Harvard in 1986, and has completed a pediatric residency at Boston Children's Hospital. Writing: Klass has published a novel, *Recombinations* (1985); a collection of short stories, *I Am Having an Adventure* (1986); a series of essays for the *New York Times*; and an autobiographical collection, *A Not Entirely Benign Procedure: Four Years as a Medical Student* (1987), of which "Learning the Language" is a chapter.

Family: Klass's concern for children is reflected not only in her choice of medical specialty, but in the dovetailing of her two careers with the demands of motherhood. She planned her pregnancy to fit in with her second-year medical school schedule, and she wrote while her son napped.

Everyone new to a group (such as a family, a fraternity), an institution (such as college), a discipline or profession (each and every one), has to learn its code, in language and in behavior, as part of the initiation process. This is how we enter and become part of a discourse community. That this is "a not entirely benign procedure," as Klass's "Learning the Language" makes clear, is partly because of the dissonance between the codes of other groups of which the learner is already a part and the new codes the learner must master to succeed in the new context. However, the newness of a language, like the newness of a love affair, leaves the initiate acutely sensitive to shades of meanings and values that with greater familiarity go unnoticed. As a medical student learning the language, Klass is aware of the dehumanizing aspects of calling an infant a "brainstem preparation," or referring to a dying patient as "CTD" (circling the drain). Although specific meanings, perhaps even the vocabulary, for our language of the future may not yet exist we can be sure that they will emerge of necessity to accommodate the inevitable changes in our culture. Klass reminds us to be sensitive to the music, as well as the words.

"Mrs. Tolstoy is your basic LOL in NAD, admitted for a soft rule-out MI," the intern announces. I scribble that on my patient list. In other words, Mrs. Tolstoy is a Little Old Lady in No Apparent Distress who is in the hospital to make sure she hasn't had a heart attack (rule out a Myocardial Infarction). And we think it's unlikely that she has had a heart attack (a *soft* rule-out).   1

If I learned nothing else during my first three months of working in the hospital as a medical student, I learned endless jargon and abbreviations. I started out in a state of primeval innocence, in which I didn't even know that "s̄ CP, SOB, N/V" meant "without chest pain, shortness of breath, or nausea and vomiting." By the end I took the abbreviations so much for granted that I would complain to my mother the English professor, "And can you believe I had to put down *three* NG tubes last night?"   2

"You'll have to tell me what an NG tube is if you want me to sympathize properly," my mother said. NG, nasogastric—isn't it obvious?   3

I picked up not only the specific expressions but also the patterns of speech and the grammatical conventions; for example, you never say that a patient's blood pressure fell or that his cardiac enzymes rose. Instead, the patient is always the subject of the verb: "He dropped his pressure." "He bumped his enzymes." This sort of construction probably reflects the profound irritation of the intern when the nurses come   4 in the middle of the night to say that Mr. Dickinson has disturbingly low blood pressure. "Oh, he's gonna hurt me bad tonight," the intern might say, inevitably angry at Mr. Dickinson for dropping his pressure and creating a problem.

5   When chemotherapy fails to cure Mrs. Bacon's cancer, what we say is, "Mrs. Bacon failed chemotherapy."

6   "Well, we've already had one hit today, and we're up next, but at least we've got mostly stable players on our team." This means that our team (group of doctors and medical students) has already gotten one new admission today, and it is our turn again, so we'll get whoever is admitted next in emergency, but at least most of the patients we already have are fairly stable, that is, unlikely to drop their pressures or in any other way get suddenly sicker and hurt us bad. Baseball metaphor is pervasive. A no-hitter is a night without any new admissions. A player is always a patient—a nitrate player is a patient on nitrates, a unit player is a patient in the intensive care unit, and so on, until you reach the terminal player.

7   It is interesting to consider what it means to be winning, or doing well, in this perennial baseball game. When the intern hangs up the phone and announces, "I got a hit," that is not cause for congratulations. The team is not scoring points; rather, it is getting hit, being bombarded with new patients. The object of the game from the point of view of the doctors, considering the players for whom they are already responsible, is to get as few new hits as possible.

8   This special language contributes to a sense of closeness and professional spirit among people who are under a great deal of stress. As a medical student, I found it exciting to discover that I'd finally cracked the code, that I could understand what doctors said and wrote, and could use the same formulations myself. Some people seem to become enamored of the jargon for its own sake, perhaps because they are so deeply thrilled with the idea of medicine, with the idea of themselves as doctors.

9   I knew a medical student who was referred to by the interns on the team as Mr. Eponym because he was so infatuated with eponymous terminology, the more obscure the better. He never said "capillary pulsations" if he could say "Quincke's pulses." He would lovingly tell over the multinamed syndromes—Wolff-Parkinson-White, Lown-Ganong-Levine, Schönlein-Henoch—until the temptation to suggest Schleswig-Holstein or Stevenson-Kefauver or Baskin-Robbins became irresistible to his less reverent colleagues.

10   And there is the jargon that you don't ever want to hear yourself using. You know that your training is changing you, but there are certain changes you think would be going a little too far.

The resident was describing a man with devastating terminal pancreatic cancer. "Basically he's CTD," the resident concluded. I reminded myself that I had resolved not to be shy about asking when I didn't understand things. "CTD?" I asked timidly.   11

The resident smirked at me. "Circling The Drain."   12

The images are vivid and terrible. "What happened to Mrs. Melville?"   13

"Oh, she boxed last night." To box is to die, of course.   14

Then there are the more pompous locutions that can make the beginning medical student nervous about the effects of medical training. A friend of mine was told by his resident, "A pregnant woman with sickle-cell represents a failure of genetic counseling."   15

Mr. Eponym, who tried hard to talk like the doctors, once explained to me, "An infant is basically a brainstem preparation." The term "brainstem preparation," as used in neurological research, refers to an animal whose higher brain functions have been destroyed so that only the most primitive reflexes remain, like the sucking reflex, the startle reflex, and the rooting reflex.   16

And yet at other times the harshness dissipates into a strangely elusive euphemism. "As you know, this is a not entirely benign procedure," some doctor will say, and that will be understood to imply agony, risk of complications, and maybe even a significant mortality rate.   17

The more extreme forms aside, one most important function of medical jargon is to help doctors maintain some distance from their patients. By reformulating a patient's pain and problems into a language that the patient doesn't even speak, I suppose we are in some sense taking those pains and problems under our jurisdiction and also reducing their emotional impact. This linguistic separation between doctors and patients allows conversations to go on at the bedside that are unintelligible to the patient. "Naturally, we're worried about adeno-CA," the intern can say to the medical student, and lung cancer need never be mentioned.   18

I learned a new language this past summer. At times it thrills me to hear myself using it. It enables me to understand my colleagues, to communicate effectively in the hospital. Yet I am uncomfortably aware that I will never again notice the peculiarities and even atrocities of medical language as keenly as I did this summer. There may be specific expressions I manage to avoid, but even as I remark them, promising myself I will never use them, I find that this language is becoming my professional speech. It no longer sounds strange in my ears—or coming from my mouth. And I am afraid that as with any new language, to use it properly you must absorb not only the vocabulary but also the   19 structure, the logic, the attitudes. At first you may notice these new and alien assumptions every time you put together a sentence, but with time and increased fluency you stop being aware of them at all. And as you lose that awareness, for better or for worse, you move closer and closer to being a doctor instead of just talking like one.

RESPONDING TO READING

1. Klass presents several different reasons for the use of medical jargon. List these reasons and develop a paper that shows how they are related to each other.

2. Klass sees value as well as danger in the use of language she presents. What is the value of this special language? What are its dangers? What does she mean when she says that absorbing a language means "you must absorb not only the vocabulary but also the structure, the logic, the attitudes." Write an essay in which you explain the structure, logic, and attitudes of the medical jargon Klass describes.

3. Consider some other specialty (such as politics, the military, education, the law, or business) with a language of its own. You may want to consult one or more additional essays dealing with language in this book, such as those by Mairs, Tan, Rodriguez, Tannen, Langer, Conroy, or Whorf. Give examples of that specialized language, and show how it implies the users' particular view of the world.

4. If the future holds increasing specialization and increasing use of jargon, as many writers predict, what will future language be like and how will that language affect the way we relate to each other? Will physicians from different nations communicate with each other more or less efficiently than lawyers speaking English to plumbers? If English becomes the international language, what logic and attitudes will that bring into relations among nations? What difference would it make if Japanese were to become the international language? What form of language lies in your own future as you become specialized? Write an essay on your vision of language in the future and how it will affect human relationships.

QUESTIONS FOR REFLECTION AND WRITING

What Is the Process of Thinking?

1. Write an essay on a characteristic or capability that you understand to be uniquely human. How have you come to know what you know on the subject? In the course of your essay, compare and contrast the ways Langer and Plato answer this question, and relate their responses to your own.

2. Can you convey in imaginative writing what you take to be "reality"? Try writing your own allegory of the cave, or of the beach, or of the lab, or of whatever scene allows you to clarify your thinking. What kinds of people mistake reality for something else? What distinguishes these people from those who see reality clearly?

3. Review the five criteria Asimov sets out for scientific creativity in "Those Crazy Ideas." To what degree do those criteria work for some of the scientists in this book, such as Angier (Chapter 1); Darwin, Gould, Goodall, Pollan, and Kuhn (this Chapter); or Gawande (Chapter 3)? You may need to look up some information on these scientists to supplement what the essays supply. If Asimov's criteria do not fit exactly, add or subtract some, or change them, so they do apply to the scientists you have chosen and their work.

4. What does Conroy mean in "Think About It" when he says that knowledge "does not always mean resolution"? Using the experiences Conroy and Fadiman (in "Under Water") relate as points of reference, write an essay on how we can come to know things that are not clear. Do you have an experience you also can narrate that enriches your perspective on the subject?

What Are Some Ways of Understanding Nature?

1. Compare and contrast Darwin's understanding of evolution in "Understanding Natural Selection" with Gould's in "Evolution as Fact and Theory." What is alike in their understanding and what is different? What are some of the reasons for these differences?

2. Jane Goodall had some difficulty being taken seriously by other scientists. To what degree does Goodall follow Kuhn's pattern or Asimov's pattern for scientific creativity? What might be added to Asimov's or Kuhn's descriptions to allow for Goodall's kind of science to be more readily accepted?

3. Pollan's "Playing God in the Garden" makes direct reference to Darwin and indirect reference to the debates about evolution that Gould focuses on. Notice when each of these essays was written, and consider the ways in which Pollan applies Darwin and Gould in a new and different context. Is this an appropriate use of science?

4. Consider the kinds of evidence used by the scientists in this section and the kinds of evidence used by some religions that dispute what these scientists say. Show how different kinds of evidence can lead to different ways of understanding nature and consider the degree to which it is possible to hold views compatible with both ways at the same time.

How Can We Explain What We Know?

1. Kuhn argued later in life that his concept of the "paradigm" was not limited to science, but could be extended to many fields of study. Certainly, language is part of his concept: "No wonder, then, that in the early stages of the development of any science different men confronting the same range of phenomena, but not usually all the same particular phenomena, describe and interpret them in different ways." Select one of the three essays on language that follow Kuhn (Tannen, Whorf, or Klass), and examine the way what Kuhn says about the language of a paradigm applies to what they have to say.

2. Compare and contrast the essays by Tannen and Whorf. In what ways are the "conversational styles" that Tannen describes similar to the language issues that Whorf sees in American Indians? In what ways are they different?

3. Klass in "Learning the Language" says that the particular uses of language by physicians that she describes serve at least two purposes: to define who is and is not a member of the group, and to protect the doctors from too much involvement in the pain and suffering they must confront. Is this use of language to help its community deal with and shape reality true in general of special language phenomena, such as those described by Tannen and Whorf?

4. Have you ever been a member of a community that uses language in the way described by Klass? If so, write an essay describing and analyzing the uses of language in that community, with reference to the insights into language as a way of knowing that you have gained from the essays in this section.

Thinking: How Do We Know What We Know?

1. Write an essay on how you have come to know something. Select a focused topic in history (the underground railway in the Civil War or oil and the Persian Gulf conflicts, for example), in science (the uses of aspirin or the meaning of a black hole), or in some other area about which you have special knowledge. Consider the normal knowledge of the field you have chosen, describing its paradigm (following Kuhn's definition). Then consider the relation of the paradigm to what you have learned and the way you learned it. To what degree is what you know exactly the same as what everyone else in the field knows? Is there something special about your way of knowing and (hence) what you know?

Ethics
*Which Principles Do
—and Should—
Govern Our Personal Lives?*

> *The bare vastness of the Hopi landscape emphasizes the visual impact of every plant, every rock, every arroyo. Nothing is overlooked or taken for granted. Each ant, each lizard, each lark is imbued with great value simply because the creature is there, simply because the creature is alive in a place where any life at all is precious.*
> LESLIE MARMON SILKO

Why Consider This Question?

We might say, with Silko, that everything is really important, since it is there. Every living thing is precious, each in its own way: The lizard is not worth more than the ant. But put a child in the picture, and a hungry mountain lion, say, and our neutrality is likely to shift; most of us would find ourselves willing to sacrifice the puma if that were necessary to save the child. Change the picture again, now adding a human family in need of food and water. How much of the landscape, if any, should we sacrifice to provide a family with necessities and comforts? Now our values conflict, with our humanity appealing for the family, but our knowledge of the fragility of the landscape asking us to leave it as it is. And so we seek ways to live in harmony with our world, as a still greater good, when we can, if we can. But the need to choose, to value one thing over another, is never far away from us. Our choices demonstrate our principles and what we think is really important.

Ethical decisions often depend on who asks the question, on who answers it, and under what circumstances it occurs. When we ask it of ourselves and answer it ourselves, the question looks very much like "What should I do now?" In this sense, principles are actions, since we

223

show that we value something by acting to support or defend it. That people are willing to die for freedom, for instance, as rebels, soldiers, authors of incendiary books, or champions of unsettling ideas (think of Gandhi or Martin Luther King, Jr.), demonstrates that they hold this principle in the highest regard. In contrast, we may say that we value something (democracy, for example) but show by our actions (neglecting to vote) that we do not, in fact, value it very much. Our actions surely speak louder than our words.

But the question is not only a personal one. We look at our friends, our family, our political representatives, and also ask, *Which principles do—and should—govern our personal lives*? How do we respond to a friend who is cheating on tests to get a good grade? A relative asks our opinion on whether it is better to stay in school or to make some good money at an unskilled job. As voters, we must choose between politicians promising low taxes and those promoting good schools and other government services—not to speak of the cynical deceivers who promise to do both. Is the competition of international free trade better than the protection of jobs at home through high tariffs on foreign goods? On what basis can we choose which is most important?

When we find ourselves puzzled about such conflicts in values, or when we find others disputing what we have simply assumed to be ethical, we need to look at and beyond our values to find out their sources. *Inquiry* has asked this kind of question before: Chapter I asked *how* we come to know who we are; Chapter 2 asked *how* we know what we know. Here, we are asking *how* we have come to value what we value. Like the other questions, this one asks us to think about our own thinking and to examine just how we have arrived at our current stand.

One way to think about our own principles is to divide them into those we have passively accepted from our society and those we have actively chosen to guide our personal lives. Of course, some ethical principles work perfectly well at both levels: We internalize and live by many of our social principles. Thus, the Ten Commandments forbid us to lie and steal, a set of values most of us accept personally—though little white lies sometimes seem necessary. Traffic laws demand that we stop at red lights, as we normally do with no pain. Such codes, rules, and regulations embody the values that let societies function. But the Ten Commandments also speak about honoring our fathers and mothers, a problem for us if they have been irresponsible or abusive. And we may be selective about which traffic laws we choose to obey; how many of us always respect the posted speed limits? And sometimes, agonizingly, our personal principles may conflict directly with society's values, as Rosa Parks experienced when she refused to ride in the back of an Alabama bus, as Henry David Thoreau demonstrated by going to jail for opposing what the felt to be an unjust war, and as

Martin Luther King, Jr. showed when he went to prison for fighting unjust racial segregation laws.

But it would be a mistake to think that there are only two kinds of ethical principles. Religion, philosophy, psychology, ecology, history, and many other fields of inquiry present us with many statements about what is important to believe and to do. And we must survive: People without basic necessities will place food, clothing, and shelter above any theoretical statements of value. John Stuart Mill argued that it is better to be "Socrates dissatisfied than a pig satisfied," but it is a sure thing that a starving Socrates would have placed a high value on a slice of ham. Nevertheless, Socrates valued his intellectual freedom enough to die for it. We are particularly likely to consider questions of value when something we cherish is absent, threatened, or taken away. The sick value good health; the hungry, food; the unemployed or underemployed, jobs; and the oppressed, liberty. We are not free agents with regard to ethical principles; our conditions of life have as much to do with what we believe and do as our abstract principles have to do with them.

The readings in this chapter focus on developing democratic principles in theory and practice, applying ethical principles to nature, and resolving conflicts of value. Since such decisions determine how we think and how we act, it is hard to imagine a more important question than "Which Principles Do—and Should—Govern Our Personal Lives?"

What Governs Ethical Behavior?

We are what we choose to do. Although we may consider ourselves free agents in our choice of what is really ethical, what we do is to a large extent determined by others whose opinions, choices, or lifestyles we admire. As our points of reference change over time, so may our principles. As young children, we are inevitably influenced by our parents and our older siblings. We are also influenced by what we like and dislike about our physical environment, our religious upbringing, and our schools. As adolescents and teenagers, we become acutely sensitive to the values of our peers; physical appearance, the "right" clothing, and popularity often seem more important than academic achievement, technical skill, or service to others. The principles that prevail into adulthood depend to an extent on what our society values, whom we choose as role models, and what rewards or other reinforcement we receive for our own behavior. Conflicting principles are the source of numerous disagreements between their respective advocates: children versus parents, students versus teachers, and one set of social or community standards versus another.

That principles are not static is clear from our continuing need to define and redefine what we mean, for instance, by "honesty" or "nature," two of the topics of this chapter. As Socrates says, "The unexamined life is not worth living"; if we take education seriously, that is, if we examine the meaning of what we believe and do, we develop our principles by testing them in situations. In the first essay in this chapter, Jeffrey Wattles tests "The Golden Rule" by asking what it actually means to treat others as we would like them to treat us—particularly if we are one of those unfortunate people who rather like bad treatment from others. Benjamin Franklin, of course, had all the answers, especially if one chooses to read his directions to "Achieving Moral Perfection" as simple good advice. But if we know much about how Franklin lived as American ambassador to France, we are entitled to wonder how seriously to take his ethical principles, particularly some that seem ironic when we look at them closely: "Humility: Imitate Jesus and Socrates."

The ability to make—and pay the price for making—morally correct decisions that are personally or politically difficult is one aspect of character as Joan Didion defines the term in "On Self Respect," in Chapter 1. For Didion, self-respect is the fundamental principle, arrived at through the practice and development of other principles—discipline, honesty, commitment to seeing one's own mistakes clearly, and willingness to accept responsibility for one's actions, good and bad.

The primary and basic principles discussed in the writings of Wattles, Didion, and the other writers in this book—honesty and self-respect—encompass a host of other ethics. It is such a composite of ethics that Atul Gawande, in "When Doctors Make Mistakes" (in the second section of this chapter), finds so difficult to untangle in the medical profession and that the Society of Professional Journalists wrestles with in its code of ethics. The journalists, well aware of the lapses that have marred their profession, seek to set out principles that somehow merge freedom, responsibility, the need to inform, and the need to withhold information until it is certifiably accurate. Ethical principles, as always, are easier to set out than to practice under situations that are anything but clear. Peter Singer, in his "Solution to World Poverty," draws that line vividly by describing just what an ordinary American's obligations to the world's poor ought to be. How many of us are ready to put our principles into action by making sacrifices in the way he proposes?

What Are Some Operative Principles of Work and Play?

Howard Gardner opens this section with "Good Work, Well Done: A Psychological Study," calling for more study by his profession, psychology, of "the place that work occupies in the overall life experiences of the individual." In particular, Gardner focuses on a special kind of work, which he and his collaborators call "good work," good in several senses of the word. Using the techniques of social science research, they surveyed many geneticists and journalists, although they assert that what they discovered applies to all of us. They conclude that it is both important and difficult to do "good work," work that is not only highly competent, but also ethically as well as financially rewarding. Gardner lists examples for us to follow: "the publisher Katharine Graham, the cellist Yo-Yo Ma, the tennis star Arthur Ashe," and others—a demanding and high standard indeed. With these models before us, Gardner maintains, we should ask ourselves such questions as "Am I doing the work that I should be doing?"

Barbara Ehrenreich, in "Serving in Florida," dramatizes what we might call "bad work." In contrast to the work Howard Gardner describes, here is the grinding work of the poor, the restaurant workers who live on the edge. Not all restaurant work is as bad as the situation that Ehrenreich describes, of course, but the work she dramatizes is neither ethically nor financially rewarding, demeaning to both body and spirit. For the workers, the goal is to get through the work shift, somehow: "The only thing to do is to treat each shift as a one-time emergency. . . . Forget that you will have to do this tomorrow, forget that you will have to be alert enough to dodge the drunks on the drive home tonight—just burn, burn, burn!" For those of us either directly or indirectly involved in the brutal treatment of such workers, the ethics of that kind of employment should perhaps cut more deeply.

When Atul Gawande considers "When Doctors Make Mistakes," he finds no easy answers. In fact, "all doctors make terrible mistakes," he points out (including the author–surgeon himself), sometimes with deadly results. What does this mean in practical terms? What are the ethical dimensions of such mistakes, given the fact that they are inevitable and an essential part of the learning process for physicians? What has medicine, using the insights of cognitive psychology and industrial error experts, been able to do to reduce mistakes? He concludes by lauding the "fierce ethic of personal responsibility for error," the willingness of physicians to acknowledge and deal with their mistakes, in full awareness of the fact that errors will occur despite all efforts to avoid them.

Deborah Fallows works as a stay-at-home mother, a profession still struggling for the dignity it deserves. She speaks of the time she "dressed for motherhood rather than for success" and debates the meaning of progress and liberation for modern mothers. Deciding to "live without a professional career but still with many of the interests and ambitions that I had before I had children" poses a serious ethical and practical dilemma. Most significantly, "it means changing the way I've been taught to think about myself and value the progress of my life." She defines what this means in complex ways: "I didn't want to become what the world kept telling me housewives are—ladies whose interests are confined to soap operas and the laundry. . . . It was possible to be a thoughtful and sensitive person and still be a mother." As she describes her life with her children, doing things no baby sitter can do, she sets out a model of ethical behavior. A decision on this matter will confront many of the readers of this book, and the ethical dimensions of the problem are crucial for whatever action one chooses.

Finally, Charles M. Young focuses on the ethical dimensions of one concept that is important in American life: losing. He points out that "to call someone a loser is probably the worst insult in the United States today" and dramatizes that assertion with his own personal experience. He is not too proud to claim that he is "the worst college football player of all time," and he is quite sure he was "the worst college football player of 1972." As he explores the principles behind losing, he touches on many aspects of American culture, most particularly the derogation of women in the male sports world. But he points out that we are all losers, living "in a country inhabited by Bill Gates and 260 million losers." To look closely at the principles behind our behavior and our language may be to demystify them (for we are all losers in a sense) and liberate ourselves.

How Can We Meet the Challenge of Creativity?

Some people believe that "creative writing" consists only of poetry and fiction. But in fact, any kind of writing can—and should—be creative. As the writers in this section make clear, the underlying principle of creativity has to do with seeing things in a fresh way. Newton's creative thinking about falling objects, as described by Jacob Bronowski in "The Reach of the Imagination," shares this fresh view with the brash student described by Alexander Calandra in "Angels on a Pin." The challenge of creativity is to find ways to express it in such a way as to demonstrate that the thinking is new and the vision is fresh; that is frequently the job of nonfiction prose, or the modern essay. If you are one of those observant and thoughtful people who try to see everything you read, everything you see, every experience of every day as if it were happening for the first time, you will not be able to avoid being creative in everything you write.

Jacob Bronowski opens this section with "The Reach of the Imagination," an essay that links creativity in art with creativity in science—imagination with the physical image. Like Susanne Langer in Chapter 2, he argues that the imagination is "a specifically *human* gift."

Imagination for Bronowski requires symbols and language, and this gift is available to all humans. Those who choose to apply their imaginations to science are not, he argues, essentially different from those who use it in the arts: "All great scientists have used their imagination freely." He sees scientific creativity and literary creativity having the same roots and tending to flower during the same historical periods.

Linda Hogan speaks as an Indian woman ("Hearing Voices") with an affinity for scientist and agricultural researcher Barbara McClintock: "It is important to me that McClintock listened to the voices of corn. It is important to the continuance of life that she told the truth of her method and it reminded us all of where our strength, our knowing, and our sustenance come from." As a poet, Hogan is concerned with "the living, breathing power of the word," which she sees as the voice of the earth itself. If we compare Hogan's view of creativity with, say, Asimov's in "Those Crazy Ideas" in Chapter 2, we see how ideas about creativity emerge from particular people writing from particular cultural contexts.

Ursula Le Guin speaks directly to the question writing students pose to her about the source of her creativity: "Where Do You Get Your Ideas From?" Her answer is equally straghtforward: "There is just the obstinate, continuous cultivation of a disposition, leading to skill in performance." No secrets, she points out, and no secret places either: no Schenectady spring of originality (referring to the writers' joke about where ideas lurk). But as a teacher, she is obliged to consider the principles behind her creativity, so she lists five "principal elements to the process" and recommends reading. But for Le Guin considerable mystery remains: "All makers must leave room for the acts of the spirit."

Physicist Alexander Calandra, in "Angels on a Pin," sees creativity as an act of rebellion against standard procedures. The student in the narrative (actually, Calandra himself as a young rebel) torments his teacher with his creative and unconventional solutions to standard problems, as a kind of playing with the world. Like Thomas Kuhn in "The Route to Normal Science" (Chapter 2), Calandra seeks new ideas in science through an unwillingness to rest content with the way things are done. And, finally, Alice Walker, in "In Search of Our Mothers' Gardens," examines the creativity that lay dormant in the oppressed black women of the past: "They waited for a day when the unknown thing that was in them would be made known; but guessed, somehow in their darkness, that on the day of their revelation they would be long dead." Focusing on two examples—her own mother and the poet Phillis Wheately—she examines the creativity that emerged in their lives and that was passed down to the present generation. The stories she tells, Walker has come to realize, are her mother's stories.

Surely, creativity is a fundamental state of awareness, made manifest in many lives in many ways. Each of the writers in this section sees it as a powerful, yet mysterious, force rooted in the physical, but transcending the physical, rooted in traditional learning, but going beyond it. There are no obvious formulas for creativity—only questions and responses. We all need creativity to keep learning from becoming rote repetition and to keep our eyes from glazing over with other people's views. How can we encourage creativity and how can we find it in ourselves?

Rhetorical Issues: Definition

Definition is central to reasoned discussions and analyses of almost any topic: literary criticism, presentations of scientific or historical information, philosophical arguments, economic interpretations, and answers to examination questions. Extended definitions may themselves be entire essays. It is appropriate to discuss definitions in a chapter on ethics because it is hard—indeed, perhaps impossible—to talk about ethics without defining the terms used to name and explain the principles behind ethical action. A principle or any other abstraction (truth, beauty, justice, love, freedom, nature) is general, yet has a multitude of connotations. There are occasions when we will avoid definition, precisely because we want readers to apply their individual perceptions and values to what we say, but this is a risky plan, used mainly by poets. Although the Trojan War was fought, claims Homer, over the beautiful Helen of Troy, possessor of "the face that launched a thousand ships," nowhere does the poet describe what she looked like. He says nothing about her height, weight, face, figure, or coloring; he can count on all who encounter Helen in his poem to endow her with their own ideals of the ultimate in female beauty, with whatever attributes they value.

But the vagueness of definition that the poet finds useful can destroy an essay. When we're writing about an abstraction or using any other term that is central to our argument or analysis, we need to stake out a claim to our point of view by defining it—our way instead of someone else's. The definition of "character," as Howard Gardner examines it in "Good Work," is crucial in determining the right way to live, both with oneself and in society. One's integrity or self-worth does not come easily or all at once, but in small increments, built through decisions and actions that cumulatively form the essential self. When you use the term "character," can you be sure that your readers will understand what you mean by it, without any explanation? When you talk about "work," will your reader understand just what you mean, and do not mean, by it? If not, and the term is essential to your discussion, then you will need to define it.

A good definition, whatever perspectives and values may be embedded in it, can forestall pages and pages of explanation and misunderstanding; definition is the writer's ounce of prevention. Definition answers the fundamental question, What is X? or, What is X not? Here are some of the more common types of definitions:

Definition According to Purpose. A definition according to purpose identifies the qualities a behavior or phenomenon (a role, a principle or policy, an activity, or a literary or artistic work) has or should have in order to fulfill its potential. Thus, such a definition might answer such questions as What is the purpose of X? ("A lie is an untruth intended to deceive.") What is X for? ("Nature exists to serve humankind" or "for its own sake.") What does X do? ("A scientist does empirical research.") and What is the role of X? ("Self-respect maintains a person's integrity.") Definitions such as these are often loaded with values, regardless of whether the definers acknowledge their biases.

Descriptive Definitions. A descriptive definition identifies the distinctive characteristics of an abstraction, an individual, or a group that set it apart from others. Thus, a descriptive definition might begin by naming something, answering the question What is X called? A possible answer might be Deborah Fallows (unique among all other women), Chaco Canyon (as opposed to all other Indian holy places), or the Brazilian film *Central Station* (and no other film from South America). A descriptive definition may also *specify the relationship among the parts of a unit or group,* addressing the question: What is the structure of X? (the universe, for instance) or How is X organized or put together? (a social system). Or it may *identify the features of something*: What does X look like? ("A nurse directed the crew into Trauma Bay 1, an examination room outfitted like an OR, with green tiles on the wall, monitoring devices, and space for portable X-ray equipment.") What is X's physical condition? ("Suffering from malnutrition and neglect and who knows what mental agonies, Phillis Wheately died.") or What is the essence—the fundamental nature—of X? (truth, beauty, or the natural world).

Process Definitions. A process definition classifies its subject according to various processes that either cause or produce it or in which it participates. Two examples are How is X produced? (Howard Gardner's "Good Work" shows what the term means by illustrating how it functions in the world.) and How does it work? (In "When Doctors Make Mistakes," Atul Gawande explains how a surgeon does his work.)

Logical Definitions. A logical definition, often used in scientific and philosophical writing, answers two related questions: Into what general category does X fit? and How does X differ from all other members of that category? For example, Charles M. Young considers "Losing" as a subcategory of low self-esteem in general (whose intent is to make people content with the destructive forces of competition); it is part of America's "state religion." The five key principles for writing logical definitions are also useful in evaluating definitions in other people's writing:

1. For economy's sake, use the most specific category, or class, to which the defined item belongs. If you're talking about losing, you can exclude other forms of low self-esteem from your discussion.

2. Any division of a class must include all members of that class. "Losing" must consider all types of failure in sports, whatever noble motives might be attributed to competition. Negative definitions explain what is *excluded* from a given classification and what is not. If all losing involves low self-esteem, then all losers share the same sense of loss and shame.

3. Subdivisions must be smaller than the class divided. In "Losing," Young discusses losing as a player, losing as a coach, losing as a lover, and losing as a business person, all aspects of the competition that is America's "national religion."

4. Categories should be mutually exclusive; that is, they should not overlap. [See Asimov's five criteria that define creativity in "Those Crazy Ideas" (Chapter 2): his last criterion, "luck," is not contained in the first four].

5. The basis for subdividing categories must be consistent throughout each stage of subdivision. Le Guin's list of elements of her writing process depends on their patterns, not on their substance.

In brief, when you are using definitions in your writing, you need to be aware of the following concerns:

- What am I defining, and why am I defining it? To explain a concept, argue a point, clear up a misconception, present a new perspective?

- What do my intended readers know about the term(s) I am defining? Enough so I can be fairly technical? Or must I stick to the fundamentals? Will my readers have a preexisting definition in mind against which I can play off mine? Can I let my own biases show, or should I aim for neutrality? Do I need to use outside authorities to reinforce my definitions?

- Where in my essay do I need definitions (every time I introduce new terms or concepts?), and how many will I need? How simple or elaborate must they be?

- How comprehensive or restrictive should my definitions be?
- What techniques of definition will I use? Labeling and categorization, description, illustration, analysis, comparison and contrast, considerations of cause and effect, argument, or analogy? Perhaps some combination of them?

QUESTIONS FOR DISCOVERY AND DISCUSSION

1. Look up the word "sophistication" in a collegiate or an unabridged dictionary. Notice the Greek root and its meaning. Then notice that the dictionary gives a series of definitions, some of which have positive connotations and some of which have negative ones. Why do you suppose that this word means such different things under different circumstances?

2. Give your own definition of "sophistication" in a particular area (e.g, clothing, wine, sports, food). Indicate whether you see the particular kind of sophistication you have chosen as positive or negative. Be explicit about the values that are important to you as you define the term.

3. Find some other words that seem to have both positive and negative connotations. Another example is "sophomore," which combines two roots expressing wisdom and foolishness. Check the dictionary for these roots, and notice the various definitions recorded there. You might even want to consult the *Oxford English Dictionary*, which will give you the meanings of the word at different periods of history. (For instance, the word "awful" had a positive connotation around 1600: It meant "awe inspiring.") Be prepared to discuss the reasons for the different definitions or for the changes in a word's meaning over time. What kinds of connotations does the word have in its various meanings.

4. What principles motivate your behavior? winning? loving? succeeding? escaping notice? Why? Can you find ways to persuade others that those principles should be important to them also? If you can, describe how; if you can't, what might make your explanation more convincing? How sure are you that what you value is indeed ethical?

5. A sarcastic bumper sticker reads, "Whoever has the most when he dies, wins." Define the meanings of "most" and "wins," and explain the principles and ethics the saying endorses.

WHAT GOVERNS ETHICAL BEHAVIOR

The Golden Rule—One or Many, Gold or Glitter?

JEFFREY WATTLES

Jeffrey Wattles was born in Chicago (1945) and studied at Stanford (B.A., 1966) and Northwestern (Ph.D., 1973). As an associate professor of philosophy at Kent State, he makes sure that his scholarship and teaching focus on universally applicable ethical standards—in particular, the Golden Rule. "We often hear that the peoples of our world share the golden rule—Do to others as you want others to do to you—as our most common moral principle," he asserts.

> The golden rule, however, is not only a unifying thread among peoples. It is also a principle with many different facets. Bring together the views of many cultures, ancient and modern, and consider the rule through psychology, philosophy, and religion, and you will find a surprisingly dynamic principle.[1]

> *The Golden Rule* (1996), Wattles's full-length study of this question, is indeed broad in its philosophical and historical range, employing theology, cultural studies, and philosophy, along with an historical perspective stretching from ancient Chinese thought to modern sociology. Wattles is also the author of numerous articles on ethics and spirituality, and he is currently at work on a book about the concepts of truth, beauty, and goodness. At Kent State, he is active in the university's service learning program, which allows students to put ethical theory into practice through charitable community work.
>   "The Golden Rule—One or Many, Gold or Glitter?" introduces some of Wattles' key ideas by examining various challenges to the rule. For example, "What if a sadomasochist goes forth to treat others as he wants to be treated?" Wattles asks. And if members of another culture possess a different set of moral values, can we be sure that we want them to treat us according to their customs? The rule thus becomes a catalyst for thinking about correct action, and as he defends the rule, Wattles introduces the reader to important ethical concepts and ways of reasoning.

1   Children are taught to respect parents and other authority figures. Adolescents are urged to control their impulses. Adults are told to conduct themselves in accord with certain moral and ethical standards.

---

[1]Quotation from Wattles' web page, http://www.personal.kent.edu/~jwattles/, 10/26/02.

Morality, then, may seem to be just an affair of imposition, a cultural voice that says "no" in various ways to our desires. To be sure, there are times when the word "no" must be spoken and enforced. But, time and again, people have discovered something more to morality, something rooted in life itself. The "no" is but one word in the voice of life, a voice that has other words, including the golden rule: Do to others as you want others to do to you. This book is about the life in that principle.

The Unity of the Rule

What could be easier to grasp intuitively than the golden rule? It has such an immediate intelligibility that it serves as a ladder that anyone can step onto without a great stretch. I know how I like to be treated; and that is how I am to treat others. The rule asks me to be considerate of others rather than indulging in self-centeredness. The study of the rule, however, leads beyond conventional interpretation, and the practice of the rule leads beyond conventional morality.

The rule is widely regarded as obvious and self-evident. Nearly everyone is familiar with it in some formulation or other. An angry parent uses it as a weapon: "Is that how you want others to treat you?" A defense attorney invites the members of the jury to put themselves in the shoes of his or her client. Noting that particular rules and interpretations do not cover every situation, a manual of professional ethics exhorts members to treat other professionals with the same consideration and respect that they would wish for themselves. Formulated in one way or another, the rule finds its way into countless speeches, sermons, documents, and books on the assumption that it has a single, clear sense that the listener or reader grasps and approves of. In an age where differences so often occasion violence, here, it seems, is something that everyone can agree on.

Promoting the notion that the golden rule is "taught by all the world's religions," advocates have collected maxims from various traditions, producing lists with entries like the following: "Hinduism: 'Let no man do to another that which would be repugnant to himself.'" "Islam: 'None of you [truly] believes until he wishes for his brother what he wishes for himself.'" The point of these lists is self-evident. Despite the differences in phrasing, all religions acknowledge the same basic, universal moral teaching. Moreover, this principle may be accepted as common ground by secular ethics as well.

Under the microscope of analysis, however, things are not so simple. Different formulations have different implications, and differences in context raise the question of whether the same concept is at work in passages where the wording is nearly identical. Is the meaning of the rule constant whenever one of these phrases is mentioned? There is a persistent debate, for example, about the relative merit of the positive formulation versus the negative one, "Do not do to others what you do not want others to do to you." Nor can the full meaning of a sentence be grasped in isolation. For example, to point to "the golden rule in Confucianism" by quoting a fifteen-word sentence from the *Analects* of Confucius does not convey the historical dynamism of the rule's evolving social, ethical, and spiritual connotations. What do the words mean in their original context? How prominent is the rule within that particular tradition? Finally, how does the rule function in a given interaction between the speaker or writer and the listener or reader? The rule may function as an authoritative reproach, a pious rehearsal of tradition, a specimen for analytic dissection, or a confession of personal commitment. Is the rule one or many? Can we even properly speak of *the* golden rule at all? Some Hindus interpret the injunction to treat others as oneself as an invitation to identify with the divine spirit within each person. Some Muslims take the golden rule to apply primarily to the brotherhood of Islam. Some Christians regard the rule as a shorthand summary of the morality of Jesus' religion. And countless people think of the rule without any religious associations at all.

6   Raising the question about the meanings of the golden rule in different contexts is not intended to reduce similarities to dust and ashes merely by appealing to the imponderable weight of cultural differences. Context is not the last word on meaning; the sentence expressing the golden rule contributes meaning of its own to its context. Meaning does involve context, but the fact that contexts differ does not prove that there is no commonality of meaning. Language and culture, moreover, are not reliable clues for identifying conceptual similarity and difference, since conceptual harmony is experienced across these boundaries.

7   The golden rule, happily, has more than a single sense. It is not a static, one-dimensional proposition with a single meaning to be accepted or rejected, defended or refuted. Nor is its multiplicity chaotic. There is enough continuity of meaning in its varied uses to justify speaking of the golden rule. My own thesis is that the rule's unity is best comprehended not in terms of a single meaning but as a symbol of a process of growth on emotional, intellectual, and spiritual levels.

The Quality of the Rule

8   "Gold is where you find it" runs a proverb coined by miners who found what they were seeking in unexpected places. So what sort of ore or alloy or sculpture is the teaching that, since the seventeenth century, has been called "the golden rule"? Is it gold or glitter? Certain appreciative remarks on the golden rule seem to bear witness to a

discovery. "Eureka!" they seem to say. "There is a supreme principle of living! It can be expressed in a single statement!"

By contrast, theologian Paul Tillich found the rule an inferior prin-   9
ciple. For him, the biblical commandment to love and the assurance that God is love "infinitely transcend" the golden rule. The problem with the rule is that it "does not tell us what we *should* wish."

Is the rule *golden*? In other words, is it worthy to be cherished as a   10
rule of living or even as *the* rule of living? The values of the rule are as much in dispute as its meanings. Most people, it seems, intuitively regard the golden rule as a good principle, and some have spoken as though there is within the rule a special kind of agency with the power to transform humankind.

It is understandable that the golden rule has been regarded as *the*   11
supreme moral principle. I do not want to be murdered; therefore I should not murder another. I do not want my spouse to commit adultery, my property to be stolen, and so forth; therefore I should treat others with comparable consideration. Others have comparable interests, and the rule calls me to treat the others as someone akin to myself. Moreover, I realize that I sometimes have desires to be treated in ways that do not represent my considered best judgment, and this reflection makes it obvious that reason is required for the proper application of the golden rule. Finally, in personal relationships, I want to be loved, and, in consequence, the rule directs me to be loving. From the perspective of someone simply interested in living right rather than in the construction and critique of theories, the rule has much to recommend it.

Some writers have put the rule on a pedestal, giving the impres-   12
sion that the rule is *sufficient* for ethics in the sense that no one could ever go wrong by adhering to it or in the sense that all duties may be inferred from it. Others have claimed that the rule is a *necessary* criterion for right action; in other words, an action must be able to pass the test of the golden rule if it is to be validated as right, and any action that fails the test is wrong. Some philosophers have hoped for an ethical theory that would be self-sufficient (depending on no controversial axioms), perfectly good (invulnerable to counterexamples), and allpowerful (enabling the derivation of every correct moral judgment, given appropriate data about the situation). They have dreamed of sculpting ethics into an independent, rational, deductive system, on the model of geometry, with a single normative axiom. However much reason may hanker for such a system, once the golden rule is taken as a candidate for such an axiom, a minor flexing of the analytic bicep is enough to humiliate it. A single counterexample suffices to defeat a pretender to this throne.

Many scholars today regard the rule as an acceptable principle for   13
popular use but as embarrassing if taken with philosophic seriousness.

Most professional ethicists rely instead on other principles, since the rule seems vulnerable to counterexamples, such as the current favorite, "What if a sadomasochist goes forth to treat others as he wants to be treated?"

14   Technically, the golden rule can defend itself from objections, since it contains within itself the seed of its own self-correction. Any easily abused interpretation may be challenged: "Would you want to be treated according to a rule construed in this way?" The recursive use of the rule—applying it to the results of its own earlier application—is a lever that extricates it from many tangles. Close examination of the counterexample of the sadomasochist [. . .] shows that to use the rule properly requires a certain degree of maturity. The counterexample does not refute the golden rule, properly understood; rather, it serves to clarify the interpretation of the rule—that the golden rule functions appropriately in a *growing* personality; indeed, the practice of the rule itself promotes the required growth. Since the rule is such a compressed statement of morality, it takes for granted at least a minimum sincerity that refuses to manipulate the rule sophistically to "justify" patently immoral conduct. Where that prerequisite cannot be assumed, problems multiply.

15   The objections that have been raised against the rule are useful to illustrate misinterpretations of the rule and to make clear assumptions that must be satisfied for the rule to function in moral theory.

16   It has been objected that the golden rule assumes that human beings are basically alike and thereby fails to do justice to the differences between people. In particular, the rule allegedly implies that what we want is what others want. As George Bernard Shaw quipped, "Don't do to others as you want them to do unto you. Their tastes may be different." The golden rule may also seem to imply that what we want for ourselves is good for ourselves and that what is good for ourselves is good for others. The positive formulation, in particular, is accused of harboring the potential for presumption; thus, the rule is suited for immediate application only among those whose beliefs and needs are similar. In fact, however, the rule calls for due consideration for any relevant difference between persons—just as the agent would want such consideration from others.

17   Another criticism is that the golden rule sets too low a standard because it makes ordinary wants and desires the criterion of morality. On one interpretation, the rule asks individuals to do whatever they imagine they might wish to have done to them in a given situation; thus a judge would be obliged by the golden rule to sentence a convicted criminal with extreme leniency. As a mere principle of sympathy, therefore, it is argued, the rule is incapable of guiding judgment in cases where the necessary action is unwelcome to its immediate recipient.

A related problem is that the rule, taken merely as a policy of sym- 18
pathy, amounts to the advice "Treat others as they want you to treat
them," as in a puzzle from the opening chapter of Herman Melville's
Moby-Dick, where Ishmael is invited by his new friend, Queequeg, to
join in pagan worship. Ishmael pauses to think it over:

> But what is worship?—to do the will of God—*that* is worship. And
> what is the will of God?—to do to my fellow man what I would have
> my fellow man to do to me—*that* is the will of God. Now, Queequeg is
> my fellow man. And what do I wish that this Queequeg would do to
> me? Why, unite with me in my particular Presbyterian form of wor-
> ship. Consequently, I must then unite with him in his; ergo, I must
> turn idolator.

If the golden rule is taken to require the agent to identify with the other
in a simplistic and uncritical way, the result is a loss of the higher perspective toward which the rule moves the thoughtful practitioner.

The next clusters of objections have a depth that a quick, initial 19
reply would betray, so I defer my response until later. If the rule is not
to be interpreted as setting up the agent's idiosyncratic desires—or
those of the recipient—as a supreme standard of goodness, then problems arise because the rule does not specify what the agent ought to
desire. The rule merely requires consistency of moral judgment: one
must apply the same standards to one's treatment of others that
one applies to others' treatment of oneself. The lack of specificity in the
rule, its merely formal or merely procedural character, allegedly renders its guidance insubstantial.

The rule seems to exhibit the limitations of any general moral prin- 20
ciple: it does not carry sufficiently rich substantive implications to be
helpful in the thicket of life's problems. Even though most people live
with some allegiance to integrating principles, action guides, mottoes,
proverbs, or commandments that serve to unify the mind, the deficiency of any principle is that it is merely a principle, merely a beginning;
only the full exposition of a system of ethics can validate the place of an
asserted principle. An appeal to a general principle, moreover, can
function as a retreat and a refusal to think through issues in their
concreteness.

There is also criticism of a practice widely associated with the 21
rule—imagining oneself in the other person's situation. The charge is
that this practice is an abstract, derivative, artificial, male, manipulative device, which can never compensate for the lack of human understanding and spontaneous goodness.

The rule has been criticized as a naively idealistic standard, unsuit- 22
ed to a world of rugged competition. The rule may seem to require that,
if I am trustworthy and want to be trusted, I must treat everyone as

being equally trustworthy. Furthermore, the broad humanitarianism of the golden rule allegedly makes unrealistic psychological demands; it is unfair to family and friends to embrace the universal concerns of the golden rule.

23   Last, some religious issues. The golden rule has been criticized for being a teaching that misleadingly lets people avoid confronting the higher teachings of religious ethics, for example, Jesus' commandment, "Love one another as I have loved you." Some find the rule of only intermediate usefulness, proposing that spiritual living moves beyond the standpoint of rules. Others have criticized the golden rule's traditional links to religion, arguing that moral intuition and moral reason can operate without reference to any religious foundation.

24   For responding to all these objections, there are three possible strategies: abandon the rule, reformulate it, or retain it as commonly worded, while taking advantage of objections to clarify its proper interpretation. I take the third way.

RESPONDING TO READING

1. What difference does Wattles see between the positive version of the Golden Rule ("Do to others as you want others to do to you") and the negative version ("Do not do to others what you do not want others to do to you")? Do you agree that there is a difference in the meaning—or possible interpretations—of these two versions?

2. Identify and explain the distinction Wattles makes between gold and glitter? How does this difference play a central role in his argument about the Golden Rule?

3. What are the rules taught to children in your culture? How many of them do connect, on a basic level, with the Golden Rule as Wattles defines it: "Do to others as you want others to do to you"? Explain your answer to these questions in a short essay.

4. Does the Golden Rule call "for due consideration for any relevant difference between persons," as Wattles argues, or is the Golden Rule always interpreted in ways that are culturally insensitive? That is, is the Golden Rule always blinded by the culture of the person applying it, or does it demand a consideration of possible cultural differences? Write an essay that serves as a wake-up call on some aspect of this issue for readers who might claim adherence to the Golden Rule, but whose behavior indicates otherwise.

5. According to Wattles, does the Golden Rule offer enough guidance to negotiate the complexities of daily life, or is it a rule that "can function as a retreat and refusal to think through issues in their concreteness"? Write an essay taking a stand on this issue. If you feel that you need to rephrase or otherwise modify the Golden Rule to accommodate your claims, restate it and explain why you've done so.

Arriving at Moral Perfection

BENJAMIN FRANKLIN

In *Becoming Benjamin Franklin*, a comparison of Benjamin Franklin's *Autobiograhy* and his actual life, scholar Ormond Seavey comments on Franklin's catalogue of virtues that present a plan for "Arriving at Moral Perfection." The virtues for which Franklin strives, are not a plan for utter moral transformation but are more like "a suit of clothes worn over the natural self." Franklin's "natural self," says Seavey, is complicated and contradictory: "one who would live according to his highest ideal himself and another who jokes too much, argues rashly, sleeps late, and leaves his papers in disarray. These two Franklins serve as opposed and coordinated principles within the same self." Thus, the list of virtues in Franklin's *Autobiography*—a work so popular that it has been continually in print from its publication three years after the author's death (1790)—itemizes the qualities necessary to succeed in business by working hard, or at least appearing to. Humility, acknowledges Franklin, was an afterthought.

Franklin, the prototype of the American self-made man, perpetrated many myths about himself in both his *Autobiography* and in *Poor Richard's Almanack*, which he wrote and published annually from 1732. Therein, he dispensed useful information and good advice that, if followed successfully, would enable readers to attain material prosperity, personal satisfaction, and public esteem. Indeed, Franklin's own life set the pace for generations to come. Born in 1706, he made enough money to retire from business at age 42, devoting the remainder of his life to science, public service, politics, and international diplomacy. Franklin the scientist made numerous discoveries in physics, navigation, and astronomy, and he applied his discoveries to practical inventions, such as the Franklin stove. Franklin the civil servant founded a public lending library, a municipal fire fighting company, the American Philosophical Society, and the University of Pennsylvania. Franklin the patriot served in the Continental Congress and as a Minister to France in the critical period during and after the Revolutionary War. Franklin, the composite of his several selves, was truly an American for all seasons.

It was about this time I conceived the bold and arduous project of   1
arriving at moral perfection. I wished to live without committing any fault at any time; I would conquer all that either natural inclination, custom, or company might lead me into. As I knew, or thought I knew, what was right and wrong, I did not see why I might not *always* do the one and avoid the other. But I soon found I had undertaken a task of more difficulty than I had imagined. While my attention was taken up and care employed in guarding against one fault, I was often surprised by another. Habit took the advantage of inattention. Inclination was

sometimes too strong for reason. I concluded at length that the mere speculative conviction that it was our interest to be completely virtuous was not sufficient to prevent our slipping, and that the contrary habits must be broken and good ones acquired and established before we can have any dependence on a steady, uniform rectitude of conduct. For this purpose I therefore contrived the following method.

2   These names of virtues with their precepts were

1. Temperance
Eat not to dulness. Drink not to elevation.

2. Silence
Speak not but what may benefit others or yourself. Avoid trifling conversation.

3. Order
Let all your things have their places. Let each part of your business have its time.

4. Resolution
Resolve to perform what you ought. Perform without fail what you resolve.

5. Frugality
Make no expence but to do good to others or yourself; i.e., waste nothing.

6. Industry
Lose no time. Be always employed in something useful. Cut off all unnecessary actions.

7. Sincerity
Use no hurtful deceit. Think innocently and justly; and, if you speak, speak accordingly.

8. Justice
Wrong none by doing injuries or omitting the benefits that are your duty.

9. Moderation
Avoid extremes. Forbear resenting injuries so much as you think they deserve.

10. Cleanliness
Tolerate no uncleanness in body, clothes or habitation.

11. Tranquillity
Be not disturbed at trifles or at accidents common or unavoidable.

12. Chastity
Rarely use venery but for health or offspring—never to dulness, weakness, or the injury of your own or another's peace or reputation.

13. Humility
Imitate Jesus and Socrates.

I made a little book in which I allotted a page for each of the   3
virtues. I ruled each page with red ink so as to have seven columns, one
for each day of the week, marking each column with a letter for the day.
I crossed these columns with thirteen red lines, marking the beginning
of each line with the first letter of one of the virtues, on which line and
in its proper column I might mark by a little black spot every fault I
found upon examination to have been committed respecting that
virtue upon that day.

I determined to give a week's strict attention to each of the virtues   4
successively. Thus in the first week my great guard was to avoid even
the least offence against temperance, leaving the other virtues to their
ordinary chance, only marking every evening the faults of the day.
Thus if in the first week I could keep my first line marked "T." clear of
spots, I supposed the habit of that virtue so much strengthened and its
opposite weakened that I might venture extending my attention to include the next, and for the following week keep both lines clear of
spots. Proceeding thus to the last, I could go thro' a course complete in
thirteen weeks, and four courses in a year.

RESPONDING TO READING

1. Franklin's definitions of the thirteen virtues are very brief. Should these be expanded? Why or Why not? Would you change his list in any way?

2. How does Franklin's list differ from modern books or articles giving good advice? How moral do you find his "virtues"?

3. Franklin is responsible only to himself for sticking to his plan of self-
   improvement. Are people more likely to succeed in making changes for
   self-improvement if they do so with group support (e.g., Weight Watchers or
   Alcoholics Anonymous) than in isolation? What can a group provide that an
   individual cannot?

4. Imagine you could follow Franklin's method for a full year. Would you then
   have achieved "moral perfection"? Why, or why not?

Society of Professional Journalists
Code of Ethics

Many professionals—including those in medicine, therapy, law, and
the academy—have professional organizations to promote high
and consistent standards of professional conduct and to advance their
own professional interests. The Society of Professional Journalists is
just such an organization. Although it has only 9000 members from

among America's numerous editors, reporters, and other news professionals, its Code of Ethics sets the model for professional conduct throughout the industry.

The Society of Professional Journalists was founded in 1909 at DePauw University (Greencastle, Indiana) as Sigma Delta Chi, an honorary journalism fraternity. In 1916, it became a professional fraternity. Its 1960 reorganization as a professional society was reflected in the 1973 name change to the Society of Professional Journalists, Sigma Delta Chi; in 1988, the "Sigma Delta Chi" was dropped. Currently based in Indianapolis, the Society of Professional Journalists has the following as its mission:

- To encourage a climate in which journalism can be practiced freely and fully
- To promote this flow of information
- To stimulate high standards and ethical behavior in the practice of journalism
- To foster excellence, encourage diversity, and inspire successive generations of talented individuals to become dedicated journalists
- To maintain constant vigilance in protection of First Amendment guarantees of freedom of speech and of the press.

Indeed, the Society of Professional Journalists is a First Amendment watchdog, tracking "administrative, legislative, and judicial developments concerning freedom of information; and filing court briefs on behalf of journalists who have been shut out of hearings, denied access to information, or forced by courts to turn over notes and research." The SPJ's Legal Defense Fund aids journalists working under these difficulties, or even jailed.

The first Code of Ethics, adopted in 1926, was borrowed from the American Society of Newspaper Editors. In 1973, Sigma Delta Chi wrote its own code, which was revised in 1984, 1987, and again in 1996. The 1996 version is the one reprinted here from the organization's website www.spj.org/ethics/, distinguished by its clarity and straightforwardness. "Embraced by thousands of writers, editors, and other news professionals," the Code of Ethics instructs journalists to "seek truth and report it, minimize harm, act independently, and be accountable."

Preamble

1   Members of the Society of Professional Journalists believe that public enlightenment is the forerunner of justice and the foundation of democracy. The duty of the journalist is to further those ends by seeking truth and providing a fair and comprehensive account of events and issues. Conscientious journalists from all media and specialties

strive to serve the public with thoroughness and honesty. Professional integrity is the cornerstone of a journalist's credibility. Members of the Society share a dedication to ethical behavior and adopt this code to declare the Society's principles and standards of practice.

Seek Truth and Report It

Journalists should be honest, fair and courageous in gathering, reporting and interpreting information.

Journalists should:

- Test the accuracy of information from all sources and exercise care to avoid inadvertent error. Deliberate distortion is never permissible.
- Diligently seek out subjects of news stories to give them the opportunity to respond to allegations of wrongdoing.
- Identify sources whenever feasible. The public is entitled to as much information as possible on sources' reliability.
- Always question sources' motives before promising anonymity. Clarify conditions attached to any promise made in exchange for information. Keep promises.
- Make certain that headlines, news teases and promotional material, photos, video, audio, graphics, sound bites and quotations do not misrepresent. They should not oversimplify or highlight incidents out of context.
- Never distort the content of news photos or video. Image enhancement for technical clarity is always permissible. Label montages and photo illustrations.
- Avoid misleading re-enactments or staged news events. If re-enactment is necessary to tell a story, label it.
- Avoid undercover or other surreptitious methods of gathering information except when traditional open methods will not yield information vital to the public. Use of such methods should be explained as part of the story.
- Never plagiarize.
- Tell the story of the diversity and magnitude of the human experience boldly, even when it is unpopular to do so.
- Examine their own cultural values and avoid imposing those values on others.
- Avoid stereotyping by race, gender, age, religion, ethnicity, geography, sexual orientation, disability, physical appearance or social status.

- Support the open exchange of views, even views they find repugnant.
- Give voice to the voiceless; official and unofficial sources of information can be equally valid.
- Distinguish between advocacy and news reporting. Analysis and commentary should be labeled and not misrepresent fact or context.
- Distinguish news from advertising and shun hybrids that blur the lines between the two.
- Recognize a special obligation to ensure that the public's business is conducted in the open and that government records are open to inspection.

Minimize Harm

2   Ethical journalists treat sources, subjects and colleagues as human beings deserving of respect.

Journalists should:

- Show compassion for those who may be affected adversely by news coverage. Use special sensitivity when dealing with children and inexperienced sources or subjects.
- Be sensitive when seeking or using interviews or photographs of those affected by tragedy or grief.
- Recognize that gathering and reporting information may cause harm or discomfort. Pursuit of the news is not a license for arrogance.
- Recognize that private people have a greater right to control information about themselves than do public officials and others who seek power, influence or attention. Only an overriding public need can justify intrusion into anyone's privacy.
- Show good taste. Avoid pandering to lurid curiosity.
- Be cautious about identifying juvenile suspects or victims of sex crimes.
- Be judicious about naming criminal suspects before the formal filing of charges.
- Balance a criminal suspect's fair trial rights with the public's right to be informed.

Act Independently

3   Journalists should be free of obligation to any interest other than the public's right to know.

Journalists should:

- Avoid conflicts of interest, real or perceived.
- Remain free of associations and activities that may compromise integrity or damage credibility.
- Refuse gifts, favors, fees, free travel and special treatment, and shun secondary employment, political involvement, public office and service in community organizations if they compromise journalistic integrity.
- Disclose unavoidable conflicts.
- Be vigilant and courageous about holding those with power accountable.
- Deny favored treatment to advertisers and special interests and resist their pressure to influence news coverage.
- Be wary of sources offering information for favors or money; avoid bidding for news.

Be Accountable

Journalists are accountable to their readers, listeners, viewers and each other.

Journalists should:

- Clarify and explain news coverage and invite dialogue with the public over journalistic conduct.
- Encourage the public to voice grievances against the news media.
- Admit mistakes and correct them promptly.
- Expose unethical practices of journalists and the news media.
- Abide by the same high standards to which they hold others.

RESPONDING TO READING

1. According to the Code of Ethics, journalists should "avoid misleading re-enactments or staged news events." When a re-enactment is used, it should be clearly labeled. At the same time, journalists "should not oversimplify or highlight incidents out of context." Can a journalist follow both of these precepts at once? Is a re-enactment, by definition, an oversimplification of certain aspects of a news story?

2. Journalists should "Distinguish news from advertising and shun hybrids that blur the lines between the two." How does this rule apply to situations such as these: (a) A story arguing that a particular car is safer than others is an advertisement implicitly advocating the purchase of that car; (b) a story about a

politician's wrongdoing is an argument against voting for that person; (c) a story about the most popular toys people are buying for their children is an advertisement for those toys. Are there other examples from local and national journalism you can think of that blur these lines between news and advertising? Can such lines even be drawn?

3. Write an essay for readers of your local paper in which you discuss the Code of Ethics' approach to the rights of individual citizens. According to the Code, when should journalists take into account an individual's right to privacy? When is the right to privacy more important than the public right to know? When is it permissible to violate an individual's right to privacy? Do you agree or disagree with the Code's rules on these issues?

4. The Code of Ethics does not offer a definition of a conflict of interest, yet it argues that journalists should "Avoid conflicts of interest, real or perceived." Lacking a clear definition, is such an injunction about behavior useful? Would a clearly stated definition make the point more clear, or would it make the rule even more difficult to follow? With other students, write a brief definition of "conflict of interest."

5. In what ways does the Code serve as an ideal to which journalists aspire rather than a reflection of the realities of journalism in America? Does the Code of Ethics seem to reflect accurately the ethics of the journalists working at your local newspaper or television stations? Watch several local news broadcasts or read several issues of a local newspaper and, in a short essay for a local audience, explain how the journalists you observe seem to be either following or not following the Code.

The Singer Solution to World Poverty

PETER SINGER

When bioethicist Peter Singer (born Melbourne, Australia, 1946) became a professor at Princeton, the president of the university tried to calm critics, stating that Singer would "Challenge students—and others—to think critically, to examine their beliefs and assumptions, to hone their abilities to identify and assess ethical issues of various kinds, and to develop both a capacity for independent thought and a set of moral values to guide them through their lives." Singer, who has an international—and controversial—reputation, studied at the University of Melbourne (B.A., 1967; M.A., 1969) and Oxford (B. Phil, 1971), taught at Oxford and New York University, and led the Centre for Human Bioethics at Monash University in Australia (1983–98). His ethical stances have indeed challenged conventional ideas; for example, he presented his opposition to "speciesism"—the idea that human rights should be valued above the rights of other species—in several books about animal rights: *Animal Liberation: A New Ethics for Our Treatment of Animals* (1975), *In Defense of Animals* (1985), *Animal*

Factories (1990), and *The Great Ape Project: Equality Beyond Humanity* (1994). Yet as a dutiful son, he supported his aging mother's long life, including nursing home care. As coauthor and editor, Singer discussed the ethics of human reproduction in *Making Babies: The New Science and Ethics of Conception* (1985) and *Rethinking Life and Death* (1995). His global perspective emerged in *How Are We to Live?* (1994), which argues for commitment to causes "larger than one-self." *One World: The Ethics of Globalization* (2002) suggests that we think beyond nationalism to solve problems such as climate change and foreign aid.

"The Singer Solution to World Poverty," from the *New York Times Magazine*, (sept. 5, 1999), presents an ethical problem: If the cost of our minor luxuries is enough to save starving children, shouldn't we take action immediately? Using imaginary scenarios to dramatize moral dilemmas, and making a direct appeal to the reader's charity, Singer brings the issues to life.

In the Brazilian film "Central Station," Dora is a retired school-teacher who makes ends meet by sitting at the station writing letters for illiterate people. Suddenly she has an opportunity to pocket $1,000. All she has to do is persuade a homeless 9-year-old boy to follow her to an address she has been given. (She is told he will be adopted by wealthy foreigners.) She delivers the boy, gets the money, spends some of it on a television set and settles down to enjoy her new acquisition. Her neighbor spoils the fun, however, by telling her that the boy was too old to be adopted—he will be killed and his organs sold for transplantation. Perhaps Dora knew this all along, but after her neighbor's plain speaking, she spends a troubled night. In the morning Dora resolves to take the boy back.

Suppose Dora had told her neighbor that it is a tough world, other people have nice new TV's too, and if selling the kid is the only way she can get one, well, he was only a street kid. She would then have become, in the eyes of the audience, a monster. She redeems herself only by being prepared to bear considerable risks to save the boy.

At the end of the movie, in cinemas in the affluent nations of the world, people who would have been quick to condemn Dora if she had not rescued the boy go home to places far more comfortable than her apartment. In fact, the average family in the United States spends almost one-third of its income on things that are no more necessary to them than Dora's new TV was to her. Going out to nice restaurants, buying new clothes because the old ones are no longer stylish, vacationing at beach resorts—so much of our income is spent on things not essential to the preservation of our lives and health. Donated to one of a number of charitable agencies, that money could mean the difference between life and death for children in need.

4   All of which raises a question: In the end, what is the ethical distinction between a Brazilian who sells a homeless child to organ peddlers and an American who already has a TV and upgrades to a better one—knowing that the money could be donated to an organization that would use it to save the lives of kids in need?

5   Of course, there are several differences between the two situations that could support different moral judgments about them. For one thing, to be able to consign a child to death when he is standing right in front of you takes a chilling kind of heartlessness; it is much easier to ignore an appeal for money to help children you will never meet. Yet for a utilitarian philosopher like myself—that is, one who judges whether acts are right or wrong by their consequences—if the upshot of the American's failure to donate the money is that one more kid dies on the streets of a Brazilian city, then it is, in some sense, just as bad as selling the kid to the organ peddlers. But one doesn't need to embrace my utilitarian ethic to see that, at the very least, there is a troubling incongruity in being so quick to condemn Dora for taking the child to the organ peddlers while, at the same time, not regarding the American consumer's behavior as raising a serious moral issue.

6   In his 1996 book, "Living High and Letting Die," the New York University philosopher Peter Unger presented an ingenious series of imaginary examples designed to probe our intuitions about whether it is wrong to live well without giving substantial amounts of money to help people who are hungry, malnourished or dying from easily treatable illnesses like diarrhea. Here's my paraphrase of one of these examples:

7   Bob is close to retirement. He has invested most of his savings in a very rare and valuable old car, a Bugatti, which he has not been able to insure. The Bugatti is his pride and joy. In addition to the pleasure he gets from driving and caring for his car, Bob knows that its rising market value means that he will always be able to sell it and live comfortably after retirement. One day when Bob is out for a drive, he parks the Bugatti near the end of a railway siding and goes for a walk up the track. As he does so, he sees that a runaway train, with no one aboard, is running down the railway track. Looking farther down the track, he sees the small figure of a child very likely to be killed by the runaway train. He can't stop the train and the child is too far away to warn of the danger, but he can throw a switch that will divert the train down the siding where his Bugatti is parked. Then nobody will be killed—but the train will destroy his Bugatti. Thinking of his joy in owning the car and the financial security it represents. Bob decides not to throw the switch. The child is killed. For many years to come, Bob enjoys owning his Bugatti and the financial security it represents.

8   Bob's conduct, most of us will immediately respond, was gravely wrong. Unger agrees. But then he reminds us that we, too, have oppor-

tunities to save the lives of children. We can give to organizations like Unicef or Oxfam America. How much would we have to give one of these organizations to have a high probability of saving the life of a child threatened by easily preventable diseases? (I do not believe that children are more worth saving than adults, but since no one can argue that children have brought their poverty on themselves, focusing on them simplifies the issues.) Unger called up some experts and used the information they provided to offer some plausible estimates that include the cost of raising money, administrative expenses and the cost of delivering aid where it is most needed. By his calculation. $200 in donations would help a sickly 2-year-old transform into a healthy 6-year-old—offering safe passage through childhood's most dangerous years. To show how practical philosophical argument can be, Unger even tells his readers that they can easily donate funds by using their credit card and calling one of these toll-free numbers: (800) 367-5437 for Unicef: (800) 693-2687 for Oxfam America.

Now you, too, have the information you need to save a child's life.   9
How should you judge yourself if you don't do it? Think again about Bob and his Bugatti. Unlike Dora, Bob did not have to look into the eyes of the child he was sacrificing for his own material comfort. The child was a complete stranger to him and too far away to relate to in an intimate, personal way. Unlike Dora, too, he did not mislead the child or initiate the chain of events imperiling him. In all these respects. Bob's situation resembles that of people able but unwilling to donate to overseas aid and differs from Dora's situation.

If you still think that it was very wrong of Bob not to throw the   10
switch that would have diverted the train and saved the child's life, then it is hard to see how you could deny that it is also very wrong not to send money to one of the organizations listed above. Unless, that is, there is some morally important difference between the two situations that I have overlooked.

Is it the practical uncertainties about whether aid will really reach   11
the people who need it? Nobody who knows the world of overseas aid can doubt that such uncertainties exist. But Unger's figure of $200 to save a child's life was reached after he had made conservative assumptions about the proportion of the money donated that will actually reach its target.

One genuine difference between Bob and those who can afford to   12
donate to overseas aid organizations but don't is that only Bob can save the child on the tracks, whereas there are hundreds of millions of people who can give $200 to overseas aid organizations. The problem is that most of them aren't doing it. Does this mean that it is all right for you not to do it?

Suppose that there were more owners of priceless vintage cars—   13
Carol, Dave, Emma, Fred and so on, down to Ziggy—all in exactly the

same situations as Bob, with their own siding and their own switch, all sacrificing the child in order to preserve their own cherished car. Would that make it all right for Bob to do the same? To answer this question affirmatively is to endorse follow-the-crowd ethics—the kind of ethics that led many Germans to look away when the Nazi atrocities were being committed. We do not excuse them because others were behaving no better.

14   We seem to lack a sound basis for drawing a clear moral line between Bob's situation and that of any reader of this article with $200 to spare who does not donate it to an overseas aid agency. These readers seem to be acting at least as badly as Bob was acting when he chose to let the runaway train hurtle toward the unsuspecting child. In the light of this conclusion, I trust that many readers will reach for the phone and donate that $200. Perhaps you should do it before reading further.

15   Now that you have distinguished yourself morally from people who put their vintage cars ahead of a child's life, how about treating yourself and your partner to dinner at your favorite restaurant? But wait. The money you will spend at the restaurant could also help save the lives of children overseas! True, you weren't planning to blow $200 tonight, but if you were to give up dining out just for one month, you would easily save that amount. And what is one month's dining out, compared to a child's life? There's the rub. Since there are a lot of desperately needy children in the world, there will always be another child whose life you could save for another $200. Are you therefore obliged to keep giving until you have nothing left? At what point can you stop?

16   Hypothetical examples can easily become farcical. Consider Bob. How far past losing the Bugatti should he go? Imagine that Bob had got his foot stuck in the track of the siding, and if he diverted the train, then before it rammed the car it would also amputate his big toe. Should he still throw the switch? What if it would amputate his foot? His entire leg?

17   As absurd as the Bugatti scenario gets when pushed to extremes, the point it raises is a serious one: only when the sacrifices become very significant indeed would most people be prepared to say that Bob does nothing wrong when he decides not to throw the switch. Of course, most people could be wrong; we can't decide moral issues by taking opinion polls. But consider for yourself the level of sacrifice that you would demand of Bob, and then think about how much money you would have to give away in order to make a sacrifice that is roughly equal to that. It's almost certainly much, much more than $200. For most middle-class Americans, it could easily be more like $200,000.

18   Isn't it counterproductive to ask people to do so much? Don't we run the risk that many will shrug their shoulders and say that morality,

so conceived, is fine for saints but not for them? I accept that we are unlikely to see, in the near or even medium-term future, a world in which it is normal for wealthy Americans to give the bulk of their wealth to strangers. When it comes to praising or blaming people for what they do, we tend to use a standard that is relative to some conception of normal behavior. Comfortably off Americans who give, say, 10 percent of their income to overseas aid organizations are so far ahead of most of their equally comfortable fellow citizens that I wouldn't go out of my way to chastise them for not doing more. Nevertheless, they should be doing much more, and they are in no position to criticize Bob for failing to make the much greater sacrifice of his Bugatti.

At this point various objections may crop up. Someone may say: "If   19 every citizen living in the affluent nations contributed his or her share I wouldn't have to make such a drastic sacrifice, because long before such levels were reached, the resources would have been there to save the lives of all those children dying from lack of food or medical care. So why should I give more than my fair share?" Another, related, objection is that the Government ought to increase its overseas aid allocations, since that would spread the burden more equitably across all taxpayers.

Yet the question of how much we ought to give is a matter to be   20 decided in the real world—and that, sadly, is a world in which we know that most people do not, and in the immediate future will not, give substantial amounts to overseas aid agencies. We know, too, that at least in the next year, the United States Government is not going to meet even the very modest United Nations-recommended target of 0.7 percent of gross national product; at the moment it lags far below that, at 0.09 percent, not even half of Japan's 0.22 percent or a tenth of Denmark's 0.97 percent. Thus, we know that the money we can give beyond that theoretical "fair share" is still going to save lives that would otherwise be lost. While the idea that no one need do more than his or her fair share is a powerful one, should it prevail if we know that others are not doing their fair share and that children will die preventable deaths unless we do more than our fair share? That would be taking fairness too far.

Thus, this ground for limiting how much we ought to give also   21 fails. In the world as it is now, I can see no escape from the conclusion that each one of us with wealth surplus to his or her essential needs should be giving most of it to help people suffering from poverty so dire as to be life-threatening. That's right: I'm saying that you shouldn't buy that new car, take that cruise, redecorate the house or get that pricey new suit. After all, a $1,000 suit could save five children's lives.

So how does my philosophy break down in dollars and cents? An   22 American household with an income of $50,000 spends around $30,000 annually on necessities, according to the Conference Board, a nonprofit economic research organization. Therefore, for a household bringing in $50,000 a year, donations to help the world's poor should be as close as possible to $20,000. The $30,000 required for necessities holds for higher incomes as well. So a household making $100,000 could cut a yearly check for $70,000. Again, the formula is simple: whatever money you're spending on luxuries, not necessities, should be given away.

23   Now, evolutionary psychologists tell us that human nature just isn't sufficiently altruistic to make it plausible that many people will sacrifice so much for strangers. On the facts of human nature, they might be right, but they would be wrong to draw a moral conclusion from those facts. If it is the case that we ought to do things that, predictably, most of us won't do, then let's face that fact head-on. Then, if we value the life of a child more than going to fancy restaurants, the next time we dine out we will know that we could have done something better with our money. If that makes living a morally decent life extremely arduous, well, then that is the way things are. If we don't do it, then we should at least know that we are failing to live a morally decent life—not because it is good to wallow in guilt but because knowing where we should be going is the first step toward heading in that direction.

24   When Bob first grasped the dilemma that faced him as he stood by that railway switch, he must have thought how extraordinarily unlucky he was to be placed in a situation in which he must choose between the life of an innocent child and the sacrifice of most of his savings. But he was not unlucky at all. We are all in that situation.

RESPONDING TO READING

1. Singer begins his essay by summarizing "Central Station," immediately generalizing from the experiences and needs of Dora, the film's main character, to American spending habits. What purpose does this generalization serve in his argument? Is it developed enough to persuade an American audience— the people he is criticizing?

2. For Singer, what moral issues are raised by the spending habits of American consumers? How does this connect with his definition of himself as a "utilitarian philosopher"?

3. Do comparisons among American consumers, fictional Brazilian schoolteachers, characters such as Bob in imaginary scenarios, and Nazis persuade readers to rethink their spending habits or attitudes towards the moral issues that Singer raises? Or are these comparisons superficial ones that serve only to make Singer's point? Do such comparisons oversimplify or complicate the issues that are raised? Why?

4. Singer's argument rests on the idea that most of his readers can afford to donate $200 to one of the two charities he names, but are unwilling to do so.

Discuss this argument with other student in your class. Are there other ways in which Singer's readers can help others—such as performing volunteer work or lobbying Congress? How does Singer's focus on donating a specific amount to one of two specific groups strengthen or weaken his argument?

5. In no uncertain terms, Singer argues that "whatever money you're spending on luxuries, not necessities, should be given away." How does the fact that he never defines *necessities* and only generally defines *luxuries* (new cars, new suits, vacations, and home redecoration) affect his argument? Based on your own experiences, how would you define these two terms? How much money would you have to give to satisfy Singer?

WHAT ARE SOME OPERATIVE PRINCIPLES OF WORK AND PLAY?

Good Work, Well Done: A Psychological Study

HOWARD GARDNER

Recognized as a gifted and creative pianist at an early age, Howard Gardner has devoted his career as a psychologist to the study of human intelligence and creativity. Born in Scranton, Pennsylvania (1943), he earned degrees from Harvard—B.A., *summa cum laude*, 1965; Ph.D., 1971. Currently a professor of cognition and education at Harvard, adjunct professor of neurology at the Boston University School of Medicine, the author of eighteen books, and the recipient of a MacArthur "genius" fellowship (1981), Gardner is widely known for *Frames of Mind: The Theory of Multiple Intelligences* (1984). This landmark study looked beyond the standard IQ numbers to locate three primary types of intelligence: perceptiveness about oneself and others ("personal intelligence"), music and language ("object-free intelligence"), and math and logic ("object-related intelligence"). Gardner continued to explore this topic in *Multiple Intelligences: The Theory in Practice* (1993) and *Intelligence Reframed: Multiple Intelligences for the 21st Century* (1999); the latter added three more kinds of intelligence: naturalistic, spiritual, and existential. His other books include *Brain Damage: Gateway to the Mind* (1975), which reports his research with aphasic adults, and *The Disciplined Mind: What All Students Should Understand* (1999), in which he argues that students should learn certain key thinking skills, instead of mastering random facts like those E.D. Hirsch, Jr., advocates in *Cultural Literacy* [to take a set of entries randomly chosen from Hirsch's list of "What Literate Americans Know": "Thirty Years War; This land is your land (song); Thoreau, Henry David; Thorpe, Jim; Three Bears, The (title)"]. Gardner argues that intelligence involves more than knowing facts like these; we must be able to connect and use them.

Recently, Gardner has turned his attention to a field that psychologists have spent surprisingly little time investigating: people's attitudes towards the work they do. Along with Mihaly Csikszentmihalyi and William Damon, he authored *Good Work: When Excellence and Ethics Meet* (2001). In the following essay, from *The Chronicle of Higher Education*, Feb. 22, 2002 (p. B7), Gardner explains the gist of his new project. That is, there are two essential characteristics of "good work": the worker uses a high amount of expertise and feels that the work relates significantly to the world.

The topic of work has long been the subject of academic study. Indeed, from their beginnings in the 18th and 19th centuries, the disciplines of economics and sociology accorded labor, production, and the organization—and organizations—of work a primary place in their firmament of concerns. Adam Smith, David Ricardo, and Karl Marx documented the opportunities and challenges faced by individual workers; Emile Durkheim and Max Weber probed the nature of bureaucracy, the division of labor, and the sense of calling. Today, when adults around the world spend about half of their waking hours at work, the topic is ever more salient.

Yet the actual experience of work has been strangely neglected by the very discipline equipped to tell us the most about it: academic psychology. Influential psychologists have had relatively little to say about the ways in which workers conceptualize their daily experiences—the goals and concerns that they bring to the workplace, the human and technical opportunities and obstacles that they encounter, the strategies that they develop to make the most of their experiences, the stances that they assume when faced with ethical dilemmas. Scanning the indexes in the psychology textbooks on my bookshelf, I find few references to work. That vast category is dwarfed by the entries for "word," on one side, and "working memory," on the other. To be sure, Freud deemed *"lieben und arbeiten"* the keys to a satisfying life; but, along with the majority of his colleagues, he directed most of his attention to sex and love, rather than to the experiences of work and the workplace.

Why have we psychologists shied away from studying something that means so much to so many of us? To be sure, any explanation is necessarily speculative. My own guess is that two facets of 20th-century psychology—particularly of the American academic variety—have militated against a holistic, experiential focus. On the one hand, psychology has suffered from a strong case of physics envy. It has sought the basic laws of the mind. The low-hanging fruit that has tempted us here are studies of sensation, perception, and the elementary operations of cognition. Indeed, those are the areas of academic psychology that have earned recognition in the National Academy of Sciences and even in the rare Nobel Prize.

The other feature of psychology has been its bias toward atomism—toward breaking down complex processes and problems into their most basic and irreducible elements. So, when psychologists turn their attention to work—or, for that matter, to play—they focus on the identification of specific skills, like typing a paragraph or playing peekaboo, where the relevant variables are most easily identified and controlled for. The complex world of work, with its welter of experiences, is too hard to pin down in the laboratory.

5   That is not to say that psychology has ignored all aspects of work. Research on how skill and expertise develop tells us about the importance of steady practice and the emergence of well-entrenched scripts to govern our daily endeavors. Studies of motivation reveal the intricate interplay between external rewards for high-level performance and those intrinsic satisfactions that can keep us engaged over the long haul, even when things are not going well. Examinations of adult development document the importance for psychic well-being of satisfaction in the workplace and the pleasures we take in passing on our skills, understandings, and passions to the younger generation. And applied industrial psychology—that exile from the university—aims to secure optimal performances from employees.

6   The scant literature on the psychology of work thus exhibits a striking schism. Arrayed on one side are studies that focus on technical excellence: what it means to be an expert or an innovator. On the other are studies that focus on the individual as a member of a working group or team. What's largely missing from the contemporary psychological literature are those topics that initially intrigued Adam Smith, above all a student of moral sentiments, and Max Weber, an explicator of work as a calling. I'm talking about the place that work occupies in the overall life experiences of the individual. It is high time that members of the psychology community attempt to bridge that schism.

7   Two other psychologists, Mihaly Csikszentmihalyi and William Damon, and I have come up with a name for the line of study that has been neglected in our profession: We call it "good work." Since 1995, we have been conducting in-depth interviews with professionals in an effort to define work that is good in two senses: It exhibits a high level of expertise, and it entails regular concern with the implications and applications of an individual's work for the wider world. We seek to understand what is good work; where it is found; how it develops and can be fostered. Most especially, we examine how individuals who wish to do good work succeed or fail in doing so, particularly in a time like our own, when conditions are changing very quickly, when market forces have enormous power over the individual (with few, if any, significant counterforces), and when our sense of time and space has been radically altered by technologies like the World Wide Web.

8   Clearly, we believe that a frontal attack by mainstream psychology on the experience of work is overdue. Equally clearly, it is especially important at this time of rapid change throughout the world. But, perhaps most important, we, as researchers, have a mission with a moral agenda. Too often, psychologists like us have studied competence purely in a technical sense—what does it mean to be intelligent, to be creative, to be a leader? What we haven't done is pay attention to the ways such tal-

ents are deployed. My colleagues and I want to see whether it is possible to understand that happy circumstance in which "good" in the technical sense converges with "good" in the moral sense.

To understand what we're after, think of two hypothetical individuals. Lawyer A wins most of her cases but cuts every possible corner and accepts only clients with deep pockets. Lawyer B defends the poor and the downtrodden, follows every regulation scrupulously, but consistently loses cases. Lawyer A is good only in the first sense of the term, of demonstrating expertise; Lawyer B only in the second sense, of showing concern for the wider world. We can all list individuals from various professions who appear to be *good* workers. My own roster would include the publisher Katharine Graham, the polio researcher Jonas Salk, the cellist Yo-Yo Ma, the tennis star Arthur Ashe, and John Gardner (no relation), the creator of many impressive institutions, to whom my colleagues and I dedicated our recent book, *Good Work: When Excellence and Ethics Meet*.   9

We are continuing our study across professions as varied as theater and philanthropy, but we initially focused on two realms of work that are crucial today: journalism and genetics. We reasoned that they deal with two vital forms of information in our lives. Journalists tell us what is happening in the world and update us as needed; in the biologist Richard Dawkins's term, they provide our "memes." Geneticists study the information that is most important for our physical existence—the code in the genes that reveals our life prospects. Until 50 years ago, genetics was carried out at some remove from our personal health. But in the wake of an epochal scientific revolution, geneticists stand poised not only to reveal our personal destinies, but also to provide the information and tools that could lead to genetic engineering, genetic therapy, and cloning of organs or entire organisms.   10

As psychologists, my colleagues and I wanted to know what it is like to work at the cutting edge of such influential professions. To find out, we conducted interviews with more than 100 geneticists and 100 journalists. Most were recognized leaders in their respective professions, but we also spoke with a number of young professionals and midlevel practitioners, those solid workers who are established but not leaders. We asked our subjects about their goals, their values, the obstacles that they encountered, the strategies that they used at such times, their backgrounds, their professional aspirations. We also posed ethical dilemmas and asked them to carry out a "Q sort," a procedure in which they rank their personal values in importance. Generally we accepted their testimony as sincere and truthful. Yet we also challenged them when it seemed appropriate—for example, if they contradicted themselves or the published record—and we reviewed each single-spaced page of each 30-to-50-page transcript in terms of our general knowledge and in light of the testimony of our subjects' professional colleagues.   11

12   At the time of our initial study, in the late 1990s, the experiences of the two groups of professionals could not have been more different. Geneticists were almost wholly a satisfied lot; they could not wait to get up in the morning and pursue their work. They felt that it was possible—even likely—that they could achieve their goals of deciphering the nature of life and catalyzing the discovery of procedures and treatments that could improve health and lengthen lives. They saw few obstacles in their paths. Nor did they express particular concern about ethical dilemmas that have since been widely reported—about, for instance, the ethics of cloning, stem-cell research, and various forms of genetic therapy. (In fact, the greatest concern they raised was about misuse of genetic data by insurance companies—the only area in which the geneticists themselves played no role.) In our terms, their domain was "highly aligned": In 1997–99, all of the principal stakeholders, from individual scientists to shareholders of biotech companies to the public, were in their corner.

13   In sharp contrast, the journalists were by and large despondent about their profession. Many had entered print or broadcast journalism armed with ideals: covering important stories, doing so in an exhaustive and fair way, relying on their own judgment about the significance of stories and the manner in which they should be presented. Instead, for the most part, our subjects reported that much of the control in journalism has passed from professionals to corporate executives and stockholders, with most of the professional decisions made less on the basis of ideals than of profits. They described what felt to them like an ineluctable trend away from stories of any complexity or sensitivity, toward material that is simple and sensational, if not of prurient interest. Journalism emerges, in our phrase, as a domain that is "poorly aligned": It is difficult to carry out good work in the profession; many individuals have left the field, and quite a few more are considering doing so.

14   While our findings might appear to be simply a "good news, bad news" story, we determined that it is more complex than that. Alignment or nonalignment are temporary conditions. Journalism was well-aligned in America in the 1950s; genetics could well become misaligned, if the research agenda comes to be set by corporate executives rather than by scientists, or if there is a major mishap in the field, a kind of genetic Three Mile Island.

15   Indeed, in the brief period since September 11, a realignment of sorts may already have commenced. The frivolous aspects of journalism have receded to some extent; readers and viewers want their news straight up, and they turn to the most reliable outlets. Genetics has not yet been directly affected. But it may be that, in the aftermath of September 11, there will be pressures to mobilize the best brains to fight bioterrorism rather than to carry out basic research in a field like genet-

ics. The recession will no doubt also put a crimp in financing. And the very specter of bioterrorism reminds us of the essential amorality of all science and technology.

Whether, and to what degree, the work experience in journalism   16 and genetics changes as a result of recent events, our study illuminates how individuals feel about good work in their fields. Consider the story Ray Suarez told us. In the early 1990s, the Chicago-based television journalist was assigned to cover a story about the possible dangers of video games; a producer had heard that such games might cause epileptic fits in children. The more that Suarez probed, however, the more he realized that the threat was not genuine. As he put it, "About halfway into the reporting of the story, I realized that we were talking about one-tenth of one one-hundredth of one one-thousandth of the kids who play video games. But TV has a tendency to play everything like '*Here's a possible danger of video games.*'" Suarez had tried to get out of covering the story, but his boss insisted that he go on and file it. "If you have a contract and a contract says certain things, you have to do what you're told," the reporter reminded us. Suarez realized that he would continue to encounter such pressures and felt that he could not tolerate them. He was considering leaving the news business altogether when he landed a job with National Public Radio. From that time on, he has worked for public broadcasting. He has opted to pursue a career in which he is able to carry out work in which he feels pride.

A very different kind of situation was faced by a young scientist (who   17 asked not to be named) who was working in a genetic-research program. To his surprise, he discovered that some of the protocols in his project were being financed twice—by the National Institutes of Health, at taxpayers expense, and by a for-profit drug company. Neither underwriter was aware of the double billing. Steeling himself, the young scientist reported what was clearly an improper situation to the dean of the medical school. The dean listened carefully and thanked the young informant. But the whistle-blower, who was trying to do good work, soon discovered that he was being moved to less sensitive positions on the team, and that nothing was being done to correct the lapse of ethics. Eventually, he realized that the dean had been the one to devise the system of double billing. The geneticist—forced to choose between probably injuring his career and tacitly condoning a scam—decided to leave the university.

The dilemmas that Suarez and the young scientist described are   18 faced by workers in every domain. Anyone can be pressured to do questionable things that promise profits; anyone can discover an illegal procedure and be penalized for reporting it to someone in authority. And, as our study confirmed, the goal of carrying out good work is harder to reach when conditions are unstable and market forces are allowed to run unchecked.

19   What does that mean—for our individual psyches and for society as a whole? In such situations, many, if not most, of us resign ourselves to our fate. It is difficult to quit one's job, let alone one's whole profession; and few in midlife, saddled with mortgage and, perhaps, tuition payments, have the fortitude to do so. As a result, we are left with a society in which profit motives reign supreme—and in which few feel in a position where they can perform good work.

20   It is worth remembering, however, Margaret Mead's famous remark: "Never doubt that a small group of committed people can change the world. Indeed, it is the only thing that ever has." Following Mead's quintessentially American sentiment, and on the basis of our study, my colleagues and I believe that the most likely path to satisfaction in good work—in the sense of developing expertise as well as helping society—is for each of us to take the initiative, one by one. We therefore call on people to focus on what we term the "three M's": Mission, Models, Mirror.

21   First: Define your mission. Whether you are a professional or a worker in a service or manufacturing industry, it is important to lay out the mission of your work. What are you trying to achieve, how does it serve society, what difference does it make? We are not speaking here about producing mission-statement boilerplate—something to be promulgated and forgotten. Rather, we are talking about identifying the reasons that one originally chose one's work and making a serious effort to determine whether that mission still stands or whether one has strayed from it—and, if so, in what direction. Evidence for the rarity of that exercise is the gratitude that many of our subjects expressed after they had taken a few hours to wrestle with the fundamental questions we had raised with them about their work experience.

22   Second: Identify role models. We probably all sense that it helps to identify individuals in our jobs whom we admire and strive to emulate. Many newspeople, for example, talk about looking up to Edward R. Murrow, Bob Woodward and Carl Bernstein, or Katharine Graham. But we were intrigued to find that individuals are also influenced by antimentors or tormentors, individuals from whom they strive to distinguish themselves. Several scientists told us that they were emboldened to pursue a certain line of work when a colleague or mentor said that it could not be done or, worse, that *they* could not do it. A few older female scientists recalled that their own professors had questioned their commitment to the field, and they said they felt a particular mission today to work with promising young women.

23   Finally: Take the mirror test. Ultimately, individuals need to be able to look at themselves objectively and see whether they are the kind of person they wish to be. When you look at yourself in the mirror, are you proud or embarrassed by what you see? How do others feel about

you? And how does your profession, as a whole, stack up—does it pass the mirror test? Quite a few journalists we interviewed expressed dismay about the way in which their profession was evolving, and a few indicated that they had voluntarily left broadcast news. We were reminded of the remark by Harold Evans, who has edited major newspapers in England and the United States: "The problem many organizations face is not to stay in business but to stay in journalism."

There is no guarantee, of course, that everyone who strives to become a good worker will succeed. Nor is there any guarantee that individuals will always assess themselves accurately; we all have a tendency to see ourselves in a positive light. Yet the research that my colleagues and I are conducting indicates that the three M's can help us and our society.   24

Anyone involved in a study of the human sphere has searched his soul in the weeks since September 11. Stacked against the enormous political, ideological, financial, and religious forces that have been unleashed, the individual human psyche seems in some ways a slender reed. Yet I've been struck by the extent to which so many of us— ranging from college students to the most experienced and successful professionals—have been jarred into posing fundamental questions to ourselves: Am I doing the work that I should be doing? If not, what should I be doing, and how should I be carrying it out?   25

As a psychologist, I had thought that most commitments to good work arise from a personal revelation or trauma, when one's life is reoriented because of a Damascene experience. But clearly, on occasion, a tremendous jolt to our wider world can also bring about reconsideration. After the detonation of nuclear weapons over Japan, for example, many particle physicists confronted agonizing questions about their work. What is unprecedented, in my experience, is a shock like September 11, which reverberates through an entire society—a shock so great that workers across the economic and political spectrum have come to pose existential questions to themselves. While such questions assuredly go beyond the hours at work, they cannot fail to ignore the substantial part of every day that is devoted to human labor. Perhaps the pervasive reflective activity of recent months may deliver a message to a discipline like my own, which has, for too long, virtually ignored the meanings of the central activity in our lives.   26

RESPONDING TO READING

1. In American culture, how are people defined by the work they do? Is this work itself judged by the salary that it pays? Do Americans evaluate the worth of an individual by the amount of money he or she makes? What are the implications of this attitude for the majority of Americans who work for minimum wage?

2. According to Gardner, how has the academic structure and focus of the field of psychology biased it against studying work, even though this is where most people spend the majority of their time?

3. How does Gardner define the concept of "good work"? Based on his definition, which jobs would be considered good? Which jobs would not be good? Does this definition bias Gardner's argument towards different kinds of work? Write an essay in which you define your ideal career or job, and show how it either reinforces or contradicts Gardner's definition of "good work."

4. Discuss with several peers the kinds of jobs each of you have held. Do these jobs have common elements? Would Gardner consider your work to be "good"? How would each of you define good work? In what ways do you consider the work you have done to be good? or not good? According to what criteria?

5. Interview one or two members of your extended family—parents, siblings, grandparents, cousins, uncles, or aunts—about their work history. Provide detailed job descriptions of the work that each person performs or has performed in his/her lifetime. (If an individual has held lots of jobs, you may want to focus on only two or three of these.) In an essay, explain how this work defines each person. Would this work be "good work" according to Gardner? Is there another definition of "good work" that you would offer based on your own experiences or those of your extended family members?

Serving in Florida

BARBARA EHRENREICH

Barbara Ehrenreich was born (1941) in Butte, Montana, to a family of "blue-eyed, Scotch–Irish Democrats" whose occupations were farming, railroad work, and mining. A graduate of highly progressive Reed College (B.A., 1963), she prepared for a career in science and health care, earning her Ph.D. in biology at Rockefeller University (1968). After working as an assistant professor of health sciences, she devoted herself full time to writing, becoming one of the most outspoken critics of American institutions and corporations. Since 1974, her journalism and books have championed the case of the working poor and of women trapped in unjust social situations. Her articles, written in a jargon-free style graced with humor and astute observation, have appeared in national magazines such as *Mother Jones* and *The Guardian*, and her essays appear regularly in *Time*. Her books include *Fear of Falling: The Inner Life of the Middle Class* (1989), *The Worst Years of Our Lives: Irreverent Notes on a Decade of Greed* (1990), *Blood Rites: The Origins and History of the Passions of War* (1997), and *Nickled and Dimed: On (Not) Getting By in American* (2001). She has also published the novel *Kipper's Game* (1993). She is an associate fellow of the New York Institute for the Humanities and a fellow of the Institute

for Policy Studies (Washington, DC), and was awarded a Guggenheim fellowship in 1987.

   Nickled and Dimed documents the living conditions of low-
salaried American workers. To research her subject, Ehrenreich
worked as a maid and a waitress in various jobs paying $6 to $7 an
hour. "Serving in Florida," from a chapter in this book, is a chronicle
of stultifying routine, squalid surroundings, and slim rewards. During this period, Ehrenreich's adult colleagues—some with families—
not only earned little, but often paid more, item per item, for food and
shelter than do most middle-class citizens.

   I could drift along like this, in some dreamy proletarian idyll, ex-   1
cept for two things. One is management. If I have kept this subject to
the margins so far it is because I still flinch to think that I spent all
those weeks under the surveillance of men (and later women) whose
job it was to monitor my behavior for signs of sloth, theft, drug abuse,
or worse. Not that managers and especially "assistant managers" in
low-wage settings like this are exactly the class enemy. Mostly, in the
restaurant business, they are former cooks still capable of pinch-hit-
ting in the kitchen, just as in hotels they are likely to be former clerks,
and paid a salary of only about $400 a week. But everyone knows they
have crossed over to the other side, which is, crudely put, corporate as
opposed to human. Cooks want to prepare tasty meals, servers want
to serve them graciously, but managers are there for only one
reason—to make sure that money is made for some theoretical entity,
the corporation, which exists far away in Chicago or New York, if a
corporation can be said to have a physical existence at all. Reflecting
on her career, Gail tells me ruefully that she swore, years ago, never to
work for a corporation again. "They don't cut you no slack. You give
and you give and they take."

   Managers can sit—for hours at a time if they want—but it's their   2
job to see that no one else ever does, even when there's nothing to do,
and this is why, for servers, slow times can be as exhausting as rushes.
You start dragging out each little chore because if the manager on duty
catches you in an idle moment he will give you something far nastier to
do. So I wipe, I clean, I consolidate catsup bottles and recheck the
cheesecake supply, even tour the tables to make sure the customer evaluation forms are all standing perkily in their places—wondering all the
time how many calories I burn in these strictly theatrical exercises. In
desperation, I even take the desserts out of their glass display case and
freshen them up with whipped cream and bright new maraschino
cherries; anything to look busy. When, on a particularly dead afternoon, Stu finds me glancing at a *USA Today* a customer has left behind,
he assigns me to vacuum the entire floor with the broken vacuum

cleaner, which has a handle only two feet long, and the only way to do that without incurring orthopedic damage is to proceed from spot to spot on your knees.

3   On my first Friday at Hearthside there is a "mandatory meeting for all restaurant employees," which I attend, eager for insight into our overall marketing strategy and the niche (your basic Ohio cuisine with a tropical twist?) we aim to inhabit. But there is no "we" at this meeting. Phillip, our top manager except for an occasional "consultant" sent out by corporate headquarters, opens it with a sneer: "The break room—it's disgusting. Butts in the ashtrays, newspapers lying around, crumbs." This windowless little room, which also houses the time clock for the entire hotel, is where we stash our bags and civilian clothes and take our half-hour meal breaks. But a break room is not a right, he tells us, it can be taken away. We should also know that the lockers in the break room and whatever is in them can be searched at any time. Then comes gossip; there has been gossip; gossip (which seems to mean employees talking among themselves) must stop. Off-duty employees are henceforth barred from eating at the restaurant, because "other servers gather around them and gossip." When Phillip has exhausted his agenda of rebukes, Joan complains about the condition of the ladies' room and I throw in my two bits about the vacuum cleaner. But I don't see any backup coming from my fellow servers, each of whom has slipped into her own personal funk; Gail, my role model, stares sorrowfully at a point six inches from her nose. The meeting ends when Andy, one of the cooks, gets up, muttering about breaking up his day off for this almighty bullshit.

4   Just four days later we are suddenly summoned into the kitchen at 3:30 P.M., even though there are live tables on the floor. We all—about ten of us—stand around Phillip, who announces grimly that there has been a report of some "drug activity" on the night shift and that, as a result, we are now to be a "drug-free" workplace, meaning that all new hires will be tested and possibly also current employees on a random basis. I am glad that this part of the kitchen is so dark because I find myself blushing as hard as if I had been caught toking up in the ladies' room myself: I haven't been treated this way—lined up in the corridor, threatened with locker searches, peppered with carelessly aimed accusations—since at least junior high school. Back on the floor, Joan cracks, "Next they'll be telling us we can't have *sex* on the job." When I ask Stu what happened to inspire the crackdown, he just mutters about "management decisions" and takes the opportunity to upbraid Gail and me for being too generous with the rolls. From now on there's to be only one per customer and it goes out with the dinner, not with the salad. He's also been riding the cooks, prompting Andy to come out of

the kitchen and observe—with the serenity of a man whose customary implement is a butcher knife—that "Stu has a death wish today."

Later in the evening, the gossip crystallizes around the theory that   5
Stu is himself the drug culprit, that he uses the restaurant phone to order up marijuana and sends one of the late servers out to fetch it for him. The server was caught and she may have ratted out Stu, at least enough to cast some suspicion on him, thus accounting for his pissy behavior. Who knows? Personally, I'm ready to believe anything bad about Stu, who serves no evident function and presumes too much on our common ethnicity, sidling up to me one night to engage in a little nativism directed at the Haitian immigrants: "I feel like I'm the foreigner here. They're taking over the country." Still later that evening, the drug in question escalates to crack. Lionel, the busboy, entertains us for the rest of the shift by standing just behind Stu's back and sucking deliriously on an imaginary joint or maybe a pipe.

The other problem, in addition to the less-than-nurturing manage-   6
ment style, is that this job shows no sign of being financially viable. You might imagine, from a comfortable distance, that people who live, year in and year out, on $6 to $10 an hour have discovered some survival stratagems unknown to the middle class. But no. It's not hard to get my coworkers talking about their living situations, because housing, in almost every case, is the principal source of disruption in their lives, the first thing they fill you in on when they arrive for their shifts. After a week, I have compiled the following survey:

> Gail is sharing a room in a well-known downtown flophouse for   7
> $250 a week. Her roommate, a male friend, has begun hitting on her, driving her nuts, but the rent would be impossible alone.

> Claude, the Haitian cook, is desperate to get out of the two-room   8
> apartment he shares with his girlfriend and two other, unrelated people. As far as I can determine, the other Haitian men live in similarly crowded situations.

> Annette, a twenty-year-old server who is six months pregnant   9
> and abandoned by her boyfriend, lives with her mother, a postal clerk.

> Marianne, who is a breakfast server, and her boyfriend are pay-   10
> ing $170 a week for a one-person trailer.

> Billy, who at $10 an hour is the wealthiest of us, lives in the trail-   11
> er he owns, paying only the $400-a-month lot fee.

> The other white cook, Andy, lives on his dry-docked boat, which,   12
> as far as I can tell from his loving descriptions, can't be more than twenty feet long. He offers to take me out on it once it's repaired, but the offer comes with inquiries as to my marital status, so I do not follow up on it.

13   Tina, another server, and her husband are paying $60 a night for a room in the Days Inn. This is because they have no car and the Days Inn is in walking distance of the Hearthside. When Marianne is tossed out of her trailer for subletting (which is against trailer park rules), she leaves her boyfriend and moves in with Tina and her husband.

14   Joan, who had fooled me with her numerous and tasteful outfits (hostesses wear their own clothes), lives in a van parked behind a shopping center at night and showers in Tina's motel room. The clothes are from thrift shops.[1]

15   It strikes me, in my middle-class solipsism, that there is gross improvidence in some of these arrangements. When Gail and I are wrapping silverware in napkins—the only task for which we are permitted to sit—she tells me she is thinking of escaping from her roommate by moving into the Days Inn herself. I am astounded: how she can even think of paying $40 to $60 a day? But if I was afraid of sounding like a social worker, I have come out just sounding like a fool. She squints at me in disbelief: "And where am I supposed to get a month's rent and a month's deposit for an apartment?" I'd been feeling pretty smug about my $500 efficiency, but of course it was made possible only by the $1,300 I had allotted myself for start-up costs when I began my low-wage life: $1,000 for the first month's rent and deposit, $100 for initial groceries and cash in my pocket, $200 stuffed away for emergencies. In poverty, as in certain propositions in physics, starting conditions are everything.

16   There are no secret economies that nourish the poor; on the contrary, there are a host of special costs. If you can't put up the two months' rent you need to secure an apartment, you end up paying through the nose for a room by the week. If you have only a room, with a hot plate at best, you can't save by cooking up huge lentil stews that can be frozen for the week ahead. You eat fast food or the hot dogs and Styrofoam cups of soup that can be microwaved in a convenience store. If you have no money for health insurance—and the Hearthside's niggardly plan kicks in only after three months—you go without routine care or prescription drugs and end up paying the price. Gail, for example, was doing fine, healthwise anyway, until she ran out of money for estrogen pills. She is supposed to be on the company health plan by now, but they claim to have lost her application form and to be beginning the paperwork all over again. So she

---

[1] I could find no statistics on the number of employed people living in cars or vans, but according to a 1997 report of the National Coalition for the Homeless, "Myths and Facts about Homelessness," nearly one-fifth of all homeless people (in twenty-nine cities across the nation) are employed in full- or part-time jobs.

spends $9 a pop for pills to control the migraines she wouldn't have, she insists, if her estrogen supplements were covered. Similarly, Marianne's boyfriend lost his job as a roofer because he missed so much time after getting a cut on his foot for which he couldn't afford the prescribed antibiotic.

My own situation, when I sit down to assess it after two weeks of 17 work, would not be much better if this were my actual life. The seductive thing about waitressing is that you don't have to wait for payday to feel a few bills in your pocket, and my tips usually cover meals and gas, plus something left over to stuff into the kitchen drawer I use as a bank. But as the tourist business slows in the summer heat, I sometimes leave work with only $20 in tips (the gross is higher, but servers share about 15 percent of their tips with the busboys and bartenders). With wages included, this amounts to about the minimum wage of $5.15 an hour. The sum in the drawer is piling up but at the present rate of accumulation will be more than $100 short of my rent when the end of the month comes around. Nor can I see any expenses to cut. True, I haven't gone the lentil stew route yet, but that's because I don't have a large cooking pot, potholders, or a ladle to stir with (which would cost a total of about $30 at Kmart, somewhat less at a thrift store), not to mention onions, carrots, and the indispensable bay leaf. I do make my lunch almost every day—usually some slow-burning, high-protein combo like frozen chicken patties with melted cheese on top and canned pinto beans on the side. Dinner is at the Hearthside, which offers its employees a choice of BLT, fish sandwich, or hamburger for only $2. The burger lasts longest, especially if it's heaped with gut-puckering jalapeños, but by midnight my stomach is growling again.

So unless I want to start using my car as a residence, I have to find 18 a second or an alternative job. I call all the hotels I'd filled out housekeeping applications at weeks ago—the Hyatt, Holiday Inn, Econo Lodge, HoJo's, Best Western, plus a half dozen locally run guest houses. Nothing. Then I start making the rounds again, wasting whole mornings waiting for some assistant manager to show up, even dipping into places so creepy that the front-desk clerk greets you from behind bullet-proof glass and sells pints of liquor over the counter. But either someone has exposed my real-life housekeeping habits—which are, shall we say, mellow—or I am at the wrong end of some infallible ethnic equation: most, but by no means all, of the working housekeepers I see on my job searches are African Americans, Spanish-speaking, or refugees from the Central European post-Communist world, while servers are almost invariably white and monolingually English-speaking. When I finally get a positive response, I have been identified once again as server material. Jerry's—again, not the real name—which is part of a well-known national chain and physically attached here to another budget hotel, is ready to use me at once. The prospect is both exciting and terrifying because, with about the same number of tables and counter seats, Jerry's attracts three or four times the volume of customers as the gloomy old Hearthside.

19   Picture a fat person's hell, and I don't mean a place with no food. Instead there is everything you might eat if eating had no bodily consequences—the cheese fries, the chicken-fried steaks, the fudge-laden desserts—only here every bite must be paid for, one way or another, in human discomfort. The kitchen is a cavern, a stomach leading to the lower intestine that is the garbage and dishwashing area, from which issue bizarre smells combining the edible and the offal: creamy carrion, pizza barf, and that unique and enigmatic Jerry's scent, citrus fart. The floor is slick with spills, forcing us to walk through the kitchen with tiny steps, like Susan McDougal in leg irons. Sinks everywhere are clogged with scraps of lettuce, decomposing lemon wedges, water-logged toast crusts. Put your hand down on any counter and you risk being stuck to it by the film of ancient syrup spills, and this is unfortunate because hands are utensils here, used for scooping up lettuce onto the salad plates, lifting out pie slices, and even moving hash browns from one plate to another. The regulation poster in the single unisex rest room admonishes us to wash our hands thoroughly, and even offers instructions for doing so, but there is always some vital substance missing—soap, paper towels, toilet paper—and I never found all three at once. You learn to stuff your pockets with napkins before going in there, and too bad about the customers, who must eat, although they don't realize it, almost literally out of our hands.

20   The break room summarizes the whole situation: there is none, because there are no breaks at Jerry's. For six to eight hours in a row, you never sit except to pee. Actually, there are three folding chairs at a table immediately adjacent to the bathroom, but hardly anyone ever sits in this, the very rectum of the gastroarchitectural system. Rather, the function of the peri-toilet area is to house the ashtrays in which servers and dishwashers leave their cigarettes burning at all times, like votive candles, so they don't have to waste time lighting up again when they dash back here for a puff. Almost everyone smokes as if their pulmonary well-being depended on it—the multi-national mélange of cooks; the dishwashers, who are all Czechs here; the servers, who are American natives—creating an atmosphere in which oxygen is only an occasional pollutant. My first morning at Jerry's, when the hypoglycemic shakes set in, I complain to one of my fellow servers that I don't understand how she can go so long without food. "Well, I don't understand how *you* can go so long without a cigarette," she responds in a tone of reproach.

Because work is what you do for others; smoking is what you do for yourself. I don't know why the antismoking crusaders have never grasped the element of defiant self-nurturance that makes the habit so endearing to its victims—as if in the American workplace, the only thing people have to call their own is the tumors they are nourishing and the spare moments they devote to feeding them.

Now, the Industrial Revolution is not an easy transition, especially, 21 in my experience, when you have to zip through it in just a couple of days. I have gone from craft work straight into the factory, from the air-conditioned morgue of the Hearthside directly into the flames. Customers arrive in human waves, sometimes disgorged fifty at a time from their tour buses, peckish and whiny. Instead of two "girls" on the floor at once, there can be as many as six of us running around in our brilliant pink-and-orange Hawaiian shirts. Conversations, either with customers or with fellow employees, seldom last more than twenty seconds at a time. On my first day, in fact, I am hurt by my sister servers' coldness. My mentor for the day is a supremely competent, emotionally uninflected twenty-three-year-old, and the others, who gossip a little among themselves about the real reason someone is out sick today and the size of the bail bond someone else has had to pay, ignore me completely. On my second day, I find out why. "Well, it's good to see *you* again," one of them says in greeting. "Hardly anyone comes back after the first day." I feel powerfully vindicated—a survivor—but it would take a long time, probably months, before I could hope to be accepted into this sorority.

I start out with the beautiful, heroic idea of handling the two jobs at 22 once, and for two days I almost do it: working the breakfast/lunch shift at Jerry's from 8:00 till 2:00, arriving at the Hearthside a few minutes late, at 2:10, and attempting to hold out until 10:00. In the few minutes I have between jobs, I pick up a spicy chicken sandwich at the Wendy's drive-through window, gobble it down in the car, and change from khaki slacks to black, from Hawaiian to rust-colored polo. There is a problem, though. When, during the 3:00–4:00 o'clock dead time, I finally sit down to wrap silver, my flesh seems to bond to the seat. I try to refuel with a purloined cup of clam chowder, as I've seen Gail and Joan do dozens of time, but Stu catches me and hisses "No *eating!*" although there's not a customer around to be offended by the sight of food making contact with a server's lips. So I tell Gail I'm going to quit, and she hugs me and says she might just follow me to Jerry's herself.

But the chances of this are minuscule. She has left the flop-house 23 and her annoying roommate and is back to living in her truck. But, guess what, she reports to me excitedly later that evening, Phillip has given her permission to park overnight in the hotel parking lot, as long as she keeps out of sight, and the parking lot should be totally safe since it's patrolled by a hotel security guard! With the Hearthside offering benefits like that, how could anyone think of leaving? This must be Phillip's theory, anyway. He accepts my resignation with a shrug, his main concern being that I return my two polo shirts and aprons.

24   Gail would have triumphed at Jerry's, I'm sure, but for me it's a crash course in exhaustion management. Years ago, the kindly fry cook who trained me to waitress at a Los Angeles truck stop used to say: Never make an unnecessary trip; if you don't have to walk fast, walk slow; if you don't have to walk, stand. But at Jerry's the effort of distinguishing necessary from unnecessary and urgent from whenever would itself be too much of an energy drain. The only thing to do is to treat each shift as a one-time-only emergency: you've got fifty starving people out there, lying scattered on the battlefield, so get out there and feed them! Forget that you will have to do this again tomorrow, forget that you will have to be alert enough to dodge the drunks on the drive home tonight—just burn, burn, burn! Ideally, at some point you enter what servers call a "rhythm" and psychologists term a "flow state," where signals pass from the sense organs directly to the muscles, bypassing the cerebral cortex, and a Zen-like emptiness sets in. I'm on a 2:00–10:00 P.M. shift now, and a male server from the morning shift tells me about the time he "pulled a triple"—three shifts in a row, all the way around the clock—and then got off and had a drink and met this girl, and maybe he shouldn't tell me this, but they had sex right then and there and it was like *beautiful*. [. . .]

RESPONDING TO READING

1. Why does Ehrenreich argue that managers and assistant managers have "crossed over to the other side"? What is "the other side"? How are managers and workers defined if we separate them into categories of "corporate" and "human"?

2. What role does Stu play in Ehrenreich's essay? What qualities of management does he represent? How does he illustrate the arguments that Ehrenreich is making about individual workers, human dignity, and the workplace?

3. How does Ehrenreich's discussion of her coworkers' living conditions support her argument? Why focus on housing? What other costs of living besides paying the rent does she connect to the problem of housing?

4. What part do issues of race and social class play in Ehrenreich's argument? Is Ehrenreich making a reasoned argument based on observations, or is she relying on stereotypes? Discuss with other students the bases on which Ehrenreich makes her observations about race and class.

5. Ehrenreich argues that "work is what you do for others; smoking is what you do for yourself." Does she refer to smoking in particular as an act of defiance, or would any other behavior forbidden on the job suffice to make her case? In a book chapter that will be read by nonsmokers and smokers

alike, how does her essay build to this statement? What connections does she implicitly and explicitly make between smoking (or other defiant acts), issues of human dignity, and management's control over individual workers? What defiant behavior or actions would you personally use to question authority? Why these?

When Doctors Make Mistakes

ATUL GAWANDE

Born in 1966, Atul Gawande received his M.D. from Harvard Medical School and, later, an M.PH. from the Harvard School of Public Health. Many of the essays in his book "Complications" (2002) have appeared in *The New Yorker*, where Gawande is a staff writer. Critic Daniel Smith argues that Gawande "has imbued his prose with physicality because medicine is predicated on exactly that: physical action. And physical action means risk, confusion, complexity, and sometimes mistakes." This focus on the ethical dilemmas of medical practitioners and patients alike suffuses Gawande's work. In "Organ Meat" (1998), Gawande argues that while selling organs may save lives, it comes at a terrible ethical price for society. He writes, "Some options are so terrible and irrevocable, so unlikely to be in a person's self-interest, and so open to exploitation and flawed decision-making that society outlaws them."

In "When Doctors Make Mistakes," from *Complications*, Gawande writes of the personal side of medicine for doctors—the trauma of making life-and-death decisions on a daily basis and of having some of those decisions be wrong. In an interview for the *Atlanticonline* (2002), he argued, "I [am] trying to demystify medicine. [. . . We] have finally come to grips with the notion that, okay, doctors are not gods. But what comes after that?"

To much of the public—and certainly to lawyers and the media— medical error is fundamentally a problem of bad doctors. The way that things go wrong in medicine is normally unseen and, consequently, often misunderstood. Mistakes do happen. We tend to think of them as aberrant. They are, however, anything but.

At 2 A.M. on a crisp Friday in winter a few years ago, I was in sterile gloves and gown, pulling a teenage knifing victim's abdomen open, when my pager sounded. "Code Trauma, three minutes," the operating room nurse said, reading aloud from my pager display. This meant that an ambulance would be bringing another trauma patient to the hospital momentarily, and, as the surgical resident on duty for emergencies, I would have to be present for the patient's arrival. I stepped back from the table and took off my gown. Two other surgeons were working on the knifing victim: Michael Ball, the attending (the staff surgeon in charge of the case), and David Hernandez, the chief resident (a general surgeon in his final year of training). Ordinarily, these two would have come to supervise and help with the trauma, but they were stuck here. Ball, a dry, cerebral forty-two-year-old, looked over at me as I headed for the door. "If you run into any trouble, you call, and one of us will peel away," he said.

3   I did run into trouble. In telling this story, I have had to change some details about what happened (including the names of those involved). Nonetheless, I have tried to stay as close to the actual events as I could while protecting the patient, myself, and the rest of the staff.

4   The emergency room was one floor up, and, taking the stairs two at a time, I arrived just as the emergency medical technicians wheeled in a woman who appeared to be in her thirties and to weigh more than two hundred pounds. She lay motionless on a hard orange plastic spinal board—eyes closed, skin pale, blood running out of her nose. A nurse directed the crew into Trauma Bay 1, an examination room outfitted like an OR, with green tiles on the wall, monitoring devices, and space for portable X-ray equipment. We lifted her onto the bed and then went to work. One nurse began cutting off the woman's clothes. Another took vital signs. A third inserted a large-bore intravenous line into her right arm. A surgical intern put a Foley catheter into her bladder. The emergency-medicine attending was Samuel Johns, a gaunt, Ichabod Crane-like man in his fifties. He was standing to one side with his arms crossed, observing, which was a sign that I could go ahead and take charge.

5   In an academic hospital, residents provide most of the "moment to moment" doctoring. Our duties depend on our level of training, but we're never entirely on our own: there's always an attending, who oversees our decisions. That night, since Johns was the attending and was responsible for the patient's immediate management, I took my lead from him. At the same time, he wasn't a surgeon, and so he relied on me for surgical expertise.

6   "What's the story?" I asked.

7   An EMT rattled off the details: "Unidentified white female unrestrained driver in high-speed rollover. Ejected from the car. Found unresponsive to pain. Pulse a hundred, BP a hundred over sixty, breathing at thirty on her own . . . ."

8   As he spoke, I began examining her. The first step in caring for a trauma patient is always the same. It doesn't matter if a person has been shot eleven times or crushed by a truck or burned in a kitchen fire. The first thing you do is make sure that the patient can breathe without difficulty. This woman's breaths were shallow and rapid. An oximeter, by means of a sensor placed on her finger, measured the oxygen saturation of her blood. The "Oz sat" is normally more than 95 percent for a

patient breathing room air. The woman was wearing a face mask with oxygen turned up full blast, and her sat was only 90 percent.

"She's not oxygenating well," I announced in the flattened-out, wake-me-up-when-something-interesting-happens tone that all surgeons have acquired by about three months into residency. With my fingers, I verified that there wasn't any object in her mouth that would obstruct her airway; with a stethoscope, I confirmed that neither lung had collapsed. I got hold of a bag mask, pressed its clear facepiece over her nose and mouth, and squeezed the bellows, a kind of balloon with a one-way valve, shooting a liter of air into her with each compression. After a minute or so, her oxygen came up to a comfortable 98 percent. She obviously needed our help with breathing. "Let's tube her," I said. That meant putting a tube down through her vocal cords and into her trachea, which would insure a clear airway and allow for mechanical ventilation. 9

Johns, the attending, wanted to do the intubation. He picked up a Mac 3 laryngoscope, a standard but fairly primitive-looking L-shaped metal instrument for prying open the mouth and throat, and slipped the shoehornlike blade deep into her mouth and down to her larynx. Then he yanked the handle up toward the ceiling to pull her tongue out of the way, open her mouth and throat, and reveal the vocal cords, which sit like fleshy tent flaps at the entrance to the trachea. The patient didn't wince or gag: she was still out cold. 10

"Suction!" he called. "I can't see a thing." 11

He sucked out about a cup of blood and clot. Then he picked up the endotracheal tube—a clear rubber pipe about the diameter of an index finger and three times as long—and tried to guide it between her cords. After a minute, her sat started to fall. 12

"You're down to seventy percent," a nurse announced. 13

Johns kept struggling with the tube, trying to push it in, but it banged vainly against the cords. The patient's lips began to turn blue. 14

"Sixty percent," the nurse said. 15

Johns pulled everything out of the patient's mouth and fitted the bag mask back on. The oximeter's luminescent-green readout hovered at 60 for a moment and then rose steadily, to 97 percent. After a few minutes, he took the mask off and again tried to get the tube in. There was more blood, and there may have been some swelling, too: all the poking down the throat was probably not helping. The sat fell to 60 percent. He pulled out and "bagged" her until she returned to 95 percent. 16

When you're having trouble getting the tube in, the next step is to get specialized expertise. "Let's call anesthesia," I said, and Johns agreed. In the meantime, I continued to follow the standard trauma protocol: completing the examination and ordering fluids, lab tests, and X rays. Maybe five minutes passed as I worked. 17

18   The patient's sats drifted down to 92 percent—not a dramatic change but definitely not normal for a patient who is being manually ventilated. I checked to see if the sensor had slipped off her finger. It hadn't. "Is the oxygen up full blast?" I asked a nurse.

19   "It's up all the way," she said.

20   I listened again to the patient's lungs—no collapse. "We've got to get her tubed," Johns said. He took off the oxygen mask and tried again.

21   Somewhere in my mind, I must have been aware of the possibility that her airway was shutting down because of vocal cord swelling or blood. If it was, and we were unable to get a tube in, then the only chance she'd have to survive would be an emergency tracheotomy: cutting a hole in her neck and inserting a breathing tube into her trachea. Another attempt to intubate her might even trigger a spasm of the cords and a sudden closure of the airway—which is exactly what did happen.

22   If I had actually thought this far along, I would have recognized how ill-prepared I was to do an emergency "trache." As the one surgeon in the room, it's true, I had the most experience doing tracheotomies, but that wasn't saying much. I had been the assistant surgeon in only about half a dozen, and all but one of them had been non-emergency cases, employing techniques that were not designed for speed. The exception was a practice emergency trache I had done on a goat. I should have immediately called Dr. Ball for backup. I should have got the trache equipment out—lighting, suction, sterile instruments—just in case. Instead of hurrying the effort to get the patient intubated because of a mild drop in saturation, I should have asked Johns to wait until I had help nearby. I might even have recognized that she was already losing her airway. Then I could have grabbed a knife and done a tracheotomy while things were still relatively stable and I had time to proceed slowly. But for whatever reasons—hubris, inattention, wishful thinking, hesitation, or the uncertainty of the moment—I let the opportunity pass.

23   Johns hunched over the patient, trying intently to insert the tube through her vocal cords. When her sat once again dropped into the 60s, he stopped and put the mask back on. We stared at the monitor. The numbers weren't coming up. Her lips were still blue. Johns squeezed the bellows harder to blow more oxygen in.

24   "I'm getting resistance," he said.

25   The realization crept over me: this was a disaster. "Damn it, we've lost her airway," I said. "Trache kit! Light! Somebody call down to OR 25 and get Ball up here!"

26   People were suddenly scurrying everywhere. I tried to proceed deliberately, and not let panic take hold. I told the surgical intern to get a sterile gown and gloves on. I took an antiseptic solution off a shelf and

dumped a whole bottle of yellow-brown liquid on the patient's neck. A nurse unwrapped the tracheostomy kit—a sterilized set of drapes and instruments. I pulled on a gown and a new pair of gloves while trying to think through the steps. This is simple, really, I tried to tell myself. At the base of the thyroid cartilage, the Adam's apple, is a little gap in which you find a thin, fibrous covering called the cricothyroid membrane. Cut through that and—*voilà!* You're in the trachea. You slip through the hole a four-inch plastic tube shaped like a plumber's elbow joint, hook it up to oxygen and a ventilator, and she's all set. Anyway, that was the theory.

I threw some drapes over her body, leaving the neck exposed. It 27 looked as thick as a tree. I felt for the bony prominence of the thyroid cartilage. But I couldn't feel anything through the layers of fat. I was beset by uncertainty—where should I cut? should I make a horizontal or a vertical incision?—and I hated myself for it. Surgeons never dithered, and I was dithering.

"I need better light," I said.   28

Someone was sent out to look for one.   29

"Did anyone get Ball?" I asked. It wasn't exactly an inspiring 30 question.

"He's on his way," a nurse said.   31

There was no time to wait. Four minutes without oxygen would 32 lead to permanent brain damage, if not death. Finally, I took the scalpel and cut. I just cut. I made a three-inch left-to-right swipe across the middle of the neck, following the procedure I'd learned for elective cases. Dissecting down with scissors while the intern held the wound open with retractors, I hit a vein. It didn't let loose a lot of blood, but there was enough to fill the wound: I couldn't see anything. The intern put a finger on the bleeder. I called for suction. But the suction wasn't working; the tube was clogged with clot from the intubation efforts.

"Somebody get some new tubing," I said. "And where's the light?" 33

Finally, an orderly wheeled in a tall overhead light, plugged it in, 34 and flipped on the switch. It was still too dim; I could have done better with a flashlight.

I wiped up the blood with gauze, then felt around in the wound 35 with my fingertips. This time, I thought I could feel the hard ridges of the thyroid cartilage and, below it, the slight gap of the cricothyroid membrane, though I couldn't be sure. I held my place with my left hand.

James O'Connor, a silver-haired, seen-it-all anesthesiologist, came 36 into the room. Johns gave him a quick rundown on the patient and let him take over ventilating her.

Holding the scalpel in my right hand like a pen, I stuck the blade 37 down into the wound at the spot where I thought the thyroid cartilage was. With small, sharp strokes—working blindly, because of the blood and the poor light—I cut down through the overlying fat and tissue until I felt the blade scrape against the almost bony cartilage. I searched with the tip of the knife, walking it along until I felt it reach a gap. I hoped it was the cricothyroid membrane, and pressed down firmly. I felt the tissue suddenly give, and I cut an inch-long opening.

38   When I put my index finger into it, it felt as if I were prying open the jaws of a stiff clothespin. Inside, I thought I felt open space. But where were the sounds of moving air that I expected? Was this deep enough? Was I even in the right place?

39   "I think I'm in," I said, to reassure myself as much as anyone else.

40   "I hope so," O'Connor said. "She doesn't have much longer."

41   I took the tracheostomy tube and tried to fit it in, but something seemed to be blocking it. I twisted it and turned it, and finally jammed it in. Just then Ball, the surgical attending, arrived. He rushed up to the bed and leaned over for a look. "Did you get it?" he asked. I said that I thought so. The bag mask was plugged onto the open end of the trache tube. But when the bellows were compressed the air just gurgled out of the wound. Ball quickly put on gloves and a gown.

42   "How long has she been without an airway?" he asked.

43   "I don't know. Three minutes."

44   Ball's face hardened as he registered that he had about a minute in which to turn things around. He took my place and summarily pulled out the trache tube. "God, what a mess," he said. "I can't see a thing in this wound. I don't even know if you're in the right place. Can we get better light and suction?" New suction tubing was found and handed to him. He quickly cleaned up the wound and went to work.

45   The patient's sat had dropped so low that the oximeter couldn't detect it anymore. Her heart rate began slowing down—first to the 60s and then to the 40s. Then she lost her pulse entirely. I put my hands together on her chest, locked my elbows, leaned over her, and started doing chest compressions.

46   Ball looked up from the patient and turned to O'Connor. "I'm not going to get her an airway in time," he said. "You're going to have to try again from above." Essentially, he was admitting my failure. Trying an oral intubation again was pointless—just something to do instead of watching her die. I was stricken, and concentrated on doing chest compressions, not looking at anyone. It was over, I thought.

47   And then, amazingly, O'Connor: "I'm in." He had managed to slip a pediatric-size endotracheal tube through the vocal cords. In thirty seconds, with oxygen being manually ventilated through the tube, her heart was back, racing at a hundred and twenty beats a minute. Her sat registered at 60 and then climbed. Another thirty seconds and it was at 97 percent. All the people in the room exhaled, as if they, too, had been denied their breath. Ball and I said little except to confer about the next

steps for her. Then he went back downstairs to finish working on the stab-wound patient still in the OR.

We eventually identified the woman, whom I'll call Louise   48 Williams; she was thirty-four years old and lived alone in a nearby sub- urb. Her alcohol level on arrival had been three times the legal limit, and had probably contributed to her unconsciousness. She had a con- cussion, several lacerations, and significant soft-tissue damage. But X rays and scans revealed no other injuries from the crash. That night, Ball and Hernandez brought her to the OR to fit her with a proper tra- cheostomy. When Ball came out and talked to family members, he told them of the dire condition she was in when she arrived, the difficulties "we" had had getting access to her airway, the disturbingly long period of time that she had gone without oxygen, and thus his uncertainty about how much brain function she still possessed. They listened with- out protest; there was nothing for them to do but wait.

Consider some other surgical mishaps. In one, a general surgeon   49 left a large metal instrument in a patient's abdomen, where it tore through the bowel and the wall of the bladder. In another, a cancer sur- geon biopsied the wrong part of a woman's breast and thereby delayed her diagnosis of cancer for months. A cardiac surgeon skipped a small but key step during a heart valve operation, thereby killing the patient. A general surgeon saw a man racked with abdominal pain in the emer- gency room and, without taking a CT scan, assumed that the man had a kidney stone; eighteen hours later, a scan showed a rupturing ab- dominal aortic aneurysm, and the patient died not long afterward.

How could anyone who makes a mistake of that magnitude be al-   50 lowed to practice medicine? We call such doctors "incompetent," "un- ethical," and "negligent." We want to see them punished. And so we've wound up with the public system we have for dealing with error: mal- practice lawsuits, media scandal, suspensions, firings.

There is, however, a central truth in medicine that complicates this   51 tidy vision of misdeeds and misdoers: all doctors make terrible mis- takes. Consider the cases I've just described. I gathered them simply by asking respected surgeons I know—surgeons at top medical schools— to tell me about mistakes they had made just in the past year. Every one of them had a story to tell.

In 1991, the *New England Journal of Medicine* published a series of   52 landmark papers from a project known as the Harvard Medical Prac- tice Study—a review of more than thirty thousand hospital admissions in New York State. The study found that nearly 4 percent of hospital patients suffered complications from treatment which either prolonged their hospital stay or resulted in disability or death, and that two-thirds of such complications were due to errors in care. One in four, or 1 percent of admissions, involved actual negligence. It was estimated that, nationwide, upward of forty-four thousand patients die each year at least partly as a result of errors in care. And subsequent investigations around the country have confirmed the ubiquity of error. In one small study of how clinicians perform when patients have a sudden cardiac arrest, twenty-seven of thirty clinicians made an error in using the defibrillator—charging it incorrectly or losing too much time trying to figure out how to work a particular model. According to a 1995 study, mistakes in administering drugs—giving the wrong drug or the wrong dose, say—occur, on average, about once every hospital admission, mostly without ill effects, but 1 percent of the time with serious consequences.

53   If error were due to a subset of dangerous doctors, you might expect malpractice cases to be concentrated among a small group, but in fact they follow a uniform, bell-shaped distribution. Most surgeons are sued at least once in the course of their careers. Studies of specific types of error, too, have found that repeat offenders are not the problem. The fact is that virtually everyone who cares for hospital patients will make serious mistakes, and even commit acts of negligence, every year. For this reason, doctors are seldom outraged when the press reports yet another medical horror story. They usually have a different reaction: That could be me. The important question isn't how to keep bad physicians from harming patients; it's how to keep good physicians from harming patients.

54   Medical malpractice suits are a remarkably ineffective remedy. Troyen Brennan, a Harvard professor of law and public health, points out that research has consistently failed to find evidence that litigation reduces medical error rates. In part, this may be because the weapon is so imprecise. Brennan led several studies following up on the patients in the Harvard Medical Practice Study. He found that fewer than 2 percent of the patients who had received substandard care ever filed suit. Conversely, only a small minority among the patients who did sue had in fact been the victims of negligent care. And a patient's likelihood of winning a suit depended primarily on how poor his or her outcome was, regardless of whether that outcome was caused by disease or unavoidable risks of care.

55   The deeper problem with medical malpractice suits is that by demonizing errors they prevent doctors from acknowledging and discussing them publicly. The tort system makes adversaries of patient and physician, and pushes each to offer a heavily slanted version of events. When things go wrong, it's almost impossible for a physician to talk to a patient honestly about mistakes. Hospital lawyers warn doctors that, although they must, of course, tell patients about injuries that occur, they are never to intimate that they were at fault, lest the "confession" wind up in court as damning evidence in a black-and-white

morality tale. At most, a doctor might say, "I'm sorry that things didn't go as well as we had hoped."

There is one place, however, where doctors can talk candidly about 56 their mistakes, if not with patients, then at least with one another. It is called the Morbidity and Mortality Conference—or, more simply, M & M—and it takes place, usually once a week, at nearly every academic hospital in the country. This institution survives because laws protecting its proceedings from legal discovery have stayed on the books in most states, despite frequent challenges. Surgeons, in particular, take the M & M seriously. Here they can gather behind closed doors to review the mistakes, untoward events, and deaths that occurred on their watch, determine responsibility, and figure out what to do differently next time.

At my hospital, we convene every Tuesday at five o'clock in a 57 steep, plush amphitheater lined with oil portraits of the great doctors whose achievements we're meant to live up to. All surgeons are expected to attend, from the interns to the chairman of surgery; we're also joined by medical students doing their surgery "rotation." An M & M can include almost a hundred people. We file in, pick up a photocopied list of cases to be discussed, and take our seats. The front row is occupied by the most senior surgeons: terse, serious men, now out of their scrubs and in dark suits, lined up like a panel of senators at a hearing. The chairman is a leonine presence in the seat closest to the plain wooden podium from which each case is presented. In the next few rows are the remaining surgical attendings; these tend to be younger, and several of them are women. The chief residents have put on long white coats and usually sit in the side rows. I join the mass of other residents, all of us in short white coats and green scrub pants, occupying the back rows.

For each case, the chief resident from the relevant service—cardiac, 58 vascular, trauma, and so on—gathers the information, takes the podium, and tells the story. Here's a partial list of cases from a typical week (with a few changes to protect confidentiality): a sixty-eight-year-old man who bled to death after heart valve surgery; a forty-seven-year-old woman who had to have a reoperation because of infection following an arterial bypass done in her left leg; a forty-four-year-old woman who had to have bile drained from her abdomen after gallbladder surgery; three patients who had to have reoperations for bleeding following surgery; a sixty-three-year-old man who had a cardiac arrest following heart bypass surgery; a sixty-six-year-old woman whose sutures suddenly gave way in an abdominal wound and nearly allowed her intestines to spill out. Ms. Williams's case, my failed tracheostomy, was just one case on a list like this. David Hernandez, the chief trauma resident, had subsequently reviewed the records and spoken to me and others involved. When the time came, it was he who stood up front and described what had happened.

59   Hernandez is a tall, rollicking, good old boy who can tell a yarn, but M & M presentations are bloodless and compact. He said something like: "This was a thirty-four-year-old female unrestrained driver in a high-speed rollover. The patient apparently had stable vitals at the scene but was unresponsive, and was brought in by ambulance unintubated. She was GCS 7 on arrival." GCS stands for the Glasgow Coma Scale, which rates the severity of head injuries, from three to fifteen. GCS 7 is in the comatose range. "Attempts to intubate were made without success in the ER and may have contributed to airway closure. A cricothyroidotomy was attempted without success."

60   These presentations can be awkward. The chief residents, not the attendings, determine which cases to report. That keeps the attendings honest—no one can cover up mistakes—but it puts the chief residents, who are, after all, underlings, in a delicate position. The successful M & M presentation inevitably involves a certain elision of detail and a lot of passive verbs. No one screws up a cricothyroidotomy. Instead, "a cricothyroidotomy was attempted without success." The message, however, was not lost on anyone.

61   Hernandez continued, "The patient arrested and required cardiac compressions. Anesthesia was then able to place a pediatric ET tube and the patient recovered stable vitals. The tracheostomy was then completed in the OR."

62   So Louise Williams had been deprived of oxygen long enough to go into cardiac arrest, and everyone knew that meant she could easily have suffered a disabling stroke or worse. Hernandez concluded with the fortunate aftermath: "Her workup was negative for permanent cerebral damage or other major injuries. The tracheostomy tube was removed on Day 2. She was discharged to home in good condition on Day 3." To the family's great relief, and mine, she had woken up in the morning a bit woozy but hungry, alert, and mentally intact. In a few weeks, the episode would heal to a scar.

63   But not before someone was called to account. A front-row voice immediately thundered, "What do you mean, 'a cricothyroidotomy was attempted without success'?" I sank into my seat, my face hot.

64   "This was my case," Dr. Ball volunteered from the front row. It is how every attending begins, and that little phrase contains a world of surgical culture. For all the talk in business schools and in corporate America about the virtues of "flat organizations," surgeons maintain an old-fashioned sense of hierarchy. When things go wrong, the attending is expected to take full responsibility. It makes no difference whether it was the resident's hand that slipped and lacerated an aorta; it doesn't matter whether the attending was at home in bed when a

nurse gave a wrong dose of medication. At the M & M, the burden of
responsibility falls on the attending.

Ball went on to describe the emergency attending's failure to intu-   65
bate Williams and his own failure to be at her bedside when things got
out of control. He described the bad lighting and her extremely thick
neck, and was careful to make those sound not like excuses but merely
like complicating factors. Some attendings shook their heads in sympathy. A couple of them asked questions to clarify certain details.
Throughout, Ball's tone was objective, detached. He had the air of a
CNN newscaster describing unrest in Kuala Lumpur.

As always, the chairman, responsible for the overall quality of our   66
surgery service, asked the final question. What, he wanted to know,
would Ball have done differently? Well, Ball replied, it didn't take long
to get the stab-wound patient under control in the OR, so he probably
should have sent Hernandez up to the ER at that point or let Hernandez close the abdomen while he himself came up. People nodded. Lesson learned. Next case.

At no point during the M & M did anyone question why I had not   67
called for help sooner or why I had not had the skill and knowledge
that Williams needed. This is not to say that my actions were seen as acceptable. Rather, in the hierarchy, addressing my errors was Ball's role.
The day after the disaster, Ball had caught me in the hall and taken me
aside. His voice was more wounded than angry as he went through my
specific failures. First, he explained, in an emergency tracheostomy it
might have been better to do a vertical neck incision; that would have
kept me out of the blood vessels, which run up and down—something
I should have known at least from my reading. I might have had a
much easier time getting her an airway then, he said. Second, and
worse to him than mere ignorance, he didn't understand why I hadn't
called him when there were clear signs of airway trouble developing. I
offered no excuses. I promised to be better prepared for such cases and
to be quicker to ask for help.

Even after Ball had gone down the fluorescent-lit hallway, I felt a   68
sense of shame like a burning ulcer. This was not guilt: guilt is what
you feel when you have done something wrong. What I felt was
shame: I was what was wrong. And yet I also knew that a surgeon can
take such feelings too far. It is one thing to be aware of one's limitations. It is another to be plagued by self-doubt. One surgeon with a national reputation told me about an abdominal operation in which he
had lost control of bleeding while he was removing what turned out to
be a benign tumor and the patient had died. "It was a clean kill," he
said. Afterward, he could barely bring himself to operate. When he did
operate, he became tentative and indecisive. The case affected his performance for months.

69   Even worse than losing self-confidence, though, is reacting defensively. There are surgeons who will see faults everywhere except in themselves. They have no questions and no fears about their abilities. As a result, they learn nothing from their mistakes and know nothing of their limitations. As one surgeon told me, it is a rare but alarming thing to meet a surgeon without fear. "If you're not a little afraid when you operate," he said, "you're bound to do a patient a grave disservice."

70   The atmosphere at the M & M is meant to discourage both attitudes—self-doubt and denial—for the M & M is a cultural ritual that inculcates in surgeons a "correct" view of mistakes. "What would you do differently?" a chairman asks concerning cases of avoidable harm. "Nothing" is seldom an acceptable answer.

71   In its way, the M & M is an impressively sophisticated and human institution. Unlike the courts or the media, it recognizes that human error is generally not something that can be deterred by punishment. The M & M sees avoiding error as largely a matter of will—of staying sufficiently informed and alert to anticipate the myriad ways that things can go wrong and then trying to head off each potential problem before it happens. It isn't damnable that an error occurs, but there is some shame to it. In fact, the M & M's ethos can seem paradoxical. On the one hand, it reinforces the very American idea that error is intolerable. On the other hand, the very existence of the M & M, its place on the weekly schedule, amounts to an acknowledgment that mistakes are an inevitable part of medicine.

72   But why do they happen so often? Lucian Leape, medicine's leading expert on error, points out that many other industries—whether the task is manufacturing semiconductors or serving customers at the Ritz-Carlton—simply wouldn't countenance error rates like those in hospitals. The aviation industry has reduced the frequency of operational errors to one in a hundred thousand flights, and most of those errors have no harmful consequences. The buzzword at General Electric these days is "Six Sigma," meaning that its goal is to make product defects so rare that in statistical terms they are more than six standard deviations away from being a matter of chance—almost a one-in-a-million occurrence.

73   Of course, patients are far more complicated and idiosyncratic than airplanes, and medicine isn't a matter of delivering a fixed product or even a catalogue of products; it may well be more complex than just about any other field of human endeavor. Yet everything we've learned in the past two decades—from cognitive psychology, from "human factors" engineering, from studies of disasters like Three Mile Island and Bhopal—has yielded the same insights: not only do all human beings err, but they err frequently and in predictable, patterned ways. And

systems that do not adjust for these realities can end up exacerbating rather than eliminating error.

The British psychologist James Reason argues, in his book *Human* 74 *Error*, that our propensity for certain types of error is the price we pay for the brain's remarkable ability to think and act intuitively—to sift quickly through the sensory information that constantly bombards us without wasting time trying to work through every situation anew. Thus systems that rely on human perfection present what Reason calls "latent errors"—errors waiting to happen. Medicine teems with examples. Take writing out a prescription, a rote procedure that relies on memory and attention, which we know are unreliable. Inevitably, a physician will sometimes specify the wrong dose or the wrong drug. Even when the prescription is written correctly, there's a risk that it will be misread. (Computerized ordering systems can almost eliminate errors of this kind, but only a small minority of hospitals have adopted them.) Medical equipment, which manufacturers often build without human operators in mind, is another area rife with latent errors: one reason physicians are bound to have problems when they use cardiac defibrillators is that the devices have no standard design. You can also make the case that onerous workloads, chaotic environments, and inadequate team communication all represent latent errors in the system.

James Reason makes another important observation: disasters do 75 not simply occur; they evolve. In complex systems, a single failure rarely leads to harm. Human beings are impressively good at adjusting when an error becomes apparent, and systems often have built-in defenses. For example, pharmacists and nurses routinely check and countercheck physicians' orders. But errors do not always become apparent, and backup systems themselves often fail as a result of latent errors. A pharmacist forgets to check one of a thousand prescriptions. A machine's alarm bell malfunctions. The one attending trauma surgeon available gets stuck in the operating room. When things go wrong, it is usually because a series of failures conspires to produce disaster.

The M & M takes none of this into account. For that reason, many 76 experts see it as a rather shabby approach to analyzing error and improving performance in medicine. It isn't enough to ask what a clinician could or should have done differently so that he and others may learn for next time. The doctor is often only the final actor in a chain of events that set him or her up to fail. Error experts, therefore, believe that it's the process, not the individuals in it, that requires closer examination and correction. In a sense, they want to industrialize medicine. [. . .]

Even in surgery there have been some encouraging developments. 77 For instance, operating on the wrong knee or foot or other body part of a patient has been a recurrent, if rare, mistake. A typical response has been to fire the surgeon. Recently, however, hospitals and surgeons have begun to recognize that the body's bilateral symmetry makes these errors predictable. In 1998, the American Academy of Orthopedic Surgeons endorsed a simple way of preventing them: make it standard practice for surgeons to initial, with a marker, the body part to be cut before the patient comes to surgery.

78   The Northern New England Cardiovascular Disease Study Group, based at Dartmouth, is another success story. Though the group doesn't conduct the sort of in-depth investigation of mishaps that Jeffrey Cooper pioneered, it has shown what can be done simply through statistical monitoring. Six hospitals belong to this consortium, which tracks deaths and other bad outcomes (such as wound infection, uncontrolled bleeding, and stroke) arising from heart surgery and tries to identify the various risk factors involved. Its researchers found, for example, that there were relatively high death rates among patients who developed anemia after bypass surgery, and that anemia developed most often in small patients. The solution used to "prime" the heart-lung machine caused the anemia, because it diluted a patient's blood, so the smaller the patient (and his or her blood supply) the greater the effect. Members of the consortium now have several promising solutions to the problem. Another study found that a group at one hospital had made mistakes in "handoffs"—say, in passing preoperative lab results to the people in the operating room. The study group solved the problem by developing a pilot's checklist for all patients coming to the OR. [. . .] Effort does matter; diligence and attention to the minutest details can save you.

79   This may explain why many doctors take exception to talk of "systems problems," "continuous quality improvement," and "process re-engineering." It is the dry language of structures, not people. I'm no exception: something in me, too, demands an acknowledgment of my autonomy, which is also to say my ultimate culpability. Go back to that Friday night in the ER, to the moment when I stood, knife in hand, over Louise Williams, her lips blue, her throat a swollen, bloody, and suddenly closed passage. A systems engineer might have proposed some useful changes. Perhaps a backup suction device should always be at hand, and better light more easily available. Perhaps the institution could have trained me better for such crises, could have required me to have operated on a few more goats. Perhaps emergency tracheostomies are so difficult under any circumstances that an automated device could have been designed to do a better job.

80   Yet although the odds were against me, it wasn't as if I had no chance of succeeding. Good doctoring is all about making the most of the hand you're dealt, and I failed to do so. The indisputable fact was that I hadn't called for help when I could have, and when I plunged the knife into her neck and made my horizontal slash my best was not

good enough. It was just luck, hers and mine, that Dr. O'Connor some-how got a breathing tube into her in time.

There are all sorts of reasons that it would be wrong to take my li-   81
cense away or to take me to court. These reasons do not absolve me. Whatever the limits of the M & M, its fierce ethic of personal responsi-bility for errors is a formidable virtue. No matter what measures are taken, doctors will sometimes falter, and it isn't reasonable to ask that we achieve perfection. What is reasonable is to ask that we never cease to aim for it.

RESPONDING TO READING

1. Gawande opens with a lengthy narrative of his own failure in surgery. How does he use this narration both to establish his own credibility and to build his argument about mistakes?

2. Discuss Gawande's narrative with classmates. Does the narrative make us sympathetic to his situation as an inexperienced doctor, or do we expect per-fection from every doctor in every emergency, even though perfection is im-possible for any individual?

3. According to Gawande, "There is [. . .] a central truth in medicine that com-plicates [our] tidy vision of misdeeds and misdoers: all doctors make terrible mistakes." Does this "central truth" make such mistakes acceptable? Should the doctors who make mistakes such as Gawande describes always be pun-ished, especially if all doctors, ultimately, make these mistakes?

4. How does the structure of the medical system in America contribute to the problem of doctors making mistakes? How does it attempt to deal with such mistakes? How does the legal system handle medical mistakes? Do the two systems—medical and legal—make dealing with mistakes easier or more dif-ficult for doctors?

5. In an essay, explain your reactions to Gawande's argument that mistakes are common, expected, and unavoidable. Is it possible for anyone practicing medicine to avoid making mistakes on living patients? Is it possible to be un-derstanding when a doctor's mistakes could, and do, lead to the death of the patient?

Why Mothers Should Stay Home

DEBORAH FALLOWS

Whether mothers should stay home and care for their young children is not an option for millions of single or less affluent parents who have to earn money to support their children. Yet for many middle-class families, including most college graduates, the choices are not as clear cut as they were a generation ago, when there was far greater social pressure for mothers to stay home. Economist Barbara Bergmann ex-plains, in *The Economic Emergence of Women* (1986), that until relatively recently, biology did indeed determine the fate of urban men and women. Men earned most of the money, often at hard physical labor, but did relatively little housework or child care. Women did the domestic tasks, but had more leisure time than women who worked outside the home. Today, as both Bergmann and Deborah Fallows point out, women who work outside the home nevertheless do most of the housework and child care, running errands and caring for dependent parents, unless they get additional assistance from paid helpers or husbands who can be convinced to assume more responsibilities than tradition and their culture have decreed.

Fallows (born 1949) clearly has an upper-middle class, traditional family in mind, and she uses herself—a well-educated (B.A., Radcliffe, 1971; Ph.D., University of Texas, 1977), talented, energetic, eager parent—as the prime example of someone who decided to stop working outside the home and stay at home with her two young children. She has become a spokesperson for full-time mothers, asserting to an audience that ranges from radical feminists to conservative traditionalists that "the choice is *not* to be either a career woman or a dumb housewife." She has expressed her views, which she characterizes as the "radical middle," in articles in *Newsweek* and *Washington Monthly*, and in her book, *A Mother's Work* (1985). Yet her essay leaves a number of questions unanswered. Is her argument applicable to less affluent families? To less capable, less engaged parents? To families of non-Western culture? To single-parent and nontraditional families, whose configurations are so varied and numerous as to outnumber the older traditional model? What principles can govern our personal lives when every family seems unique?

1   About 18 months ago, when our first son was three years old and our second was about to be born, I decided to stop working and stay at home with our children. At the time, I wrote an article about the myth of the superwoman, saying that contrary to the prevailing notion of the day, it was not possible to be both a full-time career woman and a full-fledged mother. I said that while everyone recognizes the costs a stay-at-home mother pays in terms of power, prestige, money, and advancement in traditional careers, we are not always aware of or do not so readily admit what a full-time working woman loses and gives up in terms of mothering.

2   I've been at home with our children for almost a year and a half now, and I've learned a number of things about my choice. My convictions about the importance of mothering, which were based more on intuition than experience at the time, run even deeper and stronger. Nothing means more to me now than the hours I spend with my children, but I find myself coping with a problem I hadn't fully foreseen. It is the task of regearing my life, of learning to live as a full-time mother without a professional career but still with many of the interests and ambitions that I had before I had children. And this is the hard part. It

means unraveling those long-held life plans for a certain kind of career and deciding which elements are possible to keep and which I must discard. Perhaps even more important, it means changing the way I've been taught to think about myself and value the progress of my life.

My mother became a mother in 1946; she had gone to college, stud-   3
ied music, and worked for a year at her father's office. Then she married and had my sister by the time she was 22. She wasn't expected to have a career outside the home, and she didn't. When I was growing up, the only mothers who worked were those who, as we whispered, "had to." Even the high school teachers, who we recognized probably weren't doing it just for the money, were slightly suspect.

But between my mother's time and our own, the climate of oppor-   4
tunity and expectations for women started to change. Betty Friedan and *The Feminine Mystique* came between all of those mothers and all of us daughters. The small town in northern Ohio where I grew up was not exactly a hotbed of feminist activity, but even there the signals for young women were changing in the mid-sixties. We were raised with a curious mixture of hope of becoming homecoming queen and pressure to run for student council president. When I was 11, the mothers in our neighborhood bundled off their awkward, pre-adolescent daughters to Saturday morning charm classes, where we learned how to walk on a straight line, one foot directly in front of the other, and the proper way to don a coat. We all felt a little funny and humiliated, but we didn't say anything. By the time we were 17, we were May Queens, princesses, head drum majorettes, and cheerleaders, but we were also class valedictorians, editors of the school paper and yearbook, student directors of the school band, and candidates for six-year medical programs, Seven Sisters colleges, and honors programs at the Big Ten universities. I admit with some embarrassment that my two most thrilling moments in high school were being chosen for the homecoming court and being named first-chair trumpet in the concert band.

This was the way we were supposed to achieve—to be both beauti-   5
ful and brilliant, charming and accomplished. It was one step beyond what our mothers did: we were aiming to be class presidents, not class secretaries; for medical school, not nursing school; we were building careers, not just jobs to tide us over before we landed husbands and started raising babies.

When I made my decision to stop working and stay home with our   6
children, it was with a mixture of feelings. Part was defiance of the background I've just described—how could feminism dare tell me that I couldn't choose, with *pride*, motherhood alone? Part was anxiety—how could I keep some grasp on my extra-mothering self, on the things I had really enjoyed doing before I had children? I didn't want to become what the world kept telling me housewives are—ladies whose interests are confined to soap operas and the laundry. Certainly I knew

from my own mother and from other women who had spent their middle years as full-time mothers that it was possible to be a thoughtful and sensitive person and still be a mother. But I didn't know how, and I didn't know where to turn to ask. Even my mother didn't have the answers. She was surprised when I told her I wanted to stop working and stay home with my kids. "You young women seem to handle everything so easily, so smoothly," she told me. "I never knew you were so torn between being a mother and being a professional."

7   The arrival of children in a woman's late twenties or early thirties can be handy, of course, because it means you can finish your education and start a career before taking "time out" to start your family. But it's also awkward.

8   At my tenth college reunion last June, I found that many of my friends had just become partner or vice-president of one thing or another, doctor-in-charge of some ward, tenured professor, editor-in-chief, and so forth. In these moments, I feel as if everyone is growing up around me. My reactions, though human, are not altogether pretty. I feel sorry for myself—there but for two small children go I. I feel frustrated in being passed over for things I know I could handle as well as or better than the next person. I feel anxious, wondering if I am going to "lose my touch," get rusty, boring, old, trivial too quickly. And I am afraid that in putting aside my professional ambitions just now, I may be putting aside forever the chance to attain the levels I once set for myself.

9   All of us, I think, spend time once in a while pondering the "what ifs" of our lives, and we all experience momentary pangs of self-pity over the course we've taken. I know I'm not an exception to this, but I also know that when I add up the pluses and minuses my choice was right for me, and it might be right for other women.

The Importance of "Quantity" Time

10   The first adjustment on that first morning that I dressed for motherhood rather than for success was to believe intellectually in what I felt emotionally: that it was as important, as worthy for me to spend my time with my small children as to study, do research, try cases, or invest a bank's money. Furthermore, I had to believe it was worth it to the children to have me—not someone else—there most of the time. There are a thousand small instances I have witnessed over the past year and a half that illustrate this feeling. One that stays in my mind happened last summer.

11   I had just dropped off our older son at the morning play camp at the neighborhood school. I was about to drive off when a little boy about eight years old burst out of the school and ran down the front

steps in tears. His mother was on her way down the walk and of course she saw him. She led him over to the steps, took his hands in hers, looked him directly in the eyes, and talked with him softly but deliberately for a few minutes, calming him down so he could go back inside happily and she could go on her way. What I recognized in that instant was something I'd been trying to put my finger on for months. I'd witnessed dozens of similar events, when a child was simply overwhelmed by something, and I knew there was a difference—a distinct difference in the way parents respond at such moments from the way I had seen babysitters or maids act, however loving and competent they may have been. Parents seem to have some combination of self-assurance, completeness, deliberateness, and consistency. If that boy had been my son, I would have wanted to be with him, too.

Perhaps this one episode was no more important than the many 12 reprimands or comforts I give my children during the day. But the more I'm around my children, the more such instances I happen to see and deal with. Perhaps a thousand of these episodes add up to the values and security I want to give my children.

I spend a lot of time with my children at playgrounds. We often go 13 out on nice afternoons when our older son gets home from school, sampling new ones or returning to old favorites. I particularly like playgrounds because of the balance they afford: they encourage the kids to strike out on their own but let me be there as a fallback. I've watched my older son in his share of small fistfights and scuffles, and I have been able to let him fight without intervening. He knows I'm there and runs back as often for protection as for nice things like a "Mom, see what I can do." Or our younger son toddles toward the big slide and needs me to follow him up and hold him as we slide down together. After so many hours, we've developed a style of play. I think my children know what to expect of me and I have learned their limits. I've watched the styles of many mothers and children, and you often can see, after a time, a microcosm of their lives together. I've also seen plenty of children there with full-time maids. The maids have their own styles, which usually are different from the mothers'. I've never seen a maid slide down a slide with her small charge, but I have seen plenty scold children for climbing too high on the jungle gym, and I've seen plenty step in to stop the sandfights before anyone gets dirty or hurt. There's a reason for this, of course: a maid has a lot to explain if a youngster arrives home with a bloody nose, but a mother doesn't. Sometimes, I think, the nose is worth the lesson learned from it, yet that is something only a parent—not a maid or babysitter—can take the responsibility to decide.

It has taken me a few years to realize I have very high standards for 14 my role as a mother. I don't have to be a supermom who makes my children's clothes (I really can't sew), who does all the volunteer work at school (I do my share), or who cooks gourmet meals (we eat a lot of hamburgers). But I have to be around my children—a lot. I have to know them as well as I possibly can and see them in as many different environments and moods as possible in order to know best how to help them grow up—by comforting them, letting them alone, disciplining and enjoying them, being dependable but not stifling. What I need with them is time—in quantity, not quality.

15   I'm not talking about being with my children every minute of the day. From the time they were several months old, we sent them out for short periods to the favorite neighborhood babysitter's. By the time he was two and a half, our older son was in a co-op nursery school (my husband and I would take turns doing parent duty for the 17 kids); now he's in pre-kindergarten for a full school day. These periods away from me are clearly important for my sanity, as well as for my children's socialization, their development of trust in people, and their ability to experience other ways of living. But there is a big difference between using childcare from 8 to 6, Monday through Friday, and using a babysitter or a nursery school three mornings a week.

16   I realize that not everyone enjoys the luxury of choice. Some of my female friends work because it's the only way to make ends meet. But I think a lot of people pretend they have less room for choice than they really do. For some women, the reason may be the feeling—which is widespread among men—that their dignity and success are related to how much money they earn. For others, there is a sense of independence that comes with earning money that is hard to give up. (I know that I felt freer to buy things, especially for myself, or spend money on babysitters when I was contributing to the family income.) And still others define "necessities" in an expensive way: I've heard more than one woman say she "has to work" to keep up payments on the second house. Such a woman is the parallel to the government appointee who "has to resign" from his post to return to his former profession because he "can no longer afford government service."

17   Even though some women do have a choice, I am not suggesting that all the responsibility for home and children should lie with the mother. While my husband and I are an example of a more traditional family, with a breadwinning father, a full-time mother, and two children, he shares with me many of the family responsibilities: night-tending, diapering, bathing, cooking, and playtime. A woman's decision to stay home or work is, at worst, a decision made by herself and, at best, a decision made with her spouse.

18   But with all these qualifications noted, I still know that my own choice is to stay with my children. Why does this seem to be at odds with the climate of the times, especially among certain feminists? I think it is because of a confused sense of ambition—based, in turn, on

a mistaken understanding of what being a housewife or mother actually means.

While the world's idea of the comparative importance of career 19
and motherhood may have changed a good deal since my mother's time, the general understanding of what motherhood means for those who choose it has not changed or advanced. And that may be the real problem for many women of my generation: who can blame them for shying away from a commitment to full-time motherhood if they're told, despite raising children, that motherhood is a vapid life of chores, routines, and TV? I couldn't stand motherhood myself if that were true. One of my many discoveries as a mother is that motherhood requires not the renunciation of my former ambitions but rather their refinement.

Even for those who intend to rush straight back to work, mother- 20
hood involves some interruption in the normal career plan. Separating people, even temporarily, from their professional identities, can help them see the difference between the ambition to *be*—to have an impressive job title to drop at cocktail parties—and the ambition to *do* specific things that seem satisfying and rewarding. The ambition to be is often a casualty of motherhood; the ambition to do need not be.

I see many of my friends intensely driven to keep doing things, to 21
keep involved in their former interests, or to develop entirely new ones that they can learn from and grow with. In the free time they manage to set aside—thanks to babysitters, co-op babycare, naptimes, grand-mothers' help, and husbands like mine who spend a lot of time with the children—they are thinking and doing.

Women I have talked to have described how, after some months 22
or years of settling into motherhood, their sense of what work is worth, and what they're looking for in work, has greatly changed. They are less tolerant, more selective, more demanding in what they do. One woman said that before she had children she would focus on a "cause," and was willing to do just about anything as her job toward that cause. Now she's still interested in advancing the cause, but she has no patience for busywork. In the limited time she can spare from her family, she wants to do things that really count, work in areas where her efforts make a difference. I'm not suggesting narcissism here but a clearer focus on a search for some long-range goal, some tangible accomplishment, a feeling so necessary during the season of child-raising when survival from one end of the day to the other is often the only achievement.

Each one's search is different, depending on factors like her hus- 23
band's job (if she has a husband) and the extent of his role as a caretaker, her children's needs, her family's financial situation, and her personal lifestyle.

24   One of my friends had taught English in public high schools for the last ten years. She was the kind of teacher you remember fondly from your own childhood and hope your kids are lucky enough to have because she's dedicated, demanding, and creative. She expanded her subject to include other humanities, keeping herself several steps ahead of her students by reading and studying on her own, traveling to see museums and exhibits firsthand, collecting slides and books as she goes. She has a new baby daughter now and has stopped working to stay home with her child. She's decided to go back to school next fall, taking one or two courses at a time, to pursue a master's in fine arts—a chance to study formally what she's mostly taught herself and to return to her job someday with an even better background and more ideas for her teaching.

25   Going to school can be perfect for new mothers, as many in my own mother's generation found. It requires very little time away from home, which means cutting down on time away from the children as well as on child-care costs. It can be cheap, as with my friend, who can attend a virtually tuition-free state university. You can pace your work to suit demands at home by carefully choosing the number of courses you take and the type of work required. And it's physically easy but intellectually challenging—the complement to the other demands of the early years of mothering.

26   Other mothers I know do different things with their time. One friend, formerly a practicing lawyer and now a full-time mother, volunteers some of her time to advising the League of Women Voters on legal matters. Another, formerly a producer at a big radio station, now produces her own shows, albeit at a slower pace. A third quit her job to raise her daughter but spends a lot of time on artistic projects, which she sells.

27   But if there's no real blueprint for what a modern mother should be, you wouldn't know it from what comes through in the media. On the *Today Show* last summer, for instance, Jane Pauley interviewed Felice Schwartz, the president of Catalyst, an organization that promotes career development for women. They were discussing women's changing life-styles. Ms. Schwartz said that now women are going back to work full-time four months after having children, while 15 years ago they were taking 20 years off to have them. "Isn't that fantastic progress?" she said. Fantastic it certainly is; progress it is not, except toward the narrowest and least generous notion of what achievement means for women or for humanity. Progress such as this is a step not toward "liberation" but toward the enslavement to career that has been the least attractive aspect of masculine success.

28   What it is really like to be a mother today seems to be a secret that's kept from even my contemporaries who may be considering motherhood themselves. At a dinner recently, I sat near a young woman about

my age, a New York television producer and recently anointed White House fellow. She and my husband and I were having a conversation about bureaucracy and what she found new or interesting or surprising about it in her new position. After several minutes, she turned away from my husband to me directly and said, "And how old are your children, Debbie?" It wasn't the question—not at all—but the tone that was revealing, the unattractive, condescending tone I've heard many older people use with youngsters, or doctors with patients. If I'd had her pegged as a fast-track superachiever, she had me pegged as little mother and lady of the house.

Hurt and anger were the wrong feelings at a moment like that, although I felt them. Instead, I should have felt sorry for her, not because of her own choice but because she had no sense that a choice exists— waiting to be made by women like her and like me. The choice is *not* to be either a career woman or a dumb housewife. The issue is one that she, a woman at the age when careers take off and child-bearing ability nears its eleventh hour, should be sensitive to and think about.

29

RESPONDING TO READING

1. In arguing that "it is not possible to be both a full-time career woman and a full-fledged mother," Fallows is setting herself up for the difficult task of intentionally challenging "the prevailing notion of the day" (paragraph 1). What sorts of evidence does she use to support her argument? How convincing is she?

2. To what extent can Fallows generalize from the examples she uses from her own personal experience?

3. Fallows argues her case in human terms, with little reference to the economics of earning and spending money. Does this freedom from monetary worry restrict her argument to the upper and upper-middle classes? How relevant is her argument to single parents?

4. Does Fallows's argument apply primarily to mothers of preschool children? Could an equivalent case be made for "Why Fathers Should Stay Home"?

5. What is or will your own family of the future be like? Incorporate a reply to Fallows's argument, and define your role in this family as either the father or mother of preschool children.

Losing: An American Tradition

CHARLES M. YOUNG

Young (born 1951) earned a B.A. from Macalester College in 1973 and an M.S. from Columbia University in 1975. In 1976, he began working as an associate editor of *Rolling Stone*, where he often wrote a column titled "Random Notes." As a freelance writer, Young contributes to many newspapers and to magazines such as *Crawdaddy*. "I try to write from a rock and roll sensibility," argues Young, "which at its best finds humor in the absurdity of life. A friend once accused me of liking punk rock because I never outgrew being fourteen. This is true, and there is nothing more absurd than being an adolescent in America."

"Losing: An American Tradition" was first published in *Men's Journal* (2000) and later reprinted in *Best American Sports Writing 2000*. Here, Young explores the shame and scorn American culture attaches to losing—in sports and in other areas of competition that are nevertheless set up to produce at least as many losers as winners: "Losing puts you in the center of a vast vacuum, where you are shunned by your own teammates, scorned by spectators, avoided by your friends. It's a lot like smelling bad. Nobody wants to talk about it in your presence."

1   *Somebody's got to lose. Don't we all know the feeling?*—B.C.

2   Just North of the north end zone of Blackshear Stadium at Prairie View A&M University in Texas is an unmarked grave.

3   "We buried last season," said Greg Johnson, the Prairie View Panthers' coach, during a break in football practice. "In March, just before the start of spring practice, we had them write down everything they didn't like about the past—being 0–9 last season, the record losing streak. We used the example of Superman, this guy that nobody could stop unless you got him near some green kryptonite. We asked them, 'Well, what's your green kryptonite? What is it that keeps you from doing what you need to do in the classroom and on the football field? Is it a female? Is it your friends? Is it a drug? Is it alcohol? Lack of dedication? Not enough time in the weight room? You got a nagging injury that you didn't rehab?' Whatever they wanted to bury, they wrote it down on a piece of paper. And the last thing we did, we looked at the HBO tape. The segment that Bryant Gumbel did on us for *Real Sports*, where they laughed at us and ridiculed us as the worst team in the country—'How does it feel to be 0–75 since 1989?' or whatever it was at that point. I said, 'That's the last we'll ever see of that tape,' and I put it in a big plastic trash bag with the paper. We took it to a hole I had dug near the gate, and we threw it in. All the players and all the coaches walked by. Some of them kicked dirt on it, some of them spit on it. Some of them probably thought I was crazy. I said, 'This is the last time we're going to talk about last year. This is the last time we're going to talk about the losing streak. The past is dead, and anything that's dead ought to be buried. It's history. It's gone.'"

4   That took place in September 1998, when Prairie View's NCAA-record losing streak stood at 0–77. Now skip ahead to the postgame interviews of the January 9, 1999, AFC playoff game, in which the

Denver Broncos beat the Miami Dolphins 38–3. Shannon Sharpe, the Broncos' tight end, called Miami's Dan Marino a "loser." Universally, this was viewed as a mortal insult, far beyond the bounds of acceptable trash talk.

"I cringed when I read that," said Mike Shanahan, the Broncos' coach. "I was really disappointed. Dan Marino's no loser."   5

So Sharpe, much humbled (and probably at Shanahan's insistence), groveled after the next Denver practice: "In no way, shape, or form is Dan Marino a loser. Dan, if I offended you or your family, your wife, your kids, your mother or father, your brothers or sisters, I apologize. I stand before you and sincerely apologize. I would never disrespect you as a person."   6

Which is odd. Football, along with every other major sport, is constructed to create losers. On any given game day, half the teams win, and half the teams lose. By the end of the playoffs, exactly one team can be called a winner, while thirty other teams are, literally, losers. So given that 96.7 percent of the players in the NFL can't help but be losers, why should calling somebody a loser be considered such an egregious violation of propriety that the guy who won must debase himself in public for pointing out that the guy who lost, lost?   7

Consider *Patton*, winner of the 1971 Academy Award for Best Picture and a favorite of coaches, team owners, and politicians ever since. It opens with George C. Scott standing in front of a screen-size American flag in the role of General George S. Patton, giving a pep talk to his troops. Using sports imagery to describe war (mirroring the sportswriters who use war imagery to describe sports), Patton delivers a succinct sociology lesson: "Americans love a winner, and will not tolerate a loser. Americans play to win all the time. I wouldn't give a hoot in hell for a man who lost and laughed. That's why Americans have never lost, and will never lose a war—because the very thought of losing is hateful to Americans."   8

Which is a view of most Americans that's shared by most Americans. Certain women of my acquaintance refer to men who score low on the Multiphasic Boyfriend Potentiality Scale as losers. *Cosmopolitan* has run articles on how to identify and dump losers before they have a chance to inseminate the unwary.   9

In *Jerry Maguire*, Tom Cruise suffers his worst humiliation when he spots his former girlfriend dating a rival agent at a *Monday Night Football* game. She makes an L with her fingers and mouths, "Loser."   10

In *American Beauty*, Kevin Spacey announces during his midlife crisis: "Both my wife and daughter think I'm this gigantic loser."   11

In *Gods and Monsters*, Lolita Davidovich, playing a bartender, dismisses the possibility of sex with her sometime lover, played by Brendan Fraser: "From now on, you're just another loser on the other side of the bar."   12

13   In *200 Cigarettes*, set in the ostensibly alternative subculture of Manhattan's Lower East Side, Martha Plimpton works herself into a state of despair considering the idea that no one will come to her New Year's Eve party. Then, considering an even worse possibility, she weeps: "All the losers will be here!"

14   At the real-life sentencing last February of Austin Offen for bashing a man over the head with a metal bar outside a Long Island night club, Assistant District Attorney Stephen O'Brien said that Offen was "vicious and brutal. He's a coward and a loser." Offen, displaying no shame over having crippled a man for life, screamed back: "I am not a loser!"

15   In his book *Turbo Capitalism: Winners and Losers in the Global Economy*, Edward Luttwak equates losing with poverty and observes that Americans believe that "failure is the result not of misfortune or injustice, but of divine disfavor."

16   I could list a hundred more examples, but you get the point.

17   Shannon Sharpe, in using the word *loser*, implied that Dan Marino was: unworthy of sex or love or friendship or progeny, socially clueless, stupid, parasitical, pathetic, poverty-stricken, cowardly, violent, felonious, bereft of all forms of status, beneath all consideration, hated by himself, hated by all good Americans, hated by God. And Dan Marino is one of the best quarterbacks ever to play football. [. . .]

18   The literal truth is, I may not be the worst college football player of all time. I've claimed that occasionally in the course of conversation, but I may be only the worst college football player of 1972. I was definitely the worst player on the Macalester College Scots of St. Paul, Minnesota, and we lost all of our games that season by an aggregate score of 312–46. The team went on to win one game in each of the following two seasons (after I graduated), then set the NCAA record with fifty straight losses. So, strictly speaking, the losing streak wasn't my fault. I do think I made a huge contribution to the atmosphere of despair and futility that led to the losing streak. I think that as Prairie View was to the '90s, Macalester was to the '70s. But in the final analysis, I think that over two decades at both schools, some athlete may have failed more than I did.

19   I may therefore merely be one of the worst, a weaker distinction that makes me even more pathetic than whoever it is who can make the case for sole possession of the superlative—if someone wants to make that case. [. . .]

20   A couple of weeks after I left PVU, the Panthers won a football game, 14–12, against Langston University, ending the losing streak at eighty. The campus erupted in a victory celebration that was typical of the orgiastic outpourings that people all over the world feel entitled to after an important win. I was happy for them. I felt bad for Langston, having to carry the stigma of losing to the losers of all time.

There being virtually no literature of losing, I became obsessed   21
with reading books about winning, some by coaches and some by self-
help gurus. All of them advised me to forget about losing. If you want
to join the winners, they said, don't dwell on your past humiliations.
Then I thought of George Santayana's dictum: "Those who forget the
past are condemned to repeat it." So if I remembered losing, I'd be a
loser. And if I forgot losing, I'd be a loser. Finally, I remembered a dictum of my own: "Anybody who quotes George Santayana about repeating the past will soon be repeating even worse clichés."

That Christmas, my local Barnes & Noble installed a new section   22
called "Lessons from the Winners." Publishers put out staggering numbers of books with "win" in the title (as they do with *Zen and Any Stupid Thing*), and they make money because there's a bottomless market
of losers who want to be winners. Almost all of these books are inco-
herent lists of aphorisms and advice on how to behave like a CEO
("Memorize the keypad on your cell phone so you dial and drive without taking your eyes off the road"). Most of these books are written by
men who have made vast fortunes polluting the groundwater and
screwing people who work for a living, and these men want to air out
their opinions, chiefly that they aren't admired enough for polluting
the groundwater and screwing people who work for a living. I thought
of the ultimate winner, Howard Hughes, who was once the richest man
in the world, who had several presidents catering to his every whim,
who stored his feces in jars. I got more and more depressed.

Maybe I was just hypnotized by my own history of failure, charac-   23
ter defects, and left-wing politics. Maybe what I needed was a pep talk.
Maybe what I needed was Ray Pelletier, a motivational speaker who
has made a lot of money raising morale for large corporations and athletic teams. Pelletier, a member of the National Speakers Association
Hall of Fame, wrote a book, *Permission to Win*, that Coach Johnson had
recommended to me. Basically an exhortation to feel like a winner no
matter how disastrous your circumstances happen to be, the book
deals with losing as a problem of individual psychology. I asked Pelletier if he thought that the emphasis American culture places on competition was creating vast numbers of people who, on the basis of
having lost, quite logically think of themselves as losers.

"I don't think you have to think of yourself as a loser," he said. "I   24
think competition causes you to reach down inside and challenges you
to be at your very best. The key is not to beat yourself. If you're better
than I am and you're more prepared to play that day, you deserve to
win. I have no problem with that. Every time I give a presentation, I
want it to be better than the last one. I want to be sure I'm winning in
everything that I do."

Yeah, but wasn't there a difference between excellence and   25
winning?

26   "No, that's why I say that if I get beat by a team that's more talented, I don't have a problem with that."

27   When one guy won, was he not inflicting defeat on the other guy?

28   "No. I'll give you an example. The first time I worked with a female team before a big game, I was getting them all riled up and playing on their emotions, telling them how they deserved this win and how they worked really hard. A rah-rah, goose-pimple kind of speech. Just before we went on the court, the point guard said, 'Can I ask a question? Haven't the girls in the other locker room worked really hard, too? Don't they deserve to win, too?'"

29   Pelletier then veered off into a discussion of how the game teaches you about life, of how his talks are really for fifteen years down the line when your wife leaves you, or the IRS calls for an audit, or you can't pay your mortgage. I asked him how he replied to the point guard in the locker room.

30   "I said, 'Absolutely the other team deserves to win, too. What we have to do is find out if we can play together tonight as a team.' See, that's the biggest challenge facing corporate America today. We talk about teamwork but we don't understand the concept of team. Most of us have never been coached in anything. We've been taught, but not coached. There's a big difference. Great coaches challenge you to play at your best. The key is, you're in the game, trying to better yourself."

31   But Bill Parcells, the former coach of the Jets, is famous for saying that you are what the standings say you are . . .

32   "Winning is playing at your best. Do you know the number-one reason why an athlete plays his sport? Recognition. Once you understand that, everything else becomes easy. Lou Holtz says that win means 'What's Important Now.'"

33   That's just standard practice in books about winning, I told him. They redefine the word to include all human behavior with a good connotation. In *The Psychology of Winning*, Dr. Denis Waitley writes that winning is "unconditional love." Winning could hardly be a more conditional form of love. You are loved if you win, and scorned if you lose.

34   "I don't believe that."

35   If athletes play for recognition, don't they want to be recognized as winners? And if you've lost, won't you be recognized as a loser?

36   "I don't think they're labeled that way."

37   By the press? By the fans?

38   "To me, unconditional love is an aspect of winning. The problem is that you and I have not been trained to think positively. In one of my corporate seminars, I ask people to write down all the advantages there are to being negative. I want them to think about it seriously. It's an exercise that can take fifteen or twenty minutes, and then they have the 'Aha!' There is no advantage to negative thinking. None. And yet the biggest problem we face in America is low self-esteem."

Low self-esteem has its uses, though. Whenever you see a couple   39
of male animals on a PBS nature special duking it out for the privilege
of having sex with some female of the species, one of the males is going
to dominate and the other male is either going to die or get low self-
esteem and crawl off making obsequious gestures to the winner. The
evolutionary value is obvious: Fight to the death and your genes die
with you; admit you're a loser and you may recover to fight again or
find another strategy for passing on your genes through some less selective female. Species in which one alpha male gets to have sex with
most of the females—elephant seals are a good example—need a lot of
low self-esteem among the beta males for social stability.

With 1 percent of the population possessing more wealth than the   40
bottom 95 percent, the American economy operates a lot like a bunch of
elephant seals on a rock in the ocean. And it simply must mass-produce
low self-esteem in order to maintain social stability amidst such colossal unfairness.

According to the World Health Organization, mood disorders are   41
the number-one cause worldwide of people's normal activities being
impaired. In the United States alone, the WHO estimates, depression
costs $53 billion a year in worker absenteeism and lost productivity.
While that's a hell of a market for Ray Pelletier and the National
Speakers Association, which has more than three thousand people
giving pep talks to demoralized companies and sports teams, doled-
out enthusiasm is a palliative, not a curative. In fact, demoralization is
a familiar management tool; the trick is creating just enough. Too
much and you have work paralysis, mass depression, and suicide.
Too little and you have a revolution. Ever hear a boss brag that he
doesn't *have* ulcers, he *gives* them? He's making sure his employees are
demoralized enough to stay in their place.

Consider the book *Shame and Pride*, by Dr. Donald L. Nathanson, a   42
psychiatrist and the executive director of the Silvan S. Tomkins Institute
in Philadelphia. Starting in the mid-1940s, Dr. Tomkins watched babies
for thousands of hours and made a convincing case that humans are
born preprogrammed with nine "affects"—potential states of emotion
that can be triggered by a stimulus or memory. These affects are:
interest-excitement, enjoyment-joy, surprise-startle, fear-terror, distress-
anguish, anger-rage, dissmell (*dissmell* is similar to *distaste*, but related
to the sense of smell), disgust, and shame-humiliation. These affects
"amplify" an outside stimulus or memory to give you an increase in
brain activity that eventually becomes full-blown emotion.

Until recent years, shame was the "ignored emotion" in psycholo-   43
gy. But a few people, Nathanson most prominently, built on Tomkins
and discovered the key to . . . well, not quite everything, but an awful
lot. According to Tomkins and Nathanson, shame erupts whenever
"desire outruns fulfillment." An impediment arises to the two positive

affects (interest-excitement and enjoyment-joy), and suddenly your eyes drop, your head and body slump, your face turns red, and your brain is confused to the point of paralysis. [. . .]

44   So I called up Nathanson and asked if he had any thoughts about athletes and [*Shame*. . . .]

45   Sports events are often described as a morality play, I said, but there's nothing moral about it. Sports decide who will participate in power and who will be humiliated.

46   "That's understandable when you recognize that our sense of place in society is maintained by shame. Keeping people in their place is maintaining them at certain levels of shaming interaction at which they can be controlled. This issue of winning and losing, it throws us. It defines our identity, doesn't it?"

47   Calling someone a loser is probably the worst insult in the United States today.

48   "If you're calling someone that, the person must live in a perpetual state of shame. The only way he can live with himself is to have massive denial, disavowal of his real identity. He has to make his way in the world somehow, and he can't walk around constantly thinking of himself as a loser. Yet if someone in our eyes is a loser and he refuses to admit it, this is narcissism. He has an identity that can't be sustained by consensual validation."

49   Is there some value in competition, in creating all these losers?

50   "When you're young and you're learning and it's just a bunch of guys playing a game, that's not shame. That's just figuring out that Billy is faster than Johnny. When parents and schools and bureaucracies start getting involved and demanding wins, then it gets pathological."

51   Playing for the Chicago Bears, the Philadelphia Eagles, and the Dallas Cowboys from 1961 to 1972, Mike Ditka was All-Pro five times as a tight end, won an NFL championship with the Bears in 1963, won Super Bowl VI with the Cowboys, and was elected to the Hall of Fame. As the coach of the Bears from 1982 to 1992, he won Super Bowl XX with an 18–1 team generally acknowledged as one of the greatest ever and was named Coach of the Year twice. As the coach of the New Orleans Saints for the past three seasons, he had a 15–33 record and is now most vividly remembered for flipping off the fans and grabbing his crotch during and after an especially inept defeat. (He was fined $20,000.) I asked him if he thinks that football fans are inherently interested in the game, or in the hallucination of power they get when their team wins?

52   "They relate to the winning. Well, you can't say they aren't interested in the game. They watch the game. But the excitement comes from winning."

When football players snap at journalists in the locker room after a   53
loss . . .

"That's only human nature. They probably snap at their wives   54
when they get home, too. Are you saying, Does losing bother people?
Sure it does. It's no different from a guy at IBM who loses a sale to a
competitor. You just don't like to lose. Most people want to be associated with winning. When you work your butt off and don't get the results you want, you might be a little short-tempered as a coach. That's
only life. But that's no different than any other segment of life. Football
parallels society, period."

I've noticed that the worst thing you can call somebody in the Unit-   55
ed States is a loser.

"No. The word *quitter* is the worst thing you can call somebody.   56
Lemme ask you something: If two teams play all year, and they reach
the Super Bowl, the one that loses is a loser? Come on."

"I don't like the term. . . . It's not fair. I think as long as you com-   57
pete and you do your best, if the other team is better, I don't think you
really lose. I think you lose when you quit trying."

The problem with declaring a quitter to be a lower form of dirt   58
than a loser is that you're still stigmatizing almost everybody. Studies
indicate that up to 90 percent of children drop out of organized competitive sports by the age of fifteen. Extrapolating from my own experience, I would guess that they don't enjoy feeling like losers so that the
jocks can feel like winners. Since they associate intense physical activity with feeling rotten, they grow up having problems with obesity and
depression, both of which have become epidemic in the United States.

As Mike Ditka would say, it's not fair. But I think there's a way out.   59
And I think that Alfie Kohn has seen it. Kohn, an educational philosopher, has helped inspire the opposition to standardized tests, an especially pernicious form of competition. His first book, *No Contest: The
Case Against Competition*, cites study after study demonstrating that
competition hinders work, play, learning, and creativity in people of all
ages. (In fact, there is almost no evidence to the contrary in the social
sciences.) The book is wonderfully validating for anyone who ever had
doubts about the ostensible fun of gym class and spelling bees. I told
Kohn that in my experience, people get unhinged when you question
the value of making other people fail.

"Absolutely. It calls into question America's state religion, which is   60
practiced not only on the playing field but in the classroom and the
workplace, and even in the family. The considerable body of evidence
demonstrating that this is self-defeating makes very little impression
on people who are psychologically invested in a desperate way in the
idea of winning. The real alternative to being number one is not being

number two, but being able to dispense with these pathological ratings altogether. If people accepted the research on the destructiveness of competition, you wouldn't see all these books teaching how to compete more effectively. I hear from a lot of teachers and parents whose kids fall apart after losing in spelling bees and awards assemblies, and they feel dreadful about it. The adults start to think, *Hmm, maybe competition isn't such a good thing, at least for those kids.* It took me years to see that the same harms were being visited upon the winners. The kids who win are being taught that they are good only to the extent that they continue to beat other people. They're being taught that other people are obstacles to their own success, which destroys a sense of community as effectively as when we teach losers that lesson. And finally, the winners are being taught that the point of what they are doing is to win, which leads to diminished achievement and interest in what they are doing. What's true for kids is also true for adults. It's not a problem peculiar to those who lose. We're all losers in the race to win."

61   I'm very blessed that way. I didn't have the perspective to spell it out like Alfie Kohn, but I've known I was a total loser since my first college football practice. I've admitted it here publicly, and I am free. You, you're probably holding on to some putrefying little shred of self-esteem, denying that you're a loser in a country inhabited by Bill Gates and 260 million losers. You're still hoping to beat your friend at racquetball and make him feel as bad as you do when you lose, still looking to flatten some rival with just the right factoid in an argument, still craving the sports car in the commercial that accurately announces, "There's no such thing as a gracious winner." Give up, I say. Join me. Losers of the world, unite! You have nothing to lose but your shame.

RESPONDING TO READING

1. Literally, a *loser* in a sport is simply the person or team that failed to win a given contest. But even this definition rings with more than its literal meaning; *failed* shares a root with *failure*, so a loser is, by extension, also a failure. How does Young develop both the literal and more figurative definitions of *losing/loser* in his essay? Why does the term *loser* carry connotations far beyond being bested in a contest?

2. How does Young connect definitions of *loser* to American ideas about masculinity? For a man, what does it mean to be labeled as a *loser*. Is the definition similar or different when a woman is labeled as a *loser*?

3. How does Young weave his own experiences into his essay, using himself to define what it means to be a loser? How does establishing his credentials as a loser make him an authority on the subject? Is he able to transform being a loser into a positive thing, at least at some times or in some situations?

4. Discuss American ideas about winning. Are there winners and losers in every situation and not just in sports—employment, dating, applying to college, etc.? Are there times where winners in one situation are defined as losers in another?

5. In an essay, describe an experience you have had where you (a) were labeled as a loser or (b) where you labeled someone else as a loser. What was the literal situation that led to this labeling? Now that you are reflecting on the experience from a distance, what are the connotations of labeling—or being labeled—as a loser in the situation you describe? Did loser mean more than literally losing?

How Can We Meet the Challenge
of Creativity?

The Reach of Imagination

JACOB BRONOWSKI

In "The Reach of the Imagination," first published in *The American Scholar* (1967), Jacob Bronowski (1908–74) defines the imagination with his characteristically lyrical combination of science and the arts. Imagination chimes with nature, he says, and makes a harmony that characterizes "all great acts of the imagination," whether artistic or scientific.

Bronowski himself is that rare person whose life and works, temperament and training, combine science and art in creative ways. Born in Poland, Bronowski earned a Ph.D. in mathematics from Cambridge University in 1933, and worked for the British government during World War II as a statistician interpreting the effects of bombings. As a consequence of seeing the atomic devastation at Nagasaki—"we had dehumanized the enemy and ourselves in one blow"—Bronowski realized that he had to "bear witness . . . for the foundations of human decency" and vowed to make science accessible to people in general, rather than just to specialists. He spent thirty years doing just that, the last decade as a senior fellow of the Salk Institute for Biological Studies in San Diego.

"Superbly wise" in mathematics, physical science, biology, and literature, Bronowski wrote essays and books on all these subjects, as well as radio dramas, an opera, and television documentaries. The most highly acclaimed of his works is *Science and Human Values* (1965), a soul-searching work in which he explained the connection between creativity in the sciences and the arts. The progress of science, for instance, was not "an orderly sequence of logical innovations but a shifting pattern which could be appreciated only by recognising the interwoven strands of history, art, literature and philosophy." *The Ascent of Man* (1973), a collection of essays based on a BBC-TV series, was Bronowski's last, optimistic celebration of the attempts of humans to understand and control nature, from prehistoric times to the present.

1   For three thousand years, poets have been enchanted and moved and perplexed by the power of their own imagination. In a short and summary essay I can hope at most to lift one small corner of that mystery; and yet it is a critical corner. I shall ask, What goes on in the mind when we imagine? You will hear from me that one answer to this question is fairly specific: which is to say, that we can describe the working

of the imagination. And when we describe it as I shall do, it becomes plain that imagination is a specifically *human* gift. To imagine is the characteristic act, not of the poet's mind, or the painter's, or the scientist's, but of the mind of man.

My stress here on the word *human* implies that there is a clear difference in this between the actions of men and those of other animals. Let me then start with a classical experiment with animals and children which Walter Hunter thought out in Chicago about 1910. That was the time when scientists were agog with the success of Ivan Pavlov in forming and changing the reflex actions of dogs, which Pavlov had first announced in 1903. Pavlov had been given a Nobel prize the next year, in 1904; although in fairness I should say that the award did not cite his work on the conditioned reflex, but on the digestive glands.

Hunter duly trained some dogs and other animals on Pavlov's lines. They were taught that when a light came on over one of three tunnels out of their cage, that tunnel would be open; they could escape down it, and were rewarded with food if they did. But once he had fixed that conditioned reflex, Hunter added to it a deeper idea: he gave the mechanical experiment a new dimension, literally—the dimension of time. Now he no longer let the dog go to the lighted tunnel at once; instead, he put out the light, and then kept the dog waiting a little while before he let him go. In this way Hunter timed how long an animal can remember where he has last seen the signal light to his escape route.

The results were and are staggering. A dog or a rat forgets which one of three tunnels has been lit up within a matter of seconds—in Hunter's experiment, ten seconds at most. If you want such an animal to do much better than this, you must make the task much simpler: you must face him with only two tunnels to choose from. Even so, the best that Hunter could do was to have a dog remember for five minutes which one of two tunnels had been lit up.

I am not quoting these times as if they were exact and universal: they surely are not. Hunter's experiment, more than fifty years old now, had many faults of detail. For example, there were too few animals, they were oddly picked, and they did not all behave consistently. It may be unfair to test a dog for what he *saw*, when he commonly follows his nose rather than his eyes. It may be unfair to test any animal in the unnatural setting of a laboratory cage. And there are higher animals, such as chimpanzees and other primates, which certainly have longer memories than the animals that Hunter tried.

Yet when all these provisos have been made (and met, by more modern experiments) the facts are still startling and characteristic. An animal cannot recall a signal from the past for even a short fraction of the time that a man can—for even a short fraction of the time that a child can. Hunter made comparable tests with six-year-old children and found, of course, that they were incomparably better than the best of the animals. There is a striking and basic difference between a man's ability to imagine something that he saw or experienced and an animal's failure.

7   Animals make up for this by other and extraordinary gifts. The salmon and the carrier pigeon can find their way home as we cannot; they have, as it were, a practical memory that man cannot match. But their actions always depend on some form of habit: on instinct or on learning, which reproduce by rote a train of known responses. They do not depend, as human memory does, on calling to mind the recollection of absent things.

8   Where is it that the animal falls short? We get a clue to the answer, I think, when Hunter tells us how the animals in his experiment tried to fix their recollection. They most often pointed themselves at the light before it went out, as some gun dogs point rigidly at the game they scent—and get the name *pointer* from the posture. The animal makes ready to act by building the signal into its action. There is a primitive imagery in its stance, it seems to me; it is as if the animal were trying to fix the light in its mind by fixing it in its body. And indeed, how else can a dog mark and (as it were) name one of three tunnels, when he has no such words as *left* and *right*, and no such numbers as *one, two, three*? The directed gesture of attention and readiness is perhaps the only symbolic device that the dog commands to hold on to the past, and thereby to guide himself into the future.

9   I used the verb *to imagine* a moment ago, and now I have some ground for giving it a meaning. To *imagine* means to make images and to move them about inside one's head in new arrangements. When you and I recall the past, we imagine it in this direct and homely sense. The tool that puts the human mind ahead of the animal is imagery. For us, memory does not demand the preoccupation that it demands in animals, and it lasts immensely longer, because we fix it in images or other substitute symbols. With the same symbolic vocabulary we spell out the future—not one but many futures, which we weigh one against another.

10   I am using the word *image* in a wide meaning, which does not restrict it to the mind's eye as a visual organ. An image in my usage is what Charles Peirce called a *sign*, without regard for its sensory quality. Peirce distinguished between different forms of signs, but there is no reason to make his distinction here, for the imagination works equally with them all, and that is why we call them all images.

11   Indeed, the most important images for human beings are simply words, which are abstract symbols. Animals do not have words, in our sense: there is no specific center for language, in the brain of any animal, as there is in the human brain. In this respect at least we know that

the human imagination depends on a configuration in the brain that has only evolved in the last one or two million years. In the same period, evolution has greatly enlarged the front lobes in the human brain, which govern the sense of the past and the future; and it is a fair guess that they are probably the seat of our other images. (Part of the evidence for this guess is that damage to the front lobes in primates reduces them to the state of Hunter's animals.) If the guess turns out to be right, we shall know why man has come to look like a highbrow or an egghead: because otherwise there would not be room in his head for his imagination.

The images play out for us events which are not present to our   12
senses, and thereby guard the past and create the future—a future that does not yet exist, and may never come to exist in that form. By contrast, the lack of symbolic ideas, or their rudimentary poverty, cuts off an animal from the past and the future alike, and imprisons him in the present. Of all the distinctions between man and animal, the characteristic gift which makes us human is the power to work with symbolic images: the gift of imagination.

This is really a remarkable finding. When Philip Sidney in 1580 de-   13
fended poets (and all unconventional thinkers) from the Puritan charge that they were liars, he said that a maker must imagine things that are not. Halfway between Sidney and us, William Blake said, "What is now proved was once only imagin'd." About the same time, in 1796, Samuel Taylor Coleridge for the first time distinguished between the passive fancy and the active imagination, "the living Power and prime Agent of all human Perception." Now we see that they were right, and precisely right: the human gift is the gift of imagination—and that is not just a literary phrase.

Nor is it just a literary gift; it is, I repeat, characteristically human.   14
Almost everything that we do that is worth doing is done in the first place in the mind's eye. The richness of human life is that we have many lives; we live the events that do not happen (and some that cannot) as vividly as those that do; and if thereby we die a thousand deaths, that is the price we pay for living a thousand lives. (A cat, of course, has only nine.) Literature is alive to us because we live its images, but so is any play of the mind—so is chess: the lines of play that we foresee and try in our heads and dismiss are as much a part of the game as the moves that we make. John Keats said that the unheard melodies are sweeter, and all chess players sadly recall that the combinations that they planned and which never came to be played were the best.

I make this point to remind you, insistently, that imagination is the   15
manipulation of images in one's head; and that the rational manipulation belongs to that, as well as the literary and artistic manipulation. When a child begins to play games with things that stand for other

things, with chairs or chessmen, he enters the gateway to reason and imagination together. For the human reason discovers new relations between things not by deduction, but by that unpredictable blend of speculation and insight that scientists call induction, which—like other forms of imagination—cannot be formalized. We see it at work when Walter Hunter inquires into a child's memory, as much as when Blake and Coleridge do. Only a restless and original mind would have asked Hunter's questions and could have conceived his experiments, in a science that was dominated by Pavlov's reflex arcs and was heading toward the behaviorism of John Watson.

16   Let me find a spectacular example for you from history. What is the most famous experiment that you had described to you as a child? I will hazard that it is the experiment that Galileo is said to have made in Sidney's age, in Pisa about 1590, by dropping two unequal balls from the Leaning Tower. There, we say, is a man in the modern mold, a man after our own hearts: he insisted on questioning the authority of Aristotle and St. Thomas Aquinas, and seeing with his own eyes whether (as they said) the heavy ball would reach the ground before the light one. Seeing is believing.

17   Yet seeing is also imagining. Galileo did challenge the authority of Aristotle, and he did look hard at his mechanics. But the eye that Galileo used was the mind's eye. He did not drop balls from the Leaning Tower of Pisa—and if he had, he would have got a very doubtful answer. Instead, Galileo made an imaginary experiment in his head, which I will describe as he did years later in the book he wrote after the Holy Office silenced him: the *Discorsi . . . intorno à due nuove scienze* (Discourses Concerning Two New Sciences), which was smuggled out to be printed in the Netherlands in 1638.

18   Suppose, said Galileo, that you drop two unequal balls from the tower at the same time. And suppose that Aristotle is right—suppose that the heavy ball falls faster, so that it steadily gains on the light ball, and hits the ground first. Very well. Now imagine the same experiment done again, with only one difference: this time the two unequal balls are joined by a string between them. The heavy ball will again move ahead, but now the light ball holds it back and acts as a drag or brake. So the light ball will be speeded up and the heavy ball will be slowed down; they must reach the ground together because they are tied together, but they cannot reach the ground as quickly as the heavy ball alone. Yet the string between them has turned the two balls into a single mass which is heavier than either ball—and surely (according to Aristotle) this mass should therefore move faster than either ball? Galileo's imaginary experiment has uncovered a contradiction; he says trenchantly, "You see how, from your assumption that a heavier body falls more rapidly than a lighter one, I infer that a (still) heavier

body falls more slowly." There is only one way out of the contradiction: the heavy ball and the light ball must fall at the same rate, so that they go on falling at the same rate when they are tied together.

This argument is not conclusive, for nature might be more subtle 19 (when the two balls are joined) than Galileo has allowed. And yet it is something more important: it is suggestive, it is stimulating, it opens a new view—in a word, it is imaginative. It cannot be settled without an actual experiment, because nothing that we imagine can become knowledge until we have translated it into, and backed it by, real experience. The test of imagination is experience. But then, that is as true of literature and the arts as it is of science. In science, the imaginary experiment is tested by confronting it with physical experience; and in literature, the imaginative conception is tested by confronting it with human experience. The superficial speculation in science is dismissed because it is found to falsify nature; and the shallow work of art is discarded because it is found to be untrue to our own nature. So when Ella Wheeler Wilcox died in 1919, more people were reading her verses than Shakespeare's; yet in a few years her work was dead. It had been buried by its poverty of emotion and its trivialness of thought: which is to say that it had been proved to be as false to the nature of man as, say, Jean Baptiste Lamarck and Trofim Lysenko were false to the nature of inheritance. The strength of the imagination, its enriching power and excitement, lies in its interplay with reality—physical and emotional.

I doubt if there is much to choose here between science and the 20 arts: the imagination is not much more free, and not much less free, in one than in the other. All great scientists have used their imagination freely, and let it ride them to outrageous conclusions without crying "Halt!" Albert Einstein fiddled with imaginary experiments from boyhood, and was wonderfully ignorant of the facts that they were supposed to bear on. When he wrote the first of his beautiful papers on the random movement of atoms, he did not know that the Brownian motion which it predicted could be seen in any laboratory. He was sixteen when he invented the paradox that he resolved ten years later, in 1905, in the theory of relativity, and it bulked much larger in his mind than the experiment of Albert Michelson and Edward Morley which had upset every other physicist since 1881. All his life Einstein loved to make up teasing puzzles like Galileo's, about falling lifts and the detection of gravity; and they carry the nub of the problems of general relativity on which he was working.

Indeed, it could not be otherwise. The power that man has over nature and himself, and that a dog lacks, lies in his command of imaginary experience. He alone has the symbols which fix the past and play with the future, possible and impossible. In the Renaissance, the symbolism of memory was thought to be mystical, and devices that were invented as mnemonics (by Giordano Bruno, for example, and by Robert Fludd) were interpreted as magic signs. The symbol is the tool which gives man his power, and it is the same tool whether the symbols are images or words, mathematical signs or mesons. And the symbols have a reach and a roundness that goes beyond their literal and practical meaning. They are the rich concepts under which the mind gathers many particulars into one name, and many instances into one general induction. When a man says *left* and *right*, he is outdistancing the dog not only in looking for a light; he is setting in train all the shifts of meaning, the overtones and the ambiguities, between *gauche* and *adroit* and *dexterous*, between *sinister* and the sense of right. When a man counts *one, two, three*, he is not only doing mathematics; he is on the path to the mysticism of numbers in Pythagoras and Vitruvius and Kepler, to the Trinity and the signs of the Zodiac.

22   I have described imagination as the ability to make images and to move them about inside one's head in new arrangements. This is the faculty that is specifically human, and it is the common root from which science and literature both spring and grow and flourish together. For they do flourish (and languish) together; the great ages of science are the great ages of all the arts, because in them powerful minds have taken fire from one another, breathless and higgledy-piggledy, without asking too nicely whether they ought to tie their imagination to falling balls or a haunted island. Galileo and Shakespeare, who were born in the same year, grew into greatness in the same age; when Galileo was looking through his telescope at the moon, Shakespeare was writing *The Tempest*; and all Europe was in ferment, from Johannes Kepler to Peter Paul Rubens, and from the first table of logarithms by John Napier to the authorized version of the Bible.

23   Let me end with a last and spirited example of the common inspiration of literature and science, because it is as much alive today as it was three hundred years ago. What I have in mind is man's ageless fantasy, to fly to the moon. I do not display this to you as a high scientific enterprise; on the contrary, I think we have more important discoveries to make here on earth than wait for us, beckoning, at the horned surface of the moon. Yet I cannot belittle the fascination which that ice-blue journey has had for the imagination of men, long before it drew us to our television screens to watch the tumbling of astronauts. Plutarch and Lucian, Ariosto and Ben Jonson wrote about it, before the days of Jules Verne and H. G. Wells and science fiction. The seventeenth century was heady with new dreams and fables about voyages to the moon. Kepler wrote one full of deep scientific ideas, which (alas) simply got his mother accused of witchcraft. In England, Francis Godwin wrote a wild and splendid work, *The Man in the Moone*, and the astronomer John Wilkins wrote a wild and learned one, *The Discovery of a*

New World. They did not draw a line between science and fancy; for example, they all tried to guess just where in the journey the earth's gravity would stop. Only Kepler understood that gravity has no boundary, and put a law to it—which happened to be the wrong law.

All this was a few years before Isaac Newton was born, and it was   24
all in his head that day in 1666 when he sat in his mother's garden, a young man of twenty-three, and thought about the reach of gravity. This was how he came to conceive his brilliant image, that the moon is like a ball which has been thrown so hard that it falls exactly as fast as the horizon, all the way round the earth. The image will do for any satellite, and Newton modestly calculated how long therefore an astronaut would take to fall round the earth once. He made it ninety minutes, and we have all seen now that he was right; but Newton had no way to check that. Instead he went on to calculate how long in that case the distant moon would take to round the earth, if indeed it behaves like a thrown ball that falls in the earth's gravity, and if gravity obeyed a law of inverse squares. He found that the answer would be twenty-eight days.

In that telling figure, the imagination that day chimed with nature,   25
and made a harmony. We shall hear an echo of that harmony on the day when we land on the moon, because it will be not a technical but an imaginative triumph, that reaches back to the beginning of modern science and literature both. All great acts of imagination are like this, in the arts and in science, and convince us because they fill out reality with a deeper sense of rightness. We start with the simplest vocabulary of images, with *left* and *right* and *one, two, three*, and before we know how it happened the words and the numbers have conspired to make a match with nature: we catch in them the pattern of mind and matter as one.

RESPONDING TO READING

1. Bronowski is careful to define some problematic terms. Give his definitions for the following: image, imagination, fancy, sign, words. Compare these definitions to those used by Suzanne Langer (in Chapter 2).

2. "Almost everything that we do that is worth doing is done in the first place in the mind's eye." "Nothing that we imagine can become knowledge until we have translated it into, and backed it by, real experience." Explain what Bronowski means by this. Then test its truth by examples drawn from your reading and personal experience.

3. Bronowski argues that imagination in science and in the arts turns out to be much the same. Examine the evidence he gives for this assertion. How does his evidence compare with, say, Peter Singers, Atul Gawande's, or Charles Young's earlier in this chapter or the following essay by Linda Hogan? And

how do such statements make sense in an age when many people talk about the opposition between the "two cultures" of science and humanities?

4. Consider the relationship between imagination and experience. Select an experience you have had, or that you have read about, which took place only after it had been fully imagined: some long-awaited adventure, trip, or evening that you perhaps lived out in your mind many times before it occurred. Did the experience do for you, or for your subject, what Newton's calculations did for him: "the imagination that day chimed with nature, and made a harmony"? Or were imagination and experience at odds? Describe what happened and reflect upon the way "the reach of imagination" affected what happened.

Hearing Voices

LINDA HOGAN

In the process of becoming a poet and novelist, Linda Hogan, a Chickasaw born in Denver in 1947, worked as a nurse's aide, dental assistant, waitress, homemaker, secretary, administrator, teacher's aide, and library clerk. She earned an M.A. at the University of Colorado, Boulder, in 1978, and was a professor of American and American Indian Studies at the University of Minnesota before joining the faculty of the University of Colorado. Her most recent book, *Dwellings: A Spiritual History of the Living World* (1996), is a collection of poetic musings on the nature of the natural world, as is her collection of poetry *Savings* (1988). Her fourth poetry collection, *Seeing Through the Sun* (1985), received an American Book Award.

Hogan says of her work, "My writing comes from and goes back to . . . both the human and the global community. I am interested in the deepest questions, those of spirit, of shelter, of growth and movement toward peace and liberation, inner and outer." She is also an ardent conservationist, studying the relationship between humans and other species and working as a volunteer in the conservation and rehabilitation of birds of prey. In "Hearing Voices" she amplifies these views, emphasizing how important it is to listen to the literal "language of this continent," the stories of this earth, "the stones giving guidance, the trees singing, the corn telling of inner earth, the dragonfly offering up a tongue."

1   When Barbara McClintock was awarded a Nobel Prize for her work on gene transposition in corn plants, the most striking thing about her was that she made her discoveries by listening to what the corn spoke to her, by respecting the life of the corn and "letting it come."

2   McClintock says she learned "the stories" of the plants. She "heard" them. She watched the daily green journeys of growth from

earth toward sky and sun. She knew her plants in the way a healer or mystic would have known them, from the inside, the inner voices of corn and woman speaking to one another.

As an Indian woman, I come from a long history of people who   3
have listened to the language of this continent, people who have known that corn grows with the songs and prayers of the people, that it has a story to tell, that the world is alive. Both in oral traditions and in mythology—the true language of inner life—account after account tells of the stones giving guidance, the trees singing, the corn telling of inner earth, the dragonfly offering up a tongue. This is true in the European traditions as well: Psyche received direction from the reeds and the ants, Orpheus knew the languages of earth, animals, and birds.

This intuitive and common language is what I seek for my writing,   4
work in touch with the mystery and force of life, work that speaks a few of the many voices around us, and it is important to me that McClintock listened to the voices of the corn. It is important to the continuance of life that she told the truth of her method and that it reminded us all of where our strength, our knowing, and our sustenance come from.

It is also poetry, this science, and I note how often scientific theories   5
lead to the world of poetry and vision, theories telling us how atoms that were stars have been transformed into our living, breathing bodies. And in those theories, or maybe they should be called stories, we begin to understand how we are each many people, including the stars we once were, and how we are in essence the earth and the universe, how what we do travels clear around the earth and returns. In a single moment of our living, there is our ancestral and personal history, our future, even our deaths planted in us and already growing toward their fulfillment. The corn plants are there, and like all the rest we are forever merging our borders with theirs in the world collective.

Our very lives might depend on this listening. In the Chernobyl   6
nuclear accident, the wind told the story that was being suppressed by the people. It gave away the truth. It carried the story of danger to other countries. It was a poet, a prophet, a scientist.

Sometimes, like the wind, poetry has its own laws speaking for the   7
life of the planet. It is a language that wants to bring back together what the other words have torn apart. It is the language of life speaking through us about the sacredness of life.

This life speaking life is what I find so compelling about the work   8
of poets such as Ernesto Cardenal, who is also a priest and was the Nicaraguan Minister of Culture. He writes: "The armadilloes are very happy with this government. ... Not only humans desired liberation/the whole ecology wanted it." Cardenal has also written "The Parrots," a poem about caged birds who were being sent to the United States as pets for the wealthy, how the cages were opened, the parrots

allowed back into the mountains and jungles, freed like the people, "and sent back to the land we were pulled from."

9   How we have been pulled from the land! And how poetry has worked hard to set us free, uncage us, keep us from split tongues that mimic the voices of our captors. It returns us to our land. Poetry is a string of words that parades without a permit. It is a lockbox of words to put an ear to as we try to crack the safe of language, listening for the right combination, the treasure inside. It is life resonating. It is sometimes called Prayer, Soothsaying, Complaint, Invocation, Proclamation, Testimony, Witness. Writing is and does all these things. And like that parade, it is illegitimately insistent on going its own way, on being part of the miracle of life, telling the story about what happened when we were cosmic dust, what it means to be stars listening to our human atoms.

10   But don't misunderstand me. I am not just a dreamer. I am also the practical type. A friend's father, watching the United States stage another revolution in another Third World country, said, "Why doesn't the government just feed people and then let the political chips fall where they may?" He was right. It was easy, obvious, even financially more reasonable to do that, to let democracy be chosen because it feeds hunger. I want my writing to be that simple, that clear and direct. Likewise, I feel it is not enough for me just to write, but I need to live it, to be informed by it. I have found over the years that my work has more courage than I do. It has more wisdom. It teaches me, leads me places I never knew I was heading. And it is about a new way of living, of being in the world.

11   I was on a panel recently where the question was raised whether we thought literature could save lives. The audience, book people, smiled expectantly with the thought. I wanted to say, Yes, it saves lives. But I couldn't speak those words. It saves spirits maybe, hearts. It changes minds, but for me writing is an incredible privilege. When I sit down at the desk, there are other women who are hungry, homeless. I don't want to forget that, that the world of matter is still there to be reckoned with. This writing is a form of freedom most other people do not have. So, when I write, I feel a responsibility, a commitment to other humans and to the animal and plant communities as well.

12   Still, writing has changed me. And there is the powerful need we all have to tell a story, each of us with a piece of the whole pattern to complete. As Alice Walker says, We are all telling part of the same story, and as Sharon Olds has said, Every writer is a cell on the body politic of America.

13   Another Nobel Prize laureate is Betty William, a Northern Ireland co-winner of the 1977 Peace Prize. I heard her speak about how, after witnessing the death of children, she stepped outside in the middle of the night and began knocking on doors and yelling, behaviors that

would have earned her a diagnosis of hysteria in our own medical circles. She knocked on doors that might have opened with weapons pointing in her face, and she cried out, "What kind of people have we become that we would allow children to be killed on our streets?" Within four hours the city was awake, and there were sixteen thousand names on petitions for peace. Now, that woman's work is a lesson to those of us who deal with language, and to those of us who are dealt into silence. She used language to begin the process of peace. This is the living, breathing power of the word. It is poetry. So are the names of those who signed the petitions. Maybe it is this kind of language that saves lives.

Writing begins for me with survival, with life and with freeing life,   14
saving life, speaking life. It is work that speaks what can't be easily said. It originates from a compelling desire to live and be alive. For me, it is sometimes the need to speak for other forms of life, to take the side of human life, even our sometimes frivolous living, and our grief-filled living, our joyous living, our violent living, busy living, our peaceful living. It is about possibility. It is based in the world of matter. I am interested in how something small turns into an image that is large and strong with resonance, where the ordinary becomes beautiful. I believe the divine, the magic, is here in the weeds at our feet, unacknowledged. What a world this is. Where else could water rise up to the sky, turn into snow crystals, magnificently brought together, fall from the sky all around us, pile up billions deep, and catch the small sparks of sunlight as they return again to water?

These acts of magic happen all the time; in Chaco Canyon, my sis-   15
ter has seen a kiva; a ceremonial room in the earth, that is in the center of the canyon. This place has been uninhabited for what seems like forever. It has been without water. In fact, there are theories that the ancient people disappeared when they journeyed after water. In the center of it a corn plant was growing. It was all alone and it had been there since the ancient ones, the old ones who came before us all, those people who wove dog hair into belts, who witnessed the painting of flute players on the seeping canyon walls, who knew the stories of corn. And there was one corn plant growing out of the holy place. It planted itself yearly. With no water, no person to care for it, no overturning of the soil, this corn plant rises up to tell its story, and that's what this poetry is.

RESPONDING TO READING

1. Hogan argues that poetry and science come together in important ways ("It is also poetry, this science . . ." paragraph 5). Explain what she means.
2. As a Native American, "people who have listened to the language of this continent, people who have known . . . that the world is alive," Hogan

speaks of the messages of the earth and its creatures to us. But she also cites the scientist Barbara McClintock and European myths, and she provides other arguments as well. Are you convinced by her argument that we need to listen to the "world collective" and that the source of creativity is "hearing voices"? Why, or why not?

3. Hogan sees creativity as a form of saving "spirits, maybe hearts." Explain what she means and relate her vision to that of two or three other writers in this book.

4. Write about an experience you have had, or have read about, in which some nonhuman creature or object "spoke" to a person. What is the nature of such a message? How does it arrive? What preparation is necessary? What was the result? Or, if you are skeptical about such experiences, write about the problems they cause.

Where Do You Get Your Ideas From?
URSULA K. LE GUIN

Born on October 21 (St. Ursula's Day), 1929, Le Guin received her A.B. from Radcliffe College in 1951 and her A.M. from Columbia University in 1952. She has worked as a part-time instructor of French, a creative consultant for Public Broadcasting Service, and, for most of her life, a writer. Her novels include *Planet of Exile* (1966), *City of Illusions* (1967), *Very Far Away from Anywhere Else* (1976), and *Steering the Craft: Exercises and Discussions on Story Writing for the Lone Navigator or the Mutinous Crew* (1998). Le Guin also writes children's literature, including the illustrated books *Buffalo Gals, Won't You Come Out Tonight* (1994) and *Wonderful Alexander and the Catwings* (1994).

In "Where Do You Get Your Ideas From?" Le Guin argues that there are two myths about writing fiction at the heart of this question: (1) Being a writer simply means learning the secret to being a writer and (2) a story always begins with an idea. She debunks each of these misguided assumptions in turn. Writing, she ultimately argues, is an act of collaboration between writer and reader—although the writer does "one hell of a lot of controlling" in this transaction. And all writers must accept the fact that sometimes a truly beautiful creation will, upon being read, fail utterly. This is the truth for writers, although the myths seem much less harsh.

1   *With thanks to my students in the fiction workshops at Haystack, Clarion West, and Humboldt Community College, in the summer and fall of 1987, whose work and talk enabled me to write this.*

2   Whenever I talk with an audience after a reading or lecture, somebody asks me, "Where do you get your ideas from?" A fiction writer

can avoid being asked that question only by practicing the dourest naturalism and forswearing all acts of the imagination. Science-fiction writers can't escape it, and develop habitual answers to it: "Schenectady," says Harlan Ellison. Vonda N. McIntyre takes this further, explaining that there is a mail order house for ideas in Schenectady, to which writers can subscribe for five or ten or (bargain rate) twenty-five ideas a month; then she hits herself on the head to signify remorse, and tries to answer the question seriously. Even in its most patronizing form—"Where do you get all those crazy ideas from?"—it is almost always asked seriously: the asker really wants to know.

The reason why it is unanswerable is, I think, that it involves at least two false notions, myths, about how fiction is written.   3

First myth: There is a secret to being a writer. If you can just learn the secret, you will instantly be a writer; and the secret might be where the ideas come from.   4

Second myth: Stories start from ideas; the origin of a story is an idea.   5

I will dispose of the first myth as quickly as possible. The "secret" is skill. If you haven't learned how to do something, the people who have may seem to be magicians, possessors of mysterious secrets. In a fairly simple art, such as making pie crust, there are certain teachable "secrets" of method that lead almost infallibly to good results; but in any complex art, such as housekeeping, piano-playing, clothes-making, or story-writing, there are so many techniques, skills, choices of method, so many variables, so many "secrets," some teachable and some not, that you can learn them only by methodical, repeated, long-continued practice—in other words, by work.   6

Who can blame the secret-seekers for hoping to find a shortcut and avoid all the work?   7

Certainly the work of learning any art is hard enough that it is unwise (so long as you have any choice in the matter) to spend much time and energy on an art you don't have a decided talent for. Some of the secretiveness of many artists about their techniques, recipes, etc., may be taken as a warning to the unskilled: What works for me isn't going to work for you unless you've worked for it.   8

My talent and inclination for writing stories and keeping house were strong from the start, and my gift for and interest in music and sewing were weak; so that I doubt that I would ever have been a good seamstress or pianist, no matter how hard I worked. But nothing I know about how I learned to do the things I am good at doing leads me to believe that there are "secrets" to the piano or the sewing machine or any art I'm no good at. There is just the obstinate, continuous cultivation of a disposition, leading to skill in performance.   9

10   So much for secrets. How about ideas?

11   The more I think about the word "idea," the less idea I have what it means. Writers do say things like "That gives me an idea" or "I got the idea for that story when I had food poisoning in a motel in New Jersey." I think this is a kind of shorthand use of "idea" to stand for the complicated, obscure, un-understood process of the conception and formation of what is going to be a story when it gets written down. The process may not involve ideas in the sense of intelligible thoughts; it may well not even involve words. It may be a matter of mood, resonances, mental glimpses, voices, emotions, visions, dreams, anything. It is different in every writer, and in many of us it is different every time. It is extremely difficult to talk about, because we have very little terminology for such processes.

12   I would say that as a general rule, though an external event may trigger it, this inceptive state or story-beginning phase does not come from anywhere outside the mind that can be pointed to; it arises in the mind, from psychic contents that have become unavailable to the conscious mind, inner or outer experience that has been, in Gary Snyder's lovely phrase, composted. I don't believe that a writer "gets" (takes into the head) an "idea" (some sort of mental object) "from" somewhere, and then turns it into words and writes them on paper. At least in my experience, it doesn't work that way. The stuff has to be transformed into oneself, it has to be composted, before it can grow a story.

13   The rest of this paper will be an attempt to analyze what I feel I am actually working with when I write, and where the "idea" fits into the whole process.

14   There seem to be five principal elements to the process:

15   1. The patterns of the language—the sounds of words.

16   2. The patterns of syntax and grammar; the ways the words and sentences connect themselves together; the ways their connections interconnect to form the larger units (paragraphs, sections, chapters); hence, the movement of the work, its tempo, pace, gait, and shape in time.

17   (Note: In poetry, especially lyric poetry, these first two kinds of patterning are salient, obvious elements of the beauty of the work—word sounds, rhymes, echoes, cadences, the "music" of poetry. In prose the sound patterns are far subtler and looser and must indeed avoid rhyme, chime, assonance, etc., and the patterns of sentencing, paragraphing, movement and shape in time, may be on such a large, slow scale as to escape conscious notice; the "music" of fiction, particularly the novel, is often not perceived as beautiful at all.)

18   3. The patterns of the images: what the words make us or let us see with the mind's eye or sense imaginatively.

4. The patterns of the ideas: what the words and the narration   19
of events make us understand, or use our understanding upon.

5. The patterns of the feelings: what the words and the nar-   20
ration, by using all the above means, make us experience emotionally or spiritually, in areas of our being not directly
accessible to or expressible in words.

All these kinds of patterning—sound, syntax, images, ideas, feel-   21
ings—have to work together; and they all have to be there in some degree. The inception of the work, that mysterious stage, is perhaps their
coming together: when in the author's mind a feeling begins to connect
itself to an image that will express it, and that image leads to an idea,
until now half-formed, that begins to find words for itself, and the
words lead to other words that make new images, perhaps of people,
characters of a story, who are doing things that express the underlying
feelings and ideas that are now resonating with each other . . .

If any of the processes get scanted badly or left out, in the concep-   22
tion stage, in the writing stage, or in the revising stage, the result will
be a weak or failed story. Failure often allows us to analyze what success triumphantly hides from us. I do not recommend going through a
story by Chekhov or Woolf trying to analyze out my five elements of
the writing process; the point is that in any successful piece of fiction,
they work in one insoluble unitary movement. But in certain familiar
forms of feeble writing or failed writing, the absence of one element or
another may be a guide to what went wrong.

For example: Having an interesting idea, working it up into a plot   23
enacted by stock characters, and relying upon violence to replace feeling, may produce the trash-level mystery, thriller, or science-fiction
story; but not a good mystery, thriller, or science-fiction story.

Contrariwise, strong feelings, even if strong characters enact them,   24
aren't enough to carry a story if the ideas connected with those feelings
haven't been thought through. If the mind isn't working along with the
emotions, the emotions will slosh around in a bathtub of wish fulfillment (as in most mass-market romances) or anger (as in much of the
"mainstream" genre) or hormones (as in porn).

Beginners' failures are often the result of trying to work with   25
strong feelings and ideas without having found the images to embody
them, or without even knowing how to find the words and string them
together. Ignorance of English vocabulary and grammar is a considerable liability to a writer of English. The best cure for it is, I believe, reading. People who learned to talk at two or so and have been practicing
talking ever since feel with some justification that they know their language; but what they know is their spoken language, and if they read
little, or read schlock, and haven't written much, their writing is going
to be pretty much what their talking was when they were two. It's

going to require considerable practice. The attempt to play complicated music on an instrument which one hasn't even learned the fingering of is probably the commonest weakness of beginning writers.

26   A rarer kind of failure is the story in which the words go careering around bellowing and plunging and kicking up a lot of dust, and when the dust settles you find they never got out of the corral. They got nowhere, because they didn't know where they were going. Feeling, idea, image, just got dragged into the stampede, and no story happened. All the same, this kind of failure sometimes strikes me as promising, because it reveals a writer reveling in pure language—letting the words take over. You can't go on that way, but it's not a bad place to start from.

27   The novelist-poet Boris Pasternak said that poetry makes itself from "the relationship between the sounds and the meanings of words." I think that prose makes itself the same way, if you will allow "sounds" to include syntax and the large motions, connections, and shapes of narrative. There is a relationship, a reciprocity, between the words and the images, ideas, and emotions evoked by those words: the stronger that relationship, the stronger the work. To believe that you can achieve meaning or feeling without coherent, integrated patterning of the sounds, the rhythms, the sentence structures, the images, is like believing you can go for a walk without bones.

28   Of the five kinds of patterning that I have invented or analyzed here, I think the central one, the one through which all the others connect, is the imagery. Verbal imagery (such as a simile or a description of a place or an event) is more physical, more bodily, than thinking or feeling, but less physical, more internal, than the actual sounds of the words. Imagery takes place in "the imagination," which I take to be the meeting place of the thinking mind with the sensing body. What is imagined isn't physically real, but it *feels as if it were*: the reader sees or hears or feels what goes on in the story, is drawn into it, exists in it, among its images, in the imagination (the reader's? the writer's?) while reading.

29   This illusion is a special gift of narrative, including the drama. Narration gives us entry to a shared world of imagination. The sounds and movement and connections of the words work to make the images vivid and authentic; the ideas and emotions are embodied in and grow out of those images of places, of people, of events, deeds, conversations, relationships; and the power and authenticity of the images may surpass that of most actual experience, since in the imagination we can share a capacity for experience and an understanding of truth far greater than our own. The great writers share their souls with us—"literally."

30   This brings me to the relationship of the writer to the reader: a matter I again find easiest to approach through explainable failure. The shared imaginative world of fiction cannot be taken for granted, even by a writer telling a story set right here and now in the suburbs among

people supposed to be familiar to everybody. The fictional world has to be created by the author, whether by the slightest hints and suggestions, which will do for the suburbs, or by very careful guidance and telling detail, if the reader is being taken to the planet Gzorx. When the writer fails to imagine, to *image*, the world of the narrative, the work fails. The usual result is abstract, didactic fiction. Plots that make points. Characters who don't talk or act like people, and who are in fact not imaginary people at all but mere bits of the writer's ego got loose, glibly emitting messages. The intellect cannot do the work of the imagination; the emotions cannot do the work of the imagination; and neither of them can do anything much in fiction without the imagination.

Where the writer and the reader collaborate to make the work of fiction is perhaps, above all, in the imagination. In the joint creation of the fictive world. **31**

Now, writers are egoists. All artists are. They can't be altruists and get their work done. And writers love to whine about the Solitude of the Author's Life, and lock themselves into cork-lined rooms or droop around in bars in order to whine better. But although most writing is done in solitude, I believe that it is done, like all the arts, for an audience. That is to say, with an audience. All the arts are performance arts, only some of them are sneakier about it than others. **32**

I beg you please to attend carefully now to what I am not saying. I am not saying that you should think about your audience when you write. I am not saying that the writing writer should have in mind, "Who will read this? Who will buy it? Who am I aiming this at?"—as if it were a gun. No. **33**

While *planning* a work, the writer may and often must think about readers; particularly if it's something like a story for children, where you need to know whether your reader is likely to be a five-year-old or a ten-year-old. Considerations of who will or might read the piece are appropriate and sometimes actively useful in planning it, thinking about it, thinking it out, inviting images. But once you start writing, it is fatal to think about anything but the writing. True work is done for the sake of doing it. What is to be done with it afterwards is another matter, another job. A story rises from the springs of creation, from the pure will to be; it tells itself; it takes its own course, finds its own way, its own words; and the writer's job is to be its medium. What a teacher or editor or market or critic or Alice will think of it has to be as far from the writing writer's mind as what breakfast was last Tuesday. Farther. The breakfast might be useful to the story. **34**

Once the story is written, however, the writer must forgo that divine privacy and accept the fact that the whole thing has been a performance, and it had better be a good one. **35**

When I, the writer, reread my work and settle down to reconsider it, reshape it, revise it, then my consciousness of the reader, of collaborating **36** with the reader, is appropriate and, I think, necessary. Indeed I may have to make an act of faith and declare that they will exist, those unknown, perhaps unborn people, my dear readers. The blind, beautiful arrogance of the creative moment must grow subtle, self-conscious, clear-sighted. It must ask questions, such as: Does this say what I thought it said? Does it say all I thought it did? It is at this stage that I, the writer, may have to question the nature of my relationship to my readers, as manifested in my work. Am I shoving them around, manipulating them, patronizing them, showing off to them? Am I punishing them? Am I using them as a dump site for my accumulated psychic toxins? Am I telling them what they better damn well believe or else? Am I running circles around them, and will they enjoy it? Am I scaring them, and did I intend to? Am I interesting them, and if not, hadn't I better see to it that I am? Am I amusing, teasing, alluring them? Flirting with them? Hypnotizing them? Am I giving to them, tempting them, inviting them, drawing them into the work *to work with me*—to be the one, the Reader, who completes my vision?

37   Because the writer cannot do it alone. The unread story is not a story; it is little black marks on wood pulp. The reader, reading it, makes it live: a live thing, a story.

38   A special note to the above: If the writer is a socially privileged person—particularly a White or a male or both—his imagination may have to make an intense and conscious effort to realize that people who don't share his privileged status may read his work and will not share with him many attitudes and opinions that he has been allowed to believe or to pretend are shared by "everybody." Since the belief in a privileged view of reality is no longer tenable outside privileged circles, and often not even within them, fiction written from such an assumption will make sense only to a decreasing, and increasingly reactionary, audience. Many women writing today, however, still choose the male viewpoint, finding it easier to do so than to write from the knowledge that feminine experience of reality is flatly denied by many potential readers, including the majority of critics and professors of literature, and may rouse defensive hostility and contempt. The choice, then, would seem to be between collusion and subversion; but there's no use pretending that you can get away without making the choice. Not to choose, these days, is a choice made. All fiction has ethical, political, and social weight, and sometimes the works that weigh the heaviest are those apparently fluffy or escapist fictions whose authors declare themselves "above politics," "just entertainers," and so on.

39   The writer writing, then, is trying to get all the patterns of sounds, syntax, imagery, ideas, emotions, working together in one process, in which the reader will be drawn to participate. This implies that writers do one hell of a lot of controlling. They control all their material as

closely as they can, and in doing so they are trying to control the reader, too. They are trying to get the reader to go along helplessly, putty in their hands, seeing, hearing, feeling, believing the story, laughing at it, crying at it. They are trying to make innocent little children cry.

But though control is a risky business, it need not be conceived in   40 confrontational terms as a battle with and a victory over the material or the reader. Again, I think it comes down to collaboration, or sharing the gift: the writer tries to get the reader working with the text in the effort to keep the whole story all going along in one piece in the right direction (which is my general notion of a good piece of fiction).

In this effort, writers need all the help they can get. Even under the   41 most skilled control, the words will never fully embody the vision. Even with the most sympathetic reader, the truth will falter and grow partial. Writers have to get used to launching something beautiful and watching it crash and burn. They also have to learn when to let go control, when the work takes off on its own and flies, farther than they ever planned or imagined, to places they didn't know they knew. All makers must leave room for the acts of the spirit. But they have to work hard and carefully, and wait patiently, to deserve them.

RESPONDING TO READING

1. Le Guin begins by describing two myths about writing. Are there other myths? How does Le Guin use the myths to organize and develop her essay?

2. Le Guin defines writing as an art, one with "secrets" that can be learned only through hard work. How would it change her argument if writing were defined as a science? What connotations does the term *art* have that *science* lacks? And vice versa? Are there benefits and drawbacks to each definition?

3. What secrets, techniques, and rules have you been taught about writing? Which of them agree with or contradict Le Guin's arguments about the art of writing? In your experience as a writer, which of them work or fail to work?

4. Le Guin describes the five "principal elements" of her writing process. Is the process she describes only useful to poets and writers of fiction? Compare your writing process with those of several of your classmates, for instance, in writing a paper for this course. Can your own writing process be generalized to all writers, or must it be modified to fit other writers or types of writing?

5. In an essay, compare and contrast your own writing process with Le Guin's writing process. In what ways are your ways of working similar to hers? How are your methods different from hers? Try out one of her methods and report on how it works in your own process of writing a paper.

Angels on a Pin

ALEXANDER CALANDRA

Alexander Calandra (born 1911) is professor emeritus of physical sciences at Washington University in St. Louis. He has also taught at Brooklyn College, Webster College, and the University of Chicago and has been guest lecturer at many campuses around the country.

In "Angels on a Pin," originally published in the *Saturday Review* (December 1968), Calandra uses a literary device common to social critics and satirists from Plato onward, a dialogue between a supposedly sophisticated questioner and an apparently naive respondent whose astute replies invariably outwit the questioner. In this case, the physics professor expects a prescribed, conventional answer to an exam question and the clever student offers a variety of creative alternative answers—all correct, but so unanticipated that the professor has to call in a colleague to judge their merit. The comic possibilities of the situation were exploited in a skit presented (without Calandra's permission) on *Saturday Night Live*, an ironic violation of convention which led to an out-of-court settlement.

Is it possible for truly imaginative students to surpass their professors and not only get away with their insouciance but to be rewarded for intellectual creativity?

1   Some time ago, I received a call from a colleague who asked if I would be the referee on the grading of an examination question. He was about to give a student a zero for his answer to a physics question, while the student claimed he should receive a perfect score and would if the system were not set up against the student. The instructor and the student agreed to submit this to an impartial arbiter, and I was selected.

2   I went to my colleague's office and read the examination question: "Show how it is possible to determine the height of a tall building with the aid of a barometer."

3   The student had answered: "Take the barometer to the top of the building, attach a long rope to it, lower the barometer to the street, and then bring it up, measuring the length of the rope. The length of the rope is the height of the building."

4   I pointed out that the student really had a strong case for full credit, since he had answered the question completely and correctly. On the other hand, if full credit were given, it could well contribute to a high grade for the student in his physics course. A high grade is supposed to certify competence in physics, but the answer did not confirm this. I suggested that the student have another try at answering the question. I was not surprised that my colleague agreed, but I was surprised that the student did.

5   I gave the student six minutes to answer the question, with the warning that his answer should show some knowledge of physics. At

the end of five minutes, he had not written anything. I asked if he wished to give up, but he said no. He had many answers to this problem; he was just thinking of the best one. I excused myself for interrupting him, and asked him to please go on. In the next minute, he dashed off his answer, which read:

"Take the barometer to the top of the building and lean over the   6
edge of the roof. Drop the barometer, timing its fall with a stopwatch. Then, using the formula $S = \frac{1}{2}\,at^2$, calculate the height of the building."

At this point, I asked my colleague if *he* would give up. He conceded, and I gave the student almost full credit.   7

In leaving my colleague's office, I recalled that the student had said   8
he had other answers to the problem, so I asked him what they were. "Oh, yes," said the student. "There are many ways of getting the height of a tall building with the aid of a barometer. For example, you could take the barometer out on a sunny day and measure the height of the barometer, the length of its shadow, and the length of the shadow of the building, and by the use of a simple proportion, determine the height of the building."

"Fine," I said. "And the others?"   9

"Yes," said the student. "There is a very basic measurement   10
method that you will like. In this method, you take the barometer and begin to walk up the stairs. As you climb the stairs, you mark off the length of the barometer along the wall. You then count the number of marks, and this will give you the height of the building in barometer units. A very direct method.

"Of course, if you want a more sophisticated method, you can tie   11
the barometer to the end of a string, swing it as a pendulum, and determine the value of 'g' at the street level and at the top of the building. From the difference between the two values of 'g,' the height of the building can, in principle, be calculated."

Finally, he concluded, there are many other ways of solving the   12
problem. "Probably the best," he said, "is to take the barometer to the basement and knock on the superintendent's door. When the superintendent answers, you speak to him as follows: 'Mr. Superintendent, here I have a fine barometer. If you will tell me the height of this building, I will give you this barometer.'"

At this point, I asked the student if he really did not know the con-   13
ventional answer to this question. He admitted that he did, but said that he was fed up with high school and college instructors trying to teach him how to think, to use the "scientific method," and to explore the deep inner logic of the subject in a pedantic way, as is often done in the new mathematics, rather than teaching him the structure of the subject. With this in mind, he decided to revive scholasticism as an academic lark to challenge the Sputnik-panicked classrooms of America.

RESPONDING TO READING

1. The title refers to a criticism of school learning that had no relation to experience, exemplified by a medieval argument about how many angels could stand on the head of a pin. At the end of the essay, the rebellious student claims to be reviving such scholasticism to challenge the teaching of "the scientific method." How would you characterize the conflict between the student and his physics teacher? Explain.

2. Relate the conflict between the student and the physics teacher to Thomas Kuhn's description of "The Route to Normal Science" (Chapter 2). Is the student being creative according to Kuhn's definition? Or is the student having "crazy ideas" as Isaac Asimov explains them (Chapter 2)? Is it a good idea to flout the expected and customary procedures of an institution? Consider the benefits as well as the difficulties.

3. Relate and comment upon an experience you have had in which you knew what you were supposed to do, but would have preferred to (or actually did do) something else. Did you play by the rules when you wanted to break them? Or did you break the rules, at some risk? What happened? What might have happened? As you look back now from an older and wiser stance, was the action right and creative? Duty-bound? Correct, but cowardly? Arrogant, but heroic?

In Search of Our Mothers' Gardens

ALICE WALKER

Alice Walker was born in 1944 in Eatonton, Georgia, where her parents were sharecroppers. She attended Spelman College (1961–63) and earned a B.A. at Sarah Lawrence (1965). She was active in the Civil Rights movement, registering voters in Georgia and working at Head Start in Mississippi. Since 1968, she has taught at many colleges, including Tougaloo, Brandeis, and the University of California at Berkeley. Her collections of poetry and fiction analyze the human implications of many of the social issues of her lifetime. They include *Once: Poems* (1968), *Horses Make a Landscape Look More Beautiful* (1984), *Possessing the Secret of Joy* (1992), and *Everyday Use* (1994). A writer of children's literature and nonfiction, Walker's works also include a biography of *Langston Hughes: American Poet* (1973), *Alice Walker Banned* (1996), and *Anything We Love Can Be Saved: A Writer's Activism* (1997). *The Color Purple* (1982), perhaps her most famous work, was made into a feature film by Steven Spielberg in 1985.

In "In Search of Our Mother's Gardens," Walker writes of the mothers and grandmothers who "were going nowhere immediate" and for whom "the future was not yet within their grasp"—the Black women who knew the day would come when they could speak, write, and express themselves in any way they chose without fear of reprisal from anyone. She writes especially of her own mother, an accomplished gardener who "adorned with flowers whatever shabby house [her family] was forced to live in." For this woman, beaten down by life daily in so many ways, her art was her expression of her inner self—and the legacy she left for her daughter.

I

I described her own nature and temperament. Told how   1
they needed a larger life for their expression. . . . I pointed
out that in lieu of proper channels, her emotions had
overflowed into paths and dissipated them. I talked
beautifully I thought, about an art that would be born, an
art that would open the way for women the likes of her. I
asked her to hope, and build up an inner life against the
coming of that day. . . . I sang, with a strange quiver in my
voice, a promise song.
—"Avey," JEAN TOOMER, *Cane*

The poet speaking to a prostitute who falls asleep while he's   2
talking—

When the poet Jean Toomer walked through the South in the early   3
twenties, he discovered a curious thing: Black women whose spirituality was so intense, so deep, so *unconscious*, they were themselves unaware of the richness they held. They stumbled blindly through their lives: creatures so abused and mutilated in body, so dimmed and confused by pain, that they considered themselves unworthy even of hope. In the selfless abstractions their bodies became to the men who used them, they became more than "sexual objects," more even than mere women: they became Saints. Instead of being perceived as whole persons, their bodies became shrine: what was thought to be their minds became temples suitable for worship. These crazy "Saints" stared out at the world, wildly, like lunatics—or quietly, like suicides; and the "God" that was in their gate was as mute as a great stone.

Who were these "Saints"? These crazy, loony, pitiful women?   4

Some of them without a doubt, were our mothers and grand-   5
mothers.

In the still heat of the post-Reconstruction South, this is how they   6
seemed to Jean Toomer: exquisite butterflies trapped in an evil honey, toiling away their lives in an era, a century, that did not acknowledge them, except as "the *mule* of the world." They dreamed dreams that no one knew—not even themselves, in any coherent fashion—and saw visions no one could understand. They wandered or sat about the countryside crooning lullabies to ghosts, and drawing the mother of Christ in charcoal on courthouse walls.

7   They forced their minds to desert their bodies and their striving spirits sought to rise, the frail whirlwinds from the hard red clay. And when those frail whirlwinds fell, in scattered particles, upon the ground, no one mourned. Instead, men lit candles to celebrate the emptiness that remained, as people do who enter a beautiful but vacant space to resurrect a God.

8   Our mothers and grandmothers, some of them: moving to music not yet written. And they waited.

9   They waited for a day when the unknown thing that was in them would be made known; but guessed, somehow in their darkness, that on the day of their revelation they would be long dead. Therefore to Toomer they walked, and even ran, in slow motion. For they were going nowhere immediate, and the future was not yet within their grasp. And men took our mothers and grandmothers, "but got no pleasure from it." So complex was their passion and their calm.

10   To Toomer, they lay vacant and fallow as autumn fields, with harvest time never in sight: and he saw them enter loveless marriages, without joy; and become prostitutes, without resistance; and become mothers of children without fulfillment.

11   For these grandmothers and mothers of ours were not "Saints," but Artists; driven to a numb and bleeding madness by the springs of creativity in them for which there was no release. They were Creators, who lived lives of spiritual waste, because they were so rich in spirituality—which is the basis of Art—that the strain of enduring their unused and unwanted talent drove them insane. Throwing away this spirituality was their pathetic attempts to lighten the soul to a weight their work-worn, sexually abused bodies could bear.

12   What did it mean for a Black woman to be an artist in our grandmothers' time? In our great-grandmothers' day? It is a question with an answer cruel enough to stop the blood.

13   Did you have a genius of a great-great-grandmother who died under some ignorant and depraved white overseer's lash? Or was she required to bake biscuits for a lazy backwater tramp, when she cried out in her soul to paint watercolors of sunsets, or the rain falling on the green and peaceful pasturelands? Or was her body broken and forced to bear children (who were more often than not sold away from her)— eight, ten, fifteen, twenty children—when her one joy was the thought of modeling heroic figures of Rebellion, in stone or clay?

14   How was the creativity of the Black woman kept alive, year after year and century after century, when for most of the years Black people have been in America, it was a punishable crime for a Black person to read or write? And the freedom to paint, to sculpt, to expand the mind with action, did not exist. Consider, if you can bear to imagine it, what might have been the result of singing, too, had been forbidden by law.

Listen to the voices of Bessie Smith, Billie Holiday, Nina Simone, Roberta Flack, and Aretha Franklin, among others, and imagine those voices muzzled for life. Then you may begin to comprehend the lives of our "crazy," "Sainted" mothers and grandmothers. The agony of the lives of women who might have been Poets, Novelists, Essayists, and Short Story Writers (over a period of centuries), who died with their real gifts stifled within them.

And, if this were the end of the story, we would have cause to cry   15
out in my paraphrase of Okot p'Bitek's great poem:

> O, my clanswomen
> Let us call cry together!
> Come,
> Let us mourn the death of our mother,
> The death of a Queen
> The ash that was produced
> By a great fire!
> O this homestead is utterly dead
> Close the gates
> With *lacari* thorns,
> For our mother
> The creator of the Stool is lost!
> And all the young women
> Have perished in the wilderness.[1]

But this is not the end of the story, for all the young women—our   16
mothers and grandmothers, *ourselves*—have not perished in the wilderness. And if we ask ourselves why, and search for and find the answer, we will know beyond all efforts to erase it from our minds, just exactly who, and of what, we Black American women are.

One example, perhaps the most pathetic, most misunderstood one,   17
can provide a backdrop for our mothers' work: Phillis Wheatley, a slave in the 1700s.

Virginia Woolf, in her book, *A Room of One's Own*, wrote that in   18
order for a woman to write fiction she must have two things, certainly: a room of her own (with a key and lock) and enough money to support herself.

What then are we to make of Phillis Wheatley, a slave, who owned   19
not even herself? This sickly, frail, Black girl who required a servant of her own at times—her health was so precarious—and who, had she been white, would have been easily considered the intellectual superior of all the women and most of the men in the society of her day.

---

[1]'Bitek, *Song of Lawino: An Africa Lament* (Nairobi: East African Publishing House, 1966).

20   Virginia Woolf wrote further, speaking of course not of our Phillis, that "any woman born with a great gift in the sixteenth century [insert *eighteenth century*, insert *Black woman*, insert *born or made a slave*] would certainly have gone crazed, shot herself, or ended her days in some lonely cottage outside the village, half witch, half wizard [insert *Saint,*] feared and mocked at. For it needs little skill and psychology to be sure that a highly gifted girl who had tried to use her gift for poetry would have been so thwarted and hindered by contrary instincts [add *chains, guns, the lash, the ownership of one's body by someone else, submission to an alien religion,*] that she must have lost her health and sanity to a certainty."

21   The key words, as they relate to Phillis, are "contrary instincts." For when we read the poetry of Phillis Wheatley—as when we read the novels of Nella Larsen or the oddly false-sounding autobiography of that freest of all Black women writers, Zora Hurston—evidence of "contrary instincts" is everywhere. Her loyalties were completely divided, as was, without question, her mind.

22   But how could this be otherwise? Captured at seven, a slave of wealthy, doting whites who instilled in her the "savagery" of the Africa they "rescued" her from . . . one wonders if she was even able to remember her homeland as she had known it, or as it really was.

23   Yet, because she did try to use her gift for poetry in a world that made her a slave, she was "so thwarted and hindered by . . . contrary instincts that she . . . lost her health. . . ." In the last years of her brief life, burdened not only with the need to express her gift but also with a penniless, friendless "freedom" and several small children for whom she was forced to do strenuous work to feed, she lost her health, certainly. Suffering from malnutrition and neglect and who knows what mental agonies, Phillis Wheately died.

24   So torn by "contrary instincts" was Black, kidnapped, enslaved Phillis that her description of "the Goddess"—as she poetically called the Liberty she did not have—is ironically, cruelly humorous. And, in fact, has held Phillis up to ridicule for more than a century. It is usually read prior to hanging Phillis's memory as that of a fool. She wrote:

> The Goddess comes, she moves divinely fair,
> Olive and laurel binds her *golden* hair:
> Wherever shines this native of the skies,
> Unnumber'd charms and recent graces rise.
>
> [Emphasis mine]

25

It is obvious that Phillis, the slave, combed the "Goddess's" hair every morning; prior, perhaps, to bringing in the milk, or fixing her mistress's lunch. She took her imagery from the one thing she saw elevated above all others.

With the benefit of hindsight we ask, "How could she?"   26

But at last, Phillis, we understand. No more snickering when your   27
stiff, struggling, ambivalent lines are forced on us. We know now that
you were not an idiot nor a traitor; only a sickly little Black girl,
snatched from your home and country and made a slave; a woman
who still struggled to sing the song that was your gift, although in a
land of barbarians who praised you for your bewildered tongue. It is
not so much what you sang, as that you kept alive, in so many of our
ancestors, *the notion of song.*

II

Black women are called, in the folklore that so aptly identifies one's   28
status in society, "the *mule* of the world," because we have been handed the burdens that everyone else—*everyone* else—refused to carry.
We have been called "Matriarchs," "Superwomen," and "Mean and
Evil Bitches." Not to mention "Castrators" and "Sapphire's Mama."
When we have pleaded for understanding, our character has been
distorted; when we have asked for simple caring, we have been handed empty inspirational appellations, then stuck in the farthest corner.
When we have asked for love, we have been given children. In short,
even our plainer gifts, our labors of fidelity and love, have been
knocked down our throats. To be an Artist and a Black woman, even
today, lowers our status in many respects, rather than raises it: and
yet, Artists we will be.   29

Therefore we must fearlessly pull out of ourselves and look at and
identify with our lives the living creativity some of our great-grandmothers were not allowed to know. I stress *some* of them because it is
well known that the majority of our great-grandmothers knew, even
without "knowing" it, the reality of their spirituality, even if they did-
n't recognize it beyond what happened in the singing at church—and
they never had any intention of giving it up.   30

How they did it: those millions of Black women who were not
Phillis Wheatley, or Lucy Terry or Frances Harper or Zora Hurston or
Nella Larsen or Bessie Smith—nor Elizabeth Catlett, nor Katherine
Dunham, either—brings me to the title of this essay, "In Search of Our
Mothers' Gardens," which is a personal account that is yet shared, in its
theme and its meaning, by all of us. I found, while thinking about the
far-reaching world of the creative Black woman, that often the truest
answer to a question that really matters can be found very close.   31

In the late 1920s my mother ran away from home to marry my father. Marriage, if not running away, was expected of seventeen-year-
old girls. By the time she was twenty, she had two children and was
pregnant with a third. Five children later, I was born. And this is how I

came to know my mother: she seemed a large, soft, loving-eyed woman who was rarely impatient in our home. Her quick, violent temper was on view only a few times a year, when she battled with the white landlord who had the misfortune to suggest to her that her children did not need to go to school.

32   She made all the clothes we wore, even my brothers' overalls. She made all the towels and sheets we used. She spent the summers canning vegetables and fruits. She spent the winter evenings making quilts enough to cover all our beds.

33   During the "working" day, she labored beside—not behind—my father in the fields. Her day began before sunup, and did not end until late at night. There was never a moment for her to sit down, undisturbed, to unravel her own private thoughts; never a time free from interruption—by work or the noisy inquiries of her many children. And yet, it is to my mother—and all our mothers who were not famous—that I went in search of the secret of what has fed that muzzled and often mutilated, but vibrant, creative spirit that the Black woman has inherited, and that pops out in wild and unlikely places to this day.

34   But when, you will ask, did my overworked mother have time to know or care about feeding the creative spirit?

35   The answer is so simple that many of us have spent years discovering it. We have constantly looked high, when we should have looked high—and low.

36   For example: in the Smithsonian Institution in Washington, D.C., there hangs a quilt unlike any other in the world. In fanciful, inspired, and yet simple and identifiable figures, it portrays the story of the Crucifixion. It is considered rare, beyond price. Though it follows no known pattern of quiltmaking, and though it is made of bits and pieces of worthless rags, it is obviously the work of a person of powerful imagination and deep spiritual feelings. Below this quilt I saw a note that says it was made by "an anonymous Black woman in Alabama, a hundred years ago."

37   If we could locate this "anonymous" Black woman from Alabama, she would turn out to be one of our grandmothers—an artist who left her mark in the only materials she could afford, and in the only medium her position in society allowed her to use.

38   As Virginia Woolf wrote further, in *A Room of One's Own*:

39   "Yet genius of a sort must have existed among women as it must have existed among the working class. [Change this to *slaves* and *the wives and daughters of sharecroppers*.] Now and again an Emily Brontë or a Robert Burns [change this to *a Zora Hurston or a Richard Wright*] blazes out and proves its presence. But certainly it never got itself on to paper. When, however, one reads of a witch being ducked, of a woman pos-

sessed by devils [or *Sainthood*], of a wise woman selling herbs [our root-workers], or even a very remarkable man who had a mother, then I think we are on the track of a suppressed poet, of some mute and inglorious Jane Austen. . . . Indeed, I would venture to guess that Anon, who wrote so many poems without singing them, was often a woman. . . ."

40 And so our mothers and grandmothers have, more often than not anonymously, handed on the creative spark, the seed of the flower they themselves never hoped to see: or like a sealed letter they could not plainly read.

41 And so it is, certainly, with my own mother. Unlike Ma Rainey's songs, which retained their creator's name even while blasting forth from Bessie Smith's mouth, no song or poem will bear my mother's name. Yet so many of the stories that I write, that we all write, are my mother's stories. Only recently did I fully realize this: that through years of listening to my mother's stories of her life, I have absorbed not only the stories themselves, but something of the manner in which she spoke, something of the urgency that involves the knowledge that her stories—like her life—must be recorded. It is probably for this reason that so much of what I have written is about characters whose counterparts in real life are so much older than I am.

42 But the telling of these stories, which came from my mother's lips as naturally as breathing, was not the only way my mother showed herself as an artist. For stories, too, were subject to being distracted, to dying without conclusion. Dinners must be started, and cotton must be gathered before the big rains. The artist that was and is my mother showed itself to me only after many years. This is what I finally noticed:

43 Like Mem, a character in *The Third Life of Grange Copeland*, my mother adorned with flowers whatever shabby house we were forced to live in. And not just your typical straggly country stand of zinnias, either. She planted ambitious gardens—and still does—with over fifty different varieties of plants that bloom profusely from early March until later November. Before she left home for the fields, she watered her flowers, chopped up the grass, and laid out new beds. When she returned from the fields she might divide clumps of bulbs, dig a cold pit, uproot and replant roses, or prune branches from her taller bushes or trees—until night came and it was too dark to see.

44 Whatever she planted grew as if by magic, and her fame as a grower of flowers spread over three counties. Because of her creativity with her flowers, even my memories of poverty are seen through a screen of blooms—sunflowers, petunias, roses, dahlias, forsythia, spirea, delphiniums, verbena . . . and on and on.

45   And I remember people coming to my mother's yard to be given cuttings from her flowers; I hear again the praise showered on her because whatever rocky soil she landed on, she turned into a garden. A garden so brilliant with colors, so original in its design, so magnificient with life and creativity, that to this day people drive by our house in Georgia—perfect strangers and imperfect strangers—and ask to stand or walk among my mother's art.

46   I notice that it is only when my mother is working in her flowers that she is radiant, almost to the point of being invisible—except as Creator: hand and eye. She is involved in work her soul must have. Ordering the universe in the image of her personal conception of Beauty.

47   Her face, as she prepares the Art that is her gift, is a legacy of respect she leaves to me, for all that illuminates and cherishes life. She had handed down respect for the possibilities—and the will to grasp them.

48   For her, so hindered and intruded upon in so many ways, being an artist has still been a daily part of her life. This ability to hold on, even in very simple ways, is work Black women have done for a very long time.

49   This poem is not enough, but it is something, for the woman who literally covered the holes in our walls with sunflowers:

> They were women then
> My mama's generation
> Husky of voice—Stout of
> Step
> With fists as well as
> Hands
> How they battered down
> Doors
> And ironed
> Starched white
> Shirts
> How they led
> Armies
> Headragged Generals
> Across mined
> Fields
> Booby-trapped
> Ditches
> To discover books
> Desks
> A place for us
> How they knew what we

Must know
Without knowing a page
Of it
Themselves.

Guided by my heritage of love and beauty and a respect for   50
strength—in search of my mother's garden, I found my own.

And perhaps in Africa over two hundred years ago, there was just   51
such a mother; perhaps she painted vivid and daring decorations in oranges and yellows and greens on the walls of her hut; perhaps she
sang—in a voice like Roberta Flack's—*sweetly* over the compounds of
her village; perhaps she wove the most stunning mats or told the most
ingenious stories of all the village story-tellers. Perhaps she was herself
a poet—though only her daughter's name is signed to the poems that
we know.

Perhaps Phillis Wheatley's mother was also an artist.   52

Perhaps in more than Phillis Wheatley's biological life is her moth-   53
er's signature made clear.

RESPONDING TO READING

1. How does Walker develop her idea that the women she describes are, on
   one hand, Saints and, on the other hand, are "crazy, loony, [and] pitiful"?
   What part does each of these descriptions play in her argument, and how
   does each support Walker's assertion that these women were "Artists"?

2. How much does Walker expect her audience to know about the institution
   of slavery in the American South? What must a reader know in order to understand her argument about art and abuse, spirituality and sexuality?

3. How does Walker introduce and define the idea of "contrary instincts"? How
   does this complex idea fit into her own argument about the physical bodies
   and spiritual lives of African-American women?

4. For Walker, in what ways are African-American women both trusted as spiritual guardians and, at the same time, forced into a narrowly defined role as a
   physical laborer and bearer of children?

5. Working at your school's (or town's or local historical society's) library, or
   web site(s) browse through newspapers from the eighteenth and nineteenth
   centuries, particularly newspapers printed before the American Civil War.
   In an essay, describe the representations of African-American—and particularly of African-American women—that you find. How do these representations support or contradict the arguments that Walker is making? How do
   they support or contradict your own knowledge of slavery in America? You
   could work on this in groups, with a pair of students investigating this issue
   during a particular year or span of years.

QUESTIONS FOR REFLECTION AND WRITING

What Governs Ethical Behavior?

1. Wattles's complex reading of the "golden rule" perhaps allows a careful reader to escape the moral burden that Singer places on us in his "solution to world poverty." Or perhaps not. Write an essay in which you consider the two essays together. Given the theoretical and practical imperatives of the two essays, what do you think you should do in relation to world poverty? Do you think you will do what you should? Why, or why not?

2. Choose one or two of Benjamin Franklin's 13 directives for achieving "a steady, uniform rectitude of conduct" and examine it or them closely, following the pattern used by Wattles. How is Franklin's list similar to or different from the list of rules for journalists in their code of ethics? And how useful are such lists as guides to ethical behavior?

3. Describe an experience you have had in which it was difficult to decide on an ethical course of action. What did you rely on to help you decide what to do? What in fact determined what you did? In your essay be sure to refer to several of the authors in this section and compare your decision-making process to what they recommend.

What Are Some Operative Principles of Work and Play?

1. Are there any aspects of Barbara Ehrenreich's waitressing that Howard Gardner could define as "good work"? If so, what are they? If not, what makes her job so unsatisfying? Is there anything that she could have done to make her job more like "good work"? Is there anything that anyone could have done?

2. Have you ever had a job that Gardner would define as "good work"? If so, describe it and show how and why it fits into that category. Do you expect to make your livelihood at "good work"? If so, how will you make that happen? If not, why not?

3. Gawande's job as surgeon seems to meet the test for "good work" set out by Gardner. But as he describes it, the work is so complex and difficult, so filled with possible errors, so sure to bring calamity as cure to some patients, that its goodness is at least open to question. Compare Gawande's work with the option Fallows presents, of staying at home and raising one's children. Which is better work? If you can't decide that question, what principles might help you decide it?

4. Are you a loser, as Young declares himself to be? Or a winner? Which is better? Look back to Joan Didion's "On Self Respect" in Chapter 1 and consider whether being a winner or a loser tends more to self-respect, as she defines it.

5. Who do you want to be ten years from now and what do you want to be doing? What operative principles lie behind the choices you would have to make to be that person doing those things?

How Can We Meet the Challenge of Creativity?

1. Bronowski argues that artistic and scientific creativity draw on the same sources and origins. Test his idea by determining whether it helps you understand two or three of the writers in this book, such as Angier and Welty (Chapter 1), Langer, Asimov, Conroy, Pollan, and Kuhn (Chapter 2), or any of the writers in this section. To what degree do Bronowski's ideas work out for the writers and scientists you have read?

2. Hogan, like Bronowski, sees intimate connections between creativity in different fields: "It is also poetry, this science, and I note how often scientific theories lead to the world of poetry and vision." Consider the similarities and differences between her approach to these connections and Bronowski's. What makes their essays alike? Where are the differences?

3. Notice that Le Guin, like Asimov (Chapter 2), gives a list of five ways to be creative. Compare and contrast these lists. To what degree have these creative writers and thinkers been able to pin down the route to creativity?

4. Write an essay on ways of recognizing and encouraging creativity. Can you distinguish creativity from simple egotism or blind nonconformity? Consider Calandra's "Angels On a Pin" as you make this distinction, keeping in mind that the "student" in the essay was in fact Calandra's memory of himself as a student. Use other examples from this section and from your experience. Is it always a good idea to encourage creativity?

Ethics: What Principles Do—and Should—Govern Our Personal Lives?

1. How can we best encourage ethical behavior? Write an essay in which you present the conditions that allow "good work" and ethical conditions to emerge and creativity to develop. Be sure to use examples from your reading and experience; also show what happens when creativity or ethical behavior work badly or change over time.

2. Describe an experience you have had in which your self-interest conflicted with your sense of what you ought to do. Avoid the temptation to simplify the issues and to tell a moralistic tale with a pat answer. Rather, choose a situation with enough complexity to allow for serious discussion of the choices you had to make and why you made them. Would you act in the same way now?

4

Values
What Are Human Rights and Responsibilities?

We hold these truths to be self-evident, that all men are created equal, that they are endowed by their Creator with certain unalienable Rights, that among these are Life, Liberty, and the pursuit of Happiness.
THOMAS JEFFERSON

Why Consider This Question?

The question "What are human rights and responsibilities?" is enduring and important, affecting all aspects of our lives, from daily decisions about routine matters to large philosophical and cultural issues. Our claims for certain of our rights (like making lots of money) may not be important for the larger good and, indeed, may be at odds with our responsibilities to our fellow workers. Our right to express ourselves freely may conflict with our responsibility to avoid hate speech against minorities. Our responsibility to act morally may lead us to disobey the law and land us in jail, with very few rights. Once we start trying to balance our rights against our responsibilities, we are likely to find ourselves troubled at many of the decisions we customarily make. We then must examine our values, the principles that lie behind our definitions of what we are entitled to (our rights) and what others are entitled to expect from us (our responsibilities).

On the one hand, many of the values that we act upon in our day-to-day lives emerge from received opinions we have not thought much about, and they sometimes can be as embarrassing as thumping one's masculine chest at a feminist rally. On the other hand, many of our happiest times and most successful endeavors are the result of considered values that provide guidance about what to study, where to live, whom to marry, and how to spend our lives. We are always on the lookout for ways to put our values into action: We want to elect politicians with considered and ethical plans for the future, we want to support scientists who help us understand the world and improve it, and we look to the arts for imaginative renderings of values and meaning. But we cannot expect everyone to agree with our own set of values, which are often abstract and controversial. Unless we simply accept whatever we have been told as children, we are confronted with both the right and the responsibility to think through our own value system, to defend our actions to ourselves and others in terms of our values, and to deal with others whose values differ from our own. How can we be sure that the values on which we act are indeed sound?

Not all values have to, or do not have to, lead to action, but most values have consequences, and we judge their soundness by their results. Some confirmed socialists argue that the values of Karl Marx were essentially good, even though they have worked out badly in the former Soviet Union and Eastern Europe; most observers, however, see the economic and cultural devastation of the former Soviet empire as proof that Communism was based on unrealistic values to begin with. Surely, one test of values is to examine what happens when they are applied in practice.

Some philosophers and scientists, however, maintain that the practical effects of values are irrelevant: The discovery of new knowledge is always a good thing, regardless of whether the knowledge is put into action. Still other thinkers see new knowledge as inherently dangerous, precisely because it is likely to lead to actions or thoughts that may be destructive. Was the development of atomic energy and, subsequently, atomic weapons, a good idea? Some will argue that the discovery of nuclear energy was worthy for its own sake, however such energy may be used or misused, but the argument rages on. Atomic bombs dropped on Japan in 1945 were, some will say, an unnecessary and racist expression of mindless vengeance; others claim that they saved many more lives than they cost by bringing World War II in the Pacific to a speedy end. The present use of nuclear energy leads to as much dispute: Advocates point to a limitless energy source that is relatively clean, while opponents claim that nuclear waste is dangerous and nearly impossible to dispose of and that nuclear accidents are inevitable.

Even when good ideas based on sound values seem to be working out well, we often find ourselves in trouble. Some of our best ideas seem to conflict with others of our best ideas. It is a wonderful idea to prolong life with good nutrition, healthful habits, and medical interventions, but it is also a good idea to conserve the resources of the planet, to open opportunities for the next generation, and to die with dignity. We should protect our forests and open spaces for future generations, but we should also develop our resources to create jobs and economic expansion. How can we tell which values to put into action when such conflicts occur and why we should thus put them into action?

Certainly, our perceptions about what are sound values shifts over time, and often what made perfect sense in past times seems quaint and curious now. When we speak of "an idea whose time has come," we refer to the way a new idea can overturn old habits of thought as values develop. For example, a new conception of the importance of the individual in the eighteenth century led to such changes as the end of slavery and the development of psychology. We can see such shifts in our own time, as environmentalism moves from a fringe movement to mainstream thinking and as the concept of culture moves from a European to a global context. Historians of ideas have attempted to understand just why such changes in the way people think about things take place. But no one knows exactly why values that appear strange to one generation seem simple good sense to another.

If we are willing to say that no value system is good in itself, but is good only for particular times, places, and peoples, we may have a method of thinking systematically about what makes ideas and actions derived from them good. That is, we may need to examine the particular context and consequences of a set of values in order to situate them concretely and examine their worth. The hefty female beauty painted with such gusto by artists five hundred years ago, for instance, seems as dated a value to slimmer modern Americans as one's willingness to marry the mate picked out by one's parents. We will understand that under other circumstances, times, or places, we might come to a quite different artistic or value judgment. Such relativism, however, conflicts with still another set of values: that certain enduring principles, such as truth, goodness, beauty, and justice, are eternal—applicable under all circumstances.

The readings that follow consider three aspects of the question "What are human rights and responsibilities?" The readings examine the values behind certain ideas put into action. The first section explores the vexing question, "What are the fundamental human rights?"—perhaps the most basic of all values. The second section looks at democracy from a variety of perspectives as a way of examining this powerful set of political values according to how well they work out in practice. The third section speaks to conflicts in values and ways of dealing with them. The chapter assumes that we will bring other ideas, knowledge, and experiences into play in order to test the values we hold and the opposing values we encounter.

What Are the Fundamental Human Rights?

This section opens with Wole Soyinka's "Every Dictator's Nightmare," the Nobel prize winner's overview of the concept "that certain fundamental rights are inherent to all of humanity." Soyinka points to the partial statements of this ideal in ancient, religious, and modern texts, noting that almost always there were qualifications: Some people, for example, were usually defined as more human than others. Within the last two hundred years, these rights have been seen more and more as fundamental—inherent to all humans: "The kernel of the idea, therefore, is both timeless and new." It is no wonder that this bedrock value terrifies dictators, for they cannot root it out, whatever ferocious measures they take.

Of all political ideas, that of democracy seems to have best stood the test of time, based as it is on certain fundamental human rights, namely, those explored by Soyinka. Starting with the ancient Greeks and continuing around the world with increasing power into the twenty-first century, the concept that political legitimacy must derive from the consent of the governed seems almost beyond dispute. Thomas Jefferson's "Declaration of Independence" is one of the clearest statements of this idea, and its sentences have become so familiar to most Americans that we tend not to notice its argument. Jefferson bases his argument on the "Laws of Nature and of Nature's God" and on "truths" held to be "self-evident." A careful reading of the document must inquire into what such statements mean and where they came from. Further, as the other readings in the section suggest, we must ask how well these ideas have worked out in practice.

Abraham Lincoln's speech at Gettysburg is also part of the common heritage of Americans—and once again, the familiar phrases of the "Address" do not explain themselves. Are the "liberty" of the opening paragraph and the "new birth of freedom" of the last paragraph, for instance, the same, or different in some ways? Are Lincoln's assumptions about government in his last sentence ("of the people, by the people, for the people") the same as Jefferson's? Are they the same as those we hold today? And what exactly do we mean by "liberty" and "freedom" in today's troubled times, marked by new forms of terrorism?

When we look closely at these democratic political ideas, many questions emerge. One is, who exactly are the "people" whose consent democracy requires and in whose name battles are fought? The democratic tradition does not provide comfortable answers to this question. For the Greeks, "the people" turned out to be a very limited group, with no women or slaves, for instance, as part of the electoral process.

Even for the founders of American democracy, the definition of those giving consent excluded many people, and women did not vote until well into the twentieth century. How can we reconcile these limitations with the powerful statements of Jefferson and Lincoln?

Those who have been excluded from the political process have sought to be heard and to challenge democracy in practice. Sojourner Truth's "Ain't I a Woman?" and Elizabeth Cady Stanton's "Declaration of Sentiments" responded to the ideas of Jefferson and Lincoln by protesting the obvious failure of nineteenth-century American democracy to include women. "Then that little man in black there, he says women can't have as much rights as men, 'cause Christ wasn't a woman!" Sojourner Truth states, with biting sarcasm; and Stanton echoes Jefferson's "Declaration" with one of her own, specifically including women.

What Values Govern the Common Good?

Sound values often wither if they emerge in a hostile or unreceptive environment, only to flourish when the climate is right. Although the drafters of the Declaration of Independence asserted, for example, that "all men are created equal," they actually meant free white men, not free white women, or slaves, or the original Native American settlers. That this definition has broadened over the two succeeding centuries is more the result of social and political movements and pressures than the consequence of individual enlightenment; a desire for justice for all has come to mean something new as social conditions have changed.

The notion of civil disobedience, for instance, is embedded in a number of related concepts. There has to be a civil state or other governing authority for the dissident to disobey. There has to be the opportunity for dissension; "off with his head" does not meet with argument in a totalitarian state. There has to be the belief that might does not necessarily make right, according to centuries of dissidents, from Socrates to Thoreau to Gandhi to Martin Luther King, Jr. There has to be a willingness to act on that belief, to question authority, to test the law, and, if necessary, to suffer the consequences of one's assaults on the status quo—fines, imprisonment, and even death. In America, the most notable examples of dissidents are Henry David Thoreau and Martin Luther King, Jr., both of whom went to prison for their values and who wrote the famous documents in this section defending their actions.

Thoreau's form of civil disobedience, refusing to pay the Massachusetts poll tax because of its implications for supporting the Mexican War and the existence of slavery, was technically far from heroic; he spent only a single night in jail, "the only house in a slave state in which a free man can abide with honor." But its major consequence, his

1848 essay defining and defending "Civil Disobedience," has reverberated around the world ever since. The power of his argument, not his personal suffering, has influenced political figures to follow his lead, but the fact that he did go to jail gives his essay unusual force: He not only "talked the talk," but "walked the walk."

However, violating a law to protest injustice guarantees neither exemption from the law nor the assurance that it will change. It is perhaps too easy to believe that the kind of discrimination that Richard Wright describes (and that Shelby Steele says is now in the past) in Chapter 1 ended with the civil rights movement of the 1960s or even before. But many twentieth-century autobiographies of black men and women bear painful, outraged witness to the humiliating discrimination that Martin Luther King, Jr., addresses in his "Letter from Birmingham Jail." Because of the color of their skin, King argues, twenty million "black brothers and sisters" are subject to lynching, police brutality, and discrimination in public schools and accommodations and are segregated into the "airtight cage of poverty in the midst of an affluent society." King has learned from history that privileged groups seldom give up their privileges voluntarily, which is why he is impatient with pleas to wait. Civil disobedience—the nonviolent refusal to obey the laws enforcing discrimination—is in King's view a last, but inevitable, resort in bringing about not only changes in the laws, but also changes in their enforcement.

In "Civil Disobedience: Destroyer of Democracy," Lewis H. Van Dusen, Jr,, takes issue with Dr. King's position. He distinguishes between Thoreau's civil disobedience, knowingly breaking the law from principles of moral righteousness, and Dr. King's conscientious testing of the law, violating one law while expecting support from a higher court. For Lewis, finally, the values of the law take precedence over the individual conscience.

But as Terry Tempest Williams makes clear in "The Clan of One-Breasted Women," civil disobedience remains a powerful force in American life. When the authorities are both powerful and perceived as wrong, the tradition of protest remains as a weapon for the powerless. She concludes that "to our court system it does not matter whether the United States government was irresponsible, whether it lied to its citizens, or even that citizens died from the fallout of nuclear testing. What matters is that our government is immune." To protest that immunity, Williams and nine other women committed "an act of civil disobedience." Why? "The time had come to protest with the heart, that to deny one's genealogy with the earth was to commit treason against one's soul."

The final essay in this section moves away from the tradition of protest against the abuse of power to protest against the abuse of nature. When John McPhee looks at the relation of people to nature, he sees a battle—one that nature is likely to win. We might think that a victory of nature over the well-intentioned interference of humans would be worth cheering. But in "Los Angeles Against the Mountains" it is not easy to know whom to root for. McPhee describes the attempts by residents of the Los Angeles area to build homes in the path of historic "debris flows," the thousands of tons of rock, mud, and brush that crash through mountain canyons during heavy rains. Is this deliberate attempt to control nature, this refusal to accept personal responsibility for inviting catastrophe, heroic or just plain stupid? McPhee's sarcastic laughter may not be shared by those who have lost their homes to the debris flows.

How Can Value Conflicts Be Resolved?

Most of us experience conflict and stress in our lives, and we usually attempt to resolve conflicts peacefully. But some conflicts simply cannot be resolved and must be endured. The essays in this section focus on conflicts in values that inevitably become conflicts in behavior; in a contentious world, these writers ask, how can we live harmonious lives?

Deborah Tannen, in "The Roots of Debate in Education and the Hope of Dialogue," looks at the way classrooms foster competition and an adversarial relationship between students and teachers, as well as among students themselves. The roots of this "debate format," as she calls it, come from the classical link of education to warfare in Western culture. As a result, "Knowledge was gleaned through public oral disputation and tested by combative oral performance, which carried with it the risk of public humiliation." As Tannen examines the continued use of planned conflict in education, she points out that the system particularly disadvantages women, for whom this method of learning is unnatural. While "women can learn to perform in adversarial ways," Tannen recommends that we rethink the value system that leads to such stress and conflict in our schools.

Robert Wuthnow, in "Making Choices: From Short-Term Adjustments to Principled Lives," looks at a parallel sense of conflict in the business world. There, he finds that "people are simply working too hard, taking on responsibilities that do not nurture themselves as human beings, and putting themselves under too much pressure." After listing a series of comically superficial ways in which various businesses have attempted to deal with this problem, he confronts it at a root level: The basic problem is a crisis in values, but, at the same time, "The one thing that stress relates to more powerfully than anything else, in fact, is thinking about basic values in life and trying to juggle commitments to a wide range of values." Thus, he cites survey results showing that, while 25 percent of workers complained about an "unsupportive boss," twice that number "complained about not having time enough for their family." Even the needed "new conceptions of the American Dream" that Wuthnow would like to see are not the answer, "because they can also be opposed on grounds of curbing fundamental human liberties." Even individual discretion, which appears to allow workers to opt out of the adversarial conditions of most work, turns out to be "fundamentally an illusion." With values in conflict, no easy solution will allow stressed workers to lead more satisfying lives. Wuthnow does offer some "small beacons of hope," but only a version of "moral discourse" seems likely to lead to real change.

After Wuthnow, Nelson Mandela's narrative of conflict resolution in South Africa seems like a breath of fresh hope. As he describes the "Long Walk to Freedom" he took with President F. W. de Klerk—the transition from white to black rule in South Africa—we see conflict resolution at its most historic and best. But the last essay in this section returns us to the knots of conflict in modern society, this time to the incessant noise with which we live and to which we have become accustomed. Ursula Franklin, in "Silence and the Notion of the Commons," focuses on the value of silence and its extreme rarity in America, arguing that noise should be considered a form of environmental pollution. "We have the right," she argues, "not to be assaulted by sound, and in particular, not to be assaulted by sound that is there solely for the purpose of profit. Now is the time for civic rage, as well as civic education, but also for some action." But the action she recommends is not civil disobedience, but rather two minutes of silence at the end of her talk.

Rhetorical Issues: Argument and Evidence

Many of the papers that you are asked to write have to do with examining ideas and coming to conclusions about them. The papers may be described in various ways, such as a "position paper," a "persuasion essay," an "interpretation," or an "argument," but all of them will ask you to define a topic, take a position on it, and defend that position with evidence. Our concern here is with the ways in which you can develop different kinds of evidence to support the positions you may take in such papers.

We use the term "argument" the way rhetoricians do, not as a quarrel, but as a piece of writing whose aim is both inquiry and persuasion. Most of the papers you are assigned ask you to construct an argument: "Show how . . . ," "Demonstrate that . . . ," "To what degree do you agree with. . . ." "What is the principal reason for . . . ," and so on. Note that an argument asks for more than a description, a summary, or a review of what other people have said, although all of these may be part of the argument. The inquiry represented by the writing takes place during the writing process as you work through possible answers to the questions posed by the topic; the final draft presents the results of that inquiry in as convincing a way as possible.

In most cases, you can think of your argument in terms of claims that you make about your topic and evidence that you bring to bear in support of those claims. Different kinds of claims call for different kinds of evidence, and you always need to show how the evidence supports your claims. There is a long tradition, going back to Aristotle, of describing ways of making and supporting arguments. We will summarize a few of the most useful ones.

In recent years, some new approaches to the making of arguments have become more and more acceptable both in and out of school, and these approaches are also represented in this book. The usual way of speaking about an argument, with claims and evidence, serves well for traditional essays that make a logical case, such as the readings in this chapter by Jefferson, Thoreau, or King. But arguments can also be made in untraditional ways through personal stories or folklore, for example, as Sojourner Truth and John McPhee make them. The discussion of arguments that follows is suggestive of ways to inquire into topics and to present that inquiry, rather than a blueprint to follow.

Claims. There are many kinds of claims, each of which calls for a different kind of inquiry. Here are some of the most common:

- *Claims of fact:* Did this happen? Are the numbers right?
- *Claims of value:* What is this worth? Is it good or bad?
- *Claims of interpretation:* What does this mean? What kind of thing is this?
- *Claims of policy:* What should be done?
- *Claims of cause:* What brought this about?
- *Claims of judgment:* What is my position on this problem?

Most essays will make more than one of these (or other) claims; you need not restrict yourself to only one kind of claim. But most essays will focus on one kind of claim as the principal one, and the mode of inquiry is likely to follow from that principal claim. Thus, Jefferson, in the "Declaration of Independence," makes all of the claims just listed, but his central idea is the claim of policy: "That these United Colonies are, and of Right ought to be Free and Independent States." The long list of grievances against the king are presented as claims of cause and of fact: "To prove this, let Facts be submitted to a candid world." The claim of interpretation precedes the presentation of facts: "The history of the present King of Great Britain is a history of repeated injuries and usurpations, all having in direct object the establishment of an absolute Tyranny over these States." The claim of value in the second paragraph begins "We hold these truths to be self-evident. . . ."

The claims that you make in your essays need to be arguable, that is, worthy of debate; the claims Jefferson articulated were arguable enough to lead to war. In most cases, facts are not arguable, since we need only verify them: the speed of sound or the number of days in John F. Kennedy's presidency. But as Jefferson's list of what he called "Facts" demonstrates, even if facts are not usually arguable, their interpretation almost always is. Sometimes facts become arguable when the context changes: A straight line is not necessarily the shortest distance between two points on the globe, and the weight of a liter of water changes on the moon. Again, what everybody knows (the sun rises in the east and dogs bark) is not arguable—unless what everyone "knows" happens to be wrong (Shakespeare is hard to read, mathematics is for men). Personal feelings are not arguable (I like chocolate ice cream better than vanilla), but personal opinions are if you claim that they are generally true (frozen yogurt is better than ice cream because it contains less animal fat). As you work through your planning-and-revising process, a principal goal should be to develop an arguable claim that can serve as the focus of your writing.

Claims ought to be particular, appropriate, and interesting. For example, in "Letter from Birmingham Jail," Martin Luther King, Jr., claims, not that citizens can get away with disobeying any law they choose, but rather that we must make a careful distinction between just and unjust laws: "One has not only a legal but a moral responsibility to obey just laws. Conversely, one has a moral responsibility to disobey unjust laws." Then, referring to St. Thomas Aquinas, he defines the difference: "A just law is a man-made code that squares with the moral law or the law of God. An unjust law is a code that is out of harmony with the moral law . . . a human law that is not rooted in eternal law and natural law." Then King brings in the segregation laws he was in jail for protesting as specific defining examples of unjust laws.

Evidence. Aristotle spoke of three kinds of appeals that support arguments: logos, pathos, and ethos. While these appeals are interconnected and often occur in the same argument, each of them asks for a different response from the reader. Logos is the most rational of the three; it is the logical, sequential presentation of data and argument and asks for intellectual agreement. Pathos has to do with feeling, a method of arguing that relies on emotion more than on logic. You might notice in the first section of this chapter that Jefferson's logos is responded to by Sojourner Truth's pathos. Ethos means the ethical character of the speaker or author, as perceived by the reader or audience, to support an argument. For example, politicians depend upon ethos to win approval for themselves and their programs, an appeal made easier by the media assistants who help present a winning picture on television; when ethos fails, the politician is bound to fail. President Nixon's resignation was foreshadowed by his inept attempt to reclaim his lost character: "I am not a crook!" When President Clinton confessed that he had lied about his sexual involvement with a White House intern, his impeachment for perjury was sure to follow. Ethos has considerable force in Nelson Mandela's Nobel prize acceptance speech in this chapter; he is the good man speaking well, and we respond to his goodness as much as to his speech.

While most college papers ask you to attend principally to logos, the logical argument, there are occasions on which the other kinds of appeals can be appropriate. If your learning style is relatively intuitive, you may find that evidence from your own experience or emotions—pathos—is the most powerful you can use. It might be prudent, however, to be sure that the faculty member who will be responding to the paper is open to such appeals before you pursue them.

The evidence you use ought to be appropriate to the kinds of claims you make. For example, a claim of fact needs to be supported by facts, with some further evidence that the facts are, in fact, true. Notice Jefferson's list of facts in support of the "Declaration of Independence," for example, that King George "has kept among us, in time of peace, Standing Armies without the Consent of our Legislature." At the time, that fact was obvious to all and hence required no additional support; today, however, if you were using that statement, you might provide evidence of the size and extent of those British forces. Your facts are likely to come from the Internet or the research section of the library: almanacs, encyclopedias, biographical dictionaries, and the like. You will also find facts, with sources documented, in articles in professional journals or books. Research studies will sometimes yield statistics, which are like facts in the sense that they can be instantly convincing if the source is credible. Some facts come out of personal experience ("Ain't I a Woman?"). Facts and statistics are not, however, simple proofs, for they can be interpreted in various ways. When you give factual or statistical evidence, be alert to the cautions that Linda Simon gives in "The Naked Source" in Chapter 5: The interpretation of the data determines what the facts really mean. The British government did not accept Jefferson's interpretation of the facts he cited, and that difference of interpretation led to war.

Claims of value, interpretation, or judgment will often call for a different kind of evidence. You may want to cite the opinions of authorities (see Chapter 5 on the use of sources), as well as factual material. For example, Isaac Asimov supports his claim (in "Those Crazy Ideas" in Chapter 2) that mathematical breakthroughs are made by youngsters by citing three facts: "Evariste Galois evolved group theory at twenty-one. Isaac Newton worked out calculus at twenty-three. Albert Einstein presented the theory of relativity at twenty-six." If you wanted to make the same point, you could cite Asimov as an authority, as well as the facts he accumulates. You may also use quotations and discussions of quotation as evidence for your claims, particularly if you are analyzing a text. (Notice how the use of the quotation from Asimov supports the claim that facts are powerful evidence.) Your personal experience is likely to be relevant, and you might be able to bring in an appropriate anecdote if you can connect it to the claim you are making. A personal narrative can be powerful evidence; certainly, many of the writers in *Inquiry* use such stories as compelling examples of what they seek to show. The arguments of Nancy Mairs, Shelby Steele, Frederick Douglass, Mike Rose, Eric Liu, Amy Tan, Richard Wright, and Richard Rodriguez (just to cite writers from Chapter 1) are compelling because their claims are supported by their lives; ethos and pathos are combined.

Claims of cause look to the past and hence ask for historical evidence; claims of policy look to the future and so call for evidence that a proposed change will work—perhaps because it has worked in the past. Jefferson makes both types of claim in "The Declaration of Independence": The list of abuses by the British government supports the claims of cause, and the call for independence claims that the new policy will remedy those abuses. Stanton's response in the "Declaration of Sentiments" in turn questions the policy claim with new evidence and suggests a new policy—equal treatment of women—to remedy the abuses she cites.

As you read the selections in *Inquiry*, you will find many kinds of evidence that do not fit into neat categories. The stories by Alexander Calandra ("Angels on a Pin" in Chapter 3) and by Italo Calvino ("All at One Point") in Chapter 5 use metaphor, narrative, and analogy as ways to support the claims made by the speakers. Atul Gawande, in Chapter 3, uses interviews and what anthropologists call a "thick description" (a full and detailed rendering of a phenomenon or a society) as evidence for his claims about the nature of surgical mistakes. The comic writing of Calvino (Chapter 5) uses exaggeration and an absurd premise (an entire human society existing on "one point" before the big bang) to make witty arguments. Similarly, in your own writing, you will find a wide range of possibilities for supplying evidence for your claims. What is most important is that you remain aware of the need to supply evidence—that you know that claims are not convincing unless they are supported.

How can you tell whether you have given the right kind of evidence, or enough evidence, for your claim? There is no formula to answer that question. In one sense, whether your evidence is satisfactory is a matter to be negotiated with your audience. Try out your drafts on a fellow student, with a peer group, or in a reading circle. Discuss the issue with your instructor. Keep in mind that you, as writer, are more likely to find your argument convincing than will any audience; you have already made up your mind. Your readers will not be quite so willing to credit the unstated evidence or the many sources you have read, but not quoted; the audience needs to understand your claims and to see how your evidence supports those claims in order to accept not only your argument, but your authority to make it.

Connections. The missing link between the claim and the evidence is the connection between them, called inference by logicians. You may be tempted to omit this link; if you already are convinced that your evidence supports your claims, the connection between them will seem self-evident. Thus, you are likely to assert your claim of value ("Bronowski's explanation of Newton's discovery is brilliantly clear") and follow it with a quotation from the essay giving Bronowski's explanation. But the quotation as evidence does not in itself prove your claim; it lies there, dead on the page, until you show how it relates to the claim. You need to discuss the quoted material, demonstrating where and why it is brilliant.

The same requirement for connection applies to any evidence you use. If you cite a chart, statistics, or an authority, you need to show how what you have cited relates to your claims. Personal anecdotes are in some ways the most convincing kind of evidence, because the connection of stories to claims is usually direct and emotional; but you need to be convincing enough to show how something that is true for you is not merely personal, but representative of the truth. Mike Rose, for example, is careful to point out that his experience "on the boundary" (see Chapter 1) can stand for the experience of most people with his kind of background—except that he was lucky enough and smart enough to have achieved success instead of settling for "average."

Just as with evidence, the amount of detail in the connection between evidence and claim is a matter of negotiation between you and your audience. If you are using logical appeals, you will need to make sure that you have made the connection clear and that you have been explicit about how the evidence is to be interpreted to support your claim; remember, facts and quotations do not explain themselves. Less logical or more personal appeals allow more latitude; some stories are so compelling that too much explanation might be superfluous. Alice Walker's mother is so vivid in "In Search of Our Mothers' Gardens" in Chapter 3 that she needs little clarification from the author. But if you want to convince your readers that your claims are powerful and your values are sound, you will pay attention to the nature of your claims, the kind of evidence that each claim demands you provide, and the connections that you need to make between the claims and the evidence.

QUESTIONS FOR DISCOVERY AND DISCUSSION

1. Describe a situation in which you had to deal with a conflict between your rights and your responsibilities, and tell what happened as a result of that conflict. Consider such a conflict at home, on the job, in school, at church, in a social group such as a scout troop, and the like.

2. In light of the results, what values in fact prevailed? Were they the values you had previously held? Did you change or compromise your values in order to resolve the conflict? Were you convinced that your values needed to be changed, or did you maintain your original values?

3. Excluding the political values this introduction has already discussed, pick out a fundamental value (justice, say, or fairness, or compassion, or charity) you have encountered in your reading or in your classes. What makes you think that the value you have chosen is sound? What are the arguments in its favor? What can be said in opposition to it? Under what circumstances might that value not be practical?

4. Choose a situation that seems to you to express or demonstrate a bad value system. Unfortunately, you have plenty to choose from, including the greed of some corporate managers, the hypocrisy of some self-proclaimed moral leaders, and, perhaps some educational practices (such as cheating) close to you at school. Describe the situation, give evidence to prove your claims, and connect that evidence to your claims. Then propose, if you can, a way to change the situation for the better. What people or groups would have to take what kind of action?

5. Consider the kind of claims you would have to make to convince an audience that the plan you proposed in your response to question 4 was sound. What kinds of evidence would support those claims? Can you provide a cost–benefit analysis? How much evidence would be appropriate? What explicit connections would you make between the evidence and the claims?

WHAT ARE HUMAN RIGHTS
AND RESPONSIBILITIES?

Every Dictator's Nightmare

WOLE SOYINKA

When Wole Soyinka (pronounced WO-leh Shaw-YIN-ka) received the Nobel prize for literature in 1986, the official press release observed that "his literary works . . . are vivid, often harrowing, but are also marked by an evocative, poetically intensified diction. Soyinka has been characterized as one of the finest poetical playwrights that have written in English. Born in Isara, Nigeria (1934), he was introduced to the Yoruba tribal gods and stories through his grandfather, while his mother and father lived in the colonial pattern. Soyinka's first play, *The Invention*, was produced while he was in England at the University of Leeds (B.A., 1959). Upon his return to Nigeria in 1960, shortly after independence from colonial rule had been declared, he incorporated Yoruba culture into his second play, *A Dance of the Forests. The Lion and the Jewel* (1962) was a comedy on the theme of progress, and his first novel, *The Interpreters* (1965), centered on Nigerian intellectual life. Intellectual openness was dangerous, however; Soyinka's opposition to the government's repressive policies landed him in prison. His prison diary was published as *The Man Died* (1972). In the years following the Nigerian civil war, his mood darkened; the novel *Season of Anomy* (1973) and his later plays expressed anger over widespread corruption, terrorism, and government surveillance. More recently, Soyinka has published *Isara: A Voyage around "Essay"* (1989), about his father; *The Open Sore of a Continent* (1996); *The Burden of Memory, the Muse of Forgiveness* (1998); and *Arms and the Arts* (1999) about wars of liberation and the post-colonial period.

"Every Dictator's Nightmare" displays Soyinka's passionate belief in justice, his impressive command of history, and his ear for graceful language. While the centuries may abound with examples of tyranny, bigotry, and violence, he asserts that the idea embodied in the United Nations' Universal Declaration of Human Rights deserves our attention now more than ever.

1   With the blood-soaked banner of religious fanaticism billowing across the skies as one prominent legacy of this millennium, Martin Luther's famous theses against religious absolutism struck me early as a strong candidate for the best idea of the last thousand years. By progressive association, so did the microprocessor and its implications—the liberalization of access to knowledge, and a quantum boost for the transmission of ideas. There is, however, a nobler idea that has spread

by its own power in this millennium and that has now begun to flourish: the idea that certain fundamental rights are inherent to all humanity.

Humankind has always struggled to assert certain values in their own right, values that the individual intuitively felt belonged to each person as part of natural existence. It is difficult to imagine a period when such values were not pursued in spasmodic acts of dissent from norms that appeared to govern society even in its most rudimentary form. Even after years of conformity to hallowed precedents, a few dissidents always arise, and they obtain their primary impulse in crucial instances from the individual's seizure of his or her subjective worth.   2

In the devolution of authority to one individual as the head of a collective, a system of checks on arbitrary authority is prevalent. Take, for instance, monarchical rule among the Yoruba, the people now concentrated in western Nigeria. At the apex is a quasi-deified personage, endowed with supreme authority over his subjects. To preserve the mystic aura of such a ruler, he is never seen to eat or drink. In earlier times, he was not permitted to speak directly to his people but had to employ an intermediary voice, a spokesman. For the highest-ranked kings in the Yoruban world, the *ekeji orisa* (companions to the deities), it was forbidden even to see their faces. Despite the social and psychological distance between the leader and his subjects, the monarch was pledged to rule within a strict contract of authority. Transgression of a taboo, say, or failure to fulfill ceremonial duties on time, resulted in fines, rituals of appeasement or a period of ostracism. The major crime, however, was abuse of power, excessive authoritarianism and a trampling on the rights of the citizenry. For this category of crimes, there was only one response: the king, on being found guilty, was given a covered calabash and invited to retreat to his inner chambers. He understood the sentence: he must never again be seen among the living.   3

Sometimes, of course, an individual manages to convert collective authority into a personal monopoly. In these instances, society is characterized by tensions, palpable or hidden, between the suppressed rights of the people and the power rapacity of one individual. But where does society ground its claims, its resistant will, in such circumstances? We know that rebellion may be triggered by recollections of more equitable relationships, by material expropriation or by a cultural transgression that affects the spiritual well-being of the community or individual. Such rebellion finds its authority in the belief, in one citizen after another, that the ruler has violated a fundamental condition of human existence.   4

The *droit du seigneur*, the "right" that confers on the lord the pleasure of deflowering, on her marriage night, the bride of any of his vassals—on what does the ritually cuckolded groom finally ground his rebellion other than a subjective sense of self-worth? What of the   5

Yoruban monarch who, even today in certain parts of my world, tries to exercise his "right" to *gbese le*—that is, to place his royal slipper, symbolically, on any woman who catches his fancy, and thus assign her to his harem? The manor lord's entitlement to compulsory labor from his peasants, the ownership of another being as a slave, the new age of enslavement of womanhood in countries like Afghanistan—the challenges to these and other so-called rights surely commence with the interrogation of self-worth, expanding progressively toward an examination of the common worth of the human entity as a unit of irreducible properties and rights.

6   It took centuries for societies to influence one another to the critical extent needed to incite the philosophic mind to address the concept of the human race in general, and not simply as members of a specific race or occupants of a geographical space. In its rudimentary beginnings, each society remained limited by a process that codified its own now-recognizable collective interests against all others, like the Magna Carta and the Bill of Rights. Such oaths of fealty by petty chieftains imposed duties on the suzerain but also entrenched their own equally arbitrary mechanisms of authority and coercion over the next level of society. This sometimes resulted in the bizarre alliance of the monarch with his lowest vassals against his overreaching barons and chieftains.

7   Like race and citizenship, religion was not far behind in the exclusionist philosophy of rights, formulating codes to protect the rights of the faithful but denying the same to others—the Cross against the Crescent, Buddhist versus Hindu, the believer against the infidel. Or simply religion versus secularism. Ground into powder beneath the hooves of the contending behemoths of religion, ideology and race, each social unit ponders, at least periodically, how he or she differs from cattle or sheep, from the horses that pull the carriages of majesty, even when such choices are the mere expressions of the collective will. If order alone, ornamentation, social organization, technology, bonding and even productive structures were all that defined the human species, then what significant properties marked out homo sapiens as distinct from the rest of the living species?

8   Polarizations within various micro-worlds—us versus the inferior them—have long been armed with industrious rationalizations. Christian and Islamic theologians throughout history have quarried their scriptures for passages that stress the incontestable primacy of an unseen and unknowable Supreme Deity who has conferred authority on them. And to what end? Largely to divide the world into us and the rest. The great philosophical minds of Europe, like Hume, Hegel and Kant, bent their prodigious talents to separating the species into those with rights and those with none, founded on the convenient theory

that some people were human and others less so. The Encyclopedists of France, products of the so-called Age of Reason, remain the most prolific codifiers of the human (and other) species on an ambitiously comprehensive scale, and their scholarly industry conferred a scientific benediction on a purely commercial project that saw millions of souls dragged across the ocean to serve as beasts of burden. Religion and commerce—far older professions than the one that is sometimes granted that distinction, but of an often-identical temperament—were reinforced by the authority of new scientific theories to divide humanity into higher and lower manifestations of the species. The dichotomy of the world was complete.

It took the near triumph of fascism to bring the world to its senses. The horror of the Holocaust finally took the rulers of the world back to the original question: what is the true value of humanity? It is to be doubted if the victorious three meeting in Yalta actually went into any profound philosophical niceties in the discussions that resulted in the United Nations, that partial attempt to reverse the dichotomizing course of humanity. That course, taken to its ultimate conclusion, had just resulted in an attempted purification of the species, the systematic elimination of millions in gas chambers and a war that mired the potential of Europe in the blood of its youth. After all, the concept of the master race was not new, but it was never before so obsessively articulated and systematically pursued. It was time to rethink the entire fate of humanity. The conversations at Yalta, conversations that led to the birth of the United Nations, were a partial answer to that question.

The first stage was to render the new thinking in concrete terms, to enshrine in a charter of rights the product of the bruising lessons of the immediate past: the United Nations and the Universal Declaration of Human Rights. The informing recognition is that long-suppressed extract of the intuition that humanity had guarded through evolution, one that had been proposed, compromised, amended, vitiated, subverted but never abandoned: that, for all human beings, there do exist certain fundamental rights.

The idea already exists in the Bible, in the Koran, in the Bhagavad Gita, in the Upanishads, but always in curtailed form, relativist, patriarchal, always subject to the invisible divine realms whose interpreters are mortals with distinct, secular agendas, usually allied to the very arbitrary controls that are a contradiction to such ideas. Quiet, restrained, ignored by but also blissfully indifferent to the so-called world religions, Ifa, the corpus of Yoruban spiritual precepts and secular philosophy, its origins lost in antiquity but preserved and applied till today, annunciates identical ideas through Orunmila, the god of divination:

12   *Dandan enia l'ayan ko mu ire lo s'aye . . . Ipo rere naa ni aye-amotan
ohungbogbo, ayo nnigbagbogbo, igbesi laisi ominu tabi iberu ota.*

*Certainly, it is the human being that was elected to bring values to the
world . . . and his place of good is the knowledge of all things, joy at all times,
freedom from anxiety and freedom from fear of the enemy.* [Irosu Wori]

13   Humanity has been straining to seize the fullness of this doctrine, the right to knowledge, the freedom from anxiety, the right to
security of existence as inherent to the species. It is only the process
of promulgating its pertinence to all mankind that has been long and
costly. The kernel of the idea, therefore, is both timeless and new. Its
resurrection—the concrete seizure of the idea within this millennium, answering the exigencies of politics, religion and power and securing it within the bedrock of universality—was a destiny that
would first be embraced by France.

14   There, alas, the events that gave new life to this idea did not encourage its adoption on a universal scale, indeed not even durably
within France itself. The restoration of slavery by Napoleon was surely
the most blatant contradiction of the idea, but this did not much trouble the Emperor.

15   Still, the idea had taken hold, the idea of the rights of man as a
universal principle. It certainly motored the passion of the genuine
idealists in the abolition of the slave trade, who must always be distinguished from those to whom abolition was simply a shrewd commercial calculation. The idea of the American Declaration of
Independence—an idea that still lacks full realization—that "all men
are created equal, that they are endowed by their Creator with certain
unalienable Rights" is an adumbration of that original idea from
which the French Revolution obtained its inspiration, one that has
continued to convulse the unjust order of the world wherever it has
been grasped: the fundamental rights of man.

16   It is an idea whose suppression is the main occupation of dicta-
torships—be these military or civilian, of the right or the left, secular
or theocratic. It is, however, their nightmare, their single province of
terror, one that they cannot exorcise, not even through the most un-
conscionable pogroms, scorched-earth campaigns and crimes against
humanity. It is an idea that has transformed the lives of billions and
remains poised to liberate billions more, since it is an idea that will
not settle for tokenism or for relativism—it implicitly links the liberation of one to the liberation of all. Its gospel of universalism is an-
chored in the most affective impulse that cynics attribute to the
choices made by humanity, self-love, but one that now translates humanity as one's own self.

RESPONDING TO READING

1. According to Soyinka, what idea has developed in the last thousand years that is, as his title suggests, every dictator's nightmare? How is the idea he targets one that comes out of many cultures, rather than a uniquely American idea?

2. How does Soyinka use the Holocaust to advance his argument? What is the dichotomy of human existence that he identifies and then links to the events of World War II? In what ways was that war, at its heart, about human rights, particularly regarding individual freedoms?

3. How are generalizations about human rights based on individual experiences? How is subjective individual experience transformed into a statement about the inherent rights of all people? Write an essay drawing on your own experiences that address this issue.

4. In America, are the fundamental human rights outlined in the Bill of Rights enforced selectively? Rather than being statements about the rights of all people, are the Rights, instead, only granted to some people (and perhaps only granted at some times)? Select one example from the Bill of Rights and, in an essay, explain how that right is or is not granted to all Americans. What makes it possible or impossible for that right to be applied to all Americans? Which people are or are not able to enjoy that right?

5. During a time of crisis and trauma, such as during a war, can the rights guaranteed in the Bill of Rights be taken away from everyone? From selected groups? Should they be? Explore this topic by talking with fellow students and in an essay.

Declaration of Independence

THOMAS JEFFERSON

Just two weeks before his death, which occurred on July 4, 1826—fifty years to the day after the signing of the *Declaration of Independence*—Thomas Jefferson wrote his final judgment of his "expression of the American mind":

> The Declaration will be . . . the signal of arousing men to burst the chains under which monkish ignorance and superstition had persuaded them to bind themselves, and to assume the blessings and security of self-government. That form which we have substituted, restores the free right to the unbounded exercise of reason and freedom of opinion. All eyes were opened, or opening, to the rights of man. The general spread of the light of science has already laid open to view the palpable truth, that the mass of mankind has not been born with saddles on their back, nor a few

booted and spurred, ready to ride them legitimately, by the Grace of God.

Although Benjamin Franklin and John Adams collaborated in drafting this document, its language and thought are quintessential Jefferson. He was the architect of the framework of American democracy, refusing to sign the Constitution until the Bill of Rights was added. The *Declaration* is principled and far-sighted, retaining the idealistic vision of the ultimate perfectibility of society, in which all citizens are expected to recognize the "rights of man" and act on them to secure the "unalienable rights" of "Life, Liberty, and the pursuit of Happiness."

Politician, philosopher, architect, inventor, and writer, Jefferson was born in 1743 near Charlottesville, Virginia, and was educated at the College of William and Mary. He served as a delegate to the Continental Congress in 1775, as Governor of the Commonwealth of Virginia, and as third President of the United States. His instructions for his epitaph specified only three of his many accomplishments for inclusion on his tombstone: founding of the University of Virginia and authorship of the Declaration of Independence and the Statute of Virginia for Religious Freedom.

1   When in the course of human events, it becomes necessary for one people to dissolve the political bands which have connected them with another, and to assume among the Powers of the earth, the separate and equal station to which the Laws of Nature and of Nature's God entitle them, a decent respect to the opinions of mankind requires that they should declare the causes which impel them to the separation.

2   We hold these truths to be self-evident, that all men are created equal, that they are endowed by their Creator with certain unalienable Rights, that among these are Life, Liberty and the pursuit of Happiness. That to secure these rights, Governments are instituted among Men deriving their just powers from the consent of the governed. That whenever any Form of Government becomes destructive of these ends, it is the Right of the People to alter or to abolish it, and to institute new Government, laying its foundation on such principles and organizing its powers in such form, as to them shall seem most likely to effect their Safety and Happiness. Prudence, indeed, will dictate that Governments long established should not be changed for light and transient causes; and accordingly all experience hath shown, that mankind are more disposed to suffer, while evils are sufferable, than to right themselves by abolishing the forms to which they are accustomed. But when a long train of abuses and usurpations pursuing invariably the same Object evinces a design to reduce them under absolute Despotism, it is their right, it is their duty, to throw off such government, and to provide new Guards for their future security. Such has been the patient sufferance of these Colonies; and such is now the necessity which con-

strains them to alter their former Systems of Government. The history of the present King of Great Britain is a history of repeated injuries and usurpations, all having in direct object the establishment of an absolute Tyranny over these States. To prove this, let Facts be submitted to a candid world.

He has refused his Assent to Laws, the most wholesome and necessary for the public good.   3

He has forbidden his Governors to pass Laws of immediate and pressing importance, unless suspended in their operation till his Assent should be obtained; and when so suspended, he has utterly neglected to attend them.   4

He has refused to pass other Laws for the accommodation of large districts of people, unless those people would relinquish the right of Representation in the Legislature, a right inestimable to them and formidable to tyrants only.   5

He has called together legislative bodies at places unusual, uncomfortable, and distant from the depository of their Public Records, for the sole purpose of fatiguing them into compliance with his measures.   6

He has dissolved Representative Houses repeatedly, for opposing with manly firmness his invasions on the rights of the people.   7

He has refused for a long time, after such dissolutions, to cause others to be elected; whereby the Legislative Powers, incapable of Annihilation, have returned to the People at large for their exercise; the State remaining in the mean time exposed to all the dangers of invasion from without, and convulsions within.   8

He has endeavoured to prevent the population of these States; for that purpose obstructing the Laws of Naturalization of Foreigners; refusing to pass others to encourage their migration hither, and raising the conditions of new Appropriations of Lands.   9

He has obstructed the Administration of Justice, by refusing his Assent to Laws for establishing Judiciary Powers.   10

He has made Judges dependent on his Will alone, for the tenure of their offices, and the amount and payment of their salaries.   11

He has erected a multitude of New Offices, and sent hither swarms of Officers to harass our People, and eat out their substance.   12

He has kept among us, in time of peace, Standing Armies without the Consent of our Legislature.   13

He has affected to render the Military independent of and superior to the Civil Power.   14

He has combined with others to subject us to jurisdictions foreign to our constitution, and unacknowledged by our laws; giving his Assent to their acts of pretended Legislation: 15

For quartering large bodies of armed troops among us: 16

For protecting them, by a mock Trial, from Punishment for any Murders which they should commit on the Inhabitants of these States: 17

18   For cutting off our Trade with all parts of the world:

19   For imposing Taxes on us without our Consent:

20   For depriving us in many cases, of the benefits of Trial by Jury:

21   For transporting us beyond Seas to be tried for pretended offenses:

22   For abolishing the free System of English Laws in a Neighbouring Province, establishing therein an Arbitrary government, and enlarging its boundaries so as to render it at once an example and fit instrument for introducing the same absolute rule into these Colonies:

23   For taking away our Charters, abolishing our most valuable Laws, and altering fundamentally the Forms of our Governments:

24   For suspending our own Legislatures, and declaring themselves invested with Power to legislate for us in all cases whatsoever.

25   He has abdicated Government here, by declaring us out of his Protection and waging War against us.

26   He has plundered our seas, ravaged our Coasts, burnt our towns and destroyed the Lives of our people.

27   He is at this time transporting large Armies of foreign Mercenaries to compleat works of death, desolation and tyranny, already begun with circumstances of Cruelty & perfidy scarcely paralleled in the most barbarous ages, and totally unworthy the Head of a civilized nation.

28   He has constrained our fellow Citizens taken Captive on the high Seas to bear Arms against their Country, to become the executioners of their friends and Brethren, or to fall themselves by their Hands.

29   He has excited domestic insurrections amongst us, and has endeavoured to bring on the inhabitants of our frontiers, the merciless Indian Savages, whose known rule of warfare, is an undistinguished destruction of all ages, sexes and conditions.

30   In every stage of these Oppressions We Have Petitioned for Redress in the most humble terms: Our repeated petitions have been answered only by repeated injury. A Prince, whose character is thus marked by every act which may define a Tyrant, is unfit to be the ruler of a free People.

31   Not have We been wanting in attention to our British brethren. We have warned them from time to time of attempts by their legislature to extend an unwarrantable jurisdiction over us. We have reminded them of the circumstances of our emigration and settlement here. We have appealed to their native justice and magnanimity and we have conjured them by the ties of our common kindred to disavow these usurpations, which would inevitably interrupt our connections and correspondence. They too have been deaf to the voice of justice and of consanguinity. We must, therefore acquiesce in the necessity, which denounces our Separation, and hold them, as we hold the rest of mankind, Enemies in War, in Peace Friends.

32   We, therefore, the Representatives of the United States of America, in General Congress, Assembled, appealing to the Supreme Judge of

the world for the rectitude of our intentions, do, in the Name, and by Authority of the good People of these Colonies, solemnly publish and declare, That these United Colonies are, and of Right ought to be Free and Independent States; that they are Absolved from all Allegiance to the British Crown, and that all political connection between them and the State of Great Britain, is and ought to be totally dissolved; and that as Free and Independent States, they have full power to levy War, conclude Peace, contract Alliances, establish Commerce, and to do all other Acts and Things which Independent States may of right do. And for the support of this Declaration, with a firm reliance on the protection of Divine Providence, we mutually pledge to each other our lives, our Fortunes and our sacred Honor.

[handwritten margin note: is this the definition of a sovereign state?]

RESPONDING TO READING

1. What, according to the *Declaration of Independence*, are the colonists' most significant grievances? How does the organization of the document reflect these?

2. How can revolutionaries know when the time is right to stage their coup and overthrow their government? Is the justice of one's cause measured only by the success of the coup?

3. Jefferson distrusted organized religion and believed that religion should be "subject to the laws of nature and probability, and discernible by reason" (Harold Hellenbrand, *The Unfinished Revolution*, 1990, 53). Do you see evidence for such beliefs in the *Declaration of Independence*?

4. What American values are embodied in the *Declaration of Independence*? Which of these remain important to Americans today? To you individually?

5. Define one of the values in the *Declaration of Independence*; and show its significance to some aspect of American life—such as culture, politics, economic opportunities, or education.

6. Write your own "declaration of independence," possibly in collaboration with another person, as Jefferson did, in which you justify your opposition to an oppressor or oppressive situation. Is a simple declaration of freedom sufficient? What will you have to do to enforce your claim?

Declaration of Sentiments

ELIZABETH CADY STANTON

When Elizabeth Cady (1815–1902) was ten, her brother died, and she vowed that she would fulfill the ambitions of her father, an influential lawyer and judge in Johnstown, New York. Although she studied Greek and became a top student at Emma Willard's Troy Female Seminary, her father forbade her to go to college. However, through her marriage to abolitionist agitator Henry Stanton, she was able—despite her responsibility for running a household that included the couple's seven children—to engage in social activity far more radical than attendance at college. In a public career that spanned more than fifty years, she was a militant feminist who, in collaboration with her friend, Susan B. Anthony, never stopped agitating for women's rights. These goals included the right to vote—promoted through various Woman Suffrage Associations which she helped to found—and the rights for married women to own property, to be entitled to the wages they earned, and to have equal guardianship of their children. As president of a Women's Temperance society, 1852–53, she scandalized even her ardent supporters by recommending that drunkenness be a sufficient ground for divorce. In arguing that to be truly equal with men, women have to fight for their sexual self-determination, she was a century ahead of her time.

"Declaration of Sentiments," composed in 1848, was Stanton's first theoretical political document, written for the Women's Rights Convention that she and four other feminists organized to assert that "all men and women are created equal." As political analyst Bruce Miroff has noted, through following the *Declaration of Independence* point-by-point and in parallel language, "Stanton took a classic American idiom and infused it with a radical message not contemplated by its authors," taking "the most democratic and egalitarian American values and turning them against a dominant culture that claimed to uphold them."

1   When, in the course of human events, it becomes necessary for one portion of the family of man to assume among the people of the earth a position different from that which they have hitherto occupied, but one to which the laws of nature and of nature's God entitle them, a decent respect to the opinions of mankind requires that they should declare the causes that impel them to such a course.

2   We hold these truths to be self-evident: that all men and women are created equal; that they are endowed by their Creator with certain inalienable rights; that among these are life, liberty, and the pursuit of happiness; that to secure these rights governments are instituted, deriving their just powers from the consent of the governed. Whenever any form of government becomes destructive of these ends, it is the right of those who suffer from it to refuse allegiance to it, and to insist upon the institution of a new government, laying its foundation on such principles, and organizing its powers in such form, as to them shall seem most likely to effect their safety and happiness. Prudence, indeed, will dictate that governments long established should not be changed for light and transient causes; and accordingly all experience hath shown that mankind are more disposed to suffer, while evils are sufferable, than to right themselves by abolishing the forms to which they were accustomed. But when a long train of abuses and usurpations, pursuing invariably the same object evinces a design to reduce them under absolute despotism, it is their duty to throw off such government, and to provide new guards for their future security. Such has

been the patient sufferance of the women under this government, and such is now the necessity which constrains them to demand the equal station to which they are entitled.

The history of mankind is a history of repeated injuries and usurpations on the part of man toward woman, having in direct object the establishment of an absolute tyranny over her. To prove this, let facts be submitted to a candid world. 3

He has never permitted her to exercise her inalienable right to the elective franchise. (voting) 4

He has compelled her to submit to laws, in the formation of which she had no voice. 5

He has withheld from her rights which are given to the most ignorant and degraded men—both natives and foreigners. 6

Having deprived her of this first right of a citizen, the elective franchise, thereby leaving her without representation in the halls of legislation, he has oppressed her on all sides. 7

He has made her, if married, in the eye of the law, civilly dead. 8

He has taken from her all right in property, even to the wages she earns. 9

He has made her, morally, an irresponsible being, as she can commit many crimes with impunity, provided they be done in the presence) *really?* of her husband. In the covenant of marriage, she is compelled to promise obedience to her husband, he becoming, to all intents and purposes, her master—the law giving him power to deprive her of her liberty, and to administer chastisement. 10

He has so framed the laws of divorce, as to what shall be the proper causes, and in case of separation, to whom the guardianship of the children shall be given, as to be wholly regardless of the happiness of women—the law, in all cases, going upon a false supposition of the supremacy of man, and giving all power into his hands. 11

After depriving her of all rights as a married woman, if single, and the owner of property, he has taxed her to support a government which *taxation w/out* recognizes her only when her property can be made profitable to it. *representation* 12

He has monopolized nearly all the profitable employments, and from those she is permitted to follow, she receives but a scanty remuneration. He closes against her all the avenues to wealth and distinction which he considers most honorable to himself. As a teacher of theology, medicine, or law, she is not known. 13

He has denied her the facilities for obtaining a thorough education, all colleges being closed against her. 14

He allows her in Church, as well as State, but a subordinate position, claiming Apostolic authority for her exclusion from the ministry, and, with some exceptions from any public participation in the affairs of the Church. 15

He has created a false public sentiment by giving to the world a different code of morals for men and women, by which moral delinquencies 16 which exclude women from society, are not only tolerated, but deemed of little account in man.

17   He has usurped the prerogative of Jehovah himself, claiming it as his right to assign for her a sphere of action, when that belongs to her conscience and to her God.

18   He has endeavored, in every way that he could, to destroy her confidence in her own powers, to lessen her self-respect, and to make her willing to lead a dependent and abject life.

19   Now, in view of this entire disenfranchisement of one-half the people of this country, their social and religious degradation—in view of the unjust laws above mentioned, and because women do feel themselves aggrieved, oppressed, and fraudulently deprived of their most sacred rights, we insist that they have immediate admission to all the rights and privileges which belong to them as citizens of the United States.

20   In entering upon the great work before us, we anticipate no small amount of misconception, misrepresentation, and ridicule; but we shall use every instrumentality within our power to effect our object. We shall employ agents, circulate tracts, petition the State and National legislatures, and endeavor to enlist the pulpit and the press in our behalf. We hope this Convention will be followed by a series of Conventions embracing every part of the country.

21   1898

RESPONDING TO READING

1. What, according to Stanton, are women's most significant grievances? How does the imitation of the *Declaration of Independence* make the *Declaration of Sentiments* more powerful than a mere statement of grievances?

2. What did Jefferson mean by "the laws of Nature and Nature's God"? How do these terms shift in meaning in Stanton's document?

3. How much has changed since Stanton wrote? To what degree have the underlying grievances been addressed? Can women still "anticipate no small amount of misconception, misrepresentation, and ridicule" when asserting the rights and privileges of citizens?

The Gettysburg Address

ABRAHAM LINCOLN

To understand the meaning of a speech, it is important to understand the context in which it was given. Abraham Lincoln's "Gettysburg Address" is considered "one of the greatest speeches in all history. Greatness is like granite: it is molded in fire, and lasts for centuries," says critic Gilbert Highet in "The Gettysburg Address," masterfully evoking its context:

> The dedication of the graveyard at Gettysburg was one of the *[interesting]* supreme moments of American history. The battle itself had been a turning point of the war. Losses were heavy on both sides. Thousands of dead were left on the field, and thousands of wounded died in the hot days following the battle. At first, their burial was more or less haphazard; but thoughtful men gradually came to feel that an adequate burying place and memorial were required.

At first, Lincoln, though President, was not invited to deliver the address on November 19, 1863. But when the invitation came, Lincoln was grateful for the opportunity to show that he could say something worthy of a solemn occasion. In the days when public officials still *[wouldnt that be interesting]* prepared their own speeches, Lincoln took great care in writing this address, which he began in the White House and completed at the Gettysburg hotel the night before the ceremony.

Although the contemporary press undervalued the speech, in part because it was so short, poet Carl Sandburg, a biographer of Lincoln, claims that this magnificent document portends the Emancipation Proclamation, which Lincoln in fact delivered on the following New Year's Day. In reiterating the proposition of the Declaration of Independence that "all men are created equal," Lincoln implied that the slaves were people embraced by this Declaration.

Four score and seven years ago our fathers brought forth on this continent a new nation, conceived in liberty, and dedicated to the proposition that all men are created equal.   1

Now we are engaged in a great civil war, testing whether that nation, or any nation so conceived and so dedicated, can long endure. We are met on a great battlefield of that war. We have come to dedicate a portion of that field, as a final resting place for those who here gave their lives that that nation might live. It is altogether fitting and proper that we should do this.   2

But, in a larger sense, we cannot dedicate—we cannot consecrate—we cannot hallow—this ground. The brave men, living and dead, who struggled here, have consecrated it, far above our poor power to add or detract. The world will little note, nor long remember what we say *[hehehe]* here, but it can never forget what they did here. It is for us the living, rather, to be dedicated here to the unfinished work which they who fought here have thus so far nobly advanced. It is rather for us to be here dedicated to the great task remaining before us—that from these honored dead we take increased devotion—that we here highly resolve that these dead shall not have died in vain—that this nation, under God, shall have a new birth of freedom—and that government of the people, by the people, for the people, shall not perish from the earth.   3

RESPONDING TO READING

1. What, for Lincoln, is the most significant reason for waging the Civil War? For ending it?
2. Lincoln's speech, though short, embodies a number of values both of the American culture and the Christian religion. What are these? If Lincoln had lived to act on these values, how might these have been the basis for postwar reconciliation between the North and the South?
3. Compare and contrast Lincoln's speech with Thomas Jefferson's *Declaration of Independence*.
4. What can you learn about the art of speechwriting from studying Lincoln's "Gettysburg Address"?
5. Under what circumstances is war justified? According to what principles should those contemplating war make their decision? How have these principles worked out in practice, as wars have gone on? Use the American Civil War, the second Persian War with Iraq or some other war, as your reference.

Ain't I a Woman?

SOJOURNER TRUTH

Sojourner Truth, originally named Isabella, was born into slavery (c. 1797) in Ulster County, New York, and fled to freedom in 1827. One of her first acts as a free woman was to sue for the return of one of her four children, who had been sold illegally to an Alabama slaveowner. For the next sixteen years she lived and worked as a domestic servant in New York City, becoming an active evangelist in association with a clergyman, who encouraged her efforts to convert prostitutes.

In 1843, the mystical visions and voices that had governed her life told her to adopt a new name, "Sojourner Truth," and to take to the road as an itinerant preacher. Early in her sojourn, in Northampton, Massachusetts, she encountered and became a popular champion of abolition, often sharing the platform with Frederick Douglass, whose eloquence she rivaled even though she remained illiterate throughout her life. Her speeches employed the vitality and cadences of a great Blues singer to hold the audience spellbound: "Children, I talk to God and God talks to me!" Until her death in 1883, supported by her best-selling ghostwritten *Narrative of Sojourner Truth* (1850), she promoted causes spiritual and separatist, but got nowhere with her call for a "Negro State." After the Civil War, under the influence of Elizabeth Cady Stanton, Sojourner Truth also promoted feminist causes, as "Ain't I a Woman?" reveals, reminding her audiences that half the freed slaves were women.

1   Well, children, where there is so much racket there must be something out of kilter. I think that 'twixt the negroes of the South and the

women at the North, all talking about rights, the white men will be in a fix pretty soon. But what's all this here talking about?

That man over there says women need to be helped into carriages, 2 and lifted over ditches, and to have the best place everywhere. Nobody ever helps me into carriages, or over mud-puddles, or gives me any best place! And ain't I a woman? Look at me! Look at my arm! I have ploughed and planted, and gathered into barns, and no man could head me! And ain't I a woman? I could work as much and eat as much as a man—when I could get it—and bear the lash as well! And ain't I a woman? I have borne thirteen children, and seen them most all sold off to slavery, and when I cried out with my mother's grief, none but Jesus heard me! And ain't I a woman?

Then they talk about this thing in the head; what's this they call it? 3 [Intellect, someone whispers.] That's it, honey. What's that got to do with women's rights or negro's rights? If my cup won't hold but a pint, and yours holds a quart, wouldn't you be mean not to let me have my little half-measure full? *even if we are inferior, let us too be our best?*

Then that little man in black there, he says women can't have as 4 much rights as men, 'cause Christ wasn't a woman! Where did your Christ come from? Where did your Christ come from? From God and a woman! Man had nothing to do with Him. *damn, girl!*

If the first woman God ever made was strong enough to turn the 5 world upside down all alone, these women together ought to be able to turn it back, and get it right side up again! And now they is asking to do it, the men better let them.

Obliged to you for hearing me, and now old Sojourner ain't got 6 nothing more to say.

RESPONDING TO READING

1. Identify the setting of this speech. Who are "that man over there" and "that little man in black"? What kind of talk ("all this here talking") is Sojourner Truth responding to? How does she establish her credentials as someone with authority?

2. Sojourner Truth's speech is about the same length as Lincoln's "Gettysburg Address," and the two have much else in common. The questions in this book about Lincoln's speech ask you to deduce the value system from it; do the same analysis here. Then compare the values expressed in both speeches. Could the values in this speech also serve as the basis for reconciliation, here between black and white, men and women?

3. To what degree are the grievances set out in this speech now resolved? Refer to the Alice Walker essay at the end of chapter 3, and other selections you find pertinent, as well as to your own experience as you prepare your response.

What Values Govern
the Common Good?

Civil Disobedience

Henry David Thoreau

Henry David Thoreau (1817–62), essayist, poet, and diarist, spent his life in Concord, Massachusetts. He graduated from Harvard in 1837, and thereafter worked at odd jobs while doing his real work as an original thinker. As a Transcendentalist, strongly influenced by the works of Kant, Coleridge, and Goethe, he believed that a certain kind of intuitive knowledge transcended the limits of human experience and the senses; for Thoreau, ideas and the natural world were more important and more powerful than material things. These views are reflected in his major works, *A Week on the Concord and Merrimack Rivers* (1849) and *Walden, or Life in the Woods* (1854), a record of the two years he spent at Walden Pond, in Concord. There he lived alone in a house he made and became the model of self-reliance, growing his own food, chopping his own wood, and living frugally while feasting on the bounty of nature and the cosmos.

But this self-reliance was not a means of separating himself from the pressing issues of his day; quite the reverse. As he makes clear in "Civil Disobedience," a democratic society that allows for freedom of expression embeds in that freedom the possibility of civil disobedience. He provided both inspiration and a theoretical rationale for the nonviolent protests of Gandhi in his quest to secure India's independence from British control and for the desegregation efforts of Martin Luther King, Jr.

From 1845 to 1848 the United States fought Mexico to secure annexation of Texas, a move intended to increase slave territory. Thoreau, an Abolitionist in a state where Abolitionists were harboring fugitive slaves and helping them to resettle, was profoundly committed to the position he articulates in "Civil Disobedience." He believed that any man more right than his neighbors is already a majority of one; God is a sufficient ally.

As a protest against the war, in July 1846, Thoreau refused to pay the Massachusetts poll tax, a per capita levy intended to raise money for the war, and he was jailed as a consequence. Although he spent only one night in jail, the experience moved him to examine its implications and to conclude that "Under a government which imprisons any unjustly, the true place for a just man is also a prison."

1   I heartily accept the motto, "That government is best which governs least"; and I should like to see it acted up to more rapidly and

systematically. Carried out, it finally amounts to this, which also I believe—"That government is best which governs not at all"; and when men are prepared for it, that will be the kind of government which they will have. Government is at best but an expedient; but most governments are usually, and all governments are sometimes, inexpedient. The objections which have been brought against a standing army, and they are many and weighty, and deserve to prevail, may also at last be brought against a standing government. The standing army is only an arm of the standing government. The government itself, which is only the mode which the people have chosen to execute their will, is equally liable to be abused and perverted before the people can act through it. Witness the present Mexican war, the work of comparatively a few individuals using the standing government as their tool; for, in the outset, the people would not have consented to this measure.

This American government—what is it but a tradition, though a re-   2
cent one, endeavoring to transmit itself unimpaired to posterity, but each instant losing some of its integrity? It has not the vitality and force of a single living man; for a single man can bend it to his will. It is a sort of wooden gun to the people themselves. But it is not the less necessary for this; for the people must have some complicated machinery or other, and hear its din, to satisfy that idea of government which they have. Governments show thus how successfully men can be imposed on, even impose on themselves, for their own advantage. It is excellent, we must all allow. Yet this government never of itself furthered any enterprise, but by the alacrity with which it got out of its way. *It* does not keep the country free. *It* does not settle the West. *It* does not educate. The character inherent in the American people has done all that has been accomplished; and it would have done somewhat more, if the government had not sometimes got in its way. For government is an expedient by which men would fain succeed in letting one another alone; and, as has been said, when it is most expedient, the governed are most let alone by it. Trade and commerce, if they were not made of india-rubber, would never manage to bounce over the obstacles which legislators are continually putting in their way; and, if one were to judge these men wholly by the effects of their actions and not partly by their intentions, they would deserve to be classed and punished with those mischievous persons who put obstructions on the railroads.

But, to speak practically and as a citizen, unlike those who call   3
themselves no-government men, I ask for, not at once no government, but *at once* a better government. Let every man make known what kind of government would command his respect, and that will be one step toward obtaining it.

After all, the practical reason why, when the power is once in the   4
hands of the people, a majority are permitted, and for a long period

continue, to rule is not because they are most likely to be in the right, nor because this seems fairest to the minority, but because they are physically the strongest. But a government in which the majority rule in all cases cannot be based on justice, even as far as men understand it. Can there not be a government in which majorities do not virtually decide right and wrong, but conscience?—in which majorities decide only those questions to which the rule of expediency is applicable? Must the citizen ever for a moment, or in the least degree, resign his conscience to the legislator? Why has every man a conscience, then? I think that we should be men first, and subjects afterwards. It is not desirable to cultivate a respect for the law, so much as for the right. The only obligation which I have a right to assume is to do at any time what I think right. It is truly enough said that a corporation has no conscience; but a corporation of conscientious men is a corporation *with* a conscience. Law never made men a whit more just; and, by means of their respect for it, even the well-disposed are daily made the agents of injustice. A common and natural result of an undue respect for law is, that you may see a file of soldiers, colonel, captain, corporal, privates, powder-monkeys, and all, marching in admirable order over hill and dale to the wars, against their wills, ay, against their common sense and consciences, which makes it very steep marching indeed, and produces a palpitation of the heart. They have no doubt that it is a damnable business in which they are concerned; they are all peaceably inclined. Now, what are they? Men at all? or small movable forts and magazines, at the service of some unscrupulous man in power? Visit the Navy-Yard, and behold a marine, such a man as an American government can make, or such as it can make a man with its black arts—a mere shadow and reminiscence of humanity, a man laid out alive and standing, and already, as one may say, buried under arms with funeral accompaniments, though it may be,—

> Not a drum was heard, not a funeral note,
>   As his corse to the rampart we hurried;
> Not a soldier discharged his farewell shot
>   O'er the grave where our hero was buried.[1]

5   The mass of men serve the state thus, not as men mainly, but as machines, with their bodies. They are the standing army, and the militia, jailers, constables, *posse comitatus*, etc. In most cases there is no free exercise whatever of the judgment or of the moral sense; but they put themselves on a level with wood and earth and stones; and wooden men can perhaps be manufactured that will serve the purpose as well. Such command no more respect than men of straw or a lump of dirt.

---

[1]Charles Wolfe, "Burial of Sir John Moore at Corunna" (1817). [Eds.]

They have the same sort of worth only as horses and dogs. Yet such as these even are commonly esteemed good citizens. Others—as most legislators, politicians, lawyers, ministers, and office-holders—serve the state chiefly with their heads; and, as they rarely make any moral distinctions, they are as likely to serve the devil, without *intending* it, as God. A very few—as heroes, patriots, martyrs, reformers in the great sense, and *men*—serve the state with their consciences also, and so necessarily resist it for the most part; and they are commonly treated as enemies by it. A wise man will only be useful as a man, and they will submit to be "clay," and "stop a hole to keep the wind away,"[2] but leave that office to his dust at least:—

> I am too high-born to be propertied,
> To be a secondary at control,
> Or useful serving-man and instrument
> To any sovereign state throughout the world.[3]

He who gives himself entirely to his fellow-men appears to them   6
useless and selfish; but he who gives himself partially to them is pronounced a benefactor and philanthropist.

How does it become a man to behave toward this American gov-   7
ernment today? I answer, that he cannot without disgrace be associated with it. I cannot for an instant recognize that political organization as *my* government which is the *slave's* government also.

All men recognize the right of revolution; that is, the right to refuse   8
allegiance to, and to resist, the government, when its tyranny or its inefficiency are great and unendurable. But almost all say that such is not the case now. But such was the case, they think, in the Revolution of '75. If one were to tell me that his was a bad government because it taxed certain foreign commodities brought to its ports, it is most probable that I should not make an ado about it, for I can do without them. All machines have their friction; and possibly this does enough good to counter-balance the evil. At any rate, it is a great evil to make a stir about it. But when the friction comes to have its machine, and oppression and robbery are organized, I say, let us not have such a machine any longer. In other words, when a sixth of the population of a nation which has undertaken to be the refuge of liberty are slaves, and a whole country is unjustly overrun and conquered by a foreign army, and subjected to military law, I think that it is not too soon for honest men to rebel and revolutionize. What makes this duty the more urgent is the fact that the country so overrun is not our own, but ours is the invading army.

---

[2]*Hamlet*, V, i, ll, 236–237. [Eds.]
[3]*King John*, V, ii, ll, 79–82. [Eds.]

9   Paley,[4] a common authority with many on moral questions, in his chapter on the "Duty of Submission to Civil Government," resolves all civil obligation into expediency; and he proceeds to say that "so long as the interest of the whole society requires it, that is, so long as the established government cannot be resisted or changed without public inconveniency, it is the will of God ... that the established government be obeyed—and no longer. This principle being admitted, the justice of every particular case of resistance is reduced to a computation of the quantity of the danger and grievance on the one side, and of the probability and expense of redressing it on the other." Of this, he says, every man shall judge for himself. But Paley appears never to have contemplated those cases to which the rule of expediency does not apply, in which a people, as well as an individual, must do justice, cost what it may. If I have unjustly wrested a plank from a drowning man, I must restore it to him though I drown myself.[5] This, according to Paley, would be inconvenient. But he that would save his life, in such a case, shall lose it.[6] This people must cease to hold slaves, and to make war on Mexico, though it cost them their existence as a people.

10   In their practice, nations agree with Paley; but does any one think that Massachusetts does exactly what is right at the present crisis?

> A drab of state, a cloth-o'-silver slut,
> To have her train borne up, and her soul trail in the dirt.

Practically speaking, the opponents to a reform in Massachusetts are not a hundred thousand politicians at the South, but a hundred thousand merchants and farmers here, who are more interested in commerce and agriculture than they are in humanity, and are not prepared to do justice to the slave and to Mexico, *cost what it may.* I quarrel not with far-off foes, but with those who, near at home, coöperate with, and do the bidding of, those far away, and without whom the latter would be harmless. We are accustomed to say, that the mass of men are unprepared; but improvement is slow, because the few are not materially wiser or better than the many. It is not so important that many should be as good as you, as that there be some absolute goodness somewhere; for that will leaven the whole lump.[7] There are thousands who are *in opinion* opposed to slavery and to the war, who yet in effect do nothing to put an end to them; who, esteeming themselves children of Washington and Franklin, sit down with their hands in their pockets,

---

[4]Rev. William Paley, *Principles of Moral and Political Philosophy* (1785). [Eds.]
[5]Cited by Cicero, *De Officiis,* III. [Eds.]
[6]Luke IX: 24; Matthew X: 39. [Eds.]
[7]I Corinthians V: 6. [Eds.]

and say that they know not what to do, and do nothing; who even postpone the question of freedom to the question of free trade, and quietly read the prices-current along with the latest advices from Mexico, after dinner, and, it may be, fall asleep over them both. What is the price-current of an honest man and patriot today? They hesitate, and they regret, and sometimes they petition; but they do nothing in earnest and with effect. They will wait, well disposed, for others to remedy the evil, that they may no longer have it to regret. At most, they give only a cheap vote, and a feeble countenance and God-speed, to the right, as it goes by them. There are nine hundred and ninety-nine patrons of virtue to one virtuous man. But it is easier to deal with the real possessor of a thing than with the temporary guardian of it.

All voting is a sort of gaming, like checkers or backgammon, with a   11
slight moral tinge to it, a playing with right and wrong, with moral questions; and betting naturally accompanies it. The character of the voters is not staked. I cast my vote, perchance, as I think right; but I am not vitally concerned that that right should prevail. I am willing to leave it to the majority. Its obligation, therefore, never exceeds that of expediency. Even voting *for the right* is *doing* nothing for it. It is only expressing to men feebly your desire that it should prevail. A wise man will not leave the right to the mercy of chance, nor wish it to prevail through the power of the majority. There is but little virtue in the action of masses of men. When the majority shall at length vote for the abolition of slavery, it will be because they are indifferent to slavery, or because there is but little slavery left to be abolished by their vote. *They* will then be the only slaves. Only *his* vote can hasten the abolition of slavery who asserts his own freedom by his vote.

I hear of a convention to be held at Baltimore, or elsewhere, for the   12
selection of a candidate for the Presidency, made up chiefly of editors, and men who are politicians by profession; but I think, what is it to any independent, intelligent, and respectable man what decision they may come to? Shall we not have the advantage of his wisdom and honesty, nevertheless? Can we not count upon some independent votes? Are there not many individuals in the country who do not attend conventions? But no: I find that the respectable man, so called, has immediately drifted from his position, and despairs of his country, when his country has more reason to despair of him. He forthwith adopts one of the candidates thus selected as the only *available* one, thus proving that he is himself *available* for any purposes of the demagogue. His vote is of no more worth than that of any unprincipled foreigner or hireling native, who may have been bought. O for a man who is a *man*, and, as my neighbor says, has a bone in his back which you cannot pass your hand through! Our statistics are at fault: the population has been returned too large. How many *men* are there to a square thousand miles in this country? Hardly one. Does not America offer any inducement for men

to settle her? The American has dwindled into an Odd Fellow—one who may be known by the development of his organ of gregariousness, and a manifest lack of intellect and cheerful self-reliance; whose first and chief concern, on coming into the world, is to see that the almshouses are in good repair; and, before yet he has lawfully donned the virile garb, to collect a fund for the support of the widows and orphans that may be; who, in short, ventures to live only by the aid of the Mutual Insurance company, which has promised to bury him decently.

13   It is not a man's duty, as a matter of course, to devote himself to the eradication of any, even the most enormous, wrong; he may still properly have other concerns to engage him; but it is his duty, at least, to wash his hands of it and, if he gives it no thought longer, not to give it practically his support. If I devote myself to other pursuits and contemplations, I must first see, at least, that I do not pursue them sitting upon another man's shoulders. I must get off him first, that he may pursue his contemplations too. See what gross inconsistency is tolerated. I have heard some of my townsmen say, "I should like to have them order me out to help put down an insurrection of the slaves, or to march to Mexico;—see if I would go"; and yet these very men have each, directly by their allegiance, and so indirectly, at least, by their money, furnished a substitute. The soldier is applauded who refuses to serve in an unjust war by those who do not refuse to sustain the unjust government which makes the war; is applauded by those whose own act and authority he disregards and sets at naught; as if the state were penitent to that degree that it hired one to scourge it while it sinned, but not to that degree that it left off sinning for a moment. Thus, under the name of Order and Civil Government, we are all made at last to pay homage to and support our own meanness. After the first blush of sin comes its indifference; and from immoral it becomes, as it were, *un*moral, and not quite unnecessary to that life which we have made.

14   The broadest and most prevalent error requires the most disinterested virtue to sustain it. The slight reproach to which the virtue of patriotism is commonly liable, the noble are most likely to incur. Those who, while they disapprove of the character and measures of a government, yield to it their allegiance and support are undoubtedly its most conscientious supporters, and so frequently the most serious obstacles to reform. Some are petitioning the State to dissolve the Union, to disregard the requisitions of the President. Why do they not dissolve it themselves—the union between themselves and the State—and refuse to pay their quota into its treasury? Do not they stand in the same relation to the State that the State does to the Union? And have not the same reasons prevented the State from resisting the Union which have prevented them from resisting the State?

15   How can a man be satisfied to entertain an opinion merely, and enjoy *it*? Is there any enjoyment in it, if his opinion is that he is ag-

grieved? If you are cheated out of a single dollar by your neighbor, you do not rest satisfied with knowing that you are cheated, or with saying that you are cheated, or even with petitioning him to pay you your due; but you take effectual steps at once to obtain the full amount, and see that you are never cheated again. Action from principle, the perception and the performance of right, changes things and relations; it is essentially revolutionary, and does not consist wholly with anything which was. It not only divides States and churches, it divides families; ay, it divides the *individual*, separating the diabolical in him from the divine.

Unjust laws exist: shall we be content to obey them, or shall we en-   16
deavor to amend them, and obey them until we have succeeded, or shall we transgress them at once? Men generally, under such a government as this, think that they ought to wait until they have persuaded the majority to alter them. They think that, if they should resist, the remedy would be worse than the evil. But it is the fault of the government itself that the remedy *is* worse than the evil. *It* makes it worse. Why is it not more apt to anticipate and provide for reform? Why does it not cherish its wise minority? Why does it cry and resist before it is hurt? Why does it not encourage its citizens to be on the alert to point out its faults, and *do* better than it would have them? Why does it always crucify Christ, and excommunicate Copernicus and Luther, and pronounce Washington and Franklin rebels?

One would think that a deliberate and practical denial of its au-   17
thority was the only offence never contemplated by a government; else, why has it not assigned its definite, its suitable and proportionate, penalty? If a man who has no property refuses but once to earn nine shillings for the State, he is put in prison for a period unlimited by any law that I know, and determined only by the discretion of those who placed him there; but if he should steal ninety times nine shillings from the State, he is soon permitted to go at large again.

If the injustice is part of the necessary friction of the machine of   18
government, let it go, let it go: perchance it will wear smooth—certainly the machine will wear out. If the injustice has a spring, or a pulley, or a rope, or a crank, exclusively for itself, then perhaps you may consider whether the remedy will not be worse than the evil; but if it is of such a nature that it requires you to be the agent of injustice to another, then, I say, break the law. Let your life be a counter friction to stop the machine. What I have to do is to see, at any rate, that I do not lend myself to the wrong which I condemn.

As for adopting the ways which the State has provided for reme-   19
dying the evil, I know not of such ways. They take too much time, and a man's life will be gone. I have other affairs to attend to. I came into this world, not chiefly to make this a good place to live in, but to live in it, be it good or bad. A man has not everything to do, but something;

and because he cannot do *everything*, it is not necessary that he should do *something* wrong. It is not my business to be petitioning the Governor or the Legislature any more than it is theirs to petition me; and if they should not hear my petition, what should I do then? But in this case the State has provided no way: its very Constitution is the evil. This may seem to be harsh and stubborn and unconciliatory; but it is to treat with the utmost kindness and consideration the only spirit that can appreciate or deserves it. So is all change for the better, like birth and death, which convulse the body.

20   I do not hesitate to say, that those who call themselves Abolitionists should at once effectually withdraw their support, both in person and property, from the government of Massachusetts, and not wait till they constitute a majority of one, before they suffer the right to prevail through them. I think that it is enough if they have God on their side, without waiting for that other one. Moreover, any man more right than his neighbors constitutes a majority of one already.

21   I meet the American government, or its representative, the State government, directly, and face to face, once a year—no more—in the person of its tax-gatherer; this is the only mode in which a man situated as I am necessarily meets it; and it then says distinctly, Recognize me; and the simplest, the most effectual, and, in the present posture of affairs, the indispensablest mode of treating with it on this head, of expressing your little satisfaction with and love for it, is to deny it then. My civil neighbor, the tax-gatherer, is the very man I have to deal with—for it is, after all, with men and not with parchment that I quarrel—and he has voluntarily chosen to be an agent of the government. How shall he ever know well what he is and does as an officer of the government, or as a man, until he is obliged to consider whether he shall treat me, his neighbor, for whom he has respect, as a neighbor and well-disposed man, or as a maniac and disturber of the peace, and see if he can get over this obstruction to his neighborliness without a ruder and more impetuous thought or speech corresponding with his action. I know this well, that if one thousand, if one hundred, if ten men whom I could name—if ten *honest* men only—ay, if *one* HONEST man in this State of Massachusetts, *ceasing to hold slaves*, were actually to withdraw from this copartnership, and be locked up in the county jail therefor, it would be the abolition of slavery in America. For it matters not how small the beginning may seem to be: what is once well done is done forever. But we love better to talk about it: that we say is our mission. Reform keeps many scores of newspapers in its service, but not one man. If my esteemed neighbor, the State's ambassador,[8] who will devote his days to the settlement of the question of human rights in the

---

[8]Samuel Hoar, Concord statesman, was expelled from Charleston, South Carolina where he was sent on behalf of Massachusetts black seamen in 1844. [Eds.]

Council Chamber, instead of being threatened with the prisons of Carolina, were to sit down the prisoner of Massachusets, that State which is so anxious to foist the sin of slavery upon her sister—though at present she can discover only an act of inhospitality to be the ground of a quarrel with her—the Legislature would not wholly waive the subject the following winter.

Under a government which imprisons any unjustly, the true place for a just man is also a prison. The proper place to-day, the only place which Massachusetts has provided for her freer and less desponding spirits, is in her prisons, to be put out and locked out of the State by her own act, as they have already put themselves out by their principles. It is there that the fugitive slave, and the Mexican prisoner on parole, and the Indian come to plead the wrongs of his race should find them; on that separate, but more free and honorable, ground, where the State places those who are not *with* her, but *against* her—the only house in a slave State in which a free man can abide with honor. If any think that their influence would be lost there, and their voices no longer afflict the ear of the State, that they would not be as an enemy within its walls, they do not know by how much truth is stronger than error, nor how much more eloquently and effectively he can combat injustice who has experienced a little in his own person. Cast your whole vote, not a strip of paper merely, but your whole influence. A minority is powerless while it conforms to the majority; it is not even a minority then; but it is irresistible when it clogs by its whole weight. If the alternative is to keep all just men in prison, or give up war and slavery, the State will not hesitate which to choose. If a thousand men were not to pay their tax-bills this year, that would not be a violent and bloody measure, as it would be to pay them, and enable the State to commit violence and shed innocent blood. This is, in fact, the definition of a peaceable revolution, if any such is possible. If the tax-gatherer, or any public officer, asks me, as one has done, "But what shall I do?" my answer is, "If you really wish to do anything, resign your office." When the subject has refused allegiance, and the officer has resigned his office, then the revolution is accomplished. But even suppose blood should flow. Is there not a sort of blood shed when the conscience is wounded? Through this wound a man's real manhood and immortality flow out, and he bleeds to an everlasting death. I see this blood flowing now.

I have contemplated the imprisonment of the offender, rather than the seizure of his goods—though both will serve the same purpose—because they who assert the purest right, and consequently are most dangerous to a corrupt State, commonly have not spent much time in accumulating property. To such the State renders comparatively small service, and a slight tax is wont to appear exorbitant, particularly if they are obliged to earn it by special labor with their hands. If there were one who lived wholly without the use of money, the State itself would hesitate to demand it of him. But the rich man—not to make any invidious comparison—is always sold to the institution which makes him rich. Absolutely speaking, the more money, the less virtue; for money comes between a man and his objects, and obtains them for him; and it was certainly no great virtue to obtain it. It puts to rest many questions which he would otherwise be taxed to answer; while the only new question which it puts is the hard but superfluous one, how to spend it. Thus his moral ground is taken from under his feet. The opportunities of living are diminished in proportion as what are called the "means" are increased. The best thing a man can do for his culture when he is rich is to endeavor to carry out those schemes which he entertained when he was poor. Christ answered the Herodians according to their condition. "Show me the tribute-money," said he;—and one took a penny out of his pocket;—if you use money which has the image of Caesar on it, and which he has made current and valuable, that is, *if you are men of the State*, and gladly enjoy the advantages of Caesar's government, then pay him back some of his own when he demands it. "Render therefore to Caesar that which is Caesar's, and to God those things which are God's"—leaving them no wiser than before as to which was which; for they did not wish to know.

24   When I converse with the freest of my neighbors, I perceive that, whatever they may say about the magnitude and seriousness of the question, and their regard for the public tranquillity, the long and the short of the matter is, that they cannot spare the protection of the existing government, and they dread the consequences to their property and families of disobedience to it. For my own part, I should not like to think that I ever rely on the protection of the State. But, if I deny the authority of the State when it presents its tax-bill, it will soon take and waste all my property, and so harass me and my children without end. This is hard. This makes it impossible for a man to live honestly, and at the same time comfortably, in outward respects. It will not be worth the while to accumulate property; that would be sure to go again. You must hire or squat somewhere, and raise but a small crop, and eat that soon. You must live within yourself, and depend upon yourself always tucked up and ready for a start, and not have many affairs. A man may grow rich in Turkey even, if he will be in all respects a good subject of the Turkish government. Confucius said: "If a state is governed by the principles of reason, poverty and misery are subjects of shame; if a state is not governed by the principles of reason, riches and honors are the subjects of shame." No: until I want the protection of Massachusetts to be extended to me in some distant Southern port, where my liberty is endangered, or until I am bent solely on building up an estate at home by peaceful enterprise, I can afford to refuse allegiance to Massachusetts, and her right to my property and life. It costs me less in every

sense to incur the penalty of disobedience to the State than it would to obey. I should feel as if I were worth less in that case.

Some years ago, the State met me in behalf of the Church, and com- 25 manded me to pay a certain sum toward the support of a clergyman whose preaching my father attended, but never I myself. "Pay," it said, "or be locked up in the jail." I declined to pay. But, unfortunately, another man saw fit to pay it. I did not see why the schoolmaster should be taxed to support the priest, and not the priest to the schoolmaster; for I was not the State's schoolmaster, but I supported myself by voluntary subscription. I did not see why the lyceum should not present its tax-bill, and have the State to back its demand, as well as the Church. However, at the request of the selectmen, I condescended to make some such statement as this in writing:—"Know all men by these presents, that I, Henry Thoreau, do not wish to be regarded as a member of any incorporated society which I have not joined." This I gave to the town clerk; and he has it. The State, having thus learned that I did not wish to be regarded as a member of that church, has never made a like demand on me since; though it said that it must adhere to its original presumption that time. If I had known how to name them, I should then have signed off in detail from all the societies which I never signed on to; but I did not know where to find a complete list.

I have paid no poll-tax for six years. I was put into a jail once on 26 this account, for one night; and, as I stood considering the walls of solid stone, two or three feet thick, the door of wood and iron, a foot thick, and the iron grating which strained the light, I could not help being struck with the foolishness of that institution which treated me as if I were mere flesh and blood and bones to be locked up. I wondered that it should have concluded at length that this was the best use it could put me to, and had never thought to avail itself of my services in some way. I saw that, if there was a wall of stone between me and my townsmen, there was a still more difficult one to climb or break through before they could get to be as free as I was. I did not for a moment feel confined, and the walls seemed a great waste of stone and mortar. I felt as if I alone of all my townsmen had paid my tax. They plainly did not know how to treat me, but behaved like persons who are underbred. In every threat and in every compliment there was a blunder; for they thought that my chief desire was to stand the other side of that stone wall. I could not but smile to see how industriously they locked the door on my meditations, which followed them out again without let or hindrance, and *they* were really all that was dangerous. As they could not reach me, they had resolved to punish my body; just as boys, if they cannot come at some person against whom they have a spite, will abuse his dog. I saw that the State was half-witted, that it was timid as a lone woman with her silver spoons, and that it did not know its

muses on the waste of jail

friends from its foes, and I lost all my remaining respect for it, and pitied it.

27   Thus the State never intentionally confronts a man's sense, intellectual or moral, but only his body, his senses. It is not armed with superior wit or honesty, but with superior physical strength. I was not born to be forced. I will breathe after my own fashion. Let us see who is the strongest. What force has a multitude? They only can force me who obey a higher law than I. They force me to become like themselves. I do not hear of *men* being *forced* to live this way or that by masses of men. What sort of life were that to live? When I meet a government which says to me, "Your money or your life," why should I be in haste to give it my money? It may be in a great strait, and not know what to do: I cannot help that. It must help itself; do as I do. It is not worth the while to snivel about it. I am not responsible for the successful working of the machinery of society. I am not the son of the engineer. I perceive that, when an acorn and a chestnut fall side by side, the one does not remain inert to make way for the other, but both obey their own laws, and spring and grow and flourish as best they can, till one, perchance, overshadows and destroys the other. If a plant cannot live according to its nature, it dies; and so a man.

28   The night in prison was novel and interesting enough. The prisoners in their shirt-sleeves were enjoying a chat and the evening air in the doorway, when I entered. But the jailer said, "Come, boys, it is time to lock up"; and so they dispersed, and I heard the sound of their steps returning into the hollow apartments. My room-mate was introduced to me by the jailer as "a first-rate fellow and a clever man." When the door was locked, he showed me where to hang my hat, and how he managed matters there. The rooms were whitewashed once a month; and this one, at least, was the whitest, most simply furnished, and probably the neatest apartment in the town. He naturally wanted to know where I came from, and what brought me there; and, when I had told him, I asked him in my turn how he came there, presuming him to be an honest man, of course; and, as the world goes, I believe he was. "Why," said he, "they accuse me of burning a barn; but I never did it." As near as I could discover he had probably gone to bed in a barn when drunk, and smoked his pipe there; and so a barn was burnt. He had the reputation of being a clever man, had been there some three months waiting for his trial to come on, and would have to wait as much longer; but he was quite domesticated and contented, since he got his board for nothing, and thought that he was well treated.

29   He occupied one window, and I the other; and I saw that if one stayed there long, his principal business would be to look out the window. I had soon read all the tracts that were left there, and examined where former prisoners had broken out, and where a grate had been sawed off, and heard the history of the various occupants of that room;

for I found that even here there was a history and a gossip which never circulated beyond the walls of the jail. Probably this is the only house in the town where verses are composed, which are afterward printed in a circular form, but not published. I was shown quite a long list of verses which were composed by some young men who had been detected in an attempt to escape, who avenged themselves by singing them.

I pumped my fellow-prisoner as dry as I could, for fear I should   30
never see him again; but at length he showed me which was my bed, and left me to blow out the lamp.

It was like travelling into a far country, such as I had never expect-   31
ed to behold, to lie there for one night. It seemed to me that I never had heard the town clock strike before, nor the evening sounds of the village; for we slept with the windows open, which were inside the grating. It was to see my native village in the light of the Middle Ages, and our Concord was turned into a Rhine stream, and visions of knights and castles passed before me. They were the voices of old burghers that I heard in the streets. I was an involuntary spectator and auditor of whatever was done and said in the kitchen of the adjacent village inn— a wholly new and rare experience to me. It was a closer view of my native town. I was fairly inside of it. I never had seen its institutions before. This is one of its peculiar institutions; for it is a shire town. I began to comprehend what its inhabitants were about.

In the morning, our breakfasts were put through the hole in the   32
door, in small oblong-square tin pans, made to fit, and holding a pint of chocolate, with brown bread, and an iron spoon. When they called for the vessels again, I was green enough to return what bread I had left; but my comrade seized it, and said that I should lay that up for lunch or dinner. Soon after he was let out to work at haying in a neighboring field, whither he went every day, and would not be back till noon; so he bade me good-day, saying that he doubted if he should see me again.

When I came out of prison—for some one interfered, and paid that   33
tax—I did not perceive that great changes had taken place on the common, such as he observed who went in a youth and emerged a tottering and gray-headed man; and yet a change had to my eyes come over the scene—the town, and State, and country—greater than any that mere time could effect. I saw yet more distinctly the State in which I lived. I saw to what extent the people among whom I lived could be trusted as good neighbors and friends; that their friendship was for summer weather only; that they did not greatly propose to do right; that they were a distinct race from me by their prejudices and superstitions, as the Chinamen and Malays are; that in their sacrifices to humanity they ran no risks, not even to their property; that after all they were not so noble but they treated the thief as he had treated them, and hoped, by a certain outward observance and a few prayers, and by walking in a particular straight though useless path from time to time, to save their

souls. This may be to judge my neighbors harshly; for I believe that many of them are not aware that they have such an institution as the jail in their village.

34   It was formerly the custom in our village, when a poor debtor came out of jail, for his acquaintances to salute him, looking through their fingers, which were crossed to represent the grating of a jail window, "How do ye do?" My neighbors did not thus salute me, but first looked at me, and then at one another, as if I had returned from a long journey. I was put into jail as I was going to the shoemaker's to get a shoe which was mended. When I was let out the next morning, I preceeded to finish my errand, and, having put on my mended shoe, joined a huckleberry party, who were impatient to put themselves under my conduct; and in half an hour—for the house was soon tackled—was in the midst of a huckleberry field, on one of our highest hills, two miles off, and then the State was nowhere to be seen.

35   This is the whole history of "My Prisons."

36   I have never declined paying the highway tax, because I am as desirous of being a good neighbor as I am of being a bad subject; and as for supporting schools, I am doing my part to educate my fellow-countrymen now. It is for no particular item in the tax-bill that I refuse to pay it. I simply wish to refuse allegiance to the State, to withdraw and stand aloof from it effectually. I do not care to trace the course of my dollar, if I could, till it buys a man or a musket to shoot one with—the dollar is innocent—but I am concerned to trace the effects of my allegiance. In fact, I quietly declare war with the State, after my fashion, though I will still make what use and get what advantage of her I can, as is usual in such cases.

37   If others pay the tax which is demanded of me, from a sympathy with the State, they do but what they have already done in their own case, or rather they abet injustice to a greater extent than the State requires. If they pay the tax from a mistaken interest in the individual taxed, to save his property, to prevent his going to jail, it is because they have not considered wisely how far they let their private feelings interfere with the public good.

38   This, then, is my position at present. But one cannot be too much on his guard in such a case, lest his action be biased by obstinacy or an undue regard for the opinions of men. Let him see that he does only what belongs to himself and to the hour.

39   I think sometimes, Why, this people mean well, they are only ignorant; they would do better if they knew how: why give your neighbors this pain to treat you as they are not inclined to? But I think again, This is no reason why I should do as they do, or permit others to suffer much greater pain of a different kind. Again, I sometimes say to myself, When many millions of men, without heat, without ill will, without personal feeling of any kind, demand of you a few shillings only, with-

out the possibility, such is their constitution, of retracting or altering their present demand, and without the possibility, on your side, of appeal to any other millions, why expose yourself to this overwhelming brute force? You do not resist cold and hunger, the winds and the waves, thus obstinately; you quietly submit to a thousand similar necessities. You do not put your head into the fire. But just in proportion as I regard this as not wholly a brute force, but partly a human force, and consider that I have relations to those millions as to so many millions of men, and not of mere brute or inanimate things, I see that appeal is possible, first and instantaneoulsy, from them to the Maker of them, and secondly, from them to themselves. But if I put my head deliberately into the fire, there is no appeal to fire or to the Maker of fire, and I have only myself to blame. If I could convince myself that I have any right to be satisfied with men as they are, and to treat them accordingly, and not according, in some respects, to my requisitions and expectations of what they and I ought to be, then, like a good Mussulman and fatalist, I should endeavor to be satisfied with things as they are and say it is the will of God. And, above all, there is this difference between resisting this and a purely brute or natural force, that I can resist this with some effect; but I cannot expect, like Orpheus, to change the nature of the rocks and trees and beasts.

I do not wish to quarrel with any man or nation. I do not wish to split hairs, to make fine distinctions, or set myself up as better than my neighbors. I seek rather, I may say, even an excuse for conforming to the laws of the land. I am but too ready to conform to them. Indeed, I have reason to suspect myself on this head; and each year, as the tax-gatherer comes round, I find myself disposed to review the acts and positions of the general and State governments, and the spirit of the people, to discover a pretext for conformity.

> We must affect our country as our parents,
> And if at any time we alienate
> Our love or industry from doing it honor,
> We must respect effects and teach the soul
> Matter of conscience and religion,
> And not desire of rule or benefit.

I believe that the State will soon be able to take all my work of this sort out of my hands, and then I shall be no better a patriot than my fellow-countrymen. Seen from a lower point of view, the Constitution, with all its faults, is very good; the law and the courts are very respectable; even this State and this American government are, in many respects, very admirable, and rare things, to be thankful for, such as a great many have described them; but seen from a point of view a little higher, they are what I have described them; seen from a higher still, and the highest, who shall say what they are, or that they are worth looking at or thinking of at all?

41   However, the government does not concern me much, and I shall bestow the fewest possible thoughts on it. It is not many moments that I live under a government, even in this world. If a man is thought-free, fancy-free, imagination-free, that which *is not* never for a long time appearing *to be* to him, unwise rulers or reformers cannot fatally interrupt him.

42   I know that most men think differently from myself; but those whose lives are by profession devoted to the study of these or kindred subjects content me as little as any. Statesmen and legislators, standing so completely within the institution, never distinctly and nakedly behold it. They speak of moving society, but have no resting-place without it. They may be men of a certain experience and discrimination, and have no doubt invented ingenious and even useful systems, for which we sincerely thank them; but all their wit and usefulness lie within certain not very wide limits. They are wont to forget that the world is not governed by policy and expediency. Webster never goes behind government, and so cannot speak with authority about it. His words are wisdom to those legislators who contemplate no essential reform in the existing government; but for thinkers, and those who legislate for all time, he never once glances at the subject. I know of those whose serene and wise speculations on this theme would soon reveal the limits of his mind's range and hospitality. Yet, compared with the cheap professions of most reformers, and the still cheaper wisdom and eloquence of politicians in general, his are almost the only sensible and valuable words, and we thank Heaven for him. Comparatively, he is always strong, original, and, above all, practical. Still, his quality is not wisdom, but prudence. The lawyer's truth is not Truth, but consistency or a consistent expediency. Truth is always in harmony with herself, and is not concerned chiefly to reveal the justice that may consist with wrong-doing. He well deserves to be called, as he has been called, the Defender of the Constitution. There are really no blows to be given by him but defensive ones. He is not a leader, but a follower. His leaders are the men of '87. "I have never made an effort," he says, "and never propose to make an effort; I have never countenanced an effort and never mean to countenance an effort, to disturb the arrangement as originally made, by which the various States came into the Union." Still thinking of the sanction which the Constitution gives to slavery, he says, "Because it was a part of the original compact—let it stand." Notwithstanding his special acuteness and ability, he is unable to take a fact out of its merely political relations, and behold it as it lies absolutely to be disposed of by the intellect—what, for instance, it behooves a man to do here in America today with regard to slavery—but ventures, or is driven, to make some such desperate answer as the following, while professing to speak absolutely, and as a private man—

from which what new and similar code of social duties might be inferred? "The manner," says he, "in which the governments of those States where slavery exists are to regulate it is for their own consideration, under their responsibility to their constituents, to the general laws of propriety, humanity, and justice, and to God. Associations formed elsewhere, springing from a feeling of humanity, or any other cause, have nothing whatever to do with it. They have never received any encouragement for me, and they never will." [9]

They who know of no purer sources of truth, who have traced up its   43
stream no higher, stand, and wisely stand, by the Bible and the Constitution, and drink at it there with reverence and humility; but they who behold where it comes trickling into this lake or that pool, gird up their loins once more, and continue their pilgrimage toward its fountain-head.

No man with a genius for legislation has appeared in America.   44
They are rare in the history of the world. There are orators, politicians, and eloquent men, by the thousand; but the speaker has not yet opened his mouth to speak who is capable of settling the much-vexed questions of the day. We love eloquence for its own sake, and not for any truth which it may utter, or any heroism it may inspire. Our legislators have not yet learned the comparative value of free trade and of freedom, of union, and of rectitude, to a nation. They have no genius or talent for comparatively humble questions of taxation and finance, commerce and manufactures and agriculture. If we were left solely to the wordy wit of legislators in Congress for our guidance, uncorrected by the seasonable experience and the effectual complaints of the people, America would not long retain her rank among the nations. For eighteen hundred years, though perchance I have no right to say it, the New Testament has been written; yet where is the legislator who has wisdom and practical talent enough to avail himself of the light which it sheds on the science of legislation?

The authority of government, even such as I am willing to submit   45
to—for I will cheerfully obey those who know and can do better than I, and in many things even those who neither know nor can do so well—is still an impure one: to be strictly just, it must have the sanction and consent of the governed. It can have no pure right over my person and property but what I concede to it. The progress from an absolute to a limited monarchy, from a limited monarchy to a democracy, is a progress toward a true respect for the individual. Even the Chinese philosopher was wise enough to regard the individual as the basis of the empire. Is a democracy, such as we know it, the last improvement possible in government? Is it not possible to take a step further towards recognizing and organizing the rights of man? There will never be a really free and enlightened State until the State comes to recognize the

---

[9]These extracts have been inserted since the lecture was read.

individual as a higher and independent power, from which all its own power and authority are derived, and treats him accordingly. I please myself with imagining a State at least which can afford to be just to all men, and to treat the individual with respect as a neighbor; which even would not think it inconsistent with its own repose if a few were to live aloof from it, not meddling with it, nor embraced by it, who fulfilled all the duties of neighbors and fellow-men. A State which bore this kind of fruit, and suffered it to drop off as fast as it ripened, would prepare the way for a still more perfect and glorious State, which also I have imagined, but not yet anywhere seen.

RESPONDING TO READING

1. Thoreau is arguing against two political "evils": a state that endorses slavery and uses war, and rule by majority. What are his arguments against each? To what extent do you agree with his objections?

2. To replace the rule of the state, and its majority, what does Thoreau propose as a guide? What are his arguments for relying upon that guide? What are some possible objections to using such a personal guide against the laws enacted legally? What are his replies to those arguments?

3. What are Thoreau's arguments for refusing to pay taxes to support what he claims to be evil actions? What are his arguments for breaking the law, under certain circumstances? To what degree do you support or oppose these arguments? Explain.

4. Describe Thoreau's attitude toward his night in jail. Notice his view of his cell mate, the jail routines, the effects on him of imprisonment, the moment of release. How does this attitude relate to the purpose of the essay?

5. What does Thoreau mean when he says "any man more right than his neighbors constitutes a majority of one"? Describe an example of someone else who, convinced "they have God on their side," decided to break a law. Was the person you describe "a majority of one" or just a lawbreaker?

6. The most famous sentence in this essay is "Under a government which imprisons any unjustly, the true place for a just man is also a prison." Explain what that means, and consider why that sentence has been so frequently cited in the years since Thoreau wrote. Look up the life of a prominent thinker (such as Mahatma Gandhi or Martin Luther King, Jr.), and describe how this idea has developed. Are there particular circumstances under which this idea is appropriate, or is it generally applicable?

Letter from Birmingham Jail

MARTIN LUTHER KING, JR.

Martin Luther King, Jr. (1929–68) writes as a witness to racial discrimination, in his own life and his own country. He wants his readers to put a stop to it, now and forever. In 1963, King wrote the "Letter from

Birmingham Jail" while imprisoned for "parading without a permit" in a nonviolent civil rights demonstration. Though ostensibly replying to eight clergymen who feared violence in the Birmingham desegregation demonstrations and urged him to wait, King actually intended his letter for the worldwide audience his civil rights activities commanded. Warning that America had more to fear from passive moderates ("the appalling silence of good people") than from extremists, King defended his policy of nonviolent direct action and explained why he was compelled to disobey unjust laws, just as Thoreau did: "We should never forget that everything Adolf Hitler did in Germany was 'legal'," and that it was " 'illegal' to aid and comfort a Jew in Hitler's Germany."

"Letter from Birmingham Jail" reveals why its author was the most influential leader of the American civil rights movement in the 1950s and 1960s. A forceful and charismatic leader, Dr. King was an ordained Baptist clergyman educated at Morehouse College. In 1955, he became a national spokesperson for the civil rights movement when he led a successful boycott of the segregated bus system of Montgomery, Alabama. He then became president of the Southern Christian Leadership Conference and led the sit-ins and demonstrations—including the 1964 march on Washington, D.C., where he gave his famous "I Have a Dream" speech—that helped to ensure passage of the 1964 Civil Rights Act and the Voting Rights Act of 1965. Dr. King received the Nobel Peace Prize in 1964. He was assassinated in 1968, a victim of violence during a nonviolent demonstration, but his legacy lives on.

April 16, 1963

My Dear Fellow Clergymen:

While confined here in the Birmingham city jail, I came across your   1
recent statement calling my present activities "unwise and untimely." Seldom do I pause to answer criticism of my work and ideas. If I sought to answer all the criticisms that cross my desk, my secretaries would have little time for anything other than such correspondence in the course of the day, and I would have no time for constructive work. But since I feel that you are men of genuine good will and that your criticisms are sincerely set forth, I want to try to answer your statement in what I hope will be patient and reasonable terms.[1]

---

[1]AUTHOR'S NOTE: This response to a published statement by eight fellow clergymen from Alabama (Bishop C. C. J. Carpenter, Bishop Joseph A. Durick, Rabbi Hilton L. Grafman, Bishop Paul Hardin, Bishop Holan B. Harmon, the Reverend George M. Murray, the Reverend Edward V. Ramage and the Reverend Earl Stallings) was composed under somewhat constricting circumstances. Begun on the margins of the newspaper in which the statement appeared while I was in jail, the letter was continued on scraps of writing paper supplied by a friendly Negro trusty, and concluded on a pad my attorneys were eventually permitted to leave me. Although the text remains in substance unaltered, I have indulged in the author's prerogative of polishing it for publication.

2   I think I should indicate why I am here in Birmingham, since you have been influenced by the view which argues against "outsiders coming in." I have the honor of serving as president of the Southern Christian Leadership Conference, an organization operating in every southern state, with headquarters in Atlanta, Georgia. We have some eighty-five affiliated organizations across the South, and one of them is the Alabama Christian Movement for Human Rights. Frequently we share staff, educational and financial resources with our affiliates. Several months ago the affiliate here in Birmingham asked us to be on call to engage in a nonviolent direct-action program if such were deemed necessary. We readily consented, and when the hour came we lived up to our promise. So I, along with several members of my staff, am here because I was invited here. I am here because I have organizational ties here.

3   But more basically, I am in Birmingham because injustice is here. Just as the prophets of the eighth century B.C. left their villages and carried their "thus saith the Lord" far beyond the boundaries of their home towns, and, just as the Apostle Paul left his village of Tarsus and carried the gospel of Jesus Christ to the far corners of the Greco-Roman world, so am I compelled to carry the gospel of freedom beyond my own home town. Like Paul, I must constantly respond to the Macedonian call for aid.

4   Moreover, I am cognizant of the interrelatedness of all communities and states. I cannot sit idly by in Atlanta and not be concerned about what happens in Birmingham. Injustice anywhere is a threat to justice everywhere. We are caught in an inescapable network of mutuality, tied in a single garment of destiny. Whatever affects one directly, affects all indirectly. Never again can we afford to live with the narrow, provincial "outside agitator" idea. Anyone who lives inside the United States can never be considered an outsider anywhere within its bounds.

5   You deplore the demonstrations taking place in Birmingham. But your statement, I am sorry to say, fails to express a similar concern for the conditions that brought about the demonstrations. I am sure that none of you would want to rest content with the superficial kind of social analysis that deals merely with effects and does not grapple with underlying causes. It is unfortunate that demonstrations are taking place in Birmingham, but it is even more unfortunate that the city's white power structure left the Negro community with no alternative.

6   In any nonviolent campaign there are four basic steps: collection of the facts to determine whether injustices exist; negotiation; self-purification; and direct action. We have gone through all these steps in Birmingham. There can be no gainsaying the fact that racial injustice engulfs this community. Birmingham is probably the most thoroughly segre-

gated city in the United States. An ugly record of brutality is widely known. Negroes have experienced grossly unjust treatment in the courts. There have been more unsolved bombings of Negro homes and churches in Birmingham than in any other city in the nation. These are the hard brutal facts of the case. On the basis of these conditions, Negro leaders sought to negotiate with the city fathers. But the latter consistently refused to engage in good-faith negotiation.

Then, last September, came the opportunity to talk with leaders of   7
Birmingham's economic community. In the course of the negotiations, certain promises were made by the merchants—for example, to remove the stores' humiliating racial signs. On the basis of these promises, the Reverend Fred Shuttlesworth and the leaders of the Alabama Christian Movement for Human Rights agreed to a moratorium on all demonstrations. As the weeks and months went by, we realized that we were the victims of a broken promise. A few signs, briefly removed, returned; the others remained.

As in so many past experiences, our hopes had been blasted, and   8
the shadow of deep disappointment settled upon us. We had no alternative except to prepare for direct action, whereby we would present our very bodies as a means of laying our case before the conscience of the local and the national community. Mindful of the difficulties involved, we decided to undertake a process of self-purification. We began a series of workshops on nonviolence, and we repeatedly asked ourselves: "Are you able to accept blows without retaliating?" "Are you able to endure the ordeal of jail?" We decided to schedule our direct-action program for the Easter season, realizing that except for Christmas, this is the main shopping period of the year. Knowing that a strong economic-withdrawal program would be the by-product of direct action, we felt that this would be the best time to bring pressure to bear on the merchants for the needed change.

Then it occurred to us that Birmingham's mayoralty election was   9
coming up in March, and we speedily decided to postpone action until after election day. When we discovered that the Commissioner of Public Safety, Eugene "Bull" Connor, had piled up enough votes to be in the run-off, we decided again to postpone action until the day after the run-off so that the demonstrations could not be used to cloud the issues. Like many others, we waited to see Mr. Connor defeated, and to this end we endured postponement after postponement. Having aided in this community need, we felt that our direct-action program could be delayed no longer.

You may well ask "Why direct action? Why sit-ins, marches and so   10
forth? Isn't negotiation a better path?" You are quite right in calling for negotiation. Indeed, this is the very purpose of direct action. Nonviolent direct action seeks to create such a crisis and foster such a tension

that a community which has constantly refused to negotiate is forced to confront the issue. It seeks so to dramatize the issue that it can no longer be ignored. My citing the creation of tension as part of the work of the nonviolent-resister may sound rather shocking. But I must confess that I am not afraid of the word "tension." I have earnestly opposed violent tension, but there is a type of constructive nonviolent tension which is necessary for growth. Just as Socrates felt that it was necessary to create a tension in the mind so that individuals could rise from the bondage of myths and half-truths to the unfettered realm of creative analysis and objective appraisal, so must we see the need for nonviolent gadflies to create the kind of tension in society that will help men rise from the dark depths of prejudice and racism to the majestic heights of understanding and brotherhood.

11   The purpose of our direct-action program is to create a situation so crisis-packed that it will inevitably open the door to negotiation. I therefore concur with you in your call for negotiation. Too long has our beloved Southland been bogged down in a tragic effort to live in monologue rather than dialogue.

12   One of the basic points in your statement is that the action that I and my associates have taken in Birmingham is untimely. Some have asked: "Why didn't you give the new city administration time to act?" The only answer that I can give to this query is that the new Birmingham administration must be prodded about as much as the outgoing one, before it will act. We are sadly mistaken if we feel that the election of Albert Boutwell as mayor will bring the millennium to Birmingham. While Mr. Boutwell is a much more gentle person than Mr. Connor, they are both segregationists, dedicated to maintenance of the status quo. I have hope that Mr. Boutwell will be reasonable enough to see the futility of massive resistance to desegregation. But he will not see this without pressure from devotees of civil rights. My friends, I must say to you that we have not made a single gain in civil rights without determined legal and nonviolent pressure. Lamentably, it is an historical fact that privileged groups seldom give up their privileges voluntarily. Individuals may see the moral light and voluntarily give up their unjust posture; but, as Reinhold Niebuhr has reminded us, groups tend to be more immoral than individuals.

13   We know through painful experience that freedom is never voluntarily given by the oppressor; it must be demanded by the oppressed. Frankly, I have yet to engage in a direct-action campaign that was "well-timed" in the view of those who have not suffered unduly from the disease of segregation. For years now I have heard the word "Wait!" It rings in the ear of every Negro with piercing familiarity. This "Wait" has almost always meant "Never." We must

come to see, with one of our distinguished jurists, that "justice too long delayed is justice denied."

We have waited for more than 340 years for our constitutional and   14
Godgiven rights. The nations of Asia and Africa are moving with jetlike speed toward gaining political independence, but we still creep at horse-and-buggy pace toward gaining a cup of coffee at a lunch counter. Perhaps it is easy for those who have never felt the stinging darts of segregation to say, "Wait." But when you have seen vicious mobs lynch your mothers and fathers at will and drown your sisters and brothers at whim; when you have seen hate-filled policemen curse, kick and even kill your black brothers and sisters; when you see the vast majority of your twenty million Negro brothers smothering in an airtight cage of poverty in the midst of an affluent society; when you suddenly find your tongue twisted and your speech stammering as you seek to explain to your six-year-old daughter why she can't go to the public amusement park that has just been advertised on television, and see tears welling up in her eyes when she is told that Funtown is closed to colored children, and see ominous clouds of inferiority beginning to form in her little mental sky, and see her beginning to distort her personality by developing an unconscious bitterness toward white people; when you have to concoct an answer for a five-year-old son who is asking: "Daddy, why do white people treat colored people so mean?"; when you take a cross-country drive and find it necessary to sleep night after night in the uncomfortable corners of your automobile because no motel will accept you; when you are humiliated day in and day out by nagging signs reading "white" and "colored"; when your first name becomes "nigger," your middle name becomes "boy" (however old you are) and your last name becomes "John," and your wife and mother are never given the respected title "Mrs."; when you are harried by day and haunted by night by the fact that you are a Negro, living constantly at tiptoe stance, never quite knowing what to expect next, and are plagued with inner fears and outer resentments; when you are forever fighting a degenerating sense of "nobodiness"—then you will understand why we find it difficult to wait. There comes a time when the cup of endurance runs over, and men are no longer willing to be plunged into the abyss of despair. I hope, sirs, you can understand our legitimate and unavoidable impatience.

You express a great deal of anxiety over our willingness to break   15
laws. This is certainly a legitimate concern. Since we so diligently urge people to obey the Supreme Court's decision of 1954 outlawing segregation in the public schools, at first glance it may seem rather paradoxical for us consciously to break laws. One may well ask: "How can you advocate breaking some laws and obeying others?" The answer lies in

the fact that there are two types of laws: just and unjust. I would be the first to advocate obeying just laws. One has not only a legal but a moral responsibility to obey just laws. Conversely, one has a moral responsibility to disobey unjust laws. I would agree with St. Augustine that "an unjust law is no law at all."

16   Now, what is the difference between the two? How does one determine whether a law is just or unjust? A just law is a man-made code that squares with the moral law or the law of God. An unjust law is a code that is out of harmony with the moral law. To put it in the terms of St. Thomas Aquinas: An unjust law is a human law that is not rooted in eternal law and natural law. Any law that uplifts human personality is just. Any law that degrades human personality is unjust. All segregation statutes are unjust because segregation distorts the soul and damages the personality. It gives the segregator a false sense of superiority and the segregated a false sense of inferiority. Segregation, to use the terminology of the Jewish philosopher Martin Buber, substitutes an "I-it" relationship for an "I-thou" relationship and ends up relegating persons to the status of things. Hence segregation is not only politically, economically and sociologically unsound, it is morally wrong and sinful. Paul Tillich has said that sin is separation. Is not segregation an existential expression of man's tragic separation, his awful estrangement, his terrible sinfulness? Thus it is that I can urge men to obey the 1954 decision of the Supreme Court, for it is morally right; and I can urge them to disobey segregation ordinances, for they are morally wrong.

17   Let us consider a more concrete example of just and unjust laws. An unjust law is a code that a numerical or power majority group compels a minority group to obey but does not make binding on itself. This is *difference* made legal. By the same token, a just law is a code that a majority compels a minority to follow and that it is willing to follow itself. This is *sameness* made legal.

18   Let me give another explanation. A law is unjust if it is inflicted on a minority that, as a result of being denied the right to vote, had no part in enacting or devising the law. Who can say that the legislature of Alabama which set up that state's segregation laws was democratically elected? Throughout Alabama all sorts of devious methods are used to prevent Negroes from becoming registered voters, and there are some counties in which even though Negroes constitute a majority of the population, not a single Negro is registered. Can any law enacted under such circumstances be considered democratically structured?

19   Sometimes a law is just on its face and unjust in its application. For instance, I have been arrested on a charge of parading without a permit. Now, there is nothing wrong in having an ordinance which requires a permit for a parade. But such an ordinance becomes unjust

when it is used to maintain segregation and to deny citizens the First-Amendment privilege of peaceful assembly and protest.

I hope you are able to see the distinction I am trying to point out. In 20
no sense do I advocate evading or defying the law, as would the rabid segregationist. That would lead to anarchy. One who breaks an unjust law must do so openly, lovingly, and with a willingness to accept the penalty. I submit that an individual who breaks a law that conscience tells him is unjust, and who willingly accepts the penalty of imprisonment in order to arouse the conscience of the community over its injustice, is in reality expressing the highest respect for law.

Of course, there is nothing new about this kind of civil disobedi- 21
ence. It was evidenced sublimely in the refusal of Shadrach, Meshach and Abednego to obey the laws of Nebuchadnezzar, on the ground that a higher moral law was at stake. It was practiced superbly by the early Christians, who were willing to face hungry lions and the excruciating pain of chopping blocks rather than submit to certain unjust laws of the Roman Empire. To a degree, academic freedom is a reality today because Socrates practiced civil disobedience. In our own nation, the Boston Tea Party represented a massive act of civil disobedience.

We should never forget that everything Adolf Hitler did in Ger- 22
many was "legal" and everything the Hungarian freedom fighters did in Hungary was "illegal." It was "illegal" to aid and comfort a Jew in Hitler's Germany. Even so, I am sure that, had I lived in Germany at the time, I would have aided and comforted my Jewish brothers. If today I lived in a Communist country where certain principles dear to the Christian faith are suppressed, I would openly advocate disobeying that country's anti-religious laws.

I must make two honest confessions to you, my Christian and Jew- 23
ish brothers. First, I must confess that over the past few years I have been gravely disappointed with the white moderate. I have almost reached the regrettable conclusion that the Negro's great stumbling block in his stride toward freedom is not the White Citizen's Counciler or the Ku Klux Klanner, but the white moderate, who is more devoted to "order" than to justice; who prefers a negative peace which is the absence of tension to a positive peace which is the presence of justice; who constantly says: "I agree with you in the goal you seek, but I cannot agree with your methods of direct action"; who paternalistically believes he can set the timetable for another man's freedom; who lives by a mythical concept of time and who constantly advises the Negro to wait for a "more convenient season." Shallow understanding from people of good will is more frustrating than absolute misunderstanding from people of ill will. Lukewarm acceptance is much more bewildering than outright rejection.

24   I had hoped that the white moderate would understand that law and order exist for the purpose of establishing justice and that when they fail in this purpose they become the dangerously structured dams that block the flow of social progress. I had hoped that the white moderate would understand that the present tension in the South is a necessary phase of the transition from an obnoxious negative peace, in which the Negro passively accepted his unjust plight, to a substantive and positive peace, in which all men will respect the dignity and worth of human personality. Actually, we who engage in nonviolent direct action are not the creators of tension. We merely bring to the surface the hidden tension that is already alive. We bring it out in the open, where it can be seen and dealt with. Like a boil that can never be cured so long as it is covered up but must be opened with all its ugliness to the natural medicines of air and light, injustice must be exposed, with all the tension its exposure creates, to the light of human conscience and the air of national opinion before it can be cured.

25   In your statement you assert that our actions, even though peaceful, must be condemned because they precipitate violence. But is this a logical assertion? Isn't this like condemning a robbed man because his possession of money precipitated the evil act of robbery? Isn't this like condemning Socrates because his unswerving commitment to truth and his philosophical inquiries precipitated the act by the misguided populace in which they made him drink hemlock? Isn't this like condemning Jesus because his unique God-consciousness and never-ceasing devotion to God's will precipitated the evil act of crucifixion? We must come to see that, as the federal courts have consistently affirmed, it is wrong to urge an individual to cease his efforts to gain his basic constitutional rights because the quest may precipitate violence. Society must protect the robbed and punish the robber.

26   I had also hoped that the white moderate would reject the myth concerning time in relation to the struggle for freedom. I have just received a letter from a white brother in Texas. He writes: "All Christians know that the colored people will receive equal rights eventually, but it is possible that you are in too great a religious hurry. It has taken Christianity almost two thousand years to accomplish what it has. The teachings of Christ take time to come to earth." Such an attitude stems from a tragic misconception of time, from the strangely irrational notion that there is something in the very flow of time that will inevitably cure all ills. Actually, time itself is neutral; it can be used either destructively or constructively. More and more I feel that the people of ill will have used time much more effectively than have the people of good will. We will have to repent in this generation not merely for the hateful words and actions of the bad people but for the appalling silence of the good people. Human progress never rolls in on wheels of in-

evitability; it comes through the tireless efforts of men willing to be coworkers with God, and without this hard work, time itself becomes an ally of the forces of social stagnation. We must use time creatively, in the knowledge that the time is always ripe to do right. Now is the time to make real the promise of democracy and transform our pending national elegy into a creative psalm of brotherhood. Now is the time to lift our national policy from the quicksand of racial injustice to the solid rock of human dignity.

You speak of our activity in Birmingham as extreme. At first I was   27 rather disappointed that fellow clergymen would see my nonviolent efforts as those of an extremist. I began thinking about the fact that I stand in the middle of two opposing forces in the Negro community. One is a force of complacency, made up in part of Negroes who, as a result of long years of oppression, are so drained of self-respect and a sense of "somebodiness" that they have adjusted to segregation; and in part of a few middle-class Negroes who, because of a degree of academic and economic security and because in some ways they profit by segregation, have become insensitive to the problems of the masses. The other force is one of bitterness and hatred, and it comes perilously close to advocating violence. It is expressed in the various black nationalist groups that are springing up across the nation, the largest and best-known being Elijah Muhammad's Muslim movement. Nourished by the Negro's frustration over the continued existence of racial discrimination, this movement is made up of people who have lost faith in America, who have absolutely repudiated Christianity, and who have concluded that the white man is an incorrigible "devil."

I have tried to stand between these two forces, saying that we need   28 emulate neither the "do-nothingism" of the complacent nor the hatred and despair of the black nationalist. For there is the more excellent way of love and nonviolent protest. I am grateful to God that, through the influence of the Negro church, the way of nonviolence became an integral part of our struggle.

If this philosophy had not emerged, by now many streets of the   29 South would, I am convinced, be flowing with blood. And I am further convinced that if our white brothers dismiss as "rabble-rousers" and "outside agitators" those of us who employ nonviolent direct action, and if they refuse to support our nonviolent efforts, millions of Negroes will, out of frustration and despair, seek solace and security in black-nationalist ideologies—a development that would inevitably lead to a frightening racial nightmare.

Oppressed people cannot remain oppressed forever. The yearning   30 for freedom eventually manifests itself, and that is what has happened to the American Negro. Something within has reminded him of his birthright of freedom, and something without has reminded him that it can be gained. Consciously or unconsciously, he has been caught up by the *Zeitgeist*, and with his black brothers of Africa and his brown and yellow brothers of Asia, South America and the Caribbean, the United States Negro is moving with a sense of great urgency toward the promised land of racial justice. If one recognizes this vital urge that has engulfed the Negro community, one should readily understand why public demonstrations are taking place. The Negro has many pent-up resentments and latent frustrations, and he must release them. So let him march; let him make prayer pilgrimages to the city hall; let him go on freedom rides—and try to understand why he must do so. If his re-pressed emotions are not released in nonviolent ways, they will seek expression through violence; this is not a threat but a fact of history. So I have not said to my people: "Get rid of your discontent." Rather, I have tried to say that this normal and healthy discontent can be chan-neled into the creative outlet of nonviolent direct action. And now this approach is being termed extremist.

31   But though I was initially disappointed at being categorized as an extremist, as I continued to think about the matter I gradually gained a measure of satisfaction from the label. Was not Jesus an extremist for love: "Love your enemies, bless them that curse you, do good to them that hate you, and pray for them which despitefully use you, and perse-cute you." Was not Amos an extremist for justice: "Let justice roll down like waters and righteousness like an ever-flowing stream." Was not Paul an extremist for the Christian gospel: "I bear in my body the marks of the Lord Jesus." Was not Martin Luther an extremist: "Here I stand; I cannot do otherwise, so help me God." And John Bunyan: "I will stay in jail to the end of my days before I make a butchery of my conscience." And Abraham Lincoln: "This nation cannot survive half slave and half free." And Thomas Jefferson: "We hold these truths to be self-evident, that all men are created equal. . . ." So the question is not whether we will be extremists, but what kind of extremists we will be. Will we be ex-tremists for hate or for love? Will we be extremists for the preservation of injustice or for the extension of justice? In that dramatic scene on Cal-vary's hill three men were crucified. We must never forget that all three were crucified for the same crime—the crime of extremism. Two were extremists for immorality, and thus fell below their environment. The other, Jesus Christ, was an extremist for love, truth and goodness, and thereby rose above his environment. Perhaps the South, the nation and the world are in dire need of creative extremists.

32   I had hoped that the white moderate would see this need. Perhaps I was too optimistic; perhaps I expected too much. I suppose I should have realized that few members of the oppressor race can understand the deep groans and passionate yearnings of the oppressed race, and still fewer have the vision to see that injustice must be rooted out

by strong, persistent and determined action. I am thankful, however, that some of our white brothers in the South have grasped the meaning of this social revolution and committed themselves to it. They are still all too few in quantity, but they are big in quality. Some—such as Ralph McGill, Lillian Smith, Harry Golden, James McBride Dabbs, Ann Braden and Sarah Patton Boyle—have written about our struggle in eloquent and prophetic terms. Others have marched with us down nameless streets of the South. They have languished in filthy, roach-infested jails, suffering the abuse and brutality of policemen who view them as "dirty nigger-lovers." Unlike so many of their moderate brothers and sisters, they have recognized the urgency of the moment and sensed the need for powerful "action" antidotes to combat the disease of segregation.

Let me take note of my other major disappointment. I have been so   33
greatly disappointed with the white church and its leadership. Of course, there are some notable exceptions. I am not unmindful of the fact that each of you has taken some significant stands on this issue. I commend you, Reverend Stallings, for your Christian stand on this past Sunday, in welcoming Negroes to your worship service on a non-segregated basis. I commend the Catholic leaders of this state for integrating Spring Hill College several years ago.

But despite these notable exceptions, I must honestly reiterate that   34
I have been disappointed with the church. I do not say this as one of those negative critics who can always find something wrong with the church. I say this as a minister of the gospel, who loves the church; who was nurtured in its bosom; who has been sustained by its spiritual blessings and who will remain true to it as long as the cord of life shall lengthen.

When I was suddenly catapulted into the leadership of the bus   35
protest in Montgomery, Alabama, a few years ago, I felt we would be supported by the white church. I felt that the white ministers, priests and rabbis of the South would be among our strongest allies. Instead, some have been outright opponents, refusing to understand the freedom movement and misrepresenting its leaders; all too many others have been more cautious than courageous and have remained silent behind the anesthetizing security of stained-glass windows.

In spite of my shattered dreams, I came to Birmingham with the   36
hope that the white religious leadership of this community would see the justice of our cause and, with deep moral concern, would serve as the channel through which our just grievances could reach the power structure. I had hoped that each of you would understand. But again I have been disappointed.

I have heard numerous southern religious leaders admonish their   37
worshipers to comply with a desegregation decision because it is the

law, but I have longed to hear white ministers declare: "Follow this decree because integration is morally right and because the Negro is your brother." In the midst of blatant injustices inflicted upon the Negro, I have watched white churchmen stand on the sideline and mouth pious irrelevancies and sanctimonious trivialities. In the midst of a mighty struggle to rid our nation of racial and economic injustice, I have heard many ministers say: "Those are social issues, with which the gospel has no real concern." And I have watched many churches commit themselves to a completely other-worldly religion which makes a strange, un-Biblical distinction between body and soul, between the sacred and the secular.

38   I have traveled the length and breadth of Alabama, Mississippi and all the other southern states. On sweltering summer days and crisp autumn mornings I have looked at the South's beautiful churches with their lofty spires pointing heavenward. I have beheld the impressive outlines of her massive religious-education buildings. Over and over I have found myself asking: "What kind of people worship here? Who is their God? Where were their voices when the lips of Governor Barnett dripped with words of interposition and nullification? Where were they when Governor Wallace gave a clarion call for defiance and hatred? Where were their voices of support when bruised and weary Negro men and women decided to rise from the dark dungeons of complacency to the bright hills of creative protest?"

39   Yes, these questions are still in my mind. In deep disappointment I have wept over the laxity of the church. But be assured that my tears have been tears of love. There can be no deep disappointment where there is not deep love. Yes, I love the church. How could I do otherwise? I am in the rather unique position of being the son, the grandson and the great-grandson of preachers. Yes, I see the church as the body of Christ. But, oh! How we have blemished and scarred that body through social neglect and through fear of being nonconformists.

40   There was a time when the church was very powerful—in the time when the early Christians rejoiced at being deemed worthy to suffer for what they believed. In those days the church was not merely a thermometer that recorded the ideas and principles of popular opinion; it was a thermostat that transformed the mores of society. Whenever the early Christians entered a town, the people in power became disturbed and immediately sought to convict the Christians for being "disturbers of the peace" and "outside agitators." But the Christians pressed on, in the conviction that they were "a colony of heaven," called to obey God rather than man. Small in number, they were big in commitment. They were too God-intoxicated to be "astronomically intimidated." By their effort and example they brought an end to such ancient evils as infanticide and gladiatorial contests.

Things are different now. So often the contemporary church is a   41
weak, ineffectual voice with an uncertain sound. So often it is an
archdefender of the status quo. Far from being disturbed by the presence of the church, the power structure of the average community is
consoled by the church's silent—and often even vocal—sanction of
things as they are.

But the judgment of God is upon the church as never before. If   42
today's church does not recapture the sacrificial spirit of the early
church, it will lose its authenticity, forfeit the loyalty of millions, and be
dismissed as an irrelevant social club with no meaning for the twentieth century. Every day I meet young people whose disappointment
with the church has turned into outright disgust.

Perhaps I have once again been too optimistic. Is organized reli-   43
gion too inextricably bound to the status quo to save our nation and the
world? Perhaps I must turn my faith to the inner spiritual church, the
church within the church, as the true *ekklesia* and the hope of the world.
But again I am thankful to God that some noble souls from the ranks of
organized religion have broken loose from the paralyzing chains of
conformity and joined us as active partners in the struggle for freedom.
They have left their secure congregations and walked the streets of Albany, Georgia, with us. They have gone down the highways of the
South on tortuous rides for freedom. Yes, they have gone to jail with us.
Some have been dismissed from their churches, have lost the support
of their bishops and fellow ministers. But they have acted in the faith
that right defeated is stronger than evil triumphant. Their witness has
been the spiritual salt that has preserved the true meaning of the gospel
in these troubled times. They have carved a tunnel of hope through the
dark mountain of disappointment.

I hope the church as a whole will meet the challenge of this deci-   44
sive hour. But even if the church does not come to the aid of justice, I
have no despair about the future. I have no fear about the outcome of
our struggle in Birmingham, even if our motives are at present misunderstood. We will reach the goal of freedom in Birmingham and all
over the nation, because the goal of America is freedom. Abused and
scorned though we may be, our destiny is tied up with America's destiny. Before the pilgrims landed at Plymouth, we were here. Before
the pen of Jefferson etched the majestic words of the Declaration of
Independence across the pages of history, we were here. For more
than two centuries our forebears labored in this country without
wages; they made cotton king; they built the homes of their masters
while suffering gross injustice and shameful humiliation—and yet
out of a bottomless vitality they continued to thrive and develop. If
the inexpressible cruelties of slavery could not stop us, the opposition
we now face will surely fail. We will win our freedom because the

sacred heritage of our nation and the eternal will of God are embodied in our echoing demands.

45   Before closing I feel impelled to mention one other point in your statement that has troubled me profoundly. You warmly commended the Birmingham police force for keeping "order" and "preventing violence." I doubt that you would have so warmly commended the police force if you had seen its dogs sinking their teeth into unarmed, nonviolent Negroes. I doubt that you would so quickly commend the policemen if you were to observe their ugly and inhumane treatment of Negroes here in the city jail; if you were to watch them push and curse old Negro women and young Negro girls; if you were to see them slap and kick old Negro men and young boys; if you were to observe them as they did on two occasions, refuse to give us food because we wanted to sing our grace together. I cannot join you in your praise of the Birmingham police department.

46   It is true that the police have exercised a degree of discipline in handling the demonstrators. In this sense they have conducted themselves rather "nonviolently" in public. But for what purpose? To preserve the evil system of segregation. Over the past few years I have consistently preached that nonviolence demands that the means we use must be as pure as the ends we seek. I have tried to make clear that it is wrong to use immoral means to attain moral ends. But now I must affirm that it is just as wrong, or perhaps even more so, to use moral means to preserve immoral ends. Perhaps Mr. Connor and his policemen have been rather nonviolent in public, as was Chief Pritchett in Albany, Georgia, but they have used the moral means of nonviolence to maintain the immoral end of racial injustice. As T. S. Eliot has said: "The last temptation is the greatest treason: To do the right deed for the wrong reason."

47   I wish you had commended the Negro sit-inners and demonstrators of Birmingham for their sublime courage, their willingness to suffer and their amazing discipline in the midst of great provocation. One day the South will recognize its real heroes. They will be the James Merediths, with the noble sense of purpose that enables them to face jeering and hostile mobs, and with the agonizing loneliness that characterizes the life of the pioneer. They will be old, oppressed, battered Negro women, symbolized in a seventy-two-year-old woman in Montgomery, Alabama, who rose up with a sense of dignity and with her people decided not to ride segregated buses, and who responded with ungrammatical profundity to one who inquired about her weariness: "My feet is tired, but my soul is at rest." They will be the young high school and college students, the young ministers of the gospel and a host of their elders, courageously and nonviolently sitting in at lunch counters and willingly going to jail for conscience' sake. One

day the South will know that when these disinherited children of God sat down at lunch counters, they were in reality standing up for what is best in the American dream and for the most sacred values in our Judaeo-Christian heritage, thereby bringing our nation back to those great wells of democracy which were dug deep by the founding fathers in their formulation of the Constitution and the Declaration of Independence.

48 Never before have I written so long a letter. I'm afraid it is much too long to take your precious time. I can assure you that it would have been much shorter if I had been writing from a comfortable desk, but what else can one do when he is alone in a narrow jail cell, other than write long letters, think long thoughts and pray long prayers?

49 If I have said anything in this letter that overstates the truth and indicates an unreasonable impatience, I beg you to forgive me. If I have said anything that understates the truth and indicates my having a patience that allows me to settle for anything less than brotherhood, I beg God to forgive me.

50 I hope this letter finds you strong in the faith. I also hope that circumstances will soon make it possible for me to meet each of you, not as an integrationist or a civil-rights leader but as a fellow clergyman and a Christian brother. Let us all hope that the dark clouds of racial prejudice will soon pass away and the deep fog of misunderstanding will be lifted from our feardrenched communities, and in some not too distant tomorrow the radiant stars of love and brotherhood will shine over our great nation with all their scintillating beauty.

Yours for the cause of Peace and Brotherhood,
Martin Luther King, Jr.

RESPONDING TO READING

1. Definitions are crucial to Martin Luther King, Jr.'s argument. Explain the distinctions he makes between moral law and civil law, just and unjust law. [*see* paragraphs 16–17.]

2. King grounds his argument in a long religious tradition. Why is it appropriate and necessary for him to do this? Why does he cite the theologians Aquinas (a Catholic), Buber (a Jew), and Tillich (a Protestant) (paragraph 16)?

3. In what ways is this tradition relevant to the Civil Rights movement, particularly as manifested in civil disobedience? See, for instance, King's response to the argument that civil rights activists should go slow because "It has taken Christianity almost two thousand years to accomplish what it has'" [paragraph 26].

4. King's ostensible audience is the eight Alabama clergy to whom his "Letter from Birmingham Jail" is addressed. What evidence for this do you find, besides the salutation? However, his real audience is far more extensive.

Of whom is it composed? How can you tell? Do you see yourself as part of the intended audience? Why, or why not?

5. On what grounds, under what circumstances would you be willing to go to jail? If the possibility of a prison record affected your opportunities for employment in some states (such as practicing medicine or law), would that deter you? Ultimately, what risks are you willing to take for a cause, and what price are you willing to pay?

Civil Disobedience: Destroyer of Democracy

LEWIS H. VAN DUSEN, JR.

"Civil Disobedience: Destroyer of Democracy" was originally published in the *American Bar Association Journal* in 1969, shortly after the Vietnam War protests and their accompanying civil disobedience disrupted the 1968 Democratic Convention in Chicago. Lewis H. Van Dusen, Jr., takes a predictable stance for a representative of the legal profession. He distinguishes "the conscientious law breaking of Socrates, Gandhi and Thoreau" from "the conscientious law testing" of Martin Luther King, Jr., who he claims "was not a civil disobedient." True civil disobedients, Van Dusen says, break the laws (such as by witholding taxes or violating state laws) knowing they are legally wrong, but believing they are morally right. In contrast, Dr. King's form of protest encourages the violation of one law in expectation of support from a higher jurisdictional body. Thus, Dr. King encouraged civil rights protesters to violate state laws in order to challenge the Supreme Law of the Land, and unlike true civil disobedients, he did not expect to pay a penalty. Although Van Dusen is writing for lawyers, instead of being full of the predictable legal jargon, case references, and technical legal arguments, his essay is nontechnical, an argument addressed more to general readers.

Van Dusen, born in 1910, is a graduate of Princeton and Oxford, where he was a Rhodes Scholar and earned a law degree in 1935. A lawyer in Philadelphia, he has been president and chancellor of the Philadelphia Bar Association. In the American Bar Association, he chaired the Committee on Ethics and Professional Responsibility, and served on the Committee on the Federal Judiciary.

1   As Charles E. Wyzanski, Chief Judge of the United States District Court in Boston, wrote in the February, 1968, *Atlantic* [*Monthly*]: "Disobedience is a long step from dissent. Civil disobedience involves a deliberate and punishable breach of legal duty." Protesters might prefer a different definition. They would rather say that civil disobedience is the peaceable resistance of conscience.

The philosophy of civil disobedience was not developed in our   2
American democracy, but in the very first democracy of Athens. It was
expressed by the poet Sophocles and the philosopher Socrates. In
Sophocles's tragedy, Antigone chose to obey her conscience and violate
the state edict against providing burial for her brother, who had been
decreed a traitor. When the dictator Creon found out that Antigone had
buried her fallen brother, he confronted her and reminded her that
there was a mandatory death penalty for this deliberate disobedience
of the state law. Antigone nobly replied, "Nor did I think your orders
were so strong that you, a mortal man, could overrun the gods' unwrit-
ten and unfailing laws."

Conscience motivated Antigone. She was not testing the validity   3
of the law in the hope that eventually she would be sustained. Appealing to the judgment of the community, she explained her action
to the chorus. She was not secret and surreptitious—the interment of
her brother was open and public. She was not violent; she did not
trespass on another citizen's rights. And finally, she accepted without
resistance the death sentence—the penalty for violation. By voluntarily accepting the law's sanctions, she was not a revolutionary denying
the authority of the state. Antigone's behavior exemplifies the classic
case of civil disobedience.

Socrates believed that reason could dictate a conscientious disobe-   4
dience of state law, but he also believed that he had to accept the legal
sanctions of the state. In Plato's *Crito*, Socrates from his hanging basket
accepted the death penalty for his teaching of religion to youths contrary to state laws.

The sage of Walden, Henry David Thoreau, took this philosophy of   5
nonviolence and developed it into a strategy for solving society's injustices. First enunciating it in protest against the Mexican War, he then
turned it to use against slavery. For refusing to pay taxes that would
help pay the enforcers of the fugitive slave law, he went to prison. In
Thoreau's words, "If the alternative is to keep all just men in prison or
to give up slavery, the state will not hesitate which to choose."

Sixty years later, Gandhi took Thoreau's civil disobedience as his   6
strategy to wrest Indian independence from England. The famous
salt march against a British imperial tax is his best-known example
of protest.

But the conscientious law breaking of Socrates, Gandhi and Thoreau   7
is to be distinguished from the conscientious law testing of Martin
Luther King, Jr., who was not a civil disobedient. The civil disobedient
withholds taxes or violates state laws knowing he is legally wrong, but
believing he is morally right. While he wrapped himself in the mantle
of Gandhi and Thoreau, Dr. King led his followers in violation of
state laws he believed were contrary to the Federal Constitution. But

since Supreme Court decisions in the end generally upheld his many actions, he should not be considered a true civil disobedient.

8   The civil disobedience of Antigone is like that of the pacifist who withholds paying the percentage of his taxes that goes to the Defense Department, or the Quaker who travels against State Department regulations to Hanoi to distribute medical supplies, or the Vietnam war protester who tears up his draft card. This civil disobedient has been nonviolent in his defiance of the law; he has been unfurtive in his violation; he has been submissive to the penalties of the law. He has neither evaded the law nor interfered with another's rights. He has been neither a rioter nor a revolutionary. The thrust of his cause has not been the might of coercion but the martyrdom of conscience.

Was the Boston Tea Party Civil Disobedience?

9   Those who justify violence and radical action as being in the tradition of our Revolution show a misunderstanding of the philosophy of democracy.

10   James Farmer, former head of the Congress of Racial Equality, in defense of the mass action confrontation method, has told of a famous organized demonstration that took place in opposition to political and economic discrimination. The protesters beat back and scattered the law enforcers and then proceeded to loot and destroy private property. Mr. Farmer then said he was talking about the Boston Tea Party and implied that violence as a method for redress of grievances was an American tradition and a legacy of our revolutionary heritage. While it is true that there is no more sacred document than our Declaration of Independence, Jefferson's "inherent right of rebellion" was predicated on the tyrannical denial of democratic means. If there is no popular assembly to provide an adjustment of ills, and if there is no court system to dispose of injustices, then there is, indeed, a right to rebel.

11   The seventeenth century's John Locke, the philosophical father of the Declaration of Independence, wrote in his *Second Treatise on Civil Government*: "Wherever law ends, tyranny begins . . . and the people are absolved from any further obedience. Governments are dissolved from within when the legislative [chamber] is altered. When the government [becomes] . . . arbitrary disposers of lives, liberties and fortunes of the people, such revolutions happen . . .[.]"

12   But there are some sophisticated proponents of the revolutionary redress of grievances who say that the test of the need for radical action is not the unavailability of democratic institutions but the ineffectuality of those institutions to remove blatant social inequalities. If social injustice exists, they say, concerted disobedience is required

against the constituted government, whether it be totalitarian or democratic in structure.

Of course, only the most bigoted chauvinist would claim that   13
America is without some glaring faults. But there has never been a
utopian society on earth and there never will be unless human nature
is remade. Since inequities will mar even the best-framed democracies, the injustice rationale would allow a free right of civil resistance
to be available always as a shortcut alternative to the democratic way
of petition, debate and assembly. The lesson of history is that civil insurgency spawns far more injustices than it removes. The Jeffersons,
Washingtons and Adamses resisted tyranny with the aim of promoting the procedures of democracy. They would never have resisted a
democratic government with the risk of promoting the techniques of
tyranny.

Legitimate Pressures and Illegitimate Results

There are many civil rights leaders who show impatience with the   14
process of democracy. They rely on the sit-in, boycott or mass picketing to gain speedier solutions to the problems that face every citizen.
But we must realize that the legitimate pressures that won concessions in the past can easily escalate into the illegitimate power plays
that might extort demands in the future. The victories of these civil
rights leaders must not shake our confidence in the democratic procedures, as the pressures of demonstration are desirable only if they
take place within the limits allowed by law. Civil rights gains should
continue to be won by the persuasion of Congress and other legislative bodies and by the decision of courts. Any illegal entreaty for the
rights of some can be an injury to the rights of others, for mass
demonstrations often trigger violence.

Those who advocate taking the law into their own hands should   15
reflect that when they are disobeying what they consider to be an immoral law, they are deciding on a possibly immoral course. Their answer is that the process for democratic relief is too slow, that only mass
confrontation can bring immediate action, and that any injuries are the
inevitable cost of the pursuit of justice. Their answer is, simply put, that
the end justifies the means. It is this justification of any form of demonstration as a form of dissent that threatens to destroy a society built on
the rule of law.

Our Bill of Rights guarantees wide opportunities to use mass meet-   16
ings, public parades and organized demonstrations to stimulate sentiment, to dramatize issues and to cause change. The Washington
freedom march of 1963 was such a call for action. But the rights of free
expression cannot be mere force cloaked in the garb of free speech. As

the courts have decreed in labor cases, free assembly does not mean mass picketing or sit-down strikes. These rights are subject to limitations of time and place so as to secure the rights of others. When militant students storm a college president's office to achieve demands, when certain groups plan rush-hour car stalling to protest discrimination in employment, these are not dissent, but a denial of rights to others. Neither is it the lawful use of mass protest, but rather the unlawful use of mob power.

17   Justice Black, one of the foremost advocates and defenders of the right of protest and dissent, has said:

> ... Experience demonstrates that it is not a far step from what to many seems to be the earnest, honest, patriotic, kind-spirited multitude of today, to the fanatical, threatening, lawless mob of tomorrow. And the crowds that press in the streets for noble goals today can be supplanted tomorrow by street mobs pressuring the courts for precisely opposite ends.

18   Society must censure those demonstrators who would trespass on the public peace, as it must condemn those rioters whose pillage would destroy the public peace. But more ambivalent is society's posture toward the civil disobedient. Unlike the rioter, the true civil disobedient commits no violence. Unlike the mob demonstrator, he commits no trespass on others' rights. The civil disobedient, while deliberately violating a law, shows an oblique respect for the law by voluntarily submitting to its sanctions. He neither resists arrest nor evades punishment. Thus, he breaches the law but not the peace.

19   But civil disobedience, whatever the ethical rationalization, is still an assault on our democratic society, an affront to our legal order and an attack on our constitutional government. To indulge civil disobedience is to invite anarchy, and the permissive arbitrariness of anarchy is hardly less tolerable than the repressive arbitrariness of tyranny. Too often the license of liberty is followed by the loss of liberty, because into the desert of anarchy comes the man on horseback, a Mussolini or a Hitler.

Violations of Law Subvert Democracy

20   Law violations, even for ends recognized as laudable, are not only assaults on the rule of law, but subversions of the democratic process. The disobedient act of conscience does not ennoble democracy; it erodes it.

21   First, it courts violence, and even the most careful and limited use of nonviolent acts of disobedience may help sow the dragon-teeth of

civil riot. Civil disobedience is the progenitor of disorder, and disorder is the sire of violence.

Second, the concept of civil disobedience does not invite principles 22 of general applicability. If the children of light are morally privileged to resist particular laws on grounds of conscience, so are the children of darkness. Former Deputy Attorney General Burke Marshall said: "If the decision to break the law really turned on individual conscience, it is hard to see in law how [the civil rights leader] is better off than former Governor Ross Barnett of Mississippi who also believed deeply in his cause and was willing to go to jail."

Third, even the most noble act of civil disobedience assaults the 23 rule of law. Although limited as to method, motive and objective, it has the effect of inducing others to engage in different forms of law breaking characterized by methods unsanctioned and condemned by classic theories of law violation. Unfortunately, the most patent lesson of civil disobedience is not so much nonviolence of action as defiance of authority.

Finally, the greatest danger in condoning civil disobedience as a 24 permissible strategy for hastening change is that it undermines our democratic processes. To adopt the techniques of civil disobedience is to assume that representative government does not work. To resist the decisions of courts and the laws of elected assemblies is to say that democracy has failed.

There is no man who is above the law, and there is no man who 25 has a right to break the law. Civil disobedience is not above the law, but against the law. When the civil disobedient disobeys one law, he invariably subverts all law. When the civil disobedient says that he is above the law, he is saying that democracy is beneath him. His disobedience shows a distrust for the democratic system. He is merely saying that since democracy does not work, why should he help make it work. Thoreau expressed well the civil disobedient's disdain for democracy:

> As for adopting the ways which the state has provided for remedying the evil, I know not of such ways. They take too much time and a man's life will be gone. I have other affairs to attend to. I came into this world not chiefly to make this a good place to live in, but to live in it, be it good or bad.

Thoreau's position is not only morally irresponsible but politically 26 reprehensible. When citizens in a democracy are called on to make a profession of faith, the civil disobedients offer only a confession of failure. Tragically, when civil disobedients for lack of faith abstain from democratic involvement, they help attain their own gloomy prediction. They help create the social and political basis for their own despair. By foreseeing failure, they help forge it. If citizens rely on antidemocratic means of protest, they will help bring about the undemocratic result of an authoritarian or anarchic state.

27   How far demonstrations properly can be employed to produce political and social change is a pressing question, particularly in view of the provocations accompanying the National Democratic Convention in Chicago last August and the reaction of the police to them. A line must be drawn by the judiciary between the demands of those who seek absolute order, which can lead only to a dictatorship, and those who seek absolute freedom, which can lead only to anarchy. The line, wherever it is drawn by our courts, should be respected on the college campus, on the streets and elsewhere.

28   Undue provocation will inevitably result in overreaction, human emotions being what they are. Violence will follow. This cycle undermines the very democracy it is designed to preserve. The lesson of the past is that democracies will fall if violence, including the intentional provocations that will lead to violence, replaces democratic procedures, as in Athens, Rome and the Weimar Republic. This lesson must be constantly explained by the legal profession.

29   We should heed the words of William James:

> Democracy is still upon its trial. The civic genius of our people is its only bulwark and . . . neither battleships nor public libraries nor great newspapers nor booming stocks: neither mechanical invention nor political adroitness, nor churches nor universities nor civil service examinations can save us from degeneration if the inner mystery be lost.
>
> That mystery, at once the secret and the glory of our English-speaking race, consists of nothing but two habits. . . . One of them is habit of trained and disciplined good temper towards the opposite party when it fairly wins its innings. The other is that of fierce and merciless resentment toward every man or set of men who break the public peace. (James, *Pragmatism* 1907, pages 127–128)

RESPONDING TO READING

1. Why does Van Dusen take pains to begin his argument by setting it in a long philosophical tradition and citing famous works on civil disobedience by Plato, Socrates, Sophocles, and Thoreau [paragraphs 2–6]?

2. Definitions are crucial to Van Dusen's argument. What distinctions does he make between dissent and civil disobedience? Between the nonviolent philosophy of Thoreau and Gandhi as a strategy for solving society's injustices

[paragraph 6] and "the conscientious law testing of Martin Luther King, Jr., who was not a civil disobedient" [paragraphs 5–7]?

3. On what grounds does Van Dusen distinguish between "legitimate" and "illegitimate" kinds of demonstrations [paragraphs 14–17]? Does he consider the Boston Tea Party and the American colonists' rebellion against England legitimate or illegitimate [paragraphs 10–13]? How does the authority for these differ, in Van Dusen's view, from protests against the Vietnam War (paragraphs 20–29)?

4. What is the relation of civil disobedience to democracy? Does this relationship change if you take a long-range historical view rather than considering only a single incident? Do you agree or disagree with Van Dusen? In what ways have his arguments influenced your response?

The Clan of One-Breasted Women

Terry Tempest Williams

Born (1955) in Corona, California, Terry Tempest Williams grew up in Utah, downwind of the federal government's nuclear weapons tests in Nevada. In a breach of fundamental American values, officials told residents that they were in no danger; years later, deaths from illnesses traceable to radiation numbered in the thousands. The experience shaped Williams' fundamental ambition: to celebrate and protect the environment as part of a community of friends and family. *Refuge: An Unnatural History of Family and Place* (1992), Williams' most acclaimed book, is about the Great Salt Lake and the women in her family: Both suffered greatly because of environmental abuses. As the same time that she discovered ecosystem imbalances were causing the lake to rise, her mother was approaching death from ovarian cancer, which Williams believes was linked to radioactive fallout. Williams has authored many books that similarly contemplate the delicate balance of nature, such as *The Secret Language of Snow* (1984), a children's book that earned praise from *Scientific American* magazine; *Pieces of White Shell: A Journey to Navajo Land* (1984) about Native American traditions; and *An Unspoken Hunger: Stories from the Field* (1995) about antinuclear protesting, the African Serengeti Plain, and Utah's Great Basin. In *Leap* (2000), she explores the world of art and spirituality through Hieronymus Bosch's painting "The Garden of Earthly Delights"; *Red: Passion and Patience in the Desert* (2001) is about America's Redrock Wilderness in southern Utah.

"The Clan of One-Breasted Women," from *Refuge*, portrays the women in Williams' family as stoic heroes in a battle they did not choose, but that is only the beginning. In a nightmarish sequence, her family drives through radioactive fallout from a nuclear explosion;

later she witnesses the death of one female family member after another. Yet the nightmare turns into a myth of resistance, as she and other women join in antinuclear protests.

Epilogue

1   I belong to a Clan of One-Breasted Women. My mother, my grandmothers, and six aunts have all had mastectomies. Seven are dead. The two who survive have just completed rounds of chemotherapy and radiation.

2   I've had my own problems: two biopsies for breast cancer and a small tumor between my ribs diagnosed as a "borderline malignancy."

3   This is my family history.

4   Most statistics tell us breast cancer is genetic, hereditary, with rising percentages attached to fatty diets, childlessness, or becoming pregnant after thirty. What they don't say is living in Utah may be the greatest hazard of all.

5   We are a Mormon family with roots in Utah since 1847. The "word of wisdom" in my family aligned us with good foods—no coffee, no tea, tobacco, or alcohol. For the most part, our women were finished having their babies by the time they were thirty. And only one faced breast cancer prior to 1960. Traditionally, as a group of people, Mormons have a low rate of cancer.

6   Is our family a cultural anomaly? The truth is, we didn't think about it. Those who did, usually the men, simply said, "bad genes." The women's attitude was stoic. Cancer was part of life. On February 16, 1971, the eve of my mother's surgery, I accidentally picked up the telephone and overheard her ask my grandmother what she could expect.

7   "Diane, it is one of the most spiritual experiences you will ever encounter."

8   I quietly put down the receiver.

9   Two days later, my father took my brothers and me to the hospital to visit her. She met us in the lobby in a wheelchair. No bandages were visible. I'll never forget her radiance, the way she held herself in a purple velvet robe, and how she gathered us around her.

10   "Children, I am fine. I want you to know I felt the arms of God around me."

11   We believed her. My father cried. Our mother, his wife, was thirty-eight years old.

12   A little over a year after Mother's death, Dad and I were having dinner together. He had just returned from St. George, where the Tempest Company was completing the gas lines that would service southern Utah. He spoke of his love for the country, the sandstoned

landscape, bare-boned and beautiful. He had just finished hiking the Kolob trail in Zion National Park. We got caught up in reminiscing, recalling with fondness our walk up Angel's Landing on his fiftieth birthday and the years our family had vacationed there.

Over dessert, I shared a recurring dream of mine. I told my father   13 that for years, as long as I could remember, I saw this flash of light in the night in the desert—that this image had so permeated my being that I could not venture south without seeing it again, on the horizon, illuminating buttes and mesas.

"You did see it," he said.   14

"Saw what?"   15

"The bomb. The cloud. We were driving home from Riverside,   16 California. You were sitting on Diane's lap. She was pregnant. In fact, I remember the day, September 7, 1957. We had just gotten out of the Service. We were driving north, past Las Vegas. It was an hour or so before dawn, when this explosion went off. We not only heard it, but felt it. I thought the oil tanker in front of us had blown up. We pulled over and suddenly, rising from the desert floor, we saw it, clearly, this golden-stemmed cloud, the mushroom. The sky seemed to vibrate with an eerie pink glow. Within a few minutes, a light ash was raining on the car."

I stared at my father.   17

"I thought you knew that," he said. "It was a common occurrence   18 in the fifties."

It was at this moment that I realized the deceit I had been living   19 under. Children growing up in the American Southwest, drinking contaminated milk from contaminated cows, even from the contaminated breasts of their mothers, my mother—members, years later, of the Clan of One-Breasted Women.

It is a well-known story in the Desert West, "The Day We Bombed   20 Utah," or more accurately, the years we bombed Utah: above ground atomic testing in Nevada took place from January 27, 1951 through July 11, 1962. Not only were the winds blowing north covering "low-use segments of the population" with fallout and leaving sheep dead in their tracks, but the climate was right. The United States of the 1950s was red, white, and blue. The Korean War was raging. McCarthyism was rampant. Ike was it, and the cold war was hot. If you were against nuclear testing, you were for a communist regime.

Much has been written about this "American nuclear tragedy."   21 Public health was secondary to national security. The Atomic Energy Commissioner, Thomas Murray, said, "Gentlemen, we must not let anything interfere with this series of tests, nothing."

Again and again, the American public was told by its government,   22 in spite of burns, blisters, and nausea, "It has been found that the tests may be conducted with adequate assurance of safety under conditions prevailing at the bombing reservations." Assuaging public fears was simply a matter of public relations. "Your best action," an Atomic Energy Commission booklet read, "is not to be worried about fallout." A news release typical of the times stated, "We find no basis for concluding that harm to any individual has resulted from radioactive fallout."

23   On August 30, 1979, during Jimmy Carter's presidency, a suit was filed, *Irene Allen v. The United States of America*. Mrs. Allen's case was the first on an alphabetical list of twenty-four test cases, representative of nearly twelve hundred plaintiffs seeking compensation from the United States government for cancers caused by nuclear testing in Nevada.

24   Irene Allen lived in Hurricane, Utah. She was the mother of five children and had been widowed twice. Her first husband, with their two oldest boys, had watched the tests from the roof of the local high school. He died of leukemia in 1956. Her second husband died of pancreatic cancer in 1978.

25   In a town meeting conducted by Utah Senator Orrin Hatch, shortly before the suit was filed, Mrs. Allen said, "I am not blaming the government, I want you to know that, Senator Hatch. But I thought if my testimony could help in any way so this wouldn't happen again to any of the generations coming up after us . . . I am happy to be here this day to bear testimony of this."

26   God-fearing people. This is just one story in an anthology of thousands.

27   On May 10, 1984, Judge Bruce S. Jenkins handed down his opinion. Ten of the plaintiffs were awarded damages. It was the first time a federal court had determined that nuclear tests had been the cause of cancers. For the remaining fourteen test cases, the proof of causation was not sufficient. In spite of the split decision, it was considered a landmark ruling. It was not to remain so for long.

28   In April 1987, the Tenth Circuit Court of Appeals overturned Judge Jenkins's ruling on the ground that the United States was protected from suit by the legal doctrine of sovereign immunity, a centuries-old idea from England in the days of absolute monarchs.

29   In January 1988, the Supreme Court refused to review the Appeals Court decision. To our court system it does not matter whether the United States government was irresponsible, whether it lied to its citizens, or even that citizens died from the fallout of nuclear testing. What matters is that our government is immune: "The King can do no wrong."

30   In Mormon culture, authority is respected, obedience is revered, and independent thinking is not. I was taught as a young girl not to "make waves" or "rock the boat."

"Just let it go," Mother would say. "You know how you feel, that's   31
what counts."

For many years, I have done just that—listened, observed, and qui-   32
etly formed my own opinions, in a culture that rarely asks questions
because it has all the answers. But one by one, I have watched the
women in my family die common, heroic deaths. We sat in waiting
rooms hoping for good news, but always receiving the bad. I cared for
them, bathed their scarred bodies, and kept their secrets. I watched
beautiful women become bald as Cytoxan, cisplatin, and Adriamycin
were injected into their veins. I held their foreheads as they vomited
green-black bile, and I shot them with morphine when the pain became
inhuman. In the end, I witnessed their last peaceful breaths, becoming
a midwife to the rebirth of their souls.

The price of obedience has become too high.   33

The fear and inability to question authority that ultimately killed   34
rural communities in Utah during atmospheric testing of atomic
weapons is the same fear I saw in my mother's body. Sheep. Dead
sheep. The evidence is buried.

I cannot prove that my mother, Diane Dixon Tempest, or my   35
grandmothers, Lettie Romney Dixon and Kathryn Blackett Tempest,
along with my aunts developed cancer from nuclear fallout in Utah.
But I can't prove they didn't.

My father's memory was correct. The September blast we drove   36
through in 1957 was part of Operation Plumbbob, one of the most intensive series of bomb tests to be initiated. The flash of light in the night
in the desert, which I had always thought was a dream, developed into
a family nightmare. It took fourteen years, from 1957 to 1971, for cancer
to manifest in my mother—the same time, Howard L. Andrews, an authority in radioactive fallout at the National Institutes of Health, says
radiation cancer requires to become evident. The more I learn about
what it means to be a "downwinder," the more questions I drown in.

What I do know, however, is that as a Mormon woman of the fifth   37
generation of Latter-day Saints, I must question everything, even if it
means losing my faith, even if it means becoming a member of a border
tribe among my own people. Tolerating blind obedience in the name of
patriotism or religion ultimately takes our lives.

When the Atomic Energy Commission described the country north of   38
the Nevada Test Site as "virtually uninhabited desert terrain," my family
and the birds at Great Salt Lake were some of the "virtual uninhabitants."

One night, I dreamed women from all over the world circled a   39
blazing fire in the desert. They spoke of change, how they hold the
moon in their bellies and wax and wane with its phases. They mocked
the presumption of even-tempered beings and made promises that

they would never fear the witch inside themselves. The women danced wildly as sparks broke away from the flames and entered the night sky as stars.

40　　And they sang a song given to them by Shoshone grand-mothers:

Ah ne nah, nah	Consider the rabbits
nin nah nah—	How gently they walk on the earth—
ah ne nah, nah	Consider the rabbits
nin nah nah—	How gently they walk on the earth—
Nyaga mutzi	We remember them
oh ne nay—	We can walk gently also—
Nyaga mutzi	We remember them
oh ne nay—	We can walk gently also—

The women danced and drummed and sang for weeks, preparing themselves for what was to come. They would reclaim the desert for the sake of their children, for the sake of the land.

41　　A few miles downwind from the fire circle, bombs were being tested. Rabbits felt the tremors. Their soft leather pads on paws and feet recognized the shaking sands, while the roots of mesquite and sage were smoldering. Rocks were hot from the inside out and dust devils hummed unnaturally. And each time there was another nuclear test, ravens watched the desert heave. Stretch marks appeared. The land was losing its muscle.

42　　The women couldn't bear it any longer. They were mothers. They had suffered labor pains but always under the promise of birth. The red hot pains beneath the desert promised death only, as each bomb became a stillborn. A contract had been made and broken between human beings and the land. A new contract was being drawn by the women, who understood the fate of the earth as their own.

43　　Under the cover of darkness, ten women slipped under a barbed-wire fence and entered the contaminated country. They were trespassing. They walked toward the town of Mercury, in moonlight, taking their cues from coyote, kit fox, antelope squirrel, and quail. They moved quietly and deliberately through the maze of Joshua trees. When a hint of daylight appeared they rested, drinking tea and sharing their rations of food. The women closed their eyes. The time had come to protest with the heart, that to deny one's genealogy with the earth was to commit treason against one's soul.

44　　At dawn, the women draped themselves in mylar, wrapping long streamers of silver plastic around their arms to blow in the breeze. They wore clear masks, that became the faces of humanity. And when they arrived at the edge of Mercury, they carried all the butterflies of a summer day in their wombs. They paused to allow their courage to settle.

45　　The town that forbids pregnant women and children to enter because of radiation risks was asleep. The women moved through the streets as winged messengers, twirling around each other in slow motion, peeking inside homes and watching the easy sleep of men and women. They were astonished by such stillness and periodically would utter a shrill note or low cry just to verify life.

The residents finally awoke to these strange apparitions. Some simply stared. Others called authorities, and in time, the women were apprehended by wary soldiers dressed in desert fatigues. They were taken to a white, square building on the other edge of Mercury. When asked who they were and why they were there, the women replied, "We are mothers and we have come to reclaim the desert for our children."   46

The soldiers arrested them. As the ten women were blind-folded and handcuffed, they began singing: 47

You can't forbid us everything
You can't forbid us to think—
You can't forbid our tears to flow
And you can't stop the songs that we sing.

The women continued to sing louder and louder, until they heard the voices of their sisters moving across the mesa:

Ah ne nah, nah
nin nah nah—
Ah ne nah, nah
nin nah nah—
Nyaga mutzi
oh ne nay—
Nyaga mutzi
oh ne nay—

"Call for reinforcements," one soldier said.

"We have," interrupted one woman, "we have—and you have no idea of our numbers."   48

I crossed the line at the Nevada Test Site and was arrested with nine other Utahns for trespassing on military lands. They are still conducting nuclear tests in the desert. Ours was an act of civil disobedience. But as I walked toward the town of Mercury, it was more than a gesture of peace. It was a gesture on behalf of the Clan of One-Breasted Women.   49

As one officer cinched the handcuffs around my wrists, another frisked my body. She found a pen and a pad of paper tucked inside my left boot.   50

"And these?" she asked sternly.   51

"Weapons," I replied.   52

Our eyes met. I smiled. She pulled the leg of my trousers back over my boot.   53

54   "Step forward, please," she said as she took my arm.

55   We were booked under an afternoon sun and bused to Tonopah, Nevada. It was a two-hour ride. This was familiar country. The Joshua trees standing their ground had been named by my ancestors, who believed they looked like prophets pointing west to the Promised Land. These were the same trees that bloomed each spring, flowers appearing like white flames in the Mojave. And I recalled a full moon in May, when Mother and I had walked among them, flushing out mourning doves and owls.

56   The bus stopped short of town. We were released.

57   The officials thought it was a cruel joke to leave us stranded in the desert with no way to get home. What they didn't realize was that we were home, soul-centered and strong, women who recognized the sweet smell of sage as fuel for our spirits.

RESPONDING TO READING

1. Why does Williams refer to the group to which she belongs as a "clan"? Does this world have connotations that other words, such as "family," do not have?

2. How does Williams weave her memories into an argument about family, cancer, and a duplicitous U.S. government? What is the value of using her own memories and her family's experiences to bring these separate ideas together?

3. Williams argues that in America in the 1950s, "If you were against nuclear testing, you were for a communist regime." This statement is followed closely by the argument that "Public health was secondary to national security." In what ways is this similar to U.S. attitudes in the wake of the September 11, 2001, terrorist attacks? When national security becomes of primary importance, what rights and freedoms are likely to become of secondary importance? Discuss this and the following questions with fellow students, and draft a policy statement of what principles you think should govern priorities of national security and other rights and freedoms Americans enjoy during peacetime. Should these be different during times of war?

4. Explain how the system of checks and balances among the legislative, executive, and judicial branches of the government works in reference to a particular policy issue you care about. Are these checks and balances adequate to address the case in point?

5. According to Williams, "Tolerating blind obedience in the name of patriotism or religion ultimately takes our lives." In an essay, explain how Williams reaches this conclusion. Why, for her, is obedience a step on the road to losing our lives? Do you agree or disagree with her? Why?

Los Angeles Against the Mountains
JOHN MCPHEE

John McPhee was born in Princeton, New Jersey, in 1931. He graduated from Princeton University in 1953 and still lives, writes, and teaches in his home town. Eager to publish in the *New Yorker*, he submitted his work there for twelve years before his first essay was accepted, in 1964. Since then, nearly all of his writing has appeared there before being collected in books whose subject matter ranges from Florida (*Oranges*, 1967) to Alaska (*Coming into the Country*, 1977), New York (*Giving Good Weight*, 1979) to the Great Plains and the Rocky Mountains (*Basin and Range*, 1981).

"Los Angeles Against the Mountains" was published in *The Control of Nature* (1989), a book whose ambiguous title reflects its problematic subject. Here McPhee studies in characteristic detail people's all-out battles to force nature to accommodate—beyond its capacity—high-density population and industry. In the places he analyzes, overcrowding will destroy the very features that were initially attractive: the Mississippi Delta, the volcanic islands of Iceland and Hawaii, and the steep, mountainous hillsides of Los Angeles. In "Los Angeles Against the Mountains," he shows what happens when a population surrounds "the base of Mt. Olympus demanding and expecting the surrender of the gods," and instead finds a fragile terrain vulnerable to the effects of drought and flooding rains.

1   In Los Angeles versus the San Gabriel Mountains, it is not always clear which side is losing. For example, the Genofiles, Bob and Jackie, can claim to have lost and won. They live on an acre of ground so high that they look across their pool and past the trunks of big pines at an aerial view over Glendale and across Los Angeles to the Pacific bays. The setting, in cool dry air, is serene and Mediterranean. It has not been everlastingly serene.

2   On a February night some years ago, the Genofiles were awakened by a crash of thunder—lightning striking the mountain front. Ordinarily, in their quiet neighborhood, only the creek beside them was likely to make much sound, dropping steeply out of Shields Canyon on its way to the Los Angeles River. The creek, like every component of all the river systems across the city from mountains to ocean, had not been left to nature. Its banks were concrete. Its bed was concrete. When boulders were running there, they sounded like a rolling freight. On a night like this, the boulders should have been running. The creek should have been a torrent. Its unnatural sound was unnaturally absent. There was, and had been, a lot of rain.

3   The Genofiles had two teen-age children, whose rooms were on the uphill side of the one-story house. The window in Scott's room looked straight up Pine Cone Road, a cul-de-sac, which, with hundreds like it,

defined the northern limit of the city, the confrontation of the urban and the wild. Los Angeles is overmatched on one side by the Pacific Ocean and on the other by very high mountains. With respect to these principal boundaries, Los Angeles is done sprawling. The San Gabriels, in their state of tectonic youth, are rising as rapidly as any range on earth. Their loose inimical slopes flout the tolerance of the angle of repose. Rising straight up out of the megalopolis, they stand ten thousand feet above the nearby sea, and they are not kidding with this city. Shedding, spalling, self-destructing, they are disintegrating at a rate that is also among the fastest in the world. The phalanxed communities of Los Angeles have pushed themselves hard against these mountains, an aggression that requires a deep defense budget to contend with the results. Kimberlee Genofile called to her mother, who joined her in Scott's room as they looked up the street. From its high turnaround, Pine Cone Road plunges downhill like a ski run, bending left and then right and then left and then right in steep christiania turns for half a mile above a three-hundred-foot straightaway that aims directly at the Genofiles' house. Not far below the turnaround, Shields Creek passes under the street, and there a kink in its concrete profile had been plugged by a six-foot boulder. Hence the silence of the creek. The water was now spreading over the street. It descended in heavy sheets. As the young Genofiles and their mother glimpsed it in the all but total darkness, the scene was suddenly illuminated by a blue electrical flash. In the blue light they saw a massive blackness, moving. It was not a landslide, not a mudslide, not a rock avalanche; nor by any means was it the front of a conventional flood. In Jackie's words, "It was just one big black thing coming at us, rolling, rolling with a lot of water in front of it, pushing the water, this big black thing. It was just one big black hill coming toward us."

4   In geology, it would be known as a debris flow. Debris flows amass in stream valleys and more or less resemble fresh concrete. They consist of water mixed with a good deal of solid material, most of which is above sand size. Some of it is Chevrolet size. Boulders bigger than cars ride long distances in debris flows. Boulders grouped like fish eggs pour downhill in debris flows. The dark material coming toward the Genofiles was not only full of boulders; it was so full of automobiles it was like bread dough mixed with raisins. On its way down Pine Cone Road, it plucked up cars from driveways and the street. When it crashed into the Genofiles' house, the shattering of safety glass made terrific explosive sounds. A door burst open. Mud and boulders poured into the hall. We're going to go, Jackie thought. Oh, my God, what a hell of a way for the four of us to die together.

5   The parents' bedroom was on the far side of the house. Bob Genofile was in there kicking through white satin draperies at the pan-

elled glass, smashing it to provide an outlet for water, when the three others ran in to join him. The walls of the house neither moved nor shook. As a general contractor, Bob had built dams, department stores, hospitals, six schools, seven churches, and this house. It was made of concrete block with steel reinforcement, sixteen inches on center. His wife had said it was stronger than any dam in California. His crew had called it "the fort." In those days, twenty years before, the Genofiles' acre was close by the edge of the mountain brush, but a developer had come along since then and knocked down thousands of trees and put Pine Cone Road up the slope. Now Bob Genofile was thinking, I hope the roof holds. I hope the roof is strong enough to hold. Debris was flowing over it. He told Scott to shut the bedroom door. No sooner was the door closed than it was battered down and fell into the room. Mud, rock, water poured in. It pushed everybody against the far wall. "Jump on the bed," Bob said. The bed began to rise. Kneeling on it—on a gold velvet spread—they could soon press their palms against the ceiling. The bed also moved toward the glass wall. The two teen-agers got off, to try to control the motion, and were pinned between the bed's brass railing and the wall. Boulders went up against the railing, pressed it into their legs, and held them fast. Bob dived into the muck to try to move the boulders, but he failed. The debris flow, entering through windows as well as doors, continued to rise. Escape was still possible for the parents but not for the children. The parents looked at each other and did not stir. Each reached for and held one of the children. Their mother felt suddenly resigned, sure that her son and daughter would die and she and her husband would quickly follow. The house became buried to the eaves. Boulders sat on the roof. Thirteen automobiles were packed around the building, including five in the pool. A din of rocks kept banging against them. The stuck horn of a buried car was blaring. The family in the darkness in their fixed tableau watched one another by the light of a directional signal, endlessly blinking. The house had filled up in six minutes, and the mud stopped rising near the children's chins.

Stories like that do not always have such happy endings. A man 6 went outside to pick up his newspaper one morning, heard a sound, turned, and died of a heart attack as he saw his house crushed to pieces with his wife and two children inside. People have been buried alive in their beds. But such cases are infrequent. Debris flows generally are much less destructive of life than of property. People get out of the way.

If they try to escape by automobile, they have made an obvious but 7 imperfect choice. Norman Reid backed his Pontiac into the street one January morning and was caught from behind by rock porridge. It embedded the car to the chrome strips. Fifty years of archival news photograhs show cars of every vintage standing like hippos in chunky muck. The upper halves of their headlights peep above the surface. The late Roland Case Ross, an emeritus professor at California State University, told me of a day in the early thirties when he watched a couple rushing to escape by car. She got in first. While her husband was going around to get in his side, she got out and ran into the house for more silverware. When the car at last putt-putted downhill, a wall of debris was nudging the bumper. The debris stayed on the vehicle's heels all the way to Foothill Boulevard, where the car turned left.

8   Foothill Boulevard was U.S. Route 66—the western end of the rainbow. Through Glendora, Azusa, Pasadena, it paralleled the mountain front. It strung the metropolitan border towns. And it brought in emigrants to fill them up. The real-estate line of maximum advance now averages more than a mile above Foothill, but Foothill receives its share of rocks. A debris flow that passed through the Monrovia Nursery went on to Foothill and beyond. With its twenty million plants in twelve hundred varieties, Monrovia was the foremost container nursery in the world, and in its recovery has remained so. The debris flow went through the place picking up pots and cans. It got into a greenhouse two hundred feet long and smashed out the southern wall, taking bougainvillea and hibiscus with it. Arby's, below Foothill, blamed the nursery for damages, citing the hibiscus that had come with the rocks. Arby's sought compensation, but no one was buying beef that thin.

9   In the same storm, large tree trunks rode in the debris like javelins and broke through the sides of houses. Automobiles went in through picture windows. A debris flow hit the gym at Azusa Pacific College and knocked a large hole in the upslope wall. In the words of Cliff Hamlow, the basketball coach, "If we'd had students in there, it would have killed them. Someone said it sounded like the roar of a jet engine. It filled the gym up with mud, and with boulders two and three feet in diameter. It went out through the south doors and spread all over the football field and track. Chain-link fencing was sheared off—like it had been cut with a welder. The place looked like a war zone." Azusa Pacific College wins national championships in track, but Coach Hamlow's basketball team (12–18), can't get the boulders out of its game.

10   When a debris flow went through the Verdugo Hills Cemetery, which is up a couple of switchbacks on the mountain front, two of the central figures there, resting under impressive stones, were "Hiram F. Hatch, 1st Lieut. 6th Mich. Inf., December 24, 1843–October 12, 1922," and "Henry J. Hatch, Brigadier General, United States Army, April 28, 1869–December 31, 1931." The two Hatches held the hill while many of their comrades slid below. In all, thirty-five coffins came out of the cemetery and took off for lower ground. They went down Hillrose Street and were scattered over half a mile. One came to rest in the park-

ing lot of a supermarket. Many were reburied by debris and, in various people's yards, were not immediately found. Three turned up in one yard. Don Sulots, who had moved into the fallout path two months before, said, "It sounded like thunder. By the time I made it to the front door and got it open, the muck was already three feet high. It's quite a way to start off life in a new home—mud, rocks, and bodies all around."

Most people along the mountain front are about as mindful of debris flows as those corpses were. Here today, gone tomorrow. Those who worry build barricades. They build things called deflection walls—a practice that raises legal antennae and, when the caroming debris breaks into the home of a neighbor, probes the wisdom of Robert Frost. At least one family has experienced so many debris flows coming through their back yard that they long ago installed overhead doors in the rear end of their built-in garage. To guide the flows, they put deflection walls in their back yard. Now when the boulders come they open both ends of their garage, and the debris goes through to the street.

Between Harrow Canyon and Englewild Canyon, a private street called Glencoe Heights teased the mountain front. Came a time of unprecedented rain, and the neighborhood grew ever more fearful—became in fact so infused with catastrophic anticipation that it sought the drastic sort of action that only a bulldozer could provide. A fire had swept the mountainsides, leaving them vulnerable, dark, and bare. Expecting floods of mud and rock, people had piled sandbags and built heavy wooden walls. Their anxiety was continuous for many months. "This threat is on your mind all the time," Gary Lukehart said. "Every time you leave the house, you stop and put up another sandbag, and you just hope everything will be all right when you get back." Lukehart was accustomed to losing in Los Angeles. In the 1957 Rose Bowl, he was Oregon State's quarterback. A private street could not call upon city or county for the use of heavy equipment, so in the dead of night, as steady rain was falling, a call was put in to John McCafferty—bulldozer for hire. McCafferty had a closeup knowledge of the dynamics of debris flows: he had worked the mountain front from San Dimas to Sierra Madre, which to him is Sarah Modri. ("In those canyons at night, you could hear them big boulders comin'. They sounded like thunder.") He arrived at Glencoe Heights within the hour and set about turning the middle of the street into the Grand Canal of Venice. His Cat was actually not a simple dozer but a 955 loader on tracks, with a two-and-a-quarter-yard bucket seven feet wide. Cutting water mains, gas mains, and sewers, he made a ditch that eventually extended five hundred feet and was deep enough to take in three thousand tons of debris. After working for five hours, he happened to be by John Caufield's place ("It had quit rainin', it looked like the worst was

11

12

over") when Caufield came out and said, "Mac, you sure have saved my bacon."

13   McCafferty continues, "All of a sudden, we looked up at the mountains—it's not too far from his house to the mountains, maybe a hundred and fifty feet—and we could just see it all comin'. It seemed the whole mountain had come loose. It flowed like cement." In the ditch, he put the Cat in reverse and backed away from the oncoming debris. He backed three hundred feet. He went up one side of the ditch and was about halfway out of it when the mud and boulders caught the Cat and covered it over the hood. In the cab, the mud pushed against McCafferty's legs. At the same time, debris broke into Caufield's house through the front door and the dining-room window, and in five minutes filled it to the eaves.

14   Other houses were destroyed as well. A garage left the neighborhood with a car in it. One house was buried twice. (After McCafferty dug it out, it was covered again.) His ditch, however, was effective, and saved many places on slightly higher ground, among them Gary Lukehart's and the home of John Marcellino, the chief executive officer of Mackinac Island Fudge. McCafferty was promised a lifetime supply of fudge. He was on the scene for several days, and in one span worked twenty-four hours without a break. The people of the street brought him chocolate milkshakes. He had left his lowbed parked around the corner. When at last he returned to it and prepared to go home, he discovered that a cop had given him a ticket.

15   A metropolis that exists in a semidesert, imports water three hundred miles, has inveterate flash floods, is at the grinding edges of two tectonic plates, and has a microclimate tenacious of noxious oxides will have its priorities among the aspects of its environment that it attempts to control. For example, Los Angeles makes money catching water. In a few days in 1983, it caught twenty-eight million dollars' worth of water. In one period of twenty-four hours, however, the ocean hit the city with twenty-foot waves, a tornado made its own freeway, debris flows poured from the San Gabriel front, and an earthquake shook the region. Nature's invoice was forty million dollars. Later, twenty million more was spent dealing with the mountain debris.

16   There were those who would be quick—and correct—in saying that were it not for the alert unflinching manner and imaginative strategies by which Los Angeles outwits the mountains, nature's invoices at such times would run into the billions. The rear-guard defenses are spread throughout the city and include more than two thousand miles of underground conduits and concrete-lined open stream channels—a web of engineering that does not so much reinforce as replace the natural river systems. The front line of battle is where the people

meet the mountains—up the steep slopes where the subdivisions stop and the brush begins.

Strung out along the San Gabriel front are at least a hundred and   17 twenty bowl-shaped excavations that resemble football stadiums and are often as large. Years ago, when a big storm left back yards and boulevards five feet deep in scree, one neighborhood came through amazingly unscathed, because it happened to surround a gravel pit that had filled up instead. A tungsten filament went on somewhere above Los Angeles. The county began digging pits to catch debris. They were quarries, in a sense, but exceedingly bizarre quarries, in that the rock was meant to come to them. They are known as debris basins. Blocked at their downstream ends with earthfill or concrete constructions, they are also known as debris dams. With clean spillways and empty reservoirs, they stand ready to capture rivers of boulders—these deep dry craters, lying close above the properties they protect. In the overflowing abundance of urban nomenclature, the individual names of such basins are obscure, until a day when they appear in a headline in the Los Angeles *Times*: Harrow, Englewild, Zachau, Dunsmuir, Shields, Big Dalton, Hog, Hook East, Hook West, Limekiln, Starfall, Sawpit, Santa Anita. For fifty miles, they mark the wild boundary like bulbs beside a mirror. Behind chain links, their idle ovate forms more than suggest defense. They are separated, on the average, by seven hundred yards. In aggregate, they are worth hundreds of millions of dollars. All this to keep the mountains from falling on Johnny Carson.

The principal agency that developed the debris basins was the   18 hopefully named Los Angeles County Flood Control District, known familiarly through the region as Flood Control, and even more intimately as Flood. ("when I was at Flood, one of our dams filled with debris overnight," a former employee remarked to me. "If any more rain came, we were going to have to evacuate the whole of Pasadena.") There has been a semantic readjustment, obviously intended to acknowledge that when a flood pours out of the mountains it might be half rock. The debris basins are now in the charge of the newly titled Sedimentation Section of the Hydraulic Division of the Los Angeles County Department of Public Works. People still call it Flood. By whatever name the agency is called, its essential tactic remains unaltered. This was summarized for me in a few words by an engineer named Donald Nichols, who pointed out that eight million people live below the mountains on the urban coastal plain, within an area large enough to accommodate Philadelphia, Detroit, Chicago, St. Louis, Boston, and New York. He said, "To make the area inhabitable, you had to put in lined channels on the plain and halt the debris at the front. If you don't take it out at the front, it will come out in the plain, filling up channels. A filled channel won't carry diddly-boo."

19   To stabilize mountain streambeds and stop descending rocks even before they reach the debris basins, numerous crib structures (barriers made of concrete slats) have been emplaced in high canyons—the idea being to convert plunging streams into boulder staircases, and hypothetically cause erosion to work against itself. Farther into the mountains, a dozen dams of some magnitude were built in the nineteen-twenties and thirties to control floods and conserve water. Because they are in the San Gabriels, they inadvertently trap large volumes of debris. One of them—the San Gabriel Dam, in the San Gabriel River—was actually built as a debris-control structure. Its reservoir, which is regularly cleaned out, contained, just then, twenty million tons of mountain.

20   The San Gabriel River, the Los Angeles River, and the Big Tujunga (Bigta Hung-ga) are the principal streams that enter the urban plain, where a channel that filled with rock wouldn't carry diddly-boo. Three colossal debris basins—as different in style as in magnitude from those on the mountain front—have been constructed on the plain to greet these rivers. Where the San Gabriel goes past Azusa on its way to Alamitos Bay, the Army Corps of Engineers completed in the late nineteen-forties a dam ninety-two feet high and twenty-four thousand feet wide—this to stop a river that is often dry, and trickles most of the year. Santa Fe Dam, as it is called, gives up at a glance its own story, for it is made of boulders that are shaped like potatoes and are generally the size of watermelons. They imply a large volume of water flowing with high energy. They are stream-propelled, stream-rounded boulders, and the San Gabriel is the stream. In Santa Fe Basin, behind the dam, the dry bed of the San Gabriel is half a mile wide. The boulder-strewn basin in its entirety is four times as wide as that. It occupies eighteen hundred acres in all, nearly three square miles, of what would be prime real estate were it not for the recurrent arrival of rocks. The scene could have been radioed home from Mars, whose cobbly face is in part the result of debris flows dating to a time when Mars had surface water.

21   The equally vast Sepulveda Basin is where Los Angeles receives and restrains the Los Angeles River. In Sepulveda Basin are three golf courses, which lend ample support to the widespread notion that everything in Los Angeles is disposable. Advancing this national prejudice even further, debris flows, mudslides, and related phenomena have "provided literary minds with a ready-made metaphor of the alleged moral decay of Los Angeles." The words belong to Reyner Banham, late professor of the history of architecture at University College, London, whose passionate love of Los Angeles left him without visible peers. The decay was only "alleged," he said. Of such nonsense he was having none. With his "Los Angeles: The Architecture of Four Ecologies," Banham had become to this deprecated, defamed, traduced, and

disparaged metropolis what Pericles was to Athens. Banham knew why the basins were there and what the people were defending. While all those neurasthenic literary minds are cowering somewhere in ethical crawl space, the quality of Los Angeles life rises up the mountain front. There is air there. Cool is the evening under the crumbling peaks. Cool descending air. Clean air. Air with a view. "The financial and topographical contours correspond almost exactly," Banham said. Among those "narrow, tortuous residential roads serving precipitous house-plots that often back up directly on unimproved wilderness" is "the fat life of the delectable mountains."

People of Gardena, Inglewood, and Watts no less than Azusa and   22 Altadena pay for the defense of the mountain front, the rationale being that debris trapped near its source will not move down and choke the channels of the inner city, causing urban floods. The political City of Los Angeles—in its vague and tentacular configuration— actually abuts the San Gabriels for twenty miles or so, in much the way that it extends to touch the ocean in widely separated places like Venice, San Pedro, and Pacific Palisades. Los Angeles County reaches across the mountains and far into the Mojave Desert. The words "Los Angeles" as generally used here refer neither to the political city nor to the county but to the multinamed urban integrity that has a street in it seventy miles long (Sepulveda Boulevard) and, from the Pacific Ocean at least to Pomona, moves north against the mountains as a comprehensive town.

The debris basins vary greatly in size—not, of course, in relation to   23 the populations they defend but in relation to the watersheds and washes above them in the mountains. For the most part, they are associated with small catchments, and the excavated basins are commensurately modest, with capacities under a hundred thousand cubic yards. In a typical empty reservoir—whatever its over-all dimensions may be—stands a columnar tower that resembles a campanile. Full of holes, it is known as a perforated riser. As the basin fills with a thick-flowing slurry of water, mud, and rock, the water goes into the tower, and is drawn off below. The county calls this water harvesting.

Like the freeways, the debris-control system ordinarily functions   24 but occasionally jams. When the Genofiles' swimming pool filled with cars, debris flows descended into other neighborhoods along that part of the front. One hit a culvert, plugged the culvert, crossed a road in a bouldery wave, flattened fences, filled a debris basin, went over the spillway, and spread among houses lying below, shoving them off their foundations. The debris basins have caught as much as six hundred thousand cubic yards in one storm. Over time, they have trapped some twenty million tons of mud and rock. Inevitably, sometimes something gets away.

25   At Devils Gate—just above the Rose Bowl, in Pasadena—a dam was built in 1920 with control of water its only objective. Yet its reservoir, with a surface of more than a hundred acres, has filled to the brim with four million tons of rock, gravel, and sand. A private operator has set up a sand-and-gravel quarry in the reservoir. Almost exactly, he takes out what the mountains put in. As one engineer has described it, "he pays Flood, and Flood makes out like a champ."

RESPONDING TO READING

1. How does the story of the Genofile house serve both to illustrate McPhee's concerns and to organize the essay? Select another personal story in the essay and show how it illustrates the conflict of people with nature. Whose side are you on? Why?

2. Compare and contrast the attempt to control Los Angeles floods with the attempt to control potatoes that Michael Pollan (Chapter 2) describes. What motives led to the actions that Pollan and McPhee describe? What might be better courses of action in each case? Should people ever interfere with nature? Why, or why not?

3. Describe what it was like to be caught up in some large event beyond your control: a fire, riot, hurricane, ocean tide, downhill race, illness, accident, for example. If no such event comes to mind, use an experience in which you encountered nature and felt its force. Use the narrative and detail as a way of illustrating your ideas about controlling nature.

4. Why do people persist in building houses in the path of debris flows? Select one or two other examples of people refusing to learn from the past, imagining that they can conquer nature, and so repeating mistakes that lead to serious trouble. Using these examples as your evidence, write an essay on people and the ways they encounter, and should encounter, natural forces.

How Can Value Conflicts
Be Resolved?

The Roots of Debate in Education
and the Hope of Dialogue

Deborah Tannen

For those of us who like to look at both sides of an issue, Deborah Tannen [for biography, see Chapter 2] has a suggestion: Look at *all* sides. Too much of our public debate and educational discourse, says Tannen, is founded on agonistic discourse that only aims to criticize the ideas of others and prove them wrong. The result is an argument culture in which polarized debate is ratcheted up to the point where subtleties fall by the wayside, creativity suffers, and synthesis is impossible. "The Roots of Debate," taken from Tannen's book *The Argument Culture: Moving from Debate to Dialogue* (1998), traces the adversarial model back to the writings of Plato and Aristotle and the medieval universities. If we are interested in furthering knowledge, insight, and harmony, Tannen asserts, it may be time to rethink our ways of collective inquiry. Beginning with an example of a typical classroom debate—a few students arguing loudly over extreme and oversimplified positions while the rest of the class remains silent— Tannen looks at the problem from several angles and offers some intriguing solutions.

The teacher sits at the head of the classroom, feeling pleased with herself and her class. The students are engaged in a heated debate. The very noise level reassures the teacher that the students are participating, taking responsibility for their own learning. Education is going on. The class is a success.

But look again, cautions Patricia Rosof, a high school history teacher who admits to having experienced that wave of satisfaction with herself and the job she is doing. On closer inspection, you notice that only a few students are participating in the debate; the majority of the class is sitting silently, maybe attentive but perhaps either indifferent or actively turned off. And the students who are arguing are not addressing the subtleties, nuances, or complexities of the points they are making or disputing. They do not have that luxury because they want to win the argument—so they must go for the most gross and dramatic statements they can muster. They will not concede an opponent's point, even if they can see its validity, because that would weaken their position. Anyone tempted to synthesize the varying views would not dare to do so because it would look like a "cop-out," an inability to take a stand.

3   One reason so many teachers use the debate format to promote student involvement is that it is relatively easy to set up and the rewards are quick and obvious: the decibel level of noise, the excitement of those who are taking part. Showing students how to integrate ideas and explore subtleties and complexities is much harder. And the rewards are quieter—but more lasting.

4   Our schools and universities, our ways of doing science and approaching knowledge, are deeply agonistic. We all pass through our country's educational system, and it is there that the seeds of our adversarial culture are planted. Seeing how these seeds develop, and where they came from, is a key to understanding the argument culture and a necessary foundation for determining what changes we would like to make.

Roots of the Adversarial Approach to Knowledge

5   The argument culture, with its tendency to approach issues as a polarized debate, and the culture of critique, with its inclination to regard criticism and attack as the best if not the only type of rigorous thinking, are deeply rooted in Western tradition, going back to the ancient Greeks.[1] This point is made by Walter Ong, a Jesuit professor at Saint Louis University, in his book *Fighting for Life*. Ong credits the ancient Greeks[2] with a fascination with adversativeness in language and thought. He also connects the adversarial tradition of educational institutions to their all-male character. To attend the earliest universities, in the Middle Ages, young men were torn from their families and deposited in cloistered environments where corporal, even brutal, punishment was rampant. Their suffering drove them to bond with each other in opposition to their keepers—the teachers who were their symbolic enemies. Similar in many ways to puberty rites in traditional cultures, this secret society to which young men were confined also had a private language, Latin, in which students read about military exploits. Knowledge was gleaned through public oral disputation and tested by combative oral performance, which carried with it the risk of public humiliation. Students at these institutions were trained not to discover the truth but to argue either side of an argument—in other words, to debate. Ong points out that the Latin term for school, *ludus*, also referred to play or games, but it derived from the military sense of the word—training exercises for war.

6   If debate seems self-evidently the appropriate or even the only path to insight and knowledge, says Ong, consider the Chinese approach. Disputation was rejected in ancient China as "incompatible

with the decorum and harmony cultivated by the true sage."[3] During the Classical periods in both China and India, according to Robert T. Oliver, the preferred mode of rhetoric was exposition rather than argument. The aim was to "enlighten an inquirer," not to "overwhelm an opponent." And the preferred style reflected "the earnestness of investigation" rather than "the fervor of conviction." In contrast to Aristotle's trust of logic and mistrust of emotion, in ancient Asia intuitive insight was considered the superior means of perceiving truth. Asian rhetoric was devoted not to devising logical arguments but to explicating widely accepted propositions. Furthermore, the search for abstract truth that we assume is the goal of philosophy, while taken for granted in the West, was not found in the East, where philosophy was concerned with observation and experience.

If Aristotelian philosophy, with its emphasis on formal logic, was based on the assumption that truth is gained by opposition, Chinese philosophy offers an alternative view. With its emphasis on harmony, says anthropologist Linda Young, Chinese philosophy sees a diverse universe in precarious balance that is maintained by talk. This translates into methods of investigation that focus more on integrating ideas and exploring relations among them than on opposing ideas and fighting over them.   7

Onward, Christian Soldiers

The military-like culture of early universities is also described by historian David Noble, who describes how young men attending medieval universities were like marauding soldiers: The students—all seminarians—roamed the streets bearing arms, assaulting women, and generally creating mayhem. Noble traces the history of Western science and of universities to joint origins in the Christian Church. The scientific revolution, he shows, was created by religious devotees setting up monastery-like institutions devoted to learning. Early universities were seminaries, and early scientists were either clergy or devoutly religious individuals who led monklike lives. (Until as recently as 1888, fellows at Oxford were expected to be unmarried.)   8

That Western science is rooted in the Christian Church helps explain why our approach to knowledge tends to be conceived as a metaphorical battle: The Christian Church, Noble shows, has origins and early forms rooted in the military. Many early monks[4] had actually been soldiers before becoming monks. Not only were obedience and strict military-like discipline required, but monks saw themselves as serving "in God's knighthood," warriors in a battle against evil. In later centuries, the Crusades brought actual warrior-monks.   9

10   The history of science in the Church holds the key to understanding our tradition of regarding the search for truth as an enterprise of oral disputation in which positions are propounded, defended, and attacked without regard to the debater's personal conviction. It is a notion of truth as objective, best captured by formal logic, that Ong traces to Aristotle. Aristotle regarded logic as the only trustworthy means for human judgment; emotions get in the way: "The man who is to judge would not have his judgment warped by speakers arousing him to anger, jealousy, or compassion. One might as well make a carpenter's tool crooked before using it as a measure."[5]

11   This assumption explains why Plato wanted to ban poets from education in his ideal community. As a lover of poetry, I can still recall my surprise and distress on reading this in *The Republic* when I was in high school. Not until much later did I understand what it was all about.[6] Poets in ancient Greece were wandering bards who traveled from place to place performing oral poetry that persuaded audiences by moving them emotionally. They were like what we think of as demagogues: people with a dangerous power to persuade others by getting them all worked up. Ong likens this to our discomfort with advertising in schools, which we see as places where children should learn to think logically, not be influenced by "teachers" with ulterior motives who use unfair persuasive tactics.

Sharing Time: Early Training in School

12   A commitment to formal logic as the truest form of intellectual pursuit remains with us today. Our glorification of opposition as the path to truth is related to the development of formal logic, which encourages thinkers to regard truth seeking as a step-by-step alternation of claims and counterclaims.[7] Truth, in this schema, is an abstract notion that tends to be taken of context. This formal approach to learning is taught in our schools, often indirectly. [. . .]

13   The tendency to value formal, objective knowledge over relational, intuitive knowledge grows out of our notion of education as training for debate. It is a legacy of the agonistic heritage. There are many other traces as well. Many Ph.D. programs still require public "defenses" of dissertations or dissertation proposals, and oral performance of knowledge in comprehensive exams. Throughout our educational system, the most pervasive inheritance is the conviction that issues have two sides, that knowledge is best gained through debate, that ideas should be presented orally to an audience that does its best to poke holes and find weaknesses, and that to get recognition, one has to "stake out a position" in opposition to another.

Integrating Women in the Classroom Army

If Ong is right, the adversarial character of our educational institutions   14
is inseparable from their all-male heritage. I wondered whether teaching techniques still tend to be adversarial today and whether, if they are, this may hold a clue to a dilemma that has received much recent attention: that girls often receive less attention and speak up less in class.[8] One term I taught a large lecture class of 140 students and decided to take advantage of this army (as it were) of researchers to answer these questions. Becoming observers in their own classrooms, my students found plenty of support for Ong's ideas.

I asked the students to note how relatively adversarial the teaching   15
methods were in their other classes and how the students responded. Gabrielle DeRouen-Hawkins's description of a theology class was typical:

> The class is in the format of lecture with class discussion and participation.
> There are thirteen boys and eleven girls in the class. In a fifty-minute class:
> Number of times a male student spoke: 8
> Number of times a female student spoke: 3
> . . . In our readings, theologians present their theories surrounding G-D, life, spirituality and sacredness. As the professor (a male) outlined the main ideas about the readings, he posed questions like "And what is the fault with /Smith's/ basis that the sacred is individualistic?" The only hands that went up were male. Not one female *dared* challenge or refute an author's writings. The only questions that the females asked (and all female comments were questions) involved a problem they had with the content of the reading. The males, on the other hand, openly questioned, criticized, and refuted the readings on five separate occasions. The three other times that males spoke involved them saying something like: "/Smith/ is very vague in her theory of XX. Can you explain it further?" They were openly argumentative.[9]

This description raises a number of fascinating issues. First, it gives   16
concrete evidence that at least college classrooms proceed on the assumption that the educational process should be adversarial: The teacher invited students to criticize the reading. (Theology, a required course at Georgetown, was a subject where my students most often found adversarial methods—interestingly, given the background I laid out earlier.) Again, there is nothing inherently wrong with using such methods. Clearly, they are very effective in many ways. However, among the potential liabilities is the risk that women students may be

less likely to take part in classroom discussions that are framed as arguments between opposing sides—that is, debate—or as attacks on the authors—that is, critique. (The vast majority of students' observations revealed that men tended to speak more than women in their classes—which is not to say that individual women did not speak more than individual men.)

17   Gabrielle commented that since class participation counted for 10 percent of students' grades, it might not be fair to women students that the agonistic style is more congenial to men. Not only might women's grades suffer because they speak up less, but they might be evaluated as less intelligent or prepared because when they did speak, they asked questions rather than challenging the readings.

18   I was intrigued by the student's comment "/Smith/ is very vague in her theory of XX. Can you explain it further?" It could have been phrased "I didn't understand the author's theory. Can you explain it to me?" By beginning "The author is vague in her theory," the questioner blamed the author for his failure to understand. A student who asks a question in class risks appearing ignorant. Prefacing the question this way was an excellent way to minimize that risk.

19   In her description of this class, Gabrielle wrote that not a single woman *"dared challenge or refute"* an author. She herself underlined the word "dared." But in reading this I wondered whether "dared" was necessarily the right word. It implies that the women in the class wished to challenge the author but did not have the courage. It is possible that not a single woman *cared* to challenge the author. Criticizing or challenging might not be something that appealed to them or seemed worth their efforts. Going back to the childhoods of boys and girls, it seems possible that the boys had had more experiences, from the time they were small, that encouraged them to challenge and argue with authority figures than the girls had.

20   This is not to say that classrooms are more congenial to boys than girls in every way. Especially in the lowest grades, the requirement that children sit quietly in their seats seems clearly to be easier for girls to fulfill than boys, since many girls frequently sit fairly quietly for long periods of time when they play, while most boys' idea of play involves at least running around, if not also jumping and roughhousing. And researchers have pointed out that some of the extra attention boys receive is aimed at controlling such physical exuberance. The adversarial aspect of educational traditions is just one small piece of the pie, but it seems to reflect boys' experiences and predilections more than girls'.

21   A colleague commented that he had always taken for granted that the best way to deal with students' comments is to challenge them; he took it to be self-evident that this technique sharpens their minds and helps them develop debating skills. But he noticed that women were

relatively silent in his classes. He decided to try beginning discussion with relatively open questions and letting comments go unchallenged. He found, to his amazement and satisfaction, that more women began to speak up in class.

Clearly, women can learn to perform in adversarial ways. Anyone 22 who doubts this need only attend an academic conference in the field of women's studies or feminist studies—or read Duke University professor Jane Tompkins's essay showing how a conference in these fields can be like a Western shoot-out. My point is rather about the roots of the tradition and the tendency of the style to appeal initially to more men than women in the Western cultural context. Ong and Noble show that the adversarial culture of Western science and its exclusion of women were part and parcel of the same historical roots—not that individual women may not learn to practice and enjoy agonistic debate or that individual men may not recoil from it. There are many people, women as well as men, who assume a discussion must be contentious to be interesting. Author Mary Catherine Bateson recalls that when her mother, the anthropologist Margaret Mead, said, "I had an argument with" someone, it was a positive comment. "An argument," to her, meant a spirited intellectual interchange, not a rancorous conflict. The same assumption emerged in an obituary for Diana Trilling, called "one of the very last of the great midcentury New York intellectuals."[10] She and her friends had tried to live what they called "a life of significant contention"—the contention apparently enhancing rather than undercutting the significance. [. . .]

The Culture of Critique: Attack in the Academy

The standard way of writing an academic paper is to position your 23 work in opposition to someone else's, which you prove wrong. This creates a *need* to make others wrong, which is quite a different matter from reading something with an open mind and discovering that you disagree with it. Students are taught that they must disprove others' arguments in order to be original, make a contribution, and demonstrate their intellectual ability. When there is a *need* to make others wrong, the temptation is great to oversimplify at best, and at worst to distort or even misrepresent others' positions, the better to refute them—to search for the most foolish statement in a generally reasonable treatise, seize upon the weakest examples, ignore facts that support your opponent's views, and focus only on those that support yours. Straw men spring up like scarecrows in a cornfield.

Sometimes it seems as if there is a maxim driving academic dis- 24 course that counsels, "If you can't find something bad to say, don't say anything." As a result, any work that gets a lot of attention is immediately opposed. There is an advantage to this approach: Weaknesses are exposed, and that is surely good. But another result is that it is difficult for those outside the field (or even inside) to know what is "true." Like two expert witnesses hired by opposing attorneys, academics can seem to be canceling each other out. In the words of policy analysts David Greenberg and Philip Robins:

> The process of scientific inquiry almost ensures that competing sets of results will be obtained. . . . Once the first set of findings are published, other researchers eager to make a name for themselves must come up with different approaches and results to get their studies published."[11]

How are outsiders (or insiders, for that matter) to know which "side" to believe? As a result, it is extremely difficult for research to influence public policy.

25   A leading researcher in psychology commented that he knew of two young colleagues who had achieved tenure by writing articles attacking him. One of them told him, in confidence, that he actually agreed with him, but of course he could not get tenure by writing articles simply supporting someone else's work; he had to stake out a position in opposition. Attacking an established scholar has particular appeal because it demonstrates originality and independence of thought without requiring true innovation. After all, the domain of inquiry and the terms of debate have already been established. The critic has only to say, like the child who wants to pick a fight, "Is not!" Younger or less prominent scholars can achieve a level of attention otherwise denied or eluding them by stepping into the ring with someone who has already attracted the spotlight.

Believing as Thinking

26   "The doubting game" is the name English professor Peter Elbow gives to what educators are trained to do. In playing the doubting game, you approach others' work by looking for what's wrong, much as the press corps follows the president hoping to catch him stumble or an attorney pores over an opposing witness's deposition looking for inconsistencies that can be challenged on the stand. It is an attorney's job to discredit opposing witnesses, but is it a scholar's job to approach colleagues like an opposing attorney?

27   Elbow recommends learning to approach new ideas, and ideas different from your own, in a different spirit—what he calls a "believing game." This does not mean accepting everything anyone says or writes

in an unthinking way. That would be just as superficial as rejecting everything without thinking deeply about it. The believing game is still a game. It simply asks you to give it a whirl: Read *as if* you believed, and see where it takes you. Then you can go back and ask whether you want to accept or reject elements in the argument or the whole argument or idea. Elbow is not recommending that we stop doubting altogether. He is telling us to stop doubting exclusively. We need a systematic and respected way to detect and expose strengths, just as we have a systematic and respected way of detecting faults.

Americans need little encouragement to play the doubting game because we regard it as synonymous with intellectual inquiry, a sign of intelligence. In Elbow's words, "We tend to assume that the ability to criticize a claim we disagree with counts as more serious intellectual work than the ability to enter into it and temporarily assent."[12] It is the believing game that needs to be encouraged and recognized as an equally serious intellectual pursuit.

Although criticizing is surely part of critical thinking, it is not synonymous with it. Again, limiting critical response to critique means not doing the other kinds of critical thinking that could be helpful: looking for new insights, new perspectives, new ways of thinking, new knowledge. Critiquing relieves you of the responsibility of doing integrative thinking. It also has the advantage of making the critics feel smart, smarter than the ill-fated author whose work is being picked apart like carrion. But it has the disadvantage of making them less likely to learn from the author's work.

The Socratic Method—Or Is It?

Another scholar who questions the usefulness of opposition as the sole path to truth is philosopher Janice Moulton. Philosophy, she shows, equates logical reasoning with the Adversary Paradigm, a matter of making claims and then trying to find, and argue against, counterexamples to that claim. The result is a debate between adversaries trying to defend their ideas against counterexamples and to come up with counterexamples that refute the opponent's ideas. In this paradigm, the best way to evaluate someone's work is to "subject it to the strongest or most extreme opposition."[13]

But if you parry individual points—a negative and defensive enterprise—you never step back and actively imagine a world in which a different system of ideas could be true—a positive act. And you never ask how larger systems of thought relate to each other. According to Moulton, our devotion to the Adversary Paradigm has led us to misinterpret the type of argumentation that Socrates favored: We think of the Socratic method as systematically leading an opponent into admitting error. This is primarily a way of showing up an adversary as wrong. Moulton shows that the original Socratic method—the *elenchus*—was designed to convince others, to shake them out of their habitual mode of thought and lead them to new insight. Our version of the Socratic method—an adversarial public debate—is unlikely to result in opponents changing their minds. Someone who loses a debate usually attributes that loss to poor performance or to an adversary's unfair tactics. [. . .]

Question the Basic Assumption

32   My aim is not to put a stop to the adversarial paradigm, the doubting game, debate—but to diversify: Like a well-balanced stock portfolio, we need more than one path to the goal we seek. What makes it hard to question whether debate is truly the only or even the most fruitful approach to learning is that we're dealing with assumptions that we and everyone around us take to be self-evident. A prominent dean at a major research university commented to me, "The Chinese cannot make great scientists because they will not debate publicly." Many people would find this remark offensive. They would object because it generalizes about all Chinese scientists, especially since it makes a negative evaluation. But I would also question the assumption that makes the generalization a criticism: the conviction that the only way to test and develop ideas is to debate them publicly. It may well be true that most Chinese scientists are reluctant to engage in public, rancorous debate. I see nothing insulting about such a claim; it derives from the Chinese cultural norms that many Chinese and Western observers have documented. But we also know that many Chinese have indeed been great scientists.[14] The falsity of the dean's statement should lead us to question whether debate is the only path to insight. . . .

The Cost in Human Spirit

33   Whatever the causes of the argument culture—and the many causes I have mentioned are surely not the only ones—the most grievous cost is the price paid in human spirit: Contentious public discourse becomes a model for behavior and sets the tone for how individuals experience their relationships to other people and to the society we live in.

34   Recall the way young boys on Tory Island learned to emulate their elders:

> All around milled little boys imitating their elders, cursing, fluffing, swaggering, threatening. It was particularly fascinating to see how the children learned the whole sequence of behavior. Anything that

the men did, they would imitate, shouting the same things, strutting and swaggering.[15]

Tory Island may be an especially ritualized example, but it is not a totally aberrant one. When young men come together in groups, they often engage in symbolic ritual displays of aggression that involve posturing and mock battles. Without pressing the parallel in too literal a way, I couldn't help thinking that this sounds a bit like what journalists and lawyers have observed about their own tribes: that the display of aggression for the benefit of peers is often more important than concrete results.[. . .]

Getting Beyond Dualism

At the heart of the argument culture is our habit of seeing issues and   35 ideas as absolute and irreconcilable principles continually at war. To move beyond this static and limiting view, we can remember the Chinese approach to yin and yang. They are two principles, yes, but they are conceived not as irreconcilable polar opposites but as elements that coexist and should be brought into balance as much as possible. As sociolinguist Suzanne Wong Scollon notes, "Yin is always present in and changing into yang and vice versa."[16] How can we translate this abstract idea into daily practice?

To overcome our bias toward dualism, we can make special efforts   36 not to think in twos. Mary Catherine Bateson, an author and anthropologist who teaches at George Mason University, makes a point of having her class compare *three* cultures, not two.[17] If students compare two cultures, she finds, they are inclined to polarize them, to think of the two as opposite to each other. But if they compare three cultures, they are more likely to think about each on its own terms.

As a goal, we could all try to catch ourselves when we talk about   37 "both sides" of an issue—and talk instead about "all sides." And people in any field can try to resist the temptation to pick on details when they see a chance to score a point. If the detail really does not speak to the main issue, bite your tongue. Draw back and consider the whole picture. After asking, "Where is this wrong?" make an effort to ask "What is right about this?"—not necessarily *instead*, but *in addition*.

In the public arena, producers can try to avoid, whenever possible,   38 structuring public discussions as debates. This means avoiding the format of having two guests discuss an issue, pro and con. In some cases three guests—or one—will be more enlightening than two.

An example of the advantage of adding a third guest was an   39 episode of *The Diane Rehm Show* on National Public Radio following the withdrawal of Anthony Lake from nomination as director of central intelligence. White House Communications Director Ann Lewis claimed that the process of confirming presidential appointments has become more partisan and personal.[18] Tony Blankley, former communications director for Newt Gingrich, claimed that the process has always been rancorous. Fortunately for the audience, there was a third guest: historian Michael Beschloss, who provided historical perspective. He explained that during the immediately preceding period of 1940 to 1990, confirmation hearings were indeed more benign than they have been since, but in the 1920s and the latter half of the nineteenth century, he said, they were also "pretty bloody." In this way, a third guest, especially a guest who is not committed to one side, can dispel the audience's frustration when two guests make opposite claims. [. . .]

Moving from Debate to Dialogue

40   Many of the issues I have discussed are also of concern to Amitai Etzioni and other communitarians. In *The New Golden Rule*, Etzioni proposes rules of engagement to make dialogue more constructive between people with differing views. His rules of engagement are designed to reflect—and reinforce—the tenet that people whose ideas conflict are still members of the same community.[19] Among these rules are:

- Don't demonize those with whom you disagree.
- Don't affront their deepest moral commitments.
- Talk less of rights, which are nonnegotiable, and more of needs, wants, and interests.
- Leave some issues out.
- Engage in a dialogue of convictions: Don't be so reasonable and conciliatory that you lose touch with a core of belief you feel passionately about.

41   As I stressed [. . .] earlier [. . .], producers putting together television or radio shows and journalists covering stories might consider—in at least some cases—preferring rather than rejecting potential commentators who say they cannot take one side or the other unequivocally. Information shows might do better with only one guest who is given a chance to explore an idea in depth rather than two who will prevent each other from developing either perspective. A producer who feels that two guests with radically opposed views seem truly the most appropriate might begin by asking whether the issue is being framed in the most constructive way. If it is, a third or fourth participant could be invited as well, to temper the "two sides" perspective.

Perhaps it is time to reexamine the assumption that audiences al- 42
ways prefer a fight. In reviewing a book about the history of *National
Geographic*, Marina Warner scoffs at the magazine's policy of avoiding
attack. She quotes the editor who wrote in 1915, "Only what is of a
kindly nature is printed about any country or people, everything unpleasant or unduly critical being avoided."[20] Warner describes this
editorial approach condescendingly as a "happy-talk, feel-good philosophy" and concludes that "its deep wish not to offend has often
made it dull." But the facts belie this judgment. *National Geographic* is
one of the most successful magazines of all time—as reported in the
same review, its circulation "stands over 10 million, and the readership,
according to surveys, is four times that number."

Perhaps, too, it is time to question our glorification of debate as the 43
best, if not the only, means of inquiry. The debate format leads us to regard those doing different kinds of research as belonging to warring
camps. There is something very appealing about conceptualizing differing approaches in this way, because the dichotomies appeal to our
sense of how knowledge should be organized.

Well, what's wrong with that? 44

What's wrong is that it obscures aspects of disparate work that 45
overlap and can enlighten each other.

What's wrong is that it obscures the complexity of research. Fitting 46
ideas into a particular camp requires you to oversimplify them. Again,
disinformation and distortion can result. Less knowledge is gained, not
more. And time spent attacking an opponent or defending against attacks is not spent doing something else—like original research.

What's wrong is that it implies that only one framework can apply, 47
when in most cases many can. As a colleague put it, "Most theories are
wrong not in what they assert but in what they deny."[21] Clinging to the
elephant's leg, they loudly proclaim that the person describing the elephant's tail is wrong. This is not going to help them—or their readers—
understand an elephant. Again, there are parallels in personal
relationships. I recall a man who had just returned from a weekend
human development seminar. Full of enthusiasm, he explained the
main lesson he had learned: "I don't have to make others wrong to
prove that I'm right." He experienced this revelation as a liberation; it
relieved him of the burden of trying to prove others wrong.

If you limit your view of a problem to choosing between two sides, 48
you inevitably reject much that is true, and you narrow your field of vision to the limits of those two sides, making it unlikely you'll pull back,
widen your field of vision, and discover the paradigm shift that will
permit truly new understanding.

In moving away from a narrow view of debate, we need not give 49
up conflict and criticism altogether. Quite the contrary, we can develop

more varied—and more constructive—ways of expressing opposition and negotiating disagreement.

50   We need to use our imaginations and ingenuity to find different ways to seek truth and gain knowledge, and add them to our arsenal—or, should I say, to the ingredients for our stew. It will take creativity to find ways to blunt the most dangerous blades of the argument culture. It's a challenge we must undertake, because our public and private lives are at stake.

Notes

1. This does not mean it goes back in an unbroken chain. David Noble, in *A World Without Women*, claims that Aristotle was all but lost to the West during the early Christian era and was rediscovered in the medieval era, when universities were first established. This is significant for his observation that many early Christian monasteries welcomed both women and men who could equally aspire to an androgynous ideal, in contrast to the Middle Ages, when the female was stigmatized, unmarried women were consigned to convents, priests were required to be celibate, and women were excluded from spiritual authority.

2. There is a fascinating parallel in the evolution of the early Christian Church and the Southern Baptist Church: Noble shows that the early Christian Church regarded women as equally beloved of Jesus and equally capable of devoting their lives to religious study, so women comprised a majority of early converts to Christianity, some of them leaving their husbands—or bringing their husbands along—to join monastic communities. It was later, leading up to the medieval period, that the clerical movement gained ascendancy in part by systematically separating women, confining them in either marriage or convents, stigmatizing them, and barring them from positions of power within the church. Christine Leigh Heyrman, in *Southern Cross: The Beginnings of the Bible Belt*, shows that a similar trajectory characterized the Southern Baptist movement. At first, young Baptist and Methodist preachers (in the 1740s to 1830s) preached that both women and blacks were equally God's children, deserving of spiritual authority—with the result that the majority of converts were women and slaves. To counteract this distressing demography, the message was changed: Anti-slavery rhetoric faded, and women's roles were narrowed to domesticity and subservience. With these shifts, the evangelical movement swept the South. At the same time, Heyrman shows, military imagery took over: The ideal man of God was transformed from a "willing martyr" to a "formidable fighter" led by "warrior preachers."

3. Ong, *Fighting for Life*, p. 122. Ong's source, on which I also rely, is Oliver, *Communication and Culture in Ancient India and China*. My own quotations from Oliver are from pp. 259.

4. Pachomius, for example, "the father of communal monasticism . . . and organizer of the first monastic community, had been a soldier under Constantine" and modeled his community on the military, emphasizing order,

efficiency, and military obedience. Cassian, a fourth-century proselytizer, "'likened the monk's discipline to that of the soldier,' and Chrysostom, another great champion of the movement, sternly reminded the monks that Christ had armed them to be soldiers in a noble fight" (Noble, *A World Without Women*, p. 54).

5. Aristotle, quoted in Oliver, *Communication and Culture in Ancient India and China*, p. 259.

6. I came to understand the different meaning of "poet" in Classical Greece from reading Ong and also *Preface to Plato* by Eric Havelock. These insights informed many articles I wrote about oral and literate tradition in Western culture, including "Oral and Literate Strategies in Spoken and Written Narratives" and "The Oral/Literate Continuum in Discourse."

7. Moulton, "A Paradigm of Philosophy"; Ong, *Fighting for Life*.

8. See David and Myra Sadker, *Failing at Fairness*.

9. Although my colleagues and I make efforts to refer to our students—all over the age of eighteen—as "women" and "men" and some students in my classes do the same, the majority refer to each other and themselves as "girls" and "boys" or "girls" and "guys."

10. Jonathan Alter, "*The End of the Journey*," Newsweek, Nov. 4, 1996, p. 61. Trilling died at the age of ninety-one.

11. Greenberg and Robins, "The Changing Role of Social Experiments in Policy Analysis," p. 350.

12. Elbow, *Embracing Contraries*, p. 258.

13. Moulton, "A Paradigm of Philosophy," p. 153.

14. See, for example, Needham, *Science and Civilization in China*.

15. Fox, "The Inherent Rules of Violence," p. 141.

16. Suzanne Wong Scollon: Personal communication.

17. Mary Catherine Bateson: Personal communication.

18. At the time of this show, Ms. Lewis was deputy communications director.

19. Etzioni, *The New Golden Rule*, pp. 104–106. He attributes the rule "Talk less of rights . . . and more of needs, wants, and interests" to Mary Ann Glendon.

20. Marina Warner, "High-Minded Pursuit of the Exotic," review of *Reading National Geographic* by Catherine A. Lutz and Jane L. Collins in *The New York Times Book Review*, Sept. 19, 1993, p. 13.

21. I got this from A. L. Becker, who got it from Kenneth Pike, who got it from . . . [.]

RESPONDING TO READING

1. How does Tannen connect formal, competitive debate to the history of education, particularly the education of men? What contrasting approach to education does she offer?

2. According to Tannen, how was formal education at the university level linked to religion? Does such a link limit inquiry and academic freedom?

3. In your experience, is education in America founded on "challenge and attack," as Tannen suggests? Examine a textbook or a published academic

paper in your chosen field for evidence to support or refute Tannen's assertion.

4. What role does gender play in Tannen's argument? Are her observations about how men and women behave differently in classes supported or refuted by your own experiences? (And is it even possible to ask or answer a question such as this without being adversarial towards Tannen?) In teams of two men and two women, compare your experiences and write a brief reply to Tannen.

5. For one week, keep track of how often men and women respond in one of your classes (preferably a class that involves a high level of student participation). What patterns do men and women seem to follow as they respond in class? How does the instructor respond to them? In an essay, consider the role that gender seems to play in this class you are monitoring. Do other exigencies—such as the instructor's approach or the time of day that the class meets—affect this classroom dynamic?

Making Choices: From Short-Term Adjustments to Principled Lives
ROBERT WUTHNOW

Sociologist Robert Wuthnow was born (1946) in a small Kansas town; his father was a farmer and his mother a teacher. After attending the University of Kansas (B.S., 1968), he earned graduate degrees at the University of Northern Colorado (M.A., 1969) and Berkeley (Ph.D., 1975). Currently at Princeton, as a professor of sociology and as the director of the Center for the Study of Religion, Wuthnow investigates the relationship between religion, economics, politics, art, and ethical values. A prolific author, Wuthnow has published numerous books and scholarly articles, and has edited *The Encyclopedia of Politics and Religion* (1998). His recent publications include *Quiet Hand of God: Faith-based Activism and the Public Role of Mainline Protestantism* (2002), *Creative Spirituality: The Way of the Artist* (2001), *Growing Up Religious: Christians and Jews and Their Journeys of Faith* (1999), and *Loose Connections: Joining Together in America's Fragmented Communities* (1998). A principal concern of Wuthnow's is the clash between Americans' religious values and their economic behavior. In *God and Mammon in America* (1994), he studied attitudes about workplace ethics, money, materialism, poverty, economic justice, and charity. After conducting a survey that included 175 in-depth interviews and 2000 lengthy questionnaires, he concluded that while religion helps people find meaning in their work, the basic attitudes and values of religious Americans vary little from those of their nonreligious counterparts.

"Making Choices," from *Poor Richard's Principle: Recovering the American Dream Through the Moral Dimension of Work, Business, and*

Money (1996), looks at stress, overwork, and burnout in the American workplace. Because stress is more of a philosophical problem than a physiological one, argues Wuthnow, popular remedies and quick fixes such as worker screening and fitness programs are not enough. When institutions shape our values, solutions to problems within institutions must be based on more than individual initiative.

With increasing levels of burnout, career dissatisfaction, substance 1 abuse, alcoholism, and costly job-stress suits, a growing number of American corporations have started paying attention to the possibility that people are simply working too hard, taking on responsibilities that do not nurture themselves as human beings, and putting themselves under too much pressure. General Motors has more than 100 staff psychologists dealing with problems of drugs, alcohol, burnout, and depression on the assembly line. Motorola, Xerox, Levi Strauss, and a few other large firms have initiated task forces in recent years to study the relationship between work and family problems among their employees.[1] But thus far the response from business has been mainly to invoke stricter policing in hopes of curtailing substance abuse and to encourage workers to live healthier lives through fitness programs and health evaluation clinics. Stimulating productivity while protecting their firms from undue costs has been management's top priority.

Quick-Fix Solutions

Typifying this priority is the kind of advice found routinely in manage- 2 rial columns for employers faced with stress and burnout among their employees. One such column advises readers to screen employees better for preexisting "mental maladies" and to solicit information from other workers that might be useful in warding off lawsuits. Presuming that it is the worker's own responsibility to limit stress, the column makes no mention of firms themselves trying to reduce job pressures.[2] Other columns suggest that managers deal with work-related stress by making corporate myths more visible to middle-level employees.

More generally, analyses of the work and money pressures facing 3 the American population usually take a sadly limited view, attributing them to bothersome but endemic features of corporate life, the managerial personality, and the business cycle. Most of the trouble, say the analysts, springs from crisis situations such as being laid off, landing under the thumb of a dictatorial boss, or simply having a sudden string of bad luck.[3] Others emphasize economic and demographic factors, both of which have simply made it more difficult for the present generation to realize the American Dream.

What to do? Find ways to cope. Here, for example, is the advice 4 given by a leading news magazine:

Maintain a sense of humor.
Meditate.
Get a massage.
Exercise regularly.
Eat more sensibly.
Limit intake of alcohol and caffeine.
Take refuge in family and friends.
Delegate responsibility.
Stand up to the boss.
Quit.[4] [. . .]

5   Such activities and advice may be helpful for getting through a particularly stressful day, but they will not do anything to solve the underlying problem. "Stress cannot be dealt with by psychological tricks," Sam Keen has written, "because for the most part it is a philosophical rather than a physiological problem, a matter of the wrong worldview.[5] Coming from a writer who himself has long been associated with the pop-psychology industry, this is a sobering warning indeed.

6   The reason quick-fix solutions can be of little enduring value is that stress and overwork are built into the American way of life. They are not just the nettlesome by-products of having an ill-tempered boss or seeing a prospective contract turn sour. They are rooted in endemic characteristics of the modern workplace and the international markets in which most corporations now compete. Certainly these economic realities play a significant role in the work and money pressures so many middle-class Americans are experiencing. But there is an even deeper source of many of these pressures. They are part of the values we have inherited and the way we think. They reflect both long-standing and changing conceptions of ourselves as individuals, of our responsibilities and what we most cherish in our lives.

7   Research evidence points clearly to the inadequacy of quick-fix solutions. If these ideas were really that useful, we would expect to find people faced with stress on a frequent basis using them more. If they actually worked, we might also observe that people who used them were less likely to register feelings of stress than people who didn't. But neither of these is the case. When faced with stress, large numbers of the American workforce resort to such tactics: 71 percent talk to close friends, 60 percent engage in physical exercise, 56 percent work on a hobby, 40 percent go shopping, and 30 percent take a few days off. But those faced with frequent stress are neither more nor less likely to engage in these activities than other people. Nor are those who engage in these activities any more satisfied with their work or any less likely to be worried than other people.[6]

8   The evidence also points clearly to one of the reasons why quick-fix solutions do not work. Job-related stress stems from factors other than

just those associated with unpleasant situations at work, and it raises questions about a much broader and deeper range of issues. Of people in my survey who said they experienced job-related stress almost every day, for example, only a quarter complained of conflict with co-workers (26 percent), an unsupportive boss (25 percent), or an unpleasant work environment (22 percent). In comparison, nearly half complained of not having enough time for their family (49 percent), feeling burned out (49 percent), needing more time for themselves (48 percent), and wanting other things in life (42 percent). [. . .]

Among the frequent-stress group, 53 percent had been wondering   9
if they were in the right line of work, and 55 percent had been feeling seriously burned out within the past year.

The one thing that stress relates to more powerfully than anything   10
else, in fact, is thinking about basic values in life and trying to juggle commitments to a wide range of values. In the labor force as a whole, for example, 29 percent said they think a lot about their values and priorities in life; but this proportion rose to 40 percent among persons experiencing stress almost every day in their jobs and was 56 percent among those who felt they were working themselves to death. Moreover, the more frequently respondents experienced stress, the more likely they were to say they attached value to other commitments such as family, morality, taking care of themselves, and relating to God. [. . .]

The advice columnists can think up easy solutions to our problems,   11
but they help little in thinking through the hard issues of what we really want in life. [. . .]

The Disease Model

If quick-fix solutions are too shallow, the disease model that has been   12
advanced in recent years to understand problems with work, money, and other economic commitments goes to an extreme in the other direction. Rather than linking stress and burnout to specific situations at work, it associates them with an underlying malady in the worker's personality. The problem, say proponents of this view, is "workaholism"—a malady taken to be exactly parallel with alcoholism. Suffering from some fundamental insecurity, the workaholic tries to discover true happiness by working too hard. Compulsiveness is often present, causing the individual to "binge" on day-and-night working sprees and then to feel utterly dissatisfied and unmotivated. Money problems may stem from the same problem: an insatiable longing for happiness that is wrongly pursued by trying to accumulate riches or by spending money wildly on unneeded purchases.

The disease model is valid up to a point. It does recognize the im-   13
portance of questions about personal identity, commitments, values,

and the need to settle on priorities. The compulsive behavior it describes does characterize a segment of the population. But, like so many other contemporary applications of the literature on addictions, it carries the argument too far. Workaholism may be similar to alcoholism in some respects, but its chemical basis is fundamentally different. Just how widely applicable it may be is also debatable. That it may have limited applications is suggested by the fact that only one person in six actually feels like he or she is working to death, and only one in seven claims to experience stress on a daily basis. Moreover, of this frequent-stress group, only 4 percent say they are seeing a therapist to help them with stress, and only 6 percent try to find help in a support group.

14   Proponents of the disease model, of course, argue that the fact people are not seeking help is all the more reason to be concerned. But the model ultimately suffers thereby from being impossible to confirm or disconfirm empirically. Many of its assertions focus so broadly on such "problems" as rushing, busyness, making lists, and caring about one's work that virtually everyone falls into the category of the diseased. Other assertions make valuable connections and yet lead away from a valid understanding of these connections. For example, one widely publicized book on the subject asserts that "work addicts are dishonest, controlling, self-centered, perfectionistic, and abusive to themselves and others." It is little wonder, the author expostulates, that "their morality" is askew. "You cannot lead such a life without losing your moorings. Your grounding in basic values is lost in the relentless pursuit of the addiction."[7] Clearly the important point is that basic values must somehow be brought back into focus. It helps little to describe the underlying problem as an addiction, however.

15   The broader problem is not that people who work hard have abandoned other values. Indeed, it is clearly the opposite. [Some] People [. . .] want it all. They are committed to their work and to the good life that money can buy; they also want more out of life. Indeed, when work and money are compared with other values in our society, they come out on top fairly infrequently. In my survey, for example, 29 percent of the labor force said their work was absolutely essential to their sense of personal worth, and only 15 percent said this about "making a lot of money." In comparison, 69 percent said their family was absolutely essential to their personal worth; 56 percent said this about their moral standards, 43 percent did so about taking care of themselves, and 39 percent did about their relationship to God. The study also shows that the minority who did say work and money were absolutely essential were actually *more* likely to value these other commitments, rather than less likely to value them.[8]

If something is wrong, it is that we want too much out of life, not   16
too little. And yet to say that people want to spend time with their families, that they value their moral standards and their relationship to
God, or that they want to serve the needy is surely not something to
decry. The American Dream has always championed these other pursuits as part of what the good society should encourage its members to
be doing. What has contributed to the difficulty of engaging in these
pursuits in recent years is that social conditions and cultural understandings alike have been shifting rapidly. As a result, more and more
people are having to think through their values in ways that were neither possible nor necessary in the past. [. . .]

[The] question remains whether there are principles other than   17
self-interest, pleasure, and bodily preservation that should be factored
into our thinking. The question is not simply how to rest up so we can
be more productive at work the next day. The question is how to weigh
the other priorities that have always characterized the human spirit
against those to which the dollar sign can be affixed. Should we be willing to sacrifice an hour pursuing another business deal in order to visit
a friend in the hospital? Or can we be content, as one writer discovered
when he posed this question to a class of prospective MBAs at Harvard
Business School, to regard such moral commitments as patently
absurd?

Reforming the System

Historically, the most common way of placing limits around the eco-   18
nomic system has been to invoke governmental restrictions. From early
attempts to limit the workday, pass old-age- and disability-insurance
measures, and promote greater safety in the workplace, to more recent
efforts to outlaw discrimination and implement redistributive taxation
schemes, legislation has been regarded as the principal means of com-
bating the ill effects of the marketplace. One of the major axes around
which modern political debate has revolved has thus been its position
on how much or how little the state should intervene in economic
matters.[9]

The reason why recourse to political means has so often been taken   19
is that the state's powers seem the only measure strong enough to
make a difference. Against the entrenchment of profit-motivated interests and the social influences of those in control of economic resources,
only coercion can call a halt. Pragmatic arguments, indicating that political means have in fact accomplished much in terms of ameliorating
the worst excesses of the marketplace, have often been advanced as

well. Compared with schemes for overturning capitalism itself, these reformist measures have proven decidedly more attractive. Yet political solutions can go only so far in guiding and restraining economic life.

20   Government restrictions work best within a legitimating framework of fundamental human rights, including norms of justice and equal treatment before the law. They can help prevent the worst excesses of economic production and distribution, such as the exploitation of disadvantaged minorities, conditions injurious to health, or ones that pollute the environment. Government initiatives have sometimes been able to mitigate undesirable social conditions by encouraging long-range economic growth itself. Public expenditures on transportation systems, education, and basic research are often cited as examples. Where government restrictions cannot legitimately attempt to regulate economic life is in those realms deemed to lie within the domain of individual discretion.

21   Discretion to make fundamental decisions affecting the course and quality of individual life has come to be regarded as a culturally legitimate and constitutionally guaranteed manifestation of personal freedom. Government can pass legislation prohibiting an employer from dumping toxic waste on public land or from discriminating against racial minorities, but it cannot pass laws telling that employer to be at work by a certain hour in the morning, to spend Thursday evenings at home with the family, or to give $5,000 to charity rather than purchase a new wide-screen television set. All government can do in those areas is to provide gentle nudges in one direction or another. For example, it can encourage charitable contributions by making them tax deductible or it can discourage spending on luxury items by adding a surtax.

22   Anything further violates the individual freedoms so widely cherished in democratic societies. As efforts to legislate a thirty-hour work week, add new holidays to the national calendar, and mandate social service among the young all have demonstrated, it is extremely difficult for social reformers to legislate new conceptions of the American Dream, not only because of the costs of these programs, but because they can also be opposed on grounds of curbing fundamental human liberties. [. . .]

23   Social critics are correct in suggesting that much of the public's resistance to government intervention in the economy stems from raw self-interest instead of well-schooled conceptions of civic liberty. The critics also need to be taken seriously when they point out that civic responsibility requires people to press for government solutions to such problems as discrimination in the workplace, corporate greed, exploitation of the poor and the disadvantaged, fraud, and environmental destruction. But the same critics who voice these concerns have also come increasingly to recognize that government restrictions are unlikely

to be instituted in the first place—or be effective—unless people are willing to subject themselves to some kind of moral restraint. In short, a society that places high responsibility on the individual must look not only to government to rein in its economic commitments, but to a better understanding of the ethics and values on which institutional and individual commitments are based.

The Growing Role of Discretion

In advanced industrial societies individual discretion has become increasingly significant. Not only has it been championed in various ways by conservative and liberal political theoreticians; it is also built increasingly into the fabric of economic life itself. With late-modern levels of economic development, fewer people have to work from sunrise to sunset to eke out a subsistence living, nor do people spend as large a percentage of their earnings on food, shelter, clothing, and other necessities, thus leaving a larger share of their time and money available for discretionary uses. In the workplace itself greater emphasis is likely to be placed on autonomous decision making, with fewer tasks being mandated specifically by someone in authority. The choice of careers themselves and decisions about particular places of employment have increasingly become matters of personal discretion. Indeed, the very meaning of discretion, once connoting caution and prudence, has been subtly redefined to mean the exercise of choice.   24

Discretion is part of the normative order of most institutions as well. The individual is expected to make ethical decisions and to choose how he or she will achieve desired work goals. Greater discretion is expected of individuals in their private lives, from choosing sexual and marriage partners to deciding how to school their children. With nonworking hours being defined as free time involving a wide variety of options, people are expected to exercise discretion in allocating time to various leisure activities or to community service. They are expected to exercise discretion in deciding how to allocate surplus financial resources among various consumer products and benevolent causes. All these decisions have enormous implications for the economy itself and for the quality of people's lives, but they are decisions over which most people feel government has very little rightful control. [. . .]   25

In the absence of guiding legal or coercive norms, discretionary behavior for millions of people [. . .] has increasingly become the domain in which economic influences are permitted to reign with virtually unlimited authority. Individuals define themselves as economic decision makers, allocating time and financial resources to various services,   26 leisure activities, and consumer goods. Economic institutions can right-fully try to influence these individual decisions through marketing and advertising, or in the workplace, by offering financial incentives. The individual is assumed to be free to make economic choices, so no con-stitutional issues are at stake, and is regarded as being motivated to participate in the marketplace as a consumer. Economic institutions are even said to have special claim to the individual because they are, it is sometimes claimed, the source of this discretionary time and income in the first place.[10]

How Much Freedom Do We Have?

27   To those who have considered how much economic institutions shape our lives, the claim that people are increasingly free to do whatever they want is of course recognizably overstated. They know that even the relatively affluent professionals and managers who are said to enjoy the greatest freedoms often find themselves with little room to maneuver at all. Their corporations have a rigid set of expectations to which they must conform in order to survive and succeed. These may include everything from dress codes to formal objectives to unstated rules about how to greet the boss in the morning. Professionals who work in other settings may also be subjected to bureaucratic norms re-quiring them to perform efficiently, to meet fixed work schedules, and to participate in unrewarding gatherings of their peers.

28   Sociologist Robert Jackall, in an intensive study of the work lives of corporate managers, has provided a compelling account of how the bu-reaucracies in which most people now work shape their goals, their ex-pectations, and their perceptions of themselves.[11] He argues that bureaucracy has fundamentally altered the rules by which people pur-sue the American Dream. From the outside, bureaucracies may appear as highly rational, hierarchically coordinated systems for getting the complex tasks of the modern economy done. From the inside, they ap-pear more to be what Jackall appropriately terms "moral mazes." They encourage unwavering loyalty to bosses and patrons and divide peo-ple into floating alliances among coteries and cliques. Within these un-stable networks, workers learn relativistic and often contradictory standards of trustworthiness. They turn to each other for behavioral cues, but what they experience is often too ambiguous to codify. Ethics and values take a back seat to yea-saying, pragmatism, and glib talk.

29   The result is that work gets done, but sooner or later most people begin to experience conflict between their work and the standards of value they perceive in other spheres of their lives. Jackall points espe-

cially to the tension that may arise between struggles for dominance in the bureaucracy and wider norms of friendship, honesty, and compassion. He also perceives tension between the standards of excellence that many individuals aspire to and the inevitable mediocrity that he feels plagues most organizations. Like other critics, he believes bureaucracy is fundamentally at odds with finding overall meaning at work because what is good for the organization may not be good for the individuals who work in it or for the wider society.

This line of analysis suggests that very little can be done to rectify   30 the current situation. People may think they can exercise discretion, but this perception is fundamentally an allusion. Economic institutions not only operate according to their own laws, governing our workday and our pocketbook; they also determine the way we think. Furthermore, bureaucracies are unlikely to disappear anytime soon. In the meantime, we can delude ourselves by talking about the freedom we have, but we must realize that this apparent sense of control over our lives really operates to perpetuate the institutions that dominate modern society.

The trouble with this kind of analysis is that it attributes too much   31 casual influence to the blind forces of which bureaucracy presumably consists. It buys too strongly into the kind of social structural determinism that sociologists have so often assumed they must defend in order to advance their own profession. Yet a more nuanced reading of studies like Jackall's reveals that "bureaucracy" is often little more than a metaphor for the patterns of language and behavior that are observed in the workplace. These patterns are not determined by something else; they are the stuff of which organizations are constituted. It is the conventional languages and norms that must be understood, not some deep force that exercises irresistible control over our lives.

Viewed this way, the same ambiguities that lead some observers to   32 be cynical about the modern workplace provide small beacons of hope. If bureaucracy presents people with uncertainty rather than rigid structures, then there is indeed room for discretion after all. If most people make up their moral norms to satisfy each other, then these norms are by no means fixed from on high. Moreover, the assumption that economic institutions tie people down to the point that they despair of finding any meaning in their work flies in the face of evidence we have already considered. Perhaps people are simply deluded by the organizations for which they work. They may, however, find their work sufficiently meaningful that they would like to integrate it more effectively with the other parts of their lives. Only if they assume their choices are entirely free or entirely determined by the economic realm itself will they find it impossible to pursue this integration.

The Need for Moral Discourse

33   The individual is thus left to make an increasing number of decisions about how to use his or her resources largely without any government restrictions interfering with these decisions, and yet within a normative context in which he or she is defined as an economic actor subject only to the guiding hand of economic institutions and an ethos of economic interest maximization. But how is the individual to make these decisions? On the basis of what value orientations, conceptions of the good, ethical considerations, or moral commitments does the individual decide to participate or withdraw from participating in the marketplace? Economic considerations may specify a range of options and attach various costs and benefits to these options, but they neither exhaust the range of conceivable options nor provide standards of individual or social good to be weighed in selecting among various options.

34   For this reason, all societies have in fact encouraged conceptions of the good that in one way or another limit their members' participation in the economic realm and provide autonomous moral standards for the governance of behavior within this realm. In traditional societies a minority of the population generally opted out of the so-called productive vocations to pursue careers in monastic and religious orders. In many cases people of sufficient means abandoned the pursuit of ever greater wealth in order to engage in public service, cultivate the intellectual life of the salons and universities, or participate in the leisure activities of the court. In still other instances people restricted their economic ambitions in order to raise families or to care for aging relatives. Although these activities were sometimes mandated by the state, they were more often done voluntarily. Economic interest maximization was seldom a primary consideration. A commitment to values that were deemed more basic than economic pursuits erected moral limits around the economic life.

35   In modern societies, for reasons that include the declining salience of an all-embracing conception of cosmic order and the extension of rational decision-making processes to most matters of personal life, the concept of moral limits has largely been restricted to behaviors that have little to do with the economic realm. Morality has come to focus on such issues as sexual fidelity, honesty, and propriety in personal relations, rather than referring to a deeper sense of what is fundamentally good. Indeed, we might venture to say that economic thinking has itself penetrated the moral domain to the extent that technical solutions to the perplexing questions of personal life often seem preferable to old-fashioned conceptions of duty and obligation. British sociologist Bryan Wilson observes: "As for purely personal morality, that quaint concept, so vital to communities in the past, modern man might ask

whether it has not become redundant. In modern language, to be moral is to be 'uptight'; to express moral attitudes is to inhibit people when they want—as modern men say that they have a right to want—'to do their own thing.'"[12]

But if morality connotes unwelcome strictures on personal behav-   36
ior in general, it is likely to be all the more so conceived when these activities are defined simply as consumer preferences. When someone decides to purchase a new automobile instead of spending the money on an expensive vacation, it thus seems correct to speak of the decision as one of maximizing alternative utilities, but it would seem odd to say that certain moral understandings have been expressed. That we do make decisions about economic commitments that have broader moral overtones may still be beyond dispute, but exactly how we do this is less clear. It is thus to the realm of moral discourse that we must look if we are to gain a better understanding of how the deeper commitments of the human spirit relate to the economic realm.

The Nature of Moral Discourse

Because it has so often been conceived narrowly, we need to consider   37
just what moral discourse is and how in the best of all worlds it might be constructed in order to guide and curtail our economic pursuits in effective, satisfying, and meaningful ways. Moral discourse has been the subject of growing attention in recent years, especially among ethicists, but we must select judiciously from this literature.[13]

Ethical absolutes or moral truths of the kind "courage is a virtue"   38
or "slavery is evil" will be of little concern. Ethicists worry a lot about such statements—and they think ordinary people should too—because they want to know how such claims can be defended and, if they cannot, fear there may be no basis for opposing fanatics and fools.

As one of these "ordinary people," I believe we often do not care   39
much what ethicists have to say on these questions. The problem is not, as ethicists themselves will assert, that more compelling philosophical grounds need to be discovered for making these kinds of ethical claims. Most of us ordinary people, probably to ethicists' dismay, are quite willing to accept on faith that courage is good or slavery is evil and leave the fanatics and fools for others to dispute. The problem we sense with ethicists is that none of this has very much to do with the real questions we face in our ordinary lives.

Somewhere between the absolute good and the absolute evil with   40
which ethics is concerned lie the questions we face routinely about what should be done, what is desirable or undesirable, and which of several options may be best for us to pursue. When a physician decides to take an afternoon to play golf, the issue is not one of absolute good

or evil. Even though, by some larger calculation, there may be slightly more suffering—or even death—in the world than there might have been otherwise, we would not ordinarily consider this a question of virtue or vice. Nevertheless, there is a moral dimension to such a decision, and it is this broader moral dimension that should interest us here. How does a person decide when it is preferable to spend an afternoon playing golf instead of treating the sick?

41   Moral discourse in this sense is about preferences, but not strictly so, at least not in a way that suggests applying the various models of decision-making behavior that abound in the philosophical literature. In the present case, I am not really concerned with figuring out why one physician decides to quit working at 1 p.m. and another decides to continue working till 5:30. The moral dimension of importance is concerned with broader questions about the modes of reasoning and talking that define things as legitimate.

42   In his book *Theory of the Moral Life*, John Dewey framed a conception of moral reasoning that will be useful for us to incorporate into the present discussion.[14] First published in 1908, Dewey's arguments sometimes seem overly optimistic, placing too much faith in education, reason, and scientific progress to be credible in the more complex world of today. Yet there is still much to be learned from this book. Dewey's clear-headed, moderate style resonates far more deeply with the American experience than do many of the arguments that have been borrowed in recent decades from other traditions.

43   At the heart of Dewey's conception of morality is the distinction (to which we have already referred) between right and wrong, on the one hand, and value preferences, on the other hand. Citing the case of a man torn between his religiously inspired commitment to pacifism and his sense of civic responsibility, Dewey writes: "Now he has to make a choice between competing moral loyalties and convictions. The struggle is not between a good which is clear to him and something else which attracts him but which he knows to be wrong. It is between values each of which is an undoubted good in its place but which now get in each other's way. He is forced to reflect in order to come to a decision."[15]

44   This is precisely the kind of moral dilemma most people find themselves confronted with as they consider the relationship between their economic commitments and other values. The problem generally is not choosing between something good, like working hard, and something evil, like laying around the house all day in a drunken stupor. It is usually choosing between two activities of "undoubted good" that get in each other's way, such as working hard and taking one's children to the dentist, or serving people through one's profession and being a more responsible member of one's community. These, we recognize

with Dewey, are often more difficult choices than making decisions between good and evil.

Dewey also draws a useful distinction between customary morali-   45
ty and reflective morality, The former depends on force of habit, on doing things the way they have always been done. It is the morality of the tribe, the ancestral home, the parental rules that have never been questioned. Reflective morality, in contrast, emerges from conscious deliberation. It "springs from the heart, from personal desires and affections, or from personal insight and rational choice."[16] It often requires criticizing existing customs and institutions from a new point of view.

Customary morality is of considerable importance because it often   46
provides a reliable guide in matters of right and wrong. In principle at least, long-established norms about telling the truth, not stealing from one's neighbors, and the like still pertain appropriately to most people in most situations. Customary morality also serves a positive function in everyday life simply by permitting us to *avoid* thinking about some things. Dewey suggests there is something "sick" about a person who goes through life questioning the morality of everything. But customary morality becomes a negative force when people let institutionalized norms make their basic decisions for them. The economic realm can of course be a strong source of customary morality.

Reflective morality requires conscious effort on the part of the indi-   47
vidual. It involves questioning one's behavior, knowing what options are available, thinking through the consequences of various choices, and recognizing one's responsibility to choose wisely. It comes into play most visibly when people are faced with choices about their basic values and how to realize these values in their daily lifes. Indeed, Dewey goes so far as to say that an immoral decision is one that has been made unreflectively, while a moral act takes the form of a well-considered judgment. Saying "I meant well" (when things turn out badly) is not a good excuse, Dewey asserts, because the person probably did not really pause to reflect on what he or she was about to do.

Unlike customary morality, which can often be articulated in sim-   48
ple moral dictums, *reflective morality* cannot be codified in terms of absolute rules. It is instead a matter of theory, process, and character. Theory—or, perhaps better, "outlook"—is a frame of reference, a set of beliefs and values that inform the individual's thinking. It includes a conception of individual freedom and responsibility, an understanding of the importance of reflection itself, and an awareness of the need to balance self-interest with the needs of others. Process is the ongoing act of reflection itself. It is not so much a matter of making air-tight, logical choices, but of bringing one's outlook into conscious engagement with one's experience and behavior. It requires individual soul searching,

but is also a social activity, benefiting from formal education, reading, and interacting with others. "Character" signals the fact that reflective morality is integrally rooted in the self. This means moral worth is ascribed less to single, discrete activities than to longer-term patterns of behavior. It also means that morality and the self are fundamentally intertwined in a mutually reinforcing, and hopefully upward, spiral of development. In short, moral reflection is conducive to personal growth. [. . .].[17]

49   For moral discourse to be effective, it must provide clear, unambiguous guidance about how to live individually and collectively. If it does not, people will be unable to make informed choices and in the face of uncertainty may well follow the dictates of unstated economic assumptions rather than consciously placing limits around these assumptions. But moral discourse should also provide room for a wide range of individual choices and lifestyles. Modern society is too diverse, too complex, too changeable for moral discourse to be codified as authoritative behavioral maxims. Communities of moral discourse function best when they provide opportunities for collective reflection and role models to emulate. Moral strictures may discourage greed and ambition as a general rule, yet provide arguments about individual talent or social service that legitimate exceptional endeavors for a few. Reasons for *not* following the rest of the herd, and stories of people who make a difference by leading alternative lives, may be one of the most beneficial functions moral discourse can provide.

50   In all this, it should also be evident that moral discourse, while terribly personal, must be a feature of the public life of any society. It must be codified in language, in the common stock of tradition and narrative, so that it can be communicated and provide a basis for shared understandings. Without this public dimension, moral discourse could not be transmitted intergenerationally or internalized to the point that it becomes taken for granted. This means that moral discourse, as discourse, matters in its own right and is distinguishable from ethical behavior. What people say about their lives—how they talk about greed and ambition—is at least as important as the implicit social norms that can be inferred from how they behave.

51   An ideal moral discourse, then, is one that can challenge, question, guide, and set limits around the economic sphere by giving voice to deeper considerations of what is good for the individual and the society. Rather than setting up an autonomous conception of morality that can be fulfilled entirely within the economic realm itself, it forces questions to be raised about the connections between this realm and broader conceptions of the human spirit. It provides a way of thinking and talking about what is legitimate that necessitates discussion of human

values. In doing so, it makes room for diverse talents and interests but also defines broad categories in which thinking can take place and questions of good and bad—and, even more importantly, questions of better and best—can be deliberated.

Notes

1. Hugh A. Mulligan, "Companies Give Workers Piece of the Action," *Trenton Times* (May 19, 1991).
2. La Van, Katz, and Hochwarter, "Employee Stress," 64.
3. For example, see those quoted in Annetta Miller, "Stress on the Job," *Newsweek* (April 28, 1988), 40–45.
4. *Ibid.*
5. Keen, *Fire in the Belly*, 61.
6. Economic Values Survey.
7. Diane Fassel, *Working Ourselves to Death: The High Cost of Workaholism and the Rewards of Recovery* (San Francisco: Harper San Francisco, 1990), 46.
8. Economic Values Survey.
9. Useful surveys of recent debates concerning the role of the state in regulating economic forces include Alan Wolfe, *Whose Keeper? Social Science and Moral Obligation* (Berkeley: University of California Press, 1989); Robert Dahl, *A Preface to Economic Democracy* (Berkeley: University of California Press, 1985); and Fred Block, *Post-Industrial Possibilities* (Berkeley: University of California Press, 1990).
10. The relationship between economic institutions and personal discretion is clearly described in Milton Friedman, *Capitalism and Freedom* (Chicago: University of Chicago Press, 1962); for a more recent statement, see Peter L. Berger, *The Capitalist Revolution: Fifty Propositions about Prosperity, Equality, and Liberty* (New York: Basic Books, 1986), especially chapter 5.
11. Robert Jackall, *Moral Mazes: The World of Corporate Managers* (New York: Oxford University Press, 1988). I have benefited greatly from the insightful analysis presented in this book.
12. Bryan Wilson, *Religion in Sociological Perspective* (Oxford: Oxford University Press, 1982), 161. Wilson also discusses the ways in which moral questions have been moved into the sphere of political reform.
13. As a guide to this literature, I have found especially valuable the work of my colleague Jeffrey Stout, *Ethics after Babel: The Languages of Morals and Their Discontents* (Boston: Beacon, 1988). I have also borrowed quite selectively from Alasdair MacIntyre, *After Virtue: A Study in Moral Theory*, 2d ed. (Notre Dame: University of Notre Dame Press, 1984), and Stanley Hauerwas, *Truthfulness and Tragedy* (Notre Dame: University of Notre Dame Press, 1977).
14. John Dewey, *Theory of the Moral Life* (New York: Holt, Rinehart and Winston, 1960 [1908]).
15. *Ibid.*, 6–7.
16. *Ibid.*, 3.

17. "There is not simply a succession of disconnected acts but each thing done carries forward an underlying tendency and intent, *conducting*, leading up, to further acts and to a final fulfillment or consummation" (*Ibid.*, 11).

RESPONDING TO READING

1. In what ways is on-the-job stress the responsibility of the stressed individual? When does this stress stop being the problem of the individual worker and start being the problem of the entire organization? When does stress change from a psychological problem into a philosophical problem?

2. In your opinion or experience, what sorts of stress naturally occur at work? If stress is an unavoidable facet of the modern workplace, then is it (or should it be) a company's responsibility to (a) minimize this? (b) help employees handle the stress that is actually unavoidable? Or is stress simply a way of separating employees into groups that can or cannot accomplish a given job?

3. In what ways is the quick-fix approach to stress outlined by Wuthnow inappropriate and unhelpful? How is the disease model for understanding stress also inappropriate?

4. According to Wuthnow, why is governmental control not the answer to the question of dealing with stress? What other options for improved change does he put forward?

5. In an essay, describe one or two major stresses in your own life—at work, at school, or at home. What solutions does Wuthnow offer that would be useful to you? Is there other advice you would offer about dealing with stress, strategies that Wuthnow does not address or that he does not believe in? Brainstorm these issues and solutions with a partner before you write the final draft of your paper.

The End of Apartheid

NELSON MANDELA AND FREDERIK WILLEM DE KLERK

Nelson Mandela and Frederik Willem de Klerk shared the Nobel Peace Prize in 1993 for "their work for the peaceful termination of the apartheid regime," the citation explains, "and for laying the foundations of a new democratic South Africa." Their alliance, forged largely in 1990–92, represented a unity of social and political forces unimaginable in the rigid racism that prevailed throughout the South Africa into which each was born—Mandela in Transeki, in 1918; de Klerk in Johannesberg in 1936. Each lived their entire lives, as did many if not all South Africans, in relation to their country's rigid apartheid policies, Mandela devoted to opposing them, de Klerk devoted to maintaining them.

Both were the sons of leaders. Mandela's father was Chief Henry Mandela of the Tembu Tribe; de Klerk's father was Senator Jan de

Klerk, a leading politician who became minister in the South African government. Both were educated as lawyers, Mandela at University College of Fort Hare and the University of Witwatersrand, where he qualified in law in 1942; de Klerk earned a law degree from Potchefstroom University in 1958. Whereas de Klerk practiced law for fifteen years before being elected to Parliament in 1972, as National Party member for Vereeniging, Mandela became immersed in politics immediately. He joined the African National Congress in 1944; his resistance to the National Party's apartheid policies led to a lengthy trial for treason (1956–61). By the time he was acquitted in 1961, the ANC had been banned, and Mandela established Umkhonto we Sizwe, an organization willing to resist apartheid by violent means. Mandela's freedom was short lived; in 1962, he was arrested and sentenced to five years' imprisonment with hard labor. A subsequent trial for plotting to overthrow the government by violence led in 1964 to a sentence of life imprisonment, part of which he served from 1964 to 82 at Robben Island Prison off Cape Town; thereafter, until his release in 1990, he was at Pollsmoor Prison on the mainland. His autobiography, *Long Walk to Freedom* (1994), explains, in serenely charitable language, the great physical and psychological fortitude he needed to endure the hard labor (which included several oppressive years of breaking rocks), isolation, and other deprivations of this long and harsh time. He was, however, resolute of spirit and buoyed by the international recognition his resistance to apartheid commanded.

During this time, de Klerk was active in the very government that sustained both Mandela's imprisonment and the oppressive social and economic restriction of Blacks generally. Under Prime Minister P. W. Botha, he held a succession of ministerial posts, including Posts and Telecommunications and Sports and Recreation (1978–79); Mines, Energy and Environmental Planning (1979–80); Mineral and Energy Affairs (1980–82); Internal Affairs (1982–85); and National Education and Planning (1984–89). As education minister, de Klerk supported segregated universities, although he did work for equal expenditure of funds for all racial groups. At the time of his election as the centrist Leader of the National Party in Transvaal (February 1989), he was, as his Nobel biography says, "not known to advocate reform." Nevertheless, in his first speech after being elected state president in September 1989, he called for a nonracist South Africa. In February 1990, he lifted the thirty-year ban on the ANC and released Nelson Mandela from prison: Mandela was elected ANC president in 1991. This marked the beginning of the end of apartheid, and opened the way for the drafting of a new constitution for the country based on the principle of "one person, one vote" and on the entrenchment of basic human rights. Thus, coming from very different points of departure, Mandela and de Klerk, as their Nobel Prize citation states, looked "ahead to South African reconciliation instead of back at the deep wounds of the past," showing "great integrity and great political courage."

NELSON MANDELA

1   Your Majesty the King,

2   Your Royal Highness,

3   Esteemed Members of the Norwegian Nobel Committee,

4   Honourable Prime Minister, Madame Gro Harlem Brundtland, Ministers, Members of Parliament and Ambassadors, Fellow Laureate Mr. F. W. de Klerk, Distinguished Guests,

5   Friends, Ladies and Gentlemen,

6   I extend my heartfelt thanks to the Norwegian Nobel Committee for elevating us to the status of a Nobel Peace Prize winner.

7   I would also like to take this opportunity to congratulate my compatriot and fellow laureate, State President F. W. de Klerk, on his receipt of this high honour.

8   Together, we join two distinguished South Africans, the late Chief Albert Lutulli and His Grace Archbishop Desmond Tutu, to whose seminal contributions to the peaceful struggle against the evil system of apartheid you paid well-deserved tribute by awarding them the Nobel Peace Prize.

9   It will not be presumptuous of us if we also add, among our predecessors, the name of another outstanding Nobel Peace Prize winner, the late Rev. Martin Luther King, Jr.

10   He, too, grappled with and died in the effort to make a contribution to the just solution of the same great issues of the day which we have had to face as South Africans.

11   We speak here of the challenge of the dichotomies of war and peace, violence and non-violence, racism and human dignity, oppression and repression and liberty and human rights, poverty and freedom from want.

12   We stand here today as nothing more than a representative of the millions of our people who dared to rise up against a social system whose very essence is war, violence, racism, oppression, repression and the impoverishment of an entire people.

13   I am also here today as a representative of the millions of people across the globe, the anti-apartheid movement, the governments and organisations that joined with us, not to fight against South Africa as a country or any of its peoples, but to oppose an inhuman system and sue for a speedy end to the apartheid crime against humanity.

14   These countless human beings, both inside and outside our country, had the nobility of spirit to stand in the path of tyranny and injustice, without seeking selfish gain. They recognised that an injury to one is an injury to all and therefore acted together in defense of justice and a common human decency.

15   Because of their courage and persistence for many years, we can, today, even set the dates when all humanity will join together to celebrate one of the outstanding human victories of our century.

When that moment comes, we shall, together, rejoice in a common   16
victory over racism, apartheid and white minority rule.

That triumph will finally bring to a close a history of five hundred   17
years of African colonisation that began with the establishment of the
Portuguese empire.

Thus, it will mark a great step forward in history and also serve as   18
a common pledge of the peoples of the world to fight racism, wherever
it occurs and whatever guise it assumes.

At the southern tip of the continent of Africa, a rich reward in the   19
making, an invaluable gift is in the preparation for those who suffered
in the name of all humanity when they sacrificed everything—for
liberty, peace, human dignity and human fulfillment.

This reward will not be measured in money. Nor can it be reckoned   20
in the collective price of the rare metals and precious stones that rest in
the bowels of the African soil we tread in the footsteps of our ancestors.

It will and must be measured by the happiness and welfare of the   21
children, at once the most vulnerable citizens in any society and
the greatest of our treasures.

The children must, at last, play in the open veld, no longer tortured   22
by the pangs of hunger or ravaged by disease or threatened with the
scourge of ignorance, molestation and abuse, and no longer required to
engage in deeds whose gravity exceeds the demands of their tender
years.

In front of this distinguished audience, we commit the new South   23
Africa to the relentless pursuit of the purposes defined in the World
Declaration on the Survival, Protection and Development of Children.

The reward of which we have spoken will and must also be mea-   24
sured by the happiness and welfare of the mothers and fathers of these
children, who must walk the earth without fear of being robbed, killed
for political or material profit, or spat upon because they are beggars.

They too must be relieved of the heavy burden of despair which   25
they carry in their hearts, born of hunger, homelessness and
unemployment.

The value of that gift to all who have suffered will and must be   26
measured by the happiness and welfare of all the people of our country, who will have torn down the inhuman walls that divide them.

These great masses will have turned their backs on the grave insult   27
to human dignity which described some as masters and others as servants, and transformed each into a predator whose survival depended
on the destruction of the other.

The value of our shared reward will and must be measured by the   28
joyful peace which will triumph, because the common humanity that
bonds both black and white into one human race, will have said to each
one of us that we shall all live like the children of paradise.

29   Thus shall we live, because we will have created a society which recognises that all people are born equal, with each entitled in equal measure to life, liberty, prosperity, human rights and good governance.

30   Such a society should never allow again that there should be prisoners of conscience nor that any person's human right should be violated.

31   Neither should it ever happen that once more the avenues to peaceful change are blocked by usurpers who seek to take power away from the people, in pursuit of their own, ignoble purposes.

32   In relation to these matters, we appeal to those who govern Burma that they release our fellow Nobel Peace Prize laureate, Aung San Suu Kyi, and engage her and those she represents in serious dialogue, for the benefit of all the people of Burma.

33   We pray that those who have the power to do so will, without further delay, permit that she uses her talents and energies for the greater good of the people of her country and humanity as a whole.

34   Far from the rough and tumble of the politics of our own country. I would like to take this opportunity to join the Norwegian Nobel Committee and pay tribute to my joint laureate. Mr. F. W. de Klerk.

35   He had the courage to admit that a terrible wrong had been done to our country and people through the imposition of the system of apartheid.

36   He had the foresight to understand and accept that all the people of South Africa must through negotiations and as equal participants in the process, together determine what they want to make of their future.

37   But there are still some within our country who wrongly believe they can make a contribution to the cause of justice and peace by clinging to the shibboleths that have been proved to spell nothing but disaster.

38   It remains our hope that these, too, will be blessed with sufficient reason to realise that history will not be denied and that the new society cannot be created by reproducing the repugnant past, however refined or enticingly repackaged.

39   We would also like to take advantage of this occasion to pay tribute to the many formations of the democratic movement of our country, including the members of our Patriotic Front, who have themselves played a central role in bringing our country as close to the democratic transformation as it is today.

40   We are happy that many representatives of these formations, including people who have served or are serving in the "homeland" structures, came with us to Oslo. They too must share the accolade which the Nobel Peace Prize confers.

41   We live with the hope that as she battles to remake herself, South Africa, will be like a microcosm of the new world that is striving to be born.

This must be a world of democracy and respect for human rights, a 42
world freed from the horrors of poverty, hunger, deprivation and ignorance, relieved of the threat and the scourge of civil wars and external
aggression and unburdened of the great tragedy of millions forced to
become refugees.

The processes in which South Africa and Southern Africa as a 43
whole are engaged, beckon and urge us all that we take this tide at the
flood and make of this region a living example of what all people of
conscience would like the world to be.

We do not believe that this Nobel Peace Prize is intended as a com- 44
mendation for matters that have happened and passed.

We hear the voices which say that it is an appeal from all those, 45
throughout the universe, who sought an end to the system of apartheid.

We understand their call, that we devote what remains of our lives 46
to the use of our country's unique and painful experience to demonstrate, in practice, that the normal condition for human existence is
democracy, justice, peace, non-racism, non-sexism, prosperity for
everybody, a healthy environment and equality and solidarity among
the peoples.

Moved by that appeal and inspired by the eminence you have 47
thrust upon us, we undertake that we too will do what we can to contribute to the renewal of our world so that none should, in future, be
described as the "wretched of the earth."

Let it never be said by future generations that indifference, cyni- 48
cism or selfishness made us fail to live up to the ideals of humanism
which the Nobel Peace Prize encapsulates.

Let the strivings of us all, prove Martin Luther King Jr. to have 49
been correct, when he said that humanity can no longer be tragically
bound to the starless midnight of racism and war.

Let the efforts of us all, prove that he was not a mere dreamer when 50
he spoke of the beauty of genuine brotherhood and peace being more
precious than diamonds or silver or gold.

Let a new age dawn! 51

Thank you. 52

FREDERIK WILLEM DE KLERK

Your Majesties, your Excellencies, Ladies and Gentlemen. 1

It is a little more than six years to the end of this century and to the 2
dawning of the new millennium. In three years we will mark the centenary of Alfred Nobel's death and in eight the hundredth year of this
award.

The intervening years have witnessed the most dreadful wars and 3
carnage in the long and violent history of mankind. Today as we speak,

> the shells rain down on beleaguered
> communities in Bosnia; there is bitter conflict in
> Georgia, Armenia and Azerbaijan; there are
> devastating wars and conflicts in Africa—in
> Angola, in Somalia and recently in Burundi;
> and in my own country, notwithstanding the
> tremendous progress which we have made,
> more than 3,000 people have died in political
> violence since the beginning of this year.

As always, it is the innocent—and particularly the children—who are the main victims of these conflicts.

4   Above all, we owe it to the children of the world to stop the conflicts and to create new horizons for them. They deserve peace and decent opportunities in life. I should like to dedicate this address to them and to all those—such as UNICEF—who are working to alleviate their plight.

5   The question that we must ask is whether we are making progress toward the goal of universal peace. Or are we caught up on a treadmill of history, turning forever on the axle of mindless aggression and self-destruction? Has the procession of Nobel Peace laureates since 1901 reflected a general movement by mankind toward peace?

6   When considering the great honour that has been bestowed on us as recipients of this Peace Prize, we must in all humility ask these questions. We must also consider the nature of peace. The greatest peace, I believe, is the peace which we derive from our faith in God Almighty; from certainty about our relationship with our Creator. Crises might beset us, battles might rage about us—but if we have faith and the certainty it brings, we will enjoy peace—the peace that surpasses all understanding. . . .

7   I believe that this transitional constitution ensures full participation in all fields of endeavour to all South Africans. It does not discriminate in any way on the basis of colour, creed, class or gender. It contains all the major safeguards which all our communities will need to maintain their respective identities and ways of life. It also provides adequate guarantee for the political, social, cultural and economic rights of individuals.

8   I also believe that this framework for peace will succeed if we can now establish the *frame of mind*, to which I referred, which is necessary for peace—the frame of mind which leads people to resolve differences through negotiation, compromise and agreements, instead of through compulsion and violence.

9   I believe that such a frame of mind already exists in South Africa at the moment, however fragile it might be. All our leaders, including Mr. Mandela and I, will have to lead by example in an effort to consolidate this frame of mind. We will need great wisdom to counteract the strategies

of minority elements, threatening with civil conflict. We will have to be firm and resolute in defending the framework for peace which we agreed upon.

There is no room for complacency. All of us who believe in peace   10 must redouble our efforts to reassure all our countrymen that their rights and security will be assured.

I have no doubt that we will succeed. There is growing awareness   11 among all South Africans of our interdependence—of the fact that none of us can flourish if we do not work together—that all of us will fail if we try to pursue narrow sectional interests.

Five years ago people would have seriously questioned the sanity   12 of anyone who would have predicted that Mr. Mandela and I would be joint recipients of the 1993 Nobel Peace Prize.

And yet both of us are here before you today.   13

We are political opponents.   14

We disagree strongly on key issues and we will soon fight a strenu-   15 ous election campaign against one another. But we will do so, I believe, in the frame of mind and within the framework of peace which has already been established.

We will do it—and many other leaders will do it with us—because   16 there is no other road to peace and prosperity for the people of our country. In the conflicts of the past, there was no gain for anyone in our country. Through reconciliation all of us are now becoming winners.

The compromises we have reached demand sacrifices on all sides.   17 It was not easy for the supporters of Mr. Mandela or mine to relinquish the ideals they had cherished for many decades.

But we did it. And because we did it, there is hope.   18

The coming election will not be about the past. It will be about the fu-   19 ture. It will not be about Blacks or Whites, or Afrikaners and Xhosas It will be about the best solutions for the future in the interests of all our people. It will not be about apartheid or armed struggle. It will be about future peace and stability, about progress and prosperity, about nation-building.

In my first speech after becoming Leader of the National Party, I   20 said on February the 8th, 1989:

"Our goal is a new South Africa:
A totally changed South Africa;
a South Africa which has rid itself of the
antagonism of the past;
a South Africa free of domination or oppression
in whatever form;
a South Africa within which the democratic
forces—all reasonable people—align themselves
behind mutually acceptable goals and against
radicalism, irrespective of where it comes from."

21   Since then we have made impressive progress, thanks to the cooperation of political, spiritual, business and community leaders over a wide spectrum. To Mr Mandela I sincerely say: Congratulations. And in accepting this Peace Prize today I wish to pay tribute to all who are working for peace in our land. On behalf of all South Africans who supported me, directly or indirectly, I accept it in humility, deeply aware of my own shortcomings.

22   I thank those who decided to make the award for the recognition they have granted in doing so—recognition of a mighty deed of reformation and reconciliation that is taking place in South Africa. The road ahead is still full of obstacles and, therefore, dangerous. There is, however, no question of turning back.

23   One of the great poets in Afrikaans, N. P. van Wyk Louw, wrote:

"O wye en droewe land, alleen
onder die groot suidersterre,
Sal nooit'n hoe blydskap kom
deur jou stil droefenis? . . .

Sal nooit'n magtige skoonheid kom
oor jou soos die haelwit somerwolk
wat uitbloei oor jou donker berge,
en nooit in jou'n daad geskied
wat opklink oor die aarde en
die jare in hul onmag terge. . . ."

24   Translated freely it means:

"Oh wide and woeful land, alone
Beneath the great south stars.
Will soaring joy ne'er rise above
Your silent grief?

Will ne'er mighty beauty rise
above you, like the hail-white summer clouds
that billow o'er your brooding peaks
and in you, ne'er a deed be wrought
that over the earth resounds
and mocks the ages in their impotence?"

25   What is taking place in South Africa is such a deed—a deed resounding over the earth—a deed of peace. It brings hope to all South Africans. It opens new horizons for Sub-Saharan Africa. It has the capacity to unlock the tremendous potential of our country and our region.

26   The new era which is dawning in our country, beneath the great southern stars, will lift us out of the silent grief of our past and into a future in which there will be opportunity and space for joy and beauty—for real and lasting peace.

RESPONDING TO READING

1. How do Mandela and de Klerk acknowledge and celebrate the nonviolent end of apartheid in South Africa? What connections does each make with historical figures? What connections does each make with people and movements in other nations?

2. According to Mandela, what is the reward that comes from the end of apartheid? How does he construct this reward in ways that make it more important than financial gain? How is the reward Mandela sees similar to or different from that reward identified by de Klerk?

3. How does Mandela construct apartheid as an absolute evil that had to be abolished? Does de Klerk employ similar strategies? How does each speaker characterize the other in ways that are respectful without minimizing the fact that each has a different agenda?

4. What comparisons does Mandela make between apartheid in South Africa and other "insult[s] to human dignity"? How does de Klerk describe apartheid?

5. Visit the website of a group concerned with human rights, such as Amnesty International, Doctors Without Borders, or the United Nations. Select one issue with which this group is concerned, and describe it. What is the problem, and where is it located? What are the complications and concerns that keep the problem from being resolved?

Silence and the Notion of the Commons

URSULA FRANKLIN

Born in Munich, Germany (1921), Ursula Franklin spent 18 months in a Nazi work camp with her father, a German archeologist, and her mother, a Jewish art historian; they all survived, and Franklin spent the duration of the war repairing bombed buildings. After studying experimental physics at the Technical University of Berlin (Ph.D., 1948), she and her family immigrated to Canada where she worked at the Ontario Research Foundation, becoming senior research scientist after pioneering in and inventing the field of archaeometry—the scientific study of ancient metal artifacts. In 1967, she became the first woman member of the University of Toronto's Department of Metallurgy and Materials Science, and in 1984, she became the first woman University Professor there. In 1995, the Toronto Board of Education named a new public school the Ursula Franklin Academy. Retired from academia, she currently serves as an Officer of the Order of Canada and a member of the Science Council of Canada. She has received more than ten honorary degrees and has authored or co-authored books including *Studies in Ancient Peruvian Metalworking* (1979) and *Examination of Prehistoric Copper Technology and Copper Sources* (1981). Her book *The Real World of Technology* (1992) derives from a radio lecture in which Franklin urged listeners to become "citizen scientists"—informed users of technology capable of protesting its abuse when necessary.

In "Silence and the Notion of the Commons," Franklin, who sees technology and social issues as inseparably linked, looks at something most people think they understand implicitly: quiet places. Published in the journal *Musicworks* (1994), the essay urges readers to protect the public "soundscape." In the face of boom boxes, marketing messages, and piped-in music, Franklin thinks it's time to start preserving silence—and the sanity it promotes—just as we protect resources such as clean air and water.

1   In a technological world, where the acoustic environment is largely artificial, silence takes on new dimensions, be it in terms of the human need for silence (perhaps a person's right to be free from acoustic assault), of communication, or of intentional modification of the environment.

2   This article is based on the text of a lecture given at the Banff Centre in August of 1993 as part of "The Tuning of the World" conference on acoustic ecology. It consists of two separate but interrelated parts: silence as spiritual experience (drawing largely, but not exclusively, on the Quaker tradition of religious worship) and silence as a common good. Silence is examined in terms of the general patterns of the social impact of modern technology. Silence possesses striking similarities with such aspects of life and community as unpolluted water, air, or soil, which once were taken for granted, but which have become special and precious in technologically mediated environments. The threat of a privatization of the soundscape is discussed and some immediate measures suggested.

3   I would like to thank everyone involved in this conference, and the organizers in particular, for inviting me to deliver this talk. I am very obviously an outsider and wish to come to this group to talk about something that is central to all the work that you people are doing. And so I come in a way as a friend and colleague, in a field where I am fully aware that silence has been the subject of many publications. It is the subject of more than a chapter in R. Murray Schafer's *The Tuning of the World* and John Cage and others have written books on it. I would like to examine how our concept—as well as our practice—of silence has been influenced by all the other things that have changed as our world has become what Jacques Ellul calls a "technological milieu," a world that is, in all its facets, increasingly mediated by technology.

4   Before we had a technologically mediated society, before we had electronics and electro-magnetic devices, sound was rightly seen as being ephemeral, sound was coupled to its source, and lasted only a very short time. This is very different from what we see in a landscape:

however much we feel that the landscape might be modified, however much we feel that there is a horrible building somewhere in front of a beautiful mountain, on the scale of the soundscape, the landscape is permanent. What is put up is there. That's very different from the traditional soundscape. What modern technology has brought to sound is the possibility of doing two things: to separate the sound from the source and to make the sound permanent. In addition, modern devices make it possible to decompose, recompose, analyse and mix sounds, to change the initial magnitude and sustainability of sound, as well as to change all the characteristics that link the sound with its source. R. Murray Schafer called this "schizophonia," separating the sound from the source. We now have easy access to the multitude of opportunities that result from overcoming that coupling.

The social impact of this technology is significant. Prior to these developments there was a limitation to sound and sound penetration. If you heard a bagpipe band there was a limit to the amount of time it would play; if you found it displeasing you could patiently wait until the players got exhausted. But with a recording of a bagpipe band, you are out of luck. It's never going to be exhausted. Electronics, then, have altered the modern soundscape. While modern technology is a source of joy in modern composition, through the opening of many doors for expression, it is also the source of a good number of problems related to the soundscape, problems which society as a whole must adjust to, cope with, and possibly ameliorate.   5

But then there is not only sound, there is silence. Silence is affected by these same technological developments, the same means of separating sound from source and overcoming the ephemeral nature of a soundscape. I have attempted to define silence and to analyse the attributes that make it valuable. Defining silence as the absence of external or artificially generated sound is fine, but it's a little bit shallow, because silence in many ways is very much more than the absence of sound. Absence of sound is a condition necessary to silence but it is not sufficient in itself to define what we mean by silence. When one thinks about the concept of silence, one notices that there has to be somebody who listens before you can say there is silence. Silence, in addition to being an absence of sound, is defined by a listener, by hearing.   6

A further attribute, or parameter of silence, from my point of view, comes out of the question: *why is it that we worry about silence?* I feel that one comes to the root of the meaning and practice of silence only when one asks; *why is it that we value and try to establish silence?* Because silence is an enabling environment. This is the domain that we have traditionally associated with silence, the enabling condition in which unprogrammed and unprogrammble events can take place. That is the silence of contemplation; it is the silence when people get in touch with   7 themselves; it is the silence of meditation and worship. The distinctive character of this domain of silence is that it is an enabling condition that opens up the possibility of unprogrammed, unplanned and unprogrammable happenings.

8   In this light we understand why, as Christians, traditional Quakers found it necessary in the seventeenth century, when they were surrounded by all the pomp and circumstance of the church of England, to reject it. We understand why they felt any ritual, in the sense of its programmed nature and predictability, to be a straitjacket rather than a comfort, and why they said to the amazement of their contemporaries: *we worship God in silence.* Their justification for the practice of silence was that they required it to hear God's voice. Beyond the individual's centering, beyond the individual effort of meditation, there was the need for *collective* silence. Collective silence is an enormously powerful event. There are contemporaneous accounts of Quaker meetings under heavy persecution in England, when thousands of people met silently on a hillside. Then out of the silence, one person—unappointed, unordained, unexpected, and unprogrammed—might speak, to say: *Out of the silence there can come a ministry.* The message is not essentially within that person, constructed in their intellect, but comes out of the silence to them. This isn't just history and theory. I think that if any one of you attended Quaker meetings, particularly on a regular basis, you would find that, suddenly, out of the silence, somebody speaks about something that had just entered *your* mind. It's an uncanny thing. The strength of collective silence is probably one of the most powerful spiritual forces.

9   Now, in order for something like this to happen, a lot of things are required. There is what Quakers call: *to be with heart and mind prepared.* But there is also the collective decision to be silent. And to be silent in order to let unforeseen, unforeseeable, and unprogrammed things happen. Such silence, I repeat, is the environment that enables the unprogrammed. I feel it is very much at risk.

10   I will elaborate on this, but first I want to say: there is another silence. There is the silence that enables a programmed, a planned, event to take place. There is the silence in which you courteously engage so that I might be heard: in order for one to be heard all the others have to be silent. But in many cases silence is not taken on voluntarily and it is this false silence of which I am afraid. It is not the silence only of the padded cell, or of solitary confinement; it is the silence that is enforced by the megaphone, the boom box, the PA system, and any other device that stifles other sounds and voices in order that a planned event can take place.

11   There is a critical juncture between the planned and the unplanned, the programmed and the unplannable that must be kept in

mind. I feel very strongly that our present technological trends drive us toward a decrease in the space—be it in the soundscape, the landscape, or the mindscape—in which the unplanned and unplannable can happen. Yet silence has to remain available in the soundscape, the landscape, and the mindscape. Allowing openness to the unplannable, to the unprogrammed, is the core of the strength of silence. It is also the core of our individual and collective sanity. I extend that to the collectivity because, as a community, as a people, we are threatened just as much, if not more, by the impingement of the programmed over the silent, over that which enables the unprogrammed. Much of the impingement goes unnoticed, uncommented upon, since it is much less obvious than the intrusion of a structure into the landscape. While we may not win all the battles at City Hall to preserve our trees, at least there is now a semi-consciousness that this type of struggle is important.

Where can one go to get away from the dangers of even the gentle   12 presence of programmed music, or Muzak, in our public buildings? Where do I protest that upon entering any place, from the shoe store to the restaurant, I am deprived of the opportunity to be quiet? Who has asked my permission to put that slop into the elevator I may have to use umpteen times every day? Many such "background" activities are intentionally manipulative. This is not merely "noise" that can be dealt with in terms of noise abatement. There are two aspects to be stressed in this context. One is that the elimination of silence is being done without anybody's consent. The other is that one really has to stop and think and analyse in order to see just how manipulative these interventions can be.

For instance, in the Toronto Skydome, friends tell me that the   13 sound environment is coupled and geared to the game: if the home team misses, there are mournful and distressing sounds over the PA; when the home team scores there is a sort of athletic equivalent of the Hallelujah Chorus. Again, the visitor has no choice; the programmed soundscape is part of the event. You cannot be present at the game without being subjected to that mood manipulation. I wonder if music will soon be piped into the voter's booth, maybe an upbeat, slightly military tune: "*Get on with it. Get the votes in.*" Joking aside, soundscape manipulation is a serious issue. Who on earth has given anybody the right to manipulate the sound environment?

Now, I want to come back to the definition of silence and introduce   14 the notion of the commons, because the soundscape essentially doesn't belong to anyone in particular. What we are hearing, I feel, is very much the privatization of the soundscape, in the same manner in which the enclosure laws in Britain destroyed the commons of old. There was a time when in fact every community had what was called "the commons," an area that belonged to everybody and where sheep could graze—a place important to all, belonging to all. The notion of the commons is deeply embedded in our social mind as something that all share. There are many "commons" that we take for granted and for millenia, clean air and clean water were the norm. Because of the ephemeral nature of sound in the past, silence was not considered part of the commons. Today, the technology to preserve and multiply sound and separate it from its source has resulted in our sudden awareness that silence, too, is a common good. Silence, which we need in order that unprogrammed and unprogrammable things can take place, is being removed from common access without much fuss and civic bother. It is being privatized.

15   This is another illustration of an often-observed occurrence related to the impact of technology: that things considered in the past to be normal or ordinary become rare or extraordinary, while those things once considered rare and unusual become normal and routine. Flying is no longer a big deal, but a handmade dress or a home-cooked meal may well be special. We essentially consider polluted water as normal now, and people who can afford it drink bottled water. It is hard to have bottled silence. But money still can buy distance from sound. Today, when there is civic anger, it is with respect to "noise"—like airport noise, etc. There is not yet such anger with respect to the manipulative elimination of silence from the soundscape.

16   There are those of us who have acknowledged and seen the deterioration of the commons as far as silence is concerned, who have seen that the soundscape is not only polluted by noise—so that one has to look for laws related to noise abatement—but also that the soundscape has become increasingly polluted through the private use of sound in the manipulative dimension of setting and programming moods and conditions. There is a desperate need for awareness of this, and for awareness of it in terms of the collectivity, rather than just individual needs. I feel very much that this is a time for civic anger. This is a time when one has to say: *town planning is constrained by by-laws on height, density, and other features; what are town planning's constraints in relation to silence?*

17   You may ask, what would I suggest? First of all, we must insist that, as human beings in a society, we have a right to silence. Just as we feel we have the right to walk down the street without being physically assaulted by people and preferably without being visually assaulted by ugly outdoor advertising, we also have the right not to be assaulted by sound, and in particular, not to be assaulted by sound that is there solely for the purpose of profit. Now is the time for civic rage, as well as civic education, but also for some action.

Think of the amount of care that goes into the regulation of park- 18
ing, so that our good, precious, and necessary cars have a place to be
well and safe. That's very important to society. I have yet to see, beyond hospitals, a public building that has a quiet room. Is not our sanity at least as important as the safety of our cars? One should begin to
think: are there places, even in conferences like this, that are hassle-free,
quiet spaces, where people can go? There were times when one could
say to a kid: *"Where did you go?"—"Out."—"What did you do?"—*
"Nothing." That sort of blessed time is past. The kid is programmed. We
are programmed. And we don't even ask for a quiet space anymore.

One possible measure, relatively close at hand, is to set aside, as a 19
normal matter of human rights, in those buildings over which we have
some influence, a quiet room. Further, I highly recommend starting
committee meetings with two minutes of silence, and ending them
with a few minutes of silence, too. I sit on committees that have this
practice, and find that it not only can expedite the business before the
committee, but also contributes to a certain amount of peacefulness
and sanity. One can start a lecture with a few minutes of silence, and
can close it the same way. There can be a few minutes of silence before
a shared meal. Such things help, even if they help only in small ways. I
do think even small initiatives make silence "visible" as an ever-pre-
sent part of life. I now invite you to have two minutes of silence before
we go on into the question period. Let us be quiet together.

RESPONDING TO READING

1. What value does Franklin attach to acoustic silence? Why is it important?
   How is silence contrasted with "acoustic assault"? Is this a fair comparison?

2. In what ways can sound be permanent? How is this permanence linked to
   technology? What are the effects (or possible effects) of this permanence on
   individuals who live with these sounds around them, as part of the soundscape? Do you know any people with hearing impairments? What caused
   these?

3. Why is the definition of sound as "the absence of external . . . sound" inadequate? What other definition does Franklin offer?

4. In what ways does Franklin's definition of silence transform silence into both
   a physical and spiritual phenomenon? What benefits does this spiritual silence allow?

5. Sit in the place where you normally write—at your kitchen table, your desk,
   your study carrel in the library—and listen to the soundscape around you.
   What noises break the silence? Quickly jot down each "break" as it occurs.
   In an essay, describe the soundscape around you and its effects on you. How
   are your writing and thinking affected by the sounds you hear? What role, if
   any, does silence play in your writing and thinking processes?

QUESTIONS FOR REFLECTION AND WRITING

What Are Fundamental Human Rights?

1. Is Soyinka in "Every Dictator's Nightmare" writing about an ideal that sounds great, but is not much put into practice? "The idea of the rights of man as a universal principle" is embedded in the Declaration of Independence, but it is sometimes not very apparent, either in America or abroad. Consider these rights in two or three of the essays by Douglass, Rose, and Wright in Chapter 1; Barbara Ehrenreich in Chapter 3; and Stanton and Truth in this section. Does the ideal of fundamental human rights continue to have value and meaning even if it is sometimes violated?

2. Write an essay about the relations of principle to practice in a democracy, drawing on several of the essays in this section.

3. Create a dialogue between Jefferson and Stanton. Focus on their agreement and disagreement over key terms, such as "laws of nature" or "self-evident truths" or "inalienable rights." Show both figures justifying their definitions as the basis for their political ideas. At some point, add a modern figure (such as yourself) into the conversation. The modern figure will know more about the results of these ideas than either Stanton or Jefferson could know, but will also be limited by being located in a particular time and place.

4. Create a similar dialogue between Lincoln and Sojourner Truth.

5. Lincoln's "Gettysburg Address" is sometimes seen as completing the ideas of Jefferson's Declaration of Independence. Compare the two documents, and show how Lincoln has developed some of Jefferson's ideas.

What Values Govern the Common Good?

1. Compare Thoreau's "Civil Disobedience" to King's "Letter From Birmingham Jail." What do the two essays have in common? In what ways do they differ? Focus your essay on the ways that King develops ideas that Thoreau states.

2. How is Terry Tempest Williams's "act of civil disobedience" at the end of "The Clan of One-Breasted Women" similar to, yet different from, those engaged in by Thoreau and King? She calls it "more than a gesture of peace." What does she mean by that? Can breaking the law be a peaceful gesture?

3. McPhee is not concerned with civil disobedience in "Los Angeles Against the Mountains," but rather with the responsibilities of those who disregard the most destructive forces of nature. How would you describe his attitude toward the people who build homes in the paths of slumps and then get swept away by them? Is it an appropriate attitude to take toward victims? What values lie behind this essay, with regard to the way people should interact with nature?

4. Write an essay on whether breaking the law is ever justified, using the essays by Thoreau, King, Williams, and Van Dusen as basic source material. Note that both Thoreau and King argue that we should break unjust laws, and note how they define what those laws are and how they ought to be broken. Van Dusen disagrees strongly with that view and presents arguments and evidence to support his position. Who has the best arguments?

How Can Value Conflicts Be Resolved?

1. To what degree has Tannen in "The Roots of Debate in Education . . . " accurately described the "adversarial" situation in one or two classes you have attended? What other factors might influence an adversarial classroom discussion? Examine closely her critique of that method of learning and, if it does reflect your experience, evaluate that critique. Check your responses with someone of the other sex to see if your response may be based partly on whether you are male or female. If the adversarial method is not the best one for resolving conflicts, what method would be better?

2. Select a few essays in this book that deal with education and conflict resolution, such as those by Steele, Rose, and Rodriguez in Chapter 1; Conroy, Kuhn, and Tannen in Chapter 2; and Young and Le Guin in Chapter 3. Do the essays you have chosen illustrate or deny Tannen's argument that "wonderful progress has been accompanied by more and more anonymity and disconnection, which are damaging to the human spirit and fertile ground for animosity"?

3. What common values lie behind Wuthrow's essay on leading "principled lives" and the Nobel Peace Prize acceptance speeches by Mandela and de Klerk? Although these are quite different documents, written for different kinds of occasions and audiences, what kinds of connections do they show between values in the public and private spheres? How could such common values become a source for resolving conflicts?

4. Ursula Franklin proposes a value that has become uncommon in modern American culture: silence. Do you value quiet, or does that seem to be more the province of the old than the young? How can we resolve conflicts between those who share Franklin's values and those who do not?

Values: What Are Human Rights and Responsibilities?

1. How can you tell good values from bad ones? What is the basis and procedure for making a determination about so vexed a question? Select a value you hold dear, define it, explain why you find that value important, and make an argument defending it from those who might not agree with you.

2. In the early years of the twenty-first century, a serious conflict of values has emerged between prosperous Western countries, such as the United States and Britain, and less prosperous countries with different religious, economic, and social traditions. Write an essay in which you consider the clash of values on the international scene and the ways that have been proposed to resolve the conflict. Is war one more way to resolve conflict, a failure of conflict resolution, or, perhaps, the natural result of adversarial values?

5

Reinterpretations/Contexts:
What Can We Learn from the Past?

What's past is prologue.
SHAKESPEARE, *The Tempest*

Why Consider This Question?

We come to past through the present; there is no other route. As Shakespeare knew, every yesterday promises a today and a tomorrow. So it is impossible to think of the past in the abstract, or even as a static time gone by, for the past contains the dynamics of our present and our future. As Arthur M. Schlesinger, Jr., observes in "The Challenge of Change" (*New York Times Magazine*, July 27, 1986), "Science and technology revolutionize our lives, but memory, tradition, and myth frame our response." Even when rapid changes in the present erase our sense of the past, we still cling consciously or unwittingly to our familiar habits, values, expectations, and dreams. Not even Americans, who are fond of creating themselves anew in a brave new, brand new world, can escape the powerful influence of the past on the future.

We consider the question "What can we learn from the past?" because we must understand our present and plan our future. There is no way to escape, even if we might want to. This chapter of *Inquiry* focuses on three perennial concerns—family history, environmental problems, and the evolution of ideas—all of which have implications for the future.

How Does Family Heritage Affect Who We Are?

"Happy families are all alike," begins Tolstoy's *Anna Karenina*. "Every unhappy family is unhappy in its own way." Tolstoy's arbitrary dismissal of happy families was a quick way to cut to the heart of his novel. Yet when we examine real-life families, our own included, we find that every family, like every person, both is unique and has much in common with other families, happy, unhappy, or otherwise. To understand our family history is to know better who we are and who we will become.

For a nation populated largely by immigrants, understanding family history is particularly important. Most Americans can take very little, if anything, for granted about their family's long-term past, for coming to a new country often involves losing touch with one's ancestors. Often as a result of moves, wars, fires and natural disasters, or slavery, records (of births, marriages, citizenship, and military service) were never kept or have been altered, lost, destroyed. A few letters and artifacts (the family Bible, tintypes and crumbling photographs, an item or two of furniture or clothing) survive; most do not. Only those lucky enough to be part of such longstanding cultures as the Amish or the Mormons can feel sure that family histories are secure.

Then, too, new immigrants are often working so hard to survive and trying so hard to assimilate into the mainstream culture that they suppress or deny their roots in the process. Yet their children and grandchildren want to know about their ancestors and to pass along their discoveries to succeeding generations. To ask "Where did I come from?" is a way of finding out "Who am I?" As we come to know our role models, for better and for worse, we also ask "Where am I going?" Understanding our ancestral past helps, as the essays in this section reveal, to predict our future as individuals and as members of the families that we will create.

Among the things we want to know about our ancestors, whether individuals or members of families, tribes, or nations, are such matters as What did they look like? Where did they live? How did they survive? What was their culture like? What did they do, and why? What were their values? How did they get along with one another? The authors of the essays in this section approach these questions from three perspectives, as a naturalist–anthropologist (Barry Lopez), as a family historian (Pauli Murray), and as autobiographers (Cynthia Ozick and Scott Russell Sanders).

Barry Lopez's "Searching for Ancestors" describes the quest that he and two archaeologists undertook in northern Arizona to unearth, literally and figuratively, the prehistoric Southwest Indian culture, the Anasazi. He takes pains to dispel the stereotype that equates primitive with simple and uncomplicated, showing through the evidence of their artifacts that these people were astronomers, skilled weavers, expert potters, and clever farmers. Although it is relatively easy to see what the Anasazi did, it is less obvious to know why they did these things. What were their values? Lopez concludes that we can only understand so much from the objects we find, mostly about their economic and material culture, and that it is particularly hard to reconstruct their spiritual and aesthetic life.

In *Proud Shoes*, Pauli Murray interprets her extended, multiracial family—including Cherokee Indians and prominent slave owners—in Chapel Hill, North Carolina, before and after the Civil War. In the chapter included in *Inquiry*, "The Inheritance of Values," she illustrates the character traits expected in her family: "stern devotion to duty, capacity for hard work, industry and thrift, and above all honor and courage in all things." Essayist Scott Russell Sanders interprets the four-generation "inheritance of tools" in his family, a warm, positive, and constructive (in every sense) saga. But the grim side of his inheritance emerges in his painful narrative of the effects of his father's alcoholism. As we look at both essays, we see how family history can be both commemorative and therapeutic. Yet the heritage for Sanders, like the heritage of Murray and the Anasazi, represents an embodiment of values, not only the terrible price alcoholism exacts, but also the transmission of how to read or to use tools and the reasons why these things are important, including a taste for particular books or tools, and a style of using them. Family stories are legends of human potential and limitations, precepts for survival, and parables with morals and codes of conduct. As we play out our heritage, we become who we are.

How Can We Live in Harmony with Nature?

"Those who cannot remember the past are condemned to repeat it," said philosopher George Santanyana. As Linda Simon points out at the end of this chapter, however, the reverse is not necessarily true: simply remembering the past is no assurance we will avoid repetition of it. Indeed, most learning is cumulative, for through instruction and practice we learn to correct our mistakes and, with vigilance and luck, not to make them again. Yet our nation's 50 percent divorce rate implies the truth of Samuel Johnson's assertion, that a "second marriage is a triumph of hope over experience." On a global scale, nations never seem to learn the art of peace from practicing the art of war, despite the collective wisdom of such deliberative bodies as the United Nations. To cite but two examples, the peace settlement for World War I, "the war to end all wars," prepared for the outbreak of World War II less than twenty years later; the first middle east Gulf War led the way to the second one. In the same way, the ideal of living in harmony with nature, including our fellow humans, so much a part of the American past, seems always out of reach in the present.

Other problems seem perennial, their solutions partial, temporary, or causing more problems than they solve. We have yet to eliminate poverty and its accompanying features, including malnutrition, disease, illiteracy, homelessness, unemployment, drug abuse, and child and spousal abuse. The readings in this section focus on a major problem that our society has created and has yet to solve: the destruction of the natural environment. Yet the fact that thoughtful writers from a variety of disciplines offer solutions to this problem implies that change and improvement are possible. Just because we have made mistakes does not mean that we have to go on making them. The authors write, in fact, not just to point out problems, but to point to their solutions.

Leslie Marmon Silko's "Landscape, History, and the Pueblo Imagination" explains the Pueblo Indians' world view, a way of understanding nature not through theories, mathematics, and physics, but through a belief that endows everything in the universe with "spirit and being," which remain linked in the universe even after death. Just as nothing in nature goes to waste, so the knowledge of nature and respect for its spirit are recycled in the Indian tales that affirm the powerful, loving connection between human beings and the earth. Henry David Thoreau attempted in *Walden* to reduce his needs to what he could find on the shores of the small pond where he built his cabin. In this most famous American return to nature, Thoreau sees in the environment not merely beauty and peace, but messages from the divine that echo in some ways the unity that Silko expresses. These American ideals of harmony with nature have sunk deeply into the American experience, but we are reminded of them most often by their absence, at least in modern city life.

In "The Obligation to Endure," from *Silent Spring*, biologist Rachel Carson argues that "The most alarming of all man's assaults upon the environment is the contamination," universal and irreversible, "of air, earth, rivers, and sea with dangerous and even lethal materials." Although Carson's warning had some effect, engendering legislation in the 1960s and 1970s to protect the environment and endangered species, the problems have continued, as Sandra Postel's analysis of the worldwide depletion of fresh water in "Troubled Waters" demonstrates. Postel shows how this most elemental human necessity is becoming ever scarcer and that little is being done to preserve this most precious resource. Postel's grim survey of worldwide water problems calls for a transformation in the way humanity sees water: "The fact that water is essential to life lends an ethical dimension to every decision we make about how it used, managed, and distributed. We need now technologies, to be sure, but we also need a new ethic." Both Carson and Postel reveal how our attempts to solve one set of problems can create problems as enduring as those they replace.

How Can We Interpret and Understand the Past?

It could be argued that nature, like beauty, is in the eye of the beholder. The concept of Mother Nature implies a nurturing environment, offering its bounty to the inhabitants of the Biblical Peaceable Kingdom it sustains, animals and humans alike. In contrast is the concept of "Nature red in tooth and claw" used in nineteenth-century arguments. At various times in the past, poets, philosophers, and politicians have seen the natural world as operating according to immutable—or unchanging—laws. Other contradictory interpretations regard the natural world as indifferent or inspiring to human nature; and as the source of freedom, or as a major impediment to the progress of civilization. What the nineteenth century took for granted in its vastness and abundance, the twentieth century plundered. How our new twenty-first century will treat the contaminated, ravaged natural world that extends from the depths of the seas to outer space remains to be seen. The writings of Rachel Carson and Sandra Postel in the preceding section of this chapter of *Inquiry* do not provide much of an argument for optimism.

The writings in this chapter by Stephen Hawking, Italo Calvino, Frances Fitzgerald, and Linda Simon offer views of the past ranging from the (imagined) beginning of the entire universe, to the perspective of current historians and teachers of history. The views of a physicist, a fabulist, and two historians are essentially complementary, rather than contradictory. They offer readers numerous avenues to understand and appreciate the past, which they see as a location of important knowledge and values.

In "Our Picture of the Universe," the first chapter of *A Brief History of Time*, Stephen Hawking provides an overview of the major ways that Western scientists and philosophers have conceived of the universe—whether round (Aristotle), stationary (Ptolemy), in motion (Galileo), subject to gravitational forces (Newton), or expanding (Hubble)—all ways of satisfying a natural human understanding of the "underlying order of the world." Italo Calvino's story "All at One Point"uses the scientific knowledge that Hawking summarizes, but compresses it in a fantastic fiction: the Big Bang as a warm and wonderful cosmic joke. A human society somehow exists on the point without dimension that is poised to explode into the universe. A single act of love—based on a (typically Italian vision of pasta) vision of paste—is enough to trigger creation. Finally, Frances Fitzgerald and Linda Simon speak of the ways that historians interpret and reinterpret the past. The teaching of history, they argue, has much to learn from the practise of research historians.

Rhetorical Issues: Sources

There is no special or unique way to write about what one can learn from the past any more than there is a special way to write about any other subject. The nature of the topic, however, makes it particularly appropriate to consider the sources of our information about the past and to examine ways of using sources responsibility in our writing.

Selecting Sources

Context: When psychologist Eliot Mishler titled his critique of psychological research in laboratories "Meaning in Context: Is There Any Other Kind?" he expected the answer to be an emphatic "No." His observation was radical in1979, when he published this provocative article, but it is now generally accepted. Isolated facts mean nothing without a context to help us determine which of the many possible interpretations is, or are, the best. "Best" interpretations usually mean those that accommodate all the available information and enhance our understanding of that information and the subject to which it pertains. Take for instance, the isolated facts that in the 1960s the Aral Sea was the world's fourth largest inland body of water, that thirty-five years later the Aral's volume had decreased by nearly two-thirds and its surface area by half, that sixty thousand fishing jobs had vanished, and that the remaining inhabitants were suffering from many diseases. To make sense of this information, we need to know the importance of fresh water to central Asia, the location and importance of central Asia, and the significance of this particular environmental catastrophe to the world as a whole, including your home state. If the Aral Sea, or the Brazilian rain forests, or the Florida Everglades (all in peril) were to disappear, what would be the result? To give meaning to these facts, we need enough context to understand and convey the importance they hold.

There are two categories of sources: primary (firsthand) and secondary (everything else). Primary sources include original documents by the people we are studying, such as manuscripts or books, interviews, photographs, artifacts, diaries, letters, email messages, and a person's Website. Primary sources might also be by or about people who lived during the time period or participated in the event, activity, or other phenomenon under study. Pauli Murray consulted many such documents in writing her family's history, *Proud Shoes*. These sources pertained to life and history in and around Chapel Hill, North Carolina, from its founding to early in the twentieth century, including photographs, maps, documents (such as deeds, bills of sale of slaves, or birth and marriage certificates), and records (financial statements, tax papers, court records, and wills).

Secondary sources include everyone and everything else. Secondary sources may be people: descendants, friends, and acquaintances of the original subject; experts on the subject, whether formally trained or not, including scholars, researchers, police, physicians, folklorists, and statisticians. Secondary sources also include a host of reference materials (almanacs, data banks, statistical compilations, and bibliographies) and written interpretations—scholarly articles and books, which are themselves based on a combination of primary and secondary sources. Most computer searches turn up secondary sources, of varying reliability and accuracy.

As you evaluate your materials, both primary and secondary, you will need to consider the following:

- *The date.* For primary sources, the date has to be contemporary with the subject. If you are looking for up-to-the-minute interpretations, the most recent secondary sources such as scholarly books, scientific data, or statistical compilations (identifiable by the copyright date) often supersede earlier information. But sometimes an earlier edition or work has set the standard—later editions often acknowledge their predecessors—and it's necessary to consult those as well. It sometimes saves time to begin with current materials and work backward.

- *The authority of the source.* How reliable is the author? How well qualified is he or she in terms of background and experience? One way to tell is the extent to which a given scholar is cited or quoted in others' research as long as that research is reliable.

- *Degree of generality or specialization.* How specialized is the source, and what degree of specialization is desirable? If you are discussing civil disobedience in America, what will you use to supplement primary sources, such as, say, Thoreau's "Civil Disobedience" or writings of Martin Luther King, Jr.? Would a book discussing the history of American civil disobediance, focusing on the civil rights movements in the South in the 1960s, or covering the Vietnam War protests, be the most appropriate?

- *Accuracy.* Is the source accurate, as far as you can tell? Does the author document the evidence with reliable sources that readers can check? Is appropriate evidence used and interpreted fairly?

- *Biases.* What biases does the source contain, in the sense that it emphasizes one point of view over another? Can you recognize the viewpoint? All sources are biased in some ways; many American works, for instance, are oriented toward a white, middle class North American culture. Your sources will not necessarily agree. If you are trying to interpret conflicting information, pick the least biased (most objective) sources, on the grounds that those who present or interpret the information have little or no vested interest in its use. If you are trying to interpret conflicting information from equally biased sources, rely most heavily on the source with the most authoritative reputation, the one you are most likely to trust. But you should be particularly careful not to rely uncritically, or too much, on any one source; then, you are likely to accept someone else's point of view as your own. You may well agree with one of your sources, but you need to use that source responsibly to show just how and why you agree.

Responsible Use of Sources

Suppose that you are writing a paper on American civil disobedience. You are particularly interested in the relation between idealism and lawbreaking. You decide that the following passage from Henry David Thoreau's essay in the previous chapter is relevant to your topic, and you want to use it as a source:

> Unjust laws exist: shall we be content to obey them, or shall we endeavor to amend them, and obey them until we have succeeded, or shall we transgress them at once? Men generally, under such a government as this, think that they ought to wait until they have persuaded the majority to alter them. They think that, if they should resist, the remedy would be worse than the evil. But it is the fault of the government itself that the remedy is worse than the evil. It makes it worse. Why is it not more apt to anticipate and provide for reform? Why does it not cherish its wise minority? Why does it cry and resist before it is hurt?

What Thoreau has to say is clearly useful for your topic. But how are you to use it? And how are you to avoid using it improperly?

Let's take a moment to look at the wrong ways to handle sources; many students are nervous about falling into plagiarism—using sources as if they were your own idea—by mistake. Very few students will be deliberately dishonest and foolish enough to plan plagiarism, that is, to copy what Thoreau said word for word and hand it in as if it were original. Nevertheless, honest and sensible people still have trouble using sources properly and sometimes stumble unaware into plagiarism, unless they understand clearly how to incorporate other people's ideas into their own work.

For instance, one way to misuse Thoreau's material would be to copy what he says word for word and put a note at the end of the quotation referring to the source. Sometimes plagiarism happens if you take casual notes that fail to distinguish quotations from your summaries of what you have read. There is no intention to deceive, in this case, but plagiarism is still going on, since (without quotation marks) Thoreau's words and ideas are presented as your own.

It is more responsible to put the quoted material in quotation marks, of course, but even that does not complete the job of using the source responsibly. Why is the quotation in your text? How does it relate to what you have to say?

The real point of writing a paper using sources is not just to include relevant quotations and to cite sources, but rather to demonstrate that you have thought about your quotations and your sources in relation to your topic. Quoting sources lets you engage in dialogue with others on the subject. If you just string together sources, quoted or paraphrased, with a bit of connection to hold them together, you are not accomplishing the inquiry that lies behind writing itself. Sources will help you demonstrate your ideas, and increase your authority, but they cannot substitute for your ideas.

One way many students would use this source would be to figure out what Thoreau is saying and to put it into their own words:

> People suffering under unjust laws have to decide if they should obey the laws or not. Most people decide to obey them while they work for change, since breaking the law might be worse than the unjust law itself. But it is better to break the law, since the law itself should allow the best citizens to make changes.

But inserting this rewording of Thoreau's idea into your paper, while it shows that you understand his idea, is still not by itself a responsible use of the source, particularly if you fail to cite Thoreau at the end of the paraphrase. The idea is still his, even if the words are yours, and just placing someone else's ideas into your paper represents a failure to use the source properly. Even if you do cite Thoreau after the paraphrase, your reader will not know what the citation means. How much of what you say is yours, how much is Thoreau's, or is there any difference?

The problem you must handle as a writer using sources is not only to understand Thoreau, but also to come to some personal understanding of the material at hand (here, the moral and legal problem of either obeying or disobeying unjust laws). You must regard Thoreau critically; if you end up agreeing with him, you should say so, explicitly. If not, point out where and why you differ.

So we return once more to the topic. Is Thoreau's argument (those in "a wise minority" should break laws they feel to be unjust) an idea you wish to support, in whole or in part? What does you own experience say? What do other sources, for instance, Martin Luther King, Jr., in "Letter from Birmingham Jail" (chapter 4) or Lewis H. Van Dusen (also from chapter 4), say about breaking unjust laws? Does Thoreau's living in nineteenth-century New England in any way determine what he will see? How does Thoreau's view relate to your own?

To think about your quotation in the context of your own ideas is to come to terms with the problems of writing a paper using sources. If you decide to put the whole quotation into your paper, you will need to introduce it, analyze it, comment upon it, and relate it to your own ideas. You might begin, after the quotation, with something like the following:

> When we look closely at what Thoreau has to say, we can argue that he oversimplifies the issue; as the last 150 years have made plain, it is hard to decide exactly what is an unjust law. Few of us today can be as certain as Thoreau was that any law is wrong. But Thoreau's arrogant certainty has undeniable power. . . .

But perhaps you do not want to focus so heavily on Thoreau's view; in that case, you may want to quote a small portion of what he says, as part of another argument:

> Disobedience to law in our time has proven to be a powerful force for change. The idea that we should always obey laws while seeking to change them has repeatedly been shown to be the way governments perpetuate evil; they argue that breaking laws is worse than any evil the law may bring about. But I would argue, as does Thoreau in "Civil Disobedience," that "it is the fault of the government itself that the remedy is worse than the evil." A truly democratic government will provide ways for those who object to its laws to protest legally and effectively.

Or you may just want to allude to what Thoreau says as part of a survey of various ideas on your subject:

> Among the most well-known proponents of disobeying laws they felt to be unjust are Thoreau (who briefly went to jail for opposing a government supporting slavery) and Dr. Martin Luther King, Jr., who. . . .

There are many ways to use sources responsibly, but the important principle to keep in mind is that you must understand what the source is saying and how it relates to your own ideas. In using sources, you must not simply be a sponge, soaking up uncritically everything you read. You must distinguish between the opinions of another and the opinion that you yourself, after careful consideration, come to hold. The quotation then becomes a fact, the fact that a particular writer has said something, which you as author of your own work must interpret as you would any other fact; you need to show how the evidence provided by the quotation relates to what you yourself have to say. Every writer has his or her own intellectual identity, though most ideas inevitably come from outside sources. A responsible use of sources recognizes that identity and distinguishes clearly between what you think and what the sources think. It is no sin to accept another person's idea: "But I would argue, as does Thoreau, that. . . ." But you must interpose yourself between the sources and your writing, thus making other people's ideas your own through a process of critical scrutiny.

QUESTIONS FOR DISCOVERY AND DISCUSSION

1. Interview an elderly member of your family to find out what that person remembers of particular childhood traditions, stories, rituals, or customs. What can you discover about your family's past and how your parents carried on (or modified) family traditions? Can you find family photographs that reinforce the memories? How far back can you trace your roots?

2. What stories and traditions were influential in your own childhood? Think of experiences that show the power of the past. Did your parents read to you from books they themselves used as children? Were there old places or things that embodied important memories? Can you recall experiences that you had that were the same as those your parents, grandparents, or great-grandparents had when they were children?

3. What values do you now hold that have been passed down to you from older generations? Where did they come from and what were their origins? Have you had to adjust these values to modern times, or do they still work as they did in the past?

3. To what degree did your previous schooling support or challenge the values and beliefs you received from your family? Explain to someone who does not know your family an incident that shows the way schooling related to your family traditions.

HOW DOES FAMILY HERITAGE AFFECT
WHO WE ARE?

Searching for Ancestors

archaeology

BARRY LOPEZ

In "Searching for Ancestors," from his essay collection *Crossing Open Ground* (1988), Barry Lopez explores how and why he and two archaeologists went to northern Arizona to hunt for "tangible remains" of the Indian culture, generically called Anasazi. Throughout the essay, Lopez takes pains to dispel the notion that prehistoric means either "primitive" or "uncomplicated." When we search for ancestors, whether those of our family, clan, nation, or species, we need to be aware of the relation of the people to each other, the land, the times, and the climate—intellectual and geographical. As investigators of the past, "we are takers of notes, measurers of stone, examiners of fragments in the dust. We search for order in chaos wherever we go," but we need to beware of imposing our contemporary order, *ex post facto*. "In our best moments," says Lopez, "we remember to ask ourselves what it is we are doing, whom we are benefiting from these acts. One of the great dreams of man must be to find some place between the extremes of nature and civilization where it is possible to live without regret."

Lopez was born in New York in 1945. After earning degrees from Notre Dame in 1966 and 1968, he moved to rural Oregon, where he continues to live and write. Much of his writing presents sympathetic, sometimes poetic, interpretations of animal behavior in relation to other animals or humans. Among his books are *Desert Notes: Reflections in the Eye of a Raven* (1976); *River Notes: The Dance of Herons* (1979); *Of Wolves and Men* (1979), illustrated with his own photographs; *Arctic Dreams: Imagination and Desire in a Northern Landscape* (1986), winner of the National Book Award; and *Light Action in the Caribbean* (2000), a collection of short fiction. Currently, Lopez is writing a nonfictional account of his travels in the Galápagos Islands, Kenya, Australia, and Antarctica.

biologist?

I am lying on my back in northern Arizona. The sky above, the familiar arrangement of stars at this particular latitude on a soft June evening, is comforting. I reach out from my sleeping bag, waiting for sleep, and slowly brush the Kaibab Plateau, a grit of limestone 230 million years old. A slight breeze, the settling air at dusk, carries the pungent odor of blooming cliffrose.   1

Three of us sleep in this clearing, on the west rim of Marble Canyon above the Colorado River. Two archaeologists and myself, out hunting for tangible remains of the culture called Anasazi. The Anasazi abandoned this particular area for good around A.D. 1150, because of   2

489

drought, deteriorating trade alliances, social hostilities—hard to say now. But while they flourished, both here and farther to the east in the austere beauty of canyons called de Chelly and Chaco, they represented an apotheosis in North American culture, like the Hopewell of Ohio or the horse-mounted Lakota of the plains in the last century.

3   In recent years the Anasazi have come to signify prehistoric Indians in the same way the Lakota people have been made to stand for all historic Indians. Much has been made of the "mystery" of their disappearance. And perhaps because they seem "primitive," they are too easily though of as an uncomplicated people with a comprehensible culture. It is not, and they are not. We know some things about them. From the start they were deft weavers, plaiting even the utensils they cooked with. Later they became expert potters and masons, strongly influencing cultures around them. They were clever flood-water farmers. And astronomers; not as sophisticated as the Maya, but knowledgeable enough to pinpoint the major celestial events, to plant and celebrate accordingly.

4   They were intimate with the landscape, a successful people. Around A. D. 1300 they slipped through a historical crevice to emerge (as well as we know) as the people now called Hopi and Zuni, and the pueblo peoples of the Rio Grande Valley—Keres, Tiwa, Tewa.

5   On a long, dry June day like this, hundreds of tourists wander in fascination at Mesa Verde and Pueblo Bonito; and I am out here on the land the Anasazi once walked—here with two people who squat down to look closely at the land itself before they say anything about its former inhabitants. Even then they are reticent. We are camped here amid the indigenous light siennas and dark umbers, the wild red of ripe prickly pear fruit, the dull silver of buffalo berry bushes, the dark, luminous green of a field of snakegrass.

6   We inquire after the Anasazi. Because we respect the spiritual legacy of their descendants, the Hopi. Because of the contemporary allure of Taos. Because in our own age we are "killing the hidden waters" of the Southwest, and these were a people who took swift, resourceful advantage of whatever water they could find. Because of the compelling architecture of their cliff dwellings, the stunning placement of their homes in the stone walls of Betatakin, as if set in the mouth of an enormous wave or at the bottom of a towering cumulus cloud. We make the long automobile trip to Hovenweep or the hike into Tsegi Canyon to gaze at Keet Seel. It is as though we believed *here* is a good example, here are stories to get us through the night.

7   Some eight thousand years ago, after the decline of the Folsom and Clovis hunters, whose spearpoints are still found in the crumbling arroyos of New Mexico, a culture we know very little about emerged in the Great Basin. Archaeologists call it simply the Desert Culture. Some two thousand years ago, while Rome was engaged in the Macedonian

wars, a distinct group of people emerged from this complex. They were called Anasazi from the Navajo *anaasázi,* meaning "someone's ancestors." Their culture first appeared in the Four Corners country, where Utah, Arizona, New Mexico, and Colorado meet. By this time (A.D. 1) they were already proficient weavers and basket-makers, living a mixed agricultural hunter-gatherer life and dwelling in small groups in semisubterranean houses. Archaeologists call this period, up to about A.D. 700, the Basket Maker Period. It was followed by a Pueblo Period (A.D. 700–1598), during which time the Anasazi built the great cliff and pueblo dwellings by which most of us know them.

Archaeologists divide the Anasazi occupation geographically into   8
three contemporary traditions—Kayenta, Chaco, and Mesa Verde. Here, where I have rolled my sleeping bag out this June evening, Kayenta Anasazi lived, in an area of about ten thousand square miles bounded by the Henry Mountains in Utah, the Little Colorado River to the south, Grand Canyon to the west, and Chinle Wash, near the New Mexico border, to the east. This part of the Anasazi country has long been of interest to Robert Euler, the research anthropologist at Grand Canyon National Park. He lies quietly now a few yards away from me, in the night shadow of a large juniper tree. From here, at the lip of Marble Canyon and the old edge of Anasazi territory, amid the very same plants the Anasazi took such perceptive advantage of—threads of the yucca leaf to be made into snares; the soft, shreddy bark of the cliffrose to absorb the flow of blood; delicate black seeds of rice grass to eat— from here, with the aid of an observer like Euler, it is possible to imagine who these people might have been, to make some cautious surmise about them and the meaning they may have for us, who wistfully regard them now as mysterious and vanished, like the Eskimo curlew.

We go toward sleep this evening—Euler, a colleague named Trin-   9
kle Jones, and myself—restless with the bright, looming memory of a granary we have located today, a small storage structure below a cliff edge that has been visited only by violet-green swallows and pack rats since its Anasazi owners walked away some eight hundred years ago. It is like a piece of quartz in the mind.

In a quiet corner of the national park's health clinic on the south   10
rim of the Grand Canyon, an entire wall of Euler's modest office is covered by books. A small slip of paper there reads:

> These are not books, lumps of lifeless paper, but *minds* alive on the shelves. From each of them goes out its own voice, as inaudible as the streams of sound conveyed day and night by electric waves beyond the range of our physical hearing; and just as the touch of a button on our set will fill the room with music, so by taking down one of these volumes and opening it, one can call into range the far distant voice in time and space, and hear it speaking to us, mind to mind, heart to heart.
>
> GILBERT HIGHET

11   Highet was a classics scholar. The words reflect his respect for the ideas of other cultures, other generations, and for the careful deliberations of trained minds. Euler is in this mold; keen and careful, expert in his field, but intent on fresh insight. At fifty-seven, with an ironic wit, willing to listen attentively to the ideas of an amateur, graciously polite, he is the sort of man you wish had taught you in college.

12   Of the Anasazi he says: 'It is relatively easy to see *what* they did, but why did they do these things? What were their values? What were the fundamental relationships between their institutions—their politics, economics, religion? All we can do is infer, from what we pick up on the ground."

13   To elucidate the Anasazi, Euler and his colleagues have taken several ingenious steps in recent years. In the 1920s a man named Andrew Douglass pioneered a system of dating called dendrochronology. By comparing borings from timbers used in Anasazi dwellings, Douglass and his successors eventually constructed a continuous record of tree-ring patterns going back more than two thousand years. The measurements are so precise that archaeologists can, for instance, tell that a room in a particular dwelling in Chaco Canyon was roofed over in the spring or summer of 1040 with timbers cut in the fall or winter of 1039.

14   Using dendrochronology as a parallel guide in time, archaeologists have been able to corroborate and assemble long sequences of pottery design. With the aid of radiocarbon dating, obsidian hydration dating, and a technique called thermoluminescence, they have pinned down dates for cooking fires and various tools. By determining kinds of fossil pollens and their ratios to each other, palynologists have reconstructed former plant communities, shedding light on human diets at the time and establishing a history of weather patterns.

15   With such a convergence of dates and esoteric information, archaeologists can figure out when a group of people were occupying a certain canyon, what sort of meals they were eating, what kind of animals and plants were present there, and how they were adapting their farming methods and living patterns to cope with, say, several years of heavy rainfull. With more prosaic techniques—simple excavation and observation—much more becomes clear: details and artifacts of personal adornment; locally traded items (beans and squash for tanned deerskin) and distant trade patterns (turquoise for abalone shell beads from California or copper bells from Mexico); and prevalent infirmities and diseases (arthritis, iron-deficiency anemia).

16   As much as one can learn, however—the Anasazi were a short people with straight black hair, who domesticated turkeys for a supply of feathers, which they carefully wrapped around string and wove together to make blankets—the information seems hollow when you are

standing in the cool silence of one of the great kivas at Mesa Verde. Or staring at the stone that soars like a cathedral vault above White House Ruin in Canyon de Chelly. Or turning an Anasazi flute over in your hands. The analytic tools of science can obscure the fact that these were a people. They had an obvious and pervasive spiritual and aesthetic life, as well as clothing made of feathers and teeth worn down by the grit in their cornmeal. Their abandoned dwellings and ceremonial kivas would seem to make this clear. This belief by itself—that they were a people of great spiritual strength—makes us want to know them, to understand what they understood.

The day Euler and Jones discovered the intact granary, with its   17 handful of tiny corncobs, I was making notes about the plants and animals we had encountered and trying to envision how water fell and flowed away over this parched land. Euler had told me the area we were traversing was comparable to what the Anasazi had known when they were here, though it was a little drier now. Here then was buffalo berry, which must have irritated their flesh with the white powder beneath its leaves, as it did mine. And apache plume, from whose stout twigs the Anasazi made arrows. And a species of sumac, from the fruits of which they made a sweet lemonade. Dogbane, from whose fibrous stems they wove sandals, proof against scorpions, cactus spines, and the other sharp and pointed edges of this country.

One afternoon I came on the remains of a mule deer killed by a   18 mountain lion and thought the Anasazi, eminently practical, must have availed themselves of such meat. And I considered the sheltered, well-stocked dwellings of the pack rat, who may have indicated to the newly arrived Anasazi the value of providence and storage.

Such wandering is like an interrogation of the landscape, trying by   19 means of natural history and analog to pry loose from it a sense of a people who would be intimate with it—knowledgeable of the behavior of its ground and surface water, its seven-year cycle of piñon nut production, the various subtle euphonies of whirring insects, bumblebees, and hummingbirds on a June afternoon—a people reflective of its order.

Euler stood by me at one point when I asked about a particular   20 plant—did they parch, very carefully, the tiny seeds of this desert plume in fiber baskets over their fires?—and said that their botany was so good they probably made use of everything they could digest.

They made mistakes, too, if you want to call them that: farmed one   21 area too intensively and ruined the soil; cut down too many trees with their stone axes for housing and firewood and abetted erosion; overhunted. But they survived. They lived through long droughts and took advantage of years of wetness to secure their future. One of the great lessons of the Anasazi is one of the great lessons of all aboriginal peoples, of human ecology in general: Individuals die—of starvation, disease, and injury; but the population itself—resourceful, practical, determined—carries on through nearly everything. Their indomitable fierceness is as attractive as the power we imagine concentrated in their kivas.

22   With the Anasazi, however, you must always turn back and look at the earth—the earth they farmed and hunted and gathered fruits and nuts and seeds upon—and to the weather. The Anasazi responded resourcefully and decisively to the earth and the weather that together make their land. If they were sometimes victims of their environment through drought or epidemic disease, they were more often on excellent terms with it. Given a slight advantage, as they were about A.D. 600 and again about A.D. 1150, when food was abundant at the peak of the Southwest's 550-year moisture cycle, their culture flourished. Around A.D. 600 they developed pottery, the cultivated bean, and the bow and arrow. In the bean was an important amino acid, lysine, not available in the corn they cultivated. Their diet improved dramatically. By 1150 the Anasazi were building pueblos with three-story, freestanding walls, and their crafts were resurgent during this "classic" period. We can only wonder what might have happened at the next climatic, in 1700—but by then the hostile Spanish were among them.

23   The rise and fall of Anasazi fortunes in time with the weather patterns of the region is clear to most historians. What is not clear is how much of a role weather played in the final retreat of the Anasazi in A.D. 1300 from areas they had long occupied—Mesa Verde, southern Black Mesa, Chaco Canyon. Toward the end, the Anasazi were building what seem to be defensive structures, but it is unclear against whom they were defending themselves. A good guess is that they were defending themselves against themselves, that this was a period of intense social feuding. The sudden alteration of trading relationships, social and political realignment in the communities, drought—whatever the reasons, the Anasazi departed. Their descendants took up residence along the Rio Grande, near springs on the Hopi mesas, and on tributaries of the Little Colorado where water was more dependable. Here, too, they developed farming techniques that were not so harmful to the land.

24   For many in the Southwest today the Anasazi are a vague and nebulous passage in the history of human life. For others, like Euler, they are an intense reflection of the land, a puzzle to be addressed the way a man might try to understand the now-departed curlew. For still others they are a spiritual repository, a mysterious source of strength both of their intimacy with the Colorado Plateau.

25   To wonder about the Anasazi today at a place like the Grand Canyon is to be humbled—by space and the breadth of time—to find the Anasazi neither remote nor primitive, but transcendent. The Eng-

lish novelist J. B. Priestley once said that if he were an American he would make the final test of whatever men chose to do in art and politics a comparison with this place. He believed that whatever was cheap and ephemeral would be revealed for what it was when stood up against it. Priestley was an intellectual, but he had his finger on an abiding aboriginal truth: If something will not stand up in the land, then it doesn't belong there. It is right that it should die. Most of us are now so far removed from either a practical or an aesthetic intimacy with North America that the land is no longer an arbiter for us. And a haunting sense that this arrangement is somewhat dangerous brings us to stare into the Grand Canyon and to contemplate the utter honesty of the Anasazi's life here.

In 1906, with some inkling that North America was slowly being 26 stripped of the evidence of its aboriginal life and that a knowledge of such life was valuable, Congress passed a protective Antiquities Act. The *[Legislation* impulse in 1979 to pass a much stronger Archaeological Resources Act *to protect* was different. Spurred on by escalating prices for Anasazi artifacts, *artifacts* thieves had been systematically looting sites for commercial gain. The trend continues. A second serious current threat to this human heritage is the small number of tourists who, sometimes innocently, continue to destroy structures, walk off with artifacts, and deface petroglyphs. More ominously, the national parks and monuments where most Anasazi sites are now found operate on such restricted budgets that they are unable to adequately inventory, let alone protect, these cultural resources.

Of the Grand Canyon's two thousand or more aboriginal sites only 27 three have been both excavated and stabilized. Of its 1.2 million acres, 500,000 have never even been visited by an archaeologist or historian. In the summer of 1981 an unknown person or persons pushed in the wall of an Anasazi granary on the Colorado River at the mouth of Nankoweap Canyon, one of the most famous sites in the park.

The sites, which people come so far every year to visit, are more 28 vulnerable every year.

On a helicopter reconnaissance in September 1981, part of a longterm project to locate and describe aboriginal sites in the park, Trin- 29 kle Jones found what she thought was a set of untouched ruins in the west rim of Marble Canyon. It was almost a year before she and Euler could get there to record them, on a trip on which I accompanied them.

Euler is glad to get out into the country, into the canyons that have 30 been the focus of his work since 1960. He moves easily through the juniper-piñon savannahs, around the face of a cliff and along narrow trails with a practiced stride, examining bits of stone and brush. His blue eyes often fill with wonder when he relates bits of Anasazi history, his right hand sometimes turning slowly in the air as he speaks, as if he were showing you rare fruit. He tells me one night that he reveres the land, that he thinks about his own footprints impressed in the soil and on the plants, how long before there will be no trace.

31   Euler is a former college president, an author and editor, has been on several university faculties and a codirector of the Black Mesa Archaeological Project, working one step ahead of Peabody Coal's drag buckets. The Park Service, so severely hampered by its humiliating lack of funds, is fortunate, at least, to be able to retain such men.

32   The granaries Jones found prove, indeed, to be untouched. Over a period of several days we map and describe nine new ruins. The process is somewhat mechanical, but we each take pleasure in the simple tasks. As the Anasazi had a complicated culture, so have we. We are takers of notes, measurers of stone, examiners of fragments in the dust. We search for order in chaos wherever we go. We worry over what is lost. In our best moments we remember to ask ourselves what it is we are doing, whom we are benefiting by these acts. One of the great dreams of man must be to find some place between the extremes of nature and civilization where it is possible to live without regret.

33   I lie in my sleeping bag, staring up at the Big Dipper and other familiar stars. It is surprisingly cool. The moon has risen over the land of the Navajo nation to the east. Bats flutter overhead, swooping after moths. We are the only people, I reflect, who go to such lengths to record and preserve the past. In the case of the Anasazi it is not even our own past. Until recently Indians distrusted this process. When Andrew Douglass roamed the Southwest looking for house timbers to core to establish his dendrochronologies, he was required to trade bolts of velveteen for the privilege and to close off every drill hole with a piece of turquoise.

34   I roll on my side and stare out into the canyon's abyss. I think of the astonishing variety of insects and spiders I have seen today—stinkbugs inverted in cactus flowers, butterflies, tiny biting gnats and exotic red velvet ants, and on the ceiling of an Anasazi granary a very poisonous brown recluse spider. For all the unrelieved tedium there might seem to be in the miles of juniper-piñon savannah, for all the cactus spines, sharp stones, strong light, and imagined strikes of rattlesnakes, the land is replete with creatures, and there is soft and subtle beauty here. Turn an ash-white mule deer antler over, and its underside, where it has lain against the earth, is flushed rose. Yellow pollen clings to the backs of my hands. Wild grasses roll in the wind, like the manes of horses. It is important to remember that the Anasazi lived in a place, and that the place was very much like the place I lie in tonight.

35   The Anasazi are a reminder: Human life is fundamentally diverse and finally impenetrable. That we cannot do better than a crude reconstruction of their life on the Colorado Plateau a thousand years ago is

probably to our advantage, for it steers us away from presumption and judgment.

I roll over again and look at the brightening stars. How fortunate 36 we all are, I think, to have people like Euler among us, with their long-lived inquiries; to have these bits of the Anasazi Way to provoke our speculation, to humble us in this long and endless struggle to find ourselves in the world.

The slow inhalation of light that is the fall of dusk is now complete. 37 The stars are very bright. I lie there recalling the land as if the Anasazi were something that had once bloomed in it.

RESPONDING TO READING

1. To what lengths is it appropriate to go "to record and preserve the past" (paragraph 33)? By what means can we do so? For what purposes? Suppose that preserving the past conflicts with progress, what then?

2. Why study history?

3. What sorts of evidence do archaeologists use to understand and reconstruct past civilizations?

4. "If something will not stand up in the land, then it doesn't belong there. It is right that it should die" (paragraph 25). What does Lopez mean by that? How could a natural terrain or a species (such as the buffalo or the American Eagle) protect itself against destruction by the forces of "civilization"? Yet surely Lopez does not mean that it is "right" that the land or particular species should die out. Discuss.

5. When you think of "ancestors," is your meaning the same as Lopez's? Define your meaning, and explain how you would go about studying ancestors as you define them. What would you be looking for?

The Inheritance of Values

PAULI MURRAY

In searching for her ancestors when preparing to write *Proud Shoes* (1955), of which "The Inheritance of Values" is a chapter, Pauli Murray discovered her family's history to be a microcosm of the history of America, for better and for worse. "The ideals and influences within my own family had made me a life-long fighter against all forms of inequality and injustice," says Murray. Her research was complicated because of the difficulties in tracing blacks, particularly in the South, because "the experience of slavery . . . all but wiped out the identities of black ancestors." In census records before 1870, slaves were identified not by their own names, but by the names of their owners, and usually were not named at all in public records, such as deeds, wills, or bills of sale. After the Civil War, black families, scarcely literate, were scattered, so neither oral nor written traditions preserved their histories. Former slaves and their children were reluctant to talk about their bondage, "too painful to live with." When social taboos and miscegenation laws were broken, there was additional pressure to maintain silence. Murray's people included Cherokee Indians and a prominent, white slave-owing family, whose "deep sexual and emotional involvement with slaves" leapt racial and social barriers, but created a further taboo of silence.

Despite these silences, Murray (1910–85), a lawyer who had earned her degree from Howard University in 1944, persevered in her quest for information, as she was to do in every area of her life. She found in public archives "the records of obscure citizens and the country's leaders," documents "of a common humanity" that narrowed the distances between races, classes, and political positions. Her resourceful investigation provided the basis for both her family biography, *Proud Shoes*, and for her civil rights activities.

1   There was pride on both sides of the Fitzgerald family, but my greatest inheritance, perhaps, was a dogged persistence, a granite quality of endurance in the face of calamity. There was pride in family background, of course, but my folks took greater pride in doing any kind of honest work to earn a living and remain independent. Some people thought this trait was peculiarly Grandfather's, that Grandmother was flighty and contentious. They did not know the inside story: how she had struggled to keep her home together and bring up six children with her husband going blind and losing ground most of the way. Her tenacity, like that of Grandfather, sprang partly from her deep religious faith and partly from a mulishness which refused to countenance despair.

2   "There's more ways to kill a dog beside choking him on butter," she used to say.

3   She was remembering those uncertain years when the children were growing up and Grandfather was fighting for his pension while trying to build a home. He had bought an acre of ground in Durham, planned his house on the edge of his line and used the rest of the land to dig clay for his brickyard. He made bricks by hand, the hard kind used for outer walls and guaranteed to withstand all kinds of weather. It was a slow and costly process full of setbacks and failures. His hired men were often careless and took advantage of his blindness. They'd fire the kilns with raw green wood or go to sleep on the job in the middle of a burning and let the fires go out. Grandfather's bricks would come out crumbling and useless and he'd have to start all over again.

4   Then there were his lonely pilgrimages from place to place, guided only by his cane and a kind passerby, in search of old army comrades to help reconstruct his war record twenty years after his discharge. His search frequently ended in disappointment and he'd come home dis-

couraged to make bricks for a while before starting out again. It took him almost ten years to prove his eligibility for pension payments.

During those years Grandmother was trying to educate their chil-   5
dren. Fortunately, she came into a small inheritance when Mary Ruffin Smith died around 1885. Miss Mary had not forgotten the four Smith daughters. She left each of them one hundred acres of land with provision that a house be built upon it not to cost more than $150. To ensure that the land remained free from their husbands' debts or control, she gave them only a life interest in it and provided that it should pass to their children when they died. She also left her household goods and furnishings to be divided equally among the four.

Grandmother's hundred acres came out of the old Smith planta-   6
tion near Chapel Hill. She was never entirely satisfied with this bequest; she felt Miss Mary had robbed her of the full inheritance her father had intended for her, and the restrictions of "heir property" which she did not own outright rankled. It served, however, as vindication of her own claims and was Miss Mary's backhanded recognition of their relationship. Aside from a twenty-five-acre gift to their halfbrother, Julius, who was not of Smith blood, and a few small cash bequests, the four Smith daughters and their children were the only individuals remembered in Mary Ruffin Smith's will.

Whatever Grandmother's dissatisfaction, which increased as years   7
passed, she made the most of her farm. She lived there with the children and worked the land while Grandfather was building his house in Durham. From time to time she sold off timber to help him in his brick business. She used whatever cash she could raise from her crops and fruit to send the children off to school. When she had no crops or fruit, she'd sell the chickens, the hogs or whatever else she could lay her hands on.

Aunt Sallie would never forget the time Grandmother sent Aunt   8
Maria to Hampton Institute to take up the tailoring trade. When time came for tuition, Grandmother had no money so she decided to sell her cow. Grandfather was away from home working on his pension, Aunt Pauline was off teaching and Uncle Tommie was away at school. Grandmother had no one to send to market except Sallie and Agnes, who were about twelve and eleven yars old at the time, but she was not dismayed.

"Children," she told them, "I want you to drive this cow down to   9
Durham and take her to Schwartz' market. Tell Mr. Schwartz that Cornelia Smith sent her and that she's a fine milk cow. I want a good price on her and I'm depending on you to get it."

It was a huge undertaking for two little girls—Durham was fifteen   10
miles away and the cow was none too manageable—but it would never have occurred to them that they could not deliver the cow. They started out early in the morning on a trip which took all day. The cow strayed off

the road from time to time to graze in the meadows or lie down to rest and they had to pull and tug at her to get her started again. They arrived at the market in Durham near nightfall, somewhat frightened, their clothes torn and spattered with mud. When Mr. Schwartz heard all the commotion outside and came to find two bedraggled little girls standing guard over a huge cow, he listened to their story in disbelief.

11   "You don't mean to tell me you drove that cow all the way from Chapel Hill?" he asked.

12   "Yes sir, we did."

13   "Well, I never. And you say you're Robert Fitzgerald's daughters?"

14   "Yes sir, we are."

15   "How do I know you didn't steal that cow?"

16   The little girls stood their ground.

17   "If you doubt our word, you send for our Uncle Richard Fitzgerald."

18   Mr. Schwartz finally sent for Uncle Richard, who came, took one look at them and laughed.

19   "They're my brother's children all right, and if they say their mother sent the cow to market, you can take their word for it," he told Mr. Schwartz. So the butcher bought the cow on the spot and Aunt Maria stayed in school another few months.

20   It was also part of Grandfather's creed not to coddle his daughters. He expected them to make their way in life as he had done. I found a letter he had written to Aunt Maria on September 25, 1895. She had finished her work at Hampton and gone to Philadelphia to find employment as a dressmaker, without success. She wrote to Grandfather for money to come home. He replied.

> You must not depend upon sewing. I'd go into service. You can get $12 to $15 per month and stick to work for two months without taking up your money, and you can come home independent. . . . I find many a fine mechanic tramping through the state because he cannot work at his trade. Too many people make this great mistake. You must do as I did when I first went to Philadelphia, then a boy 16. I couldn't get the kind of employment I sought so I took whatever I could get to do and stuck at it until I had accumulated enough to carry me where I wanted to go with money in my pocket. Now you are young and as able as you ever will be. You can live anywhere on the face of the earth as other people can. Take my advice, getting your board and lodging and $15 per month and you will soon be able to come home.

21   Thrift was another household god in Grandfather's home. It was not only a strong ingredient of his own children's training but it was expected of all prospective sons-in-law. When young Leon B. Jeffers wrote my grandparents for consent to marry Aunt Maria in 1901, they replied in the affirmative, saying, "From earliest acquaintance with you, you have been held in highest esteem by us. Although you

may not have money and riches to bestow upon her now, if you have that pure and undefiled love to present to her, with thrift and good management you can soon accumulate some property."

Only three of my grandparents' children were still living when I   22
was coming along—Aunt Pauline, Aunt Maria (who preferred to be called Marie) and Aunt Sallie—all schoolteachers and all having a hand in my upbringing. Their brother, Uncle Tommie, had left home before he was twenty and was never heard from again. Some thought he was lost at sea and others that he died of smallpox during the Spanish-American War. The youngest sister, Roberta, succumbed to typhoid fever when she was barely nineteen. My own mother, Agnes, who had departed from the teaching tradition to become a registered nurse, died suddenly when I was three, leaving six children and my father, who was ill. I saw him only once after that before he died.

Having no parents of my own, I had in effect three mothers, each   23
trying to impress upon me those traits of character expected of a Fitzgerald—stern devotion to duty, capacity for hard work, industry and thrift, and above all honor and courage in all things. Grandfather, of course, was their standard bearer for most of the virtues, but sometimes they talked of my own mother, who was a woman of beauty and courage and whose spirit became a guiding force in my own life although I was too young to remember her.

What happened on my mother's wedding night seemed typical of   24
her courage. Her wedding to William H. Murray, a brilliant young schoolteacher from Baltimore, was scheduled for nine o'clock on the evening of July 1, 1903, at Emanuel A.M.E. Church on Chapel Hill Road in Durham, after which the reception was to be held at Grandfather's house. Engraved invitations were sent out to numerous relatives and friends and the five Fitzgerald daughters were as excited as if all of them were brides. Will Murray was the most popular of their brothers-in-law. He had come down from Baltimore in grand style, flanked by a troupe of young men to attend him.

Preparations were in full swing; everybody was scurrying about all   25
day long. There had never been such a big wedding in the Fitzgerald household. Aunt Marie Jeffers, who was expecting a child, was putting the finishing touches on my mother's wedding gown. As family modiste, she wouldn't think of letting Aggie get married until her skillful fingers had supervised each tuck and fold.

It had been a stiflingly hot day and toward evening a thunder-   26
storm threatened. The bride was almost ready and Aunt Marie stepped back to survey her handiwork when her face went deadly pale, she screamed and fell upon her knees in her first sharp labor pains. The wedding preparations were thrown into bedlam; everything came to a standstill. People gathered at the church and the groom was waiting impatiently, but there was no bride.

27   At Grandfather's house Aunt Marie's screams could be heard all over the neighborhood. To add to the confusion the thunderstorm struck with terrifying intensity. It was the worst of all times for a child to be born in the Fitzgerald home, but if my mother was frightened she gave no sign. She slipped quietly out of her wedding clothes, put on her uniform and took her place beside the doctor who came to attend Aunt Marie. She was all nurse, coolheaded and composed. Childbirth was hazardous in those days and for a while it looked as if Aunt Marie would not make it. At the height of the storm, between sharp flashes of lightning and rolls of thunder which shook the house, the baby came. My mother's trained eye saw that the doctor's forceps were askew in the emergency and she quickly readjusted them, saving the baby's life. Even so, his head and neck were severely bruised and cut in the delivery and nobody expected him to live. He was thrown aside while doctor and nurse worked frantically to save the mother's life.

28   Somebody suggested that Agnes call off her wedding, but she shook her head and stuck to her post. When it finally appeared that Aunt Marie would survive the crisis, my mother turned to the neglected infant, bathed and bandaged him, treated his wounds, hovered over him, smacked him and almost breathed life into him. She did not turn him loose until he let out a lusty cry and she felt that he would live. She then calmly washed her hands, put on her wedding dress once more and went out into a downpour to meet her groom. Everything went off as planned, except that it was several hours later and very much subdued. The reception was switched to Uncle Richard's house and the bride received her guests as graciously as if nothing untoward had happened. The baby, Gerald, celebrated his fifty-second birthday not long ago[1] and Aunt Marie reached eighty-one before she died.

29   It was through these homespun stories, each with its own moral, that my elders sought to build their family traditions. In later years I realized how very much their wealth had consisted of intangibles. They had little of the world's goods and less of its recognition but they had forged enduring values for themselves which they tried to pass on to me. I would have need of these resources when I left the rugged security of Grandfather's house and found myself in a maze of terrifying forces which I could neither understand nor cope with. While my folks could not shield me from the impact of these forces, through their own courage and strength they could teach me to withstand them. My first experience with this outer world came the summer I was nearly seven.

---

[1]He lived to be about 70.

RESPONDING TO READING

1. This memoir is organized simply: A series of abstractions (the inherited values) are given life through a series of family anecdotes that illustrate them. Pick one of the values and show how it is illustrated by several of the stories.

2. Murray tells us that her inheritance was valuable, but not measurable in monetary terms: "In later years I realized how very much their wealth had consisted of intangibles." Describe the values she has inherited, and explain how they can be considered "wealth."

3. Murray could easily have treated this material with sentimentality and self-pity; she was orphaned early, her grandfather went blind, money was in short supply, racial prejudice was inescapable, and so on. Instead she focuses on the positive values of her inheritance. Examine the way that Murray writes, and show how her style and attitude relate to the values this essay celebrates. What has Murray learned from the past?

4. Most families have a wealth of stories, though sometimes these are not well known to all the grandchildren. Interview one or two of your oldest relatives and ask them for some stories of their youth. Then write an essay in which you interpret two or three of these tales to bring out a family value or tradition.

The Inheritance of Tools

Scott Russell Sanders

Scott Russell Sanders derives his sense of the past from two locations. Although born in Memphis in 1945, his early childhood was spent on "a scrape-dirt farm in Tennessee," where everything grew with beauty and vigor. For the next dozen years he lived on the grounds of a munitions factory in Ohio, a high security enclave of "dumps and man-made deserts, ponds once used for hatching fish and now smothered in oil, machine guns rusting in weeds." Ohio living taught him fear and the imminence of mortality. Country living taught him "not how to buy things but how to *do* things: carpentry, plumbing, grafting, gardening, pruning, sewing, making hay with or without sunshine, cooking, canning, felling and planting trees, feeding animals and fixing machines, electrical wiring, plastering, roofing."

Sanders, one of America's foremost essayists, has been an English professor at Indiana University since earning his doctorate at Cambridge (1971). His essay collections include *In Limestone Country* (1985); *The Paradise of Bombs* (1987); *Staying Put* (1993), winner of the Great Lakes Book Award for 1996; and *Force of Spirit* (2000). Sanders characteristically focuses on meaningful human relationships, the natural world, and the essence of spirituality, which links people to one another and to their environment.

In "The Inheritance of Tools," from his award-winning collection of personal essays, _The Paradise of Bombs_ (1987), Sanders examines the creative, positive aspects of his heritage, showing how tools also become extensions of the human heart, as the knowledge of how to use and care for them is transmitted from generation to generation. The ways in which people use tools, and think about tools and care for them, reflect their values and personalities, "each hammer and level and saw . . . wrapped in a cloud of knowing."

1   At just about the hour when my father died, soon after dawn one February morning when ice coated the windows like cataracts, I banged my thumb with a hammer. Naturally I swore at the hammer, the reckless thing, and in the moment of swearing I thought of what my father would say: "If you'd try hitting the nail it would go in a whole lot faster. Don't you know your thumb's not as hard as that hammer?" We both were doing carpentry that day, but far apart. He was building cupboards at my brother's place in Oklahoma; I was at home in Indiana, putting up a wall in the basement to make a bedroom for my daughter. By the time my mother called with news of his death—the long distance wires whittling her voice until it seemed too thin to bear the weight of what she had to say—my thumb was swollen. A week or so later a white scar in the shape of a crescent moon began to show above the cuticle, and month by month it rose across the pink sky of my thumbnail. It took the better part of a year for the scar to disappear, and every time I noticed it I thought of my father.

2   The hammer had belonged to him, and to his father before him. The three of us have used it to build houses and barns and chicken coops, to upholster chairs and crack walnuts, to make doll furniture and bookshelves and jewelry boxes. The head is scratched and pockmarked, like an old plowshare that has been working rocky fields, and it gives off the sort of dull sheen you see on fast creek water in the shade. It is a finishing hammer, about the weight of a bread loaf, too light, really, for framing walls, too heavy for cabinet work, with a curved claw for pulling nails, a rounded head for pounding, a fluted neck for looks, and a hickory handle for strength.

3   The present handle is my third one, bought from a lumberyard in Tennessee, down the road from where my brother and I were helping my father build his retirement house. I broke the previous one by trying to pull sixteen-penny nails out of floor joists—a foolish thing to do with a finishing hammer, as my father pointed out. "You ever hear of a crowbar?" he said. No telling how many handles he and my grandfather had gone through before me. My grandfather used to cut down hickory trees on his farm, saw them into slabs, cure the planks in his hayloft, and carve handles with a drawknife. The grain in hickory is crooked and knotty, and therefore tough, hard to split, like the grain in the two men who owned this hammer before me.

After proposing marriage to a neighbor girl, my grandfather used   4
this hammer to build a house for his bride on a stretch of river bottom
in northern Mississippi. The lumber for the place, like the hickory for
the handle, was cut on his own land. By the day of the wedding he had
not quite finished the house, and so right after the ceremony he took
his wife home and put her to work. My grandmother had worn her
Sunday dress for the wedding, with a fringe of lace tacked on around
the hem in honor of the occasion. She removed this lace and folded it
away before going out to help my grandfather nail siding on the house.
"There she was in her good dress," he told me some fifty-odd years
after that wedding day, "holding up them long pieces of clapboard
while I hammered, and together we got the place covered up before
dark." As the family grew to four, six, eight, and eventually thirteen,
my grandfather used this hammer to enlarge his house room by room,
like a chambered nautilus expanding its shell.

By and by the hammer was passed along to my father. One day he   5
was up on the roof of our pony barn nailing shingles with it, when I
stepped out the kitchen door to call him for supper. Before I could yell,
something about the sight of him straddling the spine of that roof and
swinging the hammer caught my eye and made me hold my tongue. I
was five or six years old, and the world's commonplaces were still news
to me. He would pull a nail from the pouch at his waist, bring the hammer down, and a moment later the *thunk* of the blow would reach my
ears. And that is what had stopped me in my tracks and stilled my
tongue, that momentary gap between seeing and hearing the blow. Instead of yelling from the kitchen door, I ran to the barn and climbed two
rungs up the ladder—as far as I was allowed to go—and spoke quietly
to my father. On our walk to the house he explained that sound takes
time to make its way through air. Suddenly the world seemed larger, the
air more dense, if sound could be held back like any ordinary traveler.

By the time I started using this hammer, at about the age when I   6
discovered the speed of sound, it already contained houses and mysteries for me. The smooth handle was one my grandfather had made.
In those days I needed both hands to swing it. My father would start a
nail in a scrap of wood, and I would pound away until it bent over.

"Looks like you got ahold of some of those rubber nails," he would   7
tell me. "Here, let me see if I can find you some stiff ones." And he
would rummage in a drawer until he came up with a fistful of more cooperative nails. "Look at the head," he would tell me. "Don't look at
your hands, don't look at the hammer. Just look at the head of that nail
and pretty soon you'll learn to hit it square."

Pretty soon I did learn. While he worked in the garage cutting   8
dovetail joints for a drawer or skinning a deer or tuning an engine, I
would hammer nails. I made innocent blocks of wood look like porcupines. He did not talk much in the midst of his tools, but he kept up a

nearly ceaseless humming, slipping in and out of a dozen tunes in an afternoon, often running back over the same stretch of melody again and again, as if searching for a way out. When the humming did cease, I knew he was faced with a task requiring great delicacy or concentration, and I took care not to distract him.

9   He kept scraps of wood in a cardboard box—the ends of two-by-fours, slabs of shelving and plywood, odd pieces of molding—and everything in it was fair game. I nailed scraps together to fashion what I called boats or houses, but the results usually bore only faint resemblance to the visions I carried in my head. I would hold up these constructions to show my father, and he would turn them over in his hands admiringly, speculating about what they might be. My cobbled-together guitars might have been alien spaceships, my barns might have been models of Aztec temples, each wooden contraption might have been anything but what I had set out to make.

10   Now and again I would feel the need to have a chunk of wood shaped or shortened before I riddled it with nails, and I would clamp it in a vise and scrape at it with a handsaw. My father would let me lacerate the board until my arm gave out, and then he would wrap his hand around mine and help me finish the cut, showing me how to use my thumb to guide the blade, how to pull back on the saw to keep it from binding, how to let my shoulder do the work.

11   "Don't force it," he would say, "just drag it easy and give the teeth a chance to bite."

12   As the saw teeth bit down, the wood released its smell, each kind with its own fragrance, oak or walnut or cherry or pine—usually pine because it was the softest, easiest for a child to work. No matter how weathered and gray the board, no matter how warped and cracked, inside there was this smell waiting, as of something freshly baked. I gathered every smidgen of sawdust and stored it away in coffee cans, which I kept in a drawer of the workbench. When I did not feel like hammering nails, I would dump my sawdust on the concrete flor of the garage and landscape it into highways and farms and towns, running miniature cars and trucks along miniature roads. Looming as huge as a colossus, my father worked over and around me, now and again bending down to inspect my work, careful not to trample my creations. It was a landscape that smelled dizzyingly of wood. Even after a bath my skin would carry the smell, and so would my father's hair, when he lifted me for a bedtime hug.

13   I tell these things not only from memory but also from recent observation, because my own son now turns blocks of wood into nailed porcupines, dumps cans full of sawdust at my feet and sculpts highways on the floor. He learns how to swing a hammer from the elbow instead of the wrist, how to lay his thumb beside the blade to guide a

saw, how to tap a chisel with a wooden mallet, how to mark a hole with an awl before starting a drill bit. My daughter did the same before him, and even now, on the brink of teenage aloofness, she will occasionally drag out my box of wood scraps and carpenter something. So I have seen my apprenticeship to wood and tools re-enacted in each of my children, as my father saw his own apprenticeship renewed in me.

The saw I use belonged to him, as did my level and both of my   14
squares, and all four tools had belonged to his father. The blade of the saw is the bluish color of gun barrels, and the maple handle, dark from the sweat of hands, is inscribed with curving leaf designs. The level is a shaft of walnut two feet long, edged with brass and pierced by three round windows in which air bubbles float in oil-filled tubes of glass. The middle window serves for testing if a surface is horizontal, the others for testing if a surface is plumb or vertical. My grandfather used to carry this level on the gun rack behind the seat in his pickup, and when I rode with him I would turn around to watch the bubbles dance. The larger of the two squares is called a framing square, a flat steel elbow, so beat up and tarnished you can barely make out the rows of numbers that show how to figure the cuts on rafters. The smaller one is called a try square, for marking angles, with a blued steel blade for the shank and a brass-faced block of cherry for the head.

I was taught early on that a saw is not to be used apart from a   15
square: "If you're going to cut a piece of wood," my father insisted, "you owe it to the tree to cut it straight."

Long before studying geometry, I learned there is a mystical virtue   16
in right angles. There is an unspoken morality in seeking the level and the plumb. A house will stand, a table will bear weight, the sides of a box will hold together, only if the joints are square and the members upright. When the bubble is lined up between two marks etched in the glass tube of a level, you have aligned yourself with the forces that hold the universe together. When you miter the corners of a picture frame, each angle must be exactly forty-five degrees, as they are in the perfect trangles of Pythagoras, not a degree more or less. Otherwise the frame will hang crookedly, as if ashamed of itself and of its maker. No matter if the joints you are cutting do not show. Even if you are butting two pieces of wood together inside a cabinet, where no one except a wrecking crew will ever see them, you must take pains to ensure that the ends are square and the studs are plumb.

I took pains over the wall I was building on the day my father died.   17
Not long after that wall was finished—paneled with tongue-and-groove boards of yellow pine, the nail holes filled with putty and the wood all stained and sealed—I came close to wrecking it one afternoon when my daughter ran howling up the stairs to announce that her gerbils had escaped from their cage and were hiding in my brand new

wall. She could hear them scratching and squeaking behind her bed. Impossible! I said. How on earth could they get inside my drum-tight wall? Through the heating vent, she answered. I went downstairs, pressed my ear to the honey-colored wood, and heard the *scritch scritch* of tiny feet.

18   "What can we do?" my daughter wailed. "They'll starve to death, they'll die of thirst, they'll suffocate."

19   "Hold on," I soothed. "I'll think of something."

20   While I thought and she fretted, the radio on her bedside table delivered us the headlines: Several thousand people had died in a city in India from a poisonous cloud that had leaked overnight from a chemical plant. A nuclear-powered submarine had been launched. Rioting continued in South Africa. An airplane had been hijacked in the Mediterranean. Authorities calculated that several thousand homeless people slept on the streets within sight of the Washington Monument. I felt my usual helplessness in the face of all these calamities. But here was my daughter, weeping because her gerbils were holed up in a wall. This calamity I could handle.

21   "Don't worry," I told her. "We'll set food and water by the heating vent and lure them out. And if that doesn't do the trick, I'll tear the wall apart until we find them."

22   She stopped crying and gazed at me. "You'd really tear it apart? Just for my gerbils? The *wall?*" Astonishment slowed her down only for a second, however, before she ran to the workbench and began tugging at drawers, saying, "let's see, what'll we need? Crowbar. Hammer. Chisels. I hope we don't have to use them—but just in case."

23   We didn't need the wrecking tools. I never had to assault my handsome wall, because the gerbils eventually came out to nibble at a dish of popcorn. But for several hours I studied the tongue-and-groove skin I had nailed up on the day of my father's death, considering where to begin prying. There were no gaps in that wall, no crooked joints.

24   I had botched a great many pieces of wood before I mastered the right angle with a saw, botched even more before I learned to miter a joint. The knowledge of these things resides in my hands and eyes and the webwork of muscles, not in the tools. There are machines for sale—powered miter boxes and radial-arm saws, for instance—that will enable any casual soul to cut proper angles in boards. The skill is invested in the gadget instead of the person who uses it, and this is what distinguishes a machine from a tool. If I had to earn my keep by making furniture or building houses, I suppose I would buy powered saws and pneumatic nailers; the need for speed would drive me to it. But since I carpenter only for my own pleasure or to help neighbors or to remake the house around the ears of my family, I stick with hand tools. Most of the ones I own were given to me by my father, who also taught me how

to wield them. The tools in my workbench are a double inheritance, for each hammer and level and saw is wrapped in a cloud of knowing.

All of these tools are a pleasure to look at and to hold. Merchants 25 would never paste NEW! NEW! NEW! signs on them in stores. Their designs are old because they work, because they serve their purpose well. Like folk songs and aphorisms and the grainy bits of language, these tools have been pared down to essentials. I look at my claw hammer, the distillation of a hundred generations of carpenters, and consider that it holds up well beside those other classics—Greek vases, Gregorian chants, *Don Quixote*, barbed fish hooks, candles, spoons. Knowledge of hammering stretches back to the earliest humans who squatted beside fires, chipping flints. Anthropologists have a lovely name for those unworked rocks that served as the earliest hammers. "Dawn stones," they are called. Their only qualification for the work, aside from hardness, is that they fit the hand. Our ancestors used them for grinding corn, tapping awls, smashing bones. From dawn stones to the claw hammer is a great leap in time, but no great distance in design or imagination.

On that iced-over February morning when I smashed my thumb 26 with the hammer, I was down in the basement framing the wall that my daughter's gerbils would later hide in. I was thinking of my father, as I always did whenever I built anything, thinking how he would have gone about the work, hearing in memory what he would have said about the wisdom of hitting the nail instead of my thumb. I had the studs and plates nailed together all square and trim, and was lifting the wall into place when the phone rang upstairs. My wife answered, and in a moment she came to the basement door and called down softly to me. The stillness in her voice made me drop the framed wall and hurry upstairs. She told me my father was dead. Then I heard the details over the phone from my mother. Building a set of cupboards for my brother in Oklahoma, he had knocked off work early the previous afternoon because of cramps in his stomach. Early this morning, on his way into the kitchen of my brother's trailer, maybe going for a glass of water, so early that no one else was awake, he slumped down on the linoleum and his heart quit.

For several hours I paced around inside my house, upstairs and 27 down, in and out of every room, looking for the right door to open and knowing there was no such door. My wife and children followed me and wrapped me in arms and backed away again, circling and staring as if I were on fire. Where was the door, the door, the door? I kept wondering. My smashed thumb turned purple and throbbed, making me furious. I wanted to cut it off and rush outside and scrape away the snow and hack a hole in the frozen earth and bury the shameful thing.

28   I went down into the basement, opened a drawer in my work-bench, and stared at the ranks of chisels and knives. Oiled and sharp, as my father would have kept them, they gleamed at me like teeth. I took up a clasp knife, pried out the longest blade, and tested the edge on the hair of my forearm. A tuft came away cleanly, and I saw my father testing the sharpness of tools on his own skin, the blades of axes and knives and gouges and hoes, saw the red hair shaved off in patches from his arms and the backs of hands. "That will cut bear," he would say. He never cut a bear with his blades, now my blades, but he cut deer, dirt, wood. I closed the knife and put it away. Then I took up the hammer and went back to work on my daughter's wall, snugging the bottom plate against a chalk line on the floor, shimming the top plate against the joists overhead, plumbing the studs with my level, making sure before I drove the first nail that every line was square and true.

RESPONDING TO READING

1. Show how Sanders characterizes his grandfather, his father, and himself through the continuity and transmission of their use of tools. Why does he focus on what these generations have in common and ignore any differences?

2. How does "The Inheritance of Tools" demonstrate that knowledge and skill can be transmitted from one generation to the next? What is communicated along with the specific knowledge of how to use tools?

3. Could readers who can't, don't, or won't use tools nevertheless appreciate this essay? Why or why not?

4. Tell the story of your own experience of learning to use a particular tool or collection of tools (a computer, a sewing machine, a mountain bike, a power saw, an automobile). Your explanation, including your increasing skill and ability, should also delineate your relationship with the person (family member or other) and the way(s) in which the teaching and learning were accomplished. How many generations of learners does this cumulative process involve, including people you yourself may have taught?

━━━━━━

A Drugstore Eden

Cynthia Ozick

Cynthia Ozick was born in 1928 in the Bronx, where her parents operated the drugstore she writes about in "A Drugstore Eden." She graduated with a B.A. in English from New York University in 1949 and later earned an M.A. in English from the Ohio State University. She achieved recognition as a public intellectual through publishing political and literary criticism before she achieved fame as a writer of fiction. Her second novel, *Trust*, was finished on November 22, 1963—the day of President John F. Kennedy's assassination. Beginning in this novel, Ozick's work explores Judaism, a theme central to both her writing and her life. "The term 'Jewish Writer' is," she argues, "an oxymoron," as "being a good Jew means being a person of restraint" and being a good writer means enjoying the freedom to be nasty and unkind. In her most recent book, *Quarrel* & *Quandary: Essays* (2001), Ozick ranges in topic from the Unabomber and Dostoyevsky to Henry James and Gertrude Stein.

In "A Drugstore Eden," Ozick describes The Park View, the store her parents ran during her youth—an almost idyllic setting of peace, if not prosperity, during the turbulence of the Great Depression and second World War. It was, for her, a world of "perpetual indoor sunshine" that stood in stark contrast to the terrible darkness outside its doors as "German tanks were biting into Europe," and Jewish refugees, "barred from the beaches of Haifa and Tel Aviv, [were being] returned to Nazi doom." Ozick explores the connections among history, family, memory, and the physical setting of the drugstore and the secret garden behind it that encompasses them all.

In 1929, my parents sold their drugstore in Yorkville—a neighborhood comprising Manhattan's East Eighties—and bought a pharmacy in Pelham Bay, in the northeast corner of the Bronx. It was a move from dense city to almost country. Pelham Bay was at the very end of a relatively new stretch of elevated train track that extended from the subway of the true city all the way out to a small-town enclave of little houses and a single row of local shops: shoemaker's, greengrocer, drugstore, grocery, bait store. There was even a miniature five-and-ten where you could buy pots, housedresses, and thick lisle stockings for winter. Three stops down the line was the more populous Westchester Square, with its bank and post office, which old-timers still called "the village"—Pelham Bay had once lain outside the city limits, in Westchester County.   1

This lost little finger of the borough was named for the broad but mild body of water that rippled across Long Island Sound to a blurry opposite shore. All the paths of Pelham Bay Park led down to a narrow beach of rough pebbles, and all the surrounding streets led, sooner or later, to the park, wild and generally deserted. Along many of these streets there were empty lots that resembled meadows, overgrown with Queen Anne's lace and waist-high weeds glistening with what the children termed "snake spit"; poison ivy crowded between the toes of clumps of sky-tall oaks. The snake spit was a sort of bubbly botanical excretion, but there were real snakes in those lots, with luminescent skins, brownish-greenish, crisscrossed with white lines. There were real meadows, too: acres of downhill grasses, in the middle of which you might suddenly come on a set of rusty old swings—wooden slats   2 on chains—or a broken red-brick wall left over from some ruined and forgotten Westchester estate.

3   The Park View Pharmacy—the drugstore my parents bought—stood on Colonial Avenue between Continental and Burr: Burr for Aaron Burr, the vice president who killed Alexander Hamilton in a duel. The neighborhood had a somewhat bloodthirsty Revolutionary flavor. You could still visit Spy Oak, the venerable tree, not far away, on which some captured Redcoats had been hanged; and now and then Revolutionary bullets were churned up a foot or so beneath the front lawn of the old O'Keefe house, directly across the street from the Park View Pharmacy. George Washington had watered his horses, it was believed, in the ancient sheds beyond Ye Olde Homestead, a local tavern that well after Prohibition was still referred to as "the speakeasy." All the same, there were no Daughters of the American Revolution here: Pelham Bay was populated by the children of German, Irish, Swedish, Scottish, and Italian immigrants, and by a handful of the original immigrants themselves. The greenhorn Italians, from Naples and Sicily, kept goats and pigs in their back yards and pigeons on their roofs. Pelham Bay's single Communist—you could tell from the election results that there was such a rare bird—was the Scotsman who lived around the corner, though only my parents knew this. They were privy to the neighborhood's opinions, ailments, and family secrets.

4   In those years, the drugstore seemed one of the world's permanent institutions. Who could have imagined that it would one day vanish into an aisle in the supermarket, or reemerge as a kind of supermarket itself? What passes for a pharmacy nowadays is all open shelves and ceiling racks of brilliant white neon suggesting perpetual indoor sunshine. The Park View, by contrast, was a dark cavern lined with polished wood cabinets rubbed nearly black and equipped with sliding glass doors and mirrored backs. The counters were heaped with towering ziggurats of lotions, potions, and packets, and under them ran glassed-in showcases of the same sober wood. There was a post office (designated a "substation") that sold penny postcards and stamps and money orders. The prescription area was in the rear, closed off from view: here were scores of labeled drawers of all sizes and rows of oddly shaped brown bottles. In one of those drawers traditional rock candy was stored, in two flavors, plain and maple; it dangled on long strings. And finally there was the prescription desk itself, a sloping, lecternlike affair on which the current prescription ledger always lay, like some sacred text.

5   There was also a soda fountain. A pull at a long black handle spurted out carbonated water; a push at a tiny silver spout drew forth curly drifts of whipped cream. The air in this part of the drugstore was steamy with a deep coffee fragrance, and on wintry Friday afternoons the librarians from the Travelling Library, a green truck that arrived once a week, would linger, sipping and gossiping on the high-backed

fountain chairs or else at the little glass-topped tables nearby, with their small three-cornered seats. Everything was fashioned of the same burnished chocolate-colored wood, except the fountain counters, which were heavy marble. Above the prescription area, sovereign over all, rose a symbolic pair of pharmacy globes, one filled with red fluid, the other with blue. My father's diploma, class of 1917, was mounted on a wall; next to it hung a picture of the graduates. There was my very young father, with his round pale eyes and widow's peak—a fleck in a mass of black gowns.

Sometime around 1937, my mother said to my father, "Willie, if we don't do it now we'll never do it."   6 *do what?*

It was the trough of the Great Depression. In the comics, Pete the   7 Tramp was swiping freshly baked pies set out to cool on windowsills, and in real life tramps (as the homeless were then called) were turning up in the Park View nearly every day. Sometimes they were city drunks—"Bowery bums"—who had fallen asleep downtown on the subway and ended up in Pelham Bay. Sometimes they were exhausted Midwesterners who had been riding the rails and had rolled off into the cattails of the Baychester marsh. But always my father sat them   *charity* down at the fountain and fed them a sandwich and soup. They smelled   *for the* bad, and their eyes were red and rheumy; often they were very polite.   *homeless* They never left without a meal and a nickel for carfare.

No one was worse off than the tramps, or more desolate than the   8 family who lived in an old freight car on the way to Westchester Square; but no one escaped the Depression. Seven days a week, the Park View opened at 9 A.M. and closed at two the next morning. My mother scurried from counter to counter, tended the fountain, unpacked cartons, climbed ladders; her varicose veins oozed through their strappings. My father patiently ground powders and folded the white dust into translucent paper squares with elegantly efficient motions. The drugstore was, besides, a public resource: my father bandaged cuts, took specks out of strangers' eyes, and once removed a fishhook from a man's cheek—though he sent him off to the hospital, on the other side of the Bronx, immediately afterward. My quiet father had cronies and clients, grim women and voluble men who flooded his understanding ears with the stories of their sufferings, of flesh or psy-   *privy to the* che. My father murmured and comforted, and later my parents would   *town's* whisper sadly about who had "the big C," or, with an ominous gleam,   *secrets* they would smile over a geezer certain to have a heart attack: the geezer would be newly married to a sweet young thing. (And usually they were right about the heart attack.)

Yet, no matter how hard they toiled, they were always in peril.   9 There were notes to pay off: they had bought the Park View from a pharmacist named Robbins, and every month, relentlessly, a note came due. They never fell behind, and never missed a payment (and in fact were eventually awarded a certificate attesting to this feat), but the effort—the unremitting pressure, the endless anxiety—ground them down. "The note, the note," I would hear, a refrain that shadowed my childhood, though I had no notion of what it meant.

10   What it mean was that the Depression, which had already crushed so many, was about to crush my mother and father: suddenly their troubles intensified. The Park View was housed in a building owned by a woman my parents habitually referred to, whether out of familiarity or resentment, only as Tessie. The pharmacy's lease was soon to expire, and at this moment, in the cruellest hour of the Depression, Tessie chose to raise the rent. Her tiger's eyes narrowed to slits, no appeal could soften her.

11   It was because of those adamant tiger's eyes that my mother said, "Willie, if we don't do it now we'll never do it."

12   My mother was aflame with ambition, emotion, struggle. My father was reticent and far more resigned to the world as given. Once, when the days of the Travelling Library were over and a real library had been constructed at Westchester Square—you reached it by trolley—I came home elated, carrying a pair of books I had found side by side. One was called *My Mother Is a Violent Woman*, the other was *My Father Is a Timid Man*. These seemed a comic revelation of my parents' temperaments. My mother was all heat and enthusiasm. My father was all logic and reserve. My mother, unrestrained, could have run an empire of drugstores. My father was satisfied with one.

13   Together they decided to do something revolutionary, something virtually impossible in those raw and merciless times. One street over—past McCardle's sun-baked gas station, where there was always a Model A Ford with its hood open for repair, and past the gloomy bait store, ruled over by Mr. Isaacs, a dour and reclusive veteran of the Spanish-American War, who sat reading military histories all day under a mastless sailboat suspended from the ceiling—lay an empty lot in the shape of an elongated lozenge. My parents' daring plan—for young people without means it was beyond daring—was to buy that lot and build on it, from scratch, a brand-new Park View Pharmacy.

14   They might as well have been dreaming of taking off in Buck Rogers's twenty-fifth century rocket ship. The cost of the lot was a stratospheric $13,500, unchanged from the boom of 1928, just before the national wretchedness descended. And that figure was only for the land. Then would come the digging of a foundation and the construction of a building. What was needed was a miracle.

15   One sad winter afternoon, my mother was standing on a ladder, concentrating on setting out some newly arrived drug items on a high shelf. (Although a typical drugstore stocked several thousand articles, the Park View's unit-by-unit inventory was never ample. At the end of

every week, I would hear my father's melodious, impecunious chant on the telephone, as he ordered goods from the jobber: "A sixth of a dozen, a twelfth of a dozen . . .") A stranger wearing a brown fedora and long overcoat entered, looked around, and appeared not at all interested in making a purchase; instead, he went wandering from case to case, picking things up and putting them down again, trying to be inconspicuous, asking an occasional question or two, all the while scrupulously observing my diligent parents. The stranger turned out to be a mortgage officer from the American Bible Society, and what he saw, he explained afterward, was a conscientious application of the work ethic; so it was the American Bible Society that supplied the financial foundation of my parents' Eden, the new Park View. They had entertained an angel unawares.

their miracle

The actual foundation, the one to be dug out of the ground, ran into instant biblical trouble: flood. An unemployed civil engineer named Levinson presided over the excavation; he was unemployed partly because the Depression had dried up much of the job market but mostly because engineering firms in those years were notorious for their unwillingness to hire Jews. Poor Levinson! The vast hole in the earth that was to become the Park View's cellar filled up overnight with water; the bay was near, and the water table was higher than the hapless Levinson had expected. The work halted. Along came Finnegan and rescued Levinson: Finnegan the plumber, who for a painful fee of fifty dollars (somehow squeezed out of Levinson's mainly empty pockets) pumped out the sea. 16

After the Park View's exultant move, in 1939, the shell of Tessie's old place on Colonial Avenue remained vacant for years. No one took it over; the plate-glass windows grew murkier and murkier. Dead moths were heaped in decaying mounds on the inner sills. Tessie had lost more than the heartless increase she had demanded, and more than the monthly rent the renewed lease would have brought: there was something ignominious and luckless—tramplike—about that fly-specked empty space, now dimmer than ever. But, within its freshly risen walls, the Park View redux gleamed. Overhead, fluorescent tubes—an indoor innovation—shed a steady white glow, and a big square skylight poured down shifting shafts of brilliance. Familiar objects appeared clarified in the new light: the chocolate-colored fixtures, arranged in unaccustomed configurations, were all at once thrillingly revivified. Nothing from the original Park View had been left behind—everything was just the same, yet zanily out of order: the two crystal urns with their magical red and blue fluids suggestive of alchemy; the entire stock of syrups, pills, tablets, powders, pastes, capsules; tubes and bottles by the hundred; the fountain, with its marble top; the prescription desk and its sacrosanct ledger; the stacks of invaluable cigar boxes stuffed with masses of expired prescriptions; the locked and well-guarded narcotics 17 cabinet; the post office and the safe in which the post office receipts were kept. Even the great, weighty, monosyllabically blunt hanging sign— "Drugs"—had been brought over and rehung, and it, too, looked different now. In the summer heat it dropped its black rectangular shadow over Mr. Isaac's already shadowy headquarters, where vials of live worms were crowded side by side with vials of nails and screws.

18   At around this time, my mother's youngest brother, my uncle Rubin, had come to stay with us—no one knew for how long—in our little house on St. Paul Avenue, a short walk from the Park View. Five of us lived in that house: my parents, my grandmother, my brother, and I. Rubin, who was called Ruby, was now the sixth. He was a bachelor and something of a family conundrum. He was both bitter and cheerful; effervescence would give way to lassitude. He taught me how to draw babies and bunnies, and could draw anything himself; he wrote ingenious comic jingles, which he illustrated as adroitly, it struck me, as Edward Lear; he cooked up mouthwatering corn fritters and designed fruit salads in the shape of ravishing unearthly blossoms. When now and then it fell to him to put me to bed, he always sang the same heartbreaking lullaby—Sometimes I fee-eel like a motherless child, a long, long way-ay from ho-ome"–in a deep and sweet quaver. In those days, he was mostly jobless; on occasion, he would crank up his tin lizzie and drive out to upper Westchester to prune trees. Once he was stopped at a police roadblock, under suspicion of being the Lindbergh-baby kidnapper—the back seat of his messy old Ford was strewn with ropes, hooks, and my discarded baby bottles.

19   Ruby had been disappointed in love, and was somehow a disappointment to everyone around him. When he was melancholy or resentful, the melancholy was irritable and the resentment acrid. As a very young man, he had been single-minded in a way that none of his immigrant relations, or the snobbish mother of the girlfriend who had been coerced into jilting him, could understand or sympathize with. In czarist Russia's restricted Pale of Settlement, a pharmacist was the highest vocation a Jew could attain to. In a family of pharmacists, Ruby wanted to be a farmer. Against opposition, he had gone off to farm school in New Jersey—one of several Jewish agricultural projects sponsored by the German philanthropist Baron Maurice de Hirsch. Ruby was always dreaming up one sort of horticultural improvement or another, and sometimes took me with him to visit a certain Dr. McClean, at the New York Botanical Garden, whom he was trying to interest in one of his inventions. He was kindly received, but nothing came of it. Despite his energy and originality, all Ruby's hopes and strivings collapsed in futility.

20   His presence now was fortuitous: he could assist in the move from Tessie's place to the new location. But his ingenuity, it would soon develop, was benison from the goddess Flora. The Park View occupied all

the width but not the entire depth of the lot on which it was built. It had, of course, a welcoming front door, through which customers passed, but there was also a back door, past a little aisle adjoining the prescription room in the rear of the store, and well out of sight. When you walked out this back door, you were confronted by an untamed patch of weeds and stones, some of them as thick as boulders. At the very end of it lay a large flat rock, in the center of which someone had scratched a mysterious X. The X, it turned out, was a surveyor's sign; it had been there long before my parents bought the lot. It meant that the property extended to that point and no farther.

I was no stranger either to the lot or to its big rock. It was where the 21 neighborhood children played—a sparse group in that sparsely populated place. Sometimes the rock was a pirate ship; sometimes it was a pretty room in a pretty house; in January it held a snow fort. But early one summer evening, when the red ball of the sun was very low, a little girl named Theresa, whose hair was as red as the sun's red ball, discovered the surveyor's X and warned me against stamping on it. If you stamp on a cross, she said, the Devil's helpers climb right out from inside the earth and grab you and take you away to be tortured. "I don't believe that," I said, and stamped on the X as hard as I could. Instantly, Theresa sent out a terrified shriek; chased by the red-gold zigzag of her hair, she fled. I stood there abandoned—suppose it was true? In the silence all around, the wavering green weeds seemed taller than ever before.

Looking out from the back door at those same high weeds, my 22 mother, like Theresa, saw hallucinatory shapes rising out of the ground. But it was not the Devil's minions that she imagined streaming upward; it was their very opposite—a vision of celestial growths and fragrances, brilliant botanical hues, golden pears and yellow sunflower faces, fruitful vines and dreaming gourds. She imagined an enchanted garden. She imagined a secret Eden.

What she did not imagine was that Ruby, himself so unpeaceable, 23 would turn out to be the viceroy of her peaceable kingdom. Ruby was angry at my mother; he was angry at everyone but me—I was too young to be held responsible for his lost loves and aspirations. But he could not be separated from his love of fecund dirt. Dirt—the brown dirt of the earth—inspired him; the feel and smell of dirt uplifted him; he took an artist's pleasure in the soil and all its generative properties. And though he claimed to scorn my mother, he became the subaltern of her passion. Like some wizard commander of the stones—they were scattered everywhere in a wild jumble—he swept them into orderliness. A pack of stones was marshaled into a low wall. Five stones were transformed into a perfect set of stairs. Seven stones surrounded what was to become a flower bed. Stones were borders, stones were pathways, stones—placed just so—were natural sculptures. And, finally, Ruby commanded the stones to settle in a circle in the very center of the lot. Inside the circle there was to be a green serenity of grass, invaded only by the blunders of violets and wandering buttercups. Outside the circle, the earth would be a fructifying engine. It was a dreamer's circle, like the moon or the sun, or a fairy ring, or a mystical small Stonehenge, miniaturized by a spell.

24   The back yard was cleared, but it was not yet a garden. Like a merman combing a mermaid's weedy hair, my uncle Ruby had unraveled primeval tangles and brambles. He had set up two tall metal poles to accommodate a rough canvas hammock, with a wire strung from the top of one pole to the other. Over this wire a rain-faded old shop awning has been flung, so that the hammock became a tent or cave or darkened den. A backyard hammock! I had encountered such things only in storybooks.

25   And then my uncle was gone—drafted before the garden could be dug. German tanks were biting into Europe. Weeping, my grandmother pounded her breast with her fist: the British White Paper of 1939 had declared that ships packed with Jewish refugees would be barred from the beaches of Haifa and Tel Aviv, and returned to a Nazi doom. In P.S. 71, our neighborhood school, the boys were drawing cannons and warplanes; the girls were drawing figure skaters in tutus; both boys and girls were drawing the Trylon and the Perisphere. The Trylon was a three-sided pyramid. The Perisphere was a shining globe. They were already as sublimely legendary as the Taj Mahal. The "official" colors of the 1939 World's Fair were orange and blue: everyone knew this; everyone had ridden in the noiselessly moving armchairs of the Futurama into the fair's City of Tomorrow, where the elevated highways of the impossible futuristic 1960s materialized among inconceivable suburbs. In the magical lanes of Flushing, you could watch yourself grin on a television screen as round and small as the mouth of a teacup. My grandmother, in that frail year of her dying, was taken to see the Jewish Palestine Pavilion.

26   Ruby sent a photograph of himself in army uniform and a muffled recording of his voice, all songs and jolly jingles, from a honky-tonk arcade in an unnamed Caribbean town. It was left to my mother to dig the garden. I have no inkling of when or how. I lived inside the hammock all that time, under the awning, enclosed; I read and read. Sometimes, for a treat, I would be given two nickels for carfare and a pair of quarters, and then I would climb the double staircase to the train and go all the way to Fifth-ninth Street: you could enter Bloomingdale's directly from the subway, without ever glimpsing daylight. I would run up the steps to the book department, on the mezzanine, moon over the Nancy Drew series in an agony of choosing (*Password to Larkspur Lane*, *The Whispering Statue*, each for fifty cents), and run down to the subway again with my lucky treasure. An hour and a half later I would be back in the hammock, under the awning, while the afternoon sun broiled on.

But such a trip was rare. Mostly, the books came from the Travelling Library; inside my hammock cave the melting glue of new bindings sent out a blissful redolence. And now my mother would emerge from the back door of the Park View, carrying—because it was so hot under the awning—half a cantaloupe with a hillock of vanilla ice cream in its scooped-out center. (Have I ever been so safe, so happy since? Has consciousness ever felt so steady, so unimperiled, so immortal?)

Across the ocean, synagogues were being torched, refugees were in   27 flight. On American movie screens Ginger Rogers and Fred Astaire whirled in and out of the March of Time's grim newsreels—Chamberlain with his defeatist umbrella, the Sudetenland devoured, Poland invaded. Meanwhile, my mother's garden grew. The wild raw field Ruby had regimented was ripening now into a luxuriant and powerful fertility: all around my uncle's talismanic ring of stones the ground swelled with thick, savory smells. Corn tassels hung down over the shut greenleaf lids of pearly young cobs. Fat tomatoes reddened on sticks. The bumpy scalps of cucumbers poked up. And flowers! First, as tall as the hammock poles, a flock of hunchbacked sunflowers, their heads too weighty for their shoulders—huge, heavy heads of seeds and a ruff of yellow petals. At their feet, rows of zinnias and marigolds, with tiny violets and the weedy pink buds of clover sidling between.

Now and then a praying mantis—a stiffly marching fake leaf—   28 would rub its skinny forelegs together and stare at you with two stern black dots. Or there would be a sudden blizzard of butterflies—mostly white and mothlike, but sometimes a great black-veined monarch would alight on a stone, in perfect stillness. Year by year, the shade of a trio of pear trees widened and deepened.

Did it rain? It must have rained—it must have thundered—in those   29 successive summers of my mother's garden, but I remember a perpetual sunlight, hot and honeyed, and the airless boil under the awning, and the heart-piercing scalliony odor of library glue (so explicit that I can this minute re-create it in my very tear ducts, as a kind of mourning), and the fear of bees.

No one knew the garden was there. It was utterly hidden. You   30 could not see it, or suspect it, inside the Park View, and because it was nestled in a wilderness of empty lots, it was altogether invisible from any surrounding street. It was a small secluded paradise.

And what vegetable chargings, what ferocities of growth, the tur-   31 bulent earth pushed out! Buzzings and dapplings. Birds dipping their beaks in an orgy of seed lust. It was as if the ground itself were crying peace, peace; and the war roared on. In Europe, the German death factories were pumping out smoke and human ash from a poisoned orchard of chimneys. In Pelham Bay, among bees and white-wing flutterings, the sweet brown dirt pumped ears of corn.

32   Though I was mostly alone there, I was never lonely in the garden. But, on the other side of the door, inside the Park View, an unfamiliar churning had begun—a raucous teeming, the world turning on its hinge. In the aftermath of Pearl Harbor, there was all at once a job for nearly everyone, and money to spend in any cranny of wartime leisure. The Depression was receding. On weekends, the subway spilled out mobs of city picnickers into the green fields of Pelham Bay Park, bringing a tentative prosperity to the neighborhood—especially on Sundays. I dreaded and hated this new Sunday frenzy, when the Park View seemed less a pharmacy than a carnival stand, and my isolation grew bleak. Open shelves sprouted in the aisles, laden with anomalous racks of sunglasses, ice coolers, tubes of mosquito repellent and suntan lotion, paper cups, colorful towers of hats—sailors' and fishermen's caps, celluloid visors, straw topis and sombreros, headgear of every conceivable shape. Thirsty picnickers stood three deep at the fountain, clamoring for ice cream cones or sodas. The low, serious drugstore voices that accompanied the Park View's weekly decorum were swept away by revolving, laughing crowds—carnival crowds. And at the close of these frenetic summer Sundays my parents would anxiously count up the cash register in the worn night of their exhaustion, and I would hear their joyful disbelief: unimaginable riches, almost seventy-five dollars in a single day!

33   Then, when the safe was locked up and the long cords of the fluorescent lights pulled, they would drift in the dimness into the garden to breathe the cool fragrance. At this starry hour, the katydids were screaming in chorus, and fireflies bleeped like errant semaphores. In the enigmatic dark, my mother and father, with their heads together in silhouette, looked just then as I pictured them looking on the Albany night boat, on June 19, 1921, their wedding day. There was a serial photo from that long-ago time I often gazed at—a strip taken in an automatic photo booth in fabled, faraway Albany. It showed then leaning close, my young father quizzical, my young mother trying to smile, or else trying not to; the corners of her lips wandered toward one loveliness or the other. They had brought back a honeymoon souvenir: three sandstone monkeys joined at the elbows—see no evil, hear no evil, speak no evil. And now, in their struggling forties, standing in Ruby's circle of stones, they breathed in the night smells of the garden, onion grass and honeysuckle, and felt their private triumph. Seventy-five dollars in seventeen hours.

34   Nearly all the drugstores of the old kind are gone, in Pelham Bay and elsewhere. The Park View Pharmacy lives only in a secret Eden behind my eyes. Gone are Bernardini, Pressman, Weiss, the rival druggists on the way to Westchester Square. They all, like my father, rolled suppositories on glass slabs and ground powders with brass pestles. My mother's garden has returned to its beginning: a wild patch, though enclosed now by brick house after brick house. The houses have high stoops;

they are city houses. The meadows are striped with highways. Spy Oak gave up its many ghosts long ago.

But under a matting of decayed pear pits and thriving ragweed back   35 of what used to be the Park View, Ruby's circle of stones stands frozen. The earth, I suppose, has covered them over, as—far off, in an overgrown old cemetery on Staten Island—it covers my dreaming mother, my father, my grandmother, my resourceful and embittered farmer uncle.

all dead

RESPONDING TO READING

1. What does Ozick mean by her title, "A Drugstore Eden"? What Eden do Ozick's parents seek? What prompts them to search for it, and how do they reach it? How is this Eden different—or part of—the "secret Eden" envisioned by her mother? By Ozick as a child?

2. How does Ozick use history, from the American Revolution to the Great Depression, to establish the context for her analysis of the significance of her parents' drugstore? Why is this sense of history important for her essay? In what ways does Ozick's parents' pharmacy embed this sense of history? How does it differ from modern pharmacies?

3. How does Ozick's family history, past and ongoing, relate to world history-in-the-making, the buildup to the Holocaust and World War II in Europe? How does the family pharmacy, the "Drugstore Eden," relate to its specific location? To the wider world?

4. What contrasts does Ozick build into her essay between creation and destruction, rot and growth, America and Europe? How do these contrasts develop her argument?

5. In an essay, describe a place that was important to you when you were younger, and explain its significance to you at the time. What did it look like? What sounds did you hear there? What smells do you associate with this place? If you have revisited it as you've gotten older, has it remained the same? If so, why? If not, identify its changes. Did it change because time took its toll, or did it change because you have changed as you got older?

Under the Influence: Paying the Price of My Father's Booze

SCOTT RUSSELL SANDERS

[For biographical information, see p. 503]

"Under the Influence," from *Secrets of the Universe* (1991), presents another side of Sanders's father, whom he had eulogized in "The Inheritance of Tools." This man, who died of the toxic effects of alcohol at the age of sixty-four, was "consumed by disease rather than by disappointment." Although Sanders realizes this, he writes to explain to a general audience—including some of the relatives and friends of America's "ten or fifteen million alcoholics"—"the corrosive mixture of helplessness, responsibility, and shame that I learned to feel as the son of an alcoholic." Unfortunately, Sanders can count on the story of this aspect of his family heritage to incorporate elements common to our national heritage, as well. What is a problem for one family affects us all.

1   My father drank. He drank as a gut-punched boxer gasps for breath, as a starving dog gobbles food—compulsively, secretly, in pain and trembling. I use the past tense not because he ever quit drinking but because he quit living. That is how the story ends for my father, age sixty-four, heart bursting, body cooling, slumped and forsaken on the linoleum of my brother's trailer. The story continues for my brother, my sister, my mother, and me, and will continue as long as memory holds.

2   In the perennial present of memory, I slip into the garage or barn to see my father tipping back the flat green bottles of wine, the brown cylinders of whiskey, the cans of beer disguised in paper bags. His Adam's apple bobs, the liquid gurgles, he wipes the sandy-haired back of a hand over his lips, and then, his blood-shot gaze bumping into me, he stashes the bottle or can inside his jacket, under the workbench, between two bales of hay, and we both pretend the moment has not occurred.

3   "What's up, buddy?" he says, thick-tongued and edgy.

4   "Sky's up," I answer, playing along.

5   "And don't forget prices," he grumbles. "Prices are always up. And taxes."

6   In memory, his white 1951 Pontiac with the stripes down the hood and the Indian head on the snout lurches to a stop in the driveway; or it is the 1956 Ford station wagon, or the 1963 Rambler shaped like a toad, or the sleek 1969 Bonneville that will do 120 miles per hour on straightaways; or it is the robin's-egg-blue pickup, new in 1980, battered in 1981, the year of his death. He climbs out, grinning dangerously, unsteady on his legs, and we children interrupt our game of catch, our building of snow forts, our picking of plums, to watch in silence as he weaves past us into the house, where he drops into his overstuffed chair and falls asleep. Shaking her head, our mother stubs out a cigarette he has left smoldering in the ashtray. All evening, until our bedtimes, we tiptoe past him, as past a snoring dragon. Then we curl fearfully in our sheets, listening. Eventually he wakes with a grunt, Mother slings accusations at him, he snarls back, she yells, he growls, their voices clashing. Before long, she retreats to their bedroom, sobbing—not from the blows of fists, for he never strikes her, but from the force of his words.

7   Left alone, our father prowls the house, thumping into furniture, rummaging in the kitchen, slamming doors, turning the pages of the newspaper with a savage crackle, muttering back at the late-night drivel

from television. The roof might fly off, the walls might buckle from the pressure of his rage. Whatever my brother and sister and mother may be thinking on their own rumpled pillows, I lie there hating him, loving him, fearing him, knowing I have failed him. I tell myself he drinks to ease the ache that gnaws at his belly, an ache I must have caused by disappointing him somehow, a murderous ache I should be able to relieve by doing all my chores, earning A's in school, winning baseball games, fixing the broken washer and the burst pipes, bringing in the money to fill his empty wallet. He would not hide the green bottles in his toolbox, would not sneak off to the barn with a lump under his coat, would not fall asleep in the daylight, would not roar and fume, would not drink himself to death, if only I were perfect.

I am forty-four, and I know full well now that my father was an alcoholic, a man consumed by disease rather than by disappointment. What had seemed to me a private grief is in fact, of course, a public scourge. In the United States alone, some ten or fifteen million people share his ailment, and behind the doors they slam in fury or disgrace, countless other children tremble. I comfort myself with such knowledge, holding it against the throb of memory like an ice pack against a bruise. Other people have keener sources of grief: poverty, racism, rape, war. I do not wish to compete to determine who has suffered most. I am only trying to understand the corrosive mixture of helplessness, responsibility, and shame that I learned to feel as the son of an alcoholic. I realize now that I did not cause my father's illness, nor could I have cured it. Yet for all this grownup knowledge, I am still ten years old, my own son's age, and as that boy I struggle in guilt and confusion to save my father from pain.

Consider a few of our synonyms for *drunk:* tipsy, tight, pickled, soused, and plowed; stoned and stewed, lubricated and inebriated, juiced and sluiced; three sheets to the wind, in your cups, out of your mind, under the table; lit up, tanked up, wiped out; besotted, blotto, bombed, and buzzed; plastered, polluted, putrefied; loaded or looped, boozy, woozy, fuddled, or smashed; crocked and shit-faced, corked and pissed, snockered and sloshed.

It is a mostly humorous lexicon, as the lore that deals with drunks— in jokes and cartoons, in plays, films and television skits—is largely comic. Aunt Matilda nips elderberry wine from the sideboard and burps politely during supper. Uncle Fred slouches to the table glassy-eyed, wearing a lampshade for a hat and murmuring, "Candy is dandy, but liquor is quicker." Inspired by cocktails, Mrs. Somebody recounts the events of her day in a fuzzy dialect, while Mr. Somebody nibbles her ear and croons a bawdy song. On the sofa with Boyfriend, Daughter Somebody giggles, licking gin from her lips, and loosens the bows in her hair. Junior knocks back some brews with his chums at the Leopard Lounge and stumbles home to the wrong house, wonders foggily why he cannot locate his pajamas, and crawls naked into bed with the ugliest girl in school. The family dog slurps from a neglected martini and wobbles to the nursery, where he vomits in Baby's shoe.

11   It is all great fun. But if in the audience you notice a few laughing faces turn grim when the drunk lurches onstage, don't be surprised, for these are the children of alcoholics. Over the grinning mask of Dionysus, the leering face of Bacchus, these children cannot help seeing the bloated features of their own parents. Instead of laughing, they wince, they mourn. Instead of celebrating the drunk as one freed from constraints, they pity him as one enslaved. They refuse to believe *in vino veritas*, having seen their befuddled parents skid away from truth toward folly and oblivion. And so these children bite their lips until the lush staggers into the wings.

12   My father, when drunk, was neither funny nor honest; he was pathetic, frightening, deceitful. There seemed to be a leak in him somewhere, and he poured in booze to keep from draining dry. Like a torture victim who refuses to squeal, he would never admit that he had touched a drop, not even in his last year, when he seemed to be dissolving in alcohol before our very eyes. I never knew him to lie about anything, ever, except about this one ruinous fact. Drowsy, clumsy, unable to fix a bicycle tire, balance a grocery sack, or walk across a room, he was stripped of his true self by drink. In a matter of minutes, the contents of a bottle could transform a brave man into a coward, a buddy into a bully, a gifted athlete and skilled carpenter and shrewd businessman into a bumbler. No dictionary of synonyms for *drunk* would soften the anguish of watching our prince turn into a frog.

13   Father's drinking became the family secret. While growing up, we children never breathed a word of it beyond the four walls of our house. To this day, my brother and sister rarely mention it, and then only when I press them. I did not confess the ugly, bewildering fact to my wife until his wavering and slurred speech forced me to. Recently, on the seventh anniversary of my father's death, I asked my mother if she ever spoke of his drinking to friends. "No, no, never," she replied hastily. "I couldn't bear for anyone to know."

14   The secret bores under the skin, gets in the blood, into the bone, and stays there. Long after you have supposedly been cured of malaria, the fever can flare up, the tremors can shake you. So it is with the fevers of shame. You swallow the bitter quinine of knowledge, and you learn to feel pity and compassion toward the drinker. Yet the shame lingers and, because of it, anger.

15   For a long stretch of my childhood we lived on a military reservation in Ohio, an arsenal where bombs were stored underground in bunkers and vintage airplanes burst into flames and unstable artillery shells boomed nightly at the dump. We had the feeling, as children, that we

played within a minefield, where a heedless footfall could trigger an explosion. When Father was drinking, the house, too, became a minefield. The least bump could set off either parent.   16

The more he drank, the more obsessed Mother became with stopping him. She hunted for bottles, counted the cash in his wallet, sniffed at his breath. Without meaning to snoop, we children blundered left and right into damning evidence. On afternoons when he came home from work sober, we flung ourselves at him for hugs and felt against our ribs the telltale lump in his coat. In the barn we tumbled on the hay and heard beneath our sneakers the crunch of broken glass. We tugged open a drawer in his workbench, looking for screwdrivers or crescent wrenches, and spied a gleaming six-pack among the tools. Playing tag, we darted around the house just in time to see him sway on the rear stoop and heave a finished bottle into the woods. In his goodnight kiss we smelled the cloying sweetness of Clorets, the mints he chewed to camouflage his dragon's breath.   17

I can summon up that kiss right now by recalling Theodore Roethke's lines about his own father:

> The whiskey on your breath
> Could make a small boy dizzy;
> But I hung on like death:
> Such waltzing was not easy.

Such waltzing was hard, terribly hard, for with a boy's scrawny arms I was trying to hold my tipsy father upright.   18

For years, the chief source of those incriminating bottles and cans was a grimy store a mile from us, a cinderblock place called Sly's, with two gas pumps outside and a mangy dog asleep in the window. Inside, on rusty metal shelves or in wheezing coolers, you could find pop and Popsicles, cigarettes, potato chips, canned soup, raunchy postcards, fishing gear, Twinkies, wine, and beer. When Father drove anywhere on errands, Mother would send us along as guards, warning us not to let him out of our sight. And so with one or more of us on board, Father would cruise up to Sly's, pump a dollar's worth of gas or plump the tires with air, and then, telling us to wait in the car, he would head for the doorway.

Dutiful and panicky, we cried, "Let us go with you!"   19

"No," he answered. "I'll be back in two shakes."   20

"Please!"   21

"No!" he roared." Don't you budge or I'll jerk a knot in your tails!"   22

So we stayed put, kicking the seats, while he ducked inside.   23
Often, when he had parked the car at a careless angle, we gazed in through the window and saw Mr. Sly fetching down from the shelf behind the cash register two green pints of Gallo wine. Father swigged one of them right there at the counter, stuffed the other in his

pocket, and then out he came, a bulge in his coat, a flustered look on his reddened face.

24   Because the mom and pop who ran the dump were neighbors of ours, living just down the tar-blistered road, I hated them all the more for poisoning my father. I wanted to sneak in their store and smash the bottles and set fire to the place. I also hated the Gallo brothers, Ernest and Julio, whose jovial faces beamed from the labels of their wine, labels I would find, torn and curled, when I burned the trash. I noted the Gallo brothers' address in California and studied the road atlas to see how far that was from Ohio, because I meant to go out there and tell Ernest and Julio what they were doing to my father, and then, if they showed no mercy, I would kill them.

25   While growing up on the back roads and in the country schools and cramped Methodist churches of Ohio and Tennessee, I never heard the word *alcoholic*, never happened across it in books or magazines. In the nearby towns, there were no addiction-treatment programs, no community mental-health centers, no Alcoholics Anonymous chapters, no therapists. Left alone with our grievous secret, we had no way of understanding Father's drinking except as an act of will, a deliberate folly or cruelty, a moral weakness, a sin. He drank because he chose to, pure and simple. Why our father, so playful and competent and kind when sober, would choose to ruin himself and punish his family we could not fathom.

26   Our neighborhood was high on the Bible, and the Bible was hard on drunkards. "Woe to those who are heroes at drinking wine and valiant men in mixing strong drink," wrote Isaiah. "The priest and the prophet reel with strong drink, they are confused with wine, they err in vision, they stumble in giving judgment. For all tables are full of vomit, no place is without filthiness." We children had seen those fouled tables at the local truck stop where the notorious boozers hung out, our father occasionally among them. "Wine and new wine take away the understanding," declared the prophet Hosea. We had also seen evidence of that in our father, who could multiply seven-digit numbers in his head when sober but when drunk could not help us with fourth-grade math. Proverbs warned: "Do not look at wine when it is red, when it sparkles in the cup and goes down smoothly. At the last it bites like a serpent and stings like an adder. Your eyes will see strange things, and your mind utter perverse things." Woe, woe.

27   Dismayingly often, these biblical drunkards stirred up trouble for their own kids. Noah made fresh wine after the flood, drank too much of it, fell asleep without any clothes on, and was glimpsed in the buff by his son Ham, whom Noah promptly cursed. In one passage—it was so shocking we had to read it under our blankets with flashlights—the patriarch Lot fell down drunk and slept with his daughters. The sins of the fathers set their children's teeth on edge.

Our ministers were fond of quoting St. Paul's pronouncement that 28
drunkards would not inherit the kingdom of God. These grave preachers
assured us that the wine referred to in the Last Supper was in fact grape
juice. Bible and Sermons and hymns combined to give us the impression
that Moses should have brought down from the mountain another stone
tablet, bearing the Eleventh Commandment: Thou shalt not drink.

The scariest and most illuminating Bible story apropos of drunk- 29
ards was the one about the lunatic and the swine. We knew it by heart:
When Jesus climbed out of his boat one day, this lunatic came charging
up from the graveyard, stark naked and filthy, frothing at the mouth, so
violent that he broke the strongest chains. Nobody would go near him.
Night and day for years, this madman had been wailing among the
tombs and bruising himself with stones. Jesus took one look at him and
said, "Come out of the man, you unclean spirits!" for he could see that
the lunatic was possessed by demons. Meanwhile, some hogs were
conveniently rooting nearby. "If we have to come out," begged the
demons, "at least let us go into those swine." Jesus agreed, the unclean
spirits entered the hogs, and the hogs raced straight off a cliff and
plunged into a lake, Hearing the story in Sunday school, my friends
thought mainly of the pigs. (How big a splash did they make? Who
paid for the lost pork?) But I thought of the redeemed lunatic, who
bathed himself and put on clothes and calmly sat at the feet of Jesus,
restored—so the Bible said—to "his right mind."

When drunk, our father was clearly in his wrong mind. He became 30
a stranger, as fearful to us as any graveyard lunatic, not quite frothing
at the mouth but fierce enough, quick-tempered, explosive; or else he
grew maudlin and weepy, which frightened us nearly as much. In my
boyhood despair, I reasoned that maybe he wasn't to blame for turning
into an ogre: Maybe, like the lunatic, he was possessed by demons.

If my father was indeed possessed, who would exorcise him? If he 31
was a sinner, who would save him? If he was ill, who would cure him?
If he suffered, who would ease his pain? Not ministers or doctors, for
we could not bring ourselves to confide in them; not the neighbors, for
we pretended they had never seen him drunk; not Mother, who fussed
and pleaded but could not budge him; not my brother and sister, who
were only kids. That left me. It did not matter that I, too, was only a
child, and a bewildered one at that. I could not excuse myself.

On first reading a description of delirium tremens—in a book on alco- 32
holism I smuggled from a university library—I thought immediately of
the frothing lunatic and the frenzied swine. When I read stories or
watched films about grisly metamorphoses—Dr. Jekyll and Mr. Hyde,
the mild husband changing into a werewolf, the kindly neighbor inhabited by a brutal alien—I could not help but see my own father's mutation from sober to drunk. Even today, knowing better, I am attracted by

the demonic theory of drink, for when I recall my father's transformation, the emergence of his ugly second self, I find it easy to believe in being possessed by unclean spirits. We never knew which version of Father would come home from work, the true or the tainted, nor could we guess how far down the slope toward cruelty he would slide.

33   How far a man *could* slide we gauged by observing our back-road neighbors—the out-of-work miners who had dragged their families to our corner of Ohio from the desolate hollows of Appalachia, the tight-fisted farmers, the surly mechanics, the balked and broken men. There was, for example, whiskey-soaked Mr. Jenkins, who beat his wife and kids so hard we could hear their screams from the road. There was Mr. Lavo the wino, who fell asleep smoking time and again, until one night his disgusted wife bundled up the children and went outside and left him in his easy chair to burn; he awoke on his own, staggered out coughing into the yard, and pounded her flat while the children looked on and the shack turned to ash. There was the truck driver, Mr. Sampson, who tripped over his son's tricycle one night while drunk and got mad, jumped into his semi, and drove away, shifting through the dozen gears, and never came back. We saw the bruised children of these fathers clump onto our school bus, we saw the abandoned children huddle in the pews at church, we saw the stunned and battered mothers begging for help at our doors.

34   Our own father never beat us, and I don't think he beat Mother, but he threatened often. The Old Testament Yahweh was not more terrible in His rage. Eyes blazing, voice booming, Father would pull out his belt and swear to give us a whipping, but he never followed through, never needed to, because we could imagine it so vividly. He shoved us, pawed us with the back of his hand, not to injure, just to clear a space. I can see him grabbing Mother by the hair as she cowers on a chair during a nightly quarrel. He twists her neck back until she gapes up at him, and then he lifts over her skull a glass quart bottle of milk, and milk spilling down his forearm, and he yells at her, "Say just one more word, one goddamn word, and I'll shut you up!" I fear she will prick him with her sharp tongue, but she is terrified into silence, and so am I, and the leaking bottle quivers in the air, and milk seeps through the red hair of my father's uplifted arm, and the entire scene is there to this moment, the head jerked back, the club raised.

35   When the drink made him weepy, Father would pack, kiss each of us children on the head, and announce from the front door that he was moving out. "Where to?" we demanded, fearful each time that he would leave for good, as Mr. Sampson had roared away for good in his diesel truck. "Someplace where I won't get hounded every minute," Father would answer, his jaw quivering. He stabbed a look at Mother, who might say, "Don't run into the ditch before you get there," or "Good riddance," and then he would slink away. Mother watched him

go with arms crossed over her chest, her face closed like the lid on a box of snakes. We children bawled. Where could he go? To the truck stop, that den of iniquity? To one of those dark, ratty flophouses in town? Would he wind up sleeping under a railroad bridge or on a park bench or in a cardboard box, mummied in rags like the bums we had seen on our trips to Cleveland and Chicago? We bawled and bawled, wondering if he would ever come back.

He always did come back, a day or a week later, but each time there 36
was a sliver less of him.

In Kafka's *Metamorphosis*, which opens famously with Gregor Samsa 37
waking up from uneasy dreams to find himself transformed into an insect, Gregor's family keep reassuring themselves that things will be just fine again "when he comes back to us." Each time alcohol transformed our father we held out the same hope, that he would really and truly come back to us, our authentic father, the tender and playful and competent man, and then all things would be fine. We had grounds for such hope. After his tearful departures and chapfallen returns, he would sometimes go weeks, even months, without drinking. Those were glad times. Every day without the furtive glint of bottles, every meal without a flight, every bedtime without sobs encouraged us to believe that such bliss might go on forever.

Mother was fooled by such a hope all during the forty-odd years 38
she knew Greeley Ray Sanders. Soon after she met him in a Chicago delicatessen on the eve of World War II and fell for his butter-melting Mississippi drawl and his wavy red hair, she learned that he drank heavily. But then so did a lot of men. She would soon coax or scold him into breaking the nasty habit. She would point out to him how ugly and foolish it was, this bleary drinking, and then he would quit. He refused to quit during their engagement, however, still refused during the first years of marriage, refused until my older sister came along. The shock of fatherhood sobered him, and he remained sober through my birth at the end of the war and right on through until we moved in 1951 to the Ohio arsenal. The arsenal had more than its share of alcoholics, drug addicts, and other varieties of escape artists. There I turned six and started school and woke into a child's flickering awareness, just in time to see my father begin sneaking swigs in the garage.

He sobered up again for most of a year at the height of the Korean 39
War, to celebrate the birth of my brother. But aside from that dry spell, his only breaks from drinking before I graduated from high school were just long enough to raise and then dash our hopes. Then during the fall of my senior year—the time of the Cuban Missile Crisis, when it seemed that the nightly explosions at the munitions dump and the nightly rages in our household night spread to engulf the globe—Father collapsed. His liver, kidneys, and heart all conked out. The doctors saved him, but

only by a hair. He stayed in the hospital for weeks, going through a withdrawal so terrible that Mother would not let us visit him. If he wanted to kill himself, the doctors solemnly warned him, all he had to do was hit the bottle again. One binge would finish him.

40   Father must have believed them, for he stayed dry the next fifteen years. It was an answer to prayer, Mother said, it was a miracle. I believe it was a reflex of fear, which he sustained over the years through courage and pride. He knew a man could die from drink, for his brother Roscoe had. We children never laid eyes on doomed Uncle Roscoe, but in the stories Mother told us he became a fairy-tale figure, like a boy who took the wrong turn in the woods and was gobbled up by the wolf.

41   The fifteen-year dry spell came to an end with Father's retirement in the spring of 1978. Like many men, he gave up his identity along with his job. One day he was a boss at the factory, with a brass plate on his door and a reputation to uphold; the next day he was nobody at home. He and Mother were leaving Ontario, the last of the many places to which his job had carried them, and they were moving to a new house in Mississippi, his childhood stomping ground. As a boy in Mississippi, Father sold Coca-Cola during dances while the moonshiners peddled their brew in the parking lot; as a young blade, he fought in bars and in the ring, winning a state Golden Gloves championship; he gambled at poker, hunted pheasant, raced motorcycles and cars, played semiprofessional baseball, and, along with all his buddies—in the Black Cat Saloon, behind the cotton gin, in the woods—he drank hard. It was a perilous youth to dream of recovering.

42   After his final day of work, Mother drove on ahead with a car full of begonias and violets, while Father stayed behind to oversee the packing. When the van was loaded, the sweaty movers broke open a six-pack and offered him a beer.

43   "Let's drink to retirement!" they crowed. "Let's drink to freedom! to fishing! hunting! loafing! Let's drink to a guy who's going home!"

44   At least I imagine some such words, for that is all I can do, imagine, and I see Father's hand trembling in midair as he thinks about the fifteen sober years and about the doctors' warning, and he tells himself, *Goddamnit, I am a free man*, and *Why can't a free man drink one beer after a lifetime of hard work?* and I see his arm reaching, his fingers closing, the can tilting to his lips. I even supply a label for the beer, a swaggering brand that promises on television to deliver the essence of life. I watch the amber liquid pour down his throat, the alcohol steal into his blood, the key turn in his brain.

45   Soon after my parents moved back to Father's treacherous stomping ground, my wife and I visited them in Mississippi with our four-year-old daughter. Mother had been too distraught to warn me about the return of the demons. So when I climbed out of the car that bright July

morning and saw my father napping in the hammock, I felt uneasy, and when he lurched upright and blinked his bloodshot eyes and greeted us in a syrupy voice, I was hurled back into childhood.

"What's the matter with Papaw?" our daughter asked.   46

"Nothing" I said. "Nothing!"   47

Like a child again, I pretended not to see him in his stupor, and be- 48
hind my phony smile I grieved. On that visit and on the few that remained before his death, once again I found bottles in the workbench,
bottles in the woods. Again his hands shook too much for him to run a
saw, to make his precious miniature furniture, to drive straight down
back roads. Again he wound up in the ditch, in the hospital, in jail in
the treatment center. Again he shouted and wept. Again he lied.
"I never touched a drop," he swore. "Your mother's making it up."

I no longer fancied I could reason with the men whose names I   49
found on the bottles—Jim Beam, Jack Daniel's—but I was able now to
recall the cold statistics about alcoholism: ten million victims, fifteen
million, twenty. And yet, in spite of my age, I reacted in the same blind
way as I had in childhood, by vainly seeking to erase through my efforts whatever drove him to drink. I worked on their place twelve and
sixteen hours a day in the swelter of Mississippi summers, digging
ditches, running electrical wires, planting trees, mowing grass, building sheds, as though what nagged at him was some list of chores, as
though by taking his worries upon my shoulders I could redeem him.
I was flung back into boyhood, acting as though my father would not
drink himself to death if only I were perfect.

I failed of perfection; he succeeded in dying. To the end, he consid- 50
ered himself not sick but sinful. "Do you want to kill yourself?" I asked
him. "Why not?" he answered. "Why the hell not? What's there to
save?" To the end, he would not speak about his feelings, would not or
could not give a name to the beast that was devouring him.

In silence, he went rushing off to the cliff. Unlike the biblical swine, 51
however, he left behind a few of the demons to haunt his children. Life
with him and the loss of him twisted us into shapes that will be familiar to other sons and daughters of alcoholics. My brother became a
rebel, my sister retreated into shyness, I played the stalwart and dutiful
son who would hold the family together. If my father was unstable,
I would be a rock. If he squandered money on drink, I would pinch
every penny. If he wept when drunk—and only when drunk—I would
not let myself weep at all. If he roared at the Little League umpire for
calling my pitches balls, I would throw nothing but strikes. Watching
him flounder and rage, I came to dread the loss of control. I would go
through life without making anyone mad. I vowed never to put in my
mouth or veins any chemical that would banish my everyday self.
I would never make a scene, never lash out at the ones I loved, never
hurt a soul. Through hard work, relentless work, I would achieve

something dazzling—in the classroom, on the basketball court, in the science lab, in the pages of books—and my achievement would distract the world's eyes from his humiliation. I would become a worthy sacrifice, and the smoke of my burning would please God.

52   It is far easier to recognize these twists in my character than to undo them. Work has become an addiction for me, as drink was an addiction for my father. Knowing this, my daughter gave me a placard for the wall: WORKAHOLIC. The labor is endless and futile, for I can no more redeem myself through work than I could redeem my father. I still panic in the face of other people's anger, because his drunken temper was so terrible. I shrink from causing sadness or disappointment even to strangers, as though I were still concealing the family shame. I still notice every twitch of emotion in those faces around me, having learned as a child to read the weather in faces, and I blame myself for their least pang of unhappiness or anger. In certain moods I blame myself for everything. Guilt burns like acid in my veins.

53   I am moved to write these pages now because my own son, at the age of ten, is taking on himself the griefs of the world, and in particular the griefs of his father. He tells me that when I am gripped by sadness, he feels responsible; he feels there must be something he can do to spring me from depression, to fix my life and that crushing sense of responsibility is exactly what I felt at the age of ten in the face of my father's drinking. My son wonders if I, too, am possessed. I write, therefore, to drag into the light what eats at me—the fear, the guilt, the shame—so that my own children may be spared.

54   I still shy away from nightclubs, from bars, from parties where the solvent is alcohol. My friends puzzle over this, but it is no more peculiar than for a man to shy away from the lions' den after seeing his father torn apart. I took my own first drink at the age of twenty-one, half a glass of burgundy. I knew the odds of my becoming an alcoholic were four times higher than for the children of nonalcoholic fathers. So I sipped warily.

55   I still do—once a week, perhaps, a glass of wine, a can of beer, nothing stronger, nothing more. I listen for the turning of a key in my brain.

RESPONDING TO READING

1. Sanders describes his father's alcoholism in blunt language. How, within these descriptions, does he communicate the confusing swirl of emotions that he felt when he was younger and, perhaps, still feels towards his father and his father's drinking problem?

2. Sanders lists synonyms for drunk, from "tipsy" to "sloshed." While each of these words can denote drunkenness, what different connotations does each have? Do some of them carry positive connotations, and how (or where) do

they take on those positive meanings? How does Sanders deal with these positively spun synonyms for intoxication?

3. How does Sanders construct drunkenness as a secret that everyone knows? Does this condition—a shameful public secret—continue to prevail in many families that must deal with a member who is addicted to alcohol or drugs?

4. How is religion a part of Sanders's essay about his father? What attitude(s) does Sanders manifest toward religion and its place in his family's history?

5. What other addictions are just as damaging to individuals and families as alcoholism? Are there addictions that are treated as secret or as shameful as substance abuse? Are there addictions that are socially acceptable? In an essay intended for readers not addicted to what you are discussing, describe one kind of addiction, explain its symptoms, and analyze its consequences, short and long term. If it presents problems for the addict or the addict's family, propose one or more solutions to resolve it.

HOW CAN WE LIVE IN HARMONY WITH NATURE?

Landscape, History, and the Pueblo Imagination

LESLIE MARMON SILKO

Leslie Marmon Silko opens her acclaimed novel *Ceremony* (1977) with the observation, "You don't have anything if you don't have the stories." Stories, she says, "aren't just entertainment," they are all that Native Americans have "to fight off illness and death." Silko, of Native American, Mexican, and Caucasian descent, was born in 1948 and reared on the Laguna Pueblo, New Mexico. She attended the Bureau of Indian Affairs schools at Laguna before earning a B.A. from the University of New Mexico. Although she has taught at her alma mater and at the University of Arizona, a MacArthur fellowship in 1983 provided five years' support for her writing. *Storyteller*, a collection of poems, stories, and legends was published in 1981; her second novel, *Almanac of the Dead*, which took ten years to write, was published in 1991. Critics of the novel argued that its myths were unforgettable, yet its characters were eminently forgettable. In an interview for the *Women's Review of Books*, Silko commented, "I was trying to give history a character. [. . .] I knew I was breaking rules about not doing characters in the traditional way." *Ceremony*, which depicts the struggle of Tayo, a half-breed veteran of World War II, for sanity and wholeness after returning from military service to a New Mexico Indian reservation, asserts that "the only cure . . . is a good ceremony." Tayo overcomes the ravages of alcoholism, racism, and violence through learning that ceremony is not merely a formal ritual, but a way of conducting one's life to attain the harmony that comes from an integration of human life and the cosmos.

In "Landscape, History, and the Pueblo Imagination" (1986) Silko reinforces this integrated world view. Storytelling, she says, is a communal act with everyone in the pueblo, from the youngest child to the oldest person expected to listen, remember, and tell part of the story. If even a key figure in the tribe were to die unexpectedly, the system would remain intact, the stories transcending the individual. Truth thus becomes communal, as well, living "somewhere within the web of differing versions" and outright contradictions. The narratives the Pueblos tell are linked with prominent features of the landscape; they delineate the complex relationship humans must maintain with the natural world if they are to survive in the high desert plateau. Silko's most recent work, *Gardens in the Dunes*, was published in 2000.

From a High Arid Plateau in New Mexico

You see that after a thing is dead, it dries up. It might take weeks or   1
years, but eventually if you touch the thing, it crumbles under your fingers. It goes back to dust. The soul of the thing has long since departed.
With the plants and wild game the soul may have already been borne
back into bones and blood or thick green stalk and leaves. Nothing is
wasted. What cannot be eaten by people or in some way used must
then be left where other living creatures may benefit. What domestic
animals or wild scavengers can't eat will be fed to the plants. The
plants feed on the dust of these few remains.

The ancient Pueblo people buried the dead in vacant rooms or par-   2
tially collapsed rooms adjacent to the main living quarters. Sand and
clay used to construct the roof make layers many inches deep once the
roof has collapsed. The layers of sand and clay make for easy gravedig-
ging. The vacant room fills with cast-off objects and debris. When a vacant room has filled deep enough, a shallow but adequate grave can be
scooped in a far corner. Archaeologists have remarked over formal
burials complete with elaborate funerary objects excavated in trash
middens of abandoned rooms. But the rocks and adobe mortar of collapsed walls were valued by the ancient people. Because each rock has
been carefully selected for size and shape, then chiseled to an even face.
Even the pink clay adobe melting with each rainstorm had to be
prayed over, then dug and carried some distance. Corn cobs and husks,
the rinds and stalks and animals bones were not regarded by the ancient people as filth or garbage. The remains were merely resting at a
midpoint in their journey back to dust. Human remains are not so different. They should rest with the bones and rinds where they all may
benefit living creatures—small rodents and insects—until their return
is completed. The remains of things—animals and plants, the clay and
the stones—were treated with respect. Because for the ancient people
all these things had spirit and being.

The antelope merely consents to return home with the hunter. All phas-   3
es of the hunt are conducted with love. The love the hunter and the
people have for the Antelope People. And the love of the antelope who
agree to give up their meat and blood so that human beings will not
starve. Waste of meat or even the thoughtless handling of bones cooked
bare will offend the antelope spirits. Next year the hunters will vainly
search the dry plains for antelope. Thus it is necessary to return carefully the bones and hair, and the stalks and leaves to the earth who first
created them. The spirits remain close by. They do not leave us.

The dead become dust, and in this becoming they are once more   4
joined with Mother. The ancient Pueblo people called the earth the

Mother Creator of all things in this world. Her sister, the Corn Mother, occasionally merges with her because all succulent green life rises out of the depths of the earth.

5   Rocks and clay are part of the Mother. They emerge in various forms, but at some time before, they were smaller particles or great boulders. At a later time they may again become what they once were. Dust.

6   A rock shares this fate with us and with animals and plants as well. A rock has being or spirit, although we may not understand it. The spirit may differ from the spirit we know in animals or plants or in ourselves. In the end we all originate from the depths of the earth. Perhaps this is how all beings share in the spirit of the Creator. We do not know.

From the Emergence Place

7   Pueblo potters, the creators of petroglyphs and oral narratives, never conceived of removing themselves from the earth and sky. So long as the human consciousness remains *within* the hills, canyons, cliffs, and the plants, clouds, and sky, the term *landscape*, as it has entered the English language, is misleading. "A portion of territory the eye can comprehend in a single view" does not correctly describe the relationship between the human being and his or her surroundings. This assumes the viewer is somehow *outside* or *separate from* the territory he or she surveys. Viewers are as much a part of the landscape as the boulders they stand on. There is no high mesa edge or mountain peak where one can stand and not immediately be part of all that surrounds. Human identity is linked with all the elements of Creation through the clan: you might belong to the Sun Clan or the Lizard Clan or the Corn Clan or the Clay Clan. Standing deep within the natural world, the ancient Pueblo understood the thing as it was—the squash bloosom, grasshopper, or rabbit itself could never be created by the human hand. Ancient Pueblos took the modest view that the thing itself (the landscape) could not be improved upon. The ancients did not presume to tamper with what had already been created. Thus *realism*, as we now recognize it in painting and sculpture, did not catch the imaginations of Pueblo people until recently.

8   The squash blossom itself is *one thing:* itself. So the ancient Pueblo potter abstracted what she saw to be the key elements of the squash blossom–the four symmetrical petals, with four symmetrical stamens in the center. These key elements, while suggesting the squash flower, also link it with the four cardinal directions. By representing only its intrinsic form, the squash flower is released from a limited meaning or restricted identity. Even in the most sophisticated abstract form, a squash flower or a cloud or a lightning bolt became intricately connect-

ed with a complex system of relationships which the ancient Pueblo people maintained with each other, and with the populous natural world they lived within. A bolt of lightning is itself, but at the same time it may mean much more. It may be a messenger of good fortune when summer rains are needed. It may deliver death, perhaps the result of manipulations by the Gunnadeyahs, destructive necromancers. Lightning may strike down an evil-doer. Or lightning may strike a person of good will. If the person survives, lightning endows him or her with heightened power.

Pictographs and petroglyphs of constellations or elk or antelope   9 draw their magic in part from the process wherein the focus of all prayer and concentration is upon the thing itself, which, in its turn, guides the hunter's hand. Connection with the spirit dimensions requires a figure or form which is all-inclusive. A "lifelike" rendering of an elk is too restrictive. Only the elk *is* itself. A *realistic* rendering of an elk would be only one particular elk anyway. The purpose of the hunt rituals and magic is to make contact with *all* the spirits of the Elk.

The land, the sky, and all that is within them—the landscape—   10 includes human beings. Interrelationships in the Pueblo landscape are complex and fragile. The unpredictability of the weather, the aridity and harshness of much of the terrain in the high plateau country explain in large part the relentless attention the ancient Pueblo people gave the sky and earth around them. Survival depended upon harmony and cooperation not only among human beings, but among all things—the animate and the less animate, since rocks and mountains were known to move, to travel occasionally.

The ancient Pueblos believed the Earth and the Sky were sisters (or   11 sister and brother in the post-Christian version). As long as good family relations are maintained, then the Sky will continue to bless her sister, the Earth, with rain, and the Earth's children will continue to survive. But the old stories recall incidents in which troublesome spirits or beings threaten the earth. In one story, a malicious ka'tsina, called the Gambler, seizes the Shiwana, or Rainclouds, the Sun's beloved children. The Shiwana are snared in magical power late one afternoon on a high mountain top. The Gambler takes the Rainclouds to his mountain stronghold where he locks them in the north room of his house. What was his idea? The Shiwana were beyond value. They brought life to all things on earth. The Gambler wanted a big stake to wager in his games of chance. But such greed, even on the part of only one being, had the effect of threatening the survival of all life on earth. Sun Youth, aided by old Grandmother spider, outsmarts the Gambler and the rigged game, and the Rainclouds are set free. The drought ends, and once more life thrives on earth.

Through the Stories We Hear Who We Are

12   All summer the people watch the west horizon, scanning the sky from south to north for rain clouds. Corn must have moisture at the time the tassels form. Otherwise pollination will be incomplete, and the ears will be stunted and shriveled. An inadequate harvest may bring disaster. Stories told at Hopi, Zuni, and at Acoma and Laguna describe drought and starvation as recently as 1900. Precipitation in west-central New Mexico averages fourteen inches annually. The western pueblos are located at altitudes over 5,600 feet above sea level, where winter temperatures at night fall below freezing. Yet evidence of their presence in the high desert plateau country goes back ten thousand years. The ancient Pueblo people not only survived in this environment, but many years they thrived. In A.D. 1100 the people at Chaco Canyon had built cities with apartment buildings of stone five stories high. Their sophistication as sky-watchers was surpassed only by Mayan and Inca astronomers. Yet this vast complex of knowledge and belief, amassed for thousands of years, was never recorded in writing.

13   Instead, the ancient Pueblo people depended upon collective memory through successive generations to maintain and transmit an entire culture, a world view complete with proven strategies for survival. The oral narrative, or "story," became the medium in which the complex of Pueblo knowledge and belief was maintained. Whatever the event or the subject, the ancient people perceived the world and themselves within that world as part of an ancient continuous story composed of innumerable bundles of other stories.

14   The ancient Pueblo vision of the world was inclusive. The impulse was to leave nothing out. Pueblo oral tradition necessarily embraced all levels of human experience. Otherwise, the collective knowledge and beliefs comprising ancient Pueblo culture would have been incomplete. Thus stories about the Creation and Emergence of human beings and animals into this World continue to be retold each year for four days and four nights during the winter solstice. The "hummahah" stories related events from the time long ago when human beings were still able to communicate with animals and other living things. But, beyond these two preceding categories, the Pueblo oral tradition knew no boundaries. Accounts of the appearance of the first Europeans in Pueblo country or of the tragic encounters between Pueblo people and Apache raiders were no more and no less important than stories about the biggest mule deer ever taken or adulterous couples surprised in cornfields and chicken coops. Whatever happened, the ancient people instinctively sorted events and details into a loose narrative structure. Everything became a story.

Traditionally everyone, from the youngest child to the oldest per- 15
son, was expected to listen and to be able to recall or tell a portion, if
only a small detail, from a narrative account or story. Thus the remembering and retelling were a communal process. Even if a key figure, an elder who knew much more than others, were to die
unexpectedly, the system would remain intact. Through the efforts of
a great many people, the community was able to piece together valuable accounts and crucial information that might otherwise have died
with an individual.

Communal storytelling was a self-correcting process in which lis- 16
teners were encouraged to speak up if they noted an important fact or
detail omitted. The people were happy to listen to two or three different versions of the same event or the same humma-hah story. Even
conflicting versions of an incident were welcomed for the entertainment they provided. Defenders of each version might joke and tease
one another, but seldom were there any direct confrontations. Implicit
in the Pueblo oral tradition was the awareness that loyalties, grudges,
and kinship must always influence the narrator's choices as she emphasizes to listeners this is the way *she* has always heard the story told.
The ancient Pueblo people sought a communal truth, not an absolute.
For them this truth lived somewhere within the web of differing versions, disputes over minor points, outright contradictions tangling
with old feuds and village rivalries.

A dinner-table conversation, recalling a deer hunt forty years ago 17
when the largest mule deer ever was taken, inevitably stimulates similar memories in listeners. But hunting stories were not merely after-
dinner entertainment. These accounts contained information of critical
importance about behavior and migration patterns of mule deer. Hunting stories carefully described key landmarks and locations of fresh
water. Thus a deer-hunt story might also serve as a "map." Lost travelers, and lost pinon-nut gatherers, have been saved by sighting a rock
formation they recognize only because they once heard a hunting story
describing this rock formation.

The importance of cliff formations and water holes does not end 18
with hunting stories. As offspring of the Mother Earth, the ancient
Pueblo people could not conceive of themselves without a specific
landscape. Location, or "place," nearly always plays a central role in
the Pueblo oral narratives. Indeed, stories are most frequently recalled as people are passing by a specific geographical feature or the
exact place where a story takes place. The precise date of the incident
often is less important than the place or location of the happening.
"Long, long ago," "a long time ago," "not too long ago," and "recently" are usually how stories are classified in terms of time. But the

places where the stories occur are precisely located, and prominent geographical details recalled, even if the landscape is well-known to listeners. Often because the turning point in the narrative involved a peculiarity or special quality of a rock or tree or plant found only at that place. Thus, in the case of many of the Pueblo narratives, it is impossible to determine which came first: the incident or the geographical feature which begs to be brought alive in a story that features some unusual aspect of this location.

19   There is a giant sandstone boulder about a mile north of Old Laguna, on the road to Paguate. It is ten feet tall and twenty feet in circumference. When I was a child, and we would pass this boulder driving to Paguate village, someone usually made reference to the story about Kochininako, Yellow Woman, and the Estrucuyo, a monstrous giant who nearly ate her. The Twin Hero Brothers saved Kochininako, who had been out hunting rabbits to take home to feed her mother and sisters. The Hero Brothers had heard her cries just in time. The Estrucuyo had cornered her in a cave too small to fit its monstrous head. Kochininako had already thrown to the Estrucuyo all her rabbits, as well as her moccasins and most of her clothing. Still the creature had not been satisfied. After killing the Estrucuyo with their bows and arrows, the Twin Hero Brothers slit open the Estrucuyo and cut out its heart. They threw the heart as far as they could. The monster's heart landed there, beside the old trail to Paguate village, where the sandstone boulder rests now.

20   It may be argued that the existence of the boulder precipitated the creation of a story to explain it. But sandstone boulders and sandstone formations of strange shapes abound in the Laguna Pueblo area. Yet most of them do not have stories. Often the crucial element in a narrative is the terrain—some specific detail of the setting.

21   A high dark mesa rises dramatically from a grassy plain fifteen miles southeast of Laguna, in an area known as Swanee. On the grassy plain one hundred and forty years ago, my great-grandmother's uncle and his brother-in-law were grazing their herd of sheep. Because visibility on the plain extends for over twenty miles, it wasn't until the two sheepherders came near the high dark mesa that the Apaches were able to stalk them. Using the mesa to obscure their approach, the raiders swept around from both ends of the mesa. My great-grandmother's relatives were killed, and the herd lost. The high dark mesa played a critical role: the mesa had compromised the safety which the openness of the plains had seemed to assure. Pueblo and Apache alike relied upon the terrain, the very earth herself, to give them protection and aid. Human activities or needs were maneuvered to fit existing surroundings and conditions. I imagine the last afternoon of my distant ancestors as warm and sunny for late September. They might have been traveling slowly, bringing the sheep closer to Laguna in prepara-

tion for the approach of colder weather. The grass was tall and only beginning to change from green to a yellow which matched the late-afternoon sun shining off it. There might have been comfort in the warmth and the sight of the sheep fattening on good pasture which lulled my ancestors into their fatal inattention. They might have had a rifle whereas the Apaches had only bows and arrows. But there would have been four or five Apache raiders, and the surprise attack would have canceled any advantage the rifles gave them.

Survival in any landscape comes down to making the best use of all available resources. On that particular September afternoon, the raiders made better use of the Swanee terrain than my poor ancestors did. Thus the high dark mesa and the story of the two lost Laguna herders became inextricably linked. The memory of them and their story resides in part with the high black mesa. For as long as the mesa stands, people within the family and clan will be reminded of the story of that afternoon long ago. Thus the continuity and accuracy of the oral narratives are reinforced by the landscape—and the Pueblo interpretation of that landscape is *maintained*.

The Migration Story: An Interior Journey

The Laguna Pueblo migration stories refer to specific places— mesas, springs, or cottonwood trees—not only locations which can be visited still, but also locations which lie directly on the state highway route linking Paguate village with Laguna village. In traveling this road as a child with older Laguna people I first heard a few of the stories from that much larger body of stories linked with the Emergence and Migration. It may be coincidental that Laguna people continue to follow the same route which, according to the Migration story, the ancestors followed south from the Emergence Place. It may be that the route is merely the shortest and best route for car, horse, or foot traffic between Laguna and Paguate villages. But if the stories about boulders, springs, and hills are actually remnants from a ritual that retraces the creation and emergence of the Laguna Pueblo people as a culture, as the people they became, then continued use of that route creates a unique relationship between the ritual-mythic world and the actual, everyday world. A journey from Paguate to Laguna down the long incline of Paguate Hill retraces the original journey from the Emergence Place, which is located slightly north of the Paguate village. Thus the landscape between Paguate and Laguna takes on a deeper significance: the landscape resonates the spiritual or mythic dimension of the Pueblo world even today.

Although each Pueblo culture designates a specific Emergence Place—usually a small natural spring edged with mossy sandstone and full of cattails and wild watercress—it is clear that they do not agree on any single location or natural spring as the one and only true Emergence Place. Each Pueblo group recounts its own stories about Creation, Emergence, and Migration, although they all believe that all human beings, with all the animals and plants, emerged at the same place and at the same time.

25   Natural springs are crucial sources of water for all life in the high desert plateau country. So the small spring near Paguate village is literally the source and continuance of life for the people in the area. The spring also functions on a spiritual level, recalling the original Emergence Place and linking the people and the spring water to all other people and to that moment when the Pueblo people became aware of themselves as they are even now. The Emergence was an emergence into a precise cultural identity. Thus the pueblo stories about the Emergence and Migration are not to be taken as literally as the anthropologists might wish. Prominent geographical features and landmarks which are mentioned in the narratives exist for ritual purposes, not because the Laguna people actually journeyed south for hundreds of years from Chaco Canyon or Mesa Verde, as the archaeologists say, or eight miles from the site of the natural springs at Paguate to the sandstone hilltop at Laguna.

26   The eight miles, marked with boulders, mesas, springs, and river crossings, are actually a ritual circuit or path which marks the interior journey the Laguna people made: a journey of awareness and imagination in which they emerged from being within the earth and from everything included in earth to the culture and people they became, differentiating themselves for the first time from all that had surrounded them, always aware that interior distances cannot be reckoned in physical miles or in calendar years.

27   The narratives linked with prominent features of the landscape between Paguate and Laguna delineate the complexities of the relationship which human beings must maintain with the surrounding natural world if they hope to survive in this place. Thus the journey was an interior process of the imagination, a growing awareness that being human is somehow different from all other life—animal, plant, and inanimate. Yet we are all from the same source: the awareness never deteriorated into Cartesian duality, cutting off the human from the natural world.

28   The people found the opening into the Fifth World too small to allow them or any of the animals to escape. They had sent a fly out through the small hole to tell them if it was the world which the Mother Creator had promised. It was, but there was the problem of getting out. The antelope tried to butt the opening to enlarge it, but the antelope enlarged it only a little. It was necessary for the badger with her long claws to assist the antelope, and at last the opening was enlarged

enough so that all the people and animals were able to emerge up into the Fifth World. The human beings could not have emerged without the aid of antelope and badger. The human beings depended upon the aid and charity of the animals. Only through interdependence could the human beings survive. Families belonged to clans, and it was by clan that the human being joined with the animal and plant world. Life on the high arid plateau became viable when the human beings were able to imagine themselves as sisters and brothers to the badger, antelope, clay, yucca, and sun. Not until they could find a viable relationship to the terrain, the landscape they found themselves in, could they *emerge*. Only at the moment the requisite balance between human and *other* was realized could the Pueblo people become a culture, a distinct group whose population and survival remained stable despite the vicissitudes of climate and terrain.

Landscape thus has similarities with dreams. Both have the power   29
to seize terrifying feelings and deep instincts and translate them into images—visual, aural, tactile—into the concrete where human beings may more readily confront and channel the terrifying instincts or powerful emotions into rituals and narratives which reassure the individual while reaffirming cherished values of the group. The identity of the individual as a part of the group and the greater Whole is strengthened, and the terror of facing the world alone is extinguished.

Even now, the people at Laguna Pueblo spend the greater portion   30
of social occasions recounting recent incidents or events which have occurred in the Laguna area. Nearly always, the discussion will precipitate the retelling of older stories about similar incidents or other stories connected with a specific place. The stories often contain disturbing or provocative material, but are nonetheless told in the presence of children and women. The effect of these inter-family or inter-clan exchanges is the reassurance for each person that she or he will never be separated or apart from the clan, no matter what might happen. Neither the worst blunders or disasters nor the greatest financial prosperity and joy will ever be permitted to isolate anyone from the rest of the group. In the ancient times, cohesiveness was all that stood between extinction and survival, and, while the individual certainly was recognized, it was always as an individual simultaneously bonded to family and clan by a complex bundle of custom and ritual. You are never the first to suffer a grave loss or profound humiliation. You are never the first, and you understand that you will probably not be the last to commit or be victimized by a repugnant act. Your family and clan are able to go on at length about others now passed on, others older or more experienced than you who suffered similar losses.

The wide deep arroyo near the Kings Bar (located across the reser-   31
vation borderline) has over the years claimed many vehicles. A few years ago, when a Viet Nam veteran's new red Volkswagen rolled

backwards into the arroyo while he was inside buying a six-pack of beer, the story of his loss joined the lively and large collection of stories already connected with that big arroyo. I do not know whether the Viet Nam veteran was consoled when he was told the stories about the other cars claimed by the ravenous arroyo. All his savings of combat pay had gone for the red Volkswagen. But this man could not have felt any worse than the man who, some years before, had left his children and mother-in-law in his station wagon with the engine running. When he came out of the liquor store his station wagon was gone. He found it and its passengers upside down in the big arroyo. Broken bones, cuts and bruises, and a total wreck of the car. The big arroyo has a wide mouth. Its existence needs no explanation. People in the area regard the arroyo much as they might regard a living being, which has a certain character and personality. I seldom drive past that wide deep arroyo without feeling a familiarity with and even a strange affection for this arroyo. Because as treacherous as it may be, the arroyo maintains a strong connection between human beings and the earth. The arroyo demands from us the caution and attention that constitute respect. It is this sort of respect the old believers have in mind when they tell us we must respect and love the earth.

32   Hopi Pueblo elders have said that the austere and, to some eyes, barren plains and hills surrounding their mesa-top villages actually help to nurture the spirituality of the Hopi *way*. The Hopi elders say the Hopi people might have settled in locations far more lush where daily life would not have been so grueling. But there on the high silent sandstone mesas that overlook the sandy arid expanses stretching to all horizons, the Hopi elders say the Hopi people must "live by their prayers" if they are to survive. The Hopi way cherishes the intangible: the riches realized from interaction and interrelationships with all beings above all else. Great abundances of material things, even food, the Hopi elders believe, tend to lure human attention away from what is most valuable and important. The views of the Hopi elders are not much different from those elders in all the Pueblos.

33   The bare vastness of the Hopi landscape emphasizes the visual impact of every plant, every rock, every arroyo. Nothing is overlooked or taken for granted. Each ant, each lizard, each lark is imbued with great value simply because the creature is there, simply because the creature is alive in a place where any life at all is precious. Stand on the mesa edge at Walpai and look west over the bare distances toward the pale blue outlines of the San Francisco peaks where the ka'tsina spirits reside. So little lies between you and the sky. So little lies between you and the earth. One look and you know that simply to survive is a great triumph, that every possible resource is needed, every possible ally— even the most humble insect or reptile. You realize you will be speak-

ing with all of them if you intend to last out the year. Thus it is that the Hopi elders are grateful to the landscape for aiding them in their quest as spiritual people.

Out Under the Sky

My earliest memories are of being outside, under the sky. I remem- 34
ber climbing the fence when I was three years old, and heading for the plaza in the center of Laguna village because other children passing by had told me there were ka'tsinas there dancing with pieces of wood in their mouths. A neighbor woman retrieved me before I ever saw the wood-swallowing ka'tsinas, but from an early age I knew that I wanted to be outside. Outside walls and fences.

My father had wandered all the hills and mesas around Laguna when 35
he was a child. Because the Indian School and the taunts of the other children did not set well with him. It had been difficult in those days to be part Laguna and part white, or *amedicana*. It was still difficult when I attended the Indian School at Laguna. Our full-blooded relatives and clanspeople assured us we were theirs and that we belonged there because we had been born and reared there. But the racism of the wider world we call America had begun to make itself felt years before. My father's response was to head for the mesas and hills with his older brother, their dog, and. 22 rifles. They retreated to the sandstone cliffs and juniper forests. Out in the hills they were not lonely because they had all the living creatures of the hills around them, and, whatever the ambiguities of racial heritage, my father and my uncle understood what the old folks had taught them: the earth loves all of us regardlessly, because we are her children.

I started roaming those same mesas and hills when I was nine years 36
old. At eleven I rode away on my horse, and explored places my father and uncle could not have reached on foot. I was never afraid or lonely, although I was high in the hills, many miles from home. Because I carried with me the feeling I'd acquired from listening to the old stories, that the land all around me was teeming with creatures that were related to human beings and to me. The stories had also left me with a feeling of familiarity and warmth for the mesas and hills and boulders where the incidents or action in the stories had taken place. I felt as if I had actually been to those places, although I had only heard stories about them. Somehow the stories had given a kind of being to the mesas and hills, just as the stories had left me with the sense of having spent time with the people in the stories, although they had long since passed on.

It is unremarkable to sense the presence of those long passed at the 37
locations where their adventures took place. Spirits range without boundaries of any sort. Spirits may be called back in any number of

ways. The method used in the calling also determines how the spirit manifests itself. I think a spirit may or may not choose to remain at the site of its passing or death. I think they might be in a number of places at the same time. Storytelling can procure fleeting moments to experience who they were and how life felt long ago. What I enjoyed most as a child was standing at the site of an incident recounted in one of the ancient stories Aunt Susie had told us as girls. What excited me was listening to old Aunt Susie tell us an old-time story and then for me to realize that I was familiar with a certain mesa or cave that figured as the central location of the story she was telling. That was when the stories worked best. Because then I could sit there listening and be able to visualize myself as being located *within* the story being told, within the landscape. Because the storytellers did not just tell the stories, they would in their way act them out. The storyteller would imitate voices for vast dialogues between the various figures in the story. So we sometimes say the moment is alive again within us, within our imaginations and our memory, as we listen.

38   Aunt Susie once told me how it had been when she was a child and her grandmother agreed to tell the children stories. The old woman would always ask the youngest child in the room to go open the door. "Go open the door," her grandmother would say. "Go open the door so our esteemed ancestors may bring us the precious gift of their stories." Two points seem clear: the spirits could be present and the stories were valuable because they taught us how we were the people we believed we were. The myth, the web of memories and ideas that create an identity, a part of oneself. This sense of identity was intimately linked with the surrounding terrain, to the landscape which has often played a significant role in a story or in the outcome of a conflict.

39   The landscape sits in the center of Pueblo belief and identity. Any narratives about the Pueblo people necessarily give a great deal of attention and detail to all aspects of a landscape. For this reason, the Pueblo people have always been extremely reluctant to relinquish their land for dams or highways. For this reason, Taos Pueblo fought from 1906 until 1973 to win back their sacred Blue Lake, which was illegally taken from them by the creation of Taos National Forest. For this reason, the decision in the early 1950s to begin open-pit mining of the huge uranium deposits north of Laguna, near Paguate village, has had a powerful psychological impact upon the Laguna people. Already a large body of stories has grown up around the subject of what happens to people who disturb or destroy the earth. I was a child when the mining began and the apocalyptic warning stories were being told. And I have lived long enough to begin hearing the stories which verify the earlier warnings.

40   All that remains of the gardens and orchards that used to grow in the sandy flats southeast of Paguate village are the stories of the love-

ly big peaches and apricots the people used to grow. The Jackpile Mine is an open pit that has been blasted out of the many hundreds of acres where the orchards and melon patches once grew. The Laguna people have not witnessed changes to the land without strong reactions. Descriptions of the landscape *before* the mine are as vivid as any description of the present-day destruction by the open-pit mining. By its very ugliness and by the violence it does to the land, the Jackpile Mine insures that from now on it, too, will be included in the vast body of narratives which make up the history of the Laguna people and the Pueblo landscape. And the description of what that landscape looked like *before* the uranium mining began will always carry considerable impact.

Landscape as a Character in Fiction

Drought or the disappearance of game animals may signal disharmony or even witchcraft. When the rain clouds fail to appear in time to help the corn plants, or the deer are suddenly scarce, then we know the very sky and earth are telling human beings that all is not well. A deep arroyo continues to claim victims. 41

When I began writing I found that the plots of my short stories very often featured the presence of elements out of the landscape, elements which directly influenced the outcome of events. Nowhere is landscape more crucial to the outcome than in my short story, "Storyteller." The site is southwest Alaska, near the village of Bethel, on the Kuskokwim River. Tundra country. Here the winter landscape can suddenly metamorphize into a seamless blank white so solid that pilots in aircraft without electronic instruments lose their bearings and crash their planes straight into the frozen tundra, believing down to be up. Here on the Alaska tundra, in mid-February, not all the space-age fabrics, electronics, or engines can ransom human beings from the restless shifting forces of the winter sky and winter earth. 42

The young Yupik Eskimo woman works out an elaborate yet subconscious plan to avenge the deaths of her parents. After months of baiting the trap, she lures the murderer onto the river ice where he falls through to his death. The murderer is a white man who operates the village trading post. For years the murderer has existed like a parasite, exploiting not only the fur-bearing animals and the fish, but the Yupik people themselves. When the Yupik woman kills him, the white trader has just finished cashing in on the influx of workers for the petroleum exploration and pipeline who have suddenly come to the tiny village. For the Yupik people, souls deserving punishment spend varying lengths of time in a place of freezing. The Yupik see the world's end coming with ice, not fire. Although the white trader possesses every 43 possible garment, insulation, heating fuel, and gadget ever devised to protect him from the frozen tundra environment, he still dies, drowning under the freezing river ice. Because the white man had not reckoned with the true power of that landscape, especially not the power which the Yupik woman understood instinctively and which she used so swiftly and efficiently. The white man had reckoned with the young woman and determined he could overpower her. But the white man failed to account for the conjunction of the landscape with the woman. The Yupik woman had never seen herself as anything but a part of that sky, that frozen river, that tundra. The river ice and the blinding white are her accomplices, and yet the Yupik woman never for a moment misunderstands her own relationship with that landscape. After the white trader has crashed through the river ice, the young woman finds herself a great distance from either shore of the treacherous frozen river. She can see nothing but the whiteness of the sky swallowing the earth. But far away in the distance, on the side of her log and tundra sod cabin, she is able to see the spot of bright red. A bright red marker she had nailed up weeks earlier because she was intrigued by the contrast between all that white and the spot of brilliant red. The Yupik woman knows the appetite of the frozen river. She realizes that the ice and the fog, the tundra and the snow seek constantly to be reunited with the living beings which skitter across it. The Yupik woman knows that inevitably she and all things will one day lie in those depths. But the woman is young and her instinct is to live. The Yupik woman knows how to do this.

44   Inside the small cabin of logs and tundra sod, the old Storyteller is mumbling the last story he will ever tell. It is the story of the hunter stalking a giant polar bear the color of the blue glacier ice. It is a story which the old Storyteller has been telling since the young Yupik woman began to arrange the white trader's death. But a sudden storm develops. The hunter finds himself on an ice floe off shore. Visibility is zero, and the scream of the wind blots out all sound. Quickly the hunter realizes he is being stalked. Hunted by all the forces, by all the elements of the sky and earth around him. When at last the hunter's own muscles spasm and cause the jade knife to fall and shatter the ice, the hunter's death in the embrace of the giant ice blue bear is the foretelling of the world's end. When humans have blasted and burned the last bit of life from the earth, an immeasurable freezing will descend with a darkness that obliterates the sun.

RESPONDING TO READING

1. Contrast Silko's approach to understanding nature to Hawking's (p. 572). What makes their writing so different? What assumptions about nature, human interaction with nature, and ways of understanding nature inform Silko's essay?

2. Silko values "magic" and "the spirit dimensions" (paragraph 9) as part of the interaction of land with people; the "collective memory" transmits culture and storytelling conveys knowledge. Define what Silko finds important and why.

3. The tale of Estrucuyo (paragraph 19) explains the giant sandstone boulder. Examine the tale and show how it exemplifies the Pueblo way of knowing and understanding what is important.

4. The Yupik story at the end seems to deny the point Silko makes about the uniqueness of the Pueblo way of life. Does it? What are the similarities and differences between the two cultures, as shown in their stories?

5. Silko's explanation of the relation of humans to nature suggests much about the Pueblos, Apaches, and Hopi. In what ways does this view of how people should live in time and landscape relate to issues in current America? "Survival in any landscape," Silko says, "comes down to making the best use of all available resources." What does that statement mean to you, in your particular environment? What are its implications for your survival? Your grandchildren's?

6. Tell your readers (or listeners) a story that is told in your family, and explain what it means or let the meaning emerge through the characters and actions. Assume that your audience does not know you or your family well, if at all; they may be able to respond to the story's common human elements, but you will need to supply the individualizing specific details. In what ways does this story help you "hear who [you] are" (see paragraphs 12–21)?

Where I Lived and What I Lived For

HENRY DAVID THOREAU

Although "Where I Lived and What I Lived For" by Henry David Thoreau [for biographical information, see p. 370] is famous as a philosophical manifesto and meditation on nature, it is, like its author, individualistic and highly unconventional. Thoreau describes and interprets his "experiment" in the woods as a way of raising his own consciousness and that of his readers: "I do not propose to write an ode to dejection, but to brag as lustily as chanticleer in the morning . . . if only to wake my neighbors up." He wrote to put heaven and earth in proper perspective, to find out what is essential to a good life well lived, and what is not. Thoreau's rustic, down to earth, back-to-the-woods persona is carefully contrived; his writing is always informed by classical learning, wide reading, and the philosopher's sophisticated mind.

I went to the woods because I wished to live deliberately, to front   1
only the essential facts of life, and see if I could not learn what it had to teach, and not, when I came to die, discover that I had not lived. I did not wish to live what was not life, living is so dear; nor did I wish to

practise resignation, unless it was quite necessary. I wanted to live deep and suck out all the marrow of life, to live so sturdily and Spartan-like as to put to rout all that was not life, to cut a broad swath and shave close, to drive life into a corner, and reduce it to its lowest terms, and, if it proved to be mean, why then to get the whole and genuine meanness of it, and publish its meanness to the world; or if it were sublime, to know it by experience, and be able to give a true account of it in my next excursion. For most men, it appears to me, are in a strange uncertainty about it, whether it is of the devil or of God, and have *somewhat hastily* concluded that it is the chief end of man here to "glorify God and enjoy him forever."

2   Still we live meanly, like ants; though the fable tells us that we were long ago changed into men; like pygmies we fight with cranes; it is error upon error, and clout upon clout, and our best virtue has for its occasion a superfluous and evitable wretchedness. Our life is frittered away by detail. An honest man has hardly need to count more than his ten fingers, or in extreme cases he may add his ten toes, and lump the rest. Simplicity, simplicity, simplicity! I say, let your affairs be as two or three, and not a hundred or a thousand; instead of a million count half a dozen, and keep your accounts on your thumb-nail. In the midst of this chopping sea of civilized life, such are the clouds and storms and quicksands and thousand-and-one items to be allowed for, that a man has to live, if he would not founder and go to the bottom and not make his port at all, by dead reckoning, and he must be a great calculator indeed who succeeds. Simplify, simplify. Instead of three meals a day, if it be necessary eat but one; instead of a hundred dishes, five; and reduce other things in proportion. Our life is like a German Confederacy, made up of petty states, with its boundary forever fluctuating, so that even a German cannot tell you how it is bounded at any moment. The nation itself, with all its so-called internal improvements, which, by the way are all external and superficial, is just such an unwieldy and overgrown establishment, cluttered with furniture and tripped up by its own traps, ruined by luxury and heedless expense, by want of calculation and a worthy aim, as the million households in the lands; and the only cure for it, as for them, is in a rigid economy, a stern and more than Spartan simplicity of life and elevation of purpose. It lives too fast. Men think that it is essential that the *Nation* have commerce, and export ice, and talk through a telegraph, and ride thirty miles an hour, without a doubt, whether *they* do or not; but whether we should live like baboons or like men, is a little uncertain. If we do not get out sleepers, and forge rails, and devote days and nights to the work, but go to tinkering upon our *lives* to improve *them*, who will build railroads? And if railroads are not built, how shall we get to heaven in season? But if we stay at home and mind our business, who will want rail-

roads? We do not ride on the railroad; it rides upon us. Did you ever think what those sleepers are that underlie the railroad? Each one is a man, an Irishman, or a Yankee man. The rails are laid on them, and they are covered with sand, and the cars run smoothly over them. They are sound sleepers, I assure you. And every few years a new lot is laid down and run over; so that, if some have the pleasure of riding on a rail, others have the misfortune to be ridden upon. And when they run over a man that is walking in his sleep, a supernumerary sleeper in the wrong position, and wake him up, they suddenly stop the cars, and make a hue and cry about it, as if this were an exception. I am glad to know that it takes a gang of men for every five miles to keep the sleepers down and level in their beds as it is, for this is a sign that they may sometimes get up again.

Why should we live with such hurry and waste of life? We are de- 3
termined to be starved before we are hungry. Men say that a stitch in time saves nine, and so they take a thousand stitches today to save nine to-morrow. As for *work*, we haven't any of any consequence. We have the Saint Vitus' dance, and cannot possibly keep our heads still. If I should only give a few pulls at the parish bell-rope, as for a fire, that is, without setting the bell, there is hardly a man on his farm in the outskirts of Concord, notwithstanding that press of engagements which was his excuse so many times this morning, nor a boy, nor a woman, I might almost say, but would forsake all and follow that sound, not mainly to save property from the flames, but, if we will confess the truth, much more to see it burn, since burn it must, and we, be it known, did not set it on fire,—or to see it put out, and have a hand in it, if that is done as handsomely; yes, even if it were the parish church itself. Hardly a man takes a half-hour's nap after dinner, but when he wakes he holds up his head and asks, "What's the news?" as if the rest of mankind had stood his sentinels. Some give directions to be waked every half-hour, doubtless for no other purpose; and then, to pay for it, they tell what they have dreamed. After a night's sleep the news is as indispensable as the breakfast. "Pray tell me anything new that has happened to a man anywhere on this globe,"—and he reads over his coffee and rolls, that a man has had his eyes gouged out this morning on the Wachito River; never dreaming the while that he lives in the dark unfathomed mammoth cave of this world, and has but the rudiment of an eye himself.

For my part, I could easily do without the post-office. I think that 4
there are very few important communications made through it. To speak critically, I never received more than one or two letters in my life—I wrote this some years ago—that were worth the postage. The penny-post is, commonly, an institution through which you seriously offer a man that penny for his thoughts which is so often safely offered

in jest. And I am sure that I never read any memorable news in a newspaper. If we read of one man robbed, or murdered, or killed by accident, or one house burned, or one vessel wrecked, or one steamboat blown up, or one cow run over on the Western Railroad, or one mad dog killed, or one lot of grasshoppers in the winter,—we never need read of another. One is enough. If you are acquainted with the principle, what do you care for a myriad instances and applications? To a philosopher all *news*, as it is called, is gossip, and they who edit and read it are old women over their tea. Yet not a few are greedy after this gossip. There was such a rush, as I hear, the other day at one of the offices to learn the foreign news by the last arrival, that several large squares of plate glass belonging to the establishment were broken by the pressure,—news which I seriously think a ready wit might write a twelvemonth, or twelve years, beforehand with sufficient accuracy. As for Spain, for instance, if you know how to throw in Don Carlos and the Infanta, and Don Pedro and Seville and Granada, from time to time in the right proportions,—they may have changed the names a little since I saw the papers,—and serve up a bull-fight when other entertainments fail, it will be true to the letter, and give us as good an idea of the exact state or ruin of things in Spain as the most succinct and lucid reports under this head in the newspapers: and as for England, almost the last significant scrap of news from that quarter was the revolution of 1649; and if you have learned the history of her crops for an average year, you never need attend to that thing again, unless your speculations are of a merely pecuniary character. If one may judge who rarely looks into the newspapers, nothing new does ever happen in foreign parts, a French revolution not excepted.

5   What news! how much more important to know what that is which was never old ! "Kieou-he-yu (great dignitary of the state of Wei) sent a man to Khoung-tseu to know his news. Khoung-tseu caused the messenger to be seated near him, and questioned him in these terms: What is your master doing? The messenger answered with respect: My master desires to diminish the number of his faults, but he cannot come to the end of them. The messenger being gone, the philosopher remarked: What a worthy messenger! What a worthy messenger!" The preacher, instead of vexing the ears of drowsy farmers on their day of rest at the end of the week,—for Sunday is the fit conclusion of an ill-spent week, and not the fresh and brave beginning of a new one,—with this one other draggle-tail of a sermon, should shout with thundering voice, "Pause! Avast! Why so seeming fast, but deadly slow?"

6   Shams and delusions are esteemed for soundless truths, while reality is fabulous. If men would steadily observe realities only, and not allow themselves to be deluded, life, to compare it with such things as we know, would be like a fairy tale and the Arabian Nights Entertain-

ments. If we respected only what is inevitable and has a right to be, music and poetry would resound along the streets. When we are unhurried and wise, we perceive that only great and worthy things have any permanent and absolute existence, that petty fears and petty pleasures are but the shadow of the reality. This is always exhilarating and sublime. By closing the eyes and slumbering, and consenting to be deceived by shows, men establish and confirm their daily life of routine and habit everywhere, which still is built on purely illusory foundations. Children, who play life, discern its true law and relations more clearly than men, who fail to live it worthily, but who think that they are wiser by experience, that is, by failure. I have read in a Hindoo book, that "there was a king's son, who, being expelled in infancy from his native city, was brought up by a forester, and, growing up to maturity in that state, imagined himself to belong to the barbarous race with which he lived. One of his father's ministers having discovered him, revealed to him what he was, and the misconception of his character was removed, and he knew himself to be a prince. So soul," continues the Hindoo philosopher, "from the circumstances in which it is placed, mistakes its own character, until the truth is revealed to it by some holy teacher, and then it knows itself to be *Brahme*." I perceive that we inhabitants of New England live this mean life that we do because our vision does not penetrate the surface of things. We think that that *is* which *appears* to be. If a man should walk through this town and see only the reality, where, think you, would the "Mill-dam" go to? If he should give us an account of the realities he beheld there, we should not recognize the place in his description. Look at the meeting-house, or a court-house, or a jail, or a shop, or a dwelling-house, and say what that thing really is before a true gaze, and they would all go to pieces in your account of them. Men esteem truth remote, in the outskirts of the system, behind the farthest star, before Adam and after the last man. In eternity there is indeed something true and sublime. But all these times and places and occasions are now and here. God himself culminates in the present moment, and will never be more divine in the lapse of all the ages. And we are enabled to apprehend at all what is sublime and noble only by the perpetual instilling and drenching of the reality that surrounds us. The universe constantly and obediently answers to our conceptions; whether we travel fast or slow, the track is laid for us. Let us spend our lives in conceiving then. The poet or the artist never yet had so fair and noble a design but some of his posterity at least could accomplish it.

Let us spend one day as deliberately as Nature, and not be thrown   7
off the track by every nutshell and mosquito's wing that falls on the rails. Let us rise early and fast, or breakfast, gently and without perturbation; let company come and let company go, let the bells ring and

the children cry,—determined to make a day of it. Why should we knock under and go with the stream? Let us not be upset and overwhelmed in that terrible rapid and whirlpool called a dinner, situated in the meridian shallows. Weather this danger and you are safe, for the rest of the way is down hill. With unrelaxed nerves, with morning vigor, sail by it, looking another way, tied to the mast like Ulysses. If the engine whistles, let it whistle till it is hoarse for its pains. If the bell rings, why should we run? We will consider what kind of music they are like. Let us settle ourselves, and work and wedge our feet downward through the mud and slush of opinion, and prejudice, and tradition, and delusion, and appearance, that alluvion which covers the globe, through Paris and London, through New York and Boston and Concord, through Church and State, through poetry and philosophy and religion, till we come to a hard bottom and rocks in place, which we can call *reality*, and say, This is, and no mistake; and then begin, having a *point d'appui*, below freshet and frost and fire, a place where you might found a wall or a state, or set a lamp-post safely, or perhaps a gauge, not a Nilometer, but a Realometer, that future ages might know how deep a freshet of shams and appearances had gathered from time to time. If you stand right fronting and face to face to a fact, you will see the sun glimmer on both its surfaces, as if it were a cimeter, and feel its sweet edge dividing you through the heart and marrow, and so you will happily conclude your mortal career. Be it life or death, we crave only reality. If we are really dying, let us hear the rattle in our throats and feel cold in the extremities; if we are alive, let us go about our business.

8   Time is but the stream I go a-fishing in. I drink at it; but while I drink I see the sandy bottom and detect how shallow it is. Its thin current slides away, but eternity remains. I would drink deeper; fish in the sky, whose bottom is pebbly with stars. I cannot count one. I know not the first letter of the alphabet. I have always been regretting that I was not as wise as the day I was born. The intellect is a cleaver; it discerns and rifts its way into the secret of things. I do not wish to be any more busy with my hands than is necessary. My head is hands and feet. I feel all my best faculties concentrated in it. My instinct tells me that my head is an organ for burrowing, as some creatures use their snout and fore paws, and with it I would mine and burrow my way through these hills. I think that the richest vein is somewhere hereabouts; so by the divining-rod and thin rising vapors I judge; and here I will begin to mine.

RESPONDING TO READING

1. How does Thoreau deliberate about where he might build his home? What features of the location are important to him and why? What part does imagination play in his deliberations?

2. For Thoreau, how is a poet's cultivation of a piece of land different from that of a farmer? How is the poet's work superior?

3. What events does Thoreau describe as he builds his home, as he takes possession of his property? What does he change about the land and what does he preserve? Why?

4. How does Thoreau transform his time on this land into a series of spiritual events? Select one event that he describes, and explain its significance to him. He expects the reader to share this significance; has he convinced you? Why or why not?

5. In an essay, describe for someone unfamiliar with the location either the place you live now or a place where you once lived or used as a physical or spiritual retreat. This may be a geographic location, a specific house or building, or piece of land or body of water. What was or is important about that place? How have you/did you change this place to fit your needs? How has this place changed you?

The Obligation to Endure
Rachel Carson

Rachel Carson (1907–1964), a biologist, was also an ardent conservationist. In the Cold War era, when threats of nuclear bombs and promises of "better living through chemistry" were commonplace, Carson took an environmentalist stance that at the time was considered radical and controversial. In "The Obligation to Endure," from *Silent Spring* (1962), Carson attacked the "crusade to create a chemically sterile, insect-free world" in which "many specialists and most of the so-called control [regulatory] agencies" were engaged. Throughout *Silent Spring* she contended what has since been proven, that there was an arsenal of widely used chemical pesticides and herbicides that wrought far more destruction than they prevented. Her earlier, less controversial, books were *Under the Sea Wind: A Naturalist's Picture of Ocean Life* (1941); *The Sea Around Us* (1951), winner of the National Book Award; and *The Edge of the Sea* (1955).

Carson was strongly influenced by her mother who, she said, embodied Albert Schweitzer's" "'reverence for life' more than anyone I know." She earned a bachelor's degree in biology from the Pennsylvania College for Women in 1929 and a master's degree in biology from Johns Hopkins in 1932. For fifteen years, Carson edited publications for the U.S. Fish and Wildlife Service, until 1951, when her books earned enough royalties to enable her to write full time. *Silent Spring* spoke just in time, and Carson's legacy survives her. Since her death, the federal government has passed the Endangered Species Preservation Act and other legislation requiring that all federal departments protect endangered species and their habitats, forbidding trade in such species, and regulating the uses of pesticides.

1   The history of life on earth has been a history of interaction between living things and their surroundings. To a large extent, the physical form and the habits of the earth's vegetation and its animal life have been molded by the environment. Considering the whole span of earthly time, the opposite effect, in which life actually modifies its surroundings, has been relatively slight. Only within the moment of time represented by the present century has one species—man—acquired significant power to alter the nature of his world.

2   During the past quarter century this power has not only increased to one of disturbing magnitude but it has changed in character. The most alarming of all man's assaults upon the environment is the contamination of air, earth, rivers, and sea with dangerous and even lethal materials. This pollution is for the most part irrecoverable; the chain of evil it initiates not only in the world that must support life but in living tissues is for the part irreversible. In this now universal contamination of the environment, chemicals are the sinister and little-recognized partners of radiation in changing the very nature of the world—the very nature of its life. Strontium 90, released through nuclear explosions into the air, comes to earth in rain or drifts down as fallout, lodges in soil, enters into the grass or corn or wheat grown there, and in time takes up its abode in the bones of a human being, there to remain until his death. Similarly, chemicals sprayed on croplands or forests or gardens lie long in soil, entering into living organisms, passing from one to another in a chain of poisoning and death. Or they pass mysteriously by underground streams until they emerge and, through the alchemy of air and sunlight, combine into new forms that kill vegetation, sicken cattle, and work unknown harm on those who drink from once pure wells. As Albert Schweitzer has said, "Man can hardly even recognize the devils of his own creation."

3   It took hundreds of millions of years to produce the life that now inhabits the earth—eons of time in which that developing and evolving and diversifying life reached a state of adjustment and balance with its surroundings. The environment, rigorously shaping and directing the life it supported, contained elements that were hostile as well as supporting. Certain rocks gave out dangerous radiation; even within the light of the sun, from which life draws it energy, there were shortwave radiations with power to injure. Given time—time not in years but in millennia—life adjusts, and a balance has been reached. For time is the essential ingredient; but in the modern world there is no time.

4   The rapidity of change and the speed with which new situations are created follow the impetuous and heedless pace of man rather than the deliberate pace of nature. Radiation is no longer merely the background radiation of rocks, the bombardment of cosmic rays, the ultraviolet of the sun that have existed before there was any life on earth; radiation is now the unnatural creation of man's tampering with the

atom. The chemicals to which life is asked to make its adjustment are no longer merely the calcium and silica and copper and all the rest of the minerals washed out of the rocks and carried in rivers to the sea; they are the synthetic creations of man's inventive mind, brewed in his laboratories, and having no counterparts in nature.

To adjust to these chemicals would require time on the scale that is   5 nature's; it would require not merely the years of a man's life but the life of generations. And even this, were it by some miracle possible, would be futile, for the new chemicals come from our laboratories in an endless stream; almost five hundred annually find their way into actual use in the United States alone. The figure is staggering and its implications are not easily grasped—500 new chemicals to which the bodies of men and animals are required somehow to adapt each year, chemicals totally outside the limits of biologic experience.

Among them are many that are used in man's war against nature.   6 Since the mid-1940s over 200 basic chemicals have been created for use in killing insects, weeds, rodents, and other organisms described in the modern vernacular as "pests"; and they are sold under several thousand different brand names.

These sprays, dusts, and aerosols are now applied almost univer-   7 sally to farms, gardens, forests, and homes—nonselective chemicals that have the power to kill every insect, the "good" and the "bad," to still the song of birds and the leaping of fish in the streams, to coat the leaves with a deadly film, and to linger on in soil—all this though the intended target may be only a few weeds or insects. Can anyone believe it is possible to lay down such a barrage of poisons on the surface of the earth without making it unfit for all life? They should not be called "insecticides," but "biocides."

The whole process of spraying seems caught up in an endless spi-   8 ral. Since DDT was released for civilian use, a process of escalation has been going on in which ever more toxic materials must be found. This has happened because insects, in a triumphant vindication of Darwin's principle of the survival of the fittest, have evolved super races immune to the particular insecticide used, hence a deadlier one has always to be developed—and then a deadlier one than that. It has happened because, for reasons to be described later, destructive insects often undergo a "flareback," or resurgence, after spraying, in numbers greater than before. Thus the chemical war is never won, and all life is caught in its violent crossfire.

Along with the possibility of the extinction of mankind by nuclear   9 war, the central problem of our age has therefore become the contamination of man's total environment with such substances of incredible potential for harm—substances that accumulate in the tissues of plants and animals and even penetrate the germ cells to shatter or alter the very material of heredity upon which the shape of the future depends.

10   Some would-be architects of our future look toward a time when it will be possible to alter the human germ plasm by design. But we may easily be doing so now by inadvertence, for many chemicals, like radiation, bring about gene mutations. It is ironic to think that man might determine his own future by something so seemingly trivial as the choice of an insect spray.

11   All this has been risked—for what? Future historians may well be amazed by our distorted sense of proportion. How could intelligent beings seek to control a few unwanted species by a method that contaminated the entire environment and brought the threat of disease and death even to their own kind? Yet this is precisely what we have done. We have done it, moreover, for reasons that collapse the moment we examine them. We are told that the enormous and expanding use of pesticides is necessary to maintain farm production. Yet is our real problem not one of *overproduction*? Our farms, despite measures to remove acreages from production and to pay farmers *not* to produce, have yielded such a staggering excess of crops that the American taxpayer in 1962 is paying out more than one billion dollars a year as the total carrying cost of the surplus-food storage program. And is the situation helped when one branch of the Agriculture Department tries to reduce production while another states, as it did in 1958, "It is believed generally that reduction of crop acreages under provisions of the Soil Bank will stimulate interest in use of chemicals to obtain maximum production on the land retained in crops."

12   All this is not to say there is no insect problem and no need of control. I am saying, rather, that control must be geared to realities, not to mythical situations, and that the methods employed must be such that they do not destroy us along with the insects.

13   The problem whose attempted solution has brought such a train of disaster in its wake is an accompaniment of our modern way of life. Long before the age of man, insects inhabited the earth—a group of extraordinarily varied and adaptable beings. Over the course of time since man's advent, a small percentage of the more than half a million species of insects have come into conflict with human welfare in two principal ways: as competitors for the food supply and as carriers of human disease.

14   Disease-carrying insects become important where human beings are crowded together, especially under conditions where sanitation is poor, as in time of natural disaster or war or in situations of extreme poverty and deprivation. Then control of some sort becomes necessary. It is a sobering fact, however, as we shall presently see, that the method of massive chemical control has had only limited success, and also threatens to worsen the very conditions it is intended to curb.

Under primitive agriculturel conditions the farmer had few insect   15
problems. These arose with the intensification of agriculture—the devotion of immense acreages to a single crop. Such a system set the stage
for explosive increases in specific insect populations. Single-crop farming does not take advantage of the principles by which nature works; it
is agriculture as an engineer might conceive it to be. Nature has introduced great variety into the landscape, but man has displayed a passion for simplifying it. Thus he undoes the built-in checks and balances
by which nature holds the species within bounds. One important natural check is a limit on the amount of suitable habitat for each species.
Obviously then, an insect that lives on wheat can build up its population to much higher levels on a farm devoted to wheat than on one in
which wheat is intermingled with other crops to which the insect is
not adapted.

The same thing happens in other situations. A generation or more   16
ago, the towns of large areas of the United States lined their streets with
the noble elm tree. Now the beauty they hopefully created is threatened with complete destruction as disease sweeps through the elms,
carried by a beetle that would have only limited chance to build up
large populations and to spread from tree to tree if the elms were only
occasional trees in a richly diversified planting.

Another factor in the modern insect problem is one that must be   17
viewed against a background of geologic and human history: the
spreading of thousands of different kinds of organisms from their native homes to invade new territories. This worldwide migration has
been studied and graphically described by the British ecologist Charles
Elton in his recent book *The Ecology of Invasions*. During the Cretaceous
period, some hundred million years ago, flooding seas cut many land
bridges between continents and living things found themselves confined in what Elton calls "colossal separate nature reserves." There, isolated from others of their kind, they developed many new species.
When some of the land masses were joined again, about 15 million
years ago, these species began to move out into new territories—a
movement that is not only still in progress but is now receiving considerable assistance from man.

The importation of plants is the primary agent in the modern   18
spread of species, for animals have almost invariably gone along with
the plants, quarantine being a comparatively recent and not completely effective innovation. The United States Office of Plant Introduction
alone has introduced almost 200,000 species and varieties of plants
from all over the world. Nearly half of the 180 or so major insect enemies of plants in the United States are accidental imports from abroad,
and most of them have come as hitchhikers on plants.

19   In new territory, out of reach of the restraining hand of the natural enemies that kept down its numbers in its native land, an invading plant or animal is able to become enormously abundant. Thus it is no accident that our most troublesome insects are introduced species.

20   These invasions, both the naturally occurring and those dependent on human assistance, are likely to continue indefinitely. Quarantine and massive chemical campaigns are only extremely expensive ways of buying time. We are faced, according to Dr. Elton, "with a life-and-death need not just to find new technological means of suppressing this plant or that animal"; instead we need the basic knowledge of animal populations and their relations to their surroundings that will "promote an even balance and damp down the explosure power of outbreaks and new invasions."

21   Much of the necessary knowledge is now available but we do not use it. We train ecologists in our universities and even employ them in our governmental agencies but we seldom take their advice. We allow the chemical death rain to fall as though there were no alternative, whereas in fact there are many, and our ingenuity could soon discover many more if given opportunity.

22   Have we fallen into a mesmerized state that makes us accept as inevitable that which is inferior or detrimental, as though having lost the will or the vision to demand that which is good? Such thinking, in the words of the ecologist Paul Shepard, "idealizes life with only its head out of water, inches above the limits of toleration of the corruption of its own environment. . . . Why should we tolerate a diet of weak poisons, a home in insipid surroundings, a circle of acquaintances who are not quite our enemies, the noise of motors with just enough relief to prevent insanity? Who would want to live in a world which is just not quite fatal?"

23   Yet such a world is pressed upon us. The crusade to create a chemically sterile, insect-free world seems to have engendered a fanatic zeal on the part of many specialists and most of the so-called control agencies. On every hand there is evidence that those engaged in spraying operations exercise a ruthless power. "The regulatory entomologists . . . function as prosecutor, judge and jury, tax assessor and collector and sheriff to enforce their own orders," said Connecticut entomologist Neely Turner. The most flagrant abuses go unchecked in both state and federal agencies.

24   It is not my contention that chemical insecticides must never be used. I do contend that we have put poisonous and biologically potent chemicals indiscriminately into the hands of persons largely or wholly ignorant of their potentials for harm. We have subjected enormous numbers of people to contact with these poisons, without their consent and often without their knowledge. If the Bill of Rights contains no guarantee that a citizen shall be secure against lethal poisons distrib-

uted either by private individuals or by public officials, it is surely only because our forefathers, despite their considerable wisdom and foresight, could conceive of no such problem.

I contend, furthermore, that we have allowed these chemicals to be 25 used with little or no advance investigation of their effect on soil, water, wildlife, and man himself. Future generations are unlikely to condone our lack of prudent concern for the integrity of the natural world that supports all life.

There is still very limited awareness of the nature of the threat. This 26 is an era of specialists, each of whom sees his own problem and is unaware of or intolerant of the larger frame into which it fits. It is also an era dominated by industry, in which the right to make a dollar at whatever cost is seldom challenged. When the public protests, confronted with some obvious evidence of damaging results of pesticide applications, it is fed little tranquilizing pills of half truth. We urgently need an end to these false assurances, to the sugar coating of unpalatable facts. It is the public that is being asked to assume the risks that the insect controllers calculate. The public must decide whether it wishes to continue on the present road, and it can do so only when in full possession of the facts. In the words of Jean Rostand, "The obligation to endure gives us the right to know."

RESPONDING TO READING

1. Carson refers to "man's war against nature" (paragraph 6). Indeed, people use many metaphors of combat and aggression in discussing the relation of humans to the natural world. Why do they conceive of the relationship as adversarial? Is this inevitable?

2. When she wrote "The Obligation to Endure" in 1962, Carson said, "The method of massive chemical control has had only limited success, and threatens to worsen the very conditions it is intended to curb" (paragraph 14). To what extent has her prediction come true?

3. Carson says that the "United States Office of Plant Introduction alone has introduced almost 200,000 species and varieties of plants from all over the world" into the United States (paragraph 18). What advantages can you think of in importing plant species? What disadvantages are there?

4. What are the advantages of trying to create "a chemically sterile, insect-free" world? What are the disadvantages?

5. Write an essay in which you describe an ideal relationship of people and nature. You may focus on a particular aspect of nature, such as a specific species of animal or plant; or a particular type of setting (desert, ocean) or a specific location (your state, hometown, or own backyard); or a natural phenomenon, such as the quality of air or water.

Troubled Waters

SANDRA POSTEL

In a world in which the mismanagement of water is leading to agricultural problems and even violence over water rights, Sandra Postel is a leading advocate for change: "I've been involved in water issues since I left graduate school," she told an e.magazine.com interviewer. "I've always had this fascination with water and a feeling of connection to it. Maybe it has something to do with growing up near the ocean on the south shore of Long Island, but it's been my principal passion." Her commitment has placed Postel at the forefront of the movement for water conservation and management. After studying geology and political science at Wittenberg University and resource economics and policy at Duke University, she became vice president for research at the Worldwatch Institute, a Washington-based environmental policy organization, where she retains an affiliation as senior fellow. From 1994 to 1996 she was adjunct professor of international environmental policy at the Fletcher School of Law and Diplomacy at Tufts University, and she currently serves as director of the Global Water Policy Project in Amherst, Massachusetts. Postel's books include *Last Oasis: Facing Water Scarcity* (1992), which was the basis for a 1997 PBS documentary, and *Pillar of Sand: Can the Irrigation Miracle Last?* (1999). She has published over 100 articles in periodicals including *Science, Natural History,* and *Scientific American* and has been featured on radio and television programs. Her honors include an honorary doctor-of-science degree from the Massachusetts College of Liberal Arts and a position as Pew fellow in conservation and the environment.

"Troubled Waters," originally published in *The Sciences* and collected in *Best American Science and Nature Writing* (2001), argues for a perspective on water beyond the technological and scientific: "The fact that water is essential to life lends an ethical dimension to every decision we make about how it is used, managed, and distributed." Bearing witness to disaster areas such as the Aral Sea region in central Asia and the Colorado River delta and using statistical evidence, Postel outlines the extent of the problem and some possible remedies.

1   In June 1991, after a leisurely lunch in the fashionable Washington, D.C., neighborhood of Dupont Circle, Alexei Yablokov, then a Soviet parliamentarian, told me something shocking. Some years back he had had a map hanging on his office wall depicting Soviet central Asia without the vast Aral Sea. Cartographers had drawn it in the 1960s, when the Aral was still the world's fourth-largest inland body of water.

2   I felt for a moment like a cold war spy to whom a critical secret had just been revealed. The Aral Sea, as I knew well, was drying up. The existence of such a map implied that its ongoing destruction was no acci-

dent. Moscow's central planners had decided to sacrifice the sea, judging that the two rivers feeding it could be put to more valuable use irrigating cotton in the central Asian desert. Such a planned elimination of an ecosystem nearly the size of Ireland was surely one of humanity's more arrogant acts.

Four years later, when I traveled to the Aral Sea region, the Soviet   3
Union was no more; the central Asian republics were now independent. But the legacy of Moscow's policies lived on: thirty-five years of siphoning the region's rivers had decreased the Aral's volume by nearly two thirds and its surface area by half. I stood on what had once been a seaside bluff outside the former port town of Muynak, but I could see no water. The sea was twenty-five miles away. A graveyard of ships lay before me, rotting and rusting in the dried-up seabed. Sixty thousand fishing jobs had vanished, and thousands of people had left the area. Many of those who remained suffered from a variety of cancers, respiratory ailments, and other diseases. Winds ripping across the desert were lifting tens of millions of tons of a toxic salt-dust chemical residue from the exposed seabed each year and dumping it on surrounding croplands and villages. Dust storms and polluted rivers made it hazardous to breathe the air and drink the water.

The tragedy of the Aral Sea is by no means unique. Around the world   4
countless rivers, lakes, and wetlands are succumbing to dams, river diversions, rampant pollution, and other pressures. Collectively they underscore what is rapidly emerging as one of the greatest challenges facing humanity in the decades to come: how to satisfy the thirst of a world population pushing nine billion by the year 2050, while protecting the health of the aquatic environment that sustains all terrestrial life.

The problem, though daunting, is not insurmountable. A number   5
of technologies and management practices are available that could substantially reduce the amount of water used by agriculture, industry, and households. But the sad reality is that the rules and policies that drive water-related decisions have not adequately promoted them. We have the ability to provide both people and ecosystems with the water they need for good health, but those goals need to be elevated on the political agenda.

Observed from space, our planet seems wealthy in water beyond measure.   6
sure. Yet most of the earth's vast blueness is ocean, far too salty to drink or to irrigate most crops. Only about 2.5 percent of all the water on earth is fresh water, and two thirds of that is locked away in glaciers and ice caps. A minuscule share of the world's water—less than one hundredth of 1 percent—is both drinkable and renewed each year through rainfall and other precipitation. And though that freshwater supply is renewable, it is also finite. The quantity available today is the

same that was available when civilizations first arose thousands of years ago, and so the amount of water that should be allotted to each person has declined steadily with time. It has dropped by 58 percent since 1950, as the population climbed from 2.5 billion to 6 billion, and will fall an additional 33 percent within fifty years if our numbers reach 8.9 billion, the middle of the projected range.

7   Because rainfall and river flows are not distributed evenly throughout the year or across the continents, the task of adapting water to human use is not an easy one. Many rivers are tempestuous and erratic, running high when water is needed least and low when it is needed most. Every year two thirds of the water in the earth's rivers rushes untapped to the sea in floods. An additional one fifth flows in remote areas such as the Amazon basin and the Arctic tundra. In many developing countries monsoons bring between 70 and 80 percent of the year's rainfall in just three months, greatly complicating water management. When it comes to water, it seems, nature has dealt a difficult hand.

8   As a result, the history of water management has largely been one of striving to capture, control, and deliver water to cities and farms when and where they need it. Engineers have built massive canal networks to irrigate regions that are otherwise too dry to support the cultivation and growth of crops. The area of irrigated land worldwide has increased more than thirtyfold in the past two centuries, turning near-deserts such as southern California and Egypt into food baskets. Artificial oasis cities have bloomed. In Phoenix, Arizona, which gets about seven inches of rain a year, seemingly abundant water pours from taps. With a swimming pool, lawn, and an array of modern appliances, a Phoenix household can readily consume 700 gallons of water a day.

9   But while the affluent enjoy desert swimming pools, more than a billion of the world's people lack a safe supply of drinking water, and 2.8 billion do not have even minimal sanitation. The World Health Organization estimates that 250 million cases of water-related diseases such as cholera arise annually, resulting in between 5 and 10 million deaths. Intestinal worms infect some 1.5 billion people, killing as many as 100,000 a year. Outbreaks of parasitic diseases have sometimes followed the construction of large dams and irrigation systems, which create standing bodies of water where the parasites' hosts can breed. In sub-Saharan Africa, many women and girls walk several miles a day just to collect water for their families. Tens of millions of poor farm families cannot afford to irrigate their land, which lowers their crop productivity and leaves them vulnerable to droughts.

10   Even in countries in which water and sanitation are taken for granted, there are disturbing trends. Much of the earth's stable year-round water supply resides underground in geologic formations called aquifers. Some aquifers are nonrenewable—the bulk of their water ac-

cumulated thousands of years ago and they get little or no replenishment from precipitation today. And though most aquifers are replenished by rainwater seeping into the ground, in a number of the world's most important food-producing regions farmers are pumping water from aquifers faster than nature can replace it. Aquifers are overdrawn in several key regions of the United States, including California's Central Valley, which supplies half of the nation's fruits and vegetables, and the southern Great Plains, where grain and cotton farmers are steadily depleting the Ogallala, one of the planet's greatest aquifers.

The problem is particularly severe in India, where a national assessment commissioned in 1996 found that water tables in critical   11
farming regions were dropping at an alarming rate, jeopardizing perhaps as much as one fourth of the country's grain harvest. In China's north plain, where 40 percent of that nation's food is grown, water tables are plunging by more than a meter a year across a wide area.

On the basis of the best available data, I estimate that global groundwater overpumping totals at least 160 billion cubic meters a   12
year, an amount equal to the annual flow of two Nile Rivers. Because it takes roughly 1,000 cubic meters of water to produce one ton of grain, some 160 million tons of grain—nearly 10 percent of the global food supply—depend on the unsustainable practice of depleting groundwater. That raises an unsettling question: If humanity is operating under such an enormous deficit today, where are we going to find the additional water to satisfy future needs?

Another harbinger of trouble is that many major rivers now run dry for large parts of the year. Five of Asia's great rivers—the Indus and the   13
Ganges in southern Asia, the Yellow in China, and the Amu Darya and Syr Darya in the Aral Sea basin—no longer reach the sea for months at a time. The Chinese call the Yellow River their mother river, reflecting its role as the cradle of Chinese civilization. Today the Yellow River supplies water to 140 million people and 18 million acres of farmland. Yet it has run dry in its lower reaches almost every year of this past decade, and the dry section often stretches nearly 400 miles upstream from the river's mouth. In 1997 the dry spell lasted a record 226 days.

Not surprisingly, as water becomes scarce, competition for it is intensifying. Cities are beginning to divert water from farms in north-central   14
China, southern India, the Middle East, and the western United States. Moreover, the world's urban population is expected to double to 5 billion by 2025, which will further increase the pressure to shift water away from agriculture. How such a shift will affect food production, employment in rural areas, rural-to-urban migration, and social stability are critical questions that have hardly been asked, much less analyzed.

Competition for water is also building in international river basins: 15
261 of the world's rivers flow through two or more countries. In the

vast majority of those cases there are no treaties governing how the river water should be shared. As demands tax the supply in those regions, tensions are mounting. In five water hot spots—the Aral Sea region, the Ganges, the Jordan, the Nile, and the Tigris-Euphrates—the population of the nations in each basin will probably increase by at least 30 percent and possibly by as much as 70 percent by 2025.

16   The plight of the Nile basin seems particularly worrisome. Last in line for Nile water, Egypt is almost entirely dependent on the river and currently uses two thirds of its annual flow. About 85 percent of the Nile's flow originates in Ethiopia, which to date has used little of that supply but is now constructing small dams to begin tapping the upper headwaters. Meanwhile, Egypt is pursuing two large irrigation projects that have put it on a collision course with Ethiopia. Although Nile-basin countries have been meeting regularly to discuss how they can share the river, no treaty that includes all the parties yet exists. Shortly after signing the historic peace accords with Israel in 1979, Egyptian president Anwar Sadat said that only water could make Egypt wage war again. He was referring not to another potential conflict with Israel but to the possibility of hostilities with Ethiopia over the Nile.

17   The story of the shrinking Aral Sea underscores another form of competition: the conflict between the use of water in agriculture and industry, on the one hand, and its ecological role as the basis of life and sustainer of ecosystem health, on the other. After I returned from the Aral Sea, I was tempted to view the sea and the communities around it as tragic victims of Communist central planning. A year later, however, in May 1996, I visited the delta of the Colorado River and found a depressingly similar story.

18   The Colorado delta had once been lush, supporting as many as 400 plant species and numerous birds, fish, and mammals. The great naturalist Aldo Leopold, who canoed through the delta in 1922, called it "a milk and honey wilderness," a land of "a hundred green lagoons." As I walked amid salt flats, mud-cracked earth, and murky pools, I could hardly believe I was in the same place that Leopold had described. The treaties that divide the Colorado River among seven U.S. states and Mexico had set aside nothing to protect the river system itself. More water was promised to the eight treaty parties than the river actually carries in an average year. As a result, the large dams and river diversions upstream now drain so much water that virtually nothing flows through the delta and out to the Gulf of California.

19   As in the Aral Sea basin, the Colorado predicament has caused more than an environmental tragedy. The Cocopa Indians have fished and farmed in the delta for more than 1,000 years. Now their culture faces extinction because too little river water makes it to the delta.

What was gained by despoiling such cultural and biological riches, 20
by driving long-settled people from their homes and wildlife from its
habitats? The answer seems to be more swimming pools in Los Angeles, more golf courses in Arizona, and more desert agriculture. To be
sure, the tradeoff helped boost the U.S. gross national product, but at
the untallied cost of irreplaceable natural and cultural diversity.

Given the challenges that lie ahead, how can the needs of an increas- 21
ingly thirsty world be satisfied, without further destroying aquatic
ecosystems? In my view, the solution hinges on three major components: allocating water to maintain the health of natural ecosystems,
doubling the productivity of the water allocated to human activities,
and extending access to a ready supply of water to the poor.

Just as people require a minimum amount of water to maintain 22
good health, so do ecosystems—as the Aral Sea, the Colorado delta,
and numerous other areas painfully demonstrate. As the human use of
water nears the limits of the supply in many places, we must ensure the
continued functioning of ecosystems and the invaluable services they
perform. Providing that assurance will entail a major scientific initiative, aimed at determining safe limits of water usage from aquifers,
rivers, lakes, and other aquatic systems. Laws and regulations, guaran-
teeing continued health of those ecosystems, must also be put in place.

Australia and South Africa are now leading the way in such efforts. 23
Officials in Australia's Murray-Darling River basin have placed a cap
on water extractions—a bold move aimed at reversing the decline in
the health of the aquatic environment. South Africa's new water laws
call for water managers to allocate water for the protection of ecological functions as well as for human needs.

The United States is also making efforts to heal some of its dam- 24
aged aquatic environments. A joint federal-state initiative is working to
restore the health of California's San Francisco Bay delta, which is
home to more than 120 species of fish and supports 80 percent of the
state's commercial fisheries. In Florida an $8 billion federal-state pro-
ject is attempting to repair the treasured Everglades, the famed "river
of grass," which has shrunk in half in the past century alone. And
across the country a number of dams are slated for removal in an effort
to restore fisheries and other benefits of river systems.

The second essential component in meeting water needs for the fu- 25
ture will be to maximize the use of every gallon we extract. Because
agriculture accounts for 70 percent of the world's water usage, raising
water productivity in farming regions is a top priority. The bad news
is that today less than half the water removed from rivers and aquifers
for irrigation actually benefits a crop. The good news is that there
is substantial room for improvement.

26   Drip irrigation ranks near the top of measures that offer great untapped potential. A drip system is essentially a network of perforated
plastic tubing, installed on or below the soil surface, that delivers water
at low volumes directly to the roots of plants. The loss to evaporation
or runoff is minimal. When drip irrigation is combined with the monitoring of soil moisture and other ways of assessing a crop's water
needs, the system delivers 95 percent of its water to the plant, compared with between 50 and 70 percent for the more conventional flood
or furrow irrigation systems.

27   Besides saving water, drip irrigation usually boosts crop yield and
quality, simply because it enables the farmer to maintain a nearly ideal
moisture environment for the plants. In countries as diverse as India, Israel, Jordan, Spain, and the United States, studies have consistently
shown that drip irrigation not only cuts water use by between 30 and 70
percent, but also increases crop yields by between 20 and 90 percent.
Those improvements are often enough to double the water productivity.
Lands watered by drip irrigation now account for a little more than 1 percent of all irrigated land worldwide. The potential, however, is far greater.

28   The information revolution that is transforming so many facets of society also promises to play a vital role in transforming the efficiency of
water use. The state of California operates a network of more than a
hundred automated and computerized weather stations that collect
local climate data, including solar radiation, wind speed, relative humidity, rainfall, and air and soil temperature, and then transmit the
data to a central computer in Sacramento. For each remote site, the
computer calculates an evapotranspiration rate, from which farmers
can then calculate the rate at which their crops are consuming water. In
that way they can determine, quite accurately, how much water to
apply at any given time throughout the growing season.

29   As urban populations continue expanding in the decades ahead,
household consumption of water will also need to be made more efficient. As part of the National Energy Policy Act, which was signed into
law in late 1992, the United States now has federal water standards for
basic household plumbing fixtures—toilets, faucets, and showerheads.
The regulations require that manufacturers of the fixtures meet certain
standards of efficiency—thereby building conservation into urban infra-
structure. Water usage with those fixtures will be about a third less in
2025 than it would have been without the new standards. Similar laws
could also help rapidly growing Third World cities stretch their scarce
water supplies. One of the most obvious ways to raise water productivity is to use water more than once. The Israelis, for instance, reuse two
thirds of their municipal wastewater for crop production. Because both
municipal and agricultural wastewater can carry toxic substances, reuse

must be carefully monitored. But by matching appropriate water quality to various kinds of use, much more benefit can be derived from the fresh water already under human control. And that implies that more can remain in its natural state.

The third component of the solution to water security for the future is perhaps also the greatest challenge: extending water and sanitation services to the poor. Ensuring safe drinking water is one of the surest ways to reduce disease and death in developing countries. Likewise, the most direct way of reducing hunger among the rural poor is to raise their productive capacities directly. Like trickle-down economics, trickle-down food security does not work well for the poor. Greater corn production in Iowa will not alleviate hunger among the poor in India or sub-Saharan Africa. With access to affordable irrigation, however, millions of poor farmers who have largely been bypassed by the modern irrigation age can raise their productivity and incomes directly, reducing hunger and poverty at the same time. 30

In many cases the problem is not that the poor cannot afford to pay for water but that they are paying unfair prices—often more than do residents of developed nations. It is not uncommon for poor families to spend more than a quarter of their income on water. Lacking piped-in water, many must buy from vendors who charge outrageous prices, often for poor-quality water. 31

In Istanbul, Turkey, for instance, vendors charge ten times the rate paid by those who enjoy publicly supplied water; in Bombay, the overcharge is a factor of twenty. A survey of households in Port-au-Prince, Haiti, found that people connected to the water system pay about a dollar per cubic meter ($3.78 per 1,000 gallons), whereas the unconnected must buy water from vendors for between $5.50 and $16.50 per cubic meter—about twenty times the price typically paid by urban residents in the United States. 32

Cost estimates for providing universal access to water and sanitation vary widely. But even the higher-end estimates—some $50 billion a year—amount to only 7 percent of global military expenditures. A relatively minor reordering of social priorities and investments—and a more comprehensive definition of security—could enable everyone to share the benefits of clean water and adequate sanitation. 33

Equally modest expenditures could improve the lot of poor farmers. In recent years, for instance, large areas of Bangladesh have been transformed by a human-powered device called a treadle pump. When I first saw the pump in action on a trip to Bangladesh in 1998, it reminded me of a StairMaster exercise machine, and it is operated in much the same way. The operator pedals up and down on two long poles, or treadles, each attached to a cylinder. The upward stroke sucks shallow 34 groundwater into one of the cylinders, while the downward stroke of the opposite pedal expels water from the other cylinder (that was sucked in on the preceding upward stroke) into a field channel.

35   The pump costs just thirty-five dollars, and with that purchase, farm families that previously were forced to let their land lie fallow during the dry season—and go hungry for part of the year—can grow an extra crop of rice and vegetables and take the surplus to market. Each pump irrigates about half an acre, which is appropriate for the small plots that poor farmers generally cultivate. The average net annual return on the investment has been more than $100 per pump, enabling families to recoup their outlay in less than a year.

36   So far Bangladeshi farmers have purchased 1.2 million treadle pumps, thereby raising the productivity of more than 600,000 acres of farmland and injecting an additional $325 million a year into the poorest parts of the Bangladeshi economy. A private-sector network of 70 manufacturers, 830 dealers, and 2,500 installers supports the technology, creating jobs and raising incomes in urban areas as well.

37   The treadle pump is just one of many examples of small-scale, affordable irrigation technologies that can help raise the productivity and the income of poor farm families. In areas with no perennial source of water, as in the drylands of south Asia and sub-Saharan Africa, a variety of so-called water-harvesting techniques hold promise for capturing and channeling more rainwater into the soil. In parts of India, for instance, some farmers collect rainwater from the monsoon season in earth-walled embankments, then drain the stored water during the dry season. The method, known as *haveli*, enables farmers to grow crops when their fields would otherwise be barren. Israeli investigators have found that another simple practice—covering the soil between rows of plants with polyethylene sheets—helps keep rainwater in the soil by cutting down on evaporation. The method has doubled the yields of some crops.

38 To avert much misery in this new century, the ways water is priced, supplied, and allocated must be changed. Large government subsidies for irrigation, an estimated $33 billion a year worldwide, keep prices artificially low—and so fail to penalize farmers for wasting water. Inflexible laws and regulations discourage the marketing of water, leading to inefficient distribution and use. Without rules to regulate groundwater extractions, the depletion of aquifers persists. And the failure to place a value on freshwater ecosystems—their role in maintaining water quality, controlling floods, and providing wildlife habitats—has left far too little water in natural systems.

39   Will we make the right choices in the coming age of water scarcity? Our actions must ultimately be guided by more than technology or economics. The fact that water is essential to life lends an ethical dimension to

every decision we make about how it is used, managed, and distributed. We need new technologies, to be sure, but we also need a new ethic: All living things must get enough water before some get more than enough.

RESPONDING TO READING

1. Postel opens her essay with a description of the dying Aral Sea. Why? How does this example serve as a foundation for her later argument? Why might an essay for an English-speaking, American audience open with a story about the Soviet Union?

2. How does Postel illustrate the modern problems of water management? Are there examples that every reader can connect to his or her own life? Are there examples that nearly defy comprehension? Why mix the two?

3. In what ways is competition for water a regional, national, and international problem? What other problems can occur in each of these "areas" because of this competition?

4. "The fact that water is essential to life lends an ethical dimension to every decision we make about how it is used, managed, and distributed," concludes Postel (paragraph 30). What is the cultural cost of a lack of water, according to Postel? How is this cultural cost justified by those whose consumption of water causes harm to others? What ethical decisions should be made—according to Postel or to you—in determining water use and water allocation at present? And "in the coming age of water scarcity" (which may also be now)?

5. While Postel focuses most of her essay on the use of water for agricultural purposes, the competition for this dwindling resource is clearly a problem that affects everyone. In an essay, describe, for an audience that lives either in a desert area or where you do, your own water usage and that of the people you live with over the course of one week. When do you use more water than is necessary? Can you change this? Do you already act to conserve water? Conclude your analysis with a Code of Ethics for Water Use and some rules for water conservation appropriate to the area in which you live.

How Can We Interpret
and Understand the Past?

Our Picture of the Universe
STEPHEN HAWKING

"We find ourselves in a bewildering world," writes theoretical physicist Stephen Hawking (born 1942) in his best-selling *A Brief History of Time: From the Big Bang to Black Holes* (1988). "What do we know about the universe?" he asks, in a series of fundamental questions that his work attempts to answer: "How do we know it? Where did the universe come from and where is it going? Did the universe have a beginning, and if so, what happened *before* then? What is the nature of time? Will it ever come to an end?" And, perhaps most significantly, "What is our place in the universe and where did . . . we come from?" Hawking continues his exploration of these questions in *The Theory of Everything* (2002).

Hawking is a professor at Cambridge University, from which he earned a Ph.D. in 1966, after receiving a B.A. from Oxford in 1962. Despite the physical hardship of Lou Gehrig's disease, he has consistently excelled in his chosen profession. He approaches the status of the great theoretical physicists who preceded him, holding the same position at Cambridge that Isaac Newton once had; and he is often compared with Albert Einstein. Hawking seeks a "unified theory" of the universe that will explain the behavior of everything from subatomic particles to stars and planets. In his dazzling conclusions to *A Brief History of Time*, Hawking blends Einstein's theories, atomic physics, and his own geometrical models to present a scheme that allows "the universe to begin in an explosion and end in a contraction, without ever causing time itself or the laws of physics to cease to apply." Hawking has been praised for having a "natural teacher's gifts," the rare ability to explain, in plain, nonmathematical English, a host of mathematically formidable ideas about the origin and fate of the universe. As he finished writing *Black Holes and Baby Universes*, (1993) his editor advised him that each equation included in the book would cut sales by 50%; Hawking used only $E = mc^2$.

1   A well-known scientist (some say it was Bertrand Russell) once gave a public lecture on astronomy. He described how the earth orbits around the sun and how the sun, in turn, orbits around the center of a vast collection of stars called our galaxy. At the end of the lecture, a little old lady at the back of the room got up and said: "What you have told us is rubbish. The world is really a flat plate supported on the back of a giant tortoise." The scientist gave a superior smile before replying,

"What is the tortoise standing on?" "You're very clever, young man, very clever," said the old lady. "But it's turtles all the way down!"

Most people would find the picture of our universe as an infinite   2
tower of tortoises rather ridiculous, but why do we think we know better? What do we know about the universe, and how do we know it? Where did the universe come from, and where is it going? Did the universe have a beginning, and if so, what happened *before* then? What is the nature of time? Will it ever come to an end? Recent breakthroughs in physics, made possible in part by fantastic new technologies, suggest answers to some of these longstanding questions. Someday these answers may seem as obvious to us as the earth orbiting the sun—or perhaps as ridiculous as a tower of tortoises. Only time (whatever that may be) will tell.

As long ago as 340 B.C. the Greek philosopher Aristotle, in his book   3
On the Heavens, was able to put forward two good arguments for believing that the earth was a round sphere rather than a flat plate. First, he realized that eclipses of the moon were caused by the earth coming between the sun and the moon. The earth's shadow on the moon was always round, which would be true only if the earth was spherical. If the earth had been a flat disk, the shadow would have been elongated and elliptical, unless the eclipse always occurred at a time when the sun was directly under the center of the disk. Second, the Greeks knew from their travels that the North Star appeared lower in the sky when viewed in the south than it did in more northerly regions. (Since the North Star lies over the North Pole, it appears to be directly above an observer at the North Pole, but to someone looking from the equator, it appears to lie just at the horizon.) From the difference in the apparent position of the North Star in Egypt and Greece, Aristotle even quoted an estimate that the distance around the earth was 400,000 stadia. It is not known exactly what length a stadium was, but it may have been about 200 yards, which would make Aristotle's estimate about twice the currently accepted figure. The Greeks even had a third argument that the earth must be round, for why else does one first see the sails of a ship coming over the horizon, and only later see the hull?

Aristotle thought that the earth was stationary and that the sun,   4
the moon, the planets, and the stars, moved in circular orbits about the earth. He believed this because he felt, for mystical reasons, that the earth was the center of the universe, and that circular motion was the most perfect. This idea was elaborated by Ptolemy in the second century A.D. into a complete cosmological model. The earth stood at the center, surrounded by eight spheres that carried the moon, the sun, the stars, and the five planets known at the time, Mercury, Venus, Mars, Jupiter, and Saturn (Fig. 1). The planets themselves moved on smaller circles attached to their respective spheres in order to account for their rather

complicated observed paths in the sky. The outermost sphere carried the so-called fixed stars, which always stay in the same positions relative to each other but which rotate together across the sky. What lay beyond the last sphere was never made very clear, but it certainly was not part of mankind's observable universe.

5   Ptolemy's model provided a reasonably accurate system for predicting the positions of heavenly bodies in the sky. But in order to predict these positions correctly, Ptolemy had to make an assumption that the moon followed a path that sometimes brought it twice as close to the earth as at other times. And that meant that the moon ought sometimes to appear twice as big as at other times! Ptolemy recognized this flaw, but nevertheless his model was generally, although not universally, accepted. It was adopted by the Christian church as the picture of the universe that was in accordance with Scripture, for it had the great advantage that it left lots of room outside the sphere of fixed stars for heaven and hell.

6   A simple model, however, was proposed in 1514 by a Polish priest, Nicholas Copernicus. (At first, perhaps for fear of being branded a heretic by his church, Copernicus circulated his model anonymously.) His idea was that the sun was stationary at the center and that the earth and the planets moved in circular orbits around the sun. Nearly a century passed before this idea was taken seriously. Then two astronomers—the German, Johannes Kepler, and the Italian, Galileo Galilei—started publicly to support the Copernican theory, despite the

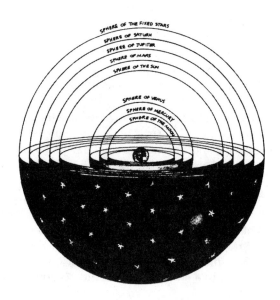

Figure 1

fact that the orbits it predicted did not quite match the ones observed. The death blow to the Aristotelian/Ptolemaic theory came in 1609. In that year, Galileo started observing the night sky with a telescope, which had just been invented. When he looked at the planet Jupiter, Galileo found that it was accompanied by several small satellites or moons that orbited around it. This implied that everything did *not* have to orbit directly around the earth, as Aristotle and Ptolemy had thought. (It was, of course, still possible to believe that the earth was stationary at the center of the universe and that the moons of Jupiter moved on extremely complicated paths around the earth, giving the *appearance* that they orbited Jupiter. However, Copernicus's theory was much simpler.) At the same time, Johannes Kepler had modified Copernicus's theory, suggesting that the planets moved not in circles but in ellipses (an ellipse is an elongated circle). The predictions now finally matched the observations.

As far as Kepler was concerned, elliptical orbits were merely an ad   7 hoc hypothesis, and a rather repugnant one at that, because ellipses were clearly less perfect than circles. Having discovered almost by accident that elliptical orbits fit the observations well, he could not reconcile them with his idea that the planets were made to orbit the sun by magnetic forces. An explanation was provided only much later, in 1687, when Sir Isaac Newton published his *Philosophiae Naturalis Principia Mathematica*, probably the most important single work ever published in the physical sciences. In it Newton not only put forward a theory of how bodies move in space and time, but he also developed the complicated mathematics needed to analyze those motions. In addition, Newton postulated a law of universal gravitation according to which each body in the universe was attracted toward every other body by a force that was stronger the more massive the bodies and the closer they were to each other. It was this same force that caused objects to fall to the ground. (The story that Newton was inspired by an apple hitting his head is almost certainly apocryphal. All Newton himself ever said was that the idea of gravity came to him as he sat "in a contemplative mood" and "was occasioned by the fall of an apple.") Newton went on to show that, according to his law, gravity causes the moon to move in an elliptical orbit around the earth and causes the earth and the planets to follow elliptical paths around the sun.

The Copernican model got rid of Ptolemy's celestial spheres, and   8 with them, the idea that the universe had a natural boundary. Since "fixed stars" did not appear to change their positions apart from a rotation across the sky caused by the earth spinning on its axis, it became natural to suppose that the fixed stars were objects like our sun but very much farther away.

Newton realized that, according to his theory of gravity, the stars   9 should attract each other, so it seemed they could not remain essentially motionless. Would they not all fall together at some point? In a letter in 1691 to Richard Bentley, another leading thinker of his day, Newton argued that this would indeed happen if there were only a finite number of stars distributed over a finite region of space. But he reasoned that if, on the other hand, there were an infinite number of stars, distributed more or less uniformly over infinite space, this would not happen, because there would not be any central point for them to fall to.

10   This argument is an instance of the pitfalls that you can encounter in talking about infinity. In an infinite universe, every point can be regarded as the center, because every point has an infinite number of stars on each side of it. The correct approach, it was realized only much later, is to consider the finite situation, in which the stars all fall in on each other, and then to ask how things change if one adds more stars roughly uniformly distributed outside this region. According to Newton's law, the extra stars would make no difference at all to the original ones on average, so the stars fall in just as fast. We can add as many stars as we like, but they will still always collapse in on themselves. We now know it is impossible to have an infinite static model of the universe in which gravity is always attractive.

11   It is an interesting reflection on the general climate of thought before the twentieth century that no one had suggested that the universe was expanding or contracting. It was generally accepted that either the universe had existed forever in an unchanging state, or that it had been created at a finite time in the past more or less as we observe it today. In part this may have been due to people's tendency to believe in eternal truths, as well as the comfort they found in the thought that even though they may grow old and die, the universe is eternal and unchanging.

12   Even those who realized that Newton's theory of gravity showed that the universe could not be static did not think to suggest that it might be expanding. Instead, they attempted to modify the theory by making the gravitational force repulsive at very large distances. This did not significantly affect their predictions of the motions of the planets, but it allowed an infinite distribution of stars to remain in equilibrium—with the attractive forces between nearby stars balanced by the repulsive forces from those that were farther away. However, we now believe such an equilibrium would be unstable: if the stars in some region got only slightly nearer each other, the attractive forces between them would become stronger and dominate over the repulsive forces so that the stars would continue to fall toward each other. On the other hand, if the stars got a bit farther away from each other, the repulsive forces would dominate and drive them farther apart.

13   Another objection to an infinite static universe is normally ascribed to the German philosopher Heinrich Olbers, who wrote about this theory in 1823. In fact, various contemporaries of Newton had raised the

problem, and the Olbers article was not even the first to contain plausible arguments against it. It was, however, the first to be widely noted. The difficulty is that in an infinite static universe nearly every line of sight would end on the surface of a star. Thus one would expect that the whole sky would be as bright as the sun, even at night. Olber's counterargument was that the light from distant stars would be dimmed by absorption by intervening matter. However, if that happened the intervening matter would eventually heat up until it glowed as brightly as the stars. The only way of avoiding the conclusion that the whole of the night sky should be as bright as the surface of the sun would be to assume that the stars had not been shining forever but had turned on at some finite time in the past. In that case the absorbing matter might not have heated up yet or the light from distant stars might not yet have reached us. And that brings us to the question of what could have caused the stars to have turned on in the first place.

The beginning of the universe had, of course, been discussed long   14 before this. According to a number of early cosmologies and the Jewish/Christian/Muslim tradition, the universe started at a finite, and not very distant, time in the past. One argument for such a beginning was the feeling that it was necessary to have "First Cause" to explain the existence of the universe. (Within the universe, you always explained one event as being caused by some earlier event, but the existence of the universe itself could be explained in this way only if it had some beginning.) Another argument was put forward by St. Augustine in his book *The City of God*. He pointed out that civilization is progressing and we remember who performed this deed or developed that technique. Thus man, and so also perhaps the universe, could not have been around all that long. St. Augustine accepted a date of about 5000 B.C. for the Creation of the universe according to the book of Genesis. (It is interesting that this is not so far from the end of the last Ice Age, about 10,000 B.C., which is when archaeologists tell us that civilization really began.)

Aristotle, and most of the other Greek philosophers, on the other   15 hand, did not like the idea of a creation because it smacked too much of divine intervention. They believed, therefore, that the human race and the world around it had existed, and would exist, forever. The ancients had already considered the argument about progress described above, and answered it by saying that there had been periodic floods or other disasters that repeatedly set the human race right back to the beginning of civilization.

The questions of whether the universe had a beginning in time and   16 whether it is limited in space were later extensively examined by the philosopher Immanuel Kant in his monumental (and very obscure) work, *Critique of Pure Reason*, published in 1781. He called these questions antinomies (that is, contradictions) of pure reason because he felt that there were equally compelling arguments for believing the thesis, that the universe had a beginning, and the antithesis, that it had existed forever. His argument for the thesis was that if the universe did not have a beginning, there would be an infinite period of time before any event, which he considered absurd. The argument for the antithesis was that if the universe had a beginning, there would be an infinite period of time before it, so why should the universe begin at any one particular time? In fact, his cases for both the thesis and the antithesis are really the same argument. They are both based on his unspoken assumption that time continues back forever, whether or not the universe had existed forever. As we shall see, the concept of time has no meaning before the beginning of the universe. This was first pointed out by St. Augustine. When asked: What did God do before he created the universe? Augustine didn't reply: He was preparing Hell for people who asked such questions. Instead, he said that time was a property of the universe that God created, and that time did not exist before the beginning of the universe.

17   When most people believed in an essentially static and unchanging universe, the question of whether or not it had a beginning was really one of metaphysics or theology. One could account for what was observed equally well on the theory that the universe had existed forever or on the theory that it was set in motion at some finite time in such a manner as to look as though it had existed forever. But in 1929, Edwin Hubble made the landmark observation that wherever you look, distant galaxies are moving rapidly away from us. In other words, the universe is expanding. This means that at earlier times objects would have been closer together. In fact, it seemed that there was a time, about ten or twenty thousand million years ago, when they were all at exactly the same place and when, therefore, the density of the universe was infinite. This discovery finally brought the question of the beginning of the universe into the realm of science.

18   Hubble's observations suggested that there was a time, called the big bang, when the universe was infinitesimally small and infinitely dense. Under such conditions all the laws of science, and therefore all ability to predict the future, would break down. If there were events earlier than this time, then they could not affect what happens at the present time. Their existence can be ignored because it would have no observational consequences. One may say that time had a beginning at the big bang, in the sense that earlier times simply would not be defined. It should be emphasized that this beginning in time is very different from those that had been considered previously. In an unchanging universe a beginning in time is something that has to be imposed by some being outside the universe; there is no physical necessity for a beginning. One can imagine that God created the universe

at literally any time in the past. On the other hand, if the universe is expanding, there may be physical reasons why there had to be a beginning. One could still imagine that God created the universe at the instant of the big bang, or even afterwards in just such a way as to make it look as though there had been a big bang, but it would be meaningless to suppose that it was created *before* the big bang. An expanding universe does not preclude a creator, but it does place limits on when he might have carried out his job!

In order to talk about the nature of the universe and to discuss   19
questions such as whether it has a beginning or an end, you have to be clear about what a scientific theory is. I shall take the simple-minded view that a theory is just a model of the universe, or a restricted part of it, and a set of rules that relate quantities in the model to observations that we make. It exists only in our minds and does not have any other reality (whatever that might mean). A theory is a good theory if it satisfies two requirements: It must accurately describe a large class of observations on the basis of a model that contains only a few arbitrary elements, and it must make definite predictions about the results of future observations. For example, Aristotle's theory that everything was made out of four elements, earth, air, fire, and water, was simple enough to qualify, but it did not make any definite predictions. On the other hand, Newton's theory of gravity was based on an even simpler model, in which bodies attracted each other with a force that was proportional to a quantity called their mass and inversely proportional to the square of the distance between them. Yet it predicts the motions of the sun, the moon, and the planets to a high degree of accuracy.

Any physical theory is always provisional, in the sense that it is   20
only a hypothesis: you can never prove it. No matter how many times the results of experiments agree with some theory, you can never be sure that the next time the result will not contradict the theory. On the other hand, you can disprove a theory by finding even a single observation that disagrees with the predictions of the theory. As philosopher of science Karl Popper has emphasized, a good theory is characterized by the fact that it makes a number of predictions that could in principle be disproved or falsified by observation. Each time new experiments are observed to agree with the predictions the theory survives, and our confidence in it is increased; but if ever a new observation is found to disagree, we have to abandon or modify the theory. At least that is what is supposed to happen, but you can always question the competence of the person who carried out the observation.

In practice, what often happens is that a new theory is devised that   21
is really an extension of the previous theory. For example, very accurate observations of the planet Mercury revealed a small difference between its motion and the predictions of Newton's theory of gravity.

Einstein's general theory of relativity predicted a slightly different motion from Newton's theory. The fact that Einstein's predictions matched what was seen, while Newton's did not, was one of the crucial confirmations of the new theory. However, we still use Newton's theory for all practical purposes because the difference between its predictions and those of general relativity is very small in the situations that we normally deal with. (Newton's theory also has the great advantage that it is much simpler to work with than Einstein's!)

22   The eventual goal of science is to provide a single theory that describes the whole universe. However, the approach most scientists actually follow is to separate the problem into two parts. First, there are the laws that tells us how the universe changes with time. (If we know what the universe is like at any one time, these physical laws tell us how it will look at any later time).) Second, there is the question of the initial state of the universe. Some people feel that science should be concerned with only the first part; they regard the question of the initial situation as a matter for metaphysics or religion. They would say that God, being omnipotent, could have started the universe off any way he wanted. That may be so, but in that case he also could have made it develop in a completely arbitrary way. Yet it appears that he chose to make it evolve in a very regular way according to certain laws. It therefore seems equally reasonable to suppose that there are also laws governing the initial state.

23   It turns out to be very difficult to devise a theory to describe the universe all in one go. Instead, we break the problem up into bits and invent a number of partial theories. Each of these partial theories describes and predicts a certain limited class of observations, neglecting the effects of other quantities, or representing them by simple sets of numbers. It may be that this approach is completely wrong. If everything in the universe depends on everything else in a fundamental way, it might be impossible to get close to a full solution by investigating parts of the problem in isolation. Nevertheless, it is certainly the way that we have made progress in the past. The classic example again is the Newtonian theory of gravity, which tells us that the gravitational force between two bodies depends only on one number associated with each body, its mass, but is otherwise independent of what the bodies are made of. Thus one does not need to have a theory of the structure and constitution of the sun and the planets in order to calculate their orbits.

24   Today scientists describe the universe in terms of two basic partial theories—the general theory of relativity and quantum mechanics. They are the great intellectual achievements of the first half of this century. The general theory of relativity describes the force of gravity and

the large-scale structure of the universe, that is, the structure on scales from only a few miles to as large as a million million million million (1 with twenty-four zeros after it) miles, the size of the observable universe. Quantum mechanics, on the other hand, deals with phenomena on extremely small scales, such as a millionth of a millionth of an inch. Unfortunately, however, these two theories are known to be inconsistent with each other—they cannot both be correct. One of the major endeavors in physics today, and the major theme of this book, is the search for a new theory that will incorporate them both—a quantum theory of gravity. We do not yet have such a theory, and we may still be a long way from having one, but we do already know many of the properties that it must have. And we shall see, in later chapters, that we already know a fair amount about the predictions a quantum theory of gravity must make.

Now, if you believe that the universe is not arbitrary, but is governed by definite laws, you ultimately have to combine the partial theories into a complete unified theory that will describe everything in the universe. But there is a fundamental paradox in the search for such a complete unified theory. The ideas about scientific theories outlined above assume we are rational beings who are free to observe the universe as we want and to draw logical deductions from what we see. In such a scheme it is reasonable to suppose that we might progress ever closer toward the laws that govern our universe. Yet if there really is a complete unified theory, it would also presumably determine our actions. And so the theory itself would determine the outcome of our search for it! And why should it determine that we come to the right conclusions from the evidence? Might it not equally well determine that we draw the wrong conclusion? Or no conclusion at all?   25

The only answer that I can give to this problem is based on Darwin's principle of natural selection. The idea is that in any population of self-reproducing organisms, there will be variations in the genetic material and upbringing that different individuals have. These differences will mean that some individuals are better able than others to draw the right conclusions about the world around them and to act accordingly. These individuals will be more likely to survive and reproduce and so their pattern of behavior and thought will come to dominate. It has certainly been true in the past that what we call intelligence and scientific discovery has conveyed a survival advantage. It is not so clear that this is still the case: our scientific discoveries may well destroy us all, and even if they don't, a complete unified theory may not make much difference to our chances of survival. However, provided the universe has evolved in a regular way, we might expect that the reasoning abilities that natural selection has given us would be valid   26 also in our search for a complete unified theory, and so would not lead us to the wrong conclusions.

27   Because the partial theories that we already have are sufficient to make accurate predictions in all but the most extreme situations, the search for the ultimate theory of the universe seems difficult to justify on practical grounds. (It is worth noting, though, that similar arguments could have been used against both relativity and quantum mechanics, and these theories have given us both nuclear energy and the microelectronics revolution!) The discovery of a complete unified theory, therefore, may not aid the survival of our species. It may not even affect our life-style. But ever since the dawn of civilization, people have not been content to see events as unconnected and inexplicable. They have craved an understanding of the underlying order in the world. Today we still yearn to know why we are here and where we came from. Humanity's deepest desire for knowledge is justification enough for our continuing quest. And our goal is nothing less than a complete description of the universe we live in.

RESPONDING TO READING

1. Hawking's narrative of how we have come to know about the structure of the universe assumes that observation and theories ideally should work together to create knowledge. But, as he points out, certain beliefs have interfered with acceptance of observation (as with Aristotle and Kepler). Identify some of the ways in which belief and observation may fail to work together; include Hawking's examples, and add others from your own reading or experience.

2. Describe the way that Hawking goes about answering the question, When did the universe begin? How does he get from that question to the concept of time and then to his assertion that "the concept of time has no meaning before the beginning of the universe." Are you surprised that he cites St. Augustine in support of his very modern idea? Why? When Hawking speaks of bringing the question of the beginning of the universe "into the realm of science," what does he mean?

3. Compare Hawking's definition of "what a scientific theory is" to Gould's in Chapter 2. How are the two definitions alike and how are they different? To what do you attribute the differences? To what degree does Kuhn's explanation (also in Chapter 2) of "normal science" help us understand the different approaches of scientists to the ideas they come up with? Why does Hawking argue for the value of "partial theories"?

4. Hawking ends the chapter by considering the "continuing quest" for a unified theory, "the ultimate theory of the universe." Explain his views and the evidence he uses. To what degree do you think that continuing this quest is really important? What answer would Hawking give to the question, "What does nature mean?" What answer would you give?

All at One Point

ITALO CALVINO

Italian novelist and short story writer Italo Calvino (1923–1985) is world renowned for his nineteen volumes of novels and short stories and for his collection of *Italian Folktales* (1980). For Calvino, to write any narrative was to write a fable, whose "irreplaceable scheme" he explained as "the child abandoned in the woods or the knight who must survive encounters with beasts and enchantments." In Calvino's fables, as in the traditional ones, the central character is either young or appears youthfully enchanted with nature, possessing "a sense of tranquility and discovery of the mysteries of life." *Cosmicomics* (1968), like *Invisible Cities* (1972) and *If on a winter's night a traveler* (1979), fuses reality and fantasy in a manner resembling that of two other master storytellers, Jorge Luis Borges and Gabriel García Márquez. *Cosmicomics*, says critic Theresa de Lauretis, is a "highly imaginative, scientifically informed, funny and inspired meditation on one insistent question: What does it mean to be human, to live and die, to reproduce and to create, to desire and to be?" This question is explored through the adventures of Qfwfq, "a strange, chameleon-like creature present at the beginning of the universe, the formation of the stars, and the disappearance of the dinosaurs."

"All at One Point" takes place at the moment—though there are no moments yet—before the Big Bang begins space and time. All future matter, including potential life forms, is jammed together at one point without dimension, poised to explode and create the universe. Naturally, in Calvino's imagination, that situation was terribly crowded, particularly so when the immigrant family (from where?) Z'Zu "wanted to hang lines across our point to dry their washing." Happily, one generous woman offers to make some noodles to share, an act of love with the most earth-shattering consequences. Though Calvino echoes the knowledge that Hawking presents, he has a different view of what is really important.

Through the calculations begun by Edwin P. Hubble on the galaxies' velocity of recession, we can establish the moment when all the universe's matter was concentrated in a single point, before it began to expand in space.

Naturally, we were all there,—*old Qfwfq said,*—where else could we   1
have been? Nobody knew then that there could be space. Or time either: what use did we have for time, packed in there like sardines?

I say "packed like sardines," using a literary image: in reality there   2
wasn't even space to pack us into. Every point of each of us coincided with every point of each of the others in a single point, which was where we all were. In fact, we didn't even bother one another, except

for personality differences, because when space doesn't exist, having somebody unpleasant like Mr. Pber^t Pber^d underfoot all the time is the most irritating thing.

3   How many of us were there? Oh, I was never able to figure that out, not even approximately. To make a count, we would have had to move apart, at least a little, and instead we all occupied that same point. Contrary to what you might think, it wasn't the sort of situation that encourages sociability; I know, for example, that in other periods neighbors called on one another; but there, because of the fact that we were all neighbors, nobody even said good morning or good evening to anybody else.

4   In the end each of us associated only with a limited number of acquaintances. The ones I remember most are Mrs. Ph(i)Nk$_o$, her friend De XuaeauX, a family of immigrants by the name of Z'zu, and Mr. Pber^t Pber^d, whom I just mentioned. There was also a cleaning woman—"maintenance staff" she was called—only one, for the whole universe, since there was so little room. To tell the truth, she had nothing to do all day long, not even dusting—inside one point not even a grain of dust can enter—so she spent all her time gossiping and complaining.

5   Just with the people I've already named we would have been overcrowded; but you have to add all the stuff we had to keep piled up in there: all the material that was to serve afterwards to form the universe, now dismantled and concentrated in such a way that you weren't able to tell what was later to become part of astronomy (like the nebula of Andromeda) from what was assigned to geography (the Vosges, for example) or to chemistry (like certain beryllium isotopes). And on top of that, we were always bumping against the Z'zu family's household goods: camp beds, mattresses, baskets; these Z'zus, if you weren't careful, with the excuse that they were a large family, would begin to act as if they were the only ones in the world: they even wanted to hang lines across our point to dry their washing.

6   But the others also had wronged the Z'zus, to begin with, by calling them "immigrants," on the pretext that, since the others had been there first, the Z'zus had come later. This was mere unfounded prejudice—that seems obvious to me—because neither before nor after existed, nor any place to immigrate from, but there were those who insisted that the concept of "immigrant" could be understood in the abstract, outside of space and time.

7   It was what you might call a narrow-minded attitude, our outlook at that time, very petty. The fault of the environment in which we had been reared. An attitude that, basically, has remained in all of us, mind you: it keeps cropping up even today, if two of us happen to meet—at the bus stop, in a movie house, at an international dentists' convention—and start reminiscing about the old days. We say hello—at times

somebody recognizes me, at other times I recognize somebody—and we promptly start asking about this one and that one (even if each remembers only a few of those remembered by the others), and so we start in again on the old disputes, the slanders, the denigrations. Until somebody mentions Mrs. $Ph(i)NK_0$—every conversation finally gets around to her—and then, all of a sudden, the pettiness is put aside, and we feel uplifted, filled with a blissful, generous emotion. Mrs. $Ph(i)NK_0$, the only one that none of us has forgotten and that we all regret. Where has she ended up? I have long since stopped looking for her: Mrs. $Ph(i)NK_0$, her bosom, her thighs, her orange dressing gown—we'll never meet her again, in this system of galaxies or in any other.

Let me make one thing clear: this theory that the universe, after   8 having reached an extremity of rarefactions, will be condensed again has never convinced me. And yet many of us are counting only on that, continually making plans for the time when we'll all be back there again. Last month, I went into the bar here on the corner and whom did I see? Mr. $Pber^t Pber^d$. "What's new with you? How do you happen to be in this neighborhood?" I learned that he's the agent for a plastic firm, in Pavia. He's the same as ever, with his silver tooth, his loud suspenders. "When we go back there," he said to me, in a whisper, "the thing we have to make sure of is, this time, certain people remain out ... You know who I mean: those Z'zus. . ."

I would have liked to answer him by saying that I've heard a number   9 of people make the same remark, concluding: "You know who I mean ... Mr. $Pber^t Pber^d$. . ."

To avoid the subject, I hastened to say: "What about Mrs.   10 $Ph(i)NK^o$? Do you think we'll find her back there again?"

"Ah, yes . . . She, by all means. . ." he said, turning purple.   11

For all of us the hope of returning to that point means, above all,   12 the hope of being once more with Mrs. $Ph(i)NK_0$. (This applies even to me, though I don't believe in it.) And in that bar, as always happens, we fell to talking about her, and were moved; even Mr. $Pber^t Pber^{d'}$s unpleasantness faded, in the face of that memory.

Mrs. $Ph(i)NK_0$'s great secret is that she never aroused any jealousy   13 among us. Or any gossip, either. The fact that she went to bed with her friend, Mr. De XuaeauX, was well known. But in a point, if there's a bed, it takes up the whole point, so it isn't a question of *going* to bed, but of *being* there, because anybody in the point is also in the bed. Consequently, it was inevitable that she should be in bed also with each of us. If she had been another person, there's no telling all the things that would have been said about her. It was the cleaning woman who always started the slander, and the others didn't have to be coaxed to imitate her. On the subject of the Z'zu family—for a change!—the horrible things we had to hear: father, daughters, brothers, sisters, mother, aunts: nobody showed any hesitation even before the most sinister insinuation. But with her it was different: the happiness I derived from her was the joy of being concealed, punctiform, in her, and of protecting her, punctiform, in me; it was at the same time vicious contemplation (thanks to the promiscuity of the punctiform convergence of us all in her) and also chastity (given her punctiform impenetrability). In short: what more could I ask?

14   And all of this, which was true of me, was true also for each of the others. And for her: she contained and was contained with equal happiness, and she welcomed us and loved and inhabited all equally.

15   We got along so well all together, so well that something extraordinary was bound to happen. It was enough for her to say, at a certain moment: "Oh, if I only had some room, how I'd like to make some noodles for you boys!" And in that moment we all thought of the space that her round arms would occupy, moving backward and forward with the rolling pin over the dough, her bosom leaning over the great mound of flour and eggs which cluttered the wide board while her arms kneaded and kneaded, white and shiny with oil up to the elbows; we thought of the space that the flour would occupy, and the wheat for the flour, and the fields to raise the wheat, and the mountains from which the water would flow to irrigate the fields, and the grazing lands for the herds of calves that would give their meat for the sauce; of the space it would take for the Sun to arrive with its rays, to ripen the wheat; of the space for the Sun to condense from the clouds of stellar gases and burn; of the quantities of stars and galaxies and galactic masses in flight through space which would be needed to hold suspended every galaxy, every nebula, every sun, every planet, and at the same time we thought of it, this space was inevitably being formed, at the same time that Mrs. $Ph(i)NK_0$ was uttering those words:" . . . ah, what noodles, boys!" the point that contained her and all of us was expanding in a halo of distance in light-years and light-centuries and billions of light-millennia, and we were being hurled to the four corners of the universe (Mr. $Pber^t$ $Pber^d$ all the way to Pavia), and she, dissolved into I don't know what kind of energy-light-heat, she, Mrs. $Ph(i)NK_0$, she who in the midst of our closed, petty world had been capable of a generous impulse, "Boys, the noodles I would make for you!," a true outburst of general love, initiating at the same moment the concept of space and, properly speaking, space itself, and time, and universal gravitation, and the gravitating universe, making possible billions and billions of suns, and of planets, and fields of wheat, and Mrs. $Ph(i)NK^0$s, scattered through the continents of the planets, kneading with floury, oil-shiny, generous arms, and she lost at that very moment, and we, mourning her loss.

RESPONDING TO READING

1. Calvino is clearly having fun with the concepts Hawking has presented. Look closely at his description of the point on which the story takes place: How fully does he understand the concepts? Show where Calvino's scientific knowledge is expressed and evaluate its adequacy as science and as a basis for fiction.

2. The story proceeds through a series of logical impossibilities, connecting the almost incomprehensible moment before space and time begin with everyday human life. Describe a few of those connections, and explain why they are logically impossible. Why is Calvino doing such fantastic things in his story?

3. No one knows why the universe began, though most religions propose reasons. What does Calvino suggest as the cause of the Big Bang? What do you think of his suggestion?

4. Do you find this kind of humor engaging? Annoying? Boring? Or what?

America Revised

FRANCES FITZGERALD

Frances Fitzgerald's work as an investigative journalist provides a constant critique of establishment America on many dimensions: social, political, religious, and intellectual. That she favors the overlooked and the oppressed is in the tradition of her public-spirited ancestors, many of them energetic, intelligent, activist women. These include Elizabeth Peabody, a notable nineteenth-century abolitionist and educator; Mary Parkman Peabody, Fitzgerald's grandmother, active in community work and once jailed for civil rights activities; and Marietta Tree, Fitzgerald's mother, appointed by President John F.Kennedy as the United States representative to the United Nations Human Rights Commission.

Fitzgerald (born 1940) writes primarily for *The New Yorker*, where all three of her books were first published serially. *Fire in the Lake: The Vietnamese and Americans in Vietnam* (1973), winner of both a Pulitzer prize and a National Book Award, made a strong antiwar protest that helped shape American opinion against military intervention in Vietnam. *Cities on a Hill: A Journey Through Contemporary American Cultures* (1986) critically examines several counterculture communities of the 1960s–80s, whose members sought to reinvent themselves, collectively and individually. Her book *Way Out there in the Blue* (2000) explores the Cold War and "Star Wars" defense system in Ronald Reagan's America. In *America Revised: A History of Schoolbooks in the Twentieth Century* (1979), Fitzgerald investigates how history books have been written and rewritten to promote what politicians and publishers believe is the national interest, irrespective of the facts, as the chapter reprinted here reveals. What schoolchildren learn about their heritage from these books is whatever version of the facts is popular or politically in fashion at the time.

1   Those of us who grew up in the fifties believed in the permanence of our American-history textbooks. To us as children, those texts were the truth of things: they were American history. It was not just that we read them before we understood that not everything that is printed is the truth, or the whole truth. It was that they, much more than other books, had the demeanor and trappings of authority. They were weighty volumes. They spoke in measured cadences: imperturbable, humorless, and as distant as Chinese emperors. Our teachers treated them with respect, and we paid them abject homage by memorizing a chapter a week. But now the textbook histories have changed, some of them to such an extent that an adult would find them unrecognizable.

2   One current junior-high-school American history begins with a story about a Negro cowboy called George McJunkin. It appears that when McJunkin was riding down a lonely trail in New Mexico one cold spring morning in 1925 he discovered a mound containing bones and stone implements, which scientists later proved belonged to an Indian civilization ten thousand years old. The book goes on to say that scientists now believe there were people in the Americas at least twenty thousand years ago. It discusses the Aztec, Mayan, and Incan civilizations and the meaning of the word "culture" before introducing the European explorers.[1]

3   Another history text—this one for the fifth grade—begins with the story of how Henry B. Gonzalez, who is a member of Congress from Texas, learned about his own nationality. When he was ten years old, his teacher told him he was an American because he was born in the United States. His grandmother, however, said, "The cat was born in the oven. Does that make him bread?" After reporting that Mr. Gonzalez eventually went to college and law school, the book explains that "the melting pot idea hasn't worked out as some thought it would," and that now "some people say that the people of the United States are more like a salad bowl than a melting pot."[2]

4   Poor Columbus! He is a minor character now, a walk-on in the middle of American history. Even those books that have not replaced his picture with a Mayan temple or an Iroquois mask do not credit him with discovering America—even for the Europeans. The Vikings, they say, preceded him to the New World, and after that the Europeans,

---

[1]Wood, Gabriel, and Biller, *America* (1975), p. 3.

[2]King and Anderson, *The United States* (sixth level), Houghton Mifflin Social Studies Program (1976), pp. 15–16.

having lost or forgotten their maps, simply neglected to cross the ocean again for five hundred years. Columbus is far from being the only personage to have suffered from time and revision. Captain John Smith, Daniel Boone, and Wild Bill Hickok—the great self-promoters of American history—have all but disappeared, taking with them a good deal of the romance of the American frontier. General Custer has given way to Chief Crazy Horse; General Eisenhower no longer liberates Europe single-handed; and, indeed, most generals, even to Washington and Lee, have faded away, as old soldiers do, giving place to social reformers such as William Lloyd Garrison and Jacob Riis. A number of black Americans have risen to prominence: not only George Washington Carver but Frederick Douglass and Martin Luther King, Jr. W. E. B. Du Bois now invariably accompanies Booker T. Washington. In addition, there is a mystery man called Crispus Attucks, a fugitive slave about whom nothing seems to be known for certain except that he was a victim of the Boston Massacre and thus became one of the first casualties of the American Revolution. Thaddeus Stevens has been reconstructed[3]—his character changed, as it were, from black to white, from cruel and vindictive to persistent and sincere. As for Teddy Roosevelt, he now champions the issue of conservation instead of charging up *San Juan Hill*. No single President really stands out as a hero, but all Presidents—except certain unmentionables in the second half of the nineteenth century—seem to have done as well as could be expected, given difficult circumstances.

Of course, when one thinks about it, it is hardly surprising that   5
modern scholarship and modern perspectives have found their way into children's books. Yet the changes remain shocking. Those who in the sixties complained of the bland optimism, the chauvinism, and the materialism of their old civics texts did so in the belief that, for all their protests, the texts would never change. The thought must have had something reassuring about it, for that generation never noticed when its complaints began to take effect and the songs about radioactive rainfall and houses made of ticky-tacky began to appear in the textbooks. But this is what happened.

The history texts now hint at a certain level of unpleasantness in   6
American history. Several books, for instance, tell the story of Ishi, the last "wild" Indian in the continental United States, who, captured in 1911 after the massacre of his tribe, spend the final four and a half years of his life in the University of California's museum of anthropology, in

---

[3]Thaddeus Stevens (1792–1868): Republican congressman from Pennsylvania. A leader in the House during and after the Civil War, he was a determined abolitionist who hated the South and violently opposed Lincoln's moderate reconstruction plan. Stevens dominated the committee that impeached Andrew Johnson.

San Francisco. At least three books show the same stunning picture of the breaker boys, the child coal miners of Pennsylvania—ancient children with deformed bodies and blackened faces who stare stupidly out from the entrance to a mine. One book quotes a soldier on the use of torture in the American campaign to pacify the Philippines at the beginning of the century. A number of books say that during the American Revolution the patriots tarred and feathered those who did not support them, and drove many of the loyalists from the country. Almost all the present-day history books note that the United States interned Japanese-Americans in detention camps during the Second World War.

7   Ideologically speaking, the histories of the fifties were implacable, seamless. Inside their covers, America was perfect: the greatest nation in the world, and the embodiment of democracy, freedom, and technological progress. For them, the country never changed in any important way: its values and its political institutions remained constant from the time of the American Revolution. To my generation—the children of the fifties—these texts appeared permanent just because they were so self-contained. Their orthodoxy, it seemed, left no handholds for attack, no lodging for decay. Who, after all, would dispute the wonders of technology or the superiority of the English colonists over the Spanish? Who would find fault with the pastorale of the West or the Old South? Who would question the anti-Communist crusade? There was, it seemed, no point in comparing these visions with reality, since they were the public truth and were thus quite irrelevant to what existed and to what anyone privately believed. They were—or so it seemed—the permanent expression of mass culture in America.

8   But now the texts have changed, and with them the country that American children are growing up into. The society that was once uniform is now a patchwork of rich and poor, old and young, men and women, blacks, whites, Hispanics, and Indians. The system that ran so smoothly by means of the Constitution under the guidance of benevolent conductor Presidents is now a rattletrap affair. The past is no highway to the present; it is a collection of issues and events that do not fit together and that led in no single direction. The word "progress" has been replaced by the word "change": children, the modern texts insist, should learn history so that they can adapt to the rapid changes taking place around them. History is proceeding in spite of us. The present, which was once portrayed in the concluding chapters as a peaceful haven of scientific advances and Presidential inaugurations, is now a tangle of problems: race problems, urban problems, foreign-policy problems, problems of pollution, poverty, energy depletion, youthful rebellion, assassination, and drugs. Some books illustrate these prob-

lems dramatically. One, for instance, contains a picture of a doll half buried in a mass of untreated sewage; the caption reads, "Are we in danger of being overwhelmed by the products of our society and wastage created by their production? Would you agree with this photographer's interpretation?"[4] Two books show the same picture of an old black woman sitting in a straight chair in a dingy room, her hands folded in graceful resignation;[5] the surrounding text discusses the problems faced by the urban poor and by the aged who depend on Social Security. Other books present current problems less starkly. One of the texts concludes sagely:

> Problems are part of life. Nations face them, just as people face them, and try to solve them. And today's Americans have one great advantage over past generations. Never before have Americans been so well equipped to solve their problems. They have today the means to conquer poverty, disease, and ignorance. The technetronic age has put that power into their hands.[6]

Such passages have a familiar ring. Amid all the problems, the deus ex machina of science still dodders around in the gloaming of pious hope.

Even more surprising than the emergence of problems is the discovery that the great unity of the texts has broken. Whereas in the fifties all texts represented the same political view, current texts follow no pattern of orthodoxy. Some books, for instance, portray civil-rights legislation as a series of actions taken by a wise, paternal government; others convey some suggestion of the social upheaval involved and make mention of such people as Stokely Carmichael and Malcolm X. In some books, the Cold War has ended; in others, it continues, with Communism threatening the free nations of the earth.   9

The political diversity in the books is matched by a diversity of pedagogical approach. In addition to the traditional narrative histories, with their endless streams of facts, there are so-called "discovery," or "inquiry," texts, which deal with a limited number of specific issues in American history. These texts do not pretend to cover the past; they focus on particular topics, such as "stratification in Colonial society" or "slavery and the American Revolution," and illustrate them with documents from primary and secondary sources. The chapters in these books amount to something like case   10

---

[4]Sellers et al., *As It Happened* (1975), p. 812.

[5]Graff, *The Free and the Brave*, 2nd ed. (1972), p. 696; and Graff and Krout, *The Adventure*, 2nd ed. (1973), p. 784.

[6]Wood, Gabriel, and Biller, *America* (1975), p. 812.

studies, in that they include testimony from people with different perspectives or conflicting views on a single subject. In addition, the chapters provide background information, explanatory notes, and a series of questions for the student. The questions are the heart of the matter, for when they are carefully selected they force students to think much as historians think: to define the point of view of the speaker, analyze the ideas presented, question the relationship between events, and so on. One text, for example, quotes Washington, Jefferson, and John Adams on the question of foreign alliances and then asks, "What did John Adams assume that the international situation would be after the American Revolution? What did Washington's attitude toward the French alliance seem to be? How do you account for his attitude?" Finally, it asks, "Should a nation adopt a policy toward alliances and cling to it consistently, or should it vary its policies toward other countries as circumstances change?"[7] In these books, history is clearly not a list of agreed-upon facts or a sermon on politics but a babble of voices and a welter of events which must be ordered by the historian.

11   In matters of pedagogy, as in matters of politics, there are not two sharply differentiated categories of books; rather, there is a spectrum. Politically, the books run from moderate left to moderate right; pedagogically, they run from the traditional history sermons, through a middle ground of narrative texts with inquiry-style questions and of inquiry texts with long stretches of narrative, to the most rigorous of case-study books. What is common to the current texts—and makes all of them different from those of the fifties—is their engagement with the social sciences. In eight-grade histories, the "concepts" of social science make fleeting appearances. But these "concepts" are the very foundation stones of various elementary-school social-studies series. The 1970 Harcourt Brace Jovanovich series, for example, boasts in its preface of "a horizontal base or ordering of conceptual schemes" to match its "vertical arm of behavioral themes."[8] What this means is not entirely clear, but the books do proceed from easy questions to hard ones, such as—in the sixth-grade book—"How was interaction between merchants and citizens different in the Athenian and Spartan social systems?" Virtually all the American-history texts for older children include discussions of "role," "status," and "culture." Some of them stage debates between eminent social scientists in roped-off sections of the text; some include essays on economics or sociology; some contain pictures and short biographies of social scientists of both sexes and di-

---

[7]Fenton, gen. ed., *A New History of the United States*, grade eleven (1969), p. 170.

[8]Brandwein et al., *The Social Sciences* (1975), introductions to all books.

verse races. Many books seem to accord social scientists a higher status than American Presidents.

Quite as striking as these political and pedagogical alterations is 12 the change in the physical appearance of the texts. The schoolbooks of the fifties showed some effort in the matter of design: they had maps, charts, cartoons, photographs, and an occasional four-color picture to break up the columns of print. But beside the current texts they look as naïve as Soviet fashion magazines. The print in the fifties books is heavy and far too black, the colors muddy. The photographs are conventional news shots—portraits of Presidents in three-quarters profile, posed "action" shots of soldiers. The other illustrations tend to be Socialist-realist-style drawings (there are a lot of hefty farmers with hoes in the Colonial-period chapters) or incredibly vulgar made-for-children paintings of patriotic events. One painting shows Columbus standing in full court dress on a beach in the New World from a perspective that could have belonged only to the Arawaks. By contrast, the current texts are paragons of sophisticated modern design. They look not like *People* or *Family Circle* but, rather, like *Architectural Digest* or *Vogue*. One of them has an Abstract Expressionist design on its cover, another a Rauschenberg-style collage, a third a reproduction of an American primitive painting. Inside, almost all of them have a full-page reproduction of a painting of the New York school—a Jasper Johns flag, say, or "The Boston Massacre," by Larry Rivers. But these reproductions are separated only with difficulty from the over-all design, for the time charts are as punctilious as Albers' squares in their color gradings. The amount of space given to illustrations is far greater than it was in the fifties; in fact, in certain "slow-learner" books the pictures far outweigh the text in importance. However, the illustrations have a much greater historical value. Instead of made-up paintings or anachronistic sketches, there are cartoons, photographs, and paintings drawn from the periods being treated. The chapters on the Colonial period will show, for instance, a ship's carved prow, a Revere bowl, a Copley painting—a whole gallery of Early Americana. The nineteenth century is illustrated with nineteenth-century cartoons and photographs—and the photographs are all of high artistic quality. As for the twentieth-century chapters, they are adorned with the contents of a modern-art museum.

The use of all this art and high-quality design contains some irony. 13 The nineteenth-century photographs of child laborers or urban slum apartments are so beautiful that they transcend their subjects. To look at them, or at the Victor Gatto painting of the Triangle shirtwaist-factory fire, is to see not misery or ugliness but an art object. In the modern chapters, the contrast between style and content is just as great: the color photographs of junkyards or polluted rivers look as enticing as

Gourmet's photographs of food. The book that is perhaps the most stark in its description of modern problems illustrates the horrors of nuclear testing with a pretty Ben Shahn picture of the Bikini explosion, and the potential for global ecological disaster with a color photograph of the planet swirling its mantle of white clouds.[9] Whereas in the nineteen-fifties the texts were childish in the sense that they were naïve and clumsy, they are now childish in the sense that they are polymorphous-perverse. American history is not dull any longer; it is a sensuous experience.

14   The surprise that adults feel in seeing the changes in history texts must come from the lingering hope that there is, somewhere out there, an objective truth. The hope is, of course, foolish. All of us children of the twentieth century know, or should know, that there are no absolutes in human affairs, and thus there can be no such thing as perfect objectivity. We know that each historian in some degree creates the world anew and that all history is in some degree contemporary history. But beyond this knowledge there is still a hope for some reliable authority, for some fixed stars in the universe. We may know journalists cannot be wholly unbiased and that "balance" is an imaginary point between two extremes, and yet we hope that Walter Cronkite will tell us the truth of things. In the same way, we hope that our history will not change—that we learned the truth of things as children. The texts, with their impersonal voices, encourage this hope, and therefore it is particularly disturbing to see how they change, and how fast.

15   Slippery history! Not every generation but every few years the content of American-history books for children changes appreciably. Schoolbooks are not, like trade books, written and left to their fate. To stay in step with the cycles of "adoption" in school districts across the country, the publishers revise most of their old texts or substitute new ones every three or four years. In the process of revision, they not only bring history up to date but make changes—often substantial changes—in the body of the work. History books for children are thus more contemporary than any other form of history. How should it be otherwise? Should students read histories written ten, fifteen, thirty years ago? In theory, the system is reasonable—except that each generation of children reads only one generation of schoolbooks. That transient history is those children's history forever—their particular version of America.

---

[9]Ver Steeg and Hofstadter, *A People* (1974), pp. 722–23.

Bibliography

Brandwein, Paul Franz, et al. *The Social Sciences: Concepts and Values.* 6 Vols., seven levels, kindergarten through grade six. New York: Harcourt Brace Jovanovich, 1975. First edition, 1957.

Fenton, Edwin. *A New History of the United States: An Inquiry Approach.* By Irwin Bartlett, Edwin Fenton, David Fowler, and Seymour Mandlebaum. New York: Holt Rinehart & Winston, 1975. In the Holt Social Studies Curriculum for grades nine through twelve: First published 1966.

Graff, Henry F. 1972. *The Free and the Brave: The Story of the American People.* Chicago: Rand MacNally. First edition 1967.

Graff, Henry F., and Krout, John A. 1973. *The Adventures of the American People.* Chicago: Rand McNally. Second edition, revised printing.

King, David C., and Anderson, Charlotte C. 1976. *The United States.* Boston: Houghton Mifflin. This is the sixth-level text in *Windows on Our World,* the Houghton Mifflin Social Studies Program, Lee F. Anderson, general editor.

Sellers, Charles G., et al. 1975. *As It Happened: A History of the United States.* New York: McGraw-Hill.

Van Steeg, Clarence L., and Hofstadter, Richard 1971. *A People and a Nation.* New York: Harper and Row. Edition used was printed in 1974.

Wood, Leonard C., Gabriel, Ralph H., and Biller, Edward L. *America: Its People and Values.* New York: Harcourt Brace Jovanovich, 1971, 1975.

RESPONDING TO WRITING

1. How does "America Revised" illustrate Fitzgerald's conclusion that history is "slippery" (paragraph 15)? In what ways, if any, are the history textbooks you have used different from the history books of the 1970s on which Fitzgerald bases her claim?

2. When you read a textbook in any subject do you hope to find "somewhere out there, an objective truth"? Has Fitzgerald's analysis of history textbooks of the 1970s convinced you that "This hope is, of course, foolish"? If so, what do you recommend that teachers and students do differently?

3. What does Fitzgerald mean by "each historian in some degree creates the world anew and all history is in some degree contemporary history" (paragraph 14)? Try to make the same claim by substituting the names of other disciplines for history and see how compelling a case you can construct.

4. Analyze an American history textbook with which you are familar, to see how it deals with a controversial topic, for example, the settlement of the West, slavery, the Vietnam War, women's suffrage, labor unions, Hispanic American culture, the Civil Rights movement. What evidence, including primary sources and photographs, does the book use to support its interpretation? From whose point of view does the author present the information? What conclusions are you as a reader supposed to draw? Or, compare two textbooks on the same point to determine where they agree and disagree, and why.

The Naked Source

Linda Simon

Linda Simon (born 1946) earned a Ph.D. from Brandeis University in
1983. A freelance writer, Simon is the author of *the Biography of Alice B.
Toklas* (1977), *Thornton Wilder: His World* (1979), *Margaret Beaufort:
Matriarch of the House of Tudor* (1982), and *Genuine Reality: A Life of
William James* (1999). As a biographer, Simon has had considerable opportunity to practice what she advocates in "The Naked Source,"
originally published in *The Michigan Quarterly Review*, 1988. *Alice B.
Toklas*, for instance, is derived from a wealth of primary sources: letters, diaries, conversations, photographs and paintings, poetry and
other creative writing, visits to the houses and locations that Toklas
shared with Gertrude Stein, as well as others' published accounts of
the pair and the period.

Students do not understand history, claims Simon, because
they lack a "real sense of the past." The way that history is taught,
with an emphasis on names and dates and others' interpretations
(secondary sources) fails to give students "a sense of historical
mindedness, a sense that lives were lived in a context." Instead of
writing term papers derived from other peoples' research, students
should be asked to write history the way real historians do it, by
consulting a variety of "naked sources"—through archives, interviews, old newspapers, and magazines. Then they should learn to
"make them speak" by the proper selection, arrangement, and emphasis required to write a historical narrative. For when they set out
to be historians, students are writing literature, not taking a test;
only then can they adequately convey a sense of the past. Currently,
Simon is working on a book about the year 1906 in which she tells
"the history of a year through the people—well-known or obscure—who lived it."

1   It is true that my students do not know history. That annals of the
American past, as students tell it, are compressed into a compact
chronicle: John Kennedy and Martin Luther King flourish just a breath
away from FDR and Woodrow Wilson, who themselves come right on
the heels of Jefferson and Lincoln. The far and distant past is more obscure still.

2   Some, because they are bright and inquistive, have learned names,
dates, and the titles of major events. But even these masters of Trivial
Pursuit often betray their ignorance of a real sense of the past. Teachers
all have favorite oneliners that point to an abyss in historical knowledge. Mine is: Sputnik *who?*

3   There is no debate here. Students do not know history. Students
should learn history. There is less agreement about what they should
know, why they should know it, and far less agreement about how
they should pursue this study of the past.

When I ask my students why they need to know history, they reply   4
earnestly: We need to learn history because those who do not know history are doomed to repeat the mistakes of the past. They have heard
this somewhere, although no one can attribute the remark. And if they
are told that George Santayana said it, they know not who Santayana
was, although if you care to inform them they will dutifully record his
name, dates (1863–1952), and the title of the work (*The Life of Reason*) in
which the remark was made.

Is that so? I ask. What will not be repeated?   5

Inevitably they respond emotionally with the example of the Holo-   6
caust. Some have watched an episode of a PBS series. Some have seen
the film *The Diary of Anne Frank*. Such genocide, they reply, will not be
repeated because we know about it. Undaunted by examples of contemporary genocide, they remain firm in their conviction. Genocide,
they maintain. And the Great Depression.

The Great Depression has made a big impact on the adolescent   7
imagination. Given any work of literature written at any time during
the 1930s, some students will explain it as a direct response to the Great
Depression. Wasn't everyone depressed, after all? And aren't most serious works of literature grim, glum, dark, and deep. There you have it.

But now we know about the Great Depression. And so it will not,   8
cannot, happen again.

I am not persuaded that requiring students to read Tacitus or   9
Thucydides, Carl Becker or Francis Parkman, Samuel Eliot Morison or
Arnold Toynbee will remedy this situation, although I believe that students, and we, might well benefit from these writers' illumination.
What students lack, after all, is a sense of historical-mindedness, a
sense that lives were lived in a context, a sense that events (the Battle of
Barnet, for example) had consequences (if men were slain on the battlefield, they could not return to the farm), a sense that answers must generate questions, more questions, and still more subtle questions.

As it is, students learning history, especially in the early grades, are   10
asked prescribed questions and are given little opportunity to pursue
their own inquiry or satisfy their own curiosity. The following questions are from current high school texts:

> Has the role of the present United Nations proved that the hopes and
> dreams of Woodrow Wilson were achievable? If so, how? If not, why?
>
> What were the advantages of an isolationist policy for the United
> States in the nineteenth century? Were there disadvantages?

Questions such as these perpetuate the idea that history is a body   11
of knowledge on which students will be tested. The first question, in
other words, asks students: Did you read the section in the text on the
role of the United Nations? Did you read the section on Wilson's aims

in proposing the League of Nations? Can you put these two sections together?

12   The second questions asks students: Did you understand the term *isolationist*? Did you read the section on U.S. foreign relations in the nineteenth century? Can you summarize the debate that the authors of the textbook recount?

13   Questions such as these perpetuate the idea that history can uncover "facts" and "truth," that history is objective, and that students, if only they are diligent, can recover "right answers" about the past. Questions such as these ignore the role of historians. Even those bright students who can recall dates and events rarely can recall the name of a historian, much less any feeling about who this particular man or woman was. For many students, historical facts are things out there, like sea shells or autumn leaves, and it hardly matters who fetches them. The sea shell will look the same whether it is gathered in Charles Beard's pocket or Henri Pirenne's.

14   What students really need to learn, more than "history," is a sense of the historical method of inquiry. They need to know what it is that historians do and how they do it. They need to understand the role of imagination and intuition in the telling of histories, they need to practice, themselves, confronting sources, making judgments, and defending conclusions.

15   When I ask my freshmen what they think historians do, they usually offer me some lofty phrases about "influencing the course of future events." But what I mean is: what do historians do after break-fast? That is a question few of my students can answer. And they are surprised when I read the following passage by British historian A. L. Rowse from his book *The Use of History*.

> You might think that in order to learn history you need a library of books to begin with. Not at all: that only comes at the end. What you need at the beginning is a pair of stout walking shoes, a pencil and a notebook; perhaps I should add a good county guide covering the area you mean to explore . . . and a map of the country . . . that gives you field footpaths and a wealth of things of interest, marks churches and historic buildings and ruins, wayside crosses and holy wells, prehistoric camps and dykes, the sites of battles. When you can't go for a walk, it is a quite a good thing to study the map and plan where you would like to go, I am all in favour of the open-air approach to history; the most delightful and enjoyable, the most imaginative and informative, and—what not everybody understands—the best training.

16   It is the best training because it gives the would-be historian an encounter with the things that all historians look at and puzzle over: primary sources about the past. Historians look at battlefields and old

buildings, read letters and diaries and documents, interview eyewitnesses or participants in events. And they ask questions of these sources. Gradually, after asking increasingly sophisticated questions, they make some sense, for themselves, of what once happened.

What professional historians do, however, is not what most students do when they set out to learn history within the confines of a course. Instead of putting students face to face with primary sources, instructors are more likely to send them to read what other people say about the past. Students begin with a library of books of secondary sources, or they may begin with a text. But that, cautions Rowse, should come "at the end." Instead of allowing students to gain experience in weighing evidence and making inferences, the structures of many courses encourage them to amass information. "I found it!" exclaim enthusiastic students. They need to ask, "But what does it mean?"   17

They need to ask that question of the kinds of sources that historians actually use. Instead of reading Morison's rendering of Columbus's voyages, for example, students might read Columbus himself: his journal, his letters to the Spanish monarchs. Then they can begin to decide for themselves what sort of man this was and what sort of experience he had. Morison—as excellent a historian as he is—comes later. With some sense of the sources that Morison used, students can begin to evaluate his contribution to history, to understand how he drew conclusions from the material available to him, to see how "facts" are augmented by historical intuition. They can begin to understand, too, that the reconstruction of the past is slow and painstaking work.   18

Courses that cover several decades or even millennia may give students a false impression of historical inquiry. Historians, like archaeologists or epidemiologists, move slowly through bumpy and perilous terrain. They are used to travelling for miles only to find themselves stranded at a dead end. Once, in the archives of Westminster Abbey, I eagerly awaited reading a fragment of a letter from King Henry VI (after all, that is how it was described in the card catalog), only to lift out of an envelope the corner of a page, about an inch across, with the faintest ink-mark the only evidence that it had, five hundred years before, been a letter at all.   19

Slowly the historian assembles pieces of the past. A household expense record might be the only artifact proving that a certain medieval woman existed. How much can be known about her? How much can be known by examining someone's checkbook today? Yet historians must make do with just such odd legacies: wills and land deeds, maps and drawings, family portraits or photographs. Can you imagine the excitement over the discovery of a diary or cache of letters? At last, a text. But the diary may prove a disappointment, a frustration. William James recorded the title of a book he may have been reading or the   20 name of a visitor. Didn't he understand that a historian or biographer would need the deep, reflective reminations of which we know he was more than capable?

21   Students have not had these experiences. When they are asked to write, they write *about* history. The research paper or the term paper seems to many of them another form of test—this time a take-home drawn out over weeks. Even if they have learned that "voice" and "audience" are important for a writer, they see history papers as different. They must be objectve; they must learn proper footnoting and documentation. They must compile an impressive bibliography. Most important, they must find something out. The research paper produces nothing so much as anxiety, and the student often feels overwhelmed by the project.

22   They might, instead, be asked to write history as historians do it. They might be introduced to archives—in their college, in their community, in their state capital. They might be encouraged to interview people, and to interview them again and again until they begin to get the kind of information that will enlighten them about a particular time or event. They might be encouraged to read newspapers on microfilm or the bound volumes of old magazines that are yellowing in the basement of their local library. And then they might be asked to write that most challenging form: the historical narrative.

23   "I can recall experiencing upon the completing of my first work of history," George Kennan wrote once, ". . . a moment of panic when the question suddenly presented itself to me: What is it that I have done here? Perhaps what I have written is not really history but rather some sort of novel, the product of my own imagination—an imagination stimulated, inspired and informed, let us hope, by the documents I have been reading, but imagination nevertheless." Most historians share Kennan's reaction.

24   Students, of course, can never discover the boundary between "fact" and imaginative construction unless they have contact with primary sources. They cannot know where the historian has intervened to analyze the information he or she has discovered. "Most of the facts that you excavate," Morison wrote in "History as A Literary Art," "are dumb things; it is for you to make them speak by proper selection, arrangement, and emphasis." Morison suggested that beginning historians look to such writers as Sherwood Anderson and Henry James for examples of the kind of palpable description and intense characterization that can make literature—historical or fictional—come alive.

25   Students need to be persuaded that they are writing literature, not taking a test, when they set out to be historians. Their writing needs to be read and evaluated not only for the facts that they have managed to compile, but for the sense of the past that they have conveyed. They

need to discover that the past was not only battles and elections, Major Forces and Charismatic Leaders, but ordinary people, growing up, courting, dancing to a different beat, camping by a river that has long since dried up, lighting out for a territory that no longer exists. Except in the imagination of historians, as they confront the naked source, unaided.

RESPONDING TO READING

1. Simon distinguishes between students who "have learned names, dates, and the titles of major events" and those who "know history." What is that distinction, and how does it compare with the "slippery history" concept of FizGerald? What does Simon mean by "historical-mindedness?"

2. What is the problem for Simon with saying that "those who do not know history are doomed to repeat the mistakes of the past"? By mocking that famous saying, she outrages a kind of proverbial wisdom. Do you agree with her objections?

3. What does Simon mean when she says that "answers must generate questions, more questions, and still more subtle questions"? If history is a matter of questions rather than merely answers, how does that change the way in which we come to know history?

4. Select a historical "fact" in dispute (such as young George Washington's chopping down the cherry tree or his later wooden teeth), and find out how it became a "fact." What is the historical method of inquiry, and how does it relate to historical fact?

5. Describe the kind of history course that Simon would prefer, and compare it to the history courses you have taken.

6. Obtain a "naked source"—an old diary, letter (or collection of letters), a birth, marriage or death certificate, a deed or property record, the memories of your oldest relative, newspapers from the distant past, or the like. If nothing old is available, use a more recent source—photographs, home movies or videos, student newspaper archives, etc. Now turn that source into history by making sense of it in context. After you have written that paper, write another about the experience you have gone through: How did you come to know what you (finally) knew about your subject?

QUESTIONS FOR REFLECTION AND WRITING

How Does Family Heritage Affect Who We Are?

1. How can you discover your family heritage? Do you need to look for artifacts, landscapes, and relics the way Lopez does in "Searching for Ancestors" and Silko in "Landscape, History, and the Pueblo Imagination? Or can you use stories from your childhood, as Murray, Sanders and Ozick do in this section? Could you locate documents, diaries, and old photos? Are there people or issues that nobody will talk about? Write an essay on how you might gather information to construct a family history.

2. Reflect on your childhood and how the history of your family affected it. Why were you treated the way you were? What songs, stories, games, traditions, and the like do you remember? Where did they come from? Do you now gain strength from that childhood, is it something you must try to overcome, or is it some kind of mixture?

3. If you have some special and wonderful memories from your childhood, as Ozick does in "A Drugstore Eden," write about both the way you remember them and whatever you now, in more mature years, believe them to have been in cold hard fact.

4. Notice that Sanders portrays his father in quite different ways in "The Inheritance of Tools": and in "Under the Influence: Paying the Price of My Father's Booze." Why do you think the writer does that? Is that dishonest? Or can very different characterizations of the same person both be true? Try writing two descriptions of a family member that portray him or her in different ways.

5. Write a history of your family, with a particular focus on how your family has helped shape who you are. Your research should include an interview with the oldest surviving member of your family, such documents as old diaries or photos or Bible records, your parents' memories of their childhoods, and family traditions. Think of your readers as your children or grandchildren in the future, wondering about how you came to be the old person they revere.

How Can We Live in Harmony with Nature?

1. Compare Silko's view of how humans do and should live with nature in "Landscape, History, and the Pueblo Imagination" with John McPhee's in "Los Angeles Against the Mountains" in Chapter 4. You can probably tell from the word "and" in Silko's title, as opposed to the word "against" in McPhee's, that they are speaking of quite different relationships. What are the similarities and differences in the authors' perspectives?

2. What does nature mean to you? Is it a specific environment (like Yosemite or the White Mountains) at the present time, or a more general concept? Pick a place (as Silko did), a phenomenon (as Hawking did), a people (as Lopez did), or even a symbolic retreat (as Thoreau did) to focus on and analyze. Include some explanation of what nature is *not* as part of your definition.

3. Pick a current problem that results from environmental mistakes in the past that affect both society at large and you as an individual. You could elaborate on one of the issues discussed in this section (as in the essays by Carson or

Postel) or elsewhere in the book (as in the essays by Goodall, Hogan, Mcphee, and Thoreau), or you could choose one that has special meaning for you (as the pollution of a favorite beach or river). Analyze the problem and interpret its consequences in a way that might enable readers to prevent comparable problems in the future. Are there solutions to the problems? If so, why have they not been implemented? If not, what should people do?

How Can We Interpret and Understand the Past?

1. Hawking and Calvino each present an explanation of how the universe began, though one does it as an astrophysicist and the other as a fiction writer. The differences between their approaches are pretty obvious, but they do share some ideas. What are they? How do they differ? Which of them offers a more satisfying explanation of the Big Bang for you? Why?

2. Fitgerald and Simon both write about issues in the teaching and learning of history in school. What problems do they see? What kinds of solutions do they propose? To what degree do their critiques describe what and how you learned about history in school?

3. Reinterpretations of history are always going on. For instance, in recent years, some scholars have proposed that Sigmund Freud's discovery of the power of the subconscious was not (as commonly believed throughout much of the twentieth century) a great psychological innovation; it was rather, they argue, Freud's own defense against believing the tales of childhood sexual abuse his patients were revealing. Again, some historians have asked us to change our opinion of England's Prime Minister Chamberlain, long believed to have mistakenly appeased Hitler at Munich and thus making World War II inevitable. These revisionist historians argue that Chamberlain actually fooled Hitler and thus gained time for England to arm itself for the inevitable war. Choose a historical controversy, and review the arguments for both traditional and revisionist interpretations. Do not overlook the possibilities of using local issues (the founding of your college or your town, for example) or family issues (why did your parents or grandparents come to America?). Then write an essay on the ways of interpreting the past that your research has turned up.

Reinterpretations/Contexts: What Can We Learn from the Past?

1. Write an essay in which you look closely at some aspect of the past either in your family or in your reading. You might, for instance, find on the Web the contents of newspapers published the day you were born. Find appropriate primary sources (documents, photographs, etc.), and help your readers to discern the meaning of what you have come to know. Your goal will be to help an audience understand what the past was really like and why it should be important to them.

2. Pick a problem in the present that only makes sense in terms of the past. Examples might be the conflict between the Israelis and the Arabs in the Middle East, the debate over affirmative action hiring and college admission policies in the United States, or the development of international terrorism as a way of channeling hostile attitudes towards the United States around the world. Write an essay in which you try to show those who are not aware of the past why such knowledge will help them understand current situations and how to act more wisely in the present and future.

6

Predictions:
What Will the Future Be Like?

> *Time present and time past*
> *Are both perhaps present in time future,*
> *And time future contained in time past.*
> T. S. ELIOT

Why Consider This Question?

The future does not exist until it happens; one thing we have learned from the past is that we cannot know what the future will be like. Yet we continue to consult scientists, doctors, science fiction writers, even astrologers, hoping to find answers to what the future may hold. Why?

One reason is that, by talking about the future, we understand better the implications of the present. Serious science fiction writers have always known this. Ray Bradbury, imagining Earth's colonization of Mars in *The Martian Chronicles*, presents the problem of humans encountering "the other," that is, those we do not understand: other species, other cultures, other social classes, or other people. Frank Herbert, in *Dune*, presents a world without water; Ursula LeGuin, in *The Left Hand of Darkness*, imagines a race without sex, or, more precisely, a world in which socially constructed meanings of sex are irrelevant. Margaret Atwood, in *The Handmaid's Tale*, presents a world dominated by a fierce and hypocritical religion. Such issues may well be of interest in the future, but we know for sure that they are crucially important to consider in the present.

Likewise, the popularity of the *Star Trek* and the *Star Wars* series has more to do with the way they speak to the present than to the credibility of their views of the future. *The Lord of the Rings* asks us to consider the corruption inherent in great power; the Harry Potter books insist that the power of the imagination is always in conflict with the Muggles, those who see only what is before their eyes. Imaginative writers have led the way into the future, but we do not judge their work according to the way their predictions work out; we ask their futures to help us imagine today more creatively.

A second reason to concern ourselves with the future is to prepare ourselves for it. What will the jobs, the educational needs, and the physical demands of the future be like? Several predictions have suggested, for example, that in our new century the United States will need more workers with Ph.D.s in all fields than we are likely to have under present policies. Such a prediction is immensely valuable for present college students thinking about going on to graduate school in the sciences or the humanities at a time when jobs are in short supply. If the prediction is sound—and this one is in some dispute—students can make plans wisely.

Despite our worries about whether even informed guesses about what is to come will work out, much about the future is predictable, or at least probable. The odds are that the sun will rise tomorrow, and for many tomorrows after that; the physical laws of attraction and repulsion will not be repealed; the human race is likely to survive in something like its present state. While the course of human events is surely not as predictable as astronomical events, or perhaps even as predictable as the weather, we have learned some ways to make informed guesses about what may happen down the road. Just as imagining the future allows us to see the present more clearly, so our ability to look closely at the present suggests what the future may be like.

Much of our speculation about the future is based on the expectation that current trends and knowledge will continue; this is called *extrapolation*, that is, extending present experience into the future. We can sometimes "change" the future by changing the present, and extrapolation gives us the information we can use to make such changes. Thus, we know enough about the effects upon the Earth's protective ozone layer of releasing certain hydrocarbons into the atmosphere to know that all life on earth is threatened by solar radiation; most nations have now banned the use of these chemicals. Several powerful extrapolations from events in the twentieth century are represented in the readings in this book: Rachel Carson's *Silent Spring* (Chapter 5), which alerted the world to the dangers of indiscriminate use of insecticides; Czeslaw Milosz's essay, "American Ignorance of War" (in this Chapter), which predicted the devastating results of a hostile attack on the United States long before the attacks on the World Trade Center and the Pentagon on September 11, 2001; and Mark Juergensmeyer's analysis of terrorism, with its almost uncanny insight into those attacks a year before they occurred. Carson's studies were based on the most careful accumulation of scientific evidence, with reasonable projections into the future, Milosz extrapolated from his own refugee experience, based on historical precedent, and Juergensmeyer brings his personal knowledge of terrorist "performances," as he puts it, and his personal interviews with agents of terror to bear on an uncertain and threatening future.

We thus find ourselves speculating about the future for at least three reasons: We want to understand our present more fully, we want to see into the future to prepare ourselves for it, and we want to imagine possible futures so that we can choose a future we will want to inhabit or to have our children inhabit. For many of us, the most immediate vision that we have of the future comes from our daily experience of technology, the computers we use almost daily and the other marvels of communication and transportation that promise a tomorrowland of plenty and ease. For this reason, the readings that follow begin with a consideration of the future of technology and its many promises. But our futures remain linked to our families as well as to our machines, so we turn as well to considerations of the modern family, most particularly, the future of women in the family and as social agents in a large religious community. But the family is not isolated; it exists within a society whose conflicts sometimes destroy families, or even (as Sanders argued in "Under the Influence" in Chapter 5) render family values destructive to the individual. Thus the second section turns to the prospects of war or peace, fear, and personal security—issues of enormous importance to all of our futures. The section concludes with several speculations about the ways that we can think about our future, now under the shadow of war and terror. The overriding question, the subject of the third section, however, remains: How can we most constructively, coherently, and creatively consider what the future will bring?

How Can We Think and Speak about Technology and Gender Roles in the Future?

Anne Fadiman in "Mail" opens this section with a loving look back at her famous father's obsession with receiving mail, old-fashioned letters brought to the mailbox at the bottom of the hill. She then takes us through a carefully detailed history of the development of the postal service in England and elsewhere, winding up with a warm and witty look at e-mail. With every gain, she points, comes some loss as well. She values e-mail for what it can do and for what it represents: "the world is a single city with a single postal rate." But she reminds us of some of the losses as well: the lack of personality, the inevitable spam, and the lack of care with the writing. The future of mail is clearly economical and efficient, but we should not forget the values that will disappear into that efficiency.

Computer scientist Paul de Palma is also no cheerleader for the future of technology; indeed, he is deeply suspicious of the commercial impulses that have so far driven the computer industry. He highly values his profession, but sees it as quite distinct from what he calls "microcomputer gadgetry," the hardware and software that most people mistakenly think is the concern of a computer scientist. The "glories of technology" have so far, he says, been in fact a diversion of huge sums from such useful purposes as education to training consumers for wasteful gadgetry: "Our brave new world, paved over with networked computers from sea to shining sea, may well be one in which we are mostly unemployed or have experienced a serious decline in living standards." He sees the incessant call for "computer literacy" as a grim joke, and the usual investment by schools in machines and training as a free benefit to the computer industry: "the costs are socialized, while the benefits are privatized." De Palma has no interest in turning the clock back—after all, as he points out, he does make a living from computer science—but he wants to "think reasonably about these machines, to recognize the hucksterism in the hysterical cries for computer literacy, to steel ourselves against the urge to keep throwing money at Redmond and Silicon Valley."

Certainly gender roles have changed greatly since the days of Sojourner Truth and Elizabeth Cady Stanton and their protests against serious inequality. (See Chapter 4.) And many observers of modern American culture expect that women will achieve full equality of opportunity with men in the near future. But when sociologist Robert S. Weiss looks at the roles of men in middle class marriages in "Marriage as Partnership," he finds rather less change than one might expect. Focusing on those he calls "occupationally successful men," Weiss tries to examine the values and attitudes they bring to their families with working wives. Surprisingly, or perhaps not so surprisingly, he finds that traditional values and traditional assumptions about family responsibilities continue to hold, despite "pride in their wives' achievements." Although some male behavior is changed, he finds that the male attitudes about roles in marriage seem quite resistant to change. When we read this essay next to those by Fallows (Chapter 3) and Tannen (Chapters 2 and 4), we must puzzle about the future of the family.

But Lettie Cottin Pogrebin speaks as the voice of the future, for Jewish women and perhaps for all people. She defines Jewish feminism as a way "to summarize a whole system of moral and political commitments. Feminists dissect privilege. We deconstruct and examine the way gender plays out in power relations, political agendas, and economic contexts. We ask, 'Who benefits? Who hurts?'" She writes, as Anzaldúa does in "Beyond Traditional Notions of Identity" in Chapter 1, expecting readers to accommodate non-English terms and phrases, to stretch their reading as they stretch their thinking, to understand and sympathize with a project "to permanently strengthen women by developing their self-esteem and marketable skills and reducing their dependence on men and social services." While Weiss has shown how difficult it is to change attitudes, Pogrebin sees a future of fully emancipated women, "for no human being can exist in one body, part slave and part free."

Will War and Terrorism Shape Our Future?

War has a way of overturning planned futures; when it comes everyone's life changes. Margaret Mead opens this section with an argument that war is not necessary; that is, it is not built into the biology of our species. The issue is significant, as she points out at the start, since some will argue that we have "such pugnacious instincts" that the best we can do is to "channel them in new directions." But Mead is more optimistic than that, and she bases her argument on anthropological knowledge of human cultures that do not practice war.

Mead's essay is more than fifty years old, and those fifty years have seen wars of every description. Czeslaw Milosz experienced some of that conflict and his gloomy essay, "American Ignorance of War," reflects that personal experience. The first encounter with war, he argues, upsets a person's belief that peace is natural: "His first stroll along a street littered with glass from bomb-shattered windows shakes his faith in the 'naturalness' of his world." Soon the conditions of war become natural, despite prior expectations that normal life is peaceful. Americans who believe that the future holds no war for them are, Milosz asserts, incredibly naive, for our turn will come.

If Milosz is right, and Mead's hopes for an invention to replace war turn out to be naive, Mark Juergensmeyer provides a blueprint for what war might look like in our future: acts of performance terrorism, spawned by religious fanaticism. Citing details of terrorist acts before the attacks of September 2001, Juergensmeyer argues that terrorist acts are not, for the most part, part of a strategic plan, to achieve a strategic goal, but rather acts of theater to make a symbolic statement. These acts create "enormous spectacles . . . as a dramatic show so powerful as to change people's perceptions of the world." It is hard to remember that Juergensmeyer was writing this before the attacks on the World Trade Center, his analysis is so clear and penetrating. He concludes his essay with speculation about why America is seen as the enemy by so many other cultures, suggesting that terrorism is likely to be with us for some time to come.

Wendell Berry reacts to the catastrophe of the terrorist attacks of 2001 with "Thoughts in the Presence of Fear," not an essay so much as a series of reflections on "the invention of a new kind of war that would turn our previous innovations against us." These reflections include a series of recommendations about what we should do in the future, such as "promote a decentralized world economy which would have the aim of assuring to every nation and region a local self-sufficiency in life-supporting goods." Further thoughts about how the future can be spared more catastrophes come from Pope John XXIII: "Justice, then, right reason and humanity urgently demand that the arms race should cease; that the stockpiles which exist in various countries should be reduced equally and simultaneously by the parties concerned; that nuclear weapons should be banned; and that a general agreement should eventually be reached about progressive disarmament and an effective method of control."

The writings in this section offer some hope for the future, but overall it is not easy to foresee just what plans or programs might ease the tensions that lead to war and terrorism. Perhaps the world will heed the warnings and predictions that writers are making. If so, then the bright promises of technology, individual and social freedoms, and self-sufficiency of nations offer a future into which we would gladly enter. If not, then the future is grim indeed.

Will a New Utopia Be Possible in the 21st Century?

It's not much of step from genetic engineering of potatoes, as we saw in Michael Pollan's "Overriding Darwin" essay in Chapter 2, to genetic engineering of people, the subject of W. French Anderson's "Genetics and Human Malleability." Or is it? Certainly, all kinds of gene therapies will soon be available to cure diseases (somatic cell gene therapy), and that "opens the door for enhancement genetic engineering," which could allow parents to insert characteristics they might desire into their children—or themselves. Anderson is opposed to genetic engineering, though not to gene therapy, because he argues that genetic engineering threatens important human values. We do not know enough, he says, comparing scientists in this field to a boy tinkering with a watch, and even if we did, we should not. Not everyone will agree with his conclusion, but the questions he raises may be more significant than the answers he puts forward.

Similar concerns are pervasive in Leigh Turner's "The Media and the Ethics of Cloning." He scorns the popular media debate, with its "hyperbolic sound bites and their print equivalents" and their focus on possible human cloning. The debate and the serious questions now should be on the cloning of what he calls "non-human animals." Not only is that debate ignorant and superficial, but it tends to ignore the most serious questions, such as "What moral obligations should extend to humans' use of other species?" Furthermore, the debate has not even begun to look at the popular and mistaken view of "DNA as destiny." Turner's call for extended and expanded public debate on these questions is a demand that we exercise "the responsibilities and obligations of citizenship." Without informed opinions, democracy cannot function.

Geneticists are fully as suspicious of the uses and misuses of altering our genes as the computer scientists are of the glories of technology. New Utopias seem to be as hard to achieve as ever, and the specialists who we think might lead us there keep asking the moral and ethical questions that we sometimes imagine we can avoid. Thus, this book concludes with the Nobel peace prize acceptance speech by Kofi Annan, secretary–general of the United Nations, and a piece by theologian Karen Armstrong. Annan reminds us all that world peace begins with individuals: "A genocide begins with the killing of one man—not for what he has done, but because of who he is. A campaign of 'ethnic cleansing' begins with one neighbour turning on another. Poverty begins when even one child is denied his or her fundamental right to education. What begins with the failure to uphold the dignity of one life, all too often ends with a calamity for entire nations." Annan issues a ringing agenda for the future: "eradicating poverty, preventing conflict, and promoting democracy." We have, Annan concludes, "no choice but cooperation at the international level." That may not be Utopia, but perhaps it is the best the future can offer.

Finally, Karen Armstrong asks, "Does God Have a Future?" She begins by entertaining the idea that "Maybe God really is an idea of the past" and presents some evidence of the loss of faith in the world as we enter the twenty-first century. She distrusts fundamentalism, whatever its religious tradition, as "literal and intolerant in its vision" and as a "retreat from God." The God that will live in the future, Armstrong argues, must be one of compassion, though also one of "uncompromising ethical demands." As she recounts the history of belief, much of it depressing, she emerges with some hope, though modest enough: "if we are to create a vibrant new faith for the twenty-first century, we should, perhaps, ponder the history of God for some lessons and warnings."

Rhetorical Issues: Discourse Communities

Perri Klass puts the issue of discourse communities most clearly in "Learning the Language" (Chapter 2); an essential part of learning to be a doctor is to learn to talk and sound like a doctor. The same goes for any profession. The first day in law school, a professor will tell the students that they have to learn how to "think like a lawyer," which means they have to stop thinking like a business or English or chemistry major; it also means that they have to learn the legal language that identifies them as lawyers, and they have to internalize that language, use it automatically. Specializing in a college major does not only mean taking advanced courses in a particular field; it means learning the way of speaking in that major, the way issues are defined, the way problems are approached. After a while, a psychology major ("Have you felt that way since you were a child?") just does not sound like a philosophy major ("What is the essential nature of being?").

Any group that has developed its own particular way of speaking can be called a "discourse community." We assert our belonging in that discourse community by speaking the language, by sounding the way a member of that community should. This is not merely a turn of phrase or a particular bit of jargon, though it may incidentally be one of those; basically, it is a sign of membership that indicates an awareness of the assumptions about the world that the group shares. Baseball fans and players, for example, know perfectly well what a "southpaw" is and why a "stolen base" is good rather than bad and why a "squeeze play" is not a sign of affection. Furthermore, such language is a way of identifying the insiders and keeping the outsiders out. When those not in the community complain that baseball is boring because there is so little action, insiders smile knowingly and murmur about the intellectual duel between the pitcher and batter that only the cognoscenti can appreciate. Some linguists talk about the "codes" of discourse communities and call our ability to move from one community to another "code switching." Most of us belong to a number of discourse communities and we switch codes effortlessly as we communicate our different memberships. Thus, we sometimes speak in the language of college students and write papers in that language. At the same time, we may be members of a family, a work group, a sports team, a religious group, a musical organization, and a club, each of which has its own language pattern. Some of us can belong to a dozen different discourse communities and switch codes so effortlessly that we are unaware of how differently we speak with different companions. Again, as we specialize in college, we start speaking and writing more and more as do those in our major field of study; if we become graduate students, we become even more "professional" in this way. We may even become so immersed in one discourse community that we forget to switch codes. If we talk to our family "like a psych major" or to our old school friends "like a philosopher," we suffer ridicule. This ridicule has the same root as the low grades some students receive on papers because they write for college in informal language or write for history courses like chemistry majors. If we fail to switch codes when called for, we are insensitive to our audience and guilty of not understanding the limitations of our own language. However rich in special meanings, nuances, and metaphors our language may be within one community, we need to be aware that other communities may not share them.

Discourse communities not only share a common vocabulary, but also common ways of presenting what they communicate. A laboratory report not only tells about an experiment; it also tells how fully we have joined those who know how to complete laboratory reports. A personal essay not only recounts an experience, but claims membership in the community of those who tell and find meaning in stories about people. We show the habits of mind of our discourse communities as we speak and write; we know what we need to say and what we need not say—because everyone in our group already knows it. We know the patterns of language and organization that are expected. And, if we are fully part of the community, we do all of this without much thought: This is how things are done. In this way, our special language expresses what Kuhn in Chapter 2 called the "paradigm," the overall pattern of thought of the group to which we belong.

How do you become part of a discourse community? You pick it up the way you picked up the language you learned as an infant. You listen hard to those who have it mastered, ask questions, and read those adept at the language. It also means trying out the language to hear how you sound and taking correction. First-year composition courses in college have many goals, but one consistent goal is to induct students into the college discourse community, to help them write "acceptable" papers. More advanced writing courses have a similar goal, though it becomes more complicated as students enter their major fields of study. This book, for example, seeks to bring together a wide range of college discourse communities to take advantage of the different ways they view common problems. This chapter gives you views of the future as seen by journalists, sociologists, computer scientists, a Jewish feminist, a fiction writer, several biologists, an international politician, and a renowned church leader.

Part of your job as a reader is to notice the discourse community of a writer. If you are not part of that discourse community, the writer must make some effort to include you rather than to exclude you. Return again to Chapter 2 and notice how careful Perri Klass, a recent medical school graduate, is to enlist you as a reader on her side as she encounters and internalizes medical language. After introducing the special language of the doctors ("Well, we've already had one hit today . . ."), she translates: "This means that our team (group of doctors and medical students) has already gotten one admission today." You might compare that article, written for the *New York Times*, with an article in a medical journal written exclusively for physicians. You might also compare the ways that the *New York Times* distinguishes itself from local newspapers. (Notice, for example, that most newspapers use one- or two-sentence paragraphs.) If you read periodicals by specialists aiming at a general audience, such as *Scientific American, National Geographic, Psychology Today,* or *The New York Review of Books,* you encounter that same problem. Can you enter into the discourse community of the writer far enough to understand what is going on and why? If not, you have lost what the writer seeks to tell you, and the writer has lost a part of the audience.

Part of our job as writers is to communicate clearly with members of our discourse community and also with those who may not be. As we all become more specialized, it becomes harder to speak to each other or to hear what others are saying. We must speak professionally to our colleagues; however, we must also know how to communicate our special knowledge to non-specialists. As writers, we need to pay special attention to the problem of making contact with those outside our own discourse communities. Some of us will read our work out loud to real or imaginary audiences to determine whether we have established the right tone and reached the right listeners. Have we defined special terms, or ordinary terms used in special ways? Are we making the right assumptions about what the audience can be expected to know? Have we edited our writing so that the audience will respect us and listen to what we have to say? This rhetorical problem, like most of the problems raised in this book, is not subject to easy answers. It is a subject for inquiry, a matter to be considered, a question to be dealt with over and over again. Unlike some problems, however, writing well for a particular audience becomes harder rather than easier as we become better educated. A wit once described specialists as those who learn more and more about less and less until they know everything about nothing. The same wit described generalists as those who learn less and less about more and more until they know nothing about everything. In both cases, the scholar, whether specialist or generalist, becomes unable to communicate at all. A principal goal of this book is to urge you to become flexible and strong readers of work in many discourse communities, while you become inquiring writers able to communicate to a wide range of audiences.

QUESTIONS FOR DISCOVERY AND DISCUSSION

1. What will you be doing ten years from now? Consider your family life, your job, your location, your living quarters, your transportation, your financial situation, and so on. Will every social or occupational community you encounter be a different discourse community or will there be some overlap?

2. What assumptions have you made about the future of the country and the world in responding to the previous question?

3. Now imagine yourself at seventy years of age looking back at your life. Try to describe what happened to you and how it related to the hopes and dreams you had when you were younger and to one or two major developments in science or society over your life span.

4. Consider the language that you have been using as you have been thinking about the future. To what degree has this language helped determine what you can imagine?

How Can We Think about Technology and Gender Roles in the Future?

———

Mail

Anne Fadiman

Anne Fadiman's extensive writing experience, wide interests, and ear for the perfect word animates her essays. [For biographical information, see p. 158.] A devotee of American essayist John McPhee, she also admires masters such as Charles Lamb, William Hazlitt, and Virginia Woolf. "The most important thing when starting out with essay writing is to find a voice with which you're comfortable," she told an *Atlantic Unbound* interviewer.* "You need to find a persona that is very much like you, but slightly caricatured. Think of it as your own voice turned up slightly in volume. That doesn't mean that the voice needs to be strident; it just needs to be a distilled version of you. Once you've found that voice, you'll discover that the essay is something you can be serious or funny with, or both." In "Mail," Fadiman's persona is both intimate and erudite, as she splices together memories of her father's passionate love affair with the daily mail, the history of the modern postal service, and her own leap into the future through e-mail.

Some years ago, my parents lived at the top of a steep hill. My father kept a pair of binoculars on his desk with which, like a pirate captain hoisting his spyglass to scan the horizon for treasure ships, he periodically inspected the mailbox to see if the flag had been raised. When it finally went up, he trudged down the driveway and opened the extra-large black metal box, purchased by my mother in the same accommodating spirit with which some wives buy their husbands extra-large trousers. The day's load—a mountain of letters and about twenty pounds of review books packed in Jiffy bags, a few of which had been pierced by their angular contents and were leaking what my father called "mouse dirt"—was always tightly wedged. But he was a persistent man, and after a brief show of resistance the mail would surrender, to be carried up the hill in a tight clinch and dumped onto a gigantic desk. Until that moment, my father's day had not truly begun.

His desk was made of steel, weighed more than a refrigerator, and bristled with bookshelves and secret drawers and sliding panels and a niche for a cedar-lined humidor. (He believed that cigar-smoking and mail-reading were natural partners, like oysters and Muscadet.) I

1

2

---

*(October 28, 1998)

think of it as less a writing surface than a mail-sorting table. He hated Sundays and holidays because there was nothing new to spread on it. Vacations were taxing, the equivalent of forced relocations to places without food. His homecomings were always followed by day-long orgies of mail-opening—feast after famine—at the end of which all the letters were answered; all the bills were paid; the outgoing envelopes were affixed with stamps from a brass dispenser heavy enough to break your toe; the books and manuscripts were neatly stacked; and the empty Jiffy bags were stuffed into an extra-large copper wastebasket, cheering confirmation that the process of postal digestion was complete.

3   "One of my unfailing minor pleasures may seem dull to more energetic souls: opening the mail," he once wrote.

> Living in an advanced industrial civilization is a kind of near-conquest over the unexpected.... Such efficiency is of course admirable. It does not, however, by its very nature afford scope to that perverse human trait, still not quite eliminated, which is pleased by the accidental. Thus to many tame citizens like me the morning mail functions as the voice of the unpredictable and keeps alive for a few minutes a day the keen sense of the unplanned and the unplannable. The letter opener is an instrument that has persisted from some antique land of chance and adventure into our ordered world of the perfectly calculated.

What chance and adventure might the day's haul contain? My brother asked him, when he was in his nineties, what kind of mail he liked best. "In my youth," he replied, "a love letter. In middle age, a job offer. Today, a check." (That was false cynicism, I think. His favorite letters were from his friends.) Whatever the accidental pleasure, it could not please until it arrived. Why were deliveries so few and so late (he frequently grumbled), when, had he lived in central London in the late seventeenth century, he could have received his mail between ten and twelve times a day?

4   We get what we need. In 1680, London had mail service nearly every hour because there were no telephones. If you wished to invite someone to tea in the afternoon, you could send him a letter in the morning and receive his reply before he showed up at your doorstep. Postage was one penny.

5   If you wished to send a letter to another town, however, delivery was less reliable and postage was gauged on a scale of staggering complexity. By the mid-1830s,

> the postage on a single letter delivered within eight miles of the office where it was posted was ... twopence, the lowest rate beyond that

limit being fourpence. Beyond fifteen miles it became fivepence; after which it rose a penny at a time, but by irregular augmentation, to one shilling, the charge for three hundred miles. There was as a general rule an additional charge of a half penny on a letter crossing the Scotch border; while letters to or from Ireland had to bear, in addition, packet rates, and rates for crossing the bridges over the Conway and the Menai.

So wrote Rowland Hill, the greatest postal reformer in history, who in 1837 devised a scheme to reduce and standardize postal rates and to shift the burden of payment from the addressee to the sender.

Until a few years ago I had no idea that if you sent a letter out of town—and if you weren't a nobleman, a member of Parliament, or other VIP who had been granted the privilege of free postal franking—the postage was paid by the recipient. This dawned on me when I was reading a biography of Charles Lamb, whose employer, the East India House, allowed clerks to receive letters gratis until 1817: a substantial perk, sort of like being able to call your friends on your office's 800 number. (Lamb, who practiced stringent economics, also wrote much of his personal correspondence on company stationery. His most famous letter to Wordsworth, for instance—the one in which he refers to Coleridge as "an Archangel a little damaged"—is inscribed on a page whose heading reads "Please to state the Weights and Amounts of the following Lots.") 6

Sir Walter Scott liked to tell the story of how he had once had to pay "five pounds odd" in order to receive a package from a young New York lady he had never met: an atrocious play called *The Cherokee Lovers*, accompanied by a request to read it, correct it, write a prologue, and secure a producer. Two weeks later another large package arrived for which he was charged a similar amount. "Conceive my horror," he told his friend Lord Melville, "when out jumped the same identical tragedy of *The Cherokee Lovers*, with a second epistle from the authoress, stating that, as the winds had been boisterous, she feared the vessel entrusted with her former communication might have foundered, and therefore judged it prudent to forward a duplicate." Lord Melville doubtless found this tale hilarious, but Rowland Hill would have been appalled. He had grown up poor, and, as Christopher Browne notes in *Getting the Message*, his splendid history of the British postal system, "Hill had never forgotten his mother's anxiety when a letter with a high postal duty was delivered, nor the time when she sent him out to sell a bag of clothes to raise 3s for a batch of letters." 7

Hill was a born Utilitarian who, at the age of twelve, had been so frustrated by the irregularity of the bell at the school where his father was principal that he had instituted a precisely timed bell-ringing 8 schedule. In 1837 he published a report called "Post Office Reform: Its Importance and Practicability." Why, he argued, should legions of accountants be employed to figure out the Byzantine postal charges? Why should Britain's extortionate postal rates persist when France's revenues had risen, thanks to higher mail volume, after its rates were lowered? Why should postmen waste precious time waiting for absent addressees to come home and pay up? A national Penny Post was the answer, with postage paid by the senders, "using a bit of paper . . . covered at the back with a glutinous wash, which the bringer might, by the application of a little moisture, attach to the back of the letter."

9   After much debate, Parliament passed a postal reform act in 1839. On January 10, 1840, Hill wrote in his diary, "Penny Postage extended to the whole kingdom this day! . . . I guess that the number despatched to-night will not be less than 100,000, or more than three times what it was this day twelve-months. If less I shall be disappointed." On January 11 he wrote, "The number of letters despatched exceeded all expectation. It was 112,000, of which all but 13,000 or 14,000 were prepaid." In May, after experimentation to produce a canceling ink that could not be surreptitiously removed, the Post Office introduced the Penny Black, bearing a profile of Queen Victoria: the first postage stamp. The press, pondering the process of cancellation, fretted about the "untoward disfiguration of the royal person," but Victoria became an enthusiastic philatelist, and renounced the royal franking privilege for the pleasure of walking to the local post office from Balmoral Castle to stock up on stamps and gossip with the postmaster. When Rowland Hill—by that time, *Sir* Rowland Hill—retired as Post Office Secretary in 1864, *Punch* asked, "SHOULD ROWLAND HILL have a Statue? Certainly, if OLIVER CROMWELL should. For one is celebrated for cutting off the head of a bad King, and the other for sticking on the head of a good Queen."

10   The Penny Post, wrote Harriet Martineau, "will do more for the circulation of ideas, for the fostering of domestic affections, for the humanizing of the mass generally, than any other single measure that our national wit can devise." It was incontrovertible proof, in an age that embraced progress on all fronts ("the means of locomotion and correspondence, every mechanical art, every manufacture, every thing that promotes the convenience of life," as Macaulay put it in a typical gush of national pride), that the British were the most civilized people on earth. Ancient Syrian runners, Chinese carrier pigeons, Persian post riders, Egyptian papyrus bearers, Greek *hemerodromes*, Hebrew dromedary riders, Roman equestrian relays, medieval monk-messengers, Catalan *troters*, international couriers of the House of Thurn and Taxis, American mail wagons—what could these all have been leading up to, like an ever-ascending staircase, but the Victorian postal system?

And yet (to raise a subversive question), might it be possible that, 11
whatever the profit in efficiency, there may have been a literary cost associated with the conversion from payment by addressee to payment
by sender? If you knew that your recipient would have to bear the cost
of your letter, wouldn't courtesy motivate you to write an extra-good
one? On the other hand, if you paid for it yourself, wouldn't you be
more likely to feel you could get away with "Having a wonderful time,
wish you were here"?

I used to think my father's attachment to the mail was strange. I now 12
feel exactly the way he did. I live in an apartment building and, with or
without binoculars, I cannot see my mailbox, one of thirteen dinky aluminum cells bolted to the lobby wall. The mail usually comes around
four in the afternoon (proving that the postal staircase that reached its
highest point with Rowland Hill has been descending ever since),
which means that at around three, *just in case*, I'm likely to visit the
lobby for the first of several reconnaissance missions. There's no flag,
but over the years my fingers have become postally sensitive, and I can
tell if the box is full by giving it the slightest of pats. If there's a hint of
convexity—it's very subtle, nothing as obvious, let us say, as the bulge
of a can that might harbor botulism—I whip out my key with the same
excitement with which my father set forth down his driveway.

There the resemblance ends. The thrill of the treasure hunt is fol- 13
lowed all too quickly by the glum realization that the box contains only
four kinds of mail: (1) junk, (2) bills, (3) work, and (4) letters that I will
read with enjoyment, place in a folder labeled "To Answer," leave there
for a geologic interval, and feel guilty about. The longer they languish,
the more I despair of my ability to live up to the escalating challenge of
their response. It is a truism of epistolary psychology that, for example,
a Christmas thank-you note written on December 26 can say any old
thing, but if you wait until February, you are convinced that nothing
less than *Middlemarch* will do.

In October of 1998 I finally gave in and signed up for e-mail. I had 14
resisted for a long time. My husband and I were proud of our retro-
grade status. Not only did we lack a modem, but we didn't have a car,
a microwave, a Cuisinart, an electric can opener, a cellular phone, a
CD player, or cable television. It's hard to give up that sort of backward image; I worried that our friends wouldn't have enough to
make fun of. I also worried that learning how to use e-mail would be
like learning how to program our VCR, an unsuccessful project that
had confirmed what excellent judgment we had shown in not pur-
chasing a car, etc.

As millions of people had discovered before me, e-mail was fast. 15
Sixteenth-century correspondents used to write "Haste, haste, haste,

for lyfe, for lyfe, haste!" on their most urgent letters; my "server," a word that conjured up a delicious sycophancy, treated *every* message as if someone's life depended on it. Not only did it get there instantly, caromed in a series of analog cyberpackets along the nodes of the Internet and reconverted to digital form via its recipient's modem. (I do not understand a word of what I just wrote, but that is immaterial. Could the average Victorian have diagrammed the mail coach route from Swansea to Tunbridge Wells?) More important, I *answered* e-mail fast— almost always on the day it arrived. No more guilt! I used to think I did not like to write letters. I now realize that what I didn't like was folding the paper, sealing the envelope, looking up the address, licking the stamp, getting in the elevator, crossing the street, and dropping the letter in the postbox.

16   At first I made plenty of mistakes. I clicked on the wrong icons, my attachments didn't stick, and, not having learned how to file addresses, I sent an X-rated message to my husband (I thought) at gcolt@aol.com instead of georgecolt@aol.com. I hope Gerald or Gertrude found it flattering. But the learning curve was as steep as my father's driveway, and pretty soon I was batting out fifteen or twenty e-mails a day in the time it had once taken me to avoid answering a single letter. My box was nearly always full—no waiting, no binoculars, no convexity checks, no tugging—and when it wasn't, the reason was not that the mail hadn't *arrived*, it was that it hadn't been *sent*. I began to look forward every morning to the festive green arrow with which AT&T WorldNet welcomed me into my father's "antique land of chance and adventure." Would I be invited to purchase Viagra, lose thirty pounds, regrow my thinning hair, obtain electronic spy software, get an EZ loan, retire in three years, or win a Pentium III 500 MHz computer (presumably in order to receive such messages even faster)? Or would I find a satisfying little clutch of friendly notes whose responses could occupy me until I awoke sufficiently to tackle something that required intelligence? As Hemingway wrote to Fitzgerald, describing the act of letter-writing: "Such a swell way to keep from working and yet feel you've done something."

17   My computer, without visible distension, managed to store a flood tide of mail that in nonvirtual form would have silted up my office to the ceiling. This was admirable. And when I wished to commune with my friend Charlie, who lives in Taipei, not only could I disregard the thirteen-hour time difference, but I was billed the same amount as if I had dialed his old telephone number on East 22nd Street. The German critic Bernhard Siegert has observed that the breakthrough concept behind Rowland Hill's Penny Post was "to think of all Great Britain as a single city, that is, no longer to give a moment's thought to what had been dear to Western discourse on the nature of the letter from the

beginning: the idea of distance." E-mail is a modern Penny Post: the world is a single city with a single postal rate.

Alas, our Penny Post, like Hill's, comes at a price. If the transfer of 18 postal charges from sender to recipient was the first great demotivator in the art of letter-writing, e-mail was the second. "It now seems a good bet," Adam Gopnik has written, "that in two hundred years people will be reading someone's collected e-mail the way we read Edmund Wilson's diaries or Pepys's letters." Maybe—but will what they read be any good? E-mails are brief. (One doesn't blather; an overlong message might induce carpal tunnel syndrome in the recipient from excessive pressure on the Down arrow.) They are also—at least the ones I receive— frequently devoid of capitalization, minimally punctuated, and creatively spelled. E-mail's greatest strength—speed—is also its Achilles' heel. In effect, it's always December 26; you are not expected to write *Middlemarch*, and therefore you don't.

In a letter to his friend William Unwin, written on August 6, 19 1780, William Cowper noted that "a Letter may be written upon any thing or Nothing." This observation is supported by the index of *The Faber Book of Letters, 1578–1939*. Let us examine some entries from the *d* section:

> damnation, 87
> dances and entertainments, 33, 48, 59, 97, 111, 275
> dentistry, 220
> depressive illness, 81, 87
> *Dictionary of the English Language*, Johnson's, 61
> Diggers, 22
> dolphins, methods of cooking, 37

I have never received an e-mail on any of these topics. Instead, I am 20 informed that Your browser is not Y2K-compliant. Your son left his Pokémon turtle under our sofa. Your column is 23 lines too long. Important pieces of news, but, as Lytton Strachey (one of the all-time great letter writers) pointed out, "No good letter was ever written to convey information, or to please its recipient: it may achieve both these results incidentally; but its fundamental purpose is to express the personality of its writer." *But wait*! you pipe up. *Someone just e-mailed me a joke*! So she did, but wasn't the personality of the sender slightly muffled by the fact that she forwarded it from an e-mail *she* received, and sent it to seventeen additional addressees?

I also take a dim, or perhaps a buffaloed, view of electronic slang. 21 Perhaps I should view it as a linguistic milestone, as historic as the evolution of Cockney rhyming slang in the 1840s. But will the future generations who reopen our hard drives be stirred by the eloquence of the e-acronyms recommended by a Web site on "netiquette"?

BTDT	been there done that
FC	fingers crossed
IITYWTMWYBMAD	
	if I tell you what this means will you buy me a drink?
MTE	my thoughts exactly
ROTFL	rolling on the floor laughing
RTFM	read the f—— manual
TAH	take a hint
TTFN	ta-ta for now

Or by the "emoticons," otherwise known as "smileys"—punctuational images, read sideways—that "help readers interpret the e-mail writer's attitude and tone"?

:-)	ha ha
:-(	boo hoo
(-:	I am left-handed
%-)	I have been staring at a green screen for 15 hours straight
:-&	I am tongue-tied
{:-)	I wear a toupee
:-[	I am a vampire
:-F	I am a bucktoothed vampire with one tooth missing
=|:-)=	I am Abraham Lincoln

22   "We are of a different race from the Greeks, to whom beauty was everything," wrote Thomas Carlyle, a Victorian progress-booster. "Our glory and our beauty arise out of our inward strength, which makes us victorious over material resistance." We have achieved a similar victory of efficiency over beauty. I wouldn't give up e-mail if you paid me, but I'd feel a pang of regret if the epistolary novels of the future were to revolve around such messages as

Subject: R U Kidding?
From: Clarissa Harlowe <claha@virtue.com>
To: Robert Lovelace <lovelaceandlovegirlz@vice.com>
hi bob, TAH. if u think i'm gonna run off w/u, :-F, do u really think
          i'm that kind of girl? if you're looking 4 a trollop, **CLICK
          HERE NOW:** *http://www.hotpix.html.* TTFN

I own a letter written by Robert Falcon Scott, the polar explorer, to G.T. Temple, Esq., who helped procure the footgear for Scott's first Antarctic expedition. The date is February 26, 1901. The envelope and octavo stationery have black borders because Queen Victoria had died in January. The paper is yellowed, the handwriting is messy, and the stamp bears the Queen's profile—and the denomination ONE PENNY. I bought the letter many years ago because, unlike a Cuisinart, which would have cost about the same, it was something I believed I could not live without. I could never feel that way about an e-mail.

I also own my father's old wastebasket, which now holds my   23
own empty Jiffy bags. Several times a day I use his stamp dispenser; it is tarnished and dinged, but still capable of unspooling its contents with a singular smoothness. And my file cabinets hold hundreds of his letters, the earliest written in his sixties in small, crabbed handwriting, the last in his nineties, after he lost much of his sight, penned with a Magic Marker in huge capital letters. I hope my children will find them someday, as Hart Crane once found his grandmother's love letters in the attic,

> pressed so long
> Into a corner of the roof
> That they are brown and soft,
> And liable to melt as snow.

RESPONDING TO READING

1. Fadiman opens her essay by describing the rituals her father would perform as he waited for and then read the daily mail. What are the components of these rituals? What purpose do these rituals seem to have for him? Are there rituals that you follow when you get and read your mail/e-mail?

2. What part does the history of mail play in Fadiman's essay? In what ways is this history contrasted with modern mailing practices?

3. In what ways does the postal system in England before January, 1840, parallel the modern use of cellular phones? What comparisons and contrasts are there between traditional mail, considering the changes it has undergone, and the modern use of e-mail? How does Fadiman feel about using e-mail?

4. According to Fadiman, what was lost when the burden of paying for mail shifted from the sender to the recipient?

5. In an essay, describe your own use of and attitudes towards mail or e-mail. How does it fit into your daily routines? If you don't use e-mail or check your mailbox regularly, then consider why you don't. What value does checking or not checking your mail or e-mail hold for you?

Http.//www.when_is_enough_enough?.com

PAUL DE PALMA

Paul de Palma is a professor of computer science at Gonzaga University. Before working in academe, he spent a decade in the computer industry. His interests include artificial intelligence and the sociology of computing. He has degrees from St. Louis University, Temple University, and the University of California at Berkeley, where he was a Woodrow Wilson Fellow. Currently, de Palma is at work on a collection of essays entitled *Dim Sum for the Mind*.

In "http://www.when_is_enough_enough?.com," originally published in *The American Scholar* (1999), de Palma argues that "The mischief is not in the computer itself, but in the ideology that surrounds it." He traces the development of the now-clichéd panacea that is the World Wide Web, dwelling specifically on the mistaken identification of the field of computer science with the technical details of "microcomputer gadgetry." In the end, de Palma asks that we, as a society, think reasonably about computers and "recognize the hucksterism in the hysterical cries for computer literacy."

1   In the misty past, before Bill Gates joined the company of the world's richest men, before the mass-marketed personal computer, before the metaphor of an information superhighway had been worn down to a cliché, I heard Roger Schank interviewed on National Public Radio. Then a computer science professor at Yale, Schank was already well known in artificial intelligence circles. Because those circles did not include me, a new programmer at Sperry Univac, I hadn't heard of him. Though I've forgotten the details of the conversation, I have never forgotten Schank's insistence that most people do not need to own computers.

2   That view, of course, has not prevailed. Either we own a personal computer and fret about upgrades, or we are scheming to own one and fret about the technical marvel yet to come that will render our purchase obsolete. Well, there are worse ways to spend money, I suppose. For all I know, even Schank owns a personal computer. They're fiendishly clever machines, after all, and they've helped keep the wolf from my door for a long time.

3   It is not the personal computer itself that I object to. What reasonable person would voluntarily go back to a typewriter? The mischief is not in the computer itself, but in the ideology that surrounds it. If we hope to employ computers for tasks more interesting than word processing, we must devote some attention to how they are actually being used, and beyond that, to the remarkable grip that the idol of computing continues to exert.

4   A distressing aspect of the media attention paid to the glories of technology is the persistent misidentification of the computing sciences with microcomputer gadgetry. This manifests itself in many ways. Once my seatmate on a plane learns that I am a computer science professor, I'm expected to chat about the glories of the new DVD-ROM as opposed to the older CD-ROM drives; or about that home shopping channel for the computer literate, the World Wide Web; or about one of

the thousand other dreary topics that fill *PC Magazine* and your daily paper, and that by and large represent computing to most Americans. On a somewhat more pernicious level, we in computer science must contend with the phenomenon of prospective employers who ask for expertise in this or that proprietary product. This has had the effect of skewing our mission in the eyes of students majoring in our field. I recently saw a student resume that listed skill with Harvard Graphics but neglected to mention course work in data communications. Another recent graduate in computer science insisted that the ability to write WordPerfect macros belonged on her résumé.

This is a sorry state. How we got there deserves some consideration.   5

A few words of self-disclosure may be in order. What I have to say   6
may strike some as churlish ingratitude to an industry that has provided me with a life of comparative ease for nearly two decades. The fact is that my career as a computer scientist was foisted upon me. When I discovered computers, I was working on a doctorate in English at Berkeley and contemplating a life not of ease but of almost certain underemployment. The computer industry found me one morning on its doorstep, wrapped me in its generous embrace, and has cared for me ever since. I am paid well to puzzle out the charming intricacies of computer programs with bright, attentive students, all happy in the knowledge that their skills will be avidly sought out the day after graduation. I can go to sleep confident that were tenure to be abolished tomorrow, the industry would welcome me back like a prodigal son.

Yet for all its largesse, I fear the computer industry has never had   7
my full loyalty. Neither did English studies, for that matter, but this probably says more about those drawn to the study of texts than about me. My memories of the time I spent in the company of the "best which has been thought and said" are hazy, perhaps because the study of literature is not so much a discipline as an attitude. The attitude that dominated all others when I was a student, that sustained my forays into the Western Americana of the Bancroft Collection, is that there is no text so dreary, so impoverished, so bereft of ideas that it does not cry out to be examined—deconstructed, as a graduate student a few years my junior might have said. But the text I now propose to examine, impelled, as it were, by early imprinting in the English department, goes beyond words on a page.

From an article here and a TV program there, from a thousand   8
conversations on commuter trains and over lunch and dinner, from the desperate scrambling of local politicians after software companies, the notion that prosperity follows computing, like the rain that was once thought to follow the settler's plow, has become a fully formed mythology.

9   In his perceptive little book *Technopoly*, Neil Postman argues that all disciplines ought to be taught as if they were history. That way, students "can begin to understand, as they now do not, that knowledge is not a fixed thing but a stage in human development, with a past and a future." I wish I'd said that first. If all knowledge has a past—and computer technology is surely a special kind of knowledge—then all knowledge is contingent. The technical landscape is not an engineering necessity. It might be other than it is. Our prospective majors might come to us, as new mathematics or physics majors come to their professors, because of an especially inspiring high school teacher, because of a flair for symbol manipulation, or even because of a (dare I use the word?) curiosity about what constitutes the discipline and its objects of study—not simply because they like gadgets and there's a ton of money to be made in computing.

10   The misidentification of computer science with microcomputer gadgetry is a symptom of a problem that goes far beyond academe. Extraordinary assertions are being made about computers in general and microcomputers in particular. These assertions translate into claims on the American purse—either directly, or indirectly through the tax system. Every dollar our school districts spend on microcomputers is a dollar not spent reducing class size, buying books for the library, reinstating art programs, hiring school counselors, and so on. In fact, every dollar that each of us spends outfitting ourselves with the year's biggest, fastest microcomputer is a dollar we might have put away for retirement, saved for our children's education, spent touring the splendors of the American West, or even chosen not to earn. In the spirit of Neil Postman, then, I'd like to speculate about how the mythology of prosperity through computing has come to be and, in the process, suggest that like the Wizard of Oz, it may be less miraculous than it looks.

11   The place to begin is the spectacular spread of microcomputers themselves. By 1993 nearly a quarter of American households owned at least one. Four years later, the *Wall Street Journal* put this figure at over 40 percent. For a home appliance that costs at least $1,000, probably closer to $2,000, this represents a substantial outlay. The home market, as it turns out, is the smaller part of the story by far. The Census Bureau tells us that in 1995, the last year for which data are available, Americans spent almost $48 billion on small computers for their homes and businesses. This figure excludes software, peripherals, and services purchased after the new machines were installed.

12   The title of an article in the *Economist*—"Personal Computers: The End of Good Times?"—hints at the extraordinary world we are trying to understand. In it we learn that annual growth in the home computer market slowed from 40 percent in 1994 to between 15 percent and 20

percent in 1995. By the fall of 1998, market analysts were predicting 16 percent growth in the industry as a whole for the current year. Those of us involved in other sectors of the economy can only look on in astonishment. When a 20 percent, or even 16 percent, growth rate—well over five times that of the economy as a whole—is "the end of good times," we know we're in the presence of an industry whose expectations and promises have left the earth's gravitational pull.

To put some flesh on these numbers, let's try a thought experiment. 13 The computer on my desk is about 16 inches by 17 inches. The Census Bureau tells us that the microcomputer industry delivered over 18 million machines in 1994, the year when, according to the *Economist*, good times ended. Of these, perhaps a third went to the home market, the balance to business. At the 40 percent growth rate in the home market cited for that year and the more modest 16 percent growth rate for the business market, the boys in Redmond and Silicon Valley will have covered the United States' 3,679,192 square miles with discarded microcomputers well before my daughter, who is now thirteen, begins to collect Social Security.

Fabulous as they seem, these figures come from only part of the 14 industry. Microcomputers do not define computing, despite their spectacular entry on the scene. The standard story goes like this: There was once a lumbering blue dinosaur called IBM that dominated the computer industry. In due course, smaller, more agile, and immensely more clever mammals appeared on the scene. The most agile and clever of these was Microsoft, which proceeded to expand its ecological niche and, in so doing, drove the feebleminded IBM to the brink of extinction.

The business history in this story is as faulty as its paleontology. 15 IBM may be lumbering and blue, but in 1997 its sales were nearly $78 billion. Compare that with Microsoft's $9 billion. The real story is not in the sales volumes of the two companies but in their profit margins. In 1997 IBM's was 7.7 percent, while Microsoft's was a spectacular 28.7 percent. This almost mythical earning capability is expressed best in *Forbes's* annual list of very rich Americans. We don't hear much about IBM billionaires these days, but Microsoft fortunes are conspicuous in the *Forbes* list, with Bill Gates's $51 billion, Paul Allen's $21 billion, and Steven Ballmer's $10.7 billion. These fortunes were accumulated in less than twenty years from manufacturing a product that requires no materials beyond the inexpensive medium it is stored on—not so different from a pickle producer, whose only cost, after the first jar comes off the line, is the jar itself. It's a tale of alchemical transmutation if ever there was one. Is it really a surprise that most people don't know that IBM is still a very successful company or that computer science does not begin and end with Windows 98?

16   This joyous account of fortunes waiting to be made in the micro-computer industry has a dark side. Just as Satan is the strongest character in *Paradise Lost*, as C.S. Lewis observed, so is popular fascination with computers due as much to the dark side as to the light. Despite generally good economic news for the past few years, Americans seem gloomy about their prospects. Our brave new world, paved over with networked computers from sea to shining sea, may well be one in which we are mostly unemployed or have experienced a serious decline in living standards. Computers, if not always at the center of the problem, are popularly thought to have been a major contributing factor.

17   Look at the substantial decline in manufacturing as a segment of the workforce in the United States. Between 1970 and 1996 (the last year for which data are available), the number of Americans employed increased by about 50 million. During this same period, the number of manufacturing jobs declined by about 200,000. The culprit here is often thought to be computer technology, through assembly line robots or through U.S.-owned (or U.S.-contracted) manufacturing facilities in developing countries. Asia and Latin America, of course, would have less appeal to American corporations without worldwide data communications networks.

18   This analysis of the decline in manufacturing employment is perhaps more appealing than true. I will return to the relationship between computers and productivity. For now it's enough to observe that most people believe there is such a relationship. So if the money to be made in the computer industry is not sufficient inducement to vote for the next school bond issue that would outfit every classroom in your city with networked computers, then the poverty your children will certainly face without such a network should do the trick. With those staggering Microsoft fortunes in the background and the threat of corporate retrenchment in the foreground, I suppose I'm naive to expect the strangers I chat with on planes to know that the computing sciences are more like mathematics and the physical sciences than like desktop publishing—or, for that matter, like the rush to the Klondike goldfields.

19   The emergence of the microcomputer as a consumer item in the past decade and a half has prompted a flood of articles in the educational literature promoting what has come to be called "computer literacy." In its most basic sense, this term appears to refer to something like a passing familiarity with microcomputers and their commercial applications, rather like the ability to drive a car and know when to get the oil changed. Sadly, the proponents of computer literacy have won the high ground by virtue of the term itself. Who would argue with literacy? It is, after all, one of the more complex human achievements. Not only is literacy a shorthand measure of a country's economic

development, but as the rhetorician Walter J. Ong has long argued, once a culture becomes generally literate, its modes of conceptualization are radically altered. Literacy—like motherhood and apple pie in the America of my youth—is unassailable.

But what about the transformative nature of literacy? I am fully aware that similar claims have been made about computers—namely, that computers, like writing, will alter our modes of conceptualization. Maybe so, but not just by running Microsoft Office. I've developed a rule of thumb about claims of this sort: If the subject matter is computers and the tense of the claim is future (and, therefore, its truth-value cannot be ascertained), look at the subtext. Is the claimant a salesman in disguise? To recognize the nonsense in the claim that computers will transform the way we think, we need only indulge in some honest self-examination. I would give up my word processor with great reluctance. This doesn't mean that my neuronal structure is somehow fundamentally different from what it was when I was writing essays similar to this one on my manual Smith Corona. It does mean that the computer industry is a smidgen richer because of my contribution. It also means, as was recently pointed out to me, that it is a good bit easier to run on at great length on a computer than on a typewriter.   20

Not surprisingly, the number of articles addressing computer literacy in the educational literature has kept pace with microcomputer developments. ERIC is a database of titles published in education journals. When I searched ERIC using the keywords *computer literacy* and *computer literate*, I found 97 articles for the years 1966–1981, or an average of about 6 per year. The decade from 1982 to 1991 produced 2,703 hits, or about 270 per year. At first glance the production of articles since 1991 shows welcome signs of dropping off. But the Internet has come to the rescue of both the microcomputer industry and its prognosticators. When I add the terms "Internet," "World Wide Web," and "information superhighway" to the mix (subtracting for duplicates), the total rises to an astonishing 4,680 articles from 1992 through the first half of 1998. This works out to about 720 articles per year. The bulk of the recent articles, of course, are full of blather about the so-called information superhighway and how all those school districts that cannot give every child access to it will be condemning the next generation to lives of poverty and ignorance.   21

Since computer literacy advocates are eloquent on the benefits of computers in our schools (and equally eloquent on the grim fate that awaits those students not so blessed), a brief look at how microcomputers are actually used in primary and secondary schools is in order. Microcomputers are now a solid presence in American education. The U.S. Census Bureau put the number at nearly 7 million in 1997, or just over 7 students per machine, compared with 11 students per machine   22 in 1994 and 63 per machine a decade earlier. Picture a classroom richly endowed with computers. Several students are bent over a machine, eyes aglow with the discoveries unfolding on the screen. Perhaps there is a kindly teacher in the portrait, pointing to some complex relationship that the computer has helped the budding physicists, social scientists, or software engineers to uncover. If this is the way you imagine primary and secondary school students using computers, you are dead wrong. Several important studies have concluded that primary and secondary school students spend more time mastering the intricacies of word processing than they do using computers for the kinds of tasks that we have in mind when we vote for a bond issue.

23   Programming, in fact, was the one area that school computer coordinators saw decline over previous years. I would be the first to acknowledge that programming does not define computer science. This simple fact is what makes the endless discussion of programming languages in computer science circles so tedious. Nevertheless, if computer science does not begin and end with programming, neither will it give up its secrets to those who cannot program. I greet the news that high school students do not program our millions of microcomputers as an English professor might greet the news that the school library is terrific but the kids don't read. Here is a puzzle worth more than a moment's thought. There is an inverse relationship between the availability of microcomputers to primary and secondary school students and the chance that those students will do something substantial with them. I am not saying that the relationship is causal, but the association is there. Draw your own conclusions. [. . .]

24   Given the several thousand articles on computer literacy and the emerging inverse relationship between productivity growth and computer expenditures, it seems reasonable to ask just who does benefit from the computer literacy movement—and who pays for it. The commonsense answer is, Students benefit. Well, common sense is right, but, as usual, only partially so. Students, of course, are served by learning how to use microcomputers. But the main beneficiaries are the major producers of hardware and software. The situation is really quite extraordinary. Schools and colleges across the country are offering academic credit to students who master the basics of sophisticated consumer products. Granted that it is more difficult to master Microsoft Office than it is to learn to use a VCR or a toaster oven, the difference is one of degree, not of kind.

25   The obvious question is why the computer industry itself does not train its customers. The answer is that it doesn't have to. Schools, at great public expense, provide this service to the computer industry free of charge. Not only do the educational institutions provide the trainers

and the setting for the training, they actually purchase the products on which the students are to be trained from the corporations that are the primary beneficiaries of that training. The story is an old but generally unrecognized one in the United States: the costs are socialized, while the benefits are privatized.

I have described a bleak landscape in this essay. Let me summarize my observations: 26

Schools and universities purchase products from the computer industry to offer training that benefits the computer industry.   27

These purchases are both publicly subsidized through tax support and paid for by students (and their parents) themselves.   28

The skill imparted is at best trivial and does not require faculty with advanced degrees in computer science—degrees acquired by and large through public, not computer industry, support.   29

As the number of microcomputers in our schools has grown, the chance that something interesting might be done with them has decreased.   30

The stunning complexity of microcomputer hardware and software has had the disastrous effect of transforming every English professor, every secretary, every engineer, every manager into a computer systems technician.   31

For all the public subsidies involved in the computer literacy movement, the evidence that microcomputers have made good on their central promise—increased productivity—is, at the very least, open to question.   32

If my argument is at least partially correct, we should begin to rethink computing. The microcomputer industry has been with us for a decade and a half. We have poured staggering sums down its insatiable maw. It is time to face an unpleasant fact: the so-called microcomputer revolution has cost much more than it has returned. One problem is that microcomputers are vastly more complex than the tasks ordinarily asked of them. To write a report on a machine with a Pentium II processor, sixty-four megabytes of memory, and an eight-gigabyte hard disk is like leasing the space shuttle to fly from New York to Boston to catch a Celtics game. Though there are those who wouldn't hesitate to do such a thing if they could afford it (or get it subsidized, which is more to the point), we follow their lead at great peril. The computer industry itself is beginning to recognize the foolishness of placing such computing power on every office worker's desk. Oracle, the world's premier manufacturer of database management systems; Sun Microsystems, a maker of powerful and highly respected engineering workstations; and IBM itself are arguing that a substantially scaled-down network computer, costing under $1,000, would serve corporate users better than the monsters necessary to run Microsoft's products.   33

34   Please don't misunderstand. This is not a neo-Luddite plea to toss computers out the window. I am, after all, a computer science professor, and I am certainly not ready (as the militias in my part of the country put it) to get off the grid. Further, the social benefits of computing—from telecommunications to business transactions to medicine to science—are well known. This essay is simply a plea to think reasonably about these machines, to recognize the hucksterism in the hysterical cries for computer literacy, to steel ourselves against the urge to keep throwing money at Redmond and Silicon Valley.

35   Putting microcomputers in their place will also have a salutary effect on my discipline. We in computer science could then begin to claim that our field—like mathematics, like English literature, like philosophy—is a marvelous human creation whose study is its own reward. To study computer science calls for concentration, discipline, even some amount of deferred gratification, but it requires neither Windows 98, nor a four-hundred-megahertz Pentium II processor, nor a graphical Web browser. Though I am tempted, I will not go so far as to say that the introductory study of computer science requires no computing equipment at all (though Alan Turing did do some pretty impressive work without a microcomputer budget). We do seem, however, to have confused the violin with the concerto, the pencil with the theorem, and the dancer with the dance.

36   I am afraid that we in computing have made a Faustian bargain. In exchange for riches, we are condemned to a lifetime of conversations about the World Wide Web. An eternity in hell with Dr. Faustus, suffering the torments of demons, would be an afternoon in the park by comparison.

RESPONDING TO READING

1. According to de Palma, what mythology surrounds computer technology in modern America? What problems does this mythology cause or contribute to?

2. How would your courses be altered if all subjects were "taught as if they were history"? What would be the benefits or drawbacks of such a change?

3. How does de Palma use history and paleontology to tell the story of the computer in America? What problem(s) does he identify with computers, and the popular understanding about them, based on these references?

4. How has the growth of the computer industry affected the realms of business, employment, and education? What positives and negatives have appeared in each because of computers? Choose one area or subfield to discuss with a group in class, and prepare topic headings for a paper on the subject that you could then write either individually or with partners.

5. In an essay, explain how computers have affected—and are affecting—the field that you plan to enter. Interview at least two people who are working in

the area in which you plan to work after graduation. How have computers changed the work these people do? Because of computers, how is the work these people do now different from the work they did when they began their careers?

Marriage as Partnership

ROBERT S. WEISS

Weiss (born 1925), a sociologist, was educated at the University of Buffalo (B.A., 1949) and the University of Michigan (Ph.D.,1955). He has taught sociology at the University of Chicago, Harvard, Brandeis, and MIT. Although Weiss's earlier publications included books on *Processes of Organization* (1956) and *Institutions and the Person* (1968), much of his recent research has focused on the relation of men's work to the rest of their lives, as exemplified by his book, *Staying the Course: The Emotional and Social Lives of Men Who Do Well at Work* (1990), in which "Marriage as Partnership" appears. In his most recent work, *Learning from Strangers* (1995), Weiss explores the "how" and "why" of using interviews to perform research.

Weiss's analysis of the work and lives of some seventy male Boston area upper-middle-class managers, administrators, and professionals, between the ages of 35 and 55, dispels a number of myths about such men—to the extent that one can generalize about an entire society on the basis of such a sample. Unlike Thoreau's "mass of men [who] lead lives of quiet desperation," Weiss's subjects "are doing as well as they can to fashion satisfactory lives for themselves and their families." They "keep society going," for they are good workers, good citizens, and good husbands and fathers according to their assumptions about marriage; they see themselves as the financial mainstays and protectors of their households. Yet Weiss's article also enables us to consider whether the traditional way is the best way for every family member, irrespective of one's age, gender, and class. What aspects of traditional roles will be viable in the future, and what should change with changing times? Why? In what ways would you expect working wives and mothers to answer?

Most marital interaction deals with issues of partnership, large 1 and small: when to have children; whether to use the money in the bank for a vacation; who will take the car in for servicing. Couples raising children together may have few discussions not concerned with partnership issues.

The understandings that inform the partnership aspect of marriage 2 are similar to those that would be found between business partners. True, a man's life is a larger and vaguer enterprise than a business. But the woman to whom the man is married contributes to life's stability of purpose, works for its success, and so deserves a share of its rewards, just as would a business partner.

3   Critical to the marital partnership is the decision of who does what—what will be the contributions of the man and of his wife to the joint enterprise that is the marital partnership?

4   The question of who does which of the chores required to keep a house orderly, the children fed, and the bills paid has lately been an area of skirmishing in that longest of wars, the War Between the Sexes. It was not, however, considered an especially troubling question by the men with whom we spoke. Virtually all of them believed that they and their wives together had established a division of marital labor that worked well enough; it was usually clear what each was to do; there rarely were arguments over tasks left undone. Most indicated that they and their wives were each grateful to the other for doing so much. A few, to be sure, harbored resentments because their wives weren't the housekeepers they thought they should be or because their wives too infrequently consulted them about the children. And at some earlier point in their marriages, several of the men seemed to have engaged in sometimes tense negotiations with their wives about how much the men were expected to help. But in most men's marriages what seemed to exist now was a division of labor that operated smoothly and with apparent acceptance by the men and their wives.

5   The division of labor in childless marriages differed from that in marriages with children. Couples without children tended to maintain a division of labor somewhere between the "everybody does everything" of roommates or cohabitants and the sexual allocation of responsibility of a traditional married pair. The men might be more responsible for the heavy tasks, the wives for domestic arrangements, but there was a great deal of sharing. Especially for marriages in which the wives' earnings were comparable to the husbands', who did what seemed to be as much a matter of personal preference as of conformity to traditional expectations.

6   But couples whose division of household labor had been roughly symmetric before the arrival of children witnessed an abrupt change once children were on the scene. The wives who had been working withdrew from the labor force so that they could look after the children. Most dropped out entirely, although a few kept some sort of part-time association, such as doing editing at home. The husbands, meanwhile, redoubled their efforts at work, since now they had a family to support.

7   Yet even after the arrival of children husbands did more than "men's work" around the house, and women more than "women's work." Husbands sometimes cooked, often helped with cleaning, and looked after the children. Wives did yard work and, when the children were nursery school age, returned to paid employment.

Despite this flexibility, husbands and wives seemed to decide who   8
would do what on the basis of underlying principles. They might not
themselves be able to say exactly what the principles were, but they
seemed nevertheless to share belief in the principles and generally to
agree on their application.

The Underlying Principles of the Marital Division of Labor

All couples began their married lives with the recognition that   9
some tasks were traditionally "men's work" and others traditionally
"women's work," an implication of principles that might be referred to
as *the traditional principles* of the marital division of labor. Most couples
used these principles to establish a basic pattern for their lives together.
They might then modify the pattern, but often enough they acted on
the principles without thinking much about the matter. Couples who
were ideologically opposed to the traditional principles were likely
nevertheless to act on them after they had children.

Whether or not they believe that their household is organized   10
along traditional lines, men know which tasks should be theirs, according to the traditional allocations, and which should be their wives'.
They may have trouble, however, in developing an adequate formulation. Asked to say what makes something men's work and what makes
something women's, they are likely to offer the rule that "Men are the
breadwinners, and their wives take care of the house and the children."
But they would agree that yardwork is men's work even though it is a
part of home maintenance, as are household repairs and fixing the gut-
ters. And they would agree that taking the children to a ballgame is
something men should do, more than women, even though it involves
child care. The traditional principles are not captured fully by "Men are
breadwinners, women are homemakers and mothers."

More nearly fundamental, for the traditional view of the marital   11
division of labor, is that men provide the household with a structure
within which to live and with the social place that comes with it. Men
are responsible for supplying the household with money, as an expression of their responsibility for the standard of living of the household
and the respect it commands in the community. They are also responsible for the integrity of the household, which is expressed as keeping
the physical structure of the household in repair and protecting its occupants. And they have first responsibility for launching their children into adulthoods in which the children have a respectable place in
the society.

In this traditional division of labor, men are responsible for much   12
of the household's relationships with the wider society. Their wives,
then, are responsible for the internal functioning of the home; for child

care and home maintenance; for relationships within the home; for the actual workings of the family.

13   The traditional principles were ordinarily augmented by an additional principle, *the principle of helping out*. No matter who is supposed to do what, the other should be willing to help out if needed. If the man is not otherwise engaged and his wife needs help putting the children to bed, the man ought to pitch in. The responsibility, however, would remain his wife's.

14   The principle of helping out is entirely consistent with the traditional principles in that it does not lead to questioning the traditional allocation of responsibilities. Quite different is another principle often invoked in debates over the marital division of labor, *the principle of equity*. This is the principle that the work of the marriage should be divided fairly between the husband and wife.

15   The principle of equity can produce results different from those of the traditional principles of the division of labor augmented by the principle of helping out. In application of the principle of equity, fairness is all. If neither the man nor his wife enjoys cleaning the house, then the husband should clean the house one week, the wife the next, or they should clean the house together, each doing half the work. Or the wife might be compensated elsewhere; perhaps the man should do some other task that neither enjoys, like laundry.

16   It is also not fair for one partner to use a labor-saving approach that is not available to the other partner. If the man and his wife decide that they will share the cooking, it is not fair for the man to do his share by ringing up the neighborhood pizza parlor. Nor is it fair for one partner to perform child care by playing with the children when the other partner performs child care by preparing their food. Nor is it fair for one partner to claim press of work when the other partner works just as hard.

17   Sometimes a man will perform a chore that is based in none of these principles. A husband will fix breakfast for his wife on a Sunday morning, although both agree that cooking is the wife's responsibility and there is no need for the husband to help or reason for him to believe that fixing her breakfast is only fair. Under such circumstances, his breakfast preparation is a gift to his wife, an expression of affection.

The Principles in Practice

18   In their division of marital labor, the men of this study largely followed traditional principles augmented by the principle of helping out, even though they were also committed to the principle of equity. This

was possible because the men felt that the arrangement they had established with their wives was fair.

With two exceptions, both in childless couples, one a man whose 19
wife earned as much as he did, the other a man whose wife earned more, the men of our sample understood themselves to be the marital partner in charge of assuring the family's income. That does not mean that they expected to be the sole earners of that income, but rather that they considered themselves to be the main earners, the partners who were ultimately responsible. The men might need their wives to help out if the household was to attain an aimed-at standard of living, but that did not diminish their responsibility for the domain. If a family's income should be too little for its bills, the fault would be the man's alone, not his wife's or his and his wife's together. He might perhaps argue that the bills were unjustified; that his wife, as the partner responsible for the family's spending, had overspent. But if he accepted that the family's income was inadequate, the failure would be entirely his.

Most men believed it was also they who were responsible for the 20
maintenance of the home and its grounds. In keeping with this, they were the ones to do whatever upkeep required building-trade skills, such as painting and carpentry, or to conduct the negotiations with the tradesmen who possessed such skills. However, maintenance of grounds, especially planting and gardening, could be assimilated to internal home care and become the woman's job, especially if the aim were decorative rather than functional. So could arranging for painting and carpentry. Indeed, men who felt they knew too little to hold their own with tradesmen, and so felt inadequate in an area that they believed to be theirs, could be relieved to have their wives take over. They could rationalize that it was easier for their wives to act as contractors because their wives were home during the day; and, in any event, their wives were only helping out.

Men believe without question that they are the ones to whom the 21
family should look for protection. It is they who should caution a daughter's boyfriend to drive carefully, should stand between an angry neighbor and one of their children who has infringed on that neighbor's territory, and, if no one else can do it, should be the one to send away a persistent door-to-door salesman. Couples so strongly committed to achieving equity that they try to ensure that the husband and wife perform the same tasks nevertheless consider it the husband's responsibility to check out a noise in the night.

Men felt strongly that it should be they who sponsored their sons 22
into the world of achievement: sports and, eventually, work. They also thought they should contribute to their daughter's movement into

adulthood, but were less certain how this was to be done, especially after the daughters became adolescent. Sometimes they acted to support their older daughters' functioning at school or in work just as they might their sons', but at other times they seemed to feel that all they could offer was protection.

23   Men believed that their wives were responsible for the quality of life inside their homes. This included all the activities necessary to the logistic support of the members of the household: keeping the household in provisions, producing meals and clean clothes, and when necessary driving the children to their various activities. It also included attending to the emotional climate of the household. The children's feelings of security, the ease with which people talked with each other, the household's sense of comfort—all these they saw as within their wives' domain. They looked to their wives for information about the emotional well-being of family members and, sometimes, for coaching in their own relationships with their children.

24   Men believed that as an extension of the wives' responsibility for relationships within the home, their wives should manage the family's relationships with couples who were friends and with the family's kin, including the man's mother and sisters. The men, of course, did their own social arranging when it involved partners in sport or in leisure activities.

25   Men believed that they, rather than their wives, should interpret the events of business and politics for the family. Managing the family's boundary with the political and economic world was in their domain of responsibility.

26   These principles of allocation of marital responsibilities are likely to appear so natural to men—and to their wives—that they become the basis for the marital division of labor without discussion or thought.

> Subconsciously, I rely on my wife to run the house, keep things organized. And so far as our social schedule, she probably takes care of that in the sense of what we're going to be doing on Friday night or Wednesday or Sunday. And I suppose she relies on me to bring the bread home and put it on the table.
>
> *Mr. Powers, businessman*

27   Mr. Abbott, a high-level technician, has been married almost thirty years. His wife is in charge of patient information at a local hospital. Their two children are now grown. Mr. Abbott said:

> We've never officially worked it out, but I think that there are things that are categorized as the man type jobs such as painting the house, making repairs. She does a very good job with the house, keeps the house very clean. Shopping is her job, obviously. She doesn't mind.

I let her pay most of the bills. She handles the budget in that sense. I take care of what I call the investing, whether it be savings or buying real estate or whatever. She won't interfere with that. We discuss major purchases. But I would have to say that she would probably leave that to me.

I don't have a great deal of difficulty in explaining myself if I want to invest in some silly stock. I tell her it's really going to become great in a short while. She'll believe me and we'll go ahead and do it. Some of my ventures haven't been that good, either. Some have been quite good.

In recent years there has been a good deal of criticism of men for insisting on a traditional division of labor within the home even when their wives work full time outside of the home. Men have been accused of using the power of their income (or of a supposed greater ability to make a life for themselves were the marriage to end) to require their wives to perform a disproportionate number of those tasks involved in running a home that are menial, repetitive, and degrading. However, this is not at all the way men feel about the traditional division of labor. Nor does it seem accurate to say that men smugly refuse to acknowledge that they have a good thing. Rather, men seem deeply invested in doing well at what they believe to be their responsibilities. Far from wanting to shirk their responsibility for income production, they will accept menial, repetitive, degrading, and dangerous work, if no better work is available. When they fail to meet what they believe to have been one of their responsibilties—providing an adequate income, protecting a child—their self-blame can be bottomless even if the fault was not theirs.   28

There is another reason men object, if only through passive resistance, to sharing tasks traditional principles would say are their wives'. So long as they—and their wives—believe the tasks to be shared are in their wives' domains of responsibility, the men are answerable to their wives. Suppose a couple should decide that the husband will supervise the children's baths. The husband is asked by the children what toys they can take into the tub. Because the husband is functioning in his wife's domain—care of the children and their possessions—his response would be subject to overrule by her. If she said, "The boy shouldn't need to take toys into the tub any more," that would be it. Men accept that in their wives' domains of responsibility, their wives are the lead partner—not quite the boss, but certainly the partner with greater authority. It's hard for a man, when doing the dishes, not to feel subordinate to his wife.   29

I tend to go along with the wife's beliefs and desires in terms of what the kids should have and what would be good for them and whether they can get along without something or not, that kind of thing. If I don't think that things are extremely wrong, and I don't find too many that are, or if I don't really feel all that strongly about them one way or the other, it's more comfortable for me to go along with it.

Mr. Draper, executive and business owner

30   One element of the traditional view of the family is that the man is the family's "head." Yet the meaning of this status is by no means immediately apparent. One meaning it does not have is that he is the family's boss.

31   For several years, when teaching courses on the family or leading workshops on family issues, I have asked people to role-play a family meeting. I cast a family of mother, father, twelve-year-old daughter, and ten-year-old son. I say that the family must work out how to arrange the family vacation. I tell the father that he is an avid fisherman and wants to vacation near a trout stream, and I tell the mother that she does not want to spend her vacation cleaning fish. I go on to tell the mother that she would prefer a beach setting where the children would have other children with whom to play, perhaps a cottage along a safe shore. And then I ask the family to resolve the dilemma.

32   Almost always when I have done this, the woman playing the mother has taken the lead. She has asked the husband for his ideas, has elicited reactions from the children, has made her own suggestions and has piloted the way to compromise. She might first gain her husband's agreement to a plan that would provide something for everyone, would then turn to the children, inform them, listen to their objections, and gain their acquiescence by diplomacy, bribery, and firmness. Sometimes the man held out stubbornly for the trout stream, but always the woman won him around. In one instance the man suggested going off by himself, but when the woman said that she wouldn't want him to do that, he immediately dropped the idea.

33   To this point the woman would be the marital partner who was really running things in the family, though she would be doing so diplomatically, with deference to her husband. But now, with a decision agreed to, something noteworthy would occur. The man would turn to me and nod, to indicate that the family had come to a resolution. Though the woman had piloted the resolution, the man would assume responsibility for presenting it to me.

34   It happened once that the man and woman turned to me together to say they had completed the exercise. I then sat stone-faced, refusing to respond. By doing this I manufactured an emergency: an instructor who seemed to have gone into a catatonic trance. Now, even though earlier it had not been the man alone who represented the family, it was

the man who took charge and said again, a bit louder, that the group had completed the exercise.

In family life, the man is not head of the family in the sense that he   35 gets his way; often enough he ends by endorsing his wife's plans. He is family head in that he represents the family in its dealings with the world.

Men who adhere to traditional principles in the allocation of mari-   36 tal responsibilities almost uniformly also adhere to the principle of helping out, though with wide variation in the extent to which they are asked to help and actually do help. The assumption that each partner will help the other underlies much of what appears to be role sharing. Should the woman be overwhelmed by tasks within the home, the man may help out by vacuuming, doing dishes, or taking the kids for a ride in the car. Should the man be unable through his own income to meet the household's bills, then the woman may, in turn, help out. Should the man be made anxious by confrontations, then the woman can represent the household in a neighborhood conflict. And should the woman hate to cook, the man may do the cooking.

In all instances of helping out, both men and women are aware of   37 whose is the initial and formal responsibility. They understand that the one who helps out is doing something extra, and a partner may decline to help out if confronted by more urgent matters in his or her own domain. Men, especially, may give helping their wives lower priority than the demands of their work.

> Along with working, she keeps the house up and does the shopping and keeps everything rolling inside, and I try to get everything outside. She takes care of the household end, I take care of the other stuff, the outside, the repairs, things like that. Paying the bills and things like that. She takes care of the food and the wash and whatever needs to be cleaned. Even though I try to help her out once in a while, I haven't been successful lately.
>
> *Mr. Brewer, owner of a catering business*

As noted previously, one problem with helping out is that the   38 helper is in a subordinate position. The domain is, after all, the spouse's. So when wives help their husbands in their husbands' work, the wives are apt to be treated as subordinates rather than partners. And when men help their wives at home, their wives are apt to give them direction.

Reliance on traditional principles plus helping out is always sub-   39 ject to criticism from the standpoint of equity. "Yes," a woman may say, "in our parents' families our mothers did the cooking and cleaning. But they didn't also work full time and bring in almost half the income. It isn't fair for me not only to work but also to have responsibility for the home and the children."

40   The principle of equity can make men uncomfortable because it implies that the men aren't meeting their obligations to their families through their work, their protectiveness, their captaining, and their helping out. Also, the men may anticipate becoming subordinates in their wives' domains of responsibility despite their wives' insistence that responsibility will be shared. The following scenario is one that some young couples report having followed.

> The wife argues, relying on the principle of equity: "You ought to share the work of the home. I work as hard at my job as you do at yours."
>
> The husband responds, rejecting the principle of equity, since he believes that he is already doing his share by meeting traditional expectations, and replacing it with the principle of helping out. "Tell me what to do and I'll do it."
>
> The wife returns to the principle of equity since use of the principle of helping out leaves her with unshared responsibility: "You live here too. You can see as well as I what has to be done. Why should I have to tell you what to do?"
>
> The husband now reminds his wife that others are likely to see the domain as hers by threatening her with inferior performance. "Well, I know your standards are different, but you'll have to put up with the way I do it."

41   The husband has a good chance of winning, because his wife is likely to agree that others will see her as the lead partner in home maintenance. In consequence it will be she who is embarrassed should a friend or relative visit and find the house scruffy.

Dual-Career Marriages

42   Mr. Foster is a former investment counselor who now, with partners, manages a program of mutual funds. His income is large. Mrs. Foster has done graduate work in business management. She holds a responsible executive position in an accounting firm that pays her well, though her income does not match her husband's. Mr. Foster told us that he admired his wife for her success and fully supported her in her commitment to work.

43   The Fosters had three children, all at home, the youngest just finishing primary school. Mr. Foster spent about as much time with the children as did his wife. When the children were smaller, Mrs. Foster had stayed at home with them. After about a year at home she had become deeply depressed, and her husband, searching for a remedy, had urged her to return to graduate school.

That time she was at home trying to deal with the kids, I think that was probably the hardest part of our marriage. She was just restless, very restless, and not feeling very accomplished. She was having a difficult time coping with being married and having kids and not having a career. At least that was my analysis.

I think that I would really say she was pretty disturbed. I remember now, the way she woke up crying a couple of times, like in bed, talking about her life. I used to get bored with it all. I'd say, "Just relax and go to sleep," that kind of thing. It was just sort of unarticulated anxiety on her part. It was a lot of self-doubt. She was not very confident, not as confident a person as she is now. And I remember it was very repetitive. It kept going around in circles. And she didn't quite know what was bugging her. But something sure as hell was bugging her. I was trying to be supportive. Trying to make it work.

What we did, she went back to school. It was a rallying point, an objective that was very definable. Everybody had a common goal to hold the thing together. And that was good. I was absolutely supportive of her going back to school. Absolutely! More than supportive, I pushed it. Because, why the hell shouldn't she? Why should she stay home? It's ridiculous.

Note how Mr. Foster applied the fundamental principles of the division of labor to his marriage. He thought of his wife as the partner primarily responsible for the children and became irritated when she could not adapt to staying at home. But he also thought of himself as responsible for making the family work. When he became aware that staying home was depressing his wife, he saw it as his place to act. 44

With his wife working, Mr. Foster began to share tasks in the home. He did some of the cooking (a bit less than his wife) and helped clean up after dinner. Most of the cooking and a good deal of child care was performed by a foreign student who acted as an au pair. While Mr. Foster's willingness to help at home was a critical element in freeing Mrs. Foster's time and energies for her job, having the foreign student may well have permitted the system to work. 45

Mr. Foster continued to define himself as the partner ultimately responsible for the family's support. As one expression of this, he made his bank account available to his wife, although his wife kept her bank account entirely to herself. 46

We've always had separate bank accounts, but I used to give Paula money before she went to work. Now Paula can sign on my account. I can't sign on hers.

Certainly Paula's working has made a very big difference in what we could do. But I'm the court of last resort. I mean, I'm the backstop.

Mr. Foster did not pay for everything. Mrs. Foster paid for items within the woman's domain: groceries and housekeeping services. Mr. 47

Foster paid for the upkeep items, the items necessary to keep the house going. As Mr. Foster put it: "Paula runs much of the house and I run other things." Mr. Foster paid for evenings out—unless he was without cash, in which case he appealed to the principle of helping out:

> Paula buys the groceries. There's a guy who comes in here once a week, and the groceries, that's a pretty good bill. And she pays for the housekeeping. And I pay for essentially everything else. I pay for the telephone and the lights and tutions and insurance. She buys a lot of stuff for the house that she wants to buy. Large furniture, that gets in a gray area. If we go out to dinner, I pay, generally. If I have money.

48   Mrs. Foster was highly successful in her work and became an important member of her firm. Her contribution to the firm was not, in Mr. Foster's view, properly recognized. Mr. Foster became outraged on his wife's behalf.

> After two years in the firm she believed she deserved a promotion and salary increase. They were refused. One reason given her was that she didn't need the status or the income since her husband was so successful.
>
> This is a textbook case, what went on there. People who don't have daughters or wives, men who don't have daughters or wives, who have gone through this, don't believe it goes on! This was so blatant it ought to be written up. I can't stand those people any more. I just absolutely see red! Just the hypocrisy! That's what it is, it's hypocrisy!

49   Mr. Foster's first thought, on hearing the story from his wife, was to provide her with understanding and support. But this was *his wife* who was being misused, and he wanted to do battle for her. Again, a traditional principle: the husband's responsibility to protect the members of his household. Mr. Foster, insofar as he did not protect his wife, was failing to behave properly, in a way he could himself respect.

50   In another dual-career family, when the wife reported harsh and unfair criticism from her boss, her husband felt almost impelled to call the boss and tell him off. The wife, alarmed, said, "Don't you dare! It means my career!" The husband reported the incident with full appreciation that his reaction had been misguided, but also with pride that he had been so strongly protective.

51   That the Fosters maintained a dual-career marriage does not mean that Mr. Foster changed his understandings of his responsibilities in his family. Rather, he adapted his understandings to his special situation. He saw himself as behaving well—indeed, unselfishly.

I think men who aren't accepting of their wives' working are probably pretty selfish. I know there are a lot of people like that. We spent Saturday night with a couple like that. He wants his wife *there*. Why the hell *should* she be *there*? At his beck and call. Women are people.

Mr. Foster viewed his acceptance of his wife's working as some- 52 thing he was doing for her. (That was why he saw himself as unselfish.) Men can also, of course, understand their wives' working as helping out. Especially if their wives are not overburdened at home, and expenses have mounted—as with children at college—men may urge their wives to work.

> We no longer have any children at home. And we will need money, at least for a couple of years, to pay two tuition bills. So those two things kind of came together at the same time. And she is going to be working and getting some money to help us over the hump with the tuition bills. After the tuition bills stop or maybe after we have only one child in school, if she wants to work, fine, if she doesn't, it is really up to her.
>
> *Mr. Ryder, department head*

At no point do men understand themselves to be no longer respon- 53 sible for income production, neither when they believe that their wives are working to help out nor when they believe their wives are working for self-realization. Nor do they stop considering their wives responsible for the domains that would be theirs were they not working.

Men are ordinarily willing to help working wives by contributing 54 to home maintenance and child care; even more, they are willing to accept that less will get done. They may, though, have moments when they regret having supported their wives' desire to work. Mr. Foster, for example, despite his insistence that he was willing to do dishes and to cook when the au pair was otherwise occupied, was irritated by evenings spent alone because his wife had to work. And though he said he didn't miss the social life that had been sacrificed to his wife's new priorities, he was thoroughly aware that it had been sacrificed.

Most of all, when men's wives work, men are likely to miss their 55 wives' solicitude should the men be stressed or fatigued by *their* work. Working wives are likely to be less attentive to careworn husbands than wives who believe their husbands to be engaged in a lone struggle for the family's subsistence. In one dual-career couple the husband and wife had agreed that neither of them would begin their evening together by burdening the other with the problems of the day. But the husband seemed wistfully to wish his wife had more tolerance for his job complaints.

RESPONDING TO READING

1. Weiss looks at the same issue that Fallows examined in Chapter 3, but from a quite different perspective. What is his angle of vision? What does he see as the significant question to deal with? Why is this question important for the future of the family?

2. Does the set of traditional assumptions about their marital responsibilities made by the men in the interviews reflect your experience? What changes in husbands' assumptions, if any, occur when wives work? What evidence does Weiss give for these conclusions and how convincing are his data? Conduct two or three interviews of your own with married men of different ages, and write an essay on the assumptions about marital responsibilities that emerge from your data; compare your conclusions to those Weiss asserts.

3. Mr. Foster sees himself as very supportive of his wife as she returns to work. But Weiss sees this support rather differently: "Mr. Foster viewed his acceptance of his wife's working as something he was doing for her." How do you think Mrs. Foster saw the situation? What distinction is Weiss drawing here? Is it important?

4. Weiss suggests that similar sets of motives lie beneath the problems that occur when wives work for their husbands and the problems that occur when husbands become protective of their wives at work. What are these motives and how do they relate to the "traditional assumptions" Weiss has defined.

5. Elsewhere, Weiss has commented that, although "men's traditional understandings of marriage are in no way modified by wives working," men's behaviors "have changed greatly." Explain what Weiss means, giving examples from his essay and, if appropriate, from your own experience. To what degree do the essays by Tannen in Chapter 4 and Fallows shed light on this interplay of traditional understandings and apparently untraditional behaviors?

Why Feminism Is Good for the Jews

LETTY COTTIN POGREBIN

"When someone attacks you as an 'outspoken intellectual female from New York,' you're not sure if they're putting you down as a feminist, a Jew, or an Easterner," might well be Pogrebin's leitmotif. Pogrebin was born (1939) and raised in New York City, where she has continued live throughout a satisfying long-term marriage, motherhood (one of her three children is now a *New York Times* reporter), and a demanding career as a journalist and—her term—"a Zionist–feminist peace activist." After graduating from Brandeis (1959), she became publicity director for the publisher Bernard Geis Associates and rose to vice president within a decade. Her strong feminist sentiments led to a career change in 1971, a pivotal year in which she became a cofounder of the National Women's Political Caucus and a founding mother and member of the editorial board of *Ms.*, a pioneering feminist magazine. Her books include *How to Make It in a [Business] Man's World* (1970); *Getting Yours: How to Make the System Work for the Working Woman* (1975), which contained practical advice for women on union membership, maternity rights, and the Equal Rights Amendment; and *Growing Up Free: Raising Your Child in the 80s* (1980), which focuses on nonsexist child rearing. She collaborated with Marlo Thomas on *Free to be You and Me*, a best-selling collection of nonsexist songs and stories for children. In recent years, her political activism has focused on Jewish–Arab peace and reconciliation and on women's rights in Israel, through leadership of a number of international peace and welfare organizations.

"Why Feminism Is Good for the Jews" is a slightly excerpted chapter from *Deborah, Golda, and Me: Being Female and Jewish in America* (1991)—Deborah being a "prophetess, military commander, and the only woman among the Bible's thirteen Judges"; Golda being Golda Meir, Prime Minister of Israel 1969–74. The book is a combination of Pogrebin's autobiography and a feminist manifesto, attempting to "illuminate in personal terms one woman's struggle to reconcile Judaism and feminism." "Anti-Semitism in the Women's Movement," first published in *Ms.* (1982) to a great outcry and reprinted in *Deborah, Golda, and Me*, prepared the intellectual ground for "Why Feminism Is Good for the Jews."

When I was in the third grade my parents enrolled me at the Yeshiva of Central Queens, where we had a full Hebrew school curriculum in the morning and "English school" until four in the afternoon. I remember little of my two years at the Yeshiva other than a teacher named Mrs. Young who wore bright red lipstick and eyeglasses to match, and the way the boys fidgeted with their tzitzit, the biblically prescribed tassel fringes that hang out from the waistline of men's pants. And I remember one particular Talmud session . . .   1

We were reading about Rabbi Akiba who insisted on studying the Torah regardless of a Roman decree forbidding it. When a friend asked him why he took such a risk, Rabbi Akiba answered with a parable about a fox on a riverbank watching fish run in a stream.   2

"Why do you run so?" asked the fox.   3

"Because we fear the fishing nets," replied the fish.   4

"Well," said the clever fox, "why not come up on dry land and live with me in safety?"   5

"Because if we are not safe in water which is supposed to be our home, how much less safe will we be on land where we shall surely die?"   6

Rabbi Akiba was talking about Jews.   7

8   "The Torah is our life," he explained to his friend. "We may study it and be in danger from our enemies; but if we give it up, we would disappear and be no more."

9   When the teacher, a visiting rabbi, finished telling the story, I raised my hand. "There must be other possibilities besides the fox or the fishnet," I insisted. "Why should Jews have the choices of a fish?"

10   "Oy!" moaned the rabbi, palms to the sky. "Who needs a girl with a boy's head?"

11   Maybe he meant it as a compliment, the way people say "She thinks like a man" with the intention of flattering a woman. But when I was nine years old, I thought he was saying there was something wrong with me. My father reassured me that my head was just fine and that the rabbi obviously thought I had asked a smart question. But since there isn't much place for smart women in Judaism, what he really meant was, "Who needs such a brain to be *wasted* on a girl?" The rabbi was telling me that I could be a brain or a girl, but not both.

12   In the Jewish world, as everywhere else, I am still hearing smart women labeled unfeminine when all they want is the right to think. Women who speak up on their own behalf are called "strident" when all they are asking is "What about us?" Women who work on women's issues are treated as traitors to Jewish solidarity when all they are saying is "We are Jews too." Women who challenge male supremacy are accused of betraying Jewish men, when all they are doing is refusing to be, in the words of Isaac Bashevis Singer, "a man's footstool." A Jewish feminist is nobody's footstool.

13   However, Jewish women are forced to make choices not required of Jews who aren't women, or women who aren't Jews. Specifically, we often are asked to choose between two movements that represent both aspects of our double identity—Judaism and feminism. Pressured to declare a priority, I feel like a child who is given the impossible task of selecting a preferred parent, or like a prisoner allowed food or water but not both. It makes no sense to ask me to side with only one half of my self interests, yet at times both camps—organized Judaism and organized feminism—expect just that. They yank and pull until I feel like the rope in a tug-of-war, frayed and frazzled both as a Jew in the women's movement and as a feminist in Judaism.

14   [. . .] Rather than assume we all understand the term "Jewish feminism" the same way, I want to explain that I use it to summarize a whole system of moral and political commitments. Feminists dissect privilege. We deconstruct and examine the way gender plays out in power relations, political agendas, and economic contexts. We ask, "Who benefits? Who hurts?" *Webster's Dictionary* defines feminism as a doctrine advocating the legal, economic, and social equality of the

sexes. *Jewish* feminism is all that plus a doctrine advocating unmitigated chutzpah within the Jewish community.

The Jewish feminist analysis begins at the beginning with Judaism's male favoritism. "The world cannot be without sons and daughters," said Rabbi Judah the Prince, who compiled the Mishnah, "yet happy is he who has sons and woe to him who has daughters." The ancient tradition of son preference continues today: nearly 92 percent of American Jewish couples say they want their firstborn to be a boy. In Israel, when a woman has just given birth to a daughter, a common response is *"Banot simon le banim"* ("Having a girl is a sign you will have a boy next"). In other words, next time you'll get it right.

To Jewish feminists, this rudimentary sexism is symptomatic of a world in need of repair. Indeed, if *tikkun olam*—the repair of the world—is an assignment Jews are supposed to take seriously, Jewish feminists add to the repair kit not just the tools of Jewish ethics but the equity blueprints of feminism. We start with Judaism's core mandate to do *tzedakah*—the Hebrew word meaning charity, caring, and "right action" whose linguistic root, *tzedek*, means justice—and we apply that mandate to gender. Although Judaism is not an egalitarian system, we believe that the theological injunction to "pursue justice" must lead ethical Jews to challenge the gender double standard. We test the fairness of a statement or policy by substituting the word "woman" wherever it says "Jew," or "Jew" wherever it says "woman." When we find inhumanity to women, we say "custom" is no substitute for decency, and when we find less justice for Jews than non-Jews, we expect reparations.

Jewish feminists believe that women should not only perform *tzedakah* and *gemilut hesed* (acts of lovingkindness), but also receive them. We ask that the Jewish community, which is so generous to the poor and hungry, be generous to women, who are spiritually impoverished and hungry for power over their lives. But we do not limit our purview to women who are victims. We celebrate women of intellectual boldness and worldly achievement. We believe that the Jewish woman who refuses to be a footstool for a man is also fortifying herself so that if need be, she can refuse to be a footstool for a Gentile.

In the United States, Jewish feminism has become almost as specialized as the field of medicine. Religious feminists target injustice in the synagogue and repair that world with new rituals and a new inclusiveness. Secular feminists monitor the world outside the synagogue, but do it with a Jewish heart and a broadened definition of "our issues."

Homelessness, for example, is both a women's and a Jewish issue. It's a women's issue because more and more mothers and children are

15

16

17

18

19

living on the streets, and because many women are just one man away from homelessness themselves. It's a Jewish issue because, whether or not Jews are personally affected, relieving human misery is a moral imperative and acting morally is what *makes* us Jews. This is not a tautology. In Leonard Fein's words, "It is the right way to live whether or not it promotes Jewish continuity or anything else outside itself."

20   Some Jewish feminists do their caring in the world outside the Jewish community. Every Saturday morning, for instance, a group of women wearing prayer shawls and *kipot* on their heads meet in front of an abortion clinic and say a prayer to help each other endure the day ahead. They are volunteer escorts who will stand between taunting, shrieking "Operation Rescue" bullies and the frightened pregnant women who come to the clinic to exercise their right to reproductive choice.

21   Other Jewish feminists direct their caring to the struggle for disarmament and environmental sanity, to the sanctuary movement, to antiracism work, gay and lesbian rights, the national campaign for child care, hunger projects, and AIDS activism—and they bring their feminist values and their Judaism with them wherever they go.

22   In Natan Sharansky's autobiography, *Fear No Evil*, one splendid passage describes the way a developed Jewish identity can expand rather than contract one's political commitments:

> While my own focus was on Jewish emigration, I was also active on behalf of people from many national and religious groups whose rights were brutally violated by the Soviet regime, including Pentecostals and Catholics, Ukrainians and Crimean Tatars....My interest in helping other persecuted peoples was an important part of my own freedom—a freedom that became real only after I returned to my Jewish roots.

Sharansky's next paragraph (absent the masculine pronouns) could have been written by a young Jewish feminist:

> For the activist Jews of my generation, our movement represented the exact opposite of what our parents had gone through when they were young. But we saw what had happened to their dreams, and we understood that the path to liberation could not be found in denying our own roots while pursuing universal goals. On the contrary: we had to deepen our commitment, because only he who understands his own identity and has already become a free person can work effectively for the human rights of others.

23 There are also Jewish feminists who choose to focus their efforts on the needs of Jews. They help Jewish institutions establish child-care cen-

ters, parenting classes, support groups for Jewish lesbians, social programs that break the Noah's Ark syndrome and welcome Jewish singles one by one. They promote lectures, films, and courses that reflect feminist perspectives on issues of concern to Jews—like the environmental crisis, or the morality of surrogate motherhood. They introduce nonsexist books and biographies of achieving Jewish women into Hebrew schools. They collect women's oral histories so that female reality will be part of the Jewish master story for future generations.

Along with a wider definition of "our issues," Jewish feminists also 24
broaden the concept of *tzedakah*. They support not just traditional Jewish causes like Hadassah Hospital or Yeshiva University, but progressive social justice groups like New Jewish Agenda, American Jewish World Service, New Israel Fund, the Shalom Center, the Jewish Fund for Justice, and projects that specifically benefit women—such as *Lilith*, the magazine of Jewish feminism; or the Israel Women's Network; or the battered women's shelters here and in Israel. Traditional Jews have no trouble contributing to Hadassah Hospital or Yeshiva University, but if Jewish feminists do not support women's empowerment projects few others will.

When it comes to philanthropy, I have begun to ask my audiences 25
to take a cue from our mothers' warning that we had better wear clean underwear in case we get hit by a truck. I ask that we look at our checkbook stubs instead. If you got hit by a truck, and someone found your checkbook, what would it tell the world about you and your values? Are you buying too much clothing, jewelry, vacations, more pleasures than you need? Are you giving only to "safe" causes like the library, symphony, cancer, or heart disease? Or are you developing the habit of *feminist* philanthropy—giving independently of your husband if you have a husband—and are you funding change, not charity, especially for women?

Of the eight degrees of *tzedakah* described by Maimonides, the 26
highest is that form of assistance we give to enable the weak to raise themselves. Likewise, feminism's goal is not to "help" but to permanently strengthen women by developing their self-esteem and marketable skills and reducing their dependence on men or social services. Feminists search out projects that directly benefit and empower *women*, because we see women as both the subject and the instrument of our efforts.

Jewish feminists also serve as watchdogs within the community. We 27
complain when other Jews subvert women's issues. We fuss when Jewish men treat child care, parental leave, domestic violence, or sexual harassment as trivial sidelines to the main battles on the Jewish agenda. We fault the men who have opposed affirmative action—who worry about its impact on Jewish *men* and ignore the fact that many Jewish

women lawyers, doctors, engineers, students, and executives have affirmative action to thank for their education or their job. We criticize Jewish agencies because more than half their staffs but only 2 percent of their executive directors are women. We protest when the Jewish establishment makes politically pragmatic alliances with Evangelical Christians and right-wing conservatives, selling out women's rights in return for lip service to Israel's security. We want our agenda to be a priority for Jewish men too, and we deplore those whose loyalty to Israel becomes an excuse for bedding down with the reactionaries. [. . .]

28   In the personal sphere, we want girl babies and boy babies to be greeted as equally precious Jewish lives and we want those lives to be made equally meaningful and satisfying. We are not happy when parents spend more money to celebrate a Bar Mitzvah than a Bat Mitzvah. We ask friends of the family to choose an appropriate coming-of-age gift to give to both sexes, rather than codify sex-specific rituals by giving a boy a kiddush cup or a prayer book, while a girl gets a *challah* knife or candlesticks. [. . .]

29   Jewish feminists talk back. We are not always polite. We make other Jews uncomfortable. We openly rebuke a wide variety of Jewish men—the comedian who gets laughs at our expense; the liberal man who boasts of being a supportive mate and "letting" his wife work, but never makes it any easier for her by doing the laundry; the screenwriter who blames his mother for everything; the novelist who makes Jewish women unlovable; the mythographer who glorifies only the *ayshet chayil* (the wife who "watches her family's comings and goings") and not our activist heroines.

30   That's a pretty wide-ranging definition of Jewish feminism, but let's assume you go along with it. Okay, feminism is good for women, you say, but you're still worried. Is it good for the Jews? you ask. To this I would respond talmudically by posing a question of my own: What do you mean by *the* Jews?

31   We've seen that feminism's preeminent goal is to grant full humanity to the female of the species from the moment when the doctor says, "It's a girl!" Can full humanity for the other half of the Jewish people be bad for "the Jews"?

32   Feminism envisions a world in which women can be more in control of the forces that affect their lives. How can that be bad for "the Jews"?

33   Feminists are also challenging the equation of masculinity and dominance, trying to enlarge men's capacity for emotional expression and family caregiving, and to expand children's options regardless of their gender. Is it possible that greater opportunities for children, more loving men, and more competent, confident women could not be good for "the Jews"?

34   If we understand the word "feminism" in this way, the original question loses all possible logic unless—*unless* the flaw lies with one's concept of "the Jews." Jewish feminists define women as Jews, but

some others define us only as Jewish *women*. To them, "Jews" means *men* the way "everyone" means men in the New Square Talmud class.

For instance, when the media quote "American Jewish reaction" to   35
Yasir Arafat's latest pronouncement, they do not quote the presidents of B'nai B'rith Women, National Council of Jewish Women, Federation of Temple Sisterhoods, or Amit Women. They quote the chair*men* of the boards of the Conference of Presidents of Major Jewish Organizations, or the male heads of B'nai B'rith, American Jewish Congress, or American Jewish Committee. For the most part, "Jewish opinion" is the opinion of Jewish men. [. . .]

Some of all women are Jews and half of all Jews are women, and   36
those of us who are both cannot always be single-issue advocates. Jewish women may not be able to support a pro-choice candidate who is anti-Israel, any more than African-American women could support a pro-choice candidate who fails to protest apartheid. Rather than espouse a utopian universalism, today's feminists must make room for ethnic and cultural priorities. The Women's Movement's political comfort zone must widen so that Jewish women can be female-identified when it comes to fighting male domination in B'nai B'rith, and Jewish-identified when it comes to marching with our brothers against the convent in Auschwitz.

Because I want to be able to march in both directions, I continue to   37
insist that forced choices are false choices. No Jewish woman can let herself be divided either by other women or other Jews. She cannot emancipate the Jew within and leave the woman shackled, any more than she can emancipate the woman within and leave the Jew at risk— for no human being can exist in one body, part slave and part free. I reject freedom in half measures. I've come a long way from the third grade of the Yeshiva but I still refuse the limited choices of a fish.

RESPONDING TO READING

1. Pogrebin opens her essay with a parable, a short story with an instructive moral. How does this parable apply, according to Pogrebin, to the Jews?

2. According to Pogrebin, in what ways is Judaism unfriendly to women?

3. Why does Pogrebin argue that feminism is good for Judaism? How does she define feminism? How does she support her argument about the value of feminism for Judaism?

4. In what ways, according to Pogrebin, are Jewish feminists like other Jews? How are they unlike other Jews?

5. In an essay, describe a group to which you belong, religious or secular. Does it treat both sexes the same? If not, in what ways does this group treat men and women differently? How does this equal/unequal treatment affect the entire group? Would the kind of feminism that Pogrebin describes be acceptable in that group? Valuable?

WILL WAR AND TERRORISM
SHAPE THE FUTURE?

Warfare Is Only an Invention—Not a Biological Necessity

MARGARET MEAD

Margaret Mead (1901–78) was a woman of enormous energy, stamina, and creativity. She has received numerous awards for her revolutionary anthropology, particularly for her pioneering field work in the ethnography of women and children. When Mead began her studies with Franz Boas at Columbia University in the 1920s (she earned a Ph.D. in 1929), anthropology was dependent on rigid, statistical analysis. But Boas, Mead, and other noted researchers between World Wars I and II regarded small, homogeneous, tribal societies as "natural laboratories," says anthropologist Clifford Geertz, and conceived of anthropology "as uniquely positioned to find out the essentials of social life that are disguised or covered over in complex, modern societies." Mead's method of understanding the Balinese, the Samoans, the New Guineans, and others was to learn the native language quickly and immerse herself in the society that she was studying, using psychology, extensive interviews, and careful observation of the artifacts and customs of the culture to record (in copious notes) the tribal character. Then, to convey what she had learned to outsiders, she contextualized her information in a colorful, thickly descriptive style easy for general readers to understand.

Mead's prodigious effort resulted in thirty-nine books; the best known are *Coming of Age in Samoa* (1928), *Sex and Temperament in Three Primitive Societies* (1935), and her autobiography, *Blackberry Winter* (1972). In addition, she published nearly fourteen hundred other articles, interpreting and offering advice on an enormous range of issues in contemporary Western society, including cultural stability, adolescence, sex differences, education and culture, family life, child rearing, national character, international relationships, and cooperation and competition. The following article, originally published in *Asia* magazine (1940), illustrates both Mead's characteristic method of arguing—to use numerous parallel examples from diverse societies—and her anthropologist's justification for pacifism: "warfare is a defective social institution."

1   Is war a biological necessity, a sociological inevitability or just a bad invention? Those who argue for the first view endow man with such pugnacious instincts that some outlet in aggressive behavior is

necessary if man is to reach full human stature. It was this point of view which lay back of William James's famous essay, "The Moral Equivalent of War," in which he tried to retain the warlike virtues and channel them in new directions. A similar point of view has lain back of the Soviet Union's attempt to make competition between groups rather than between individuals. A basic, competitive, aggressive, warring human nature is assumed, and those who wish to outlaw war or outlaw competitiveness merely try to find new and less socially destructive ways in which these biologically given aspects of man's nature can find expression. Then there are those who take the second view: warfare is the inevitable concomitant of the development of the state, the struggle for land and natural resources of class societies springing, not from the nature of man, but from the nature of history. War is nevertheless inevitable unless we change our social system and outlaw classes, the struggle for power, and possessions; and in the event of our success warfare would disappear, as a symptom vanishes when the disease is cured.

One may hold a sort of compromise position between these two extremes; one may claim that all aggression springs from the frustration of man's biologically determined drives and that, since all forms of culture are frustrating, it is certain each new generation will be aggressive and the aggression will find its natural and inevitable expression in race war, class war, nationalistic war, and so on. All three of these positions are very popular today among those who think seriously about the problems of war and its possible prevention, but I wish to urge another point of view, less defeatist perhaps than the first and third, and more accurate than the second: that is, that warfare, by which I mean recognized conflict between two groups *as groups*, in which each group puts an army (even if the army is only fifteen pygmies) into the field to fight and kill, if possible, some of the members of the army of the other group—that warfare of this sort is an invention like any other of the inventions in terms of which we order our lives, such as writing, marriage, cooking our food instead of eating it raw, trial by jury or burial of the dead, and so on. Some of this list any one will grant are inventions: trial by jury is confined to very limited portions of the globe; we know that there are tribes that do not bury their dead but instead expose or cremate them; and we know that only part of the human race has had the knowledge of writing as its cultural inheritance. But, whenever a way of doing things is found universally, such as the use of fire or the practice of some form of marriage, we tend to think at once that it is not an invention at all but an attribute of humanity itself. And yet even such universals as marriage and the use of fire are inventions like the rest, very basic ones, inventions which were perhaps necessary if human history was to take the turn that it has taken, but nevertheless inventions. At some point in his social development man was undoubtedly without the institution of marriage or the knowledge of the use of fire.

3   The case for warfare is much clearer because there are peoples even today who have no warfare. Of these the Eskimos are perhaps the most conspicuous examples, but the Lepchas of Sikkim described by Geoffrey Gorer in *Himalayan Village* are as good. Neither of these peoples understands war, not even defensive warfare. The idea of warfare is lacking, and this idea is as essential to really carrying on war as an alphabet, or a syllabary is to writing. But whereas the Lepchas are a gentle, unquarrelsome people, and the advocates of other points of view might argue that they are not full human beings or that they had never been frustrated and so had no aggression to expand in warfare, the Eskimo case gives no such possibility of interpretation. The Eskimo are not a mild and meek people; many of them are turbulent and troublesome. Fights, theft of wives, murder, cannibalism, occur among them— all outbursts of passionate men goaded by desire or intolerable circumstance. Here are men faced with hunger, men faced with loss of their wives, men faced with the threat of extermination by other men, and here are orphan children, growing up miserably with no one to care for them, mocked and neglected by those about them. The personality necessary for war, the circumstances necessary to goad men to desperation are present, but there is no war. When a traveling Eskimo entered a settlement he might have to fight the strongest man in the settlement to establish his position among them, but this was a test of strength and bravery, not war. The idea of warfare, of one *group* organizing against another *group* to maim and wound and kill them was absent. And without that idea passions might rage but there was no war.

4   But, it may be argued, isn't this because the Eskimo have such a low and undeveloped form of social organization? They own no land, they move from place to place, camping, it is true, season after season on the same site, but this is not something to fight for as the modern nations of the world fight for land and raw materials. They have no permanent possessions that can be looted, no towns that can be burned. They have no social classes to produce stress and strains within the society which might force it to go to war outside. Doesn't the absence of war among the Eskimo, while disproving the biological necessity of war, just go to confirm the point that it is the state of development of the society which accounts for war, and nothing else?

5   We find the answer among the pygmy peoples of the Andaman Islands in the Bay of Bengal. The Andamans also represent an exceedingly low level of society; they are a hunting and food-gathering people; they live in tiny hordes without any class stratification; their houses are simpler than the snow houses of the Eskimo. But they knew about war-

fare. The army might contain only fifteen determined pygmies marching in a straight line, but it was the real thing none the less. Tiny army met tiny army in open battle, blows were exchanged, casualities suffered, and the state of warfare could only be concluded by a peacemaking ceremony.

Similarly, among the Australian aborigines, who built no permanent dwellings but wandered from water hole to water hole over their almost desert country, warfare—and rules of "international law"— were highly developed. The student of social evolution will seek in vain for his obvious causes of war, struggle for lands, struggle for power of one group over another, expansion of population, need to divert the minds of a populace restive under tyranny, or even the ambition of a successful leader to enhance his own prestige. All are absent, but warfare as a practice remained, and men engaged in it and killed one another in the course of a war because killing is what is done in wars.

From instances like these it becomes apparent that an inquiry into the cause of war misses the fundamental point as completely as does an insistence upon the biological necessity of war. If people have an idea of going to war and the idea that war is the way in which certain situations, defined within their society, are to be handled, they will sometimes go to war. If they are a mild and unaggressive people, like the Pueblo Indians, they may limit themselves to defensive warfare; but they will be forced to think in terms of war because there are peoples near them who have warfare as a pattern, and offensive, raiding, pillaging warfare at that. When the pattern of warfare is known, people like the Pueblo Indians will defend themselves, taking advantage of their natural defenses, the *mesa* village site, and people like the Lepchas, having no natural defenses and no idea of warfare, will merely submit to the invader. But the essential point remains the same. There is a way of behaving which is known to a given people and labeled as an appropriate form of behavior; a bold and warlike people like the Sioux or the Maori may label warfare as desirable as well as possible; a mild people like the Pueblo Indians may label warfare as undesirable; but to the minds of both peoples the possibility of warfare is present. Their thoughts, their hopes, their plans are oriented about this idea, that warfare may be selected as the way to meet some situation.

So simple peoples and civilized peoples, mild peoples and violent, assertive peoples, will all go to war if they have the invention, just as those peoples who have the custom of dueling will have duels and peoples who have the pattern of vendetta will indulge in vendetta. And, conversely, peoples who do not know of dueling will not fight duels, even though their wives are seduced and their daughters ravished; they may on occasion commit murder but they will not fight duels. Cultures which lack the idea of the vendetta will not meet every quarrel in this way. A people can use only the forms it has. So the Balinese have their special way of dealing with a quarrel between two individuals: if the two feel that the causes of quarrel are heavy they may go and register their quarrel in the temple before the gods, and, making offerings, they may swear never to have anything to do with each other again. Today they register such mutual "not-speaking" with the Dutch government officials. But in other societies, although individuals might feel as full of animosity and as unwilling to have any further contact as do the Balinese, they cannot register their quarrel with the gods and go on quietly about their business because registering quarrels with the gods is not an invention of which they know.

9   Yet, if it be granted that warfare is after all an invention, it may nevertheless be an invention that lends itself to certain types of personality, to the exigent needs of autocrats, to the expansionist desires of crowded peoples, to the desire for plunder and rape and loot which is engendered by a dull and frustrating life. What, then, can we say of this congruence between warfare and its uses? If it is a form which fits so well, is not this congruence the essential point? But even here the primitive material causes us to wonder, because there are tribes who go to war merely for glory, having no quarrel with the enemy, suffering from no tyrant within their boundaries, anxious neither for land nor loot nor women, but merely anxious to win prestige which within that tribe has been declared obtainable only by war and without which no young man can hope to win his sweetheart's smile of approval. But if, as was the case with the Bush Negroes of Dutch Guiana, it is artistic ability which is necessary to win a girl's approval, the same young man would have to be carving rather than going out on a war party.

10   In many parts of the world, war is a game in which the individual can win counters—counters which bring him prestige in the eyes of his own sex or of the opposite sex; he plays for these counters as he might, in our society, strive for a tennis championship. Warfare is a frame for such prestige-seeking merely because it calls for the display of certain skills and certain virtues; all of these skills—riding straight, shooting straight, dodging the missiles of the enemy, and sending one's own straight to the mark—can be equally well exercised in some other framework, and, equally, the virtues—endurance, bravery, loyalty, steadfastness—can be displayed in other contexts. The tie-up between proving oneself a man and proving this by a success in organized killing is due to a definition which many societies have made of manliness. And often, even in those societies which counted success in warfare a proof of human worth, strange turns were given to the idea, as when the plains Indians gave their highest awards to

the man who touched a live enemy rather than to the man who brought in a scalp—from a dead enemy—because the latter was less risky. Warfare is just an invention known to the majority of human societies by which they permit their young men either to accumulate prestige or avenge their honor or acquire loot or wives or slaves or sago lands or cattle or appease the blood lust of their gods or the restless souls of the recently dead. It is just an invention, older and more widespread than the jury system, but none the less an invention.

But, once we have said this, have we said anything at all? Despite a   11 few instances, dear to the hearts of controversialists, of the loss of the useful arts, once an invention is made which proves congruent with human needs or social forms, it tends to persist. Grant that war is an invention, that it is not a biological necessity nor the outcome of certain special types of social forms, still, once the invention is made, what are we to do about it? The Indian who had been subsisting on the buffalo for generations because with his primitive weapons he could slaughter only a limited number of buffalo did not return to his primitive weapons when he saw that the white man's more efficient weapons were exterminating the buffalo. A desire for the white man's cloth may mortgage the South Sea Islander to the white man's plantation, but he does not return to making bark cloth, which would have left him free. Once an invention is known and accepted, men do not easily relinquish it. The skilled workers may smash the first steam looms which they feel are to be their undoing, but they accept them in the end, and no movement which has insisted upon the mere abandonment of usable inventions has ever had much success. Warfare is here, as part of our thought; the deeds of warriors are immortalized in the words of our poets; the toys of our children are modeled upon the weapons of the soldier; the frame of reference within which our statesmen and our diplomats work always contains war. If we know that it is not inevitable, that it is due to historical accident that warfare is one of the ways in which we think of behaving, are we given any hope by that? What hope is there of persuading nations to abandon war, nations so thoroughly imbued with the idea that resort to war is, if not actually desirable and noble, at least inevitable whenever certain defined circumstances arise?

In answer to this question I think we might turn to the history of   12 other social inventions, and inventions which must once have seemed as firmly entrenched as warfare. Take the methods of trial which preceded the jury system: ordeal and trial by combat. Unfair, capricious, alien as they are to our feeling today, they were once the only methods open to individuals accused of some offense. The invention of trial by jury gradually replaced these methods until only witches, and finally not even witches, had to resort to the ordeal. And for a long time the jury system seemed the one best and finest method of settling legal disputes, but today new inventions, trial before judges only or before commissions, are replacing the jury system. In each case the old method was replaced by a new social invention; the ordeal did not go out because people thought it unjust or wrong, it went out because a method more congruent with the institutions and feelings of the period was invented. And, if we despair over the way in which war seems such an ingrained habit of most of the human race, we can take comfort from the fact that a poor invention will usually give place to a better invention.

13   For this, two conditions at least are necessary. The people must recognize the defects of the old invention, and someone must make a new one. Propaganda against warfare, documentation of its terrible cost in human suffering and social waste, these prepare the ground by teaching people to feel that warfare is a defective social institution. There is further needed a belief that social invention is possible and the invention of new methods which will render warfare as out-of-date as the tractor is making the plow, or the motor car the horse and buggy. A form of behavior becomes out-of-date only when something else takes its place, and in order to invent forms of behavior which will make war obsolete, it is a first requirement to believe that an invention is possible.

RESPONDING TO READING

1. What are the logical consequences of each of the deterministic conclusions Mead summarizes in the first paragraph? What is the "sort of compromise position" that Mead proposes between them and what are the implications of that position? Why does Mead reject all three positions? Has new evidence appeared during the fifty or so years since the essay was written to support any of these positions?

2. Why is it important to decide whether war is biologically determined or only a human invention?

3. How much and what kind of evidence is necessary or required to disprove assertions of biological necessity? What, for example, is shown by the contrast between the Eskimo and the pygmy people? Is Mead asserting that less well-developed tribes do not know war or have the idea of war? Evaluate the evidence that Mead presents to determine whether it is sufficient to prove her argument.

4. List the various purposes for war that Mead cites. As the list accumulates, do you notice the author's attitude towards war? Describe Mead's view of war and of its goals. Why does she feel that people will not abandon this "invention" readily?

5. Give Mead's response to her own question, "What hope is there of persuading nations to abandon war?" Using your knowledge of all that has happened since 1940, evaluate her answer. Then speculate about the next fifty years: Will war be replaced by a better invention or will it continue to exist?

American Ignorance of War

CZESLAW MILOSZ

Czeslaw Milosz (pronounced *Ches*-law *Mee*-wosh), poet, critic, novelist, essayist, and translator, was born in 1911 in Lithuania. During his first forty years he lived under three repressive political systems: as a child in Czarist Russia; in Poland as a member of the underground resistance during the Nazi occupation, during which time he taught himself English in order to read William Blake. After World War II he worked in Paris as a cultural attaché representing Communist Poland. He defected to the West in 1951 ("socialist realism is nothing more than a different name for a lie") and has written ever since of the central issues of our time: the impact of history upon moral being, the search for ways to survive spiritual ruin in a ruined world. In 1960, he accepted a professorship at the University of California, Berkeley, where he has lived ever since, becoming an American citizen in 1970. His wide-ranging writings include *Native Realm: A Search for Self-Definition* (1968), *The History of Polish Literature* (1983), two novels, and eighteen volumes of poetry. His most recent work, *To Begin Where I Am* (2002) contains essays that span the length of Milosz's career and the depths of his wide-ranging interests. His work was denied publication in his native land until he was awarded the Noble Prize for Literature in 1980.

"American Ignorance of War," translated from the Polish by Jane Zielonko, is a section of Milosz's first American publication, *The Captive Mind* (1953), in which he examines the artist's life under Communism and explains why he defected. The book, praised as "a brilliant and original study of the totalitarian mentality," is still fresh and relevant fifty years later. In "American Ignorance of War," Milosz warns his new fellow citizens to learn from the history of other countries. The current generations of Americans, having never experienced the mammoth upheaval of full-scale war on their own shores, regard their culture, their customs, their ways of thinking about life, as *natural*. Yet in a totalitarian regime, especially during wartime, all is utterly changed. What was once inconceivable—repression, humiliation, genocide—becomes the new norm, natural. Considering other major changes that have occurred in the past fifty years, among them two wars in the Persian Gulf, the AIDS epidemic, and the events of (and following) September 11, 2001, is it possible to deny that Milosz's bleak vision of the future might occur?

"Are Americans *really* stupid?" I was asked in Warsaw. In the voice of the man who posed the question, there was despair, as well as the hope that I would contradict him. This question reveals the attitude of the average person in the people's democracies toward the West: it is despair mixed with a residue of hope.

During the last few years, the West has given these people a number of reasons to despair politically. In the case of the intellectual, other,

1

2

more complicated reasons come into play. Before the countries of Central and Eastern Europe entered the sphere of the Imperium, they lived through the Second World War. That war was much more devastating there than in the countries of Western Europe. It destroyed not only their economies, but also a great many values which had seemed till then unshakable.

3   Man tends to regard the order he lives in as *natural*. The houses he passes on his way to work seem more like rocks rising out of the earth than like products of human hands. He considers the work he does in his office or factory as essential to the harmonious functioning of the world. The clothes he wears are exactly what they should be, and he laughs at the idea that he might equally well be wearing a Roman toga or medieval armor. He respects and envies a minister of state or a bank director, and regards the possession of a considerable amount of money as the main guarantee of peace and security. He cannot believe that one day a rider may appear on a street he knows well, where cats sleep and children play, and start catching passersby with his lasso. He is accustomed to satisfying those of his physiological needs which are considered private as discreetly as possible, without realizing that such a pattern of behavior is not common to all human societies. In a word, he behaves a little like Charlie Chaplin in *The Gold Rush*, bustling about in a shack poised precariously on the edge of a cliff.

4   His first stroll along a street littered with glass from bomb-shattered windows shakes his faith in the "naturalness" of his world. The wind scatters papers from hastily evacuated offices, papers labeled "Confidential" or "Top Secret" that evoke visions of safes, keys, conferences, couriers, and secretaries. Now the wind blows them through the street for anyone to read; yet no one does, for each man is more urgently concerned with finding a loaf of bread. Strangely enough, the world goes on even though the offices and secret files have lost all meaning. Farther down the street, he stops before a house split in half by a bomb, the privacy of people's homes—the family smells, the warmth of the beehive life, the furniture preserving the memory of loves and hatreds—cut open to public view. The house itself, no longer a rock, but a scaffolding of plaster, concrete, and brick; and on the third floor, a solitary white bathtub, rain-rinsed of all recollection of those who once bathed in it. Its formerly influential and respected owners, now destitute, walk the fields in search of stray potatoes. Thus overnight money loses its value and becomes a meaningless mass of printed paper. His walk takes him past a little boy poking a stick into a heap of smoking ruins and whistling a song about the great leader who will preserve the nation against all enemies. The song remains, but the leader of yesterday is already part of an extinct past.

5   He finds he acquires new habits quickly. Once, had he stumbled upon a corpse on the street, he would have called the police. A crowd

would have gathered, and much talk and comment would have ensued. Now he knows he must avoid the dark body lying in the gutter, and refrain from asking unnecessary questions. The man who fired the gun must have had his reasons; he might well have been executing an Underground sentence.

Nor is the average European accustomed to thinking of his native   6
city as divided into segregated living areas, but a single decree can force him to this new pattern of life and thought. Quarter A may suddenly be designated for one race; B, for a second; C, for a third. As the resettlement deadline approaches, the streets become filled with long lines of wagons, carts, wheelbarrows, and people carrying bundles, beds, chests, caldrons, and bird cages. When all the moves are effected, 2,000 people may find themselves in a building that once housed 200, but each man is at last in the proper area. Then high walls are erected around quarter C, and daily a given lot of men, women, and children are loaded into wagons that take them off to specially constructed factories where they are scientifically slaughtered and their bodies burned.

And even the rider with the lasso appears, in the form of a military   7
van waiting at the corner of a street. A man passing that corner meets a leveled rifle, raises his hands, is pushed into the van, and from that moment is lost to his family and friends. He may be sent to a concentration camp, or he may face a firing squad, his lips sealed with plaster lest he cry out against the state; but, in any case, he serves as a warning to his fellow men. Perhaps one might escape such a fate by remaining at home. But the father of a family must go out in order to provide bread and soup for his wife and children; and every night they worry about whether or not he will return. Since these conditions last for years, everyone gradually comes to look upon the city as a jungle, and upon the fate of twentieth-century man as identical with that of a caveman living in the midst of powerful monsters.

It was once thought obvious that a man bears the same name and   8
surname throughout his entire life; now it proves wiser for many reasons to change them and to memorize a new and fabricated biography. As a result, the records of the civilian state become completely confused. Everyone ceases to care about formalities, so that marriage, for example, comes to mean little more than living together.

Respectable citizens used to regard banditry as a crime. Today,   9
bank robbers are heroes because the money they steal is destined for the Underground. Usually they are young boys, mothers' boys, but their appearence is deceiving. The killing of a man presents no great moral problem to them.

The nearness of death destroys shame. Men and women change as   10
soon as they know that the date of their execution has been fixed by a fat little man with shiny boots and a riding crop. They copulate in public,

on the small bit of ground surounded by barbed wire—their last home on earth. Boys and girls in their teens, about to go off to the barricades to fight against tanks with pistols and bottles of gasoline, want to enjoy their youth and lose their respect for standards of decency.

11   Which world is "natural"? That which existed before, or the world of war? Both are natural, if both are within the realm of one's experience. All the concepts men live by are a product of the historic formation in which they find themselves. Fluidity and constant change are the characteristics of phenomena. And man is so plastic a being that one can even conceive of the day when a thoroughly self-respecting citizen will crawl on all fours, sporting a tail of brightly colored feathers as a sign of conformity to the order he lives in.

12   The man of the East cannot take Americans seriously because they have never undergone the experiences that teach men how relative their judgements and thinking habits are. Their resultant lack of imagination is appalling. Because they were born and raised in a given social order and in a given system of values, they believe that any other order must be "unnatural," and that it cannot last because it is incompatible with human nature. But even they may one day know fire, hunger, and the sword. In all probability this is what will occur; for it is hard to believe that when one half of the world is living through terrible disasters, the other half can continue a nineteenth-century mode of life, learning about the distress of its distant fellow men only from movies and newspapers. Recent examples teach us that this cannot be. An inhabitant of Warsaw or Budapest once looked at newsreels of bombed Spain or burning Shanghai, but in the end he learned how these and many other catastrophes appear in actuality. He read gloomy tales of the NKVD until one day he found he himself had to deal with it. *If something exists in one place, it will exist everywhere.* This is the conclusion he draws from his observations, and so he has no particular faith in the momentary prosperity of America. He suspects that the years 1933–1945 in Europe prefigure what will occur elsewhere. A hard school, where ignorance was punished not by bad marks but by death, has taught him to think sociologically and historically. But it has not freed him from irrational feelings. He is apt to believe in theories that foresee violent changes in the countries of the West, for he finds it unjust that they should escape the hardships he had to undergo.

RESPONDING TO READING

1. Give the several definitions of "natural" that Milosz uses in this essay. How can he argue that war is natural? Why is it natural that Americans should be ignorant of war? Why does he argue that it is natural that war will come to America?

2. Examine closely the details that Milosz uses to support his argument. Notice the irony in the details, such as the "top secret" papers blowing in the street that nobody cares to read. Why does he select these details, why does he present them the way he does, and how do they affect you?

3. Compare and contrast Milosz's essay with Mead's. Note the different experiences of the two writers, the dates of their essays, and the different examples they cite. Whose conclusions do you find most comfortable? Whose conclusions do you find most compelling?

4. Will there be a war in America in your lifetime? If so, what would be the causes, the forces in opposition, the results? If not, argue against Milosz's essay, particularly his assertion that "If something exists in one place, it will exist everywhere."

Terror in the Mind of God

MARK JUERGENSMEYER

Juergensmeyer, born 1940, in Carlinsville, Illinois, earned a B.A. from the University of Illinois at Urbana–Champaign (1962); an M.A. (1968) and, later, a Ph.D. (1974) from the University of California, Berkeley. His career as an academic winds through a number of universities, from Punjab University in Chandigarh, India, and the Berkeley Urdu Program in Lahore, Pakistan, to the University of Hawaii and the Pacific Rim Research Program in the University of California system. Like his travels as a teacher, his explorations as a writer cover numerous topics: *Ethics in the Corporate Decision-making Process* (written with Charles McCoy and Fred Twining, 1975), *The New Cold War?: Religious Nationalism Confronts the Secular State* (1993), and *Terror in the Mind of God: The Global Rise of Religious Violence* (2000).

In both *The New Cold War?* and *Terror in the Mind of God*, Juergensmeyer follows the same thread: the tendency of religious fundamentalists to turn to violence as a response to perceived threats of cultural assimilation and annihilation. Researching his topic, Juergensmeyer interviewed individuals involved in terrorist events of the last decade, including the man responsible for the (first) bombing of the World Trade Center. As a reviewer for the *Los Angeles Times* commented, "Juergensmeyer is ultimately serving the highest aspirations of organized religion when he insists on shedding light on the darker corners of human belief and human conduct."

[. . . Instances] of exaggerated violence are constructed events: they   1
are mind-numbing, mesmerizing theater. At center stage are the acts themselves—stunning, abnormal, and outrageous murders carried out in a way that graphically displays the awful power of violence—set

within grand scenarios of conflict and proclamation. Killing or maiming of any sort is violent, of course, but these acts surpass the wounds inflicted during warfare or death delivered through capital punishment, in large part because they have a secondary impact. By their demonstrative nature, they elicit feelings of revulsion and anger in those who witness them.

Performance Violence

2   How do we make sense of such theatrical forms of violence? One way of answering this is to view dramatic violence as part of a strategic plan. This viewpoint assumes that terrorism is always part of a political strategy—and, in fact, some social scientists have defined terrorism in just that way: "the use of covert violence by a group for political ends." In some cases this definition is indeed appropriate, for an act of violence can fulfill political ends and have a direct impact on public policy.

3   The Israeli elections in 1996 provided a case in point. Shortly after the assassination of Yitzhak Rabin, his successor, Shimon Peres, held a 20 percent lead in the polls over his rival, Benjamin Netanyahu, but this lead vanished following a series of Hamas suicide attacks on Jerusalem buses. Netanyahu narrowly edged out Peres in the May elections. Many observers concluded that Netanyahu—no friend of Islamic radicals—had the terrorists of Hamas to thank for his victory.

4   When the Hamas operative who planned the 1996 attacks was later caught and imprisoned, he was asked whether he had intended to affect the outcome of the elections. "No," he responded, explaining that the internal affairs of Israelis did not matter much to him. This operative was a fairly low-level figure, however, and one might conjecture that his superiors had a more specific goal in mind. But when I put the same question to the political leader of Hamas, Dr. Abdul Aziz Rantisi, his answer was almost precisely the same: these attacks were not aimed at Israeli internal politics, since Hamas did not differentiate between Peres and Netanyahu. In the Hamas view, the two Israeli leaders were equally opposed to Islam. "Maybe God wanted it," the Hamas operative said of Netanyahu's election victory. Even if the Hamas leaders were being disingenuous, the fact remains that most of their suicide bombings have served no direct political purpose.

5   Other examples of religious terrorism have also shown little strategic value. The release of nerve gas in the Tokyo subways and the bombing of the World Trade Center did not provide any immediate political benefits to those who caused them. Although Mahmud Abouhalima, convicted for his part in the World Trade Center bombing, told me that assaults on public buildings did have a long-range strategic value in that they helped to "identify the government as

enemy," in general the "political ends" for which these acts were committed seemed distant indeed.

A political scientist, Martha Crenshaw, has shown that the notion   6
of "strategic" thinking can be construed in a broad sense to cover not just immediate political achievements but also the internal logic that propels a group into perpetrating terrorist acts. As Abouhalima said, many of those who committed them felt they were justified by the broad, long-range benefits to be gained. My investigations indicate that Crenshaw is right—acts of terrorism are usually the products of an internal logic and not of random or crazy thinking—but I hesitate to use the term *strategy* for all rationales for terrorist actions. *Strategy* implies a degree of calculation and an expectation of accomplishing a clear objective that does not jibe with such dramatic displays of power as the World Trade Center bombing. These creations of terror are done not to achieve a strategic goal but to make a symbolic statement.

By calling acts of religious terrorism "symbolic," I mean that they   7
are intended to illustrate or refer to something beyond their immediate target: a grander conquest, for instance, or a struggle more awesome than meets the eye. As Abouhalima said, the bombing of a public building may dramatically indicate to the populace that the government or the economic forces behind the building were seen as enemies, to show the world that they were targeted as satanic foes. The point of the attack, then, was to produce a graphic and easily understandable object lesson. Such explosive scenarios are not *tactics* directed toward an immediate, earthly, or strategic goal, but *dramatic events* intended to impress for their symbolic significance. As such, they can be analyzed as one would any other symbol, ritual, or sacred drama.

I can imagine a line with "strategic" on the one side and "symbolic"   8
on the other, with various acts of terrorism located in between. The hostage taking in the Japanese embassy by the Tupac Amaru in Peru in 1997—clearly an attempt to leverage power in order to win the release of members of the movement held prisoner by the Peruvian government— might be placed closer to the political, strategic side. The Aum Shinrikyo nerve gas attack in 1995 might be closer to the symbolic, religious side. Each was the product of logical thought, and each had an internal rationale. In cases such as the Tokyo nerve gas attack that were more symbolic than strategic, however, the logic was focused not on an immediate political acquisition, but at a larger, less tangible goal.

The very adjectives used to describe acts of religious terrorism—   9
symbolic, dramatic, theatrical—suggest that we look at them not as tactics but as *performance violence*. In speaking of terrorism as "performance," I am not suggesting that such acts are undertaken lightly or capriciously. Rather, like religious ritual or street theater, they are dramas designed to have an impact on the several audiences that they affect. Those who witness the violence—even at a distance, via the

news media—are therefore a part of what occurs. Moreover, like other forms of public ritual, the symbolic significance of such events is multi-faceted; they mean different things to different observers. [. . .]

10   In addition to referring to drama, the term *performance* also implies the notion of "performative"—as in the concept of "performative acts." This is an idea developed by language philosophers regarding certain kinds of speech that are able to perform social functions: their very utterance has a transformative impact. Like vows recited during marriage rites, certain words not only represent reality but also shape it: they contain a certain power of their own. The same is true of some nonverbal symbolic actions, such as the gunshot that begins a race, the raising of a white flag to show defeat, or acts of terrorism.

11   Terrorist acts, then, can be both *performance events*, in that they make a symbolic statement, and *performative acts*, insofar as they try to change things. When Yigal Amir aimed his pistol at Israel's prime minister, Yitzhak Rabin, and when Sikh activists targeted Punjab's chief minister with a car bomb in front of the state's office buildings, the activists were aware that they were creating enormous spectacles. They probably also hoped that their actions would make a difference—if not in a direct, strategic sense, then in an indirect way as a dramatic show so powerful as to change people's perceptions of the world.

12   But the fact that the assassins of Prime Minister Rabin and Chief Minister Beant Singh hoped that their acts would make such a statement does not mean that they in fact did. As I noted, public symbols mean different things to different people, and a symbolic performance may not have the intended effect. The way the act is perceived—by both the perpetrators and those who are affected by it—makes all the difference. In fact, the same is true of performative speech. One of the leading language philosophers, J. L. Austin, has qualified the notion that some speech acts are performative by observing that the power of the act is related to the perception of it. Children, for example, playing at marriage are not wedded by merely reciting the vows and going through the motions, nor is a ship christened by just anyone who gives it a name.[1]

13   The French sociologist Pierre Bourdieu, carrying further the idea that statements are given credibility by their social context, has insisted that the power of performative speech—vows and christenings—is rooted in social reality and is given currency by the laws and social customs that stand behind it.[2] Similarly, an act of terrorism usually implies an underlying power and legitimizing ideology. But whether the power and legitimacy implicit in acts of terrorism are like play-acted marriage vows or are the real thing depends in part on how the acts are perceived. It depends, in part, on whether their significance is believed.

14   This brings us back to the realm of faith. Public ritual has traditionally been the province of religion, and this is one of the reasons

that performance violence comes so naturally to activists from a religious background. In a collection of essays on the connection between religion and terrorism published some years ago, one of the editors, David C. Rapoport, observed—accurately, I think—that the two topics fit together not only because there is a violent streak in the history of religion, but also because terrorist acts have a symbolic side and in that sense mimic religious rites. The victims of terrorism are targeted not because they are threatening to the perpetrators, he said, but because they are "symbols, tools, animals or corrupt beings" that tie into "a special picture of the world, a specific consciousness" that the activist possesses.[3]

The street theater of performance violence forces those who witness it directly or indirectly into that "consciousness"—that alternative view of the world. This gives the perpetrators of terrorism a kind of celebrity status and their actions an illusion of importance. The novelist Don DeLillo goes so far as to say that "only the lethal believer, the person who kills and dies for faith," is taken seriously in modern society.[4] When we who observe these acts take them seriously—are disgusted and repelled by them, and begin to distrust the peacefulness of the world around us—the purposes of this theater are achieved.   15

Setting the Stage

In looking at religious terrorism as theater, the appropriate place to begin is the stage—the location where the acts are committed, or rather, performed. When followers of an expatriate Muslim sheik living in New Jersey chose to make a statement about their unhappiness with American and Jewish support for Middle East leaders whom they perceived to be enemies of Islam, they found the most dramatic stage in sight: the World Trade Center. It turned out to be an apt location for a variety of symbolic reasons.   16

Designed to be the tallest buildings in New York City, and at one time the highest in the world, the 110-story twin towers of the World Trade Center house the headquarters of international businesses and financial corporations. Among its many offices are quarters for the federal Secret Service and the governor of the state of New York. More than fifty thousand employees daily enter the huge edifice, which also includes a hotel, shops, and several restaurants. From the windows of the penthouse restaurant, Windows on the World, the executives who come to lunch can scarcely identify Jersey City and the other industrial areas stretched out across the Hudson River in a distant haze.   17

From across the river in Jersey City, the twin towers of the building are so tall that when no other part of the skyline in New York City is visible, the tower tops are seen ethereally suspended above the eastern   18 horizon. When Muhammad A. Salameh came to the Ryder Truck Rental lot on Jersey City's busy Kennedy Boulevard on Wednesday, February 24, 1993, to rent a ten-foot Ford Econoline van, therefore, he could catch glimpses of the World Trade Center in the distance.

19   Two days later, at noon, shortly after the van was driven to level B2 of the parking basement of the World Trade Center, an enormous blast shuddered through the basement levels, collapsing several floors, killing several workers instantly, and ripping a 180-foot hole in the wall of the underground Port Authority Trans-Hudson train station. On the 110th floor, in the Windows on the World restaurant, young executives who were attending a career-launching lunch felt a thump and heard what seemed to be a mild earthquake or a clap of thunder. When the electricity went off and they were told to evacuate the building, they headed downstairs jauntily singing "One Hundred Bottles of Beer on the Wall." Their joviality turned to nervous apprehension when they were greeted with clouds of soot and smoke as they groped their way down 110 flights of stairs into a scene of confusion and suffering on the ground floor.

20   Throughout the world the news media projected images of American power and civic order undermined. Based on the belief by government officals that the World Trade Center was targeted primarily as a public symbol, security was rushed to federal monuments and memorials in Washington, DC, later that afternoon. Although six people were killed in the blast, it was the assault on the building itself that received the most prominent reportage. Within an hour of the World Trade Center bombing, a coffeehouse in Cairo was attacked—allegedly by the same group implicated in the World Trade Center incident. This bombing killed more people but garnered very little attention outside of Cairo. Regardless of the number killed, a coffeehouse is not the World Trade Center. The towers are in their own way as American as the Statue of Liberty or the Washington Monument, and by assaulting them activists put their mark on a visibly American symbol.

21   The same can be said about the bombing of the Alfred P. Murrah Federal Building in Oklahoma City on April 19, 1995, by Timothy McVeigh and Terry Nichols. In this case the number killed was much greater than at the World Trade Center, and an enormous outpouring of public sympathy for the victims overhadowed any concern about damage done to the building. Yet there were several similarities between the two events: McVeigh and Nichols used a mixture of ammonium nitrate fertilizer and diesel fuel not unlike that used in the World Trade Center blast, and they mimicked the World Trade Center bombers by employing a Ryder rental truck. Like Mahmud Abouhalima and his colleages, these self-designated soldiers were fighting a quasi-religious war against the American government, and they chose

a building that symbolized what they regarded as an oppressive government force. [. . .]

If one had to choose a single building that symbolized the presence 22
of centralized federal governmental power in this region of mid-America, the Murrah building in Oklahoma City would be it. When the dust settled after the devastating roar of the enormous explosion on Wednesday morning, April 19, 1995, the entire front of the building had been sheared off, killing 168 and injuring more than five hundred. Among the dead and injured were scores of children in the building's day care center, but only four ATF officials were injured, and none were killed. Clearly, the target of the attack was not so much the government agents, or even an agency such as the ATF, as it was the building itself and its everyday staff of government workers.

What was targeted was a symbol of normal government opera- 23
tions. In this scenario of terrorism, the lives of the workers were, like the building, a part of the scenery: they and the edifice constituted the stage on which the dramatic act was to be performed. If the building were attacked at night without the workers present, the explosion would not have been a serious blow to government operations, nor would the pain of the event be felt as acutely by society at large. If the building's employees had been machine-gunned as they left their offices, with the building itself left unscathed, the symbolism of an attack on normal government operations would have been incomplete. Such targets as the World Trade Center and the Oklahoma City federal building have provided striking images of a stable, seemingly invulnerable economic and political power. Yet all buildings are ultimately vulnerable, a fact that performers of terror such as Abouhalima and McVeigh have been eager to demonstrate. [. . .]

Because air traffic itself is indicative of a society's economic vitali- 24
ty, often airplanes rather than airports have provided terrorism's stage. The most dramatic example is Ramzi Yousef's Bojinka plot, aimed at eleven U.S. trans-Pacific passenger airplanes and alleged to have been funded by Saudi millionaire Osama bin Laden, which would have created a catastrophic event on one fateful day in 1995. The term *Bojinka* was one that Yousef himself had chosen and was the label for the file in the hard disk of his white Toshiba laptop computer that listed the details of the plot—where flights would depart, what routes they would take, and where the participants in the plot should deplane in order to escape the explosions caused by the bombs that they were to leave behind. In the trial that convicted him of conspiring to commit these acts of terrorism, Yousef, acting as his own lawyer, offered as his main defense the notion that anyone with computer expertise could have planted such information on his hard disk. Yet he was not able to refute the testimony of witnesses who heard him talk

about the plot and the Philippines airline stewardess who saw him sitting in the very seat under which a bomb exploded on a later leg of the flight, after Yousef had departed. In December 1994, Yousef is said to have boarded the plane and, once it was aloft, entered one of the bathrooms and mixed a highly inflammable cocktail involving a liquid form of nitroglycerin. He sealed it in a container and attached a blasting cap and a timer. Returning to his seat, he strapped the device underneath the cushion and departed the plane at its next stop, leaving the bomb beneath the seat to explode in midair as the plane journeyed on to its next destination. [. . .]

25   According to a chronology of terrorist acts maintained by Bruce Hoffman at the RAND Corporation and St. Andrews University, twenty-two airlines were bombed worldwide from 1969 to 1996, and many others were hijacked. A nation can feel dishonored by the bombing of one of its airlines even when the plane, such as the downed Pan Am 103, is far from home. In that case the bomb—plastic explosives hidden in a portable radio-tape player, allegedly placed by Libyan intelligence agencies operating out of Malta—blew up the aircraft as it flew above Scotland in 1988, the shredded pieces of the plane landing near the small town of Lockerbie. [. . .]

26   The symbolism of other locations has been more general: the locations represented the power and stability of the society itself. As we have seen, buildings such as the World Trade Center and the Oklahoma City federal building, along with transportation systems, are examples of such general symbols. [. . .] Computer networks and Internet channels are also symbols of a society's centrality—its central communication system. As the Melissa virus in 1999 demonstrated, acts of sabotage can cripple large corporations and government agencies. In response to NATO's bombing in Serbia and Kosovo in May 1999, hackers electronically entered the computer systems of several United States government agencies, leaving antiwar messages in their wake.

27   By revealing the vulnerability of a nation's most stable and powerful entities, movements that undertake these acts of sabotage have touched virtually everyone in the nation's society. Any person in the United States could have been riding the elevator in the World Trade Center, visiting the Oklahoma City federal building, traveling on Pan Am 103, or using a computer when a virus invaded it, and everyone in the United States will look differently at the stability of public buildings, transportation networks, and communication systems as a result of these violent incidents.

28   Why is the location of terrorist events—of performance violence— so important?

29   Such central places—even if they exist only in cyberspace—are symbols of power, and acts of terrorism claim them in a symbolic way.

That is, they express for a moment the power of terrorist groups to control central locations—by damaging, terrorizing, and assaulting them—even when in fact most of the time they do not control them at all. Even before the smoke had cleared at the World Trade Center, life inside was returning to normal. Although the Murrah Federal Building was destroyed, the governmental functions that had been conducted there continued unabated. Yet during that brief dramatic moment when a terrorist act levels a building or damages some entity that a society regards as central to its existence, the perpetrators of the act assert that they—and not the secular government—have ultimate control over that entity and its centrality.

The very act, however, is sometimes more than symbolic: by   30 demonstrating the vulnerability of governmental power, to some degree it weakens that power. Because power is largely a matter of perception, symbolic statements can lead to real results. On the whole, however, the small degree to which a government's authority is discredited by a terrorist act does not warrant the massive destructiveness of the act itself. More significant is the impression—in most cases it is simply an illusion—that the movements perpetrating the acts have enormous power and that the ideologies behind them have cosmic importance. In the war between religious and secular authority, the loss of a secular government's ability to control and secure public spaces, even for a terrible moment, is ground gained for religion's side. [. . .]

More than any other government, America has been assigned the   31 role of primary or secondary foe. The wrath has been directed largely toward political leaders and governmental symbols, but the wider circle has included American businessmen, American culture, and the American "system"—a generic term that has included all responsible persons and every entity that has kept the country functioning as a political, economic, and social unit. According to the RAND Chronicle of International Terrorism, since 1968 the United States each year has headed the list of countries whose citizens and property were most frequently attacked. The U.S. State Department's counterterrorism unit reported that during the 1990s, 40 percent of all acts of terrorism worldwide have been against American citizens and facilities.[5]

Mahmud Abouhalima has said that he regards America as a world-   32 wide enemy. The reason, he says, is not only because the United States supports the secular Egyptian government that he and his colleagues find directly oppressive, but also because of its history of terrorist acts. The bombing of Hiroshima, for instance, Abouhalima compared with the bombing of the Oklahoma City federal building.[6] Abouhalima's spiritual leader, Sheik Omar Abdul Rahman, during a lengthy courtroom speech at the end of the trial convicting him of conspiring to bomb the World Trade Center, predicted that a "revengeful" God would "scratch" America from the face of the earth.[7]

33   Osama bin Ladin, implicated in the bombing of the American embassies in Kenya and Tanzania in 1998, explained in an interview a year before the bombing that America deserved to be targeted because it was "the biggest terrorist in the world."[8] It may be only coincidence that after the embassy bombings U.S. National Security Advisor Samuel Berger called Osama "the most dangerous nonstate terrorist in the world."[9] The reason bin Laden gave for targeting America was its list of "crimes," which included "occupying the lands of Islam in the holiest of places, the Arabian Peninsula, plundering its riches, dictating to its rulers, humiliating its people, terrorizing its neighbors and turning its bases in the peninsula into a spearhead through which to fight the neighboring Muslim peoples."[10] In response to what bin Laden regarded as a declaration of war on Muslims by America, he issued a fatwa calling on "every Muslim" as "an individual duty" to join him in a righteous war "to kill the Americans and their allies." Their obligation was not only "to kill the Americans" but also to "plunder their money wherever and whenever they find it." He sealed his fatwa with the reassurance that "this is in accordance with the words of Almighty God" and that "every Muslim who believes in God and wishes to be rewarded" should "comply with God's order."[11]

34   Why is America the enemy? This question is hard for observers of international politics to answer, and harder still for ordinary Americans to fathom. Many have watched with horror as their compatriots and symbols of their country have been destroyed by people whom they do not know, from cultures they can scarcely identify on a global atlas, and for reasons that do not seem readily apparent. From the frames of reference of those who regard America as enemy, however, several motives appear.

35   One reason we have already mentioned: America is often a secondary enemy. In its role as trading partner and political ally, America has a vested interest in shoring up the stability of regimes around the world. This has often put the United States in the unhappy position of being a defender and promoter of secular governments regarded by their religious opponents as primary foes. Long before the bombing of the World Trade Center, Sheik Omar Abdul Rahman expressed his disdain for the United States because of its role in propping up the Mubarak regime in Egypt. "America is behind all these un-Islamic governments," the Sheik explained, arguing that the purpose of American political and economic support was "to keep them strong" and to try to "defeat the Islamic movements."[12] In the case of Iran prior to the Islamic revolution, Ayatollah Khomeini saw the shah and the American government linked as evil twins: America was tarred by its association

with the shah, and the shah, in turn, was corrupted by being a "companion of satanic forces"—that is, of America.[13] When Khomeini prayed to his "noble God for protection from the evil of every wicked traitor" and asked Him to "destroy the enemies," the primary traitor he had in mind was the shah and the chief enemy America.[14]

A second reason America is regarded as enemy is that both directly   36
and indirectly it has supported modern culture. In a world where villagers in remote corners of the world increasingly have access to MTV, Hollywood movies, and the Internet, the images and values that have been projected globally have been American. It was this cultural threat that brought an orthodox rabbi, Manachem Fruman, who lived in a Jewish settlement on the West Bank of Israel near Hebron, to regular meetings with Hamas-related mullahs in nearby villages. What they had in common, Rabbi Fruman told me, was their common dislike of the "American-style" traits of individualism, the abuse of alcohol, and sexy movies that were widespread in modern cities such as Tel Aviv. Rabbi Fruman told me that "when the mullahs asked, who brought all this corruption here, they answered, 'the Jews.' But," Fruman continued, "rabbis like me don't like this corruption either." Hence the rabbi and the mullahs agreed about the degradation of modern urban values, and they concurred over which country was ultimately responsible. When the mullahs asserted that the United States was the "capital of the devil," Rabbi Fruman told me, he could agree.[15] In a similar vein, Mahmud Abouhalima told me he was bitter that Islam did not have influence over the global media the way that secular America did. America, he believed, was using its power of information to promote the immoral values of secular society.[16]

The third reason for the disdain of America is economic. Although   37
most corporations that trade internationally are multinational, with personnel and legal ties to more than one country, many are based in the United States or have American associations. Even those that were identifiably European or Japanese are thought to be American-like and implicitly American in attitude and style. When Ayatollah Khomeini identified the "satanic" forces that were out to destroy Islam, he included not only Jews but also the even "more satanic" Westerners—especially corporate leaders with "no religious belief" who saw Islam as "the major obstacle in the path of their materialistic ambitions and the chief threat to their political power."[17] The ayatollah went on to claim that "all the problems of Iran" were due to the treachery of "foreign colonialists."[18] On another occasion, the ayatollah blended political, personal, and spiritual issues in generalizing about the cosmic foe—Western colonialism—and about "the black and dreadful future" that "the agents of colonialism, may God Almighty abandon them all," have in mind for Islam and the Muslim people.[19]

38   What the ayatollah was thinking of when he prophesied a "black and dreadful future" for Islam was the global domination of American economy and culture. This fear of globalization is the fourth reason America is often targeted as an enemy. The apprehensions of Ayatollah Khomeini were shared by many not only in the Muslim world but elsewhere, including the United States. There right-wing militias were convinced that the "new world order" proclaimed by President George Bush was more than a mood of global cooperation: it was a conspiratorial plot to control the world. Accepting this paranoid vision of American leaders' global designs, the Aum Shinrikyo master Shoko Asahara linked the U.S. army with the Japanese government, Freemasons, and Jews in the image of a global conspiratorial band.

39   Like all stereotypes, each of these characterizations holds a certain amount of truth. America's culture and economy have dominated societies around the world in ways that have caused concern to protectors of local societies. The vast financial and media networks of American-backed corporations and information systems have affected the whole of the globe. There has indeed been a great conflict between secular and religious life throughout the world, and America does ordinarily support the secular side of the fight. Financial aid provided to leaders such as Israel's Benjamin Netanyahu and Egypt's Hosni Mubarak has shored up the political power of politicians opposed to religious nationalism. Moreover, after the fall of the Soviet Union, the United States has been virtually the only coherent military power in the world. Hence it has been an easy target for blame when people have felt that their lives were going askew or were being controlled by forces they could not readily see. Yet to dislike America is one thing; to regard it as a cosmic enemy is quite another.

40   When the United States has been branded as an enemy in a cosmic war, it has been endowed with superhuman—or perhaps subhuman—qualities, ones that have had little to do with the people who actually live in America. It is the image of the country that has been despised—a reified notion of Americanism, not its people. Individual Americans have often been warmly accepted by those who hate the collective image that they hold as cosmic enemy. This was brought home to me in Gaza when I talked with Dr. Abdul Aziz Rantisi about the Hamas movement's attitude toward America and its pro-Israeli stance. As Dr. Rantisi offered me coffee in the comfortable living room of his home, he acknowledged that the United States was a secondary enemy because of its complicity in Israel's existence and its oppression of Palestinian Arabs. From his point of view, it deserved to be treated as an enemy. What about individual Americans, I cautiously asked him, raising the example of American professors. Would such people be targeted?

41   "You?" Rantisi responded, somewhat surprised. "You don't count. You're our guest."[20]

Notes

1. For a discussion of Girard's theories, and an alternative to certain aspects of it, see my article "Sacrifice and Cosmic War" in Mark Juergensmeyer, ed., *Violence and the Sacred in the Modern World* (London: Frank Cass, 1991), 101–17, and the concluding reply from Girard in the same volume.
2. See the essays in John Stratton Hawley, ed., *Sati, the Blessing and the Curse: The Burning of Wives in India* (New York: Oxford University Press, 1994).
3. Anthony F. C. Wallace, *The Death and Rebirth of the Seneca* (New York: Random House, 1969) 102–7.
4. For a summary of the project, see John Stratton Hawley, "Introduction: Saints and Virtues," in J. S. Hawley, ed., *Saints and Virtues* (Berkeley: University of California Press, 1987), xi–xxiv.
5. Robin Wright, "Prophetic 'Terror 2000' Mapped Evolving Threat," *Los Angeles Times*, August 9, 1998, A16.
6. Interview with Abouhalima, September 30, 1997.
7. John J. Goldman, "Defendants Given 25 years to Life in New York Terror Plot," *Los Angeles Times*, January 18, 1996, A1.
8. Osama bin Laden, interviewed on an ABC News report rebroadcast on August 9, 1998.
9. Samel Berger, quoted in *"Jihad* Is an Individual Duty," B9.
10. *"Jihad* Is an Individual Duty," B9.
11. *"Jihad* Is an Individual Duty," B9.
12. Sheik Omar Abdul Rahman, quoted in Kim Murphy, "Have the Islamic Militants Turned to a New Battlefront in the US?" *Los Angeles Times*, March 3, 1993, A20.
13. Ayatollah Khomeini, *Collection of Speeches, Position Statements* (Arlington, VA: Joint Publications Research Service, 1979), 24.
14. Khomeini, *Collection*, 30.
15. Interview with Rabbi Manachem Fruman, Tuqua settlement, West Bank, Israel, August 14, 1995.
16. Interview with Abouhalima, September 30, 1997.
17. Imam [Ayatollah] Khomeini, *Islam and Revolution: Writings and Declarations*, Hamid Algar, trans., annot. (London: Routledge and Kegan Paul, 1985) (orig. published by Mizan Press, Berkeley, in 1981), 27–28.
18. Khomeini, *Collection*, 3.
19. Khomeini, *Collection*, 25.
20. Interview with Rantisi, March 2, 1989.

RESPONDING TO READING

1. In what ways is an act of terrorism a dramatic, theatrical act? What are the positive and negative effects of such a definition?

2. Why is Juergensmeyer reluctant to think of terrorist acts as strategic acts? According to Juergensmeyer, what is the "logic" of terrorism?

3. What distinction does Juergensmeyer draw between "performance events" and "performative acts"? How do these distinctions apply to terrorism?

4. Juergensmeyer describes the 1993 bombing of the World Trade Center. How does an awareness of the second terrorist attacks, in September of 2001, affect your reading of this example?

5. Select an act of terror that has occurred during your lifetime, and find two separate stories about the event—from newspapers, magazines, Web sites, etc. In an essay, describe how each story explains the act of terror. Is it a performative act or a performance event? Does the story focus on religion, politics, or some other ideological system of values?

Thoughts in the Presence of Fear

WENDELL BERRY

Berry, a native Kentuckian born in 1934 on a farm in Henry County, writes, lives, and farms with a "land ethic." After earning a B.A. (1956) and M.A. in English (1957) from the University of Kentucky, Berry spent a year at Stanford (1958–59) on a creative-writing fellowship before returning to Kentucky, where he taught at his alma mater from 1964 to 1977. Since then he has lived his philosophy as a writer, conservationist, farmer, and philosopher both in words and on the land. He works his land with horses and uses only organic methods of fertilization and pest control; he is growing trees which he expects to mature into an "old growth forest" as part of his heritage, "if somebody doesn't cut them down." He has received Guggenheim and Rockefeller fellowships and the Thomas Merton Award, given to people who "advance the transformation of the world."

Berry's love of the land and the community is reflected in novels (*Remembering*, 1988; *A World Lost*, 1996), poetry (*The Country of Marriage*, 1973; *The Kentucky River: Two Poems, 1975*), and essays (*The Unsettling of America: Culture and Agriculture*, 1977). His social philosophy is discussed in his writings, such as "Thoughts in the Presence of Fear," which appeared in the fall of 2001 on the OrionOnline.org Web site as "Thoughts on America" and was published in the *South Atlantic Quarterly*, Spring 2002. This thoughtful, wide-ranging response to "the horrors of September 11" represents a distillation of Berry's philosophical principles. He told interviewer Jordan Fisher-Smith that "The old have an obligation to be exemplary, if they can . . . [and] they also have an obligation to be intelligent about their failings . . . . they have an obligation to see that they're remembered not as a liability or a great burden, but as a help. And of course the young, the inheritors, have an obligation to remember these people and live up to them—be worthy of them." The principles expressed in "Thoughts in the Presence of Fear" reflect Berry's understanding that the obligation "goes both ways. . . . You inherit, and in turn you bequeath an inheritance of some kind." Thus, he explores the largely undesirable consequences of the belief that "we should go on and on from one technological innovation to the next, which would cause the economy to 'grow' and make everything better and better. This of course implied at every point a hatred of the past, of all things inherited and free" (paragraph 5). He patiently explains why these values are wrong, and makes the case for a peaceable, self-sufficient economy, based on "thrift and care, on saving and conserving, not on excess and waste" (paragraph 27).

I. The time will soon come when we will not be able to remember   1
the horrors of September 11 without remembering also the unquestioning technological and economic optimism that ended on that day.[1]

II. This optimism rested on the proposition that we were living in a   2
"new world order" and a "new economy" that would "grow" on and on, bringing a prosperity of which every new increment would be "unprecedented."

III. The dominant politicians, corporate officers, and investors who   3
believed this proposition did not acknowledge that the prosperity was limited to a tiny percent of the world's people, and to an ever smaller number of people even in the United States; that it was founded upon the oppressive labor of poor people all over the world; and that its ecological costs increasingly threatened all life, including the lives of the supposedly prosperous.

IV. The "developed" nations had given to the "free market" the sta-   4
tus of a god, and were sacrificing to it their farmers, farmlands, and communities, their forests, wetlands, and prairies, their ecosystems and watersheds. They had accepted universal pollution and global warming as normal costs of doing business.

V. There was, as a consequence, a growing worldwide effort on be-   5
half of economic decentralization, economic justice, and ecological responsibility. We must recognize that the events of September 11 make this effort more necessary than ever. We citizens of the industrial countries must continue the labor of self-criticism and self-correction. We must recognize our mistakes.

VI. The paramount doctrine of the economic and technological eu-   6
phoria of recent decades has been that everything depends on innovation. It was understood as desirable, and even necessary, that we should go on and on from one technological innovation to the next, which would cause the economy to "grow" and make everything better and better. This of course implied at every point a hatred of the past, of all things inherited and free. All things superceded in our progress of innovations, whatever their value might have been, were discounted as of no value at all.

VII. We did not anticipate anything like what has now happened.   7
We did not foresee that all our sequence of innovations might be at once overridden by a greater one: the invention of a new kind of war that would turn our previous innovations against us, discovering and

exploiting the debits and the dangers that we had ignored. We never considered the possibility that we might be trapped in the webwork of communication and transport that was supposed to make us free.

8   VIII. Nor did we foresee that the weaponry and the war science that we marketed and taught to the world would become available, not just to recognized national governments, which possess so uncannily the power to legitimate large-scale violence, but also to "rogue nations," dissident or fanatical groups and individuals—whose violence, though never worse than that of nations, is judged by the nations to be illegitimate.

9   IX. We had accepted uncritically the belief that technology is only good; that it cannot serve evil as well as good; that it cannot serve our enemies as well as ourselves; that it cannot be used to destroy what is good, including our homelands and our lives.

10   X. We had accepted too the corollary belief that an economy (either as a money economy or as a life-support system) that is global in extent, technologically complex, and centralized is invulnerable to terrorism, sabotage, or war, and that it is protectable by "national defense."

11   XI. We now have a clear, inescapable choice that we must make. We can continue to promote a global economic system of unlimited "free trade" among corporations, held together by long and highly vulnerable lines of communication and supply, but now recognizing that such a system will have to be protected by a hugely expensive police force that will be worldwide, whether maintained by one nation or several or all, and that such a police force will be effective precisely to the extent that it oversways the freedom and privacy of the citizens of every nation.

12   XII. Or we can promote a decentralized world economy which would have the aim of assuring to every nation and region a local self-sufficiency in life-supporting goods. This would not eliminate international trade, but it would tend toward a trade in surpluses after local needs had been met.

13   XIII. One of the gravest dangers to us now, second only to further terrorist attacks against our people, is that we will attempt to go on as before with the corporate program of global "free trade," whatever the cost in freedom and civil rights, without self-questioning or self-criticism or public debate.

14   XIV. This is why the substitution of rhetoric for thought, always a temptation in a national crisis, must be resisted by officials and citizens alike. It is hard for ordinary citizens to know what is actually happening in Washington in a time of such great trouble; for all we know, serious and difficult thought may be taking place there. But the talk that we are hearing from politicians, bureaucrats, and commentators has so far tended to reduce the complex problems now facing us to issues of unity, security, normality, and retaliation.

XV. National self-righteousness, like personal self-righteousness, is a   15
mistake. It is misleading. It is a sign of weakness. Any war that we may
make now against terrorism will come as a new installment in a history of
war in which we have fully participated. We are not innocent of making
war against civilian populations. The modern doctrine of such warfare
was set forth and enacted by General William Tecumseh Sherman, who
held that a civilian population could be declared guilty and rightly subjected to military punishment. We have never repudiated that doctrine.

XVI. It is a mistake also—as events since September 11 have   16
shown—to suppose that a government can promote and participate in
a global economy and at the same time act exclusively in its own interest by abrogating its international treaties and standing apart from international cooperation on moral issues.

XVII. And surely, in our country, under our Constitution, it is a fun-   17
damental error to suppose that any crisis or emergency can justify any
form of political oppression. Since September 11, far too many public
voices have presumed to "speak for us" in saying that Americans will
gladly accept a reduction of freedom in exchange for greater "security."
Some would, maybe. But some others would accept a reduction in security (and in global trade) far more willingly than they would accept
any abridgement of our Constitutional rights.

XVIII. In a time such as this, when we have been seriously and   18
most cruelly hurt by those who hate us, and when we must consider
ourselves to be gravely threatened by those same people, it is hard to
speak of the ways of peace and to remember that Christ enjoined us to
love our enemies, but this is no less necessary for being difficult.

XIX. Even now we dare not forget that since the attack on Pearl   19
Harbor—to which the present attack has been often and not usefully
compared—we humans have suffered an almost uninterrupted sequence
of wars, none of which has brought peace or made us more peaceable.

XX. The aim and result of war necessarily is not peace but victory,   20
and any victory won by violence necessarily justifies the violence that
won it and leads to further violence. If we are serious about innovation,
must we not conclude that we need something new to replace our perpetual "war to end war"?

XXI. What leads to peace is not violence but peaceableness, which   21
is not passivity, but an alert, informed, practiced, and active state of
being. We should recognize that while we have extravagantly subsidized the means of war, we have almost totally neglected the ways of
peaceableness. We have, for example, several national military acade-
mies, but not one peace academy. We have ignored the teachings and
the examples of Christ, Gandhi, Martin Luther King, and other peaceable leaders. And here we have an inescapable duty to notice also that
war is profitable, whereas the means of peaceableness, being cheap or
free, make no money.

22   XXII. The key to peaceableness is continuous practice. It is wrong to suppose that we can exploit and impoverish the poorer countries, while arming them and instructing them in the newest means of war, and then reasonably expect them to be peaceable.

23   XXIII. We must not again allow public emotion or the public media to caricature our enemies. If our enemies are now to be some nations of Islam, then we should undertake to know those enemies. Our schools should begin to teach the histories, cultures, arts, and language of the Islamic nations. And our leaders should have the humility and the wisdom to ask the reasons some of those people have for hating us.

24   XXIV. Starting with the economies of food and farming, we should promote at home, and encourage abroad, the ideal of local self-sufficiency. We should recognize that this is the surest, the safest, and the cheapest way for the world to live. We should not countenance the loss or destruction of any local capacity to produce necessary goods.

25   XXV. We should reconsider and renew and extend our efforts to protect the natural foundations of the human economy: soil, water, and air. We should protect every intact ecosystem and watershed that we have left, and begin restoration of those that have been damaged.

26   XXVI. The complexity of our present trouble suggests as never before that we need to change our present concept of education. Education is not properly an industry, and its proper use is not to serve industries, either by job-training or by industry-subsidized research. It's proper use is to enable citizens to live lives that are economically, politically, socially, and culturally responsible. This cannot be done by gathering or "accessing" what we now call "information"—which is to say facts without context and therefore without priority. A proper education enables young people to put their lives in order, which means knowing what things are more important than other things; it means putting first things first.

27   XXVII. The first thing we must begin to teach our children (and learn ourselves) is that we cannot spend and consume endlessly. We have got to learn to save and conserve. We do need a "new economy," but one that is founded on thrift and care, on saving and conserving, not on excess and waste. An economy based on waste is inherently and hopelessly violent, and war is its inevitable by-product. We need a peaceable economy.

Note

1. We gratefully acknowledge Wendell Berry and the editors of OrionOnline for allowing us to reproduce this article, which originally appeared on OrionOnline.org, the Web site of *Orion* and *Orion Afield* magazines, under the feature headline "Thoughts on America."

RESPONDING TO READING

1. According to Berry, the idea that the American economy must constantly grow leads to many negative effects, in America and throughout the world. What negative impacts does economic growth lead to? How does growth imply "a hatred of the past"?

2. In what ways does the "new kind of war" that Berry describes turn new technologies against the people who use them? Do new methods of making war always do this?

3. Berry describes two possible choices, between a global economy run by large corporations and a decentralized global economy. What are the positives and negatives of each? Which choice does Berry prefer?

4. How does Berry support his claim that the United States is "not innocent of making war against civilian populations"? Do you agree or disagree with his claim? Are all wars, at heart, wars against civilians?

5. Berry argues that no "crisis or emergency can justify any form of political oppression." In an essay, argue for or against this claim. Are there times when individual freedoms must be sacrificed for the common good? Or does the common good never outweigh the rights of the individual?

Disarmament

POPE JOHN XXIII

Angelo Giuseppe Roncalli was born in 1881 at Sotto il Monte (Bergamo), Italy, the third of a sharecropper's family of thirteen children. At the age of twelve, he enrolled in the seminary in Bergamo; at twenty, he began doctoral studies in theology at the Apollinaris in Rome. Despite time out for service in the Italian army, he completed his doctorate and was ordained in 1904. For the next nine years, until he was recalled to military service in 1915–18 as a chaplain, Roncalli served as secretary to the bishop of Bergamo, Giacomo Radini-Tedeschi, a compassionate, social-minded prelate who concentrated on problems of the working class. Returning to Bergamo after World War I ended, Roncalli served as spiritual director of the seminary until 1921, when he was called to Rome to reorganize the Society for the Propagation of the Faith—whereupon began his active involvement with the wider world. Appointed apostolic visitor to Bulgaria (1925), and in 1934 transferred to Turkey and Greece as apostolic delegate, he established an office in Istanbul for locating prisoners of war. From 1944 to 1952, he served as papal nuncio to Paris, assisting in the Church's postwar work in France-and then became the first permanent observer of the Holy See at UNESCO. When he was 72, he returned to Italy as cardinal-patriarch of Venice, where he expected to spend his last years in pastoral work.

However, in 1958 he was elected Pope. Although the conclave of cardinal electors may have regarded him, because of his advanced age—76—as a transitional figure, his election in fact marked, as the Vatican acknowledges, "a turning point in history and a new age for the Church." While maintaining the pastoral orientation he announced in his coronation address, since "all other human gifts and accomplishments—learning, practical experience, diplomatic finesse—can broaden and enrich pastoral work but they cannot replace it," the activist John XXIII dramatically modernized the Roman Catholic Church. He enlarged the College of Cardinals from 70 to 87, with the largest international membership in its history. He initiated a groundbreaking revision of the Code of Canon Law, convening the first diocesan synod in the history of Rome in 1960, followed by Vatican Council II in 1962; the Pontifical Commission for the Revision of the Code was appointed in 1963. John XXIII was considered an exceptionally warm humanitarian; the world's testimony at his death in 1963 was epitomized in a newspaper drawing of the Earth, shrouded in mourning, captioned "A Death in the Family."

Pacem in terris (Peace on Earth), the Encyclical Letter of John XXII, of which "Disarmament" is a section, was also published in 1963. In scope, stature, and significance it has been compared to Beethoven's Ninth Symphony, "the symphony of peace," and praised worldwide as "one of the strongest and most eloquent papal statements on peace ever made." Addressed to "all men of good will," as commentator Peter Riga notes in *Peace on Earth* (1964), "its firm basis is taken from political and moral philosophy." "Peace among all peoples requires," said John XXIII, "Truth as its foundation, justice as its rule, love as its driving force, liberty as its atmosphere." Its central idea is "direct and clear," says Riga, "the freedom, dignity, rights, and responsibilities of each human person are the only valid foundation upon which any national or international organization can be built. Universal peace is primarily a question of law, and this law, properly understood, must embody in concrete and operative structures the inalienable rights possessed by every human being." With this broad, ecumenical approach, John XXIII put an end, "at least in theory," says Riga, "to the Catholic ghetto mentality which has been prevalent since the reformation. The concept of the Church as an armed fortress fighting off the onslaughts of the enemy is a thing of the past. The Pope tells Catholics that they must become involved in the modern world, with all of its particular problems."

Disarmament

1   109. On the other hand, it is with deep sorrow that We note the enormous stocks of armaments that have been and still are being made in more economically developed countries, with a vast outlay of intellectual and economic resources. And so it happens that, while the people of

these countries are loaded with heavy burdens, other countries as a result are deprived of the collaboration they need in order to make economic and social progress.

110. The production of arms is allegedly justified on the grounds that in present-day conditions peace cannot be preserved without an equal balance of armaments. And so, if one country increases its armaments, others feel the need to do the same; and if one country is equipped with nuclear weapons, other countries must produce their own, equally destructive.

111. Consequently, people live in constant fear lest the storm that every moment threatens should break upon them with dreadful violence. And with good reason, for the arms of war are ready at hand. Even though it is difficult to believe that anyone would deliberately take the responsibility for the appalling destruction and sorrow that war would bring in its train, it cannot be denied that the conflagration may be set off by some unexpected and obscure event. And one must bear in mind that, even though the monstrous power of modern weapons acts as a deterrent, it is to be feared that the mere continuance of nuclear tests, undertaken with war in mind, will prove a serious hazard for life on earth.

112. Justice, then, right reason and humanity urgently demand that the arms race should cease; that the stockpiles which exist in various countries should be reduced equally and simultaneously by the parties concerned; that nuclear weapons should be banned; and that a general agreement should eventually be reached about progressive disarmament and an effective method of control. In the words of Pius XII, Our Predecessor of happy memory: *The calamity of a world war, with the economic and social ruin and the moral excesses and dissolution that accompany it, must not be permitted to envelop the human race for a third time.*[1]

113. All must realize that there is no hope of putting an end to the building up of armaments, nor of reducing the present stocks, nor, still less, of abolishing them altogether, unless the process is complete and thorough and unless it proceeds from inner conviction: unless, that is, everyone sincerely co-operates to banish the fear and anxious expectation of war with which men are oppressed. If this is to come about, the fundamental principle on which our present peace depends must be replaced by another, which declares that the true and solid peace of nations consists not in equality of arms but in mutual trust alone. We believe that this can be brought to pass, and We consider that it is something which reason requires, that it is eminently desirable in itself and that it will prove to be the source of many benefits.

---

[1] Cf. Pius XII's *Radio Broadcast*, Christmas Eve, 1941, *A.A.S.*, XXXIV (1942), p. 17; and Benedict XV's *Adhortatio* to the rulers of peoples at war, August 1, 1917, *A.A.S.*, IX (1917), p. 418.

6   114. In the first place, it is an objective demanded by reason. There can be, or at least there should be, no doubt that relations between States, as between individuals, should be regulated not by the force of arms but by the light of reason, by the rule, that is, of truth, of justice and of active and sincere co-operation.

7   115. Secondly, We say that it is an objective earnestly to be desired in itself. Is there anyone who does not ardently yearn to see war banished, to see peace preserved and daily more firmly established?

8   116. And finally, it is an objective which will be a fruitful source of many benefits, for its advantages will be felt everywhere, by individuals, by families, by nations, by the whole human family. The warning of Pius XII still rings in our ears: *Nothing is lost by peace; everything may be lost by war.*[2]

9   117. Since this is so, We, the Vicar on earth of Jesus Christ, Savior of the World and Author of Peace, and as interpreter of the very profound longing of the entire human family, following the impulse of Our heart, seized by anxiety for the good of all, We feel it Our duty to beseech men, especially those who have the responsibility of public affairs, to spare no labor in order to ensure that world events follow a reasonable and humane course.

10   118. In the highest and most authoritative assemblies, let men give serious thought to the problem of a peaceful adjustment of relations between political communities on a world level: an adjustment founded on mutual trust, on sincerity in negotiations, on faithful fulfillment of obligations assumed. Let them study the problem until they find that point of agreement from which it will be possible to commence to go forward towards accords that will be sincere, lasting and fruitful.

11   119. We, for Our part, will not cease to pray God to bless these labors so that they may lead to fruitful results.

RESPONDING TO READING

1. What percentage of its annual budget does your nation spend on its military? How does this compare to amounts spent on other necessities, such as health care and education?

2. According to Pope John XXIII, why does equality among nations—in regards to weapons of war—lead to a more dangerous world? Do you agree, or is the old paradox true: If you want peace, then you must prepare for war?

3. Is it possible "that the stockpiles [of weapons] which exist in various countries should be reduced equally and simultaneously," or is this an unworkable solution to the problem identified in this essay?

---

[2]Cf. Pius XII's *Radio Broadcast*, August 24, 1939, *A.A.S.*, XXXI (1939), p. 334.

4. Pope John XXIII asks, "Is there anyone who does not ardently yearn to see war banished, to see peace preserved and daily more firmly established?" Is there? Who benefits most from war? Who benefits least from times of peace?

5. In an essay, explain who the audience is for Pope John XXIII's essay. How does he present his arguments, and who would be persuaded by the arguments he makes? How would his arguments have to change for a different audience?

WILL A NEW UTOPIA BE POSSIBLE IN THE 21ST CENTURY?

Genetics and Human Malleability

W. FRENCH ANDERSON

More than forty years ago, when W. French Anderson raised the idea of gene therapy at a college seminar, the visiting lecturer told him it was a worthless line of inquiry.* Now, however, Anderson is considered "the father of gene therapy," at the forefront of efforts to turn genetic research into cures for diseases. Born (1936) and raised in Tulsa Oklahoma, Anderson was a child prodigy: He learned math before kindergarten, devoured science books at the age of eight, overcame a stutter by learning to talk with pebbles in his mouth, joined the school debating team, and won a track scholarship to Harvard. After earning his B.A. (1958), he went on to an M.A. at Cambridge (1960) and an M.D. at Harvard (1963). There followed twenty-seven years of research with the National Heart, Lung and Blood Institute at the National Institutes of Health, where he also served as chairman of the Department of Medicine and Physiology in the graduate program. In 1990, he led the team that performed the first approved gene transplant to treat a human genetic disease. Currently, as director of the Gene Therapy Laboratories at the University of Southern California Keck School of Medicine, he works to save patients from life-threatening diseases such as X-SCID, a deadly immune system defect. Anderson is editor-in-chief of the journal *Human Gene Therapy* and has published over 350 articles in scientific journals. He is a popular scientific spokesperson in the media, and has earned many honors and prizes, including an Award for Excellence in Technology Transfer from the U.S. government.

In "Genetics and Human Malleability" Anderson addresses the ethical dimension of gene therapy. Considering the fact that there could be a substantial market for "enhancement" therapy—genetic improvement of human memory or body size, for instance—scientists should consider the implications of such practices. Anderson argues firmly against genetic intervention unless human lives are at stake and also explores some of the subtle distinctions that doctors will have to make as gene therapy comes into the medical mainstream.

1   Just how much can, and should we change human nature . . . by genetic engineering? Our response to that hinges on the answers to three further questions: (1) What *can* we do now? Or more precisely,

---

Time, Jan 17, 1994 v143 n3 p56(2).

what *are* we doing now in the area of human genetic engineering? (2) What *will* we be able to do? In other words, what technical advances are we likely to achieve over the next five to ten years? (3) What *should* we do? I will argue that a line can be drawn and should be drawn to use gene transfer only for the treatment of serious disease, and not for any other purpose. Gene transfer should never be undertaken in an attempt to enhance or "improve" human beings. . . .

It is clear that there are several applications for gene transfer that probably will be carried out over the next five to ten years. Many genetic diseases that are caused by a defect in a single gene should be treatable, such as ADA deficiency (a severe immune deficiency disease of children), sickle cell anemia, hemophilia, and Gaucher disease. Some types of cancer, viral diseases such as AIDS, and some forms of cardiovascular disease are targets for treatment by gene therapy. In addition, germline gene therapy, that is, the insertion of a gene into the reproductive cells of a patient, will probably be technically possible in the foreseeable future. . . .

But successful somatic cell gene therapy also opens the door for enhancement genetic engineering, that is, for supplying a specific characteristic that individuals might want for themselves (somatic cell engineering) or their children (germline engineering) which would not involve the treatment of a disease. The most obvious example at the moment would be in the insertion of a growth hormone gene into a normal child in the hope that this would make the child grow larger. Should parents be allowed to choose (if the science should ever make it possible) whatever useful characteristics they wish for their children?

No Enhancement Engineering

A line can and should be drawn between somatic cell therapy and enhancement genetic engineering. Our society has repeatedly demonstrated that it can draw a line in biomedical research when necessary. The [1978] Belmont Report [a government-sponsored study on the protection of human research subjects] illustrates how guidelines were formulated to delineate ethical from unethical clinical research and to distinguish clinical research from clinical practice. Our responsibility is to determine how and where to draw lines with respect to genetic engineering.

Somatic cell gene therapy for the treatment of severe disease is considered ethical because it can be supported by the fundamental moral principle of beneficence: It would relieve human suffering. Gene therapy would be, therefore, a moral good. Under what circumstances would human genetic engineering not be a moral good? In the broadest sense, when it detracts from, rather than contributes to, the dignity of man. Whether viewed from a theological perspective or a secular humanist one, the justification for drawing a line is founded on the argument that, beyond the line, human values that our society considers important for the dignity of man would be significantly threatened.

6   Somatic cell enhancement engineering would threaten important human values in two ways: It could be medically hazardous, in that the risks could exceed the potential benefits and the procedure therefore could cause harm. And it would be morally precarious, in that it would require moral decisions our society is not now prepared to make, and it could lead to an increase in inequality and discriminatory practices.

7   Medicine is a very inexact science. We understand roughly how a simple gene works and that there are many thousands of housekeeping genes, that is, genes that do the job of running a cell. We predict that there are genes which make regulatory messages that are involved in the overall control and regulation of the many housekeeping genes. Yet we have only limited understanding of how a body organ develops into the size and shape it does. We know many things about how the central nervous system works—for example, we are beginning to comprehend how molecules are involved in electric circuits, in memory storage, in transmission of signals. But we are a long way from understanding thought and consciousness. And we are even further from understanding the spiritual side of our existence.

8   Even though we do not understand how a thinking, loving, interacting organism can be derived from its molecules, we are approaching the time when we can change some of those molecules. Might there be genes that influence the brain's organization or structure or metabolism or circuitry in some way so as to allow abstract thinking, contemplation of good and evil, fear of death, awe of a "God"? What if in our innocent attempts to improve our genetic make-up we alter one or more of those genes? Could we test for the alteration? Certainly not at present. If we caused a problem that would affect the individual or his or her offspring, could we repair the damage? Certainly not at present. Every parent who has several children knows that some babies accept and give more affection than others, in the same environment. Do genes control this? What if these genes were accidentally altered? How would we even know if such a gene were altered?

Tinkering with the Unknown

9   My concern is that, at this point in the development of our culture's scientific expertise, we might be like the young boy who loves to take things apart. He is bright enough to disassemble a watch, and maybe even bright enough to get it back together again so that it works. But what if he tries to "improve" it? Maybe put on bigger hands so that the

time can be read more easily. But if the hands are too heavy for the mechanism, the watch will run slowly, erratically, or not at all. The boy can understand what is visible, but he cannot comprehend the precise engineering calculations that determined exactly how strong each spring should be, why the gears interact in the ways that they do, etc. Attempts on his part to improve the watch will probably only harm it. We are now able to provide a new gene so that a property involved in a human life would be changed, for example, a growth hormone gene. If we were to do so simply because we could, I fear we would be like that young boy who changed the watch's hands. We, too, do not really understand what makes the object we are tinkering with tick. . . .

Yet even aside from the medical risks, somatic cell enhancement   10
engineering should not be performed because it would be morally precarious. Let us assume that there were no medical risks at all from somatic cell enhancement engineering. There would still be reasons for objecting to this procedure. To illustrate, let us consider some example. What if a human gene were cloned that could produce a brain chemical resulting in markedly increased memory capacity in monkeys after gene transfer. Should a person be allowed to receive such a gene on request? Should a pubescent adolescent whose parents are both five feet tall be provided with a growth hormone gene on request? Should a worker who is continually exposed to an industrial toxin receive a gene to give him resistance on his, or his employer's request?

Three Problems

These scenarios suggest three problems that would be difficult to re-   11
solve: What genes should be provided; who should receive a gene; and, how to prevent discrimination against individuals who do or do not receive a gene.

We allow that it would be ethically appropriate to use somatic cell   12
gene therapy for treatment of serious disease. But what distinguishes a serious disease from a "minor" disease from cultural "discomfort"? What is suffering? What is significant suffering? Does the absence of growth hormone that results in a growth limitation to two feet in height represent a genetic disease? What about a limitation to a height of four feet, to five feet? Each observer might draw the lines between serious disease, minor disease, and genetic variation differently. But all can agree that there are extreme cases that produce significant suffering and premature death. Here then is where an initial line should be drawn for determining what genes should be provided: treatment of serious disease.

If the position is established that only patients suffering from seri-   13
ous diseases are candidates for gene insertion, then the issues of patient

selection are no different than in other medical situations: the determination is based on medical need within a supply and demand framework. But if the use of gene transfer extends to allow a normal individual to acquire, for example, a memory-enhancing gene, profound problems would result. On what basis is the decision made to allow one individual to receive the gene but not another: Should it go to those best able to benefit society (the smartest already?) To those most in need (those with low intelligence? But how low? Will enhancing memory help a mentally retarded child?) To those chosen by a lottery? To those who can afford to pay? As long as our society lacks a significant consensus about these answers, the best way to make equitable decisions in this case should be to base them on the seriousness of the objective medical need, rather than on the personal wishes or resources of an individual.

14   Discrimination can occur in many forms. If individuals are carriers of a disease (for example, sickle cell anemia), would they be pressured to be treated? Would they have difficulty in obtaining health insurance unless they agreed to be treated? These are ethical issues raised also by genetic screening and by the Human Genome Project. But the concerns would become even more troublesome if there were the possibility for "correction" by the use of human genetic engineering.

15   Finally, we must face the issue of eugenics, the attempt to make hereditary "improvements." The abuse of power that societies have historically demonstrated in the pursuit of eugenic goals is well documented. Might we slide into a new age of eugenic thinking by starting with small "improvements"? It would be difficult, if not impossible, to determine where to draw a line once enhancement engineering had begun. Therefore, gene transfer should be used only for the treatment of serious disease and not for putative improvements.

16   Our society is comfortable with the use of genetic engineering to treat individuals with serious disease. On medical and ethical grounds we should draw a line excluding any form of enhancement engineering. We should not step over the line that delineates treatment from enhancement.

RESPONDING TO READING

1.   According to Anderson, in what ways do the things we *are* doing with genetic engineering hinder discussions about what we *should* be doing? Are these discussions further hindered by a focus on what *might* be possible in some near or far future?

2.   What physical, moral, and spiritual threats are inherent in any genetic engineering? What types of engineering are less threatening than others? Why?

3.   How does Anderson's example of a young boy disassembling, assembling, and improving a watch metaphorically support his argument? That is, what

are the implicit and explicit parallels Anderson draws between the example and his larger point?

4. How does Anderson define "discrimination"? What part does this definition play in his deliberations on the problems of genetic engineering?

5. At the end of his essay, Anderson makes a clear, unambiguous pronounce- ment: "We should not step over the line that delineates treatment from en- hancement." In an essay, explain whether you agree or disagree with this statement and why. Is treatment always positive and enhancement always negative for Anderson? Is it for you?

The Media and the Ethics of Cloning

LEIGH TURNER

An advocate for informed public debate about science and ethics, Leigh Turner was educated at the University of Winnipeg (B.A, M.A.) and at the School of Religion and Social Ethics at the University of Southern California (M.A., Ph.D.), where he wrote his doctoral disser- tation on "Bioethics in a Pluralistic World." After working at the Hast- ings Center in New York, as a research associate studying ethical issues in science and medicine, he joined the faculty of the University of Toronto Joint Centre for Bioethics (1998–2000) as assistant profes- sor. Simultaneously, he held the position of clinical ethicist at Baycrest Centre for Geriatric Care and Sunnybrook & Women's College Health Sciences Centre. Since 2000, Turner has been on the faculty of McGill University both in the Biomedical Ethics Unit and the Department of Social Studies of Medicine. Taking his inspiration in part from sociol- ogist of science Robert K. Merton, Turner studies issues such as assist- ed suicide and cross-cultural attitudes to end-of-life care; recently, he has looked at conflicts of interest in biomedical science and the growth of global, venture-capital driven, biotechnology businesses.

"The Media and the Ethics of Cloning," from the *Chronicle of Higher Education*, criticizes our sound-bite-driven discourse about complex issues such as cloning. For example, Turner points out that sensationalistic media reports about human cloning dominate the dis- cussion, while the question of animal cloning is shunted aside. Mean- while, biotechnology firms pursue plans to turn animals into "pharmaceutical factories." Important ethical concepts are being ig- nored, and basic scientific concepts misunderstood, Turner argues, and he suggests several ways that scientists and nonscientists could become active participants in a more meaningful debate.

If the contemporary debate on cloning has a patron saint, surely it   1 is Andy Warhol.[1] Not only did Warhol assert that everyone would have

---

[1]American artist (1928–1987) who mass-produced images by silk-screening.

15 minutes of fame—witness the lawyers, philosophers, theologians, and bioethicists who found their expertise in hot demand on the nightly morality plays of network television following Ian Wilmut's cloning of the sheep Dolly—but he also placed "clones," multiple copies of the same phenomenon, at the heart of popular culture. Instead of multiple images of Marilyn Monroe and Campbell's soup cans, we now have cloned sheep. Regrettably, it is Warhol's capacity for hyperbole rather than his intelligence and ironic vision that permeates the current debate on cloning.

2   It would be unfair to judge hastily written op-ed pieces, popular talk shows, and late-night radio programs by the same standards that one would apply to a sustained piece of philosophical or legal analysis. But the popular media could do more to foster thoughtful public debate on the legal, moral, political, medical, and scientific dimensions of the cloning of humans and non-human animals.

3   As did many of my colleagues at the Hastings Center,[2] I participated in several interviews with the media following Ian Wilmut's announcement in *Nature*[3] that he had succeeded in cloning Dolly from a mammary cell of an adult sheep. After clearly stating to one Los Angeles radio broadcaster before our interview that I was not a theologian and did not represent a religious organization, I was rather breathlessly asked during the taping what God's view on cloning is and whether cloning is "against creation." Predictably, the broadcaster didn't want to discuss how religious ethicists are contributing to the nascent public discourse about the ethics of cloning. Instead, he wanted me to provide a dramatic response that would get the radio station's phones ringing with calls from atheists, agnostics, and religious believers of all stripes.

4   In addition to inundating the public with hyperbolic sound bites and their print equivalents, the media have overwhelmingly emphasized the issues involved in cloning humans, paying almost no attention to the moral implications of cloning non-human animals. While the ethics of cloning humans clearly need to be debated, the cloning of non-human animals has already taken place and deserves to be treated as a meaningful moral concern.

5   Although I suspect that a compelling argument for the cloning of animals can be made, we should not ignore the difference between actually formulating such arguments and merely presuming that non-human cloning is altogether unproblematic. Admittedly, humans already consider non-human animals as commodities in many ways, including as a source of food. Yet perhaps cloning animals with the in-

---

[2]A nonprofit institute that supports research on ethical issues in medicine, health care, and science.

[3]An important scientific journal published in Great Britain.

tent of using them as "pharmaceutical factories," to produce insulin and other substances to treat human illnesses, should raise questions about how far such an attitude ought to extend. What moral obligations should extend to humans' use of other species? Do the potential medical benefits for humans outweigh the dangers of encouraging people to think of non-human animals as machines to be manipulated to fulfill human goals? These kinds of questions deserve to be part of the public discussion about cloning. Given some people's concerns about the use of traps to catch wild animals, the living conditions of farm animals, and the treatment of animals used in medical and pharmaceutical research, I find this gap in public discourse perplexing.

But perhaps the most significant problem with the media hyper-   6
bole concerning cloning is the easy assumption that humans simply are a product of their genes—a view usually called "genetic essentialism." Television hosts and radio personalities have asked whether it would be possible to stock an entire basketball team with clones of Michael Jordan. In response, philosophers, theologians, and other experts have reiterated wearily that, although human behavior undeniably has a genetic component, a host of other factors—including uterine environment, family dynamics, social setting, diet, and other personal history—play important roles in an individual's development. Consequently, a clone produced from the DNA of an outstanding athlete might not even be interested in sports.

While this more-sophisticated message has received some media   7
attention, we continue to see stories emphasizing that the wealthy might some day be able to produce copies of themselves, or that couples with a dying infant might create an identical copy of the child. The popular media seem to remain transfixed by what Dorothy Nelkin, the New York University sociologist of science, refers to as "DNA as destiny."

What's more, the cloning issue reveals the way in which the mass   8
media foster attitudes of technological and scientific determinism by implying that scientific "progress" cannot be halted. Of course, many scientists share these attitudes, and, too often, they refuse to accept moral responsibility for their participation in research that may contribute to human suffering. But scientists should not merely ply their craft, leaving moral reasoning to others. They should participate in public debates about whether certain scientific projects are harmful and should not be allowed to continue because they have unjustifiable, dehumanizing implications. A good model is the outspoken criticism of nuclear weapons by many nuclear physicists, who have helped limit research intended to produce more effective nuclear devices.

Scientists are not riding a juggernaut capable of crushing every-   9
thing in its path simply because mass cloning of animals, and possibly

eventually humans, may be technically possible. There is no reason to think that scientific research has a mandate that somehow enables it to proceed outside the web of moral concerns that govern all other human endeavors; it does not exist above the law or outside the rest of society. To think otherwise is to succumb to a technological determinism that denies the responsibilities and obligations of citizenship.

10   Despite the media's oversimplifications, citizens have an obligations to scrutinize carefully all of the issues involved and, if necessary, to regulate cloning through laws, professional codes of behavior, and institutional policies. I want to suggest three ways that scholars, policy makers, and concerned citizens can, in fact, work to improve public debate about ethical issues related to new developments in science and technology.

11   First, scientists and ethicists need a fuller understanding of each other's work. Scientists must recognize the moral implications of their research and address those implications when they discuss the research in public. The formal education of most scientists does not encourage them to consider ethical issues. Whereas courses in bioethics are now found in most school of medicine and nursing, graduate students in such disciplines as human genetics, biochemistry, and animal physiology are not encouraged to grapple with the ethical aspects of their research. Similarly, most ethicists have very little knowledge of science, although many of them feel perfectly entitled to comment on the moral issues of new scientific discoveries.

12   This gap in understanding fosters an inaccurate, unrealistic conception of what the most pressing ethical issues are. For example, the real challenges for researchers today involve the cloning of non-human animals for use in developing pharmaceutical products. Sustained study of non-human clones will be needed before researchers can even begin to seriously consider research involving human subjects. Rather than encouraging the media's interest in cloning humans, ethicists more knowledgeable about the science involved might have been able to shift the public debate toward the moral questions raised by cloning sheep, pigs, and other animals, questions that need immediate public debate.

13   Thus, we need to include more courses in various scientific departments on the ethics of contemporary scientific research; offer courses for ethicists on the basics of human genetics, anatomy, and physiology; and establish continuing-education courses and forums that bring together scientists and scholars in the humanities.

14   Second, ethicists need to do a better job of presenting their concerns in the popular media. Scientific journals written for a popular audience—such as *Scientific American, New Scientist, Discover,* and *The Sciences*—provide excellent popular accounts of scientific research and technological developments, but they rarely specifically address the

moral implications of the discoveries they report. Regrettably, most of the academic journals that do address the ethical aspects of scientific topics—such as the *Hastings Center Report*, the *Journal of Medical Ethics*, and the *Cambridge Quarterly of Healthcare Ethics*—lack the broad readership of the popular-science magazines. Right now, perhaps the best "popular" source of sustained ethical analysis of science, medicine, and health care is *The New York Times Magazine*.

If ethicists hope to reach larger audiences with more than trivial   15 sound bites, they need to establish and promote appropriate outlets for their concerns. For example, Arthur Caplan, director of the Center for Bioethics at the University of Pennsylvania, wrote a regular weekly newspaper column for the *St. Paul Pioneer Press* when he directed a bioethics center at the University of Minnesota. His column addressed the ethical implications of medical and scientific research. Other scholars have yet to follow his example—perhaps, in part, because many academics feel that writing for the mass media is unworthy of their time. They are wrong.

One way of improving public debate on these important issues is   16 for universities to encourage their faculty members to write for newspapers, popular magazines, and even community newsletters. Such forms of communication should be viewed as an important complement to other forms of published research. Leon Kass's writing on cloning in *The New Republic* and Michael Walzer's and Michael Sandel's writing on assisted suicide in the same publication should not be considered any less significant simply because the work appears in a magazine intended for a wide audience. After all, if universities are to retain their public support, they must consistently be seen as important players in society, and one easy way to do this is to encourage their faculty members to contribute regularly to public discussion.

Finally, we need to expand public debate about ethical issues in sci-   17 ence beyond the mass media. To complement the activities of the National Bioethics Advisory Commission and the projects on ethics at universities and research centers, we should create forums at which academics and citizens from all walks of life could meet to debate the issues. Instead of merely providing a gathering place for scholars pursuing research projects, institutions such as the Hastings Center, Georgetown University's Kennedy Institute of Ethics, and the University of Pennsylvania's Center for Bioethics need to foster outreach programs and community-discussion groups that include non-specialists. My experience suggests that members of civic organizations and community-health groups, such as the New York Citizens' Committee on Health Care Decisions, are quite eager to discuss the topic of cloning.

What we need are fewer commentaries by self-promoting experts on   18 network television, and more intelligent discussions by scholars and citizens in local media including local public-television stations. We need creative alternatives to the onslaught of talking heads, all saying much the same thing (as though they themselves were clones) to docile, sheep-like audiences waiting for others to address the most pressing moral issues of the day.

RESPONDING TO READING

1. Turner argues that "the popular media could do more to foster thoughtful public debate on the legal, moral, political, medical, and scientific dimensions of the cloning of humans and non-human animals." In your experience of popular media, particularly television, is this true? Is it possible to sustain "thoughtful public debate" on any issue, given the reality that television is, primarily, a medium of entertainment?

2. What concerns does Turner raise about the cloning of nonhuman animals? How are his concerns affected by the fact that nonhuman animals have already been cloned successfully? Is it desirable to argue about what *should* be done after it already has been done?

3. Why is the cloning of nonhuman animals (such as Dolly the sheep) more acceptable to the general public than the cloning of a human?

4. How does Turner define "genetic essentialism"? In what ways does this definition influence discussions of cloning, of either humans or nonhuman animals?

5. Turner argues that scientists should always confront—or be forced to confront—the moral implications of their work. In an essay, explain whether you agree or disagree with this idea. Would scientific developments be unduly hampered if scientists were made to consider every possible implication of their work? Is there scientific research that should never have occurred?

The United Nations in the 21st Century
KOFI ANNAN

Kofi Annan was born in Kumasi, Ghana (1938). Educated internationally after beginning work at the University of Science and Technology in Kumasi, he completed his undergraduate work in economics at Macalester College in St. Paul, Minnesota, in 1961. From 1961 to 1962, he studied economics at the Institut Universitaire des Hautes Études Internationales in Geneva. And in 1971–72, as a Sloan Fellow at M.I.T., he earned an M.S. in management. His work with the United Nations began in 1962 as a budget officer with the World Health Organization in Geneva. He later served with the UN Economic Commission for Africa in Addis Ababa; the UN Emergency Force in Ismailia; and the Office of the UN High Commissioner for Refugees in Geneva. At the UN in New York, he held a variety of posts, among them assistant secretary–general for human resources management; controller; assistant secretary–general for peacekeeping; and under secretary–general during an unprecedented growth in UN peacekeeping operations around the world. He was chosen as the seventh secretary–general of the UN in January 1997. In December 2001, Annan received the Nobel peace prize. The Nobel Committee said that Mr. Annan "had been preeminent in bringing new life to the [United Nations] and in [proclaiming] that the only negotiable road to global peace and cooperation goes by way of the United Nations."

In his lecture from December 2001, Annan speaks of the trauma facing children in Afghanistan, then embriled in the first stage of the U.S. War on Terror, as trauma that could be said to face children across the world. Borders, he argues, are no longer between nations but are, instaed, "between powerful and powerless, free and fettered, privileged and humiliated." While past aggressions led the world to this time of violence and terror—compounded by the ever-increasing gulf between those who have and those who want—this progression need not continue, argues Annan. Challenges face the nations of the world, but the United Nations exists to face and overcome those challenges through cooperation, understanding, and peaceful resolution.

Today, in Afghanistan, a girl will be born. Her mother will hold her and feed her, comfort her and care for her—just as any mother would anywhere in the world. In these most basic acts of human nature, humanity knows no divisions. But to be born a girl in today's Afghanistan is to begin life centuries away from the prosperity that one small part of humanity has achieved. It is to live under conditions that many of us in this hall would consider inhuman.   1

I speak of a girl in Afghanistan, but I might equally well have mentioned a baby boy or girl in Sierra Leone. No one today is unaware of this divide between the world's rich and poor. No one today can claim ignorance of the cost that this divide imposes on the poor and dispossessed who are no less deserving of human dignity, fundamental freedoms, security, food and education than any of us. The cost, however, is not borne by them alone. Ultimately, it is borne by all of us—North and South, rich and poor, men and women of all races and religions.   2

Today's real borders are not between nations, but between powerful and powerless, free and fettered, privileged and humiliated. Today, no walls can separate humanitarian or human rights crises in one part of the world from national security crises in another.   3

Scientists tell us that the world of nature is so small and interdependent that a butterfly flapping its wings in the Amazon rainforest can generate a violent storm on the other side of the earth. This principle is known as the "Butterfly Effect." Today, we realize, perhaps more than ever, that the world of human activity also has its own "Butterfly Effect"—for better or for worse.   4

5   Ladies and Gentlemen,

6   We have entered the third millennium through a gate of fire. If today, after the horror of 11 September, we see better, and we see further—we will realize that humanity is indivisible. New threats make no distinction between races, nations or regions. A new insecurity has entered every mind, regardless of wealth or status. A deeper awareness of the bonds that bind us all—in pain as in prosperity—has gripped young and old.

7   In the early beginnings of the 21st century—a century already violently disabused of any hopes that progress towards global peace and prosperity is inevitable—this new reality can no longer be ignored. It must be confronted.

8   The 20th century was perhaps the deadliest in human history, devastated by innumerable conflicts, untold suffering, and unimaginable crimes. Time after time, a group or a nation inflicted extreme violence on another, often driven by irrational hatred and suspicion, or unbounded arrogance and thirst for power and resources. In response to these cataclysms, the leaders of the world came together at mid-century to unite the nations as never before.

9   A forum was created—the United Nations—where all nations could join forces to affirm the dignity and worth of every person, and to secure peace and development for all peoples. Here States could unite to strengthen the rule of law, recognize and address the needs of the poor, restrain man's brutality and greed, conserve the resources and beauty of nature, sustain the equal rights of men *and* women, and provide for the safety of future generations.

10   We thus inherit from the 20th century the political, as well as the scientific and technological power, which—if only we have the will to use them—give us the chance to vanquish poverty, ignorance and disease.

11   In the 21st Century I believe the mission of the United Nations will be defined by a new, more profound, awareness of the sanctity and dignity of every human life, regardless of race or religion. This will require us to look beyond the framework of States, and beneath the surface of nations or communities. We must focus, as never before, on improving the conditions of the individual men and women who give the state or nation its richness and character. We must begin with the young Afghan girl, recognizing that saving that one life is to save humanity itself.

12   Over the past five years, I have often recalled that the United Nations' Charter begins with the words: "We the peoples." What is not always recognized is that "we the peoples" are made up of individuals whose claims to the most fundamental rights have too often been sacrificed in the supposed interests of the state or the nation.

A genocide begins with the killing of one man—not for what he   13
has done, but because of who he is. A campaign of 'ethnic cleansing'
begins with one neighbour turning on another. Poverty begins when
even one child is denied his or her fundamental right to education.
What begins with the failure to uphold the dignity of one life, all too
often ends with a calamity for entire nations.

In this new century, we must start from the understanding that   14
peace belongs not only to states or peoples, but to each and every member of those communities. The sovereignty of States must no longer be
used as a shield for gross violations of human rights. Peace must be
made real and tangible in the daily existence of every individual in
need. Peace must be sought, above all, because it is the condition for
every member of the human family to live a life of dignity and security.

The rights of the individual are of no less importance to immi-   15
grants and minorities in Europe and the Americas than to women in
Afghanistan or children in Africa. They are as fundamental to the poor
as to the rich; they are as necessary to the security of the developed
world as to that of the developing world.

From this vision of the role of the United Nations in the next century   16
flow three key priorities for the future: eradicating poverty, preventing
conflict, and promoting democracy. Only in a world that is rid of poverty can all men and women make the most of their abilities. Only where
individual rights are respected can differences be channelled politically
and resolved peacefully. Only in a democratic environment, based on respect for diversity and dialogue, can individual self-expression and self-
government be secured, and freedom of association be upheld.

Throughout my term as Secretary-General, I have sought to place   17
human beings at the centre of everything we do—from conflict prevention to development to human rights. Securing real and lasting improvement in the lives of individual men and women is the measure of
all we do at the United Nations.

It is in this spirit that I humbly accept the Centennial Nobel Peace   18
Prize. Forty years ago today, the Prize for 1961 was awarded for the
first time to a Secretary-General of the United Nations—posthumously,
because Dag Hammarskjöld had already given his life for peace in
Central Africa. And on the same day, the Prize for 1960 was awarded
for the first time to an African—Albert Luthuli, one of the earliest leaders of the struggle against apartheld in South Africa. For me, as a young
African beginning his career in the United Nations a few months later,
those two men set a standard that I have sought to follow throughout
my working life.

This award belongs not just to me. I do not stand here alone. On be-   19
half of all my colleagues in every part of the United Nations, in every

corner of the globe, who have devoted their lives—and in many instances risked or given their lives in the cause of peace—I thank the Members of the Nobel Committee for this high honour. My own path to service at the United Nations was made possible by the sacrifice and commitment of my family and many friends from all continents—some of whom have passed away—who taught me and guided me. To them, I offer my most profound gratitude.

20   In a world filled with weapons of war and all too often words of war, the Nobel Committee has become a vital agent for peace. Sadly, a prize for peace is a rarity in this world. Most nations have monuments or memorials to war, bronze salutations to heroic battles, archways of triumph. But peace has no parade, no pantheon of victory.

21   What it does have is the Nobel Prize—a statement of hope and courage with unique resonance and authority. Only by understanding and addressing the needs of individuals for peace, for dignity, and for security can we at the United Nations hope to live up to the honour conferred today, and fulfill the vision of our founders. This is the broad mission of peace that United Nations staff members carry out every day in every part of the world [. . .]

22   The idea that there is one people in possession of the truth, one answer to the world's ills, or one solution to humanity's needs, has done untold harm throughout history—especially in the last century. Today, however, even amidst continuing ethnic conflict around the world, there is a growing understanding that human diversity is both the reality that makes dialogue necessary, and the very basis for that dialogue.

23   We understand, as never before, that each of us is fully worthy of the respect and dignity essential to our common humanity. We recognize that we are the products of many cultures, traditions and memories; that mutual respect allows us to study and learn from other cultures; and that we gain strength by combining the foreign with the familiar.

24   In every great faith and tradition one can find the values of tolerance and mutual understanding. The Qur'an, for example, tells us that "We created you from a single pair of male and female and made you into nations and tribes, that you may know each other." Confucius urged his followers: "when the good way prevails in the state, speak boldly and act boldly. When the state has lost the way, act boldly and speak softly." In the Jewish tradition, the injunction to "love thy neighbour as thyself," is considered to be the very essence of the Torah.

25   This thought is reflected in the Christian Gospel, which also teaches us to love our enemies and pray for those who wish to persecute us. Hindus are taught that "truth is one, the sages give it various names." And in the Buddhist tradition, individuals are urged to act with compassion in every facet of life.

Each of us has the right to take pride in our particular faith or her- 26
itage. But the notion that what is ours is necessarily in conflict with
what is theirs is both false and dangerous. It has resulted in endless en-
mity and conflict, leading men to commit the greatest of crimes in the
name of a higher power.

It need not be so. People of different religions and cultures live side 27
by side in almost every part of the world, and most of us have overlapping identities which unite us with very different groups. We *can* love
what we are, without hating what—and who—we are *not*. We can
thrive in our own tradition, even as we learn from others, and come to
respect their teachings.

This will not be possible, however, without freedom of religion, of 28
expression, of assembly, and basic equality under the law. Indeed, the
lesson of the past century has been that where the dignity of the individual has been trampled or threatened—where citizens have not enjoyed the basic right to choose their government, or the right to change
it regularly—conflict has too often followed, with innocent civilians
paying the price, in lives cut short and communities destroyed.

The obstacles to democracy have little to do with culture or reli- 29
gion, and much more to do with the desire of those in power to maintain their position at any cost. This is neither a new phenomenon nor
one confined to any particular part of the world. People of all cultures
value their freedom of choice, and feel the need to have a say in decisions affecting their lives.

The United Nations, whose membership comprises almost all the 30
States in the world, is founded on the principle of the equal worth of
every human being. It is the nearest thing we have to a representative
institution that can address the interests of all states, and all peoples.
Through this universal, indispensable instrument of human progress,
States can serve the interests of their citizens by recognizing common
interests and pursuing them in unity. No doubt, that is why the Nobel
Committee says that it "wishes, in its centenary year, to proclaim that
the only negotiable route to global peace and cooperation goes by way
of the United Nations".

I believe the Committee also recognized that this era of global chal- 31
lenges leaves no choice but cooperation at the global level. When States
undermine the rule of law and violate the rights of their individual citizens, they become a menace not only to their own people, but also to
their neighbours, and indeed the world. What we need today is better
governance—legitimate, democratic governance that allows each individual to flourish, and each State to thrive. [. . .]

You will recall that I began my address with a reference to the girl 32
born in Afghanistan today. Even though her mother will do all in her
power to protect and sustain her, there is a one-in-four risk that she will

not live to see her fifth birthday. Whether she does is just one test of our common humanity—of our belief in our individual responsibility for our fellow men and women. But it is the only test that matters.

33   Remember this girl and then our larger aims—to fight poverty, prevent conflict, or cure disease—will not seem distant, or impossible. Indeed, those aims will seem very near, and very achievable—as they should. Because beneath the surface of states and nations, ideas and language, lies the fate of individual human beings in need. Answering their needs will be the mission of the United Nations in the century to come.

34   Thank you very much.

RESPONDING TO READING

1. How does Annan use specific examples to illustrate his generalizations, and to connect his audience both with individuals and with all people?

2. What is the "Butterfly Effect"? How does it apply both to nature and to human politics?

3. How does Annan use history to make his argument? What specific events does he refer to, and how do these specifics support his views on the United Nations and any hope for peace?

4. Annan states that "there is a growing understanding that human diversity is both the reality that makes dialogue necessary, and the very basis for that dialogue." What are his explanations of each of these realities? Do you agree with his belief in the value of diversity? Why, or why not?

5. Annan argues that "The obstacles to democracy have little to do with culture or religion, and much more to do with the desire of those in power to maintain their position at any cost." In an essay, explain whether you agree or disagree with this statement. Is the maintenance of power the only obstacle to democracy? Is the maintenance of power always—or necessarily—an obstacle to the development of democracy?

Does God Have a Future?

KAREN ARMSTRONG

Karen Armstrong, an English historian of ideas, entered a Roman Catholic convent as a novitiate in 1965, at the age of 17. She spent seven years with this order before making an agonizing decision to leave it for a more secular life. After earning a B.A. in literature from St. Anne's College, Oxford University, she taught modern literature at the University of London and headed the English department at a private girls' school before becoming a freelance writer and broadcaster in 1982. There she focused on religious subjects, including a six-part documentary on the life and work of Saint Paul, and worked on Bill Moyers' PBS series on *Genesis: A Living Conversation*. She currently teaches at the Leo Baeck School for the Study of Judaism and the Training of Rabbis and Teachers and is also—because of her extensive writing on the Middle East—an honorary member of the Association of Muslim Social Sciences. Armstrong considers herself an unaffiliated monotheist who appreciates many aspects of Eastern Orthodoxy, but finds it easier to pray with Jews and Muslims than with Christians. In her view, modern monotheism has two main flaws. One is a tendency toward "belligerent righteousness," which results in pogroms, inquisitions, and other shameful manifestations of intolerance. The other, particularly apparent in Western Christianity, is the propensity for defining God in secular terms; treating the deity as "just another provable fact" marginalizes God and makes it easier for unbelievers to claim he doesn't exist. "Only Western Christianity makes a song and dance about creeds and beliefs," she explains. "The authentic test of a religion is not what you believe. It's what you do, and unless your religion expresses itself in compassion for all living things, it is not authentic."

Armstrong's ecumenical orientation informs her many books on religion: *Through the Narrow Gate* (an account of her life in the convent, 1981), *The Gospel According to Woman* (1987), *Holy War—The Crusades and Their Impact on Today's World* (1991), *Muhammed: A Biography of the Prophet* (1992), and the bestselling *A History of God: The 400-Year Quest of Judaism, Christianity, and Islam* (1993), in which "Does God Have a Future?" appears. "All religions change and develop," she writes. "If they do not, they will become obsolete." Consequently, "each generation has to create its own imaginative conception of God."

As we approach the end of the second millennium, it seems likely   1
that the world we know is passing away. For decades we have lived with the knowledge that we have created weapons that could wipe out human life on the planet. The Cold War may have ended, but the new world order seems no less frightening than the old. We are facing the possibility of ecological disaster. The AIDS virus threatens to bring a plague of unmanageable proportions. Within two or three generations, the population will become too great for the planet to support. Thousands are dying of famine and drought. Generations before our own have felt that the end of the world is nigh, yet it does seem that we are facing a future that is unimaginable. How will the idea of God survive in the years to come? For 4000 years it has constantly adapted to meet the demands of the present, but in our own century, more and more people have found that it no longer works for them, and when religious ideas cease to be effective they fade away. Maybe God really is an idea of the past. The American scholar Peter Berger notes that we often have a double standard when we compare the past with our own time. Where the past is analyzed and made relative, the present is rendered

immune to this process and our current position becomes an absolute: thus "the New Testament writers are seen as afflicted with a false consciousness rooted in *their* time, but the analyst takes the consciousness of *his* time as an unmixed intellectual blessing."[1] Secularists of the nineteenth and early twentieth centuries saw atheism as the irreversible condition of humanity in the scientific age.

2   There is much to support this view. In Europe, the churches are emptying; atheism is no longer the painfully acquired ideology of a few intellectual pioneers but a prevailing mood. In the past it was always produced by a particular idea of God, but now it seems to have lost its inbuilt relationship to theism and become an automatic response to the experience of living in a secularized society. Like the crowd of amused people surrounding Nietzsche's madman, many are unmoved by the prospect of life without God. Others find his absence a positive relief. Those of us who have had a difficult time with religion in the past find it liberating to be rid of the God who terrorized our childhood. It is wonderful not to have to cower before a vengeful deity, who threatens us with eternal damnation if we do not abide by his rules. We have a new intellectual freedom and can boldly follow up our own ideas without pussyfooting around difficult articles of faith, feeling all the while a sinking loss of integrity. We imagine that the hideous deity we have experienced is the authentic God of Jews, Christians and Muslims and do not always realize that it is merely an unfortunate aberration.

3   There is also desolation. Jean-Paul Sartre (1905–80) spoke of the God-shaped hole in the human consciousness, where God had always been. Nevertheless, he insisted that even if God existed, it was still necessary to reject him, since the idea of God negates our freedom. Traditional religion tells us that we must conform to God's idea of humanity to become fully human. Instead, we must see human beings as liberty incarnate. Sartre's atheism was not a consoling creed, but other existentialists saw the absence of God as a positive liberation. Maurice Merleau-Ponty (1908–61) argued that instead of increasing our sense of wonder, God actually negates it. Because God represents absolute perfection, there is nothing left for us to do or achieve. Albert Camus (1913–60) preached a heroic atheism. People should reject God defiantly in order to pour out all their loving solicitude upon mankind. As always, the atheists have a point. God had indeed been used in the past to stunt creativity; if he is made a blanket answer to every possible problem and contingency, he can indeed stifle our sense of wonder or achievement. A passionate and committed atheism can be more religious than a weary or inadequate theism. [. . .]

4   The fact that people who have no conventional religious beliefs should keep returning to central themes that we have discovered in

the history of God indicates that the idea is not as alien as many of us assume. Yet during the second half of the twentieth century, there has been a move away from the idea of a personal God who behaves like a larger version of us. There is nothing new about this. As we have seen, the Jewish scriptures, which Christians call their "Old" Testament, show a similar process; the Koran saw al-Lah in less personal terms than the Judeo-Christian tradition from the very beginning. Doctrines such as the Trinity and the mythology and symbolism of the mystical systems all strove to suggest that God was beyond personality. Yet this does not seem to have been made clear to many of the faithful. When John Robinson, Bishop of Woolwich, published *Honest to God* in 1963, stating that he could no longer subscribe to the old personal God "out there," there was uproar in Britain. A similar furor has greeted various remarks by David Jenkins, Bishop of Durham, even though these ideas are commonplace in academic circles. Don Cupitt, Dean of Emmanuel College, Cambridge, has also been dubbed "the atheist priest": he finds the traditional realistic God of theism unacceptable and proposes a form of Christian Buddhism, which puts religious experience before theology. Like Robinson, Cupitt has arrived intellectually at an insight that mystics in all three faiths have reached by a more intuitive route. Yet the idea that God does not really exist and that there is Nothing out there is far from new.

There is a growing intolerance of inadequate images of the Absolute. This is a healthy iconoclasm, since the idea of God has been used in the past to disastrous effect. One of the most characteristic new developments since the 1970s has been the rise of a type of religiosity that we usually call "fundamentalism" in most of the major world religions, including the three religions of God. A highly political spirituality, it is literal and intolerant in its vision. In the United States, which has always been prone to extremist and apocalyptic enthusiasm, Christian fundamentalism has attached itself to the New Right. Fundamentalists campaign for the abolition of legal abortion and for a hard line on moral and social decency. Jerry Falwell's Moral Majority achieved astonishing political power during the Reagan years. Other evangelists such as Maurice Cerullo, taking Jesus' remarks literally, believe that miracles are an essential hallmark of true faith. God will give the believer anything that he asks for in prayer. In Britain, fundamentalists such as Colin Urquhart have made the same claim. Christian fundamentalists seem to have little regard for the loving compassion of Christ. They are swift to condemn the people they see as the "enemies of God." Most would consider Jews and Muslims destined for hellfire, and Urquhart has argued that all oriental religions are inspired by the devil.

6   There have been similar developments in the Muslim world, which have been much publicized in the West. Muslim fundamentalists have toppled governments and either assassinated or threatened the enemies of Islam with the death penalty. Similarly, Jewish fundamentalists have settled in the Occupied Territories of the West Bank and the Gaza Strip with the avowed intention of driving out the Arab inhabitants, using force if necessary. Thus they believe that they are paving a way for the advent of the Messiah, which is at hand. In all its forms, fundamentalism is a fiercely reductive faith. Thus Rabbi Meir Kahane, the most extreme member of Israel's Far Right until his assassination in New York in 1990:

> There are not several messages in Judaism. There is only one. And this message is to do what God wants. Sometimes God wants us to go to war, sometimes he wants us to live in peace. . . . But there is only one message: God wanted us to come to this country to create a Jewish state.[2]

This wipes out centuries of Jewish development, returning to the Deuteronomist perspective of the Book of Joshua. It is not surprising that people who hear this kind of profanity, which makes "God" deny other people's human rights, think that the sooner we relinquish him the better.

7   Yet [. . .], this type of religiosity is actually a retreat from God. To make such human, historical phenomena as Christian "Family Values," "Islam" or "the Holy Land" the focus of religious devotion is a new form of idolatry. This type of belligerent righteousness has been a constant temptation to monotheists throughout the long history of God. It must be rejected as inauthentic. The God of Jews, Christians and Muslims got off to an unfortunate start, since the tribal deity Yahweh was murderously partial to his own people. Latter-day crusaders who return to this primitive ethos are elevating the values of the tribe to an unacceptably high status and substituting man-made ideals for the transcendent reality which should challenge our prejudices. They are also denying a crucial monotheistic theme. Ever since the prophets of Israel reformed the old pagan cult of Yahweh, the God of monotheists has promoted the ideal of compassion.

8   [. . .] Compassion was a characteristic of most of the ideologies that were created during the Axial Age. The compassionate ideal even impelled Buddhists to make a major change in their religious orientation when they introduced devotion (*bhakti*) to the Buddha and *bodhisattvas*. The prophets insisted that cult and worship were useless unless society as a whole adopted a more just and compassionate ethos. These insights were developed by Jesus, Paul and the Rabbis, who all shared the same Jewish ideals and suggested major changes in Judaism in

order to implement them. The Koran made the creation of a compassionate and just society the essence of the reformed religion of al-Lah. Compassion is a particularly difficult virtue. It demands that we go beyond the limitations of our egotism, insecurity and inherited prejudice. Not surprisingly, there have been times when all three of the God-religions have failed to achieve these high standards. During the eighteenth century, deists rejected traditional Western Christianity largely because it had become so conspicuously cruel and intolerant. The same will hold good today. All too often, conventional believers, who are not fundamentalists, share their aggressive righteousness. They use "God" to prop up their own loves and hates, which they attribute to God himself. But Jews, Christians and Muslims who punctiliously attend divine services yet denigrate people who belong to different ethnic and ideological camps deny one of the basic truths of their religion. It is equally inappropriate for people who call themselves Jews, Christians and Muslims to condone an inequitable social system. The God of historical monotheism demands mercy not sacrifice, compassion rather than decorous liturgy.

There has often been a distinction between people who practice a 9 cultic form of religion and those who have cultivated a sense of the God of compassion. The prophets fulminated against their contemporaries who thought that temple worship was sufficient. Jesus and St. Paul both made it clear that external observance was useless if it was not accompanied by charity: it was little better than sounding brass or a tinkling cymbal. Muhammad came into conflict with those Arabs who wanted to worship the pagan goddesses alongside al-Lah in the ancient rites, without implementing the compassionate ethos that God demanded as a condition of all true religion. There had been a similar divide in the pagan world of Rome: the old cultic religion celebrated the status quo, while the philosophers preached a message that they believed would change the world. It may be that the compassionate religion of the One God has only been observed by a minority; most have found it difficult to face the extremity of the God-experience with its uncompromising ethical demands. Ever since Moses brought the tablets of the Law from Mount Sinai, the majority have preferred the worship of a Golden Calf, a traditional, unthreatening image of a deity they have constructed for themselves, with its consoling, time-honored rituals. Aaron, the high priest, presided over the manufacture of the golden effigy. The religious establishment itself is often deaf to the inspiration of prophets and mystics who bring news of a much more demanding God.

God can also be used as an unworthy panacea, as an alternative to 10 mundane life and as the object of indulgent fantasy. The idea of God has frequently been used as the opium of the people. This is a particular danger when he is conceived as an-other Being—just like us, only bigger and better—in his own heaven, which is itself conceived as a paradise of earthly delights. Yet originally, "God" was used to help people to concentrate on this world and to face up to unpleasant reality. Even the pagan cult of Yahweh, for all its manifest faults, stressed his involvement in current events in profane time, as opposed to the sacred time of rite and myth. The prophets of Israel forced their people to confront their own social culpability and impending political catastrophe in the name of the God who revealed himself in these historical occurrences. The Christian doctrine of Incarnation stressed the divine immanence in the world of flesh and blood. Concern for the here and now was especially marked in Islam: nobody could have been more of a realist than Muhammad, who was a political as well as a spiritual genius. As we have seen, later generations of Muslims have shared his concern to incarnate the divine will in human history by establishing a just and decent society. From the very beginning, God was experienced as an imperative to action. From the moment when—as either El or Yahweh—God called Abraham away from his family in Haran, the cult entailed concrete action in this world and often a painful abandonment of the old sanctities.

11   This dislocation also involved great strain. The Holy God, who was wholly other, was experienced as a profound shock by the prophets. He demanded a similar holiness and separation on the part of his people. When he spoke to Moses on Sinai, the Israelites were not allowed to approach the foot of the mountain. An entirely new gulf suddenly yawned between humanity and the divine, rupturing the holistic vision of paganism. There was, therefore, a potential for alienation from the world, which reflected a dawning consciousness of the inalienable autonomy of the individual. It is no accident that monotheism finally took root during the exile to Babylon, when the Israelites also developed the ideal of personal responsibility, which has been crucial in both Judaism and Islam.[3] [. . .] The Rabbis used the idea of an immanent God to help Jews to cultivate a sense of the sacred rights of the human personality. Yet alienation has continued to be a danger in all three faiths: in the West the experience of God was continually accompanied by guilt and by a pessimistic anthropology. In Judaism and Islam there is no doubt that the observance of Torah and Shariah has sometimes been seen as a heteronymous compliance with an external law, even though we have seen that nothing could have been further from the intention of the men who compiled these legal codes.

12   Those atheists who preached emancipation from a God who demands such servile obedience were protesting against an inadequate but unfortunately familiar image of God. Again, this was based on a conception of the divine that was too personalistic. It interpreted the scriptural image of God's judgment too literally and assumed that God was a sort of Big Brother in the sky. This image of the divine Tyrant im-

posing an alien law on his unwilling human servants has to go. Terrorizing the populace into civic obedience with threats is no longer acceptable or even practicable, as the downfall of communist regimes demonstrated so dramatically in the autumn of 1989. The anthropomorphic idea of God as Law-giver and Ruler is not adequate to the temper of post-modernity. Yet the atheists who complained that the idea of God was unnatural were not entirely correct. [. . .] Jews, Christians and Muslims have developed remarkably similar ideas of God, which also resemble other conceptions of the Absolute. When people try to find an ultimate meaning and value in human life, their minds seem to go in a certain direction. They have not been coerced to do this; it is something that seems natural to humanity.

Yet if feelings are not to degenerate into indulgent, aggressive or 13 unhealthy emotionalism, they need to be informed by the critical intelligence. The experience of God must keep abreast of other current enthusiams, including those of the mind. The experiment of Falsafah was an attempt to relate faith in God with the new cult of rationalism among Muslims, Jews and, later, Western Christians. Eventually Muslims and Jews retreated from philosophy. Rationalism, they decided, had its uses, especially in such empirical studies as science, medicine and mathematics, but it was not entirely appropriate in the discussion of a God who lay beyond concepts. The Greeks had already sensed this and developed an early distrust of their native metaphysics. One of the drawbacks of the philosophic method of discussing God was that it could make it sound as though the Supreme Deity were simply another Being, the highest of all the things that exist, instead of a reality of an entirely different order. Yet the venture of Falsafah was important, since it showed an appreciation of the necessity of relating God to other experiences—if only to define the extent to which this was possible. To push God into intellectual isolation in a holy ghetto of his own is unhealthy and unnatural. It can encourage people to think that it is not necessary to apply normal standards of decency and rationality to behavior supposedly inspired by "God."

From the first, Falsafah had been associated with science. It was 14 their initial enthusiasm for medicine, astronomy and mathematics which had led the first Muslim Faylasufs to discuss al-Lah in metaphysical terms. Science had effected a major change in their outlook, and they found that they could not think of God in the same way as their fellow Muslims. The philosophic conception of God was markedly different from the Koranic vision, but Faylasufs did recover some insights that were in danger of being lost in the *ummah* at that time. Thus the Koran had an extremely positive attitude to other religious traditions: Muhammad had not believed that he was founding a new, exclusive religion and considered that all rightly guided faith came from the One God. By the ninth century, however, the *ulema* were beginning to lose sight of this and were promoting the cult of Islam as the one true religion. The Faylasufs reverted to the older universalist approach, even though they reached it by a different route. We have a similar opportunity today. In our scientific age, we cannot think about God in the same way as our forebears, but the challenge of science could help us to appreciate some old truths.

15   [. . .] Albert Einstein had an appreciation of mystical religion. Despite his famous remarks about God not playing dice, he did not believe that his theory of relativity should affect the conception of God. During a visit to England in 1921, Einstein was asked by the Archbishop of Canterbury what were its implications for theology. He replied: "None. Relativity is a purely scientific matter and has nothing to do with religion."[4] When Christians are dismayed by such scientists as Stephen Hawking, who can find no room for God in his cosmology, they are perhaps still thinking of God in anthropomorphic terms as a Being who created the world in the same way as we would. Yet creation was not originally conceived in such a literal manner. Interest in Yahweh as Creator did not enter Judaism until the exile to Babylon. It was a conception that was alien to the Greek world: creation *ex nihilo* was not an official doctrine of Christianity until the Council of Nicaea in 341. Creation is a central teaching of the Koran, but, like all its utterances about God, this is said to be a "parable" or a "sign" (*aya*) of an ineffable truth. Jewish and Muslim rationalists found it a difficult and problematic doctrine, and many rejected it. Sufis and Kabbalists all preferred the Greek metaphor of emanation. In any case, cosmology was not a scientific description of the origins of the world but was originally a symbolic expression of a spiritual and psychological truth. There is consequently little agitation about the new science in the Muslim world: [. . .] the events of recent history have been more of a threat than has science to the traditional conception of God. In the West, however, a more literal understanding of scripture has long prevailed. When some Western Christians feel their faith in God undermined by the new science, they are probably imagining God as Newton's great Mechanick, a personalistic notion of God which should, perhaps, be rejected on religious as well as on scientific grounds. The challenge of science might shock the churches into a fresh appreciation of the symbolic nature of scriptural narrative.

16   The idea of a personal God seems increasingly unacceptable at the present time for all kinds of reasons: moral, intellectual, scientific and spiritual. Feminists are also repelled by a personal deity who, because of "his" gender, has been male since his tribal, pagan days. Yet to talk about "she"—other than in a dialectical way—can be just as limiting, since it confines the illimitable God to a purely human category. The old metaphysical notion of God as the Supreme Being, which has long

been popular in the West, is also felt to be unsatisfactory. The God of the philosophers is the product of a now outdated rationalism, so the traditional "proofs" of his existence no longer work. The widespread acceptance of the God of the philosophers by the deists of the Enlightenment can be seen as the first step to the current atheism. Like the old Sky God, this deity is so remote from humanity and the mundane world that he easily becomes *Deus Otiosus* and fades from our consciousness.

The God of the mystics might seem to present a possible alterna-   17 tive. The mystics have long insisted that God is not an-Other Being; they have claimed that he does not really exist and that it is better to call him Nothing. This God is in tune with the atheistic mood of our secular society, with its distrust of inadequate images of the Absolute. Instead of seeing God as an objective fact, which can be demonstrated by means of scientific proof, mystics have claimed that he is a subjective experience, mysteriously experienced in the ground of being. This God is to be approached through the imagination and can be seen as a kind of art form, akin to the other great artistic symbols that have expressed the ineffable mystery, beauty and value of life. Mystics have used music, dancing, poetry, fiction, stories, painting, sculpture and architecture to express this Reality that goes beyond concepts. Like all art, however, mysticism requires intelligence, discipline and self-criticism as a safeguard against indulgent emotionalism and projection. The God of the mystics could even satisfy the feminists, since both Sufis and Kabbalists have long tried to introduce a female element into the divine.

There are drawbacks, however. Mysticism has been regarded with   18 some suspicion by many Jews and Muslims since the Shabbetai Zevi fiasco and the decline of latter-day Sufism. In the West, mysticism has never been a mainstream religious enthusiasm. The Protestant and Catholic Reformers either outlawed or marginalized it, and the scientific Age of Reason did not encourage this mode of perception. Since the 1960s, there has been a fresh interest in mysticism, expressed in the enthusiasm for Yoga, meditation and Buddhism, but it is not an approach that easily consorts with our objective, empirical mentality. The God of the mystics is not easy to apprehend. It requires long training with an expert and a considerable investment of time. The mystic has to work hard to acquire this sense of the reality known as God (which many have refused to name). Mystics often insist that human beings must deliberately create this sense of God for themselves, with the same degree of care and attention that others devote to artistic creation. It is not something that is likely to appeal to people in a society which has become used to speedy gratification, fast food and instant communication. The God of the mystics does not arrive readymade and prepackaged.

He cannot be experienced as quickly as the instant ecstasy created by a revivalist preacher, who quickly has a whole congregation clapping its hands and speaking in tongues.

19   It is possible to acquire some of the mystical attitudes. Even if we are incapable of the higher states of consciousness achieved by a mystic, we can learn that God does not exist in any simplistic sense, for example, or that the very word "God" is only a symbol of a reality that ineffably transcends it. The mystical agnosticism could help us to acquire a restraint that stops us rushing into these complex matters with dogmatic assurance. But if these notions are not felt upon the pulse and personally appropriated, they are likely to seem meaningless abstractions. Secondhand mysticism could prove to be as unsatisfactory as reading the explanation of a poem by a literary critic instead of the original. [. . .] Mysticism was often seen as an esoteric discipline, not because the mystics wanted to exclude the vulgar herd but because these truths could only be perceived by the intuitive part of the mind after special training. They mean something different when they are approached by this particular route, which is not accessible to the logical, rationalist faculty.

20   Ever since the prophets of Israel started to ascribe their own feelings and experiences to God, monotheists have in some sense created a God for themselves. God has rarely been seen as a self-evident fact that can be encountered like any other objective existent. Today many people seem to have lost the will to make this imaginative effort. This need not be a catastrophe. When religious ideas have lost their validity, they have usually faded away painlessly: if the human idea of God no longer works for us in the empirical age, it will be discarded. Yet in the past people have always created new symbols to act as a focus for spirituality. Human beings have always created a faith for themselves, to cultivate their sense of the wonder and ineffable significance of life. The aimlessness, alienation, anomie and violence that characterize so much of modern life seem to indicate that now that they are not deliberately creating a faith in "God" or anything else—it matters little what—many people are falling into despair.

21   In the United States, [. . .] ninety-nine percent of the population claim to believe in God, yet the prevalence of fundamentalism, apocalypticism and "instant" charismatic forms of religiosity in America is not reassuring. The escalating crime rate, drug addiction and the revival of the death penalty are not signs of a spiritually healthy society. In Europe there is a growing blankness where God once existed in the human consciousness. One of the first people to express this dry desolation—quite different from the heroic atheism of Nietzsche—was Thomas Hardy. In "The Darkling Thrush," written on December 30,

1900, at the turn of the twentieth century, he expressed the death of spirit that was no longer able to create a faith in life's meaning:

> I leant upon a coppice gate
>   When Frost was spectre-grey
> And Winter's dregs made desolate
>   The weakening eye of day.
> The tangled bine-stems scored the sky
>   Like strings of broken lyres,
> And all mankind that haunted nigh
>   Had sought their household fires.
>
> The land's sharp features seemed to be
>   The Century's corpse outleant,
> His crypt the cloudy canopy,
>   The wind his death-lament.
> The ancient pulse of germ and birth
>   Was shrunken hard and dry,
> And every spirit upon earth
>   Seemed fervourless as I.
>
> At once a voice arose among
>   The bleak twigs overhead
> In a full-hearted evensong
>   Of joy illimited;
> An aged thrush, frail, gaunt, and small,
>   In blast-beruffled plume,
> Had chosen thus to fling his soul
>   Upon the growing gloom.
>
> So little cause for carolings
>   Of such ecstatic sound
> Was written on terrestrial things
>   Afar or nigh around,
> That I could think there trembled through
>   His happy good-night air
> Some blessed Hope, whereof he knew
>   And I was unaware.

Human beings cannot endure emptiness and desolation; they will fill the vacuum by creating a new focus of meaning. The idols of fundamentalism are not good substitutes for God; if we are to create a vibrant new faith for the twenty-first century, we should, perhaps, ponder the history of God for some lessons and warnings.

Notes

1. Peter Berger, *A Rumour of Angels* (London, 1970), p. 58.
2. Quoted in Raphael Mergui and Philippa Simmonot, *Israel's Ayatollahs; Meir Kahane and the Far Right in Israel* (London, 1987), p. 43.
3. Personal responsibility is also important in Christianity, of course, but Judaism and Islam have stressed it by their lack of a mediating priesthood, a perspective that was recovered by the Protestant Reformers.
4. Philipp Frank, *Einstein: His Life and Times* (New York, 1947), pp. 189–90.

RESPONDING TO READING

1. As she ponders the future of God, how does Armstrong talk about His past? What connections does she make between the two, between the past and the future?

2. Armstrong cites many experts as she develops her ideas in this essay. Pick three of the sources that she cites and summarize the view of each. How does each expert's opinion fit into Armstrong's argument?

3. How does Armstrong describe a view of God that is different from "the personal God of traditional Western theism"? How does such a description/definition of God challenge traditional Western views?

4. On what major religions does Armstrong focus her analysis? How would you summarize the differences and similarities she describes in each religion's conception of God? Does God have a future? If you say yes, what is it to be? If you say no, what will replace Him?

5. In an essay, consider your responses to Armstrong's arguments about God's past and future. What were your feelings about her argument? What, in your own background or religious training, led you to react as you did? How did your own views of religion affect your reading of Armstrong's text?

QUESTIONS FOR REFLECTION AND WRITING

How Can We Think about Technology and Gender Roles in the Future?

1. What attitudes do both Fadiman in "Mail" and de Palma in "http" share about the advances in technology they describe? We might expect Fadiman, a literary type, whose father was a popular literary figure, to be less than enthusiastic about e-mail, but it does seem odd that a professional computer scientist should be skeptical about the blessings of technology. How convincing do you find their arguments? Will the future of technology render their arguments irrelevant?

2. De Palma's discomfort with the way technology is being used in the schools echoes several other essays about schooling in this book, most particularly those by Rose in Chapter 1, Calandra in Chapter 3, Tannen in Chapter 4, and Fitgerald and Simon in Chapter 5. Are the schools just an easy target, or do these writers see something consistently wrong with our schools? If so, what is it? Do their descriptions of what happens in school ring true for you in terms of your own experience? In particular, does de Palma describe the way technology was used in the schools you attended? What might our schools do to prepare the next generation to use technology more effectively? Or is attention to technology a waste of precious school time and resources?

3. Just as Fadiman and de Palma raise questions about the claimed benefits of technology, Weiss questions whether despite all the talk about changed roles in marriage, the roles of husbands and wives have actually changed much. Consider his conclusions, the date of his study, and the value of his evidence, and then write an essay about the future of marriage—the institution itself and whether you see yourself inside or outside of it.

4. Consider Pogrebin's "Why Feminism Is Good for the Jews" in the context of other essays in this book on the role of women: Select from those by Kingston, Angier, and Anzaldúa in Chapter 1; Tannen in Chapter 2; Ehrenreich, Fallows, and Walker in Chapter 3; Stanton, Truth, Williams, and Tannen in Chapter 4; Murray in Chapter 5. Are Pogrebin's arguments restricted to Jews or can they apply as well, or as badly, to other groups or to the society as a whole? In your experience, have women's roles changed as much as these essays suggest, or (as Weiss proposes) is this change just skin deep? Does the future promise genuine equality, or are gender differences so profound that changes will be more talked about than actually enacted?

Will War and Terrorism Shape Our Future?

1. Examine the arguments summarized by Mead, that humans are so aggressive by nature that war is inevitable. Mead goes on to refute these arguments, but others do not. Bring to bear upon the discussion whatever evidence you can find from your reading and experience, including the essay by Milosz and, perhaps, Gulliver's explanation of war to the pacifist horses who rule the fourth book of Jonathan Swift's *Gulliver's Travels*. Then write an essay addressed to others in this class defending your conclusions about the inevitability of war. Finally, abstract and alter your argument so that it would be suitable for a short "think piece" or "opinion article" in your local newspaper.

2. Do you expect to see a war in your future? Do you expect to experience additional terrorism in the United States? If not, on what sorts of evidence do you base your hopes? If so, what will it be like and who will participate? Be sure to refer to several of the essays in this section as you develop your scenario for the future.

3. Is the statement "Disarmament" by Pope John XXIII an abstract and unlikely hope, or is it possible to implement? What would Mead say about that statement? Milosz? Juergensmeyer? Berry? Write an essay in which you examine the role of religious leaders in the quest for world peace.

Will a New Utopia Be Possible in the 21st Century?

1. Write an essay on human and nonhuman cloning in the future, starting with either the Anderson or the Turner essay (or both). If you choose to take a position on the subject, what arguments, evidence, and tone will be appropriate for an audience made up of this writing class? If you choose to speculate about the possibilities, without taking a position, what discourse community will you address? Twenty years from now, will your subject, argument, and evidence be different from what it is today? How and why, or why not?

2. Read, or reread, Mary Shelley's *Frankenstein*, one of the first works of fiction to anticipate artificial human creation of life. How is Dr. Frankenstein's creative method like and unlike cloning? What moral questions does Frankenstein have to confront as a result of his creative success? Do the same questions arise with cloning?

3. Write an essay or story about your own version of a perfect society, a "utopia" (the word comes from two Greek terms meaning "nowhere"). You may wish to read some of the long line of published utopias beginning with Thomas More's sixteenth century version or even the equally long line of "dystopias," stories of utopias gone bad, such as George Orwell's *1984*. What would a perfect society look like, feel like, be like?

Predictions: What Will the Future Be Like?

1. Create a dialogue—an imaginative fiction—about the past that you will have with your grandchildren someday. They will be asking about how you have come to know so much and what caused you to do what you have done. You will probably exaggerate the degree of planning and logic that went into your life, but will want them to understand what happened. Since this scene is set in the distant future, imagine what your life will be (has been) like and what the family you establish will be like. Was the world experiencing "good old days" when you were in college, or did things get better during your lifetime?

2. Write an essay about the future of this year's college graduates. Twenty years from now, what will be some of their major concerns? Their values? What are they likely to be doing, saying, thinking? Will they be working or replaced by computers? How will they communicate? What will their future be like?

3. Write an essay about the graduating class of twenty years from now. Be sure to refer to predictions of the future contained in some of the essays in this chapter. What will those graduates have studied and what will be some of their major concerns? Their values? What will their future be like?

Acknowledgments

FRENCH W. ANDERSON *Genetics and Human Malleability* by W. French Anderson. Hastings Center Report, Jan/Feb 1990, 3 pgs. Reprinted by permission.

NATALIE ANGIER "Estrogen, Desire and Puberty" from *Woman* by Natalie Angier, pp. 193–206. © 1999 by Natalie Angier. Reprinted by permission of Houghton Mifflin Company. All rights reserved.

GLORIA ANZALDÚA "Beyond Traditional Notions of Identity" Copyright © 2002. From *This Bridge We Call Home: Radical Visions for Transformation* by Gloria Anzaldúa, editor; Louise Keating, editor. Reproduced by permission of Routledge, Inc., part of The Taylor & Francis Group.

KAREN ARMSTRONG "Does God Have a Future?" From *A History of God* © 1993 by Karen Armstrong. Used by permission of Alfred A. Knopf, a division of Random House, Inc.

ISAAC ASIMOV *Those Crazy Ideas* by Dr. Isaac Asimov. © Dr. Isaac Asimov. Reprinted by permission.

WENDELL BERRY "Thoughts in the Presence of Fear" originally published in Orion Online's *Thoughts on America* series and subsequently in book form in *In the Presence of Fear: Three Essays for a Changed World* by Wendell Berry, December 2001, The Orion Society.

JACOB BRONOWSKI "The Reach of the Imagination" by Jacob Bronowski, delivered as "The Blashfield Address," May 1996. From *The Proceedings of the American Academy of Arts and Letters and the National Institute of Arts and Letters*, Second Series #17, 1967. Reprinted by permission of the American Academy of Arts and Letters, New York City.

ALEXANDER CALANDRA *Angels on the Head of a Pin* by Alexander Calandra. © Alexander Calandra. Reprinted by permission.

ITALO CALVINO "All at One Point" from *Cosmicomics* by Italo Calvino. Copyright © 1965 by Giulio Einaudi Editore, S.p.A. Torino. English translation by William Weaver copyright © 1968 and renewed 1996 by Harcourt, Inc. and Jonathon Cape Ltd. Reprinted by permission of Harcourt Inc. and The Wylie Agency.

RACHEL CARSON "The Obligation to Endure" from *Silent Spring* by Rachel Carson. Copyright © 1962 by Rachael l. Carson. Copyright renewed 1990 by Roger Christie. Reprinted by permission of Houghton Mifflin Company. All rights reserved.

FRANK CONROY "Think About It" by Frank Conroy. Copyright © 1988 by *Harper's Magazine*. All rights reserved. Reprinted from the November issue by special permission.

PAUL DE PALMA http//www.when_is_enough_enough?.com "When Is Enough Enough.com" by Paul de Palma. Reprinted from *The American Scholar*, Volume 68, No. 1, Winter 1999. Copyright © Paul de Palma. Reprinted by permission.

JOAN DIDION "On Self Respect" from *Slouching Towards Bethlehem* by Joan Didion. Copyright © 1966, 1968, renewed 1996 by Joan Didion. Reprinted by permission of Farrar, Strauss and Giroux, LLC.

BARBARA EHRENREICH "Serving in Florida" Excerpt from *Nickel and Dimed: On (Not) Getting By In America* by Barbara Ehrenreich. © 2001 by Barbara Ehrenreich. Reprinted by permission of Henry Holt & Company, LLC.

ANNE FADIMAN "Under Water" by Anne Fadiman. Originally appeared in *The New Yorker*, August 23, 1999, pp. 152–153. Copyright © 1999 by Anne Fadiman. Reprinted by permission of Lescher & Lescher, Ltd. All rights reserved.

ANNE FADIMAN "Mail" by Anne Fadiman. Originally appeared in *The American Scholar*, Vol. 69, No. 1, Winter 2000. Copyright © Annie Fadiman. Reprinted by permission of Lescher & Lescher, Ltd. All rights reserved.

DEBORAH FALLOWS "Why Mothers Should Stay Home" by Deborah Fallows. Reprinted with permission from *The Washington Monthly*. Copyright by Washington Monthly Publishing, LLC, 733–15th Street NW, Suite 1000, Washington, DC 20005. (202) 393–5155. Web site: www.washingtonmonthly.com.

FRANCES FITZGERALD "America Revised" from *America Revised: History Schoolbooks in the 20th Century* by Frances Fitzgerald. Published by Little, Brown and Company. Copyright © 1979, 1980 by Frances Fitzgerald. Reprinted by permission of Lescher & Lescher Ltd. All rights reserved.

URSULA FRANKLIN *Silence and the Notion of the Commons* by Ursula Franklin. Musicworks, Summer 1994, p. 59. © Ursula Franklin. Reprinted by permission.

HOWARD GARDNER "Good Work, Well Done: A Psychological Study" by Howard Gardner from *The Chronicle of Higher Education*, February 22, 2002, B7-9. Reprinted by permission of the author.

ATUL GAWANDE "When Doctors Make Mistakes" Excerpt from *When Doctors Make Mistakes* from *Complications: A Surgeon's Notes on an Imperfect Science* by Atul Gawande. © 2002 by Atul Gawande. Reprinted by permission of Henry Holt & Company, LLC.

JANE GOODALL "First Observations" from *In the Shadow of Man* by Jane Goodall. San Diego, San Diego State University Press, 1988. Reprinted by permission.

STEPHEN JAY GOULD "Evolution as Fact and Theory" from *Hen's Teeth and Horse's Toes: Further Reflections in Natural History*, by Stephen Jay Gould, pp. 253–262. Copyright © 1983 by Stephen Jay Gould. Reprinted by permission of W.W. Norton & Company.

STEPHEN HAWKING "Our Picture of the Universe" from *A Brief History of Time* by Stephen W. Hawking. Copyright © 1988, 1996 by Stephen W. Hawking. Used by permission of Bantam Books, a division of Random House, Inc.

LINDA HOGAN *Hearing Voices* by Linda Hogan. © Linda Hogan. Used by permission.

MARK JUERGENSMEYER "Theater of Terror or Expand America as Enemy" from *Terror in the Mind of God: The Global Rise of Religious Violence* by Mark Juergensmeyer. © 1999 by The Regents of the University of California.

MARTIN LUTHER JR. KING *Letter from Birmingham Jail* Copyright © 1963 Dr. Martin Luther King, Jr., copyright renewed 1991 Coretta Scott King. Reprinted by arrangement with the Estate of Martin Luther King, Jr., c/o Writers House as agent for the proprietor, New York, NY.

MAXINE HONG KINGSTON "On Discovery" Excerpt from *China Men* by Maxine Hong Kingston. Copyright © 1977, 1978, 1979, 1980 by Maxine Hong Kingston. Reprinted by permission of Alfred A. Knopf, Inc., a division of Random House, Inc.

PERRI KLASS "Learning the Language" from *A Not Entirely Benign Procedure* by Perri Klass. Copyright © 1987 by Perri Klass. Used by permission of G.P. Putnam's Sons, a division of Penguin Putnam Inc.

THOMAS KUHN *The Route to Normal Science* by Thomas Kuhn. Reprinted by permission of The University of Chicago Press.

SUSANNE LANGER *Sign and Symbols* by Susanne Langer. © Susanne Langer. Reprinted by permission.

URSULA LE GUIN "Where Do You Get Your Ideas From?" Copyright © 1987 by Ursula Le Guin; first appeared in *Dancing at the Edge of the World*. Permission granted by the author and the author's agents, Virginia Kidd Agency, Inc.

ERIC LIU "Notes of a Native Speaker" from *The Accidental Asian: Notes of a Native Speaker* by Eric Liu. Copyright © 1998 by Eric Liu. Used by permission of Crown Publishers, a division of Random House, Inc.

BARRY LOPEZ "Searching for Ancestors" from *Crossing Open Ground* by Barry Lopez. First appeared in *Outside Magazine*. Copyright © 1983, 1988 by Barry Lopez. Reprinted by permission.

NANCY MAIRS "On Being a Cripple" from *Plaintext* by Nancy Mairs. © 1986 The Arizona Board of Regents. Reprinted by permission of the University of Arizona Press.

JOHN MCPHEE "Los Angeles Against the Mountains." Excerpt from *Los Angeles Against the Mountains* from *The Control of Nature* by John McPhee. Copyright © 1989 by John McPhee. Reprinted by permission of Farrar, Strauss & Giroux, Inc. and Macfarlane Walter & Ross.

MARGARET MEAD *Warfare is Only an Invention—Not a Biological Necessity*. Courtesy of the Institution for Intercultural Studies, Inc. New York.

PAULI MURRAY "The Inheritance of Values" from *Proud Shoes* by Pauli Murray. Copyright © 1956, 1978 by the Estate of Pauli Murray. Reprinted by permission of the Charlotte Sheedy Literary Agency.

CYNTHIA OZICK *A Drugstore Eden* by Cynthia Ozick. © 1996 Cynthia Ozick. Reprinted by permission.

LETTY COTTIN POGREBIN "Why Feminism of Good for the Jews" from *Deborah, Golda and Me* by Letty Cottin Pogrebin. © 1991 by Letty Cottin Pogrebin. Used by permission of Crown Publishers, a division of Random House, Inc.

MICHAEL POLLAN "Overriding Darwin: Genetically Engineered Potatoes" 27 para. excerpt from Chapter 5 [on potatoes] 10 pp. From *The Botany of Desire* by Michael Pollan. Copyright © 2001 by Michael Pollan. Used by permission of Random House, Inc.

SANDRA POSTEL "Troubled Waters" from *Dividing the Waters: Food, Security, Ecosystem, Health & the New Politics* (Worldwatch Paper, 132). Worldwatch Institute, June 1996. Reprinted by permission.

SOCIETY OF PROFESSIONAL JOURNALISTS *Society of Professional Journalists Code of Ethics*, 2 pp. Reprinted with permission of the Society of Professional Journalists, 3909 N. Meridian St., Indianapolis, IN 46208.

RICHARD RODRIGUEZ   "Aria" from *Hunger of Memory* by Richard Rodriguez. Copyright © 1982 by Richard Rodriguez. Reprinted by permission of David R. Godine, publisher.

MIKE ROSE   "I Just Wanna Be Average" Reprinted with the permission of The Free Press, a imprint of Simon & Schuster Adult Publishing Group, from *Lives on The Boundary: The Struggles and Achievements of America's Underprepared* by Mike Rose. Copyright © 1989 by Mike Rose.

SCOTT RUSSELL SANDERS   "The Inheritance of Tools" by Scott Russell Sanders. Copyright © 1984 by Scott Russell Sanders. First appeared in *Milkweed Chronicle*. Reprinted by permission of the author and Virginia Kidd, Literary Agent.

SCOTT RUSSELL SANDERS   "Under the Influence: Paying the Price of My Father's Booze" from *Secrets of the Universe* by Scott Russell Sanders. Copyright © by Scott Russell Sanders. Reprinted by permission of the author.

LESLIE MARMON SILKO   *Landscape, History and the Pueblo Imagination* by Leslie Marmon Silko. Reprinted by permission of The Wylie Agency, Inc.

LINDA SIMON   *The Naked Source* by Linda Simon. © Linda Simon. Reprinted by permission.

PETER SINGER   "The Singer Solution to World Poverty" by Peter Singer. *New York Times Magazine*, September 5, 1999, pp. 60–63. © 1999 The New York Times. Reprinted by permission.

WOLE SOYINKA   "Every Dictator's Nightmare" by Wole Soyinka. First appeared in *The New York Times Magazine* April 19th, 2000. Reprinted by permission of Melanie Jackson Agency, L.L.C.

SHELBY STEELE   "The Age of White Guilt and the Disappearance of the Black Individual" by Shelby Steele. *Harper's Magazine*, November 2002, pp. 31–39 (49 paragraphs). Copyright © 2002 by *Harper's Magazine*. Reprinted from the November 2002 issue by special permission.

AMY TAN   "Mother Tongue" by Amy Tan. © Amy Tan. First appeared in *The Three Penny Review*. Reprinted by permission of the Sandra Dijkstra Literary Agency.

DEBORAH TANNEN   "Conversational Styles" "Teacher's Classroom Strategies Should Recognize That Men and Women Use Language Differently" by Deborah Tannen, *The Chronicle of Higher Education*, June 19, 1991. Copyright © 1991 Deborah Tannen. Reprinted by permission of the author.

DEBORAH TANNEN   "The Roots of Debate in Education and the Hope of Dialogue" From *The Argument Culture* by Deborah Tannen. Copyright © 1997 by Deborah Tannen. Used by permission of Random House, Inc.

LEIGH TURNER   "The Media and Ethics of Cloning" by Leigh Turner. *Chronicle of Higher Education*, September 27, 1997, 4 pgs. Reprinted by permission of the author.

LEWIS H. JR. VAN DUSEN   *Civil Disobedience: Destroyer of Democracy* by Lewis H. Van Dusen, Jr.. 26 A.B.A.J. 1969. Used by permission of the Journal of the American Bar Association.

ALICE WALKER   *In Search of Our Mothers' Garden: Womanist Prose* by Alice Walker. © 1974 by Alice Walker. Reprinted by permission of Harcourt, Inc.

JEFFREY WATTLES   "The Golden Rule—One or Many, Gold or Glitter?" From *The Golden Rule* by Jeffrey Wattles. Copyright © 1996 by Jeffrey Wattles. Used by permission of Oxford University Press, Inc.

ROBERT WEISS   "Marriage as Partnership" Reprinted with the permission of The Free Press, a imprint of Simon & Schuster Adult Publishing Group, from *Staying The Course: The Emotional Lives of Men Who Do Well at Work* by Robert S. Weiss, pp. 119–129. Copyright © 1990 by Robert S. Weiss.

EUDORA WELTY   "Listening" from *One Writer's Beginnings* by Eudora Welty. Cambridge, MA: Harvard University Press. Copyright © 1983, 1984 by Eudora Welty. Reprinted by permission.

BENJAMIN LEE WHORF   "An American Indian Model of the Universe" by Benjamin Lee Whorf. *International Journal of American Linguistics*, 16 (1950) pp. 67–72.

TERRY TEMPEST WILLIAMS   "The Clan of One-Breasted Women" From *Refuge: An Unnatural History of Family and Place* by Terry Tempest Williams. Copyright © 1991 by Terry Tempest Williams. Used by permission of Pantheon Books, a division of Random House, Inc.

RICHARD WRIGHT   *The Power of Books* by Richard Wright. © Mrs. Ellen Wright. Reprinted by permission.

ROBERT WUTHNOW   "Making Choices: from Short-Term Adjustments to Principled Lives" from *Poor Richard's Principle: Recovering the American Dream Through the Moral Dimension of Work, Business, Money* by Robert Wuthnow, pp. 37–58, 15 pp. excerpt. © 1996 by Princeton University Press. Reprinted by permission.

CHARLES M. YOUNG   "Losing: An American Tradition" Adapted from *Losing: An American Tradition* by Charles M. Young. Men's Journal, April 2000. Reprinted by permission.

CZESLAW MILOSZ, TRANS. ZIELONKO   "American Ignorance of War" from *The Captive Mind* by Czeslaw Milosz, trans. J. Zielonko. Copyright © 1951, 1953 by Czeslaw Milosz. Reprinted by permission of Alfred A. Knopf, division of Random House, Inc.

Index by Field of Inquiry

Rhetorical Index

Autobiography

Comparison and Contrast

Index of Authors and Titles